Linux+ Guide to
Linux® Certification

Jason W. Eckert
M. John Schitka

THOMSON

COURSE TECHNOLOGY

Australia • Canada • Mexico • Singapore • Spain • United Kingdom • United States

THOMSON

COURSE TECHNOLOGY

Linux+ Guide to Linux® Certification

By Jason W. Eckert and M. John Schitka

Senior Editor:
William Pitkin III

Product Manager:
Laura Hildebrand

Production Editor:
Elena Montillo

Technical Reviewers:
Robert Guess, Ray Esparza, Robert
Koch, Tim Chappell, Randy Weaver

Development Editor:
Dave George

Quality Assurance Manager:
John Bosco

MQA Project Leader:
Nicole Ashton

Associate Product Manager:
Tim Gleeson

Editorial Assistant:
Nick Lombardi

Marketing Manager:
Jason Sakos

Text Designer:
GEX Publishing Services

Compositor:
GEX Publishing Services

Cover Design:
Steve Deschene

BRIEF
Contents

PREFACE   xi

CHAPTER ONE
Introduction to Linux   1

CHAPTER TWO
Preparing for Linux Installation   47

CHAPTER THREE
Linux Installation and Usage   77

CHAPTER FOUR
Exploring Linux Filesystems   125

CHAPTER FIVE
Linux Filesystem Management   187

CHAPTER SIX
Linux Filesystem Administration   243

CHAPTER SEVEN
Advanced Installation   301

CHAPTER EIGHT
Working with the BASH Shell   357

CHAPTER NINE
System Initialization   409

CHAPTER TEN
The X Window System   449

CHAPTER ELEVEN
Managing Linux Processes   491

CHAPTER TWELVE
Common Administrative Tasks   531

CHAPTER THIRTEEN
Compression, System Back-up, and Software Installation   593

CHAPTER FOURTEEN
Troubleshooting and Performance   641

CHAPTER FIFTEEN
Linux Networking   689

APPENDIX A
Certification   745

APPENDIX B
GNU Public License   753

APPENDIX C
Finding Linux Resources on the Internet   759

GLOSSARY   763

INDEX   785

TABLE OF

Contents

PREFACE   xi

CHAPTER ONE
Introduction to Linux   1
    Operating Systems   2
    The Linux Operating System   4
        Versions of the Linux Operating System   4
        Identifying Kernel Versions   5
        Licensing Linux   6
        Linux Advantages   10
    The History of Linux   16
        UNIX   16
        The Hacker Culture   17
        Linux   19
    Linux Distributions   20
    Common Uses of Linux   24
        Internet Servers   24
        File and Print Servers   28
        Application Servers   29
        Supercomputers   30
        Scientific / Engineering Workstations   31
        Office Workstations   33
    Chapter Summary   36
    Key Terms   36
    Review Questions   41
    Discovery Exercises   44

CHAPTER TWO
Preparing for Linux Installation   47
    Understanding Hardware   48
        Central Processing Units (CPUs)   48
        Physical Memory   50
        Disk Drives   52
        Mainboards and Peripheral Components   55
        Video Adapter Cards and Monitors   58
        Keyboards and Mice   59
    Gathering Pre-Installation Information   60
        Gathering Hardware Information   61
        Gathering Software Information   65
    Chapter Summary   67
    Key Terms   67
    Review Questions   71
    Hands-on Projects   74
    Discovery Exercises   75

CHAPTER THREE
Linux Installation and Usage   77
Installing Linux   78
    Installation Methods   78
    Creating Boot Disks   78
    Performing the Installation   79
Basic Linux Usage   99
    Shells, Terminals, and the Kernel   99
    Basic Shell Commands   103
    Shell Metacharacters   105
    Getting Command Help   106
    Shutting Down the Linux System   111
Chapter Summary   112
Key Terms   112
Review Questions   114
Hands-on Projects   117
Discovery Exercises   123

CHAPTER FOUR
Exploring Linux Filesystems   125
The Linux Directory Structure   126
    Changing Directories   127
Viewing Files and Directories   129
    File Types   129
    Filenames   130
    Listing Files   132
    Wildcard Metacharacters   137
Displaying the Contents of Text Files   138
Displaying the Contents of Binary Files   145
Searching for Text within Files   147
    Regular Expressions   148
    The grep Command   149
Editing Text Files   152
    The vi Editor   152
    Other Common Text Editors   161
Chapter Summary   167
Key Terms   167
Review Questions   170
Hands-on Projects   174
Discovery Exercises   184

CHAPTER FIVE
Linux Filesystem Management   187
The Filesystem Hierarchy Standard   188
Managing Files and Directories   189
Finding Files   194
Linking Files   199
File and Directory Permissions   203
    File and Directory Ownership   203
    Managing File and Directory Permissions   206
    Default Permissions   214
    Special Permissions   216

Chapter Summary   220
Key Terms   221
Review Questions   223
Hands-on Projects   228
Discovery Exercises   239

CHAPTER SIX
Linux Filesystem Administration   **243**
The /dev Directory   244
Filesystems   247
    Filesystem Types   247
    Mounting   249
Working with Floppy Disks   250
Working with CD-ROMs   259
Working with Hard Disks   262
    Hard Disk Partitioning   262
    Working with Hard Disk Partitions   266
Monitoring Filesystems   272
    Disk Usage   272
    Checking Filesystems for Errors   275
Hard Disk Quotas   278
Chapter Summary   282
Key Terms   282
Review Questions   284
Hands-on Projects   291
Discovery Exercises   298

CHAPTER SEVEN
Advanced Installation   **301**
Advanced Hardware Configuration   302
    SCSI Hard Disk Drive Configuration   302
    Mainboard Flow Control: IRQs, DMAs, and I/O Addresses 305
    Plug-and-Play   308
    RAID Configuration   309
Advanced Installation Methods   311
    Text-Based CD-ROM Installation   311
    Hard Disk Installation   316
    Network-Based Installations   319
    Installing Linux on Non-Intel Architectures   327
Troubleshooting Installation   330
    Problems Starting the Installation   331
    Problems During Installation   331
    Problems After Installation   332
Chapter Summary   343
Key Terms   344
Review Questions   346
Hands-on Projects   351
Discovery Exercises   356

CHAPTER EIGHT
Working with the BASH Shell   **357**
Command Input and Output   358
    Redirection   359
    Pipes   363

Shell Variables   369
    Environment Variables   369
    User-Defined Variables   375
    Other Variables   377
    Environment Files   378
Shell Scripts   379
    Escape Sequences   381
    Reading Standard Input   382
    Decision Constructs   382
Chapter Summary   390
Key Terms   391
Review Questions   392
Hands-on Projects   398
Discovery Exercises   405

CHAPTER NINE
System Initialization   **409**
The Boot Process   410
Boot Loaders   411
    LILO   411
    GRUB   415
    Dual Booting Linux   419
Linux Initialization   427
    Runlevels   427
    The /etc/inittab File   429
    Configuring Daemon Startup   434
Chapter Summary   436
Key Terms   437
Review Questions   438
Hands-on Projects   442
Discovery Exercises   448

CHAPTER TEN
The X Window System   **449**
Linux GUI Components   450
    X Windows   450
    Window Managers and Desktop Environments   451
Starting and Stopping X Windows   455
Configuring X Windows   457
Chapter Summary   475
Key Terms   476
Review Questions   477
Hands-on Projects   483
Discovery Exercises   489

CHAPTER ELEVEN
Managing Linux Processes   **491**
Linux Processes   492
Viewing Processes   493
Killing Processes   500
Process Execution   502
Running Processes in the Background   503
Process Priorities   506

Scheduling Commands 509
   Scheduling Commands with atd 509
   Scheduling Commands with crond 512
Chapter Summary 516
Key Terms 517
Review Questions 518
Hands-on Projects 523
Discovery Exercises 528

CHAPTER TWELVE
Common Administrative Tasks 531
Printer Administration 532
   The Print Process 532
   Managing Print Jobs 534
   Configuring Printers 537
Log File Administration 548
   The System Log Daemon 549
   Managing Log Files 552
Administering Users and Groups 555
   Creating User Accounts 561
   Modifying User Accounts 564
   Deleting User Accounts 565
   Managing Groups 566
   Using the Red Hat User Manager 568
Chapter Summary 573
Key Terms 574
Review Questions 576
Hands-on Projects 581
Discovery Exercises 591

CHAPTER THIRTEEN
Compression, System Back-up, and Software Installation ... 593
Compression 594
   The compress Utility 594
   The gzip Utility 596
   The bzip2 Utility 599
System Back-up 601
   The tar Utility 602
   The cpio Utility 607
   The dump/restore Utility 610
Software Installation 615
   Compiling Source Code into Programs 615
   Installing Programs using RPM 622
Chapter Summary 628
Key Terms 628
Review Questions 629
Hands-on Projects 633
Discovery Exercises 639

CHAPTER FOURTEEN
Troubleshooting and Performance 641
Troubleshooting Methodology 642
Resolving Common System Problems 644
   Hardware-Related Problems 645
   Software-Related Problems 648

Performance Monitoring 653
    Monitoring Performance with sysstat Utilities 654
    Other Performance Monitoring Utilities 662
Customizing the Kernel 664
    Kernel Modules 664
    Compiling a New Linux Kernel 666
    Patching the Linux Kernel 671
Chapter Summary 672
Key Terms 672
Review Questions 674
Hands-on Projects 680
Discovery Exercises 686

CHAPTER FIFTEEN
Linux Networking **689**
Networks and TCP/IP 690
    The TCP/IP Protocol 691
Configuring a NIC Interface 692
Configuring a PPP Interface 699
Name Resolution 708
Connecting to Network Resources 711
    Downloading Files using FTP 711
    Accessing Files with NFS 714
    Accessing Windows Files 715
    Running Remote Applications 717
    Accessing E-mail 719
Common Network Services 723
Chapter Summary 729
Key Terms 730
Review Questions 732
Hands-on Projects 737
Discovery Exercises 743

APPENDIX A
Certification **745**
    Why Get Certified? 745
    Linux+ Certification Objectives 746

APPENDIX B
GNU Public License **753**

APPENDIX C
Finding Linux Resources on the Internet **759**

GLOSSARY **763**

INDEX **785**

Preface

...In a future that includes competition from open source, we can expect that the eventual destiny of any software technology will be to either die or become part of the open infrastructure itself.

Eric S. Raymond, The Cathedral and the Bazaar

As Eric S. Raymond reminds us, Open Source Software will continue to shape the dynamics of the computer software industry for the next long while, just as it has done for the last decade. Created and perpetuated by hackers, Open Source Software refers to software in which the source code is freely available to anyone who wishes to improve it (usually through collaboration). And, of course, at the heart of Open Source Software lies Linux — an operating system whose rapid growth has shocked the world by demonstrating the nature and power of the Open Source model.

However, as Linux continues to grow, so must the number of Linux-educated users, administrators, developers, and advocates. Thus we find ourselves in a time when Linux education is of great importance to the Information Technology industry. Key to demonstrating Linux ability is the certification process. The *Linux+ Guide to Linux® Certification* uses carefully constructed examples, questions, and practical exercises to prepare readers with the necessary information to obtain the sought after Linux+ certification from CompTIA. The Linux+ certification may also be used to fulfill the UNIX module of the cSAGE certification, which is geared toward junior level system engineers. Once candidates pass the Linux+ exam, they are required only to pass the cSAGE core exam to earn the cSAGE Certification designation. Whatever your ultimate goal, you can be assured that reading this book in combination with study, creativity, and practice, will make the Open Source world come alive for you as it has for many others.

The Intended Audience

Simply put, this book is intended for those who wish to learn the Linux operating system and pass the Linux+ certification exam from CompTIA. It does not assume any prior knowledge of Linux or of computer hardware. Also, the topics introduced in this book, and covered in the certification exam, are geared towards systems administration, yet are also well suited for those who will use or develop programs for Linux systems.

Chapter 1, "Introduction to Linux" introduces operating systems as well as the features, benefits, and uses of the Linux operating system. As well, this chapter discusses the history and development of Linux and Open Source Software.

Chapter 2, "Preparing for Linux Installation" introduces the various hardware components inside a computer, as well as methods that can be used to collect hardware and software information prior to installing the Linux operating system.

Chapter 3, "Linux Installation and Usage" walks through a typical Linux installation given the hardware and software information collected in the previous chapter. As well, this chapter describes how to interact with a Linux system via a terminal and enter basic commands into a Linux shell such as those used to obtain help and properly shutdown the system.

Chapter 4, "Navigating the Linux Filesystem" outlines the Linux filesystem structure, and the types of files that can be found within it. As well, this chapter discusses commands that can be used to view and edit the content of those files.

Chapter 5, "Linux Filesystem Management" covers those commands which can be used to locate and manage files and directories on a Linux filesystem. Furthermore, this chapter outlines the different methods used to link files as well as how to interpret and set file and directory permissions.

Chapter 6, "Linux Filesystem Administration" discusses how to create, mount, and manage filesystems in Linux. This chapter also discusses the various filesystems available for Linux systems and the device files that are used to refer to the devices which may contain these filesystems.

Chapter 7, "Advanced Installation" introduces advanced hardware concepts and configurations that may prove useful when installing Linux. As well, this chapter discusses different methods that may be used to install Linux as well as common problems that may occur during installation, and their resolutions.

Chapter 8, "Working with the BASH Shell" covers the major features of the BASH shell including redirection, piping, variables, aliases, and environment files. Also, this chapter details the syntax of basic shell scripts.

Chapter 9, "System Initialization" covers the different bootloaders that may be used to start the Linux kernel and dual-boot the Linux operating system with other operating systems such as Windows. This chapter also discusses how daemons are started during system initialization as well as how to start and stop them afterwards.

Chapter 10, "The X Window System" discusses the structure of Linux Graphical User Interfaces as well as their configuration and management.

Chapter 11, "Managing Linux Processes" covers the different types of processes, as well as how to view their attributes, change their priority, and kill them. Furthermore, this chapter discusses how to schedule processes to occur in the future using various utilities.

Chapter 12, "Common Administrative Tasks" details three important areas of system administration: printer administration, log file administration, and user administration.

Chapter 13, "Compression, System Backup, and Software Installation" describes utilities that are commonly used to compress or back up files on a Linux filesystem. As well, this chapter discusses how to install software from source code as well as using the Red Hat Package Manager (RPM).

Chapter 14, "Troubleshooting and Performance" discusses the system maintenance cycle as well as good troubleshooting procedures for solving hardware and software problems. Also, this chapter outlines utilities that can be used to monitor and pinpoint the cause of performance problems, as well as how to patch and recompile the kernel to fix software, hardware, and performance problems.

Chapter 15, "Linux Networking" introduces networks, network utilities, and the TCP/IP protocol, as well as how to configure the TCP/IP protocol on a NIC or PPP interface. In addition, this chapter details the configuration of name resolution and common networking services.

Additional information is also contained in the appendices at the rear of the book. **Appendix A** discusses the certification process with emphasis on the Linux+ certification and how the objective list for the Linux+ certification matches each chapter in the textbook. **Appendix B** is a copy of the GNU Public License. **Appendix C** explains how to find Linux resources on the Internet and lists some common resources by category.

Features

To ensure a successful learning experience, this book includes the following pedagogical features:

- **Chapter Objectives**: Each chapter in this book begins with a detailed list of the concepts to be mastered within that chapter. This list provides you with a quick reference to the contents of that chapter, as well as a useful study aid.

- **Screenshots, Illustrations, and Tables**: Wherever applicable, screenshots and illustrations are used to aid you in the visualization of common installation, administration and management steps, theories, and concepts. In addition, many tables provide command options that may be used in combination with the specific command being discussed.

- **End-of-Chapter Material**: The end of each chapter includes the following features to reinforce the material covered in the chapter:
  - Chapter Summary: Gives a brief but complete summary of the chapter
  - Key Terms List: Lists all new terms and their definitions
  - Review Questions: Test your knowledge of the most important concepts covered in the chapter

- Hands-on Projects: Are preceded by the Hands-on icon and a description of the exercise that follows. These projects contain specific step-by-step instructions that enable you to apply the knowledge gained in the chapter

  - Discovery Exercises: Include theoretical, research, or scenario-based projects

- **On the CD-ROM**: On the two CD-ROMs included with this text you will find a copy of Red Hat® Linux® Publisher's Edition, Version 7.2.

Text and Graphic Conventions

Wherever appropriate, additional information and exercises have been added to this book to help you better understand what is being discussed in the chapter. Icons throughout the text alert you to additional materials. The icons used in this textbook are as follows:

 Tips are included from the authors' experiences that provide additional real-world insights into the topic being discussed.

 Notes are used to present additional helpful material related to the subject being described.

Instructor's Materials

The following supplemental materials are available when this book is used in a classroom setting. All of the supplements available with this book are provided to the instructor on a single CD-ROM.

- **Electronic Instructor's Manual**: The Instructor's Manual that accompanies this textbook includes additional instructional material to assist in class preparation, including suggestions for classroom activities, discussion topics, and additional projects.

- **Solutions**: Answers to all end-of-chapter materials are provided, including the Review Questions, and, where applicable, Hands-on Projects and Discovery Exercises.

- **ExamView®**: This textbook is accompanied by ExamView, a powerful testing software package that allows instructors to create and administer printed, computer (LAN-based), and Internet exams. ExamView includes hundreds of questions that correspond to the topics covered in this text, enabling students to generate detailed study guides that include page references for further review. The computer-based and Internet testing components allow students to take exams at their computers, and also save the instructor time by grading each exam automatically.

- **PowerPoint presentations**: This textbook comes with Microsoft PowerPoint slides for each chapter. These are included as a teaching aid for classroom presentation, to make available to students on the network for chapter review, or to be printed for classroom distribution. Instructors, please feel at liberty to add your own slides for additional topics you introduce to the class.

- **Figure Files**: All of the figures in this textbook are reproduced on the Instructor's Resource CD in bit-mapped format. Similar to the PowerPoint presentations, these are included as a teaching aid for classroom presentation, to make available to students for review, or to be printed for classroom distribution.

- **MeasureUp™ Test Prep Software**: Test preparation software for the Linux+ Certification Exam is available. You can download copies of this software free of charge at Course Technology's Web site at: *www.course.com/comptia*. Click the link for Linux+ Test Prep. The user name and password is: testprep. This password is case sensitive and does not contain a space between the two words.

ACKNOWLEDGMENTS

First, we wish to thank the staff at Course Technology for an overall enjoyable experience writing a textbook on Linux that takes a fundamentally different approach than traditional textbooks. More specifically, we wish to thank our Project Manager, Laura Hildebrand, for her coordination and insight, as well as our Developmental Editor, Dave George, for working through all of our comments and code samples to transform the text into its current state. As well, we wish to thank Moirag Haddad at Digital Content Factory for her advice and guidance, and our Director, Roy Cleeves, of TriOS College for freeing us up to write this textbook.

Jason W. Eckert: I must take this time to thank my co-author, M. John Schitka for the hard work, long hours, and dedication he spent on this book. As well, I thank Starbucks Coffee for keeping me on schedule, and most importantly, my daughter Mackenzie for providing me with many of the examples used in this textbook as well as teaching me that having fun playing a Harry Potter game is more important than writing a textbook.

M. John Schitka: First I want to thank my mentor and co-author Jason W. Eckert for his insight, patience, and wisdom during the long hours and late nights that went into the creation of this textbook. More importantly I must thank my family, my wife Jill, and children Kyra, Luke, and Noah for their support, tolerance, and patience during the time it took to write this textbook. Hopefully readers will find it enlightening and of benefit in their educational journey.

Finally, we wish to acknowledge the encouragement of our colleagues Mitch Mijailovic and Tonio Mladineo; if it were not for them, I doubt we would love the Linux operating system as much as we do today.

Readers are encouraged to e-mail comments, questions, and suggestions regarding *Linux+ Guide to Linux® Certification* to the authors:

- Jason W. Eckert: jasonec@trios.com
- M. John Schitka: johnsc@trios.com

Before You Begin

Linux can be a large and intimidating topic if poorly organized. As a result, each concept introduced in this textbook has been carefully planned and introduced in sequence. To ensure that you gain a solid understanding of core Linux concepts, you must read this book in consecutive order since each chapter builds upon previous ones. As well, we recommend that you participate in a local Linux Users Group (LUG) and explore the Internet for Web sites, FAQs, HOWTOs, and newsgroups that will expand your knowledge of Linux.

Lab Requirements

The following hardware is required for the Hands-on Projects at the end of each chapter and should be listed on the Hardware Compatibility List available at *www.redhat.com*:

- Pentium II 200 or higher CPU
- 64 MB RAM (128 MB RAM recommended)
- 4 GB hard disk
- CD-ROM drive
- 3.5" floppy diskette drive
- Network Interface Card
- Internet connection

Similarly, the following lists the software required for the Hands-on Projects at the end of each chapter:

- Red Hat® Linux® Publisher's Edition, Version 7.2
- Ethereal 0.8 or greater source code in tarball format (available from *www.ethereal.com*)
- Nmap 2.53 or greater in RPM format (available from *www.nmap.org*)

1

INTRODUCTION TO LINUX

**After completing this chapter,
you will be able to:**

♦ Understand the purpose of an operating system

♦ Outline the key features of the Linux operating system

♦ Describe the origins of the Linux operating system

♦ Identify the characteristics of various Linux distributions and where to find them

♦ Explain the common uses of Linux in industry today

Linux technical expertise has quickly become significant in the computer workplace as more and more companies have switched to using Linux to meet their computing needs. Thus, it is important today to understand how Linux can be used, what benefits Linux offers to a company, and how Linux has developed and continues to develop. In the first half of this chapter, you learn about operating system terminology and features of the Linux operating system, as well as the history and development of Linux. Later in this chapter, you learn about the various types of Linux and situations in which Linux is used.

OPERATING SYSTEMS

Every computer has two fundamental types of components: hardware and software. **Hardware** consists of the physical components inside a computer and are electrical in nature; they contain a series of circuits that are used to manipulate the flow of information. There can be many different pieces of hardware in a computer, including:

- A processor, which computes information (also known as the Central Processing Unit or CPU)
- Physical memory, which stores information needed by the processor (also known as Random Access Memory or RAM)
- Hard disk drives, which store most of the information that one uses
- Floppy disk drives, which store information on floppy disks
- CD-ROM drives, which read information from CD-ROMs
- Sound cards, which provide sound to external speakers
- Video cards, which display results to the computer monitor
- Circuit boards, which hold and provide electrical connections between various hardware components (also known as mainboards or motherboards)

Software, on the other hand, refers to the sets of instructions or **programs** that understand how to use the hardware of the computer in a meaningful way; they allow different hardware to interact with, as well as manipulate, data (or files) commonly used with programs. When a bank teller types information into the computer behind the counter at a bank, for example, that bank teller is using a program that understands what to do with your bank records. Programs and data are usually stored on hardware media such as CD-ROMs, hard disks, or floppy disks, although they can also be stored on other media or even embedded in computer chips. Some of these programs are loaded into various parts of your computer hardware (such as your computer's memory and processor) when you first turn your computer on; others are loaded when you start additional software such as word processors or **Internet** browsers. Once a program is executed on your computer's hardware, that program is referred to as a **process**. (Thus, the difference between a program and a process is small. A program is a file stored on your computer, whereas a process is that file in action, performing a certain task.)

There are two different types of programs that are executed on a computer: **applications**, which include those programs designed for a specific use and that we commonly interact with, such as word processors, computer games, graphical manipulation programs, and computer system utilities; and **operating system (OS)** software, which consists of a series of software components used to control the hardware of your computer directly.

Without an operating system, you would not be able to use your computer. Turning on a computer loads the operating system into the computer hardware, which loads and centrally controls all other application software in the background. Applications then take the information that users send them and relay that information to the operating system. The operating system then uses the computer hardware to carry out the requests. The relationship among users, application software, operating system software, and computer hardware is illustrated in Figure 1-1.

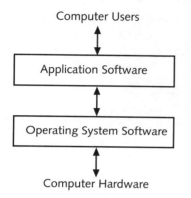
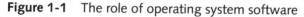

Figure 1-1   The role of operating system software

The operating system carries out many different tasks by interacting with many different types of computer hardware. In order for the operating system to accomplish this, it must contain the appropriate **device driver** software for every hardware device in your computer. Each device driver tells the operating system how to use that specific device. The operating system also provides a **user interface**, which is an application program that accepts user input indicating what is to be done, forwards this input to the operating system for completion, and, once completed, gives the results back to the user. The user interface can be a command line prompt, where the user must type a command to tell the operating system what to do; or it may be a **graphical user interface (GUI)**, which consists of a series of visual depictions of tasks, known as icons, that the user can use to control the operating system, as depicted in Figure 1-2.

Finally, operating systems offer **system services**, which are applications that handle system-related tasks such as printing, scheduling programs, and network access. These system services determine most of the functionality that is seen in an operating system. Different operating systems offer different system services, and many operating systems allow users to customize the services they offer.

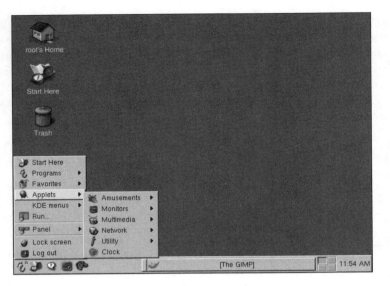

Figure 1-2   A Linux graphical user interface

THE LINUX OPERATING SYSTEM

Linux (pronounced "Líh-nucks") is an operating system that is used today to run a variety of applications on a variety of different hardware. Similar to other operating systems, the Linux operating system loads into computer memory when you first turn on your computer and initializes all of the hardware components. Next it loads the programs required to give the user an interface that you may use to enter commands that tell the operating system other applications to load to perform specific tasks. In the usual way, the operating system then uses the computer hardware to perform the tasks required by the applications.

Linux has the ability to manage thousands of tasks at the same time, including allowing multiple users to access the system simultaneously. Hence we refer to Linux as a **multi-user** and **multitasking** operating system.

Versions of the Linux Operating System

The core component of the Linux operating system is called the Linux **kernel**. The Linux kernel and supporting function libraries are written almost entirely in the C programming language, which is one of the most common languages that software developers use when creating programs.

Although a variety of different software can be used to modify the appearance of Linux, the underlying kernel is common to all Linux. The Linux kernel is developed continuously, and thus it is important to understand the different version numbers of the Linux

1

kernel in order to decide which kernel version is appropriate for certain needs. Since the Linux kernel is directly responsible for controlling the hardware (via device drivers) in your computer, upgrading the Linux kernel may be necessary to take advantage of new technologies such as USB (Universal Serial Bus), or fix problems (also known as bugs) the present kernel has with existing hardware. Consequently, a good understanding of what hardware features your system needs to use is important in deciding which kernel to use.

 A complete list of kernels, kernel versions, and their respective improvements can be found on the Internet at *http://www.kernel.org*.

In some cases a kernel module or a kernel patch can be used to provide or fix kernel support for hardware supported by the kernel. Kernel modules and kernel patches will be discussed later in this book.

Identifying Kernel Versions

Linux kernel versions are comprised of the following three components:

- Major number
- Minor number
- Revision number

Let's look at an example of a current Linux kernel version, 2.3.9. In this example, the **major number** is the number 2, which indicates the major revision to the Linux kernel. The **minor number,** represented by the number 3, indicates the minor revision and stability of the Linux kernel. If the minor number is odd, it is referred to as a **developmental kernel**, whereas if the minor number is even, it is referred to as a **production kernel**. Developmental kernels are not fully tested and imply instability; they are later tested for vulnerabilities by people who develop Linux software. Production kernels are developmental kernels that have been thoroughly tested by several Linux developers and are declared to be stable. In the example above, the kernel has a major number of 2 and a minor number of 3. Since the minor number is odd, this indicates a developmental kernel. This kernel will eventually be improved by Linux developers, tested, and declared stable. When this happens, the version of this kernel will change to 2.4 (indicating a production kernel).

Linux kernel changes occur frequently. Those changes that are very minor are represented by a **revision number** indicating the most current changes to the version of the particular kernel that is being released. For example, a 2.4.12 kernel has a major number of 2, a minor number of 4, and a revision number of 12. This kernel is the 12th release of the 2.4 kernel. Some kernels may have over one hundred different revisions as a result of developers making constant improvements to the kernel code.

When choosing a kernel for a mission-critical computer such as an e-mail server, ensure that the minor number is even. This reduces the chance that you will encounter a bug in the kernel and hence saves you the time needed to change kernels.

Table 1-1 shows the latest revisions of each major and minor kernel released since the initial release of Linux.

Table 1-1   Latest revisions of common Linux kernels

Kernel Version	Date Released	Type
0.01	September 1991	First Linux kernel
0.12	January 1992	Production (Stable)
0.95	March 1992	Developmental
0.98.6	December 1992	Production (Stable)
0.99.15	March 1994	Developmental
1.0.8	April 1994	Production (Stable)
1.1.95	March 1995	Developmental
1.2.12	July 1995	Production (Stable)
1.3.100	May 1996	Developmental
2.0.36	November 1998	Production (Stable)
2.1.132	December 1998	Developmental
2.2.20	November 2001 (latest release—was developed concurrently with newer kernels)	Production (Stable)
2.3.99	May 2000	Developmental
2.4.17	December 2001	Production (Stable)
2.5.3	January 2002	Developmental

Licensing Linux

The method of Linux licensing is one of the major reasons why companies choose Linux as their operating system. As an operating system, Linux is unique compared to most other operating systems because it is freely developed and continuously improved by a large community of software developers. For this reason, it is referred to as **Open Source Software (OSS)**. In order to understand what OSS is, one must understand how source code is used to create programs. **Source code** refers to the list of instructions that a software developer writes to make up a program; an example of source code is depicted in Figure 1-3.

1

```
#define MODULE
#include <linux/module.h>
int init_module(void)
{
printk("My module has been activated\n");
return 0;
}
void cleanup_module(void)
{
printk("My module has been de-activated\n");
}
```

Figure 1-3   An example of source code

Once the instructions are finished, the source code is compiled into a format (called machine language) that only your microprocessor can understand and execute. To edit an existing program, one must edit the source code and then recompile it.

The format and structure of source code follows certain rules defined by the **programming language** in which it was written. There are many different programming languages available that one can use to write source code for Linux. Once compiled into machine language, all programs look the same to the computer operating system, regardless of the programming language from which they were created. As a result, software developers choose a programming language to create source code based on ease of use, functionality, and comfort level.

The concept of Open Source Software enables software developers to read the source code of other people's software, modify that source code to make the program better, and redistribute that source code to other developers who may improve it further. Also, software made in this fashion must be distributed free of charge, regardless of the number of modifications made to it. People who develop Open Source Software commonly use the Internet to share their source code, manage software projects, and submit comments and fixes for bugs (flaws). In this way, the Internet acts as the glue that binds Open Source Software developers together.

 The complete Open Source definition can be found on the Internet at *http://www.opensource.org*.

Some implications of Open Source Software are as follows:

- Software is developed very rapidly through widespread collaboration.
- Software bugs are promptly noted and fixed.
- Software features evolve very quickly based on users' needs.
- The perceived value of the software increases, as it is based on usefulness and not price.

It is not difficult to understand why the sharing of ideas and source code is beneficial to software development, since sharing is beneficial to projects of any kind; however, the business model is very different. Open Source Software uses a non-traditional business model and, as a result, many find it difficult to understand how a product that is distributed freely can generate revenue. After all, without revenue any company will go out of business.

Open Source Software products were never intended to generate revenue directly; they were designed only with the betterment of software in mind. Software creation is an art, not a specific procedure. Programs made to perform the same task may be created in several different ways. For example, while one software developer may create a program that measures widgets using four pages of source code, another developer may create a program that does the same task in one page of source code. Because of this, software development has the potential to be haphazard if poorly managed. Open Source Software eliminates many of the problems associated with traditional software development by pooling the talent of many individual software developers to improve the quality and direction that software creation takes through the free sharing of ideas. There exists no single corporate purpose or deadline. Also, as Open Source Software developers contribute their strengths to a project, they learn new techniques from other developers at the same time.

Since the selling of software for profit would discourage the free sharing of source code, Open Source Software generates revenue indirectly. Companies usually make money by selling computer hardware that runs Open Source Software, by selling customer support for Open Source Software, or by creating **closed source software** programs that run on Open Source products such as Linux.

The key element to Open Source Software is the fact that it is software development for the sake of software development; the users of the program determine how it is developed and, as a result, the development of the software is rapid and efficient.

The features of Open Source Software may be beneficial, but legal licenses must exist to keep OSS definitions from changing. Before learning about some of the common licenses available, examine the following table, which defines some general terms used to describe the types of software that exist:

Table 1-2   Software types

Open Source	Software in which the source code and software may be obtained free of charge and modified
Closed Source	Software in which the source code is not available; although this type of software may be distributed free of charge it is usually quite costly
Freeware	Closed source software that is given out free of charge
Shareware	Closed source software that is initially given out free of charge but requires payment after a certain period of use

1

Types of Open Source Licenses

Linux adheres to the **GNU Public License (GPL)**, which was developed by the **Free Software Foundation (FSF)**. The GPL stipulates that the source code of any software published under its license must be freely available. If someone modifies that source code, then that person must also redistribute that source code freely, thereby keeping the source code free forever.

GNU stands for "GNU's Not UNIX."

The GPL is freely available on the Internet at *http://www.gnu.org* and in Appendix A of this book.

Another type of Open Source license is the **Artistic License**, which ensures that the source code of the program is freely available, yet allows the original author of the source code some control over the changes made to it. Thus, if one developer obtains and improves the source code of a program, the original author has the right to reject those improvements. As a result of this restriction, artistic licenses are rarely used because many developers do not wish to work on potentially futile projects.

In addition to the two different Open Source licenses mentioned, there are many types of Open Source licenses available that differ only slightly from one another. Those licenses must adhere to the Open Source definition but may contain extra conditions that the Open Source definition does not.

A list of approved Open Source licenses can be found on the Internet at *http://www.opensource.org.*

Types of Closed Source Licenses

Closed source software may be distributed for free or for a cost; either way, the source code for the software is unavailable from the original developers. The majority of closed source software is sold commercially and bears the label of its manufacturer. Each of these software packages may contain a separate license that restricts free distribution of the program and its source code in many different ways.

An example of closed source software is software made by companies such as Microsoft, Novell, or Electronic Arts.

One type of closed source software is **freeware**, in which the software program is distributed free of charge, yet the source code is unavailable. Freeware may also contain licenses that restrict the distribution of source code. Another approach to this style of closed source licensing is **shareware**, which is distributed free of charge, yet after a certain number of hours of usage—or to gain certain features of the program—payment is required. Although both freeware and shareware do not commonly distribute their source code under an Open Source license, some people incorrectly refer to OSS as freeware, assuming that the source code is free as well.

Linux Advantages

There are many operating systems in use today; the main ones include Linux, Microsoft Windows, Novell Netware, UNIX, and Mac OS. Notably, Linux is the fastest growing operating system released to date. Though Linux was only created in 1991, the number of Linux users estimated by Red Hat in 1998 was 7.5 million, and Linux growth has increased dramatically each year since then. Many large companies, including IBM, Hewlett-Packard, Intel, and Dell, have announced support for Linux and OSS. In the year 2000, IBM announced that it would spend one billion dollars on Linux and Linux development alone. There are a multitude of reasons why so many people have begun using Linux. The advantages listed below are examined in the sections that follow:

- Risk reduction
- Meeting business needs
- Stability and security
- Flexibility for different hardware platforms
- Ease of customization
- Ease of obtaining support
- Cost reduction

Risk Reduction

Companies invest in software to perform mission-critical tasks such as database tracking, Internet business (e-commerce), and data manipulation. However, changes in customer needs and market competition may cause the software a company uses to change frequently. This can be very costly and time consuming, but is a risk that companies must take. Imagine that a fictitious company, ABC Inc., buys a piece of software from a fictitious software vendor, ACME Inc., to integrate its sales and accounting information with customers via the Internet. What would happen if ACME Inc. goes out of business or stops supporting the software due to lack of sales? In either case, ABC Inc. would be using a product that has no software support, and any problems that ABC has with the software after that time would go unsolved and could result in lost revenue. Additionally, all closed source software is eventually retired some time after it was purchased, forcing companies to buy new software every so often in order to obtain new features and maintain software support.

Instead, if ABC Inc. chose to use an OSS product and the original developers become unavailable to maintain it, then ABC Inc. is free to take the source code, add features to it, and maintain it themselves provided the source code is redistributed free of charge. Also, most OSS does not retire after a short period of time because collaborative Open Source development results in constant software improvement geared to the needs of the users.

Meeting Business Needs

Recall that Linux is merely one product of Open Source development. There are many thousands of OSS programs in existence, and new ones are created daily by software developers worldwide. Most Open Source Internet tools have been developed for quite some time now, and the focus in the Linux community in the past few years has been on developing application software for Linux, such as databases and office productivity suites. Almost all of this software is Open Source and freely available, compared to other operating systems, in which most software is closed source and costly.

OSS is easy to locate, as there are several Web sites on the Internet that allow Linux developers space to host their software for others to download; SourceForge at *http://www.sourceforge.net*, FreshMeat at *http://www.freshmeat.net*, and Ibiblio at *http://www.ibiblio.org* are some of the most common. New software is published to these sites daily; SourceForge alone hosts over 35,000 different software developments. Some common software available for Linux includes, but is not limited to:

- Scientific and engineering software
- Software emulators
- Web servers, Web browsers, and e-commerce suites
- Desktop productivity software (e.g., word processors, presentation software, spreadsheets)
- Graphics manipulation software
- Database software
- Security software

In addition to this, companies that run the UNIX operating system may find it easy to migrate to Linux. For those companies, Linux supports most UNIX commands and standards, which makes transitioning to Linux very easy since the company would likely not need to purchase additional software or retrain staff. Take for example a company that tests scientific products, which has spent much time and energy developing custom software that ran on the UNIX operating system. If this company transitions to another operating system, staff would need to be retrained or hired and much of the custom software would need to be rewritten and retested, which could result in a loss of customer confidence. If, however, that company transitioned to Linux, then the staff would require little retraining, and little of the custom software would need to be rewritten and retested, hence saving money and minimizing the impact on consumer confidence. Also, for companies that require a certain development environment or need to support previous custom software developed in the past, Linux provides support for most programming languages.

Stability and Security

OSS is developed by those people who have a use for it. This collaboration between several developers with a common need speeds up software creation, and when bugs in the software are found by these users, bug fixes are created very quickly. Often the users who identify the bugs can fix the problem because they have the source code, or they can provide detailed descriptions of their problems such that other developers may fix them.

By contrast, customers using closed source operating systems must rely on the operating system vendor to fix any bugs. Users of closed source operating systems must report the bug to the manufacturer and wait for the manufacturer to develop, test, and release a solution to the problem known as a **hot fix**. This process may take weeks or even months to occur. For most companies and individuals, this process is slow and costly. The thorough and collaborative Open Source approach to testing software and fixing software bugs increases the stability of Linux; it is not uncommon to find a Linux system that has been running continuously for months or even years without being turned off.

Security is also a vital concern for many companies and individuals. Linux source code is freely available and publicly scrutinized. Like bugs, security loopholes are quickly identified and fixed, usually by several different developers. In contrast, the source code for closed source operating systems is not released to the public for scrutiny, which means customers must rely on the vendor of that closed source operating system to provide security. As a result, security breaches may go un-reported if discovered by the wrong person. This situation is demonstrated by the number of computer viruses (destructive programs that exploit security loopholes) that are available for a closed source operating system such as Windows as compared to the number of viruses available to Linux. As of 2001, there were 18 known Linux viruses and more than 30,000 Windows viruses.

 A complete list of computer viruses can be found on the Internet at *http://www.viruslist.com.*

Flexibility for Different Hardware Platforms

Another important feature of Linux is that it can run on a variety of different computer **hardware platforms** frequently found in different companies. Although Linux is most commonly installed on the Intel x86 platform, it may also be installed on other types of hardware, such as the DEC Alpha. This means that companies can run Linux on very large and expensive hardware for big tasks such as graphics rendering or chemical

1

molecular modeling, as well as on older hardware—such as an old Sun SPARC computer—to extend its lifetime in a company. Few other operating systems run on more than two different hardware platforms, making Linux the ideal choice for companies that use a variety of different or specialized hardware.

Following is a partial list of hardware platforms on which Linux can run:

- Intel
- Itanium
- Mainframe (S/390)
- Cirrus Logic ARM
- DEC Alpha
- MIPS
- M68K
- PA-RISC
- SPARC
- Ultra-SPARC
- PowerPC (Macintosh)

In addition to the above platforms, Linux can be customized to work on most hardware, including embedded devices such as watches or microwaves. This embedded operating system technology will become more important in the future as the need increases for new functionality in present day products. Many high-tech companies rely on embedded operating system technology to drive their systems—the NASA space shuttles for example. Currently there are over 100 different companies that embed Linux in their products.

 A list of embedded Linux vendors can be found on the Internet at *http://www.embedded-linux.org.*

Ease of Customization

Being able to control the inner workings of the operating system is another attractive feature of Linux, particularly for companies that need it to perform specialized functions. If you desire to use Linux as an Internet Web server, then you may simply recompile the Linux kernel to include only the support needed to be an Internet Web server. This will result in a much smaller and faster kernel.

 A small kernel performs faster than a large kernel, as there is less code for the processor in the computer to analyze. Generally, you should take out any unnecessary support in the kernel to improve performance.

Today, customizing and recompiling the Linux kernel is a well-documented and easy process; however, it is not the only way to customize Linux. Only software packages necessary to perform certain tasks need to be installed; thus each Linux system may have a unique configuration and set of applications available to the user. Linux also supports the Shell and PERL programming languages, which can be utilized to automate tasks or create custom tasks that are then invoked as needed.

Consider a company that needs an application to copy a database file from one computer to another computer, yet also requires that the database file be manipulated in a specific way, tested by another program for duplicate records, summarized, and then finally printed as a report. This may seem like a task requiring expensive software; however, in Linux one can simply write a short PERL script that uses common Linux commands and programs together to achieve this task in only a few minutes. This type of customization is invaluable to companies, as it allows them to combine several existing applications together to perform a certain task that may be specific only to that company and hence not previously developed by another free software developer. Most Linux configurations present hundreds of small utilities, which, combined with Shell or PERL programming, can quickly and easily make new programs to meet many business needs.

Ease of Obtaining Support

For those who are new to Linux, the Internet offers a world of Linux documentation. **Frequently Asked Questions (FAQs)** and easy-to-read instructions known as **HOWTO** documents are arranged by topic and are available to anyone. HOWTO documents are maintained by their authors, yet centrally collected by the **Linux Documentation Project (LDP)**, which has over 250 Web sites worldwide that allow one to search or download HOWTO documents.

A search of the word HOWTO on a typical Internet **search engine** such as *http://www.google.com* will display thousands of results, or you can download the worldwide collection of HOWTO documents at *http://www.linuxdoc.org*.

In addition, there are several Internet newsgroups that allow Linux users to post messages and reply to previously posted messages. If someone has a specific problem with Linux, that person can simply post the problem on an Internet newsgroup and receive help from those who know the solution. Messages to Linux newsgroups are posted often, thus one can usually expect a solution to a problem within hours. A list of common Linux newsgroups can be found on the Internet at *http://groups.google.com*.

Appendix C describes how to navigate Internet resources and lists some common resources useful throughout this textbook.

Although online support is the most common method of getting help, there are other methods. Most Linux distributions provide professional telephone support services for a modest fee, and many organizations exist to give free support to those who ask. The most common of these groups are referred to as **Linux User Groups (LUGs)**, and most large cities across the globe have at least one. LUGs are groups of Linux users who meet regularly to discuss Linux-related issues and problems. An average LUG meeting consists of several new Linux users (also known as Linux newbies), administrators, developers, and experts (also known as Linux GURUs). LUG meetings are a place to solve problems, as well as learn about the local Linux community.

 To find a list of available LUGs in your region, search for the words LUG *<city-name>* in an Internet search engine such as *http://www.google.com*. When searching for a LUG, also keep in mind that LUGs may go by several different names; for example, the LUG in Hamilton, Ontario, Canada is known as HLUG (Hamilton Linux Users Group).

Cost Reduction

Linux is cheaper than alternative operating systems such as Windows, because there is no cost associated with acquiring the software. There is also a wealth of OSS that can run on a variety of different hardware platforms running Linux, and there is a large community of developers who diagnose and fix bugs in a short period of time for free. However, although Linux and the Linux source code are distributed freely, implementing Linux is not cost free. Costs include purchasing the computer hardware necessary for the computers hosting Linux, hiring people to install and maintain Linux, and training users of Linux software.

The largest costs that companies face with Linux are those for the people involved in maintaining the Linux system. When using a closed source operating system, however, this administrative cost is also necessary, alongside the costs of the hardware, the operating system, additional software, and bug fixing. The overall cost of using a particular operating system is known as the **Total Cost of Ownership (TCO)**. An example of the factors involved in calculating the TCO for operating systems can be seen in Table 1–3.

Table 1-3   Calculating the Total Cost of Ownership

Operating System	Linux	Closed Source Operating System
Operating System Cost	$0	Greater than $0
Cost of Administration	Low: Stability is high and bugs are fixed quickly by Open Source Developers.	Moderate/High: Bug fixes are created by the vendor of the operating system, which could result in costly downtime.
Cost of Additional Software	Low/None: Most software available for Linux is also Open Source.	High: Most software available for closed source operating systems is also closed source.
Cost of Software Upgrades	Low/None	Moderate/High: Closed source software is eventually retired and companies must buy upgrades or new products to gain functionality and stay competitive.

THE HISTORY OF LINUX

Linux is based on the UNIX operating system developed by Ken Thompson and Dennis Ritchie of AT&T Bell Laboratories in 1969 and was developed through the efforts of many people as a result of the "hacker culture" that formed in the 1980s. Therefore, in order to understand how and why Linux emerged on the operating system market, one must first understand UNIX and the hacker culture. A timeline representing the history of the UNIX and Linux operating systems can be found in Figure 1-4.

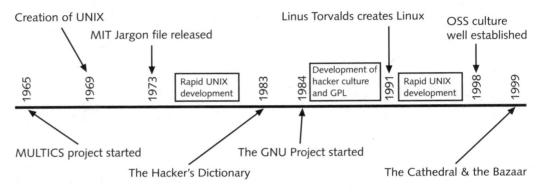

Figure 1-4   Timeline of UNIX and Linux development

UNIX

The UNIX operating system has roots running back to 1965 when the Massachusetts Institute of Technology (MIT), General Electric, and Bell Labs began development on an operating system called **Multiplexed Information and Computing Service (MULTICS)**. MULTICS was a test project intended to reveal better ways of developing time-sharing operating systems, in which the operating system regulates the amount of time each process has to use the processor; however the project was abandoned in 1969.

Ken Thompson, who had worked on the MULTICS operating system, continued to experiment with operating system development after the project was abandoned and developed an operating system called **UNIX** in 1969 that ran on the DEC (Digital Equipment Corporation) PDP-7 computer. Shortly thereafter, Dennis Ritchie invented the C programming language that was to be used on Ken Thompson's UNIX operating system. The C programming language was a revolutionary language. Most programs at the time needed to be written specifically for the hardware of the computer, which involved referencing volumes of information regarding the hardware in order to write a simple program. However, the C programming language was much easier to use to write programs, and it was possible to run a program on several different machines without having to rewrite the code for each machine. The UNIX operating system was rewritten in the C programming language, and by the late 1970s, UNIX ran on different hardware platforms, something that the computing world had never seen until that time. Hence people called UNIX a portable operating system.

Unfortunately, the company Ken Thompson and Dennis Ritchie worked for (AT&T Bell Laboratories) was restricted by a federal court order from marketing UNIX, and the solution AT&T put into action involved selling off the UNIX source code to several different companies and encouraging standards between them. Each of these companies developed its own "flavor" of UNIX, yet adhered to standards agreed upon by all. AT&T also gave away free copies of the UNIX source code to certain universities to promote widespread development of UNIX; the University of California at Berkeley **BSD (Berkeley Software Distribution)** UNIX is one result of this. It entered the computing scene in the early 1980s. In 1982, one of the companies that AT&T sold UNIX source code to (Sun Microsystems) marketed UNIX on relatively cheaper hardware and sold thousands of computers that ran UNIX to various companies and universities.

Throughout the 1980s, UNIX found its place primarily in large corporations that had enough money to purchase the expensive computing equipment needed to run it (usually a DEC PDP-11, VAX, or Sun Microsystems computer). A typical UNIX system in the 1980s could cost over $100,000US, yet performed thousands of tasks for client computers or "dumb terminals." Today, UNIX still functions in that environment; most large companies employ different flavors of UNIX for their heavy-duty, mission-critical tasks such as e-commerce and database hosting. Some common flavors of UNIX today include Sun Microsystems's **Solaris** UNIX, Hewlett-Packard's **HP-UX**, and IBM's **AIX** UNIX.

The Hacker Culture

The term **hacker** refers to someone with the intent of expanding their knowledge of computing through experimentation. This should not be confused with the term **cracker**, which specifies someone who illegally uses computers for personal benefit or to cause damage.

Most hackers in the early days of UNIX came primarily from engineering or scientific backgrounds, because those were the fields in which most UNIX development occurred. Fundamental to hacking was the idea of sharing knowledge. A famous hacker, Richard Stallman, promoted the free sharing of ideas while he worked at the Artificial Intelligence lab at MIT. He believed that free sharing of all knowledge in the computing industry would promote development. In the mid 1980s, Richard formed the Free Software Foundation (FSF) to encourage free software development. This movement was quickly accepted by the academic community in universities around the world, and many university students and other hackers participated in making free software, most of which ran on UNIX. As a result, the hacker culture was commonly identified alongside the UNIX operating system.

Unfortunately, UNIX was not free software, and by the mid 1980s some of the collaboration seen earlier by different UNIX vendors diminished and UNIX development fragmented into different streams. As a result, UNIX did not represent the ideals of the Free Software Foundation, and so Richard Stallman founded the **GNU Project** in 1984 to promote free development for a free operating system that was not UNIX.

GNU stands for "GNU's Not UNIX."

 A description of the Free Software Foundation and GNU can be found on the Internet at *http://www.gnu.org*.

This development eventually led to the publication of the GNU Public License (GPL), which legalized free distribution of source code and encouraged collaborative development. As mentioned earlier in this chapter, any software published under this license must be freely available with its source code; any modifications made to the source code must then be redistributed free as well, keeping the software development free forever.

As more and more hackers worked together developing software, a hacker culture developed with its own implied rules and conventions. Most developers worked together without ever meeting each other; they communicated primarily via newsgroups and e-mail. In addition, *The Hacker's Dictionary* was published in 1983 by MIT and detailed terminology collected since the mid 1970s regarding computing and computing culture. The FSF, GNU, GPL, and *The Hacker's Dictionary* were all tangible parts of the hacker culture, yet no tangible definition of this culture existed until the hacker Eric S. Raymond published his book *The Cathedral and the Bazaar* in 1999. In this book, Raymond describes several aspects of the hacker culture:

- Software users are treated as co-developers.

- Software is developed primarily for peer recognition and not for money.

- The original author of a piece of software is regarded as the owner of that software and coordinates the cooperative software development.

- The use of a particular piece of software determines its value, not its cost.

- Attacking the author of source code is never done. Instead, bug fixes are either made or recommended.

- Developers must understand the implied rules of the hacker culture before being accepted into it.

This hacker culture proved to be very productive, and several thousand free tools and applications were made in the 1980s, including the famous EMACS editor, which is a common tool used in Linux today. During this time period, many programming function libraries and UNIX-like commands also appeared as a result of the work on the GNU project. Hackers became accustomed to working together via newsgroup and e-mail correspondence. In short, this hacker culture, which supported free sharing of source code and collaborative development, set the stage for Linux.

1

Linux

Although Richard Stallman started the GNU Project to make a free operating system, the GNU operating system never took off. But much of the experience gained by hackers developing the GNU project was later pooled into Linux. A Finnish student named **Linus Torvalds** first developed Linux in 1991 when he was experimenting with improving **MINIX** (Mini-UNIX, a small educational version of UNIX developed by Andrew Tannenbaum) for the Intel x86 platform. The Intel x86 platform was fast becoming standard in homes and businesses across the world, and was a good choice for any free development at the time. The key feature of the Linux operating system that attracted the development efforts of the hacker culture was the fact that Linus Torvalds had published Linux under the GNU Public License.

Since 1991, when the source code for Linux was released, the number of software developers dedicated to improving Linux has increased each year. The Linux kernel was developed collaboratively and centrally managed; however, many Linux add-on packages were developed freely worldwide by those members of the hacker culture who were interested in their release. Linux was a convenient focal point on which free software developers could concentrate. During the early and mid 1990s, Linux development was radical; hackers used this time to experiment with a development project of this size. Also during this time, several **distributions** of Linux appeared. A distribution of Linux used the commonly developed Linux operating system kernel and libraries, yet was packaged with add-on software specific to a certain use.

There were many distributions of Linux formed, such as **Red Hat**, **Caldera**, and **SuSE**, yet this branding of Linux did not imply the fragmentation that UNIX experienced in the late 1980s. All distributions of Linux shared a common kernel and utilities; the fact that they contained different add-on packages simply made them look different on the surface. Linux still derived its usefulness from collaborative development, and in 1998 the term Open Source Software (OSS) development was put into place for this type of collaborative software development. OSS was created and advocated by the hacker culture, and by 1998 there were many thousands of OSS developers worldwide. Many small companies that offered Linux solutions for business were formed, people invested in these companies, and many were released publicly on the stock market. Unfortunately, this trend was short-lived, and by the year 2000 most of these companies vanished. At the same time, the OSS movement caught the attention and support of many large companies (such as IBM, Compaq, Dell, and Hewlett-Packard), and there was a shift in Linux development to support the larger computing environments and embedded Linux.

It is important to note that Linux is simply a by-product of OSS development. Recall that the OSS developers are still members of the hacker culture and as such are intrinsically motivated to develop software that has an important use. Thus, OSS development has changed over time; in the 1980s, the hacker culture concentrated on developing Internet and programming tools, whereas in the 1990s, the hacker culture focused on Linux operating system development. Since the year 2000, there has been great interest in developing application programs for use on the Linux operating system. Graphics programs, games, and custom business tools are only some of the popular developments that OSS developers have released in the past couple of years. Because Linux is currently very well developed, more application development can be expected from the OSS community in the next decade.

LINUX DISTRIBUTIONS

It is time consuming and inefficient to obtain Linux by first downloading and installing the Linux kernel and then adding desired Open Source Software packages afterwards. As a rule, one downloads a distribution of Linux containing the Linux kernel, common function libraries, and a series of Open Source Software packages.

 Remember that although different Linux distributions appear different on the surface, they run the same kernel and contain many of the same packages.

Despite the fact that varied distributions of Linux are essentially the same under the surface, they do have important differences. Different distributions may support different hardware platforms. Also, Linux distributions ship with predefined sets of software; some Linux distributions ship with a large number of server-related tools such as Web servers and database servers, while others ship with a large number of workstation and development software applications. Still others may ship with a complete set of Open Source tools from which one can customize their Linux system; one simply chooses a subset of these Open Source tools to install in order to perform specific functions, such as a database server.

Linux distributions that ship with many specialized tools may not contain a Graphical User Interface (GUI); an example of this would be a Linux distribution that fits on a floppy and can be used as a **router**. Most distributions, however, do ship with a GUI which can be further customized to suit the needs of the user. The core component of the GUI in Linux is referred to as **X Windows** and can be obtained from the Internet at *http://www.XFree86.org*. There are several window managers and desktop environments, which together affect the look and feel of this GUI, and these components can differ from distribution to distribution. X Windows in combination with a window manager and desktop environment is referred to as a **GUI environment**. There are two competing GUI environments in Linux: the **GNU Object Model Environment (GNOME)** and the **Kommon Desktop Environment (KDE)**. Both these GUI environments are more or less comparable in functionality, though users may have a personal preference for one desktop over the other. This is often the case when a company wishes to do a great deal of software development in the GUI environment; the GNOME desktop written in the C programming language uses the widely available gtk toolkit whereas the KDE desktop written in the C++ programming language uses the qt toolkit. Whichever language and tool kit best fits the need will be the one preferred at that time. Most common Linux distributions ship with both GNOME and KDE GUI environments, while others offer support for both so that either GUI environment can be easily downloaded and installed. A comparison of these two GUI environments can be seen in Figure 1-5 and 1-6.

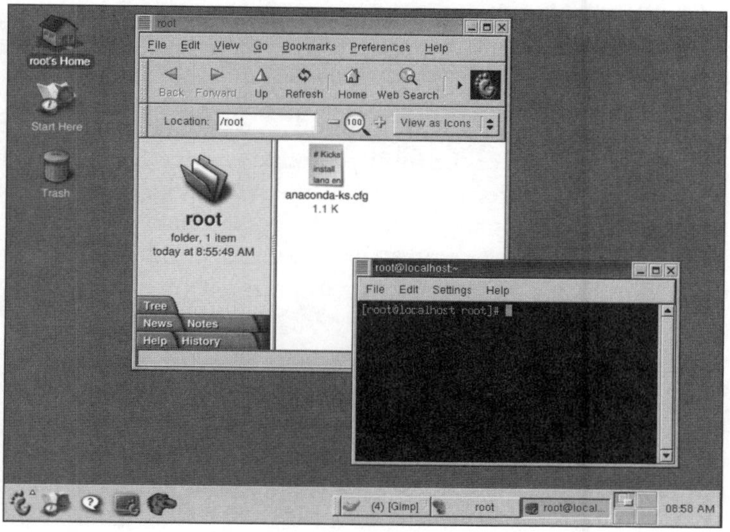

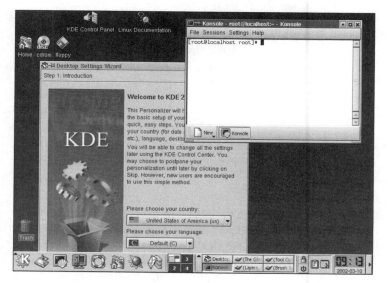

Figure 1-5   The GNOME Desktop

Figure 1-6   The KDE Desktop

Another difference between Linux distributions is language support. Certain distributions are available with more support for certain languages than others. Two examples are SuSE Linux, which has increased support for the German language, and TurboLinux, which has increased support for Japanese and Chinese. As a result, these two distributions of Linux are most popular in countries with populations who speak those languages primarily. There are many Linux distributions specialized for different languages, and most Linux documentation, such as HOWTO documents, are available in many different languages.

Although these differences between Linux distributions can help narrow down the choice of Linux distributions to install, one of the most profound reasons companies choose one distribution over another is support for package managers. A **package manager** is a software system that installs and maintains software. It keeps track of installed software, requires a standard format and documentation, and can manage and remove software from a system by recording all relevant software information in a central software database on your computer.

A package manager in Linux is similar to the "Add/Remove Programs" applet in the Windows Control Panel.

The most widely supported package manager is the Red Hat Package Manager (RPM). Most Linux software is available in RPM format, and the Red Hat Package Manager is standard on many Linux distributions. The Debian Package Manager offers the same advantages as the Red Hat Package Manager, yet few distributions offer it. In addition to obtaining software in package manager format, one can also download software in tarball format. A **tarball** is merely a compressed archive of files, like Winzip or RAR, which usually contain scripts that will install the software contents to the correct location on the system. Unfortunately, tarballs do not update a central software database and as a result are very difficult to manage, upgrade, or remove from the system. Traditionally, most Linux software was available in tarball format, but more and more people are using package managers to install software.

A complete listing of Linux distributions can be found on the Internet at *http://www.linux.org*, and this list can be searched by hardware platform, software category, or language.

Anyone can create a Linux distribution by packaging Open Source Software with the Linux kernel. As a result, there are over 150 publicly registered Linux distributions. Many of these are small, specialized distributions designed to fulfill certain functions, but some are mainstream Linux distributions commonly used in most situations. Each distribution usually has an associated Web site from which the distribution can be downloaded for free. Additionally, most Linux distributions can be obtained from several different Web sites such as *http://www.linuxiso.org*. Many distributions of Linux are also available on

CD-ROM for a small fee from various computer stores and Web sites; however down-loading from the Internet is the most common method of obtaining Linux.

A brief list of some mainstream Linux distributions, their features, and where to find them on the Internet is given in Table 1–4.

Table 1-4   Common Linux distributions

Distribution	Features	Platforms	Location
Red Hat Linux	The most common Linux distribution used today with tools useful in any Linux environment. Ships with GNOME, KDE, and RPM.	X86 Itanium Alpha SPARC mainframe M68K MIPS Embedded	*http://www.redhat.com*
Caldera Linux	Linux geared toward the business environment with several server management products. Ships with KDE and RPM.	x86	*http://www.caldera.com*
SuSE Linux	The most common Linux distribution in Europe, SuSE offers software packages for almost any business needs. Ships with GNOME, KDE, and RPM.	x86 Itanium Alpha PPC SPARC mainframe embedded	*http://www.suse.com*
Slackware Linux	With many features similar to UNIX, it is commonly used in multiprocessor environments due to its enhanced multiprocessor support. It ships with GNOME and KDE.	x86 Alpha SPARC	*http://www.slackware.com*
Debian Linux	Offers the largest number of packages of all Linux—it contains software packages for any use and ships with GNOME, KDE, the Debian Package Manager, and RPM.	x86 Alpha SPARC ARM M68K PPC	*http://www.debian.org*
TurboLinux	The most common distribution of Linux in Asia, it is famous for its clustering abilities. It ships with GNOME, KDE, and RPM.	x86 Itanium Alpha mainframe	*http://www.turbolinux.com*
Mandrake Linux	A user-oriented distribution very similar to Red Hat with enhancements for ease of use. It ships with GNOME, KDE, and RPM	x86 PPC	*http://www.linux-mandrake.com*

COMMON USES OF LINUX

As discussed earlier, an important feature of Linux is its versatility. Linux can provide services meeting the needs of differing companies in a variety of situations. Furthermore, configuring these services is straightforward given the wide range of documentation freely available on the Internet; one simply chooses the services that are required and then customizes Linux to provide those services. These services may be used on the local computer **workstation**, or they may be configured to allow other computers to connect to it across a network. Services that are used on the local computer are referred to as **workstation services**, whereas services that are made available for other computers across a network are known as **server services**.

 A computer that hosts a server service is commonly referred to as a **server**.

Although there are thousands of different server and workstation services that one may use to customize Linux, some configurations of Linux that are commonly used today include:

- Internet servers
- File & print servers
- Application servers
- Supercomputers
- Scientific/Engineering workstations
- Office workstations

Internet Servers

Linux hosts a wide range of Internet services, and it was from these services that Linux gained much popularity in the 1990s. All of these services are available free of charge and like all Open Source Software undergo constant improvement, which makes Linux an attractive choice when planning for the use of Internet services in a company. Companies that use services on a computer to serve client computers are said to have an Internet server. Linux offers hundreds of network services that provide the framework for an internet server; the most common of these services include:

- Mail services
- Routing
- FTP services
- Firewalls & proxy services

- Web services
- News services
- DNS services

These applications will be discuissed in more detail later in this book.

Mail Services

In the 1980s and early 1990s, e-mail (or electronic mail) was a service that was found primarily in universities. Today, almost every Internet user has an e-mail account and uses e-mail on a regular basis. E-mail addresses are easy to acquire and can be obtained free of charge.

 Free e-mail addresses can be acquired from several different Web sites; one such well-known Web site is *http://www.hotmail.com.*

E-mail is distributed via a network of e-mail servers, also known as **mail transfer agents (MTAs)**. There are many mail transfer agents freely available for Linux including sendmail, postfix, smail, and qmail. Before the user can access the e-mail, it must be downloaded from a mail transfer agent; the service that provides this is known as a **mail delivery agent (MDA)**. Linux also provides several of these services; procmail and fetchmail are two of the most common. Finally, e-mail must be viewed using a program known as a **mail user agent (MUA)**. Common MUAs available for Linux include mutt, pine, printmail, elm, mail, Netscape, and Eudora.

Routing

Routing is a core service that is necessary for the Internet to function. The Internet is merely a large network of interconnected smaller networks. In other words, the Internet connects company networks, home networks, and institutional networks together so that they can communicate to each other. A router is a computer or special hardware device that provides this interconnect; it contains information regarding the structure of the Internet and sends information from one network to another. Companies can use routers to connect their internal networks to the Internet as well as to connect their networks together inside the company. Linux is a good choice for this, as it provides support for routing and is easily customizable. There are many Linux distributions that can fit on a single floppy disk that provide routing capabilities.

 An example of a Linux distribution that can fit on a floppy and is customized to perform routing is the Linux Router Project, which can be downloaded from the Internet at *http://www.linuxrouter.org.*

FTP Services

The most common and efficient method for transferring files over the Internet is by using the File Transfer Protocol (FTP). FTP is also commonplace when transferring files on an internal company network, as it is very quick and robust. One simply starts the FTP service on their computer (now known as an FTP server) and allows users to connect; users on other computers then to connect to this server using an FTP client program and download any desired files. Most FTP servers available on the Internet allow any user to connect and are hence called anonymous FTP servers. Furthermore, most operating systems—such as Linux, UNIX, Microsoft Windows, and MacOS—are distributed with an FTP client program, making it easy for users to connect to these FTP servers.

Although there are several FTP service software programs available for Linux, the most commonly used is the Washington University FTP Server (wu-ftp), which can be downloaded from the Internet at *http://www.wu-ftpd.org*.

Firewalls and Proxy Services

The term "firewall" originates in the automobile industry. A firewall protects the passengers in a car if a fire breaks out in the engine compartment. Just as an automobile firewall protects passengers, a computer firewall protects companies from outside intruders on the Internet. Most firewalls are computers, which are placed between the company network and the company's connection to the Internet. All traffic must then pass through this firewall, allowing the company to control traffic at this point, using a complex set of rules. Linux has firewall support built directly into the kernel; utilities such as ipchains and netfilter/iptables, which ship with most distributions, can be used to configure the rules necessary to make a system a firewall.

One may find out more about using netfilter/iptables to configure Linux firewalls on the Internet at *http://netfilter.samba.org*.

Since firewalls are usually located between a company's internal network and the Internet, they often provide other services that allow computers inside the company easy access to the Internet. The most common of these services are known as proxy services; a proxy server requests Internet resources such as Web sites and FTP sites on behalf of the computer inside the company. In other words, a workstation computer inside the company simply sends a request to the proxy server connected to the Internet, and the proxy server obtains and returns the requested information to the workstation computer. In addition to this, one proxy server can allow thousands of company workstation computers access to the Internet simultaneously without lengthy configuration of the workstation computers. Proxy servers keep track of the information passed to each client by maintaining a Network Address Translation (NAT) table. Although ipchains and netfilter/iptables can both perform some proxy server functions, the most common proxy server used on Linux is Squid, which also retains a copy of any requested Internet resources (a process known as caching) such that it may respond quicker to future requests for the same resources.

 To obtain or find information regarding the Squid proxy server on the Internet, visit *http://www.squid-cache.org.*

Web Services

While many Internet tools and services are available, the most popular is the Internet browser, which can connect client computers to servers worldwide hosting information of many types: text, pictures, music, binary data, video, and much more. The community of servers that hosts this information is known as the World Wide Web, and a server hosting information is known as a Web server. On a basic level, a Web server is just a server using Hyper Text Transfer Protocol (HTTP) to provide information to requesting Web browsers running on client computers; however, Web servers can also process programs known as Common Gateway Interface (CGI) scripts and provide secure connections such as Secure Socket Layer (SSL). A CGI is a program that runs on the Web server and enables connection to a resource, such as a database, that is running on another server on the network not connected to the Internet. This is very useful because not all information provided over the Internet needs to reside on Web servers. CGIs can be written in several programming languages including C and C++, making them readily compatible with Linux. SSL is a method of communicating with a Web server in which the information passing between the client computer and the Web server is encrypted to keep it secure. This form of transmission is widely used any time confidentiality is required, such as in Internet banking or e-commerce to get a client's credit card information; it is indicated by a change in the browser's address bar from http:// to https://.

There are many Open Source Web server software packages available for Linux. The most widely used is the Apache Web server comprising more than 60% of all Web servers in the world during 2001.

 For more information about the Apache Web server on the Internet, visit *http://www.apache.org.*

News Services

Web servers host valuable information, but most do not provide any means for users to communicate with each other. This functionality is provided by a news server, which allows users to post messages in forums called **newsgroups** and allows other users to read and reply to those messages. Newsgroups are sometimes referred to as computer bulletin boards and are similar to bulletin boards seen around a school campus and in other public places. Persons having or requiring information or services post a notice advertising this that others see and respond to. Newsgroup forums are grouped according to topic and posting to a newsgroup is often a very quick way to find the solution to a problem, since people who read the posting are likely to have had the same problem and found the solution. Many Open Source Software developers use newsgroups to exchange information and coordinate software creation. As with e-mails, a special program called a newsreader is necessary to access newsgroups and read postings hosted on news servers. Common Linux newsreaders include Gnews, Knews, Gnus, Netscape, and pine. The most popular Open Source news server software available for Linux is called InterNetworkNews (INN) and is shipped with most common Linux distributions. INN is maintained by an Open Source organization called the Internet Software Consortium, which continually develops and improves several Open Source Internet technologies.

To obtain a newsreader for Linux from the Internet, visit *http://linux.tucows.com/internet/news.html*. To obtain a copy of INN for Linux from the Internet, visit the Internet Software Consortium at *http://www.isc.org/products/INN.*

DNS Services

Computers communicating on a network need to be uniquely identified. This is accomplished by assigning each computer a number called an **Internet Protocol (IP) address** to allow them to identify and reference each other. Each computer that uses the Internet must have an IP address. An IP address is a long string of numbers, which are meaningless to users and very hard to remember. To make them easier to remember, IP addresses are masked by strings of user-friendly names such as www.linux.org, referred to as a **Fully Qualified Domain Name (FQDN)**. When using a Web browser such as Internet Explorer or Netscape Navigator to request information from a Web server, the address typed into the address box of the browser (i.e., http://www.linux.org) is converted to an IP address before it is sent onto the Internet. In order to translate computer names such as www.linux.org to IP addresses, a server hosting the Domain Naming Service (DNS) is contacted. The DNS server, which has been supplied with the proper FQDN to IP mappings, then returns the correct IP address for the requested server, and the Internet Web browser then uses this IP address to connect to the target Web site. For companies wishing to create a DNS server, Linux is an inexpensive solution, as many distributions of Linux ship with a Domain Name Service known as BIND (Berkeley Internet Name Daemon).

One can find the latest version of BIND on the Internet at the Internet Software Consortium Web site, *http://www.isc.org.*

File and Print Servers

Networks were created to share resources, primarily printers and information. In business, it is not cost effective to purchase and install a printer on the computer of every user who needs to print. It is far easier and cheaper to install one central printer on a server and let multiple users print to it across the computer network. Often, information must also be commonly available to users in order to let them collaborate on projects or perform their daily jobs. Duplicating data on every user machine would consume too much hard drive space, and coordinating changes to this data would be nearly impossible. By employing the use of a network, this information can be made available to all that need it and easily kept up-to-date. Another benefit to this central storage of information is that a user can access data regardless of the computer that he or she logs in to. Central storage also allows a company to safeguard its information by using devices to back up or make copies of stored data on a regular basis in case a computer failure occurs. Most companies perform backups of data at least every week to ensure that if data is lost on the central server, it may be restored from a backup copy quickly.

Linux is well-suited to the task of centrally sharing resources. It is inherently a fast, light operating system, and a distribution specific to a certan task can be installed on the central server. Linux is not only able to share information with other Linux and UNIX machines using services such as Network File System (NFS), but is able to share resources with computers running other operating systems such as Microsoft Windows, MacOS, or IBM OS/2. Client computers are able to access a shared resource on a server running Linux, provided that server has the appropriate service available. The most common service used to allow clients to connect to shared information and printers on a Linux server is Samba, which makes a Linux server appear as a Windows server to Windows clients.

 Samba can be found on the Internet at *http://www.samba.org*.

Application Servers

An application server is one running a program that acts as an intermediary between a client computer and information, normally stored in a database.

A **database** is an organized collection of data that is arranged into tables of related information. The client requests some data to be changed or displayed, and the application server interacts with the database to manipulate and retrieve the required information. This is often described as a front-end / back-end relationship. The front end runs on the client computer and is the interface the user sees and interacts with to request data. The front end takes this request, formulates it such that the server can understand it, and passes the request along to the back-end application running on the server. This back-end application then interacts with the database and returns the results to the front-end application on the client computer, which then puts it into a user-friendly format and displays it to the user. With the rapid development of the Internet in the 1990s, many companies began centralizing their key software elements on Internet application servers, which can serve client computers worldwide; this approach saves both time and money when changes need to be made to the software. It also means only one central database need be maintained. **Database Management Systems (DBMS)** are a collection of programs and tools designed to allow for the creation, modification, manipulation, maintenance, and access of information from databases.

There are several free Open Source DBMS programs and tools to facilitate creation, management, and retrieval of data from a database as well as interaction with a variety of closed source databases including those from Microsoft and Oracle.

For a list of Open Source DBMS software available for Linux on the Internet, visit *http://scilinux.sourceforge.net/database.html*.

The most popular and widely used database software available for Linux today is MySQL (My Structured Query Language). Powerful, fast, and light, it can interact with other databases such as Oracle, and be integrated with most Web servers via CGI scripts for use as an application server on the Internet. Most other Open Source technology has support for MySQL.

To learn more about MySQL on the Internet, visit *http://www.mysql.com*.

Application servers need not only be used for interaction with databases, but can provide management functionality as well, allowing access and administration from anywhere in the world via the Internet. Management interfaces have taken advantage of the comprehensive development surrounding client Web browsers and Internet technologies and now offer a full range of computer management abilities from the comfortable and standard interface of the client Web browser. One common Open Source management interface for Linux is Webmin, which is a customizable application server that gives users the ability to manage almost all services available in Linux from anywhere on the Internet.

Webmin can be found on the Internet at *http://www.webmin.com*.

Supercomputers

Many companies and institutions need to perform extra-ordinarily large calculations that would be unsuitable for most computers. To satisfy these tasks, companies either buy computers having multiple processors or use specialized services to combine several smaller computers together, allowing them to function as one large supercomputer.

Combining several smaller computers together is called **clustering**. Companies and individuals requiring this type of computing are called the supercomputing community, and this community is growing quickly today as technology advances in new directions.

Although it may seem logical to purchase computers that have a large number of processors, the performance of a computer relative to the number of processors decreases as you add processors to a computer. In other words, a computer with 64 processors does not handle 64 times as much work as one processor due to physical limitations within the computer hardware itself; a computer with 64 processors may only perform 50 times as much work as a single processor. The ability of a computer to increase workload as the number of processors increases is known as **scalability**, and most computers, regardless of the operating system used, do not scale well when there are more than 32 processors. As a result of this limitation, many people in the supercomputing community **cluster** several smaller computers together to work as one large computer. This approach results in much better scalability; 64 computers with one processor each working towards a common goal can handle close to 64 times as much as a single processor.

Most of the supercomputing community has focused on Linux when developing clustering technology; the most common method of Linux clustering is known as **Beowulf clustering**, which is easy to configure and well documented. Although there are many different ways to implement a Beowulf cluster, the most common method is to have one master computer send instructions to several slave computers, which compute parts of the calculation concurrently and send their results back to the master computer. This type of supercomputing breaks tasks down into smaller units of execution and executes them in parallel on many machines at once; thus it is commonly referred to as parallel supercomputing, and there are many free programs available written to run on parallelized computers. Beowulf parallel supercomputer technology has been aggressively developed since the mid 1990s and has been tested in various environments; there are currently thousands of Beowulf clusters worldwide in various institutions, companies, and universities.

For more information on the Internet about Beowulf clusters, visit *http://www.beowulf.org*.

Scientific / Engineering Workstations

Many of the developers from Richard Stallman's Free Software Foundation came from the scientific and engineering community, which needed to develop many programs to run analyses. In the 1980s and early 1990s this scientific and engineering community largely developed software for the UNIX operating system that was common in universities around the world. However, today this community is focusing on developing software for Linux; any software previously made for UNIX can be ported to Linux easily. Scientists and engineers often use parallel supercomputers to compute large tasks, and

Open Source Software developers, with a background in scientific computing, have done much of the development on Beowulf technology. One example of this is SHARCnet (Shared Hierarchical Academic Research Computing Network) in Ontario, Canada, in which several universities have developed and tested supercomputing technology and parallel programs for use in the scientific and engineering fields.

 One can find more information about SHARCnet from the Internet at *http://www.sharcnet.ca.*

Often the programs required by the scientific and engineering community must be custom developed to suit the needs of the people involved; however, there are many Open Source Software programs freely available in many different scientific and engineering fields that one can use or modify, including, but not limited to:

- Physics, astrophysics, & biophysics
- Fluid dynamics & geophysics
- Biocomputation
- Materials & polymer chemistry
- General mathematics & optimization
- Data mining
- Number theory
- Computer / linear / array algebra
- Mathematical visualization & modeling
- Statistics & regression analysis
- Data plotting & processing
- Computer graphics generation
- Computer modeling
- Paleontology
- Molecular modeling
- Electrical engineering
- Artificial intelligence
- Geographic modeling & earth sciences
- Oceanography

Office Workstations

Server services for Linux have been the primary focus of Open Source Software development for Linux in the 1990s, but recently this focus has been expanded to many other types of software, including workstation software designed to be of benefit to end users in office and home environments. By definition, a workstation is a single-user computer, more powerful than a typical home system; however, people commonly call any single-user computer that is not a server a workstation. It is where users work and interact, running programs and connecting to servers. Today, one can find many different Open Source Software packages allowing the ability to create, organize, and manipulate office documents and graphic art, including, but not limited to:

- Text editors
- Word processors
- Graphic editing software
- Desktop publishing software
- Financial software
- Office productivity suites

Text Editors

A **text editor** is a program that can create and edit text files. Many text editors offer extra features such as indexing, Linux command input, and automatic color coding for source code constructs in various programming languages such as HTML, PERL, and Python. One of the most popular Open Source text editors available for Linux is the vim (vi improved) editor, which is based on the vi editor for UNIX. The vim editor is small and is shipped with almost every Linux distribution; if one is familiar with using vim, then one will likely find it easy to manipulate files on any Linux computer. Other popular editors include nedit, which is an easy editor for use in GUI environments, and the GNU emacs editor, which also allows one to customize its features using the Lisp programming language designed for artificial intelligence.

 One may find more information about the aforementioned text editors at *http://www.vim.org, http://www.gnu.org,* and *http://www.nedit.org.*

Word Processors

Like text editors, word processors allow the creation and manipulation of text files, but are typically GUI-based, are easier to use, and provide additional functionality when working with documents such as letters, essays, and memos. This added functionality is seen in formatting and additional features such as, but not limited to:

- Margins, tables, and columns
- Page and paper size
- Common style rules
- Font type, size, and special features (bold, italicize, etc.)
- Embedded graphics
- Spelling and grammar checkers
- Page layout and print previews
- Text manipulation tools (find, replace, undo, and redo functions)

Word processors achieve this functionality using special control characters used to send formatting information to a printer. Most word processors hide this information from the user and simply display the text information in a What You See Is What You Get (WYSIWYG) format, meaning the way the information is viewed on the screen is what the output will be when printed to paper. This allows the user to easily create and arrange the document with the appearance of the final printed version in mind. As with most Linux applications there is a host of word processing programs available, however, different word processing programs will store the documents they create in different formats. Fortunately, most current popular word processing programs will recognize and convert for use files stored in a variety of commonplace formats.

One of the most popular and widely used Linux word processors is Abiword, a multi-platform multi-feature application associated with the GNOME user interface, available on the Internet from *http://www.abisource.com*. Another popular word processing program for Linux associated with KDE is Kword, available for download from the Internet through the KDE project Web site at *http://www.kde.org*.

Graphics Editing Software

Graphics editing software includes applications specifically designed to create and manipulate graphical images, such as artwork, photographs, and logos. Images can be cropped and rotated, and colors or color pallettes can be created or modified, among other things. For example, the eye color of a subject in a photograph can be changed and wrinkles erased from the face. There are a number of powerful graphics manipulation tools available for Linux, including kdegraphics, a suite of graphics editors for the KDE interface, and killustrator, also for KDE, which are available for download from the KDE project Web site at *http://www.kde.org*. Another very powerful and extremely popular graphics editor is the GNU Image Manipulation Program (GIMP), which was used to take the screen shots for this book. The latest version of GIMP is available for download on the Internet at *http://www.gimp.org*.

Desktop Publishing Software

Desktop publishing software combines text and graphics editing software together and adds features that allow one to control format and layout. This software is usually used to produce high quality products such as brochures, newsletters, advertising flyers, invitations, and tickets, which once were only available from commercial printing or typesetting companies. Since it is relatively inexpensive to purchase computers and high quality printers, people commonly use desktop publishing software to create these products at home. LyX is an example of a powerful Open Source Software program that allows one to lay out their document according to structure; LyX then uses a program called Latex to create the visual layout. LyX is very popular in academic circles, as it allows researchers the ability to easily organize their findings without having to concentrate on layout.

 LyX can be downloaded from the Internet at *http://www.lyx.org*.

Since many word processors today can also manipulate and embed graphical objects, these word processors are also referred to as desktop publishing software. Most users today simply utilize graphic editing software to manipulate images they have scanned in or otherwise uploaded to their computers and then import and embed these images into documents they manipulate and format with word processing applications.

Financial Software

Financial software describes a family of applications designed to track financial transactions and perform bookkeeping and accounting procedures, in areas of both personal and business finances. From balancing a checkbook to running a business and keeping its books balanced, there are numerous applications designed to meet the purpose, some even providing database integration. Examples include programs such as Kfinance and Kmymoney2 for the KDE interface, or Gnucash for the GNOME interface, all available for download from the Internet through Sourceforge at *http://www.sourceforge.net*.

Office Productivity Suites

A suite is a collection of things, as in a suite of rooms or a musical suite. Office productivity suites are merely collections of applications offered in combination to meet a variety of standard needs seen in business or the home, ranging from word processing and graphics manipulation to project management, presentation, and spreadsheet and database tools. We have discussed word processors, databases, and graphics manipulation applications. Project management utilities include schedulers, timesheets, and project status, tracking, and e-mail tools. Presentation utilities allow for the compilation of slide shows, graphs, and various audio-visual aids to be used during seminars or presentations. Spreadsheets display numerical information, normally arranged in rows and columns, and allow calculations and other manipulations to be performed on the data, as well as the creation of charts and graphs.

There are office productivity suites available for both of the Linux GUI interfaces. The KDE suite is called Koffice and, along with support and documentation, is available on the Internet at *http://www.koffice.org*. The GNOME office productivity suite called Gnome Office is available on the Internet at *http://www.gnome.org/gnome-office*. Both of these are powerful and free Open Source tools; however, there is another common office suite available for Linux: Sun Microsystem's StarOffice. While it is not OSS, it is free and probably the most powerful and versatile of the free office suites available for Linux. It is available for a variety of different operating systems and supports many different languages; one can download it from the Internet at *http://www.sun.com/staroffice*.

CHAPTER SUMMARY

- ❏ Linux is an operating system whose kernel and many additional software packages are freely developed and improved upon by a large community of software developers in collaboration. It is based on the UNIX operating system and has roots in the hacker culture perpetuated by the Free Software Foundation.

- ❏ Since Linux is published under the GNU Public License we refer to it as Open Source Software. Most additional software that is run on Linux is also Open Source Software.

- ❏ Companies find Linux a stable, low-risk, and flexible alternative to other operating systems, which can be installed on several different hardware platforms to meet business needs and result in a lower Total Cost of Ownership.

- ❏ Linux is available in different distributions, all of which have a common kernel but are packaged with different Open Source Software applications.

- ❏ There exists a wide variety of documentation and resources for Linux in the form of Internet Web sites, HOWTOs, FAQs, newsgroups, and LUGs.

- ❏ Linux is an extremely versatile operating system that can provide a wide range of workstation and server services to meet most computing needs of companies and individuals.

KEY TERMS

AIX — A version of UNIX developed by IBM.

application — Software that runs on an operating system and provides the user with specific functionality (e.g., word processing or financial calculation).

artistic license — An Open Source license that allows source code to be distributed freely, but changed only at the discretion of the original author.

Beowulf cluster — A popular and widespread method of clustering computers together to perform useful tasks using Linux.

BSD (Berkeley Software Distribution) — A version of UNIX, developed out of the original UNIX source code, and given away free by AT&T to the University of California at Berkeley.

Caldera — A version of Linux supported and distributed by Caldera Systems Inc.

closed source software — Software whose source code is not freely available from the original author. Windows 98 is an example of closed source software.

cluster —Several smaller computers that function as one large supercomputer.

clustering — The act of making a cluster. *See* cluster.

cracker — Someone who uses computer software maliciously for personal profit.

database — An organized set of data.

Database Management System (DBMS) — Software that manages databases.

developmental kernel — A Linux kernel whose minor number is odd and has been recently developed, but not thoroughly tested.

device driver — A piece of software that contains instructions that the kernel of an operating system uses to control and interact with a specific type of computer hardware.

distribution — A complete set of Linux operating system software including the kernel, supporting function libraries, and a variety of Open Source Software packages that can be downloaded from the Internet free of charge. These Open Source Software packages are what differentiate the various distributions of Linux.

Free Software Foundation — An organization started by Richard Stallman that promotes and encourages the collaboration of software developers worldwide allowing the free sharing of source code and software programs.

freeware — Computer software programs distributed and made available at no cost to the user by the developer.

Frequently Asked Questions (FAQ) — An area on a Web site where answers to commonly posed questions can be found.

Fully Qualified Domain Name (FQDN) — A string of words identifying a server on the Internet.

GNU Object Model Environment (GNOME) — One of the two competing Graphical User Interface (GUI) environments for Linux.

GNU Project — A free operating system project started by Richard Stallman.

GNU Public License — A software license, ensuring that the source code for any Open Source Software will remain freely available to anyone who wants to examine, build on, or improve upon it.

graphical user interface (GUI) — The component of an operating system that provides a user-friendly interface comprising graphics or icons to represent desired tasks. Users can point and click to execute a command rather than having to know and use proper command line syntax.

GUI environment —A GUI core component such as X Windows, combined with a window manager and desktop environment, which provides the look and feel of the GUI. Although functionality may be similar among GUI environments, users may prefer one environment to another due to its ease of use.

hacker — Someone who explores computer science to gain knowledge. Not to be confused with cracker.

hardware — Tangible parts of a computer, such as the network boards, video card, hard disk drives, printers, and keyboards.

hardware platform — A particular configuration and grouping of computer hardware, normally centered on and determined by processor type and architecture.

hot fix — A solution for a software bug made by a closed source vendor.

HOWTO — A task-specific instruction guide to performing any of a wide variety of tasks; freely available from the Linux Documentation Project at *http://www.linuxdoc.org.*

HP-UX — A version of UNIX developed by Hewlett-Packard.

Internet — A large network of interconnected networks connecting company networks, home computers, and institutional networks together so that they can communicate with each other.

Internet Protocol (IP) address — A unique string of numbers assigned to a computer to uniquely identify it on the Internet.

kernel — The central, core program of an operating system. The shared commonality of the kernel is what defines Linux, the differing Open Source Software applications that can interact with the common kernel is what differentiates Linux distributions.

Kommon Desktop Environment (KDE) — One of the two competing Graphical User Interfaces (GUI) available for Linux.

Linus Torvalds — Finnish graduate student who coded and created the first version of Linux and subsequently distributed it under the GNU Public License.

Linux — A software operating system originated by Linus Torvalds. The common core, or kernel, continues to evolve and be revised. Differing Open Source Software bundled with the Linux kernel is what defines the wide variety of distributions now available.

Linux Documentation Project (LDP) — A large collection of Linux resources, information, and help files, supplied free of charge and maintained by the Linux community.

Linux User Group (LUG) — An open forum of Linux users who discuss and assist each other in using and modifying the Linux operating system and the Open Source Software run on it. There are LUGs worldwide.

mail delivery agent (MDA) — The service that downloads e-mail from a mail transfer agent.

1

mail transfer agent (MTA) — An e-mail server.

mail user agent (MUA) — A program that allows e-mail to be read by a user.

major number — The number preceding the first dot in the number used to identify a Linux kernel version. It is used to denote a major change or modification.

MINIX — Mini-UNIX, created by Andrew Tannenbaum. Instructions on how to code the kernel for this version of the UNIX operating system were publicly available. Using this as a starting point, Linus Torvalds improved this version of UNIX for the Intel platform and created the first version of Linux.

minor number — The number following the first dot in the number used to identify a Linux kernel version, denoting a minor modification. If odd, it is a version under development and not yet fully tested. *See* developmental kernel and production kernel.

Multiplexed Information and Computing Service (MULTICS) — A prototype time-sharing operating system that was developed in the late 1960's by AT&T Bell Laboratories.

multitasking — A type of operating system that has the ability to manage multiple tasks simultaneously.

multiuser — A type of operating system that has the ability to provide access to multiple users simultaneously.

newsgroup — An Internet protocol service accessed via an application program called a newsreader. This service allows access to postings (e-mails in a central place accessible by all newsgroup users) normally organized along specific themes. Users with questions on specific topics can post messages, which may be answered by other users.

Open Source Software (OSS) — Programs distributed and licensed so that the source code making up the program is freely available to anyone who wants to examine, utilize, or improve upon it.

operating system (OS) — Software used to control and directly interact with the computer hardware components.

package manager — Software used to install, maintain, and remove other software programs by storing all relevant information in a central software database on the computer.

process — A program loaded into memory and running on the processor performing a specific task.

production kernel — A Linux kernel whose minor number (the number after the dot in the version number) is even and deemed stable for use through widespread testing.

program — Sets of instructions that know how to interact with the operating system and computer hardware to perform specific tasks, stored as a file on some media (i.e., hard disk drive).

programming language — The syntax used for developing a program. There are different programming languages that use different syntax.

Red Hat — One of the most popular and prevalent distributions of Linux in North America, distributed and supported by Red Hat Inc.

revision number — The number after the second dot in the version number of a Linux kernel, which identifies the certain release number of a kernel.

router — A computer running routing software, or a special function hardware device, providing interconnection between networks; it contains information regarding the structure of the networks and sends information from one component network to another.

scalability — The ability of computers to increase workload as the number of processors increases.

search engine — An Internet Web site that allows one to search the World Wide Web for specific information using keywords to conduct a search.

server — A computer configured to allow other computers to connect to it from across a network.

server services — Services that are made available for other computers across a network.

shareware — Programs developed and provided at minimal cost to the end user. These programs are initially free but require payment after a period of time or usage.

software — Programs stored on a storage device in a computer that provide a certain function when executed.

Solaris — A version of UNIX developed by Sun Microsystems from AT&T source code.

source code — The sets of organized instructions on how to function and perform tasks that defines or constitutes a program.

SuSE — One of the most popular and prevalent distributions of Linux in Europe.

system service — Additional functionality provided by a program that has been incorporated into and started as part of the operating system.

tarball — A compressed archive of files that contain scripts that install Linux software to the correct locations on a computer system.

text editor — A program that allows the creation, modification, and manipulation of a text file.

Total Cost of Ownership (TCO) — The full sum of all accumulated costs, over and above the simple purchase price of utilizing a product. It includes such sundries as training, maintenance, additional hardware, and downtime.

UNIX — The first true multitasking, multiuser operating system, developed by Ken Thompson and Dennis Ritchie, from which Linux originated.

user interface —What the user sees and uses to interact with the operating system and application programs.

workstation — A computer used to connect to services on a server.

workstation services — Services that are used on a local computer.

X Windows — The core component of the GUI in Linux.

REVIEW QUESTIONS

1. Every computer consists of physical components and logical components. The logical components of a computer, which understand how to work with the physical components, are referred to as:

   a. hardware

   b. records

   c. software

   d. processors

2. The operating system software is necessary for a computer to function. True or False?

3. Linux is a _____ and _____ operating system.

   a. production, stable

   b. multiuser, multitasking

   c. processing, operating

   d. large, useful

4. The core component of the Linux operating system is the Linux kernel. If you were a Linux systems administrator for a company, when would you need to upgrade your Linux kernel? (Choose all that apply.)

   a. when you need to have support in Linux for new hardware

   b. when you need another user interface

   c. when you need to increase the stability of Linux

   d. when you need to use kernel modules

5. Which of the following kernels are developmental kernels? (Choose all that apply.)

   a. 2.3.4

   b. 2.5.5

   c. 2.2.7

   d. 2.4.4

6. A production kernel refers to a kernel whose:

   a. revision number is even

   b. minor number is odd

   c. major number is odd

   d. minor number is even

7. There are many types of software today. Which type of software does Linux represent?

   a. Open Source Software

   b. closed source software

   c. freeware

   d. shareware

8. Which of the following are characteristics of Open Source Software? (Choose all that apply.)

   a. The value of the software is directly related to its price.

   b. Software is developed collaboratively.

   c. Source code for software is available for a small fee.

   d. Any bugs are fixed quickly.

9. Which license does Linux adhere to?

   a. Open license

   b. Artistic license

   c. GNU Public License

   d. Free Source License

10. What are some good reasons for using Linux in a corporate environment? (Choose all that apply.)

    a. Linux software is unlikely to become abandoned by its developers.

    b. Linux is secure and has a lower Total Cost of Ownership than other operating systems.

    c. Linux is widely available for many platforms and supports many programming languages.

    d. Most Linux software is closed source.

11. Which of the following are common methods for gaining support for Linux?

    a. HOWTO documents at *http://www.linuxdoc.org*

    b. A local Linux User Group

    c. Internet newsgroups

    d. All the above

12. Which two people are accredited with creating the UNIX operating system? (Choose both that apply.)

    a. Dennis Ritchie

    b. Richard Stallman

    c. Linus Torvalds

    d. Ken Thompson

13. Who formed the Free Software Foundation to promote open development?

 a. Dennis Ritchie

 b. Richard Stallman

 c. Linus Torvalds

 d. Ken Thompson

14. Which culture embraced the term GNU (GNU's Not UNIX) and laid the free software groundwork for Linux?

 a. the hacker culture

 b. the MIT culture

 c. the cracker culture

 d. the Artificial Intelligence culture

15. Linux was developed by _____ to resemble the _____ operating system.

 a. Linus Torvalds, MINIX

 b. Linus Torvalds, GNU

 c. Richard Stallman, GNU

 d. Richard Stallman, MINIX

16. When the core components of the Linux operating system are packaged together with other Open Source Software, we call this a:

 a. new kernel

 b. new platform

 c. Linux distribution

 d. GNU Project

17. Which common GUI environments are available in most Linux distributions? (Choose all that apply.)

 a. GNOME

 b. CDE

 c. KDE

 d. RPM

18. Which of the following are factors that determine which Linux distribution one will use? (Choose all that apply.)

 a. Package manager support

 b. Hardware platform

 c. Kernel features

 d. Language support

19. What is the most common Open Source Web server available for Linux?

    a. Samba

    b. Apache

    c. Quid

    d. Pine

20. Which of the following can be used on Linux to provide file and print services?

    a. Samba

    b. Apache

    c. Quid

    d. Pine

21. Joe wishes to create documents such as memos, letters, charts, and presentations. What type of program does Joe need?

    a. Desktop publishing software

    b. Text editor

    c. Office productivity suite

    d. Word processor

22. Linux can be used to restrict other computers on the Internet from accessing your company network. What do we call such a Linux server?

    a. an FTP server

    b. a supercomputer

    c. a DNS server

    d. a firewall

23. Which of the following Internet Web site addresses is likely an Open Source Project Web site?

    a. *www.crazy.net*

    b. *www.appserv.org*

    c. *www.ftp.com*

    d. *www.google.com*

DISCOVERY EXERCISES

1. You work for a large manufacturing company, which is considering Linux as a solution for some or all servers in its IT department. The company hosts an Oracle database on UNIX, and the UNIX servers that host this database contain several small programs that were custom made. Furthermore, Windows 98 is currently used on desktops throughout the company, and users store their data on

Windows NT file servers. What considerations must you keep in mind before migrating your company's servers to Linux? Which distribution(s) and Open Source Software would you choose to accomplish this? If you needed to create a report detailing the benefits of moving to an Open Source solution using Linux, what benefits would you list in the report to persuade others in the company that Linux lowers the Total Cost of Ownership

2. While attending a local Linux User Group (LUG) meeting you are asked by some people who are unfamiliar with Linux to explain what a GPL is and how it relates to Open Source Software. These people also find it difficult to understand how Open Source Software generates profit, and have heard from others that Open Source Software is of poor quality compared to commercial software and as a result may not be predominant in the future. How will you formulate your answer to these people and what examples will you use to demonstrate your points? Which Web sites can you direct them to for further information?

3. As a software developer working for a large clothing store chain, you are responsible for creating software used to connect retail store computers to a central database at the head office. Recently, some friends of yours have suggested that you publish your software under the GPL. What are some direct benefits to publishing your software under the GPL? To publish software made for a company under the GPL, one will need the permission of the company, as the company currently owns any software that it pays developers to create. When you approach people in your company regarding Open Source Software and explain how companies benefit from releasing software Open Source, you are asked what benefits the company will receive from funding an Open Source project over time (i.e., paying your salary) and what the procedure is for releasing and maintaining Open Source Software. What benefits will you offer them, and where could you send them to gain more information on procedures involved in the Open Source community?

4. You are a network administrator who is in charge of a medium-sized Linux network. The company you work for asks you to implement routing in the network, which is a topic that you are unfamiliar with. Where could you go to learn what you must obtain to enable routing on your Linux network? Provided that you have a functional Web browser and an Internet connection, explore this topic on the Internet and list the Web sites that you used to obtain the information required. This information may range from broad descriptions of what you need to do to accomplish a certain task to detailed guides and instructions on putting your plan into action. From these sources of information, devise a report outlining the major steps necessary to implement routing on your network.

5. At a company function a top executive corners you and complains that your department is wasting too much money. The executive demands to know why the company must spend so much money on computers and software, especially operating systems and related licenses (for closed source programs and operating systems). Write a report that defends your department by explaining the nature of

hardware, software, and operating systems. In the report, be sure to explain how Open Source Software and the Linux operating system can be used to reduce this cost in the long term.

6. You are contacted by a project organizer for a university computer science fair. The project organizer asks you to hold a forum that discusses the origins of the Linux operating system, how it has evolved, and how it continues to develop. The main focus of this forum is to encourage university students towards participating in the Open Source community and as a result should also detail the philosophy, major features, and methods of the hacker culture. Prepare a point-form list of the major topics that you will discuss, and write down some sample questions that you anticipate from the participants as well as your responses.

7. Provided that you have a functional Web browser and an Internet connection, research three different distributions of Linux on the Internet. Record where you went to obtain your information, and compare and contrast the different distributions with regard to the strengths of each and available packages. Once finished, locate and visit two Linux newsgroups. How did you locate them and where did you obtain the information? What are the topic areas specific to each? Find two questions per newsgroup posted by a user in need of a solution to a problem and follow the thread of responses suggested by others to solve that problem.

2

PREPARING FOR LINUX INSTALLATION

After completing this chapter, you will be able to:

♦ Describe common types of central processing units
♦ Describe common types of physical memory
♦ Describe common types of disk drives and other storage devices
♦ Describe mainboards and peripheral devices
♦ Describe video adapter cards and monitors
♦ Describe keyboards and mice
♦ Obtain the hardware information necessary to install Linux
♦ Obtain the software information necessary to install Linux

A computer is composed of hardware, which is simply a collection of switches and circuits that require operating system software to function in a meaningful way. This chapter introduces you to the hardware and software terminology necessary to install a Linux system and discusses how to obtain this information from several sources.

Understanding Hardware

Fundamental to the installation of Linux is an understanding of the various hardware components of the computer. This allows the user to make certain that any hardware detected automatically during installation was detected correctly and that the hardware meets any installation requirements. The hardware components necessary to understand prior to installing Linux include:

- Central processing units (CPUs)
- Physical memory
- Disk drives
- Mainboards & peripheral components
- Video adapter cards
- Keyboards & mice

Central Processing Units (CPUs)

The core component of any computer is the **central processing unit (CPU)**, also known as the microprocessor or processor; it is where the vast majority of all calculations and processing of information takes place. Processors are integrated circuit boards consisting of millions of transistors forming electrical pathways through which electricity is channeled. They consist of two main components: the **arithmetic logic unit** and the **control unit**. The arithmetic logic unit is where all the mathematical calculations and logic-based operations are executed. The control unit is where instruction code or commands are loaded and carried out, and it also often sends information to the arithmetic logic unit for execution.

Processors can have their integral electronics arranged in different ways; this is referred to as the processor's **architecture** or platform. Recall from Chapter 1 that the Linux operating system is available for many different platforms including SPARC (Scaleable Processor ARChitecture), Alpha, and Intel. These different arrangements of electrical circuits can have a determined effect on the processor's speed of executing certain types of instructions. Hence, we categorize processors based on the types of instructions they execute. The two main categories of processor architectures are **Complex Instruction Set Computer (CISC) processors** and **Reduced Instruction Set Computer (RISC) processors**. CISC processors normally execute more complex commands than RISC processors; however, since complex commands take longer to execute on a processor, RISC processors tend to be faster than CISC processors. We shall limit our discussion to the Intel processor architecture throughout the remainder of this text, as it is the most common CISC processor available in homes and businesses around the world.

The speed at which a processor can execute commands is related to an internal time cycle referred to as **clock speed**. Similar to the way a quartz watch keeps time, the

2

processor has a crystal that oscillates at a determinable frequency when current is passed though it. This is the drumbeat to which the processor keeps time and by which all actions are measured. The clock speed is measured in Megahertz (MHz), or millions of cycles per second; a processor running at 200MHz has a clock speed or oscillation frequency of 200 million cycles per second. A processor may require one cycle to complete a command or may be **superscalar**, that is, able to complete more than one command in any given cycle. In either case, the faster the clock speed of the processor, the greater the number of commands it can execute in a given span of time.

The clock speed of the processor in a computer is separate from and does not need to match the clock speed of other hardware components in the computer; in most cases the clock speed of the processor is the fastest of any hardware component inside the computer.

Clock speed alone is not the sole determination of the speed at which a processor can work. The amount of information a processor can work with or process at any given time, measured in binary digits **(bits)**, is also a major factor. Hence, processors are also classified by how much information they can work with at a given time; the more information that can be moved or worked on at once the faster data can be manipulated. A computer able to process 16 bits of information at a time is over twice as fast as one that can process 8 bits of information at a time; an 8-bit processor running at 800MHz would be comparable to a 16-bit processor running at 350MHz. Processors today typically work with 32 or 64 bits of information at a time; most Intel processors available today such as the Pentium Processor series are 32-bit processors and much cheaper than their 64-bit counterparts, such as the Intel Itanium, SPARC, and Alpha processors.

In addition to the number of bits a processor can handle at one time, a computer's cache size and location also affect a processor's ability to calculate larger volumes of data. A **cache** is a temporary store of information; processors can use cache to store recently used instruction sets or information for future use. The more information a processor can store on its local circuit board in a processor cache, the faster it will be able to execute repetitive or frequently used instruction sets. A cache stored in the processor itself is referred to as **Level 1 (L1) cache**. Not all processors have Level 1 caches, and if they do they are not necessarily the same size. In place of, or in addition to, Level 1 cache, processors can utilize **Level 2 (L2) cache**, which is information stored for retrieval in a separate computer chip that is connected to the processor via a high speed link. Although not as fast as Level 1 cache, Level 2 cache is a much cheaper alternative and more common.

In a situation that requires more processing ability than can be provided by a single processor, one may choose to add more than one processor to a system. Multiple processors can then work together to distribute the load and perform the same tasks faster; however, multiprocessor support must be incorporated into the Linux kernel during installation. The most common kernel configuration for using multiple processors is called **Symmetric Multi-Processing (SMP)** and allows the same operating system and memory use of both processors simultaneously for any task. Another configuration called

ASymmetric Multi-Processing (ASMP) refers to a system where each processor is given a certain role or set of tasks to complete independent of the other processors.

Physical Memory

Physical memory is a storage area for information that is directly wired through circuit boards to the processor. Physical memory is divided into two major categories: **Random Access Memory (RAM)** and **Read Only Memory (ROM)**. Both RAM and ROM are stored on computer chips and allow access to information. However, RAM requires a constant supply of electricity to maintain stored information whereas ROM is static in nature and able to store information even when there is no power to the system. Following this, we refer to RAM as **volatile** memory since its contents are lost when one turns the computer off, whereas ROM is labeled as non-volatile memory.

RAM

As discussed in Chapter 1, software programs are files that contain instructions to be executed by the processor and are loaded into RAM physical memory upon execution; the processor can then work with the instructions in memory. The amount of RAM is directly related to computer performance, since greater amounts of RAM memory allow more programs to run simultaneously on the system. Different programs require different amounts of memory to execute properly; thus software programs, including operating systems, specify a minimum amount of RAM in their documentation. A Linux machine running the GNOME desktop GUI environment requires more memory than a Linux machine that does not use any GUI environments.

RAM is classified into two major types: **Dynamic RAM (DRAM)** and **Static RAM (SRAM)**. DRAM is the cheaper of the two types and thus the most common. It has a slower access speed compared to SRAM and the information store it holds must be refreshed thousands of times a second, necessitating a continuous, uninterrupted flow of electricity. If the flow of electricity to the DRAM chip is disrupted even for the briefest of moments, the information store will be lost. DRAM is the type of physical memory commonly referred to simply as computer memory and is seen as an array of integrated circuits (chips) arranged on a small board called a stick, which in turn is connected into the computer's main circuit board via slots. The number of transistors making up the chips on a stick of DRAM determines the amount of information that can be stored, measured in megabytes (MB).

Two different sticks of DRAM may have the same physical dimensions, but could hold vastly different amounts of information. There are two main types of DRAM sticks: **Single In-line Memory Modules (SIMM)** and **Dual In-line Memory Modules (DIMM)**. SIMMs are the older of the two and connect the array of integrated circuits comprising it to the motherboard via a connection having connectors (pins) along only one edge; SIMMs are no longer produced and are not commonly seen today. DIMM are widely used today and connect the array of integrated circuits comprising them to the motherboard via a connection having pins along both edges; having more connections, DIMMs are able to store more information and transfer it more rapidly than SIMMs.

As technology changes, so does the nature of DRAM and the speed at which it works. Two recent DIMM technologies include **Synchronous Dynamic Random Access Memory (SDRAM)** and **Rambus Dynamic Random Access Memory (RDRAM)**. SDRAM uses the standard DIMM connector on the motherboard and transfers data to and from the store on the memory module in bursts and at a higher speed than traditional DRAM. RDRAM is a proprietary product that uses a RIMM connection, which is a DIMM with different pin settings, and runs at a very high clock speed, thus transferring data at a rapid rate. RIMM is not an acronym, but a trademarked word of the Rambus Corporation.

The second major type of RAM, Static RAM (SRAM), is more expensive to produce and allows faster access time to stored information since the information store does not need constant refreshing and can go for short periods without a flow of electricity. Nonetheless, this interruption in electrical flow must be brief, and the information store is lost when the computer is powered down. SRAM is the type of physical memory used for Level 2 processor caches and any memory chips attached directly to the main circuit boards of the computer.

ROM

Read Only Memory (ROM) is physical memory that can be read but not written to, and is stored in a permanent, non-volatile manner on integrated circuits (computer chips) inside the computer. Unlike RAM, this memory store is not reliant on the flow of electricity and will remain intact for an indefinite period on the computer in the absence of power. Due to this property, ROM is often used to store the programs used to initialize hardware components when starting a computer; this is known as **BIOS (Basic Input/Output System) ROM**. While true ROMs are still in use, the fact that the information store in a ROM computer chip is immutable led to variants that are maintained in the absence of electrical flow but can be altered if need be. These ROM variants include:

- **Programmable Read Only Memory (PROM)**, which consists of a blank ROM computer chip that can be written to once and never rewritten again.

- **Erasable Programmable Read Only Memory (EPROM)**, in which the information contents can be erased and rewritten repeatedly. The contents of EPROM must be erased and rewritten as a whole; individual parts cannot be singly modified. An example of EPROM memory is the **Complementary Metal–Oxide Semiconductor (CMOS)** computer chip in a computer, which stores the configuration information used by the BIOS ROM when the system is first powered on.

- **Electronically Erasable Programmable Read Only Memory (EEPROM)**, which maintains an information store that can not only be erased and rewritten as a whole, but can be modified singly leaving other portions intact. This ability to store information statically in the absence of electricity yet modify it if needed is why EEPROM chips are popular in many peripheral computer components.

Disk Drives

Most information in a computer is maintained using media that is non-volatile and does not consist of integrated circuits; the most common media of this type used today include **hard disks**, which are stored in **hard disk drives** (also referred to as hard drives or HDDs); **Compact Disk-Read Only Memory (CD-ROM)** disks, which are inserted into CD-ROM disk drives; and **floppy disks**, which are inserted into floppy disk drives. **Disk drive** devices do not transfer data as fast as RAM or ROM can, but can store vast amounts of modifiable information in a cost effective manner on the disks they contain for later use. When information is needed by the processor, it is transferred from the disk drive to RAM, such as when the operating system starts during system startup or when application programs are executed on a running system.

Hard Disk Drives

Traditionally, most information was stored on magnetic tape by magnetic tape devices; this use of a magnetic medium was quickly transferred to the floppy drives and hard disk drives we use today. The process works similar to the way audio and video tapes are recorded and played back. A surface is covered with a ferrous material, and the constituent particles of this ferrous material can be rearranged by electro-magnetic heads to record data and then read by detecting the pattern of arrangement using the same equipment. Unlike magnetic tape devices, which must fast-forward or rewind magnetic tape in order to read or write data, HDDs read and write information to and from magnetic material coating rigid metal platters by spinning these platters rapidly under moveable arms holding electro-magnetic heads. HDDs are not directly wired to the processor, but must pass through a hard disk controller card that controls the flow of information to and from the HDD. These controller cards come in two general types: **Integrated Drive Electronics (IDE)** and **Small Computer Systems Interface (SCSI)**. Hard drives that connect to these controllers must be of the same type; one must use IDE hard disks with an IDE controller card and SCSI hard disks with a SCSI controller card.

IDE controllers, also known as **Advanced Technology Attachment (ATA)** controllers, are usually circuit boards found on the bottom of an IDE hard drive and connect to the mainboard via a ribbon cable. Most mainboards contain two slots for IDE ribbon cables (a primary controller slot and a secondary controller slot), and each IDE ribbon cable can have up to two IDE hard drives attached to it; thus most computers are limited to four IDE hard drives. Since each IDE ribbon cable can have two IDE hard drives attached to it, there must be a method that can uniquely identify each IDE hard drive. This method involves setting jumper switches on the physical IDE hard drive such that one IDE hard drive is called "master" and one IDE hard drive is called "slave" on the same ribbon cable. Hence we may call the master hard drive connected to the primary IDE controller slot a "primary master IDE HDD." The four possible IDE hard drive configurations and their Linux names are listed in Table 2-1.

Table 2-1 IDE HDD configurations

Description	Linux Name
Primary Master IDE HDD	hda
Primary Slave IDE HDD	hdb
Secondary Master IDE HDD	hdc
Secondary Slave IDE HDD	hdd

Unlike IDE, SCSI controllers are physically separate from the HDD and are usually attached to the mainboard via slots on the mainboard itself. SCSI hard drives are able to transfer data at much faster rates than IDE hard drives, and the SCSI controller card can interact with more than one HDD at a time. However, IDE hard drives and controllers are cheaper to manufacture than their SCSI counterparts and thus are the most common hard drive technology in homes and small-to-medium sized businesses. For the purposes of this chapter, we will restrict our discussion to IDE hard disks.

Hard drives manufactured today can store over 80 Gigabytes (GB) of data, and are often divided up into small, more manageable sections called **partitions**. Each partition must then be prepared to store files. To do this, you must format each partition with a **filesystem** that specifies how data should reside on the hard disk itself.

In the Windows operating system, each drive letter (C:, D:, E:) may correspond to a separate filesystem that resides on a partition on the hard drive.

There are limits to the number and type of partitions into which an HDD can be divided. Hard disk drives can contain a maximum of four major partitions (called **primary partitions**). To overcome this limitation, you may optionally label one of these primary partitions as "extended;" this **extended partition** can then contain an unlimited number of smaller partitions called **logical drives**. Each logical drive within the extended partition and all other primary partitions may contain its own filesystem and be used to store data. The table of all partition information for a given hard disk is stored in the first readable sector, called the **Master Boot Record (MBR)**, which is outside all partitions. Recall that a primary master IDE HDD is referred to as hda in Linux; the first primary partition on this drive would be labeled hda1, the second hda2, and so on. Since there may be four primary partitions on a hard disk, logical drives inside the extended partition are labeled hda5, hda6, and so on, regardless of which primary partition is labeled as extended. An example of this partition strategy is listed in Table 2-2.

Table 2-2   Example partitioning scheme for a primary master IDE HDD

Description	Linux Name	Windows Name
First primary partition on the primary master HDD	hda1	C:
Second primary partition on the primary master HDD	hda2	D:
Third primary partition on the primary master HDD	hda3	E:
Fourth primary partition on the primary master HDD (EXTENDED)	hda4	F:
First logical drive in the extended partition on the primary master HDD	hda5	G:
Second logical drive in the extended partition on the primary master HDD	hda6	H:
Third logical drive in the extended partition on the primary master HDD	hda7	I:

Other Information Storage Devices

In addition to HDDs there are other information stores available including floppy disks, CD-ROM disks, and zip disks. These are often referred to as **removable media**, because the medium used to store the information is not fixed in the computer as with an HDD, but removable and transferable between computers.

Floppy disks store information electro-magnetically like hard disks and are traditionally the most common removable medium; they are referred to as floppy because the medium covered with ferrous material used to store information is flexible (or floppy) in contrast to the rigid metal platters used in HDDs. Floppy drives, also referred to as 3½-inch floppy drives in reference to the size of the removable storage unit, can hold much less data than HDDs (only 1.44MB) and have much slower data transfer rates.

Zip disks are an evolution of floppy disks and, although they look physically similar, they differ from regular floppies in that they can hold considerably more information (up to 250MB). These sophisticated floppy disks cannot use regular 3½-inch floppy disk drive units; they need to be used with special zip drives, yet are commonly used to transport large files or make back-up copies of important information in many homes and small offices.

CD-ROM disks differ from all other disk media mentioned insofar as they do not use ferrous material and electro-magnetic heads to store and retrieve data, but instead use lasers to read reflected light pulses. A pitted layer of reflective material, normally aluminum, is sandwiched between layers of clear plastic and laser pulses are bounced off it. The pits in the surface deflect the laser pulses hitting them and the resulting pattern of disruption in reflection of laser pulses is read as stored information. This technology gives CD-ROMs some advantages over other removable storage devices, including greater data transfer speed, larger storage capacity, and more resistance to data loss. This makes them very useful in storing large amounts of data, and as a result are the choice medium for distributing software such as the Linux operating system.

CD-ROM drives are rated by the speed at which they can read data from the CD-ROM disc compared to the speed of a regular audio Compact Disc (CD); typical CD-ROMs today can read data over 50 times (50X) the speed of an audio CD. Most CD-ROM drives are connected to the main circuit boards in a computer via an Advanced Technology Attachment Packet Interface (ATAPI) that allows them to act like an IDE HDD. Typically, one of the four possible IDE devices in a computer is a CD-ROM drive, and this drive must be configured using jumper switches on the CD-ROM drive itself in the same fashion as IDE hard disk drives.

Although the data transfer rate of a CD-ROM drive is faster than that of a floppy or zip drive, it is still slower than that of an HDD. If a CD-ROM drive is placed on the same IDE channel as an HDD it will impact and slow down the effective data transfer rate of the HDD; as a result, it is wise to place CD-ROM drives on an IDE controller separate from any IDE HDDs.

Many CD-ROM drives today can also write information to CD-ROM disks; these devices are called Compact Disk ReWritable (CD-RW) drives.

Mainboards and Peripheral Components

Programs are loaded into physical memory and executed by the processor; however, there must exist some device that provides the interconnect between these hardware devices. This interconnect (also called a **bus**) is provided by a circuit board called the **mainboard** or **motherboard**. The bus serves to connect common hardware components such as the processor, physical memory, and disk drives, but also connects **peripheral components** such as video cards, sound cards, and **network interface cards (NICs)**. Peripheral components commonly connect to the rest of the system by means of an Input/Output bus (also known as an I/O bus or expansion bus) that is represented by different slots or ports on the mainboard itself. The three most common slots for peripheral devices include:

- ISA
- PCI
- AGP

Industry Standard Architecture (ISA) slots only allow peripheral components an interconnect that transfers information at a speed of 8MHz and are much less common than other slots, as they are used to connect older components. **Peripheral Component Interconnect (PCI)** is a much newer bus connection that was introduced in 1995 and is the most common type of slot found in computers today; it can transfer information at a speed of 33MHz and can use **Direct Memory Access (DMA)**. DMA allows a peripheral to bypass the CPU and talk directly with other peripheral components to enhance performance; there are 8 DMA channels one can configure to allow this ability. **Accelerated Graphics Port (AGP)** is designed for video card peripherals and allows a transfer speed of over 66MHz. It was not designed to replace PCI, but to enhance video card operations and allow for faster access to system memory for graphical functions. A mainboard with these slots can be seen in Figure 2-1.

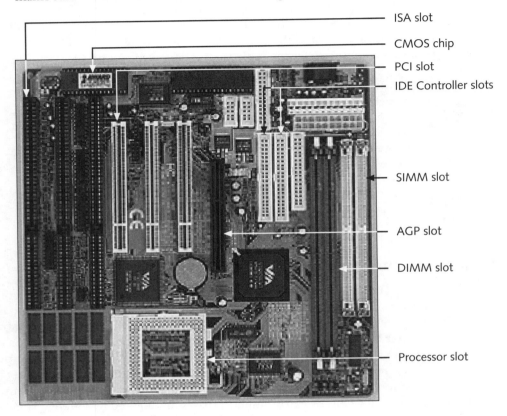

Figure 2-1   Mainboard components

Other peripherals may not have slots on the mainboard; instead they may connect via a cable to a port on the edge of the mainboard that is visible from the exterior of the computer (and hence difficult to see in Figure 2-1). These ports include:

- PS/2
- COM (Serial)
- LPT
- USB
- IEEE1394 (Firewire)
- PCMCIA

2

PS/2 ports are small round connectors with 6 pins that typically connect keyboards and mice to the computer. Some computers may instead use a larger 5-pin port to connect the keyboard; this port is called an AT port and was used prior to PS/2 ports.

COM ports (also called **serial ports**) are rectangular nine-pin connectors that can be used to connect a variety of different peripherals to the mainboard including mice, serial printers, scanners, and digital cameras. Today, COM ports are used far less than in the past as their transfer speed is quite slow; as a result, of the four COM ports commonly used (COM1, COM2, COM3, and COM4), today there are ports for only COM1 and COM2 on most mainboards.

In the past, printers have commonly used a rectangular 25-pin **LPT port** (also called a **parallel port**) for connection to the mainboard. Although there are two commonly used LPT ports (LPT1 and LPT2), most computers today typically only have LPT1 available on their mainboards.

Most peripheral components such as keyboards, mice, printers, digital cameras, and scanners now connect to the mainboard by means of a **Universal Serial Bus (USB)** port rather than a serial or parallel port. USB allows a transfer speed of up to 480Mb per second (most USB supports up to 12Mb per second) and can be used with a device called a USB hub to allow up to 127 different devices to connect to one USB port on the mainboard. Most computers come with two USB ports on the mainboard, and almost all USB devices can be attached to the computer for the operating system to detect and use while the computer is powered on. This feature is called hot-swapping, and any device that can be attached to the mainboard of a running computer is referred to as a **hot-swappable** device.

Another hot-swappable variant of USB is **Firewire (IEEE1394)**, which was developed by Apple Computer, Inc. in 1995 and supports a transfer speed of up to 400Mb per second. As a result of supporting such high transfer speeds, Firewire is commonly used to connect SCSI hard disks, scanners, digital cameras, and CD-RW drives to the computer.

When considering laptop portable computers, a large number of connectors or ports may increase the physical size of the computer and decrease its portability. For these computers, **Personal Computer Memory Card International Association (PCMCIA)** ports allow a small card to be inserted into the computer (usually less than 10.5mm thick) with the electronics necessary to provide a certain function. PCMCIA slots do not require much electricity, are hot-swappable, and are commonly used for network interface cards, modems, and expansion memory. Another feature of laptop portable computers is **Advanced Power Management (APM)**, which shuts off power to components such as PCMCIA devices if they are not being used, to save electricity.

There are a wide variety of ways to connect peripheral components to a computer via slots or ports on the mainboard; however, each peripheral device must be maintained separately from other devices on the system so that information does not cross paths when calculated by the CPU. This separation is obtained by two features of each peripheral component: the **Interrupt Request Line (IRQ)** and the **Input/Output (I/O) address**. The IRQ specifies a unique channel to the CPU itself, and these channels are labeled using the numbers 0 to 15. If two devices try to use the same IRQ a conflict will occur and neither device will work (however, some devices can share IRQs if they are configured to do so). Each device must also have a small working area of RAM where the CPU can pass information to and receive information from the device; this working area is known as the I/O address and must be unique for each device. I/O addresses are written in hexadecimal notation and indicate the range of memory used; an example of an I/O address is 0x300–31F.

On older equipment (usually ISA), one had to manually configure the IRQ and I/O address; however, most peripherals today are **Plug-and-Play (PnP)** and can automatically assign the correct IRQ, I/O address, and DMA channel (if used) without any user intervention. For Plug-and-Play to work properly, the BIOS and operating system must support Plug-and-Play configurations. Today, Plug-and-Play support is standard on most computers and operating systems such as Linux.

Video Adapter Cards and Monitors

Video adapter cards (commonly referred to as video cards) are one of the most vital peripheral components in a computer, because they provide a graphical display for the user when connected to a monitor device. Video cards typically plug into a slot on the motherboard (ISA, PCI, AGP) but can also be part of the motherboard itself (the latter are called integrated video cards and are common today because they are cheaper to produce).

Every display is made up of tiny dots or pixels; the more pixels that can be displayed, the sharper the image. Typical systems today display a minimum of 800 pixels horizontally and 600 pixels vertically; this is called the **resolution** of the screen and can be simplified to 800 x 600. Each pixel can also represent a color. The total set of colors that one can display on the screen is referred to as the **color depth**, and most systems today display a color depth of at least 16 million colors (also called 24-bit color depth).

Both the color depth and resolution depend on how much RAM is on the video card. Most video cards today come with 16MB of RAM on the card itself, which is enough to support most resolutions, but some video cards are configured to borrow RAM from the system mainboard. A list of maximum resolutions and color depths available with certain amounts of RAM is seen in Table 2-3.

Table 2-3   Memory requirements for screen resolutions & color depths

Video RAM	Resolution	Color Depth
1MB	1024 × 768 800 × 600	256 colors (8-bit color) 65,536 colors (16-bit color)
2MB	1024 × 768 800 × 600	65,536 colors (16-bit color) 16 million colors (24-bit color)
4MB	1024 × 768	16 million colors (24-bit color)

2

The screen image is refreshed several times a second to allow for changes or animation on the screen; a higher **refresh rate** will reduce the chances of images flickering on the screen. It is important to note that a refresh rate that is set too high can damage the monitor itself; always ensure that the monitor can support the refresh rate configured on the video card. There are two types of refresh rates: **HSync (horizontal refresh)** and **VSync (vertical refresh)**, which are measured in Hertz (Hz).

Keyboards and Mice

Video cards and monitors provide a method of viewing output, but there must be some means of providing user input and direction; keyboards and mice are two such devices. Keyboards are one of the oldest and most common input devices, consisting of a normal typewriter key set combined with special function keys allowing input to be sent to the computer. The number of additional function keys varies, giving keyboards anywhere from eighty-four to over one hundred and four different keys in total. Most keyboards follow the standard QWERTY typewriter layout, but others offer a different key arrangement call Dvorak. Still others offer a split set of key arrangement, one set for each hand, and are termed ergonomic keyboards. Regardless of layout or number of keys, keyboards connect to the motherboard in a variety of ways including:

- A large circular AT 5-pin connector
- A small circular PS/2 6-pin connector
- A USB connection
- A wireless infrared or radio connection

A relatively newer device used with most computer systems is the computer mouse, developed by Douglas C. Engelbart in the 1960s. Slow to gain popularity, mice are as common today as keyboards, and in many cases offer a faster and more versatile interface, which has led to the term "point and click." Without a mouse, one could communicate with a computer via a keyboard device only; a user could only submit tasks for the computer to perform by typing in commands into a command-line interface. Mice allow users versatility when using programs that are graphical in nature; moving a mouse across a desk surface moves a cursor on the video screen in a similar path, and pressing one of the buttons displays action choices or executes tasks. Mice can connect to the motherboard in a variety of ways including:

- A serial port
- A small circular PS/2 6-pin connector
- A USB connection
- A wireless infrared or radio connection

GATHERING PRE-INSTALLATION INFORMATION

All operating systems require a certain minimum set of computer hardware requirements to function properly, since an operating system is merely a series of software programs that interact with and control the computer hardware. Although most hardware purchased today will be sufficient to run the Linux operating system, it is nonetheless important to ensure that a computer meets the minimum hardware requirements before performing an installation.

These minimum installation requirements can be obtained from several sources. If the operating system was obtained on CD-ROM, then a printed manual or file on the CD-ROM may specify these requirements, but one may also find the minimum hardware requirements for most operating systems on the vendor's Web site. For the RedHat Linux 7.2 operating system, one may find the minimum hardware requirements at *http://www.redhat.com* or in Table 2-4.

Table 2-4   Red Hat 7.2 hardware requirements

Central Processing Unit (CPU)	Minimum: Pentium-class Recommended: Pentium II 200 Megahertz or higher
Random Access Memory (RAM)	Minimum for text-mode: 32MB Minimum for graphical: 64MB Recommended for graphical: 128MB
Disk Space Free (Hard Disk Drive)	Minimum: 650MB free space Recommended: 2.5GB free space Full Installation: 4.5GB free space *Additional free space will be required for any file storage or the installation of other software programs
Additional Drives	CD-ROM drive 3.5-inch floppy disk drive
Peripheral Devices	All peripheral devices (i.e., video cards, sound cards, network cards) must be Red Hat 7.2-compliant

Furthermore, each operating system supports only particular types of hardware components. Although some operating systems such as Linux support a wider variety of hardware components than other operating systems, each individual hardware component in your computer should be checked against a **Hardware Compatibility List (HCL)** readily found on the vendor's Web site.

For Red Hat Linux, the HCL can be found alongside the minimum installation requirements on the Internet at *http://www.redhat.com*.

As well as identifying hardware components to ensure that they are supported by the Linux operating system and meet minimum requirements, one should also identify the software components that will be used in the Linux operating system. This includes the computer's hostname, Internet or network configuration parameters, and the software packages that need to be installed to satisfy a certain use. Each of these will be discussed in the following chapter.

Since there are many pieces of hardware and software information to document, it is good form to complete a pre-installation checklist that contains all important installation information. At minimum, a pre-installation checklist should contain the information seen in Table 2-5.

Table 2-5 Sample pre-installation checklist

CPU (Type & MHz)	Intel Pentium III 800Mhz
RAM (MB)	256MB
Keyboard model & layout	101-key keyboard connected to PS/2 port
Mouse model & device	2-button Microsoft Intellimouse connected to COM1 port
Hard disk type (Primary Master, etc.)	Primary Master
Hard disk size (Gb)	40GB
Hostname	localhost.localdomain
Network Card Internet Protocol Configuration (IP Address, Netmask, Gateway, DNS Servers, DHCP)	DHCP: not used IP Address: 192.168.6.188 Netmask: 255.255.255.0 Gateway: 192.168.6.1 DNS Servers: 200.10.2.1, 200.10.82.79
Packages to install	GNOME desktop Samba Squid Apache GIMP Emacs
Video card make & model	Cirrus Logic GD 5446—Revision u
Video card RAM (MB)	2MB
Monitor make & model	Samsung Syncmaster 551s
Monitor VSync & HSync ranges	HSync: 30–55KHz VSync: 50–20Hz

Gathering Hardware Information

One can use several tools and resources to fill in the hardware information sections of the pre-installation checklist. The computer manuals that are shipped with the computer system are one such resource; most computer manuals have the specifications of each computer component listed in a table at the rear of the book or inside the front cover. Also, one may already have the Windows operating system installed on the computer prior to installing Linux; in this case, one may use common Windows utilities to view hardware information. The most comprehensive of these utilities is the System Information Tool seen in Figure 2-2.

To access the Windows System Information Tool, simply navigate to Start Menu, Programs, Accessories, System Tools, System Information.

Figure 2-2   The Windows System Information tool

The Windows Device Manager (in the System applet of the Windows Control Panel) is another utility that can display most of the required hardware information as seen in Figure 2-3.

To access the Windows 95/98/Me Device Manager, simply navigate to Start Menu, Settings, Control Panel, System, Device Manager. To access the Windows 2000/XP Device Manager, simply navigate to Start Menu, Settings, Control Panel, System, Hardware, Device Manager.

Another Windows utility useful for gaining hardware information regarding your video card and monitor is the Display applet of the Windows Control Panel as seen in Figure 2-4.

To access the Windows Display applet information regarding your video card and monitor, simply navigate to Start Menu, Settings, Control Panel, Display, Settings, Advanced.

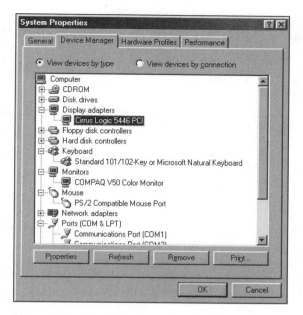

Figure 2-3   The Windows Device Manager

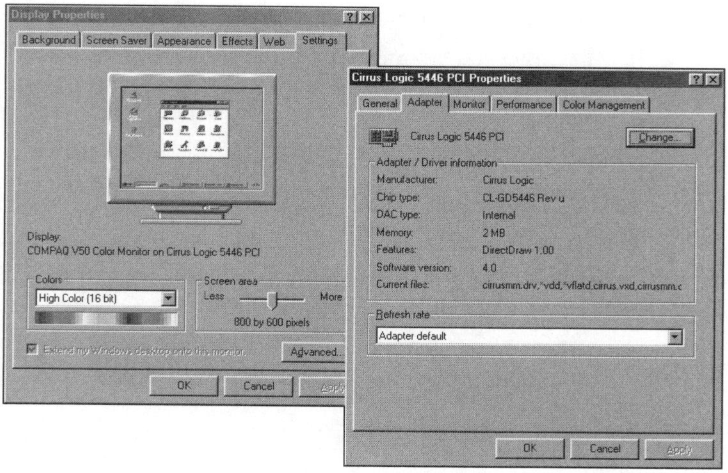

Figure 2-4   The Windows Display applet

Although system manuals and the Windows Control Panel can be used to find information about your computer, recall that each computer stores configuration information in a CMOS chip on the computer mainboard. This information in the CMOS chip is read by the BIOS ROM chip when the computer is first turned on in order to initialize peripherals and perform a **Power-On Self Test (POST)**. The POST displays output similar to Figure 2-5 when one first powers on the computer.

```
Award Modular BIOS v4.51PG, AN Energy Star Ally
Copyright © 1984-98, Award Software, Inc.

ASUS P2L-B ACPI BIOS Revision 1008

Award Plug and Play BIOS Extension v1.0A
Initializing Plug and Play Cards
Card-01: D-Link DE-220P PnP ISA Card
Card-01: Creative SB AWE64 PnP

PNP Init Completed

Detecting HDD Primary Master    ... QUANTUM FIREBALL CX6.4A
Detecting HDD Primary Slave     ... None
Detecting HDD Secondary Master  ... ATAPI CDROM
Detecting HDD Secondary Slave   ... None



Press DEL to enter SETUP
01/28/99-i440LX-<P2L-B7>
```

Figure 2-5   System POST

After the POST has completed, the BIOS looks for an operating system on a floppy, CD-ROM, or hard disk. Most settings used by the BIOS are configurable as they are stored on the CMOS chip, and most BIOSs allow one to choose these settings after the POST has completed by pressing the Delete key, as seen in Figure 2-5 above. If a user enters the BIOS setup utility, a screen such as the one seen in Figure 2-6 shall appear where one may configure devices and observe hardware settings.

```
                    ROM PCI/ISA BIOS (<P2L-B>)
                       CMOS SETUP UTILITY
                      AWARD SOFTWARE, INC.

   STANDARD CMOS SETUP              SUPERVISOR PASSWORD

   BIOS FEATURES SETUP              USER PASSWORD

   CHIPSET FEATURES SETUP           IDE HDD AUTO DETECTION

   POWER MANAGEMENT SETUP           SAVE & EXIT SETUP

   PNP AND PCI SETUP                EXIT WITHOUT SAVING

   LOAD BIOS DEFAULTS

   LOAD SETUP DEFAULTS

   Esc : Quit
   F10 : Save & Exit Setup
```

Figure 2-6   BIOS Setup Utility

The system BIOS setup utility looks very different from manufacturer to manufacturer; however, each utility contains roughly the same general types of information and configurations.

Gathering Software Information

Although hardware information is valuable to obtain prior to installing Linux, the Linux installation program will also ask for several software settings such as the time zone and language support, and most of these software settings need not be documented prior to installation as they can be added during the installation at the discretion of the user. Some settings, however, should be researched before starting the installation; these settings include the system network configuration and the package selections.

Identifying System Network Configuration

If one is installing a Linux system to use or provide network services, then the installation program will prompt for the necessary values to complete the configuration of the NIC in the computer. These values are usually assigned by the network administrator or Internet Service Provider for the company. A summary of these settings is described below:

- **Hostname**—The name of the computer, which is registered in DNS (Domain Name Service) such that others can connect to it by name.

- **IP address**—The unique number assigned to the computer, which allows it to participate on an Internet Protocol (IP) network such as the Internet.

- **Netmask**—Also known as the Network Mask or Subnet Mask, it specifies which portion of the IP address identifies which logical network the computer is on.

- **Gateway**—Also known as the default gateway or gateway of last resort, it specifies the address of a computer that accepts information from the local computer and sends it to other computers if the local computer can not.

- **DNS servers**—These servers resolve **Fully Qualified Domain Names (FQDNs)** such as *www.linux.org* to IP addresses such that one can connect to them across the Internet. One may list more than one DNS server; the local computer will then try the second server in the list if the first one is unavailable, and so on.

One may configure the above settings manually during the installation program or have the settings automatically configured provided there exists a **Dynamic Host Configuration Protocol (DHCP) server** on the network. If you select the option to use DHCP during installation, the Linux computer will attempt to get these settings from a DHCP server on the network. One may also choose to configure the aforementioned network settings later, after the installation has completed.

Software Package Selection

By far the most important software information required before installation comes from the software packages needed to customize the Linux system to perform certain tasks. These software packages require disk space, and as a result you should keep available disk space in mind when choosing from among them. Since you are given the option to choose from hundreds of individual packages during installation, you can only estimate the disk space needed for common Linux uses. Typically, a Red Hat Linux installation may require anywhere from 350MB of hard disk space for software during basic installation to 2.8GB for software during a full installation. A Linux workstation with either the KDE or GNOME desktop should require about 1.5GB of hard disk space, whereas a Linux workstation with both KDE and GNOME desktops will require about 1.8GB of hard disk space. Most specialized servers such as Linux Web servers and Linux DNS servers require about 1.3 GB of free hard disk space. During the installation program, sets of packages grouped by function are displayed; however, you may choose to customize this list and select only the individual packages needed. A list of common packages and their descriptions, valuable when choosing to customize packages, is found in Table 2-6.

Table 2-6   Common Linux packages

X Windows	The core component of Graphical User Interface (GUI) in Linux, which is required by the KDE and GNOME GUI environments
GNOME desktop	A GUI environment available for Linux
KDE desktop	A GUI environment available for Linux
Samba (SMB) server	Allows easy integration of Linux and Windows for file and printer sharing
NIS (Network Information Services) server	Centralizes and coordinates the changing of configuration files across Linux computers
NFS (Network File System) server	Allows Linux systems to share files across a network
GIMP (GNU Image Manipulation Program)	Graphical manipulation program
BIND / DNS server	Contains a table mapping IP addresses to FQDNs for use by client computers on the Internet
Apache server	The most common Web server available for Linux
MySQL server	A database management system
Postgres SQL server	A database management system
TeX	A program that processes text for desktop publishing
Emacs	A common text editor
Squid proxy server	Allows several computers access to the Internet via one Internet connection
Mozilla	A common Internet Web browser
FTP server (wu-ftpd)	Allows quick transfer of files across the Internet independent of the operating system
InterNetworkNews (INN) server	Hosts and manages newsgroup postings
Netfilter / iptables / ipchains	Allow Linux to function as a network firewall server

2

Chapter Summary

❑ An understanding of the various hardware components of a computer before a Linux installation will allow one to make the appropriate choices during installation and verify that the Linux installation was successful.

❑ CPUs process most instructions in a computer and come in two different architectures: RISC and CISC.

❑ Computer memory may be volatile (RAM) or non-volatile (ROM).

❑ Most information is stored on hard disks, floppy disks, and CD-ROM disks in a non-volatile manner. There are two main types of hard disks: SCSI and IDE.

❑ Peripheral components such as video adapter cards, sound cards, mice, keyboards, and NICs attach to the mainboard via an expansion slot or port.

❑ Common expansion slots include ISA, PCI, and AGP.

❑ Common ports include PS/2, serial, parallel, USB, Firewire, and PCMCIA.

❑ All peripheral components must have a unique IRQ and I/O address to communicate with the processor. They may optionally use DMA to bypass certain processor operations.

❑ Hardware information can be gathered from computer manuals, the system BIOS, or other operating systems such as Windows.

❑ Most software information can be specified at the time of installation; however, the network configuration and package selection should be carefully planned before installation.

Key Terms

Accelerated Graphics Port (AGP) — A motherboard connection slot designed for video card peripherals allowing data transfer speeds of over 66MHz.

Advanced Power Management (APM) — A BIOS feature that shuts off power to peripheral devices not in use to save electricity; this feature is commonly used on laptop computers.

Advanced Technology Attachment (ATA) — *See* Integrated Device Electronics.

architecture — The method employed of arranging a computer's integral electronics.

arithmetic logic unit — The section of the CPU where all the mathematical calculations and logic-based operations are executed.

ASymmetric Multi-Processing (ASMP) — A system containing more than one processor where each processor is given a certain role or set of tasks to complete independent of the other processors.

Basic Input/Output System (BIOS) ROM — The computer chips on a computer mainboard that contain the programs used to initialize hardware components at boot time.

bit — The smallest unit of information that a computer can compute.

bus — A term that represents the pathway information takes from one hardware device to another via a mainboard.

cache — A temporary store of information used by the processor.

central processing unit (CPU) — Integrated circuit board used to perform the majority of all calculations on a computer system; also known as a processor or microprocessor.

clock speed—The speed at which a processor (or any other hardware device) can execute commands related to an internal time cycle.

color depth—The total set of colors that can be displayed on a computer video screen.

COM ports — Rectangular nine-pin connectors that can be used to connect a variety of different peripherals to the mainboard including mice, serial printers, scanners, and digital cameras; also called serial ports.

Compact Disk–Read Only Memory (CD-ROM) — Physically durable removable storage media resistant to data corruption used in CD-ROM drives and CD-RW drives.

Complex Instruction Set Computer (CISC) processors — Processors that execute complex instructions on each time cycle.

Complimentary Metal-Oxide Semiconductor (CMOS) — A computer chip used to store the configurable information used by the BIOS ROM.

control unit — The area in a processor where instruction code or commands are loaded and carried out.

Direct Memory Access (DMA) — Allows peripheral devices to bypass the CPU and talk directly with other peripheral components, enhancing performance.

disk drive — A device that contains either a hard disk, floppy disk, CD-ROM, CD-RW disk, or zip disk.

DNS servers — Servers that resolve Fully Qualified Domain Names (FQDNs) such as *www.linux.org* to IP addresses such that one can connect to them across the Internet.

Dual In-line Memory Modules (DIMM) — A newer connection slot having connectors (pins) along both edges allowing the array of integrated circuits comprising a stick of RAM to connect the motherboard.

Dynamic Host Configuration Protocol (DHCP) server — A server on the network that hands out Internet Protocol (IP) configuration to computers that request it.

Dynamic RAM (DRAM) — A type of Random Access Memory that needs to refresh its store of information thousands of times a second and is available as a SIMM or DIMM stick.

Electronically Erasable Programmable Read Only Memory (EEPROM) — A type of ROM whose information store can not only be erased and rewritten as a whole, but can be modified singly leaving other portions intact.

Erasable Programmable Read Only Memory (EPROM) — A type of ROM whose information store can be erased and rewritten, but only as a whole.

extended partition — A partition on an HDD that can be further subdivided into components called logical drives.

filesystem — The way in which an HDD partition is formatted to allow data to reside on the physical media; common Linux filesystems include ext2, ext3, REIS-ERFS, and vfat.

Firewire (IEEE1394) — A mainboard connection technology developed by Apple Computer, Inc. in 1995 that supports data transfer speeds of up to 400Mb per second.

floppy disks — Removable storage media that consist of a flexible medium coated with a ferrous material that are read by floppy disk drives.

Fully Qualified Domain Names (FQDN) — User-friendly names used to identify machines on networks and the Internet.

gateway — Also known as default gateway or gateway of last resort, it specifies the address of a computer that accepts information from the local computer and will send it to other computers if the local computer cannot.

hard disk drive (HDD) — A device used to write and read data to and from a hard disk.

hard disks — Non-removable storage media consisting of a rigid disk coated with a ferrous material and used in hard disk drives (HDD).

Hardware Compatibility List (HCL) — A list of hardware components that have been tested and deemed compatible with a given operating system.

hostname — A user-friendly name used to uniquely identify a computer on a network; this name is usually a FQDN.

hot-swappable — The ability to add or remove hardware to or from a computer while the computer and operating system are functional.

HSync (horizontal refresh) — The rate at which horizontal elements of the video screen image are refreshed allowing for changes or animation on the screen, measured in Hertz (Hz).

Industry Standard Architecture (ISA) — An older motherboard connection slot designed to allow peripheral components an interconnect that transfers information at a speed of 8MHz.

Input/Output (I/O) address — The small working area of RAM where the CPU can pass information to and receive information from a device.

Integrated Drive Electronics (IDE) — Controllers that control the flow of information to and from up to 4 hard disks connected to the mainboard via a ribbon cable; also known as Advanced Technology Attachment (ATA).

Internet Protocol (IP) address — The unique number that each computer participating on the Internet must have.

Interrupt Request Line (IRQ) — Specifies a unique channel from a device to the CPU.

Level 1 (L1) cache — Cache memory stored in the processor itself.

Level 2 (L2) cache — Cache memory stored in a computer chip on the motherboard for use by the processor.

logical drives — The smaller partitions contained within an extended partition on an HDD.

LPT port — A rectangular 25-pin connection to the mainboard used to connect peripheral devices such as printers; also called parallel ports.

mainboard — A circuit board that connects all other hardware components together via slots or ports on the circuit board; also called a motherboard.

Master Boot Record (MBR) — The area of a hard disk outside of a partition, which stores partition information and boot loaders.

motherboard — *See* mainboard.

netmask — Specifies which portion of the IP address identifies the logical network the computer is on; also known as network mask or subnet mask.

network interface card (NIC) — A hardware device used to connect a computer to a network of other computers and communicate or exchange information on it.

parallel port — *See* LPT port.

partitions — Used to divide up a hard disk into smaller areas for ease of use; partitions may be primary or extended.

peripheral component — A component that attaches to the mainboard of a computer and provides a specific function such as a video card, mouse, or keyboard.

Peripheral Component Interconnect (PCI) — The most common motherboard connection slot found in computers today, which can transfer information at a speed of 33MHz and use DMA (Direct Memory Access).

Personal Computer Memory Card International Association (PCMCIA) — A mainboard connection technology that allows a small card to be inserted with the electronics necessary to provide a certain function.

physical memory — A storage area for information that is directly wired through circuit boards to the processor.

Plug-and-Play (PnP) — Operating system and peripheral devices that can automatically assign the correct IRQ, I/O address, and DMA settings without any user intervention.

Power-On Self Test (POST) — The initialization of hardware components by the ROM BIOS when the computer is first powered on.

primary partitions — The major unique and separate divisions into which an HDD can be divided (up to four are allowed per HDD).

Programmable Read Only Memory (PROM) — A blank ROM computer chip that can be written to once and never rewritten again.

PS/2 ports — Small round mainboard connectors developed by IBM with six pins that typically connect keyboards and mice to the computer.

Rambus Dynamic Random Access Memory (RDRAM) — A proprietary type of RAM developed by the Rambus Corporation.

Random Access Memory (RAM) — A computer chip able to store information, which is then lost when there is no power to the system.

Read Only Memory (ROM) — A computer chip able to store information in a static permanent manner, even when there is no power to the system.

Reduced Instruction Set Computer (RISC) processors — Relatively fast processors that understand small instruction sets.

refresh rate — The rate at which information displayed on a video screen is refreshed, measured in Hertz (Hz).

removable media — Information storage media that can be removed from a computer allowing transfer of data between machines.

resolution — The total number of pixels that can be displayed on a computer video screen horizontally and vertically.

serial port — *See* COM port.

Single In-line Memory Modules (SIMM) — An older type of memory stick that connects to the mainboard using connectors along only one edge.

Small Computer Systems Interface (SCSI) — Consists of controllers that can connect several SCSI HDDs to the mainboard and control the flow of data to and from the SCSI HDDs.

Static RAM (SRAM) — An expensive type of RAM commonly used in computer chips on the mainboard and which has a fast access speed.

superscalar — Refers to the ability of a computer processor to complete more than one command in a single cycle.

Symmetric Multi-Processing (SMP) — Refers to a system containing more than one processor in which each processor shares tasks and memory space.

Synchronous Dynamic Random Access Memory (SDRAM) — A form of RAM that uses the standard DIMM connector and transfers data at a very fast rate.

Universal Serial Bus (USB) — A mainboard connection technology that allows data transfer speeds of up to 480Mb per second and is used for many peripheral components today such as mice, printers, and scanners.

video adapter card — A peripheral component used to display graphical images to a computer monitor.

volatile — Refers to information storage devices that store information only when there is electrical flow; conversely, non-volatile information storage devices store information even when there is no electrical flow.

VSync (vertical refresh) — The rate at which vertical elements of the video screen image are refreshed, measured in Hertz (Hz.)

zip disk — A removable information storage unit similar to a floppy disk that can store much more information than floppy disks and are used in zip drives.

REVIEW QUESTIONS

1. RAM and ROM are both forms of Random Access Memory. True or False?

2. The arrangement of the integral components of a CPU is referred to as the processor's _____.

    a. structure

    b. architecture

    c. design

    d. layout

3. Complex Instruction Set Computer (CISC) processors are generally faster than Reduced Instruction Set Computer (RISC) processors. True or False?

4. A(n) _____ uses optics instead of magnetism to store information.

   a. ATAPI HDD

   b. RDRAM

   c. CD-RAM

   d. CD-ROM

5. How many IDE devices can a typical mainboard support?

   a. two

   b. one

   c. as many as there are free expansion slots for

   d. four

6. There can be _____ primary partition(s) on an HDD.

   a. two

   b. three

   c. one

   d. four

7. hdc6 refers to:

   a. clock speed on an HDD

   b. the second logical drive in the extended partition on the primary slave HDD

   c. the extended partition on the primary slave HDD

   d. the second logical drive in the extended partition on the secondary master HDD

8. CD-ROMs, floppy disks, and zip disks are referred to as:

   a. slow media

   b. backup media

   c. removable media

   d. durable media

9. The three most common slots for peripheral device connections are _____, _____, and _____.

   a. ISA, PDI, AGE

   b. PCI, ISA, AGP

   c. IMA, APG, PIC

   d. DMA, IRQ, PCI

2

10. If a hardware component is not listed on the HCL for the operating system it
   _____.

   a. needs to be made hot-swappable

   b. must be added to this list by the user before it will function

   c. will function without concern

   d. may not function or be recognized by the operating system

11. EEPROM stands for:

   a. Erratic Extensible Program Random Object Memory

   b. Elastic Erasable Project Read Only Memory

   c. Electronically Erasable Programmable Read Only Memory

   d. Easily Erasable Programmable Read Only Memory

12. Static Dynamic Random Access Memory (SDRAM) is a permanent memory store that requires no flow of electricity to be maintained. True or False?

13. A user normally accesses the BIOS (Basic Input/Output System) of a computer after powering it on by pressing:

   a. the F8 key

   b. the BIOS key

   c. the DEL key

   d. any key

14. Every computer connected to and communicating on an Internet Protocol (IP) network must have a unique _____.

   a. IP address

   b. node name

   c. subnet mask

   d. gateway

15. _____ is/are directly wired to the processor.

   a. Physical Memory

   b. Hard Disk Drives

   c. Random Object Memory

   d. Keyboards

   e. All of the above

16. There are normally four LPT ports and two COM ports on most mainboards. True or False?

17. The System Monitor in the Windows Control Panel can be used to determine the hardware configuration of a computer system. True or False?

18. The peripheral component used to attach a computer to a network is called a NIC. True or False?

19. The BIOS configuration of a computer is typically stored on a(n) _____ chip on the mainboard.

    a. AGP

    b. CMOS

    c. EEPM

    d. ROM

20. Hard disks are typically divided into _____ which contain _____.

    a. partitions, filesystems

    b. filesystems, partitions

    c. extentions, logical drives

    d. logical drives, extentions

HANDS-ON PROJECTS

Project 2-1

In this hands-on project, you will fill in a pre-installation checklist.

1. Fill in the following pre-installation checklist for your computer by supplying the appropriate information.

CPU (Type & MHz)	
RAM (Mb)	
Language support	English
Keyboard model & layout	
Mouse model & device	
Hard disk type (Primary Master, etc.)	
Hard disk size	
Space required for swap partition (Mb) *this should be equal to the amount of RAM (Mb)!	
Space available for filesystems (Mb) *this should be equal to the Hard disk size (Mb) less the amount of RAM (Mb) less 50Mb!	
Boot loader	LILO
Hostname	localhost.localdomain

Network Card Internet Protocol Configuration (IP Address, Netmask, Gateway, DNS Servers, DHCP) *values here are usually assigned by your Internet Service Provider	
Time zone	
Root password	Secret
Additional user account name	user1
Additional user account password	Secret
Packages to install	All packages
Video card make & model	
Video card RAM (Mb)	
Monitor make & model	
Monitor VSync & HSync ranges	

2. For any hardware components listed above, ensure that the hardware is listed on the HCL available on the Internet at *http://www.redhat.com* (provided that you have a functional Web browser and Internet access).

DISCOVERY EXERCISES

1. You work for the Nimbus Corporation as a network administrator. You have been instructed to install Red Hat Linux 7.2 on a multi-processor computer with a Cirrus Logic video card. Upon further examination, you note that it uses a GD5434 chip set. Will this be a problem? Provided that you have a functional Web browser and an Internet connection, where on the Internet could you go to confirm this? List 2 Internet sources for information on this issue.

2. You are asked to install Linux on a computer in your office to provide file and print services. The IT manager is unfamiliar with Linux and purchases a computer without checking the specific hardware inside, since the company has purchased several of these computers in the past and has had no problems with the Windows operating system automatically detecting the hardware inside them. Prepare a list of reasons that you could give the IT manager outlining why understanding the hardware components of a computer is valuable for a Linux installation. What problems could you encounter when installing on this hardware? Furthermore, design an installation checklist and fill in sample values that are reasonable for a file and print server that will support 100 users. Remember that all processes on a computer exist in RAM, and the more RAM a computer has, the more it is able do at any one time. Also remember that there are different types of processor architecture and that some are faster than others. You may even want to consider more than one processor. Also consider what packages you would consider installing. On this sample checklist, state rationales for each choice (processor, memory, disk space, packages, etc.) given your knowledge of each of these requirements.

3. Boot your computer, and as the BIOS information comes up press the **Pause/ Break** key and observe the output on the screen. From this output, record:

   ❏ The kind of processor in your computer

   ❏ The kind of HDD in your computer

   Use the appropriate key on your keyboard (usually Del) to access the BIOS settings on your machine. Navigate through the menus and record:

   ❏ The boot order for your computer (e.g., floppy then CD-ROM then HDD)

   ❏ 4 other pieces of information that you found interesting or useful

4. You work for Jimslim, a peripheral device company that has developed a new video card and has done extensive testing to ensure that is it is fully compatible with the Red Hat 7.2 Linux operating system. As an employee of Jimslim, and assuming that you have access to a functional Web browser and the Internet, what would you do to get it approved and placed on the HCL by Red Hat?

5. Provided that you have access to a computer with the Windows operating system, use the mouse to navigate to the System Information tool (**Start Menu → Programs → Accessories → System Tools → System Information**) and answer the following:

   ❏ IRQs presently in use

   ❏ DMAs presently in use

   ❏ The type of display or video card you have

   ❏ What kind of input devices you have

   ❏ Applications that are registered

3

LINUX INSTALLATION AND USAGE

**After completing this chapter,
you will be able to:**

♦ Install Red Hat Linux 7.2 using good practices

♦ Outline the structure of the Linux interface

♦ Enter basic shell commands and find command documentation

♦ Properly shut down the Linux operating system

This chapter explores the steps involved during a Red Hat Linux 7.2 installation using the hardware and software information that you obtained in Chapter 2. The latter half of the chapter presents an overview of the various components that you will use when interacting with the operating system, as well as how to enter basic shell commands, obtain help, and properly shut down the Linux system.

INSTALLING LINUX

Although the installation of Linux requires careful planning in addition to the gathering of hardware and software information, it also requires the selection of an installation method, the optional creation of installation boot floppy disks, and the configuration of various parts of the Linux operating system via an installation program.

Installation Methods

Before performing a Linux installation, you must choose the method of installation. The installation method simply specifies the source of the Linux packages and the installation program itself. Although using CD-ROMs that contain the appropriate packages is the most common method of installation, there are many different methods of installation available to those installing Linux, including:

- Installation from an FTP server across the network
- Installation from an HTTP Web server across the network
- Installation from an NFS server across the network
- Installation from packages located on the hard disk

The CD-ROM installation method is discussed in this chapter; other methods will be discussed in Chapter 7. To install from a CD-ROM, you simply place the Linux CD-ROM in the CD-ROM drive and turn on the computer. Most computers automatically search for a startup program on the CD-ROM immediately after being turned on, which can then be used to start the installation of Linux.

 Turning on a computer to load an operating system is commonly referred to as booting a computer. Since the Linux installation program on Linux CD-ROMs can be loaded when you first turn on a computer, they are referred to as bootable CD-ROMs.

Creating Boot Disks

If the installation of Linux does not start when the CD-ROM is placed in the CD-ROM drive during computer startup, you should first check to make sure that the system BIOS settings allow the CD-ROM to be searched at boot time. However, if the system BIOS allows booting from the CD-ROM and the Linux installation program still fails to start, you must make a floppy **boot disk** that can be inserted into the floppy disk drive at boot time and used to load the installation program, which will later find the appropriate packages on the CD-ROM.

Since most computers contain the Windows operating system on them before Linux is installed, there is a Windows utility called **rawrite** in the dosutils directory on the first Red Hat Linux installation CD-ROM, which you may use to create a boot disk. The rawrite program requires an image file that contains the information needed to create the floppy boot disk; Red Hat supplies many floppy boot disk images in the images folder on the first Red Hat Linux installation CD-ROM:

- boot.img—used to create a floppy boot disk for a CD-ROM or hard disk installation

- bootnet.img—used to create a floppy boot disk for an installation from a server across the network

- pcmcia.img—used to create a floppy boot disk for an installation on portable laptop computers

To create a floppy boot disk from inside the Windows operating system, you may perform the following steps:

1. Insert the first Red Hat 7.2 installation CD-ROM disk into your CD-ROM drive.

2. Double-click My Computer and choose your CD-ROM drive (D: for example).

3. Double-click the dosutils directory on your first Red Hat 7.2 installation CD-ROM.

4. Double-click the rawrite program to execute it. When prompted for the source image file, type D:\images\boot.img (assuming D: is your CD-ROM drive in Windows) and press Enter. When prompted for the destination drive, place a blank, formatted floppy disk in your floppy drive, type A: and press Enter.

 The images directory on the first Red Hat 7.2 installation CD-ROM also contains images that can be used to create floppy disks with extra drivers for uncommon hardware devices. These images are:
- drvblock.img—extra block device drivers
- drvnet.img—extra network card drivers
- oldcdrom.img—extra drivers for older CD-ROM devices
- pcmciadd.img—drivers for PCMCIA (laptop portable computer) devices

Performing the Installation

Installing the Linux operating system involves interacting with an installation program that prompts the user for information regarding the nature of the Linux system being installed. This installation program also allows a user to identify or change hardware components that are detected automatically by the installation program. More specifically, the installation procedure involves the following stages:

- Starting the installation

- Choosing the language, keyboard, and mouse

- Providing installation options

- Partitioning the hard disk

- Configuring the boot loader
- Configuring the network and firewall
- Choosing a system language and time zone
- Creating user accounts and configuring authentication
- Selecting packages
- Configuring the video hardware
- Installing packages and creating boot disks
- Selecting monitor and X Windows settings

Starting the Installation

As mentioned earlier, to perform a CD-ROM-based installation of Red Hat Linux 7.2, you simply place the first Red Hat Linux 7.2 CD-ROM in the CD-ROM drive and turn the computer on. Alternatively, you may also use a floppy boot disk to start the installation program if the CD-ROM device is not bootable. Whether using a floppy boot disk or CD-ROM to start the installation, an initial welcome screen appears that indicates that the installation program has loaded, as seen in Figure 3-1.

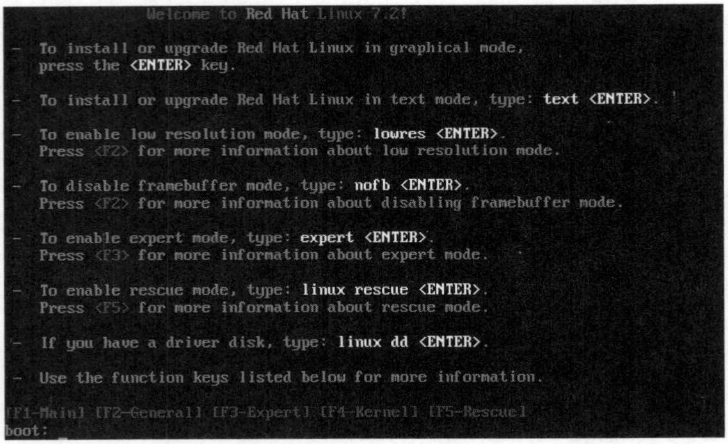

Figure 3-1   Beginning a Red Hat installation

3

Pressing the Enter key at this screen performs a default graphical installation that automatically detects hardware and suits most hardware configurations that are present on the HCL. This is the method that will be discussed in this chapter. However, you may also pass information to the installation program to alter the type of installation that occurs if the installation program cannot successfully detect hardware components. By far, the largest problem during installation is initiating a graphical installation; some video cards that are not on the HCL may result in a black or distorted screen during the default graphical installation. If this is the case, simply restart the installation and follow the instructions on the welcome screen to disable framebuffer support for a graphical installation. **Framebuffers** are abstract representations of video adapter card hardware that programs may use instead of directly communicating with the video adapter card hardware. If disabling framebuffer support does not allow a graphical install, you may restart the installation and choose to perform either a low screen resolution installation or a text-based install, again by simply following the instructions on the Welcome screen.

 Although most prefer to perform a graphical install for ease of use, a text-based installation is faster, as the graphical user interface need not be loaded. Text-based installations are the standard for the hard disk and network installations discussed in Chapter 7.

In the event that the Red Hat Linux installation detects hardware incorrectly, you may also choose to perform an expert installation after restarting the installation program; no hardware will then be detected automatically, and you must select your hardware from a list. If uncommon or older hardware components exist in the computer, you may also need to create a driver disk as discussed in the previous section and load those drivers at the boot: prompt.

Choosing the Language, Keyboard, and Mouse

Once a user presses Enter at the boot: prompt, a graphical installation starts and the user is prompted to answer a series of questions to complete the installation. The first screen allows you to choose the installation language, as seen in Figure 3-2.

After the language selection screen, you are asked to choose the keyboard and mouse configurations as seen in Figure 3-3 and Figure 3-4, respectively. The default model and layout of your keyboard as well as the model and device of your mouse are automatically detected, and as a result they are seldom changed. It is good practice, however, to verify that the information on the screen is correct before continuing. When in doubt, choose a Generic 101-key PC keyboard with U.S. English layout and a Generic mouse device, as they are likely to work in most situations. To support special characters, choose Enable dead keys in the Keyboard Configuration. Similarly, to accommodate programs that can make use of the third mouse button, ensure that Emulate 3 Buttons is checked if the mouse currently does not have a third mouse button. This option, if selected, lets a user simulate a third mouse button by pressing both mouse buttons simultaneously.

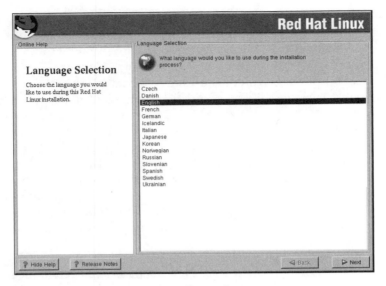

Figure 3-2   Selecting an installation language

Figure 3-3   Verifying keyboard configuration

On the left-hand side of most Red Hat installation screens there is a description of the current screen and common selections.

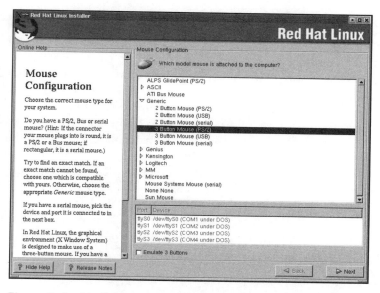

Figure 3-4   Verifying mouse configuration

Once the keyboard and mouse configurations are verified, you are presented with another welcome screen, which identifies sources of installation documentation, as seen in Figure 3–5.

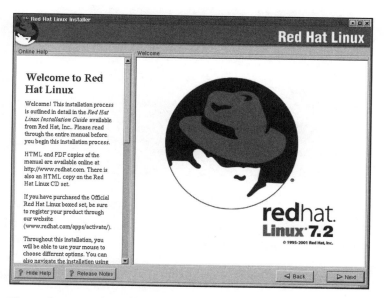

Figure 3-5   Welcome screen

Providing Installation Options

Next, you must choose whether to upgrade a previous installation of Red Hat Linux (version 3.03 or greater) that exists on the hard drive or perform a fresh installation (Figure 3-6). Typically, you only perform an upgrade if there are data and configurations on the previous installation of Red Hat Linux that are difficult to recreate or back-up. If choosing a fresh install (the first option), you are presented with four more options that allow you to simplify package selection. If you choose to perform a Workstation installation, then a set of packages most common to workstation users will be installed, including a GUI environment and common applications. Conversely, a Server installation contains few workstation packages, several server services, and typically does not contain a GUI environment. If installing Red Hat Linux on a laptop computer, choose Laptop to ensure that those packages required for PCMCIA and other laptop devices are available. Although these selections may simplify the selection of packages, it is commonplace to choose Custom, which allows you to select only the packages needed to suit your computing needs.

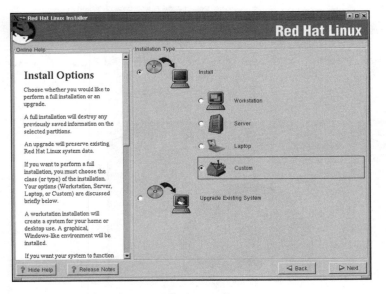

Figure 3-6   Choosing installation options

Although the user chooses an installation method here defining a general set of packages, a detailed package selection will be entered later during the installation process.

It is important to consider available hard disk space when planning package selection. A typical workstation, server, or laptop installation places about 1.5GB of data on the hard disk, whereas a full installation may place almost 3GB of data on the hard disk. If you are installing a large number of packages, ensure that you have enough free space on the hard disk for log files that will be generated in the future, and working space for the packages installed. Generally, you should ensure that you have at least one-and-a-half times the space required on the hard disk for the packages required prior to installation. Because server packages generally require more working space, it is good form when installing a Linux server to ensure that you have at least twice the hard disk space required before packages are installed.

Partitioning the Hard Disk

The next screen displayed after you choose the install options allows you to choose your partitioning strategy (Figure 3-7). Recall that partitioning divides a hard disk into adjacent sections, each of which can contain a separate filesystem used to store data. Each of these filesystems may then be accessed by Linux if they are attached (or mounted) to a certain directory. When data is stored in that particular directory, it is physically stored on the respective filesystem on the hard drive. The Red Hat installation program can automatically create partitions based on common configurations; however, it is generally good practice to partition manually in order to suit the needs of the specific Linux system.

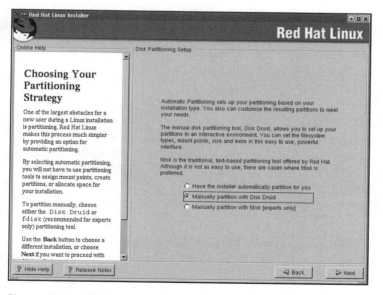

Figure 3-7   Choosing a partitioning method

At minimum, Linux requires only two partitions to be created: a partition that is mounted to the root directory in Linux (/) and that may contain all of the files used by the operating system, applications, and users; and a partition used for virtual memory (also known as **swap memory**). **Virtual memory** consists of an area on the hard disk that can be used to store information that would normally reside in physical memory (RAM), if the physical memory is being used excessively. When programs are executed that require a great deal of resources on the computer, information is continuously swapped from physical memory to virtual memory on the hard disk, and vice versa. Typically a swap partition should be at least the size of the physical RAM, but can be much larger if the Linux system is intended to run large applications. Many users make the swap partition twice the size of physical RAM to avoid any problems later on after installation. A swap partition does not contain a filesystem and is never mounted to a directory, as it is the Linux operating system that is ultimately responsible for swapping information.

Although you may choose to create only root and swap partitions, extra partitions make Linux more robust against filesystem errors. For example, if the filesystem on one partition encounters an error, only data on one part of the system is affected and not the entire system (other filesystems). Since there are some common directories in Linux that are used vigorously and as a result more prone to failure, it is good practice to mount these directories to their own filesystem. Directories that are commonly mounted to separate partitions, as well as their recommended sizes, are listed in Table 3-1.

Table 3-1   Common Linux filesystems and sizes

Directory	Description	Recommended Size
/boot	Contains the Linux kernel and boot files	50MB
/home	Default location for user home directories	200MB per user
/usr	System commands and utilities	Depends on the packages installed—typically 2GB
/usr/local	Location for most additional programs	Depends on the packages installed—typically 4GB
/opt	An alternate location for additional programs	Depends on the packages installed—typically 4GB
/var	Contains log files and spools	2GB
/tmp	Holds temporary files created by programs	500MB

Each of these filesystems may be of different types. The most common types used today are the **ext2**, **ext3**, **vfat**, and **REISER** filesystems, although Linux can support upwards of 50 different filesystems presently. Each filesystem essentially performs the same function, which is to store files on a partition; however, each offers different features and as such are specialized for different uses. The ext2 filesystem is the traditional filesystem still used on most Linux computers, and the vfat (Virtual File Allocation Table) filesystem is one that is compatible with the FAT filesystem in Windows. The ext3 and REISER filesystems, however, are much more robust than the ext2 and vfat filesystems, as they perform a function called journaling. A **journaling** filesystem is one that keeps track of the information written to the hard drive in a journal. If you copy a file on the hard drive from one directory to another, that file must pass into physical memory and then be written to the new location on the hard disk. If the power to the computer is turned off during this process, information may not be transmitted as expected and data may be lost or corrupted. With a journaling filesystem, each step required to copy the file to the new location is first written to a journal, so that the system can retrace the steps the system took prior to a power outage and complete the file copy. Both of these filesystems also host a variety of additional improvements compared to ext2 and vfat including faster data transfer and indexing, and as a result are common choices for Linux servers today.

Once the number and types of filesystems required for the installation have been determined, you may choose to allow the Red Hat Linux installation program to partition automatically based on the total amount of hard disk space on your system, or you may choose to partition manually using either the Disk Druid tool or fdisk.

Disk Druid is an easy-to-use graphical partitioning program and as such is the recommended tool to use. Using Disk Druid, you can delete existing partitions, create and edit new ones, or even create a **Redundant Array of Inexpensive Disks (RAID)** volume to prevent data loss if any hard disks break down. RAID will be discussed later in the book.

An example of using Disk Druid to create /boot, /, and swap partitions on a primary master IDE hard disk (/dev/hda) is displayed in Figures 3-8 and 3-9. Figure 3-8 shows Disk Druid after the three partitions were created, and Figure 3-9 shows the dialog box displayed when you choose to create a new partition.

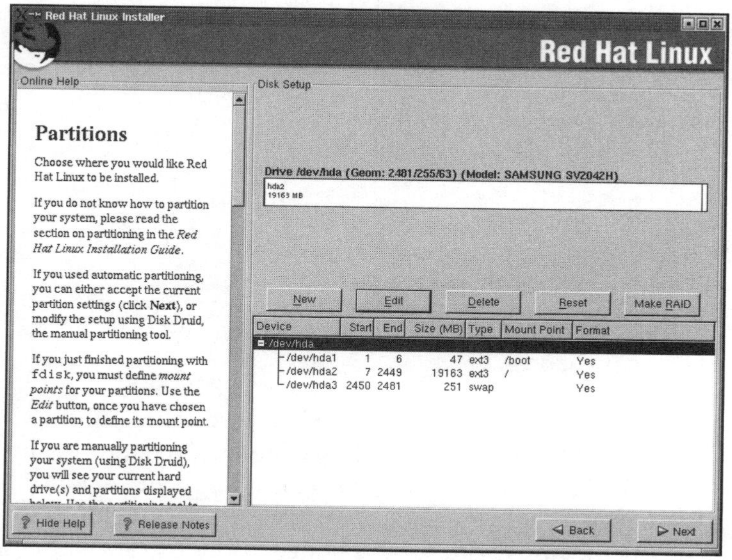

Figure 3-8 Disk Druid

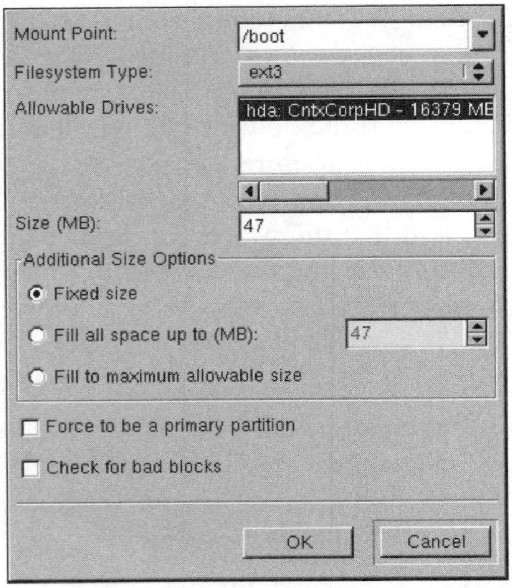

Figure 3-9   Adding a partition

Once the partitions have been created with Disk Druid, they must be formatted with a filesystem. Figure 3-10 displays the dialog box confirming this action.

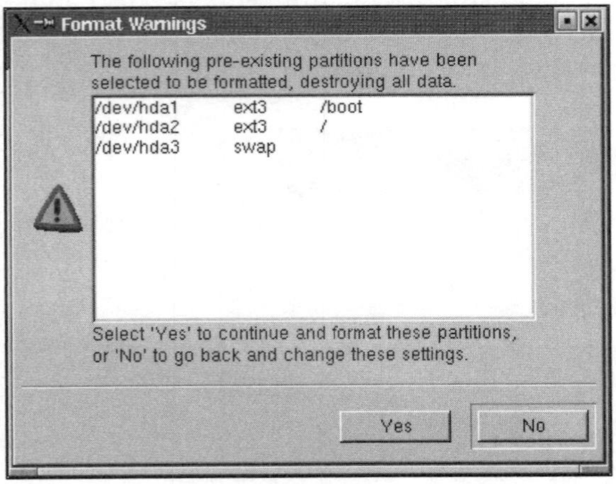

Figure 3-10   Formatting partitions

Although Disk Druid is the most common method of partitioning during installation, you may instead choose the fdisk utility to create partitions, as seen in Figure 3-11. The fdisk utility is the traditional partitioning tool in Linux; it gives the user a command line interface for entering in partition commands and allows greater functionality than Disk Druid. This utility will be discussed later in the book.

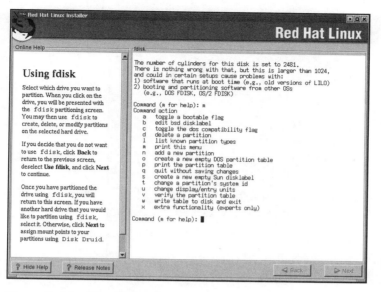

Figure 3-11   The fdisk utility

Configuring the Boot Loader

Once partitions and filesystems have been specified during the installation program, you are prompted to configure the boot loader, as seen in Figure 3-12. A **boot loader** is a program started by the BIOS ROM after POST, which loads the Linux kernel into memory from a hard disk partition inside the computer, yet can also be used to boot (start) other operating systems such as Windows if they exist on the hard drive. There are two available boot loaders that one may choose during the Red Hat Linux installation: **LInux LOader (LILO)**, which is the traditional and most common boot loader, and **GRand Unified Bootloader (GRUB)**, which is a recent boot loader that offers several features LILO does not. Boot loaders will be discussed in Chapter 8.

The most common place for the boot loader to reside is on the Master Boot Record (MBR); however, you can also place it on the first hard disk sector of the / or /boot filesystem partition if you wish to use a boot loader from another operating system to boot Linux. In addition to this, you may choose which operating system name (Boot label) to load by default upon system startup; you may pass certain information to the Linux operating system kernel via the boot loader; or you may force the use of a certain parameter called **Large Block Addressing 32-bit (LBA32)**. (LBA32 is only required if the / or /boot partition starts after the 1024th cylinder of the hard disk (after the first 8GB) and the system BIOS does not advertise this information to the boot loader.)

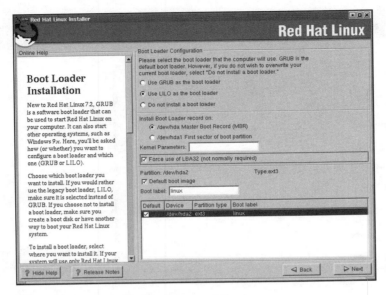

Figure 3-12   Configuring the boot loader

Configuring the Network and Firewall

If the Network Interface Card (NIC) was detected by the Red Hat installer, you will see a network configuration screen similar to the one shown in Figure 3–13, which allows you to configure whether the NIC will be activated at boot time and what configuration information it will use (manually defined or via DHCP). If you are configuring IP manually, you need to enter the IP address, netmask (or subnet mask), hostname, gateway (or default gateway), and primary DNS only; the network and broadcast addresses are automatically generated from the IP address/netmask pair, and the secondary and ternary DNS addresses are for backup purposes in the event the primary DNS is unavailable.

Once the NIC has been configured, you are prompted to choose which network traffic to allow into the Linux system (called an incoming firewall) as seen in Figure 3–14. Choosing High allows only DNS and DHCP traffic into the computer and should only be used for computers that contain sensitive information that is not shared with other computers on the network, whereas Medium allows DNS, DHCP, FTP, Telnet, HTTP, SSH, and X Windows traffic. You may also choose to customize which traffic is allowed by choosing Customize when a firewall setting is selected.

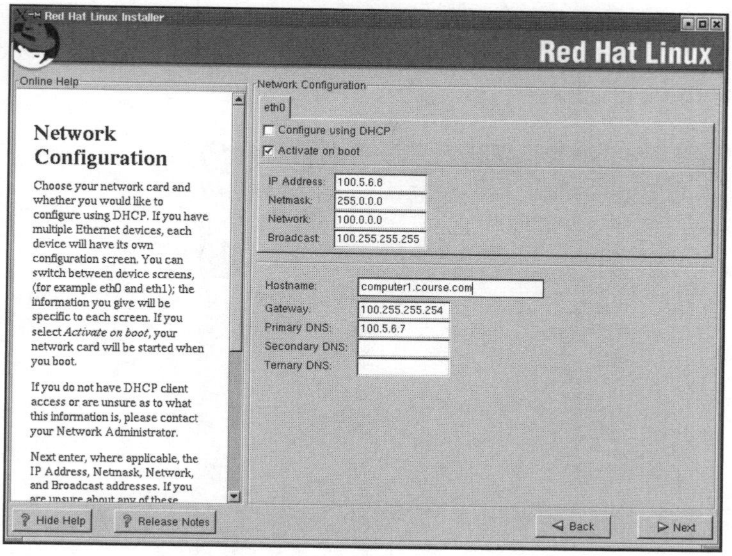

Figure 3-13　Configuring the network

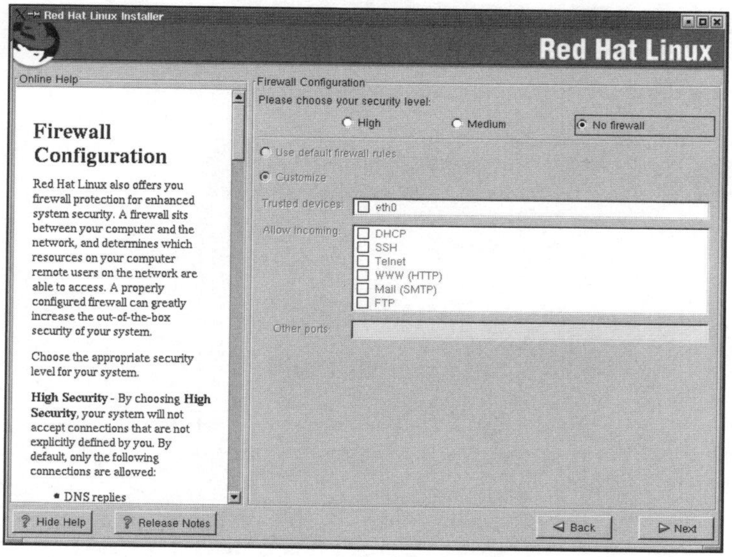

Figure 3-14　Configuring a firewall

Choosing a System Language and Time Zone

Earlier during the installation, you were prompted to choose a language for the installation process itself; however, Linux allows the support of multiple languages after installation.

Thus, you must choose the language(s) that will be supported by the Linux operating system, as shown in Figure 3-15. You must also choose the appropriate time zone for your region, as depicted in Figure 3-16.

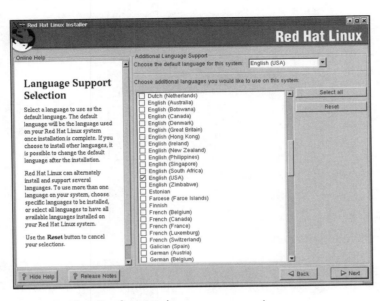

Figure 3-15   Configuring language support

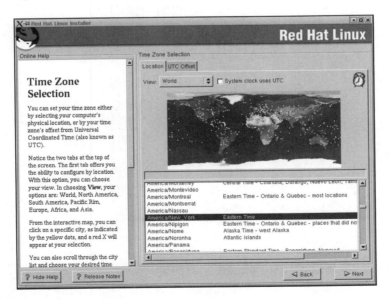

Figure 3-16   Selecting a time zone

Creating User Accounts and Configuring Authentication

All Linux systems require secure access, which means that each user must log in with a valid username and password before gaining access to a user interface. This process is called **authentication**. During installation, two user accounts should be configured: the administrator account (root), which has full rights to the system; and at least one regular user account. To accomplish this, you simply specify a password that is at least six characters long for the root user account, as seen in Figure 3-17, and then add another user account to the system, as seen in Figure 3-18.

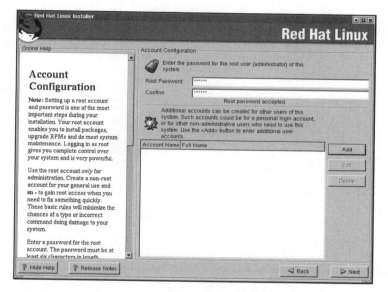

Figure 3-17   Configuring the root password

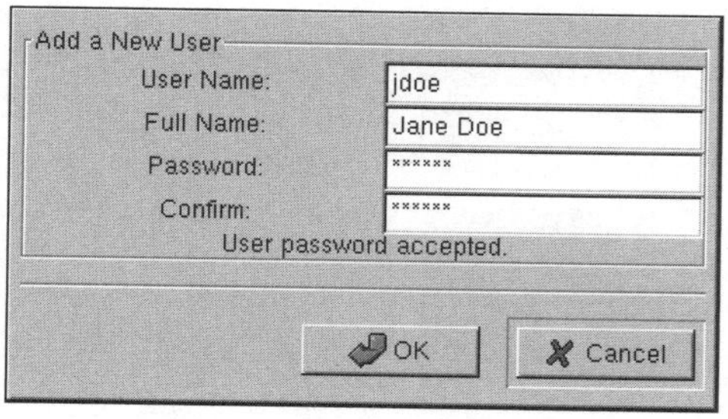

Figure 3-18   Configuring a regular user account

You must also configure the password database used to store user account information, as depicted in Figure 3-19. Message Digest 5 (MD5) passwords support a length of up to 256 characters and are encrypted using an MD5 hash algorithm, and shadow passwords are passwords that are stored in a separate database from the user account information for better security. You may also choose to authenticate some or all users based on a database that resides on another server on the network. Network Information System (NIS) shares password databases amongst Linux systems, whereas Lightweight Directory Access Protocol (LDAP), Kerberos, and Server Message Blocks (SMB) represent types of authentication services that may be present on other servers on the network. You will be prompted for this information during installation; many of these terms will be fully explained later in this book.

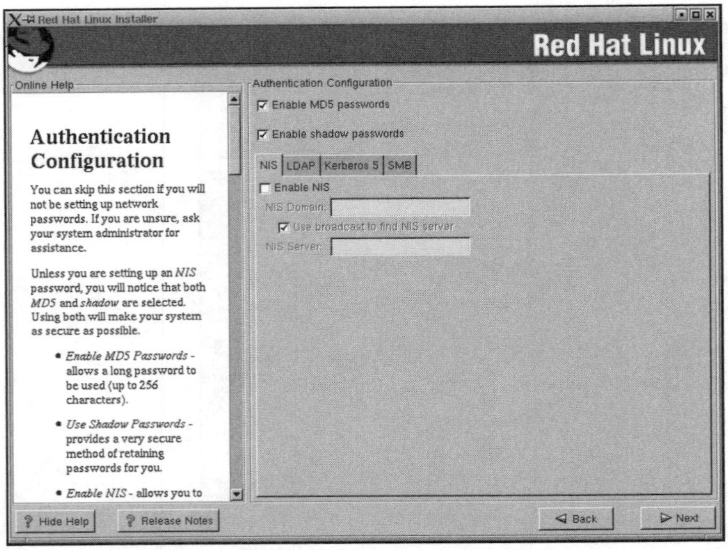

Figure 3-19   Configuring the type of authentication

Selecting Packages

Next, the Red Hat installer provides a list of packages based on the installation options chosen earlier in Figure 3-6. You can choose the general packages required for certain functionality as seen in Figure 3-20, or you may choose to refine the list of packages by placing a check in the Select individual packages box at the bottom of the screen, which results in a screen similar to Figure 3-21.

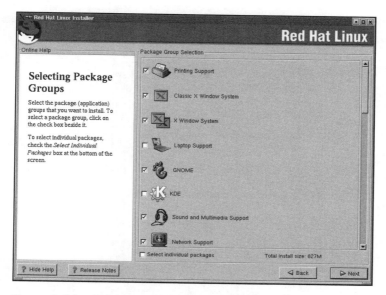

Figure 3-20   Selecting packages to install

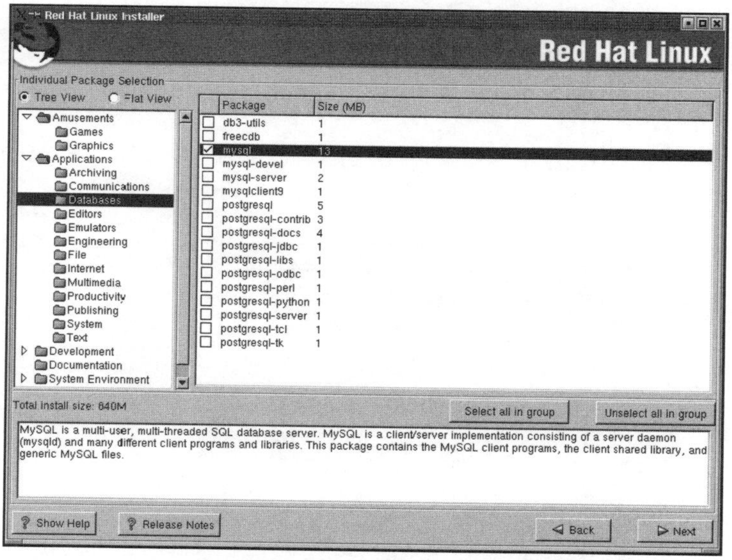

Figure 3-21   Refining individual package selection

Configuring the Video Hardware

The next step prior to copying packages to the hard drive is the configuration of video adapter hardware. If your video hardware is listed on the HCL, the Red Hat Linux installer usually detects the model and amount of video RAM automatically; however, it is safe practice to verify that the values detected are correct to avoid problems after installation. A sample video hardware selection can be seen in Figure 3-22.

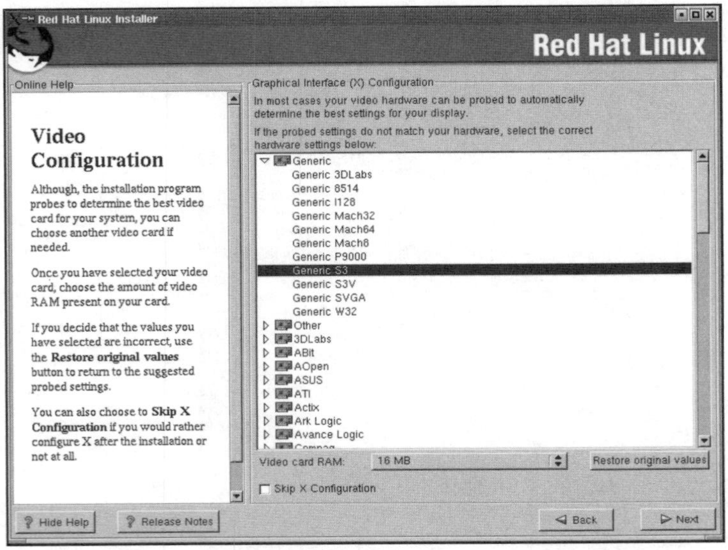

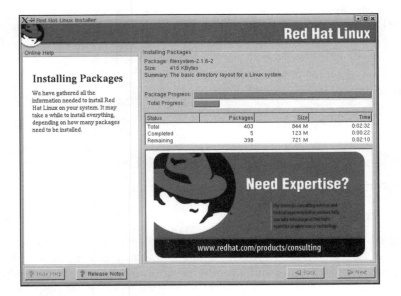

Figure 3-22   Verifying video hardware

Installing Packages and Creating Boot Disks

After the video hardware has been configured, the packages selected for installation are copied to filesystems created on the hard disk, as seen in Figure 3-23.

Figure 3-23   Copying packages to the hard disk

Once the package installation is finished, you have the option to create a boot disk, as depicted in Figure 3-24. Unlike the installation floppy disk that you may create to start a Linux installation, this floppy contains a boot loader configured with the information regarding your newly created system structure. If the boot loader configured on the MBR fails to load Linux or is improperly configured, you may simply place this boot floppy in the floppy disk drive and boot into the Linux operating system on the hard drive.

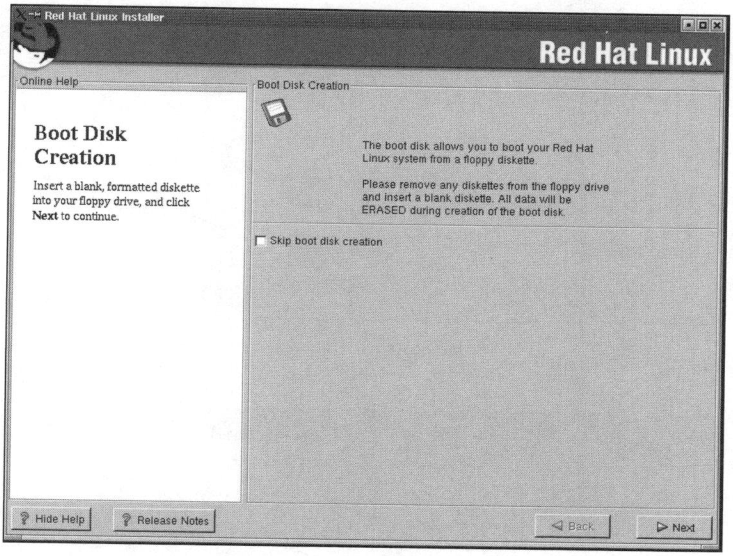

3

Figure 3-24   Creating a boot disk

Selecting Monitor and X Windows Settings

It is very important to select the correct monitor settings, as seen in Figure 3-25, since incorrect settings may cause damage to the monitor. Most monitors available today are automatically detected; you simply need to verify the correct model and horizontal and vertical sync ranges detected before continuing. However, if the monitor was not automatically detected, you should try to locate it on the list of monitor models or use a generic model with the correct horizontal and vertical sync ranges.

The final step to complete during installation is the configuration of X Windows, as seen in Figure 3-26. The Red Hat installation program presents the user with a series of color depths (the number of different colors that can be displayed) and resolutions (the number of pixels on the screen, which affects screen size). Choosing a higher color depth and screen resolution results in more available colors and smaller icons, respectively. You are also allowed to choose the default GUI environment (KDE or GNOME), if both are installed, and prompted whether to display a graphical login screen upon boot-up. Once finished, clicking Exit at the congratulations screen seen in Figure 3-27 ejects the CD-ROM from the CD-ROM drive and reboots the system so that one may use the Linux operating system.

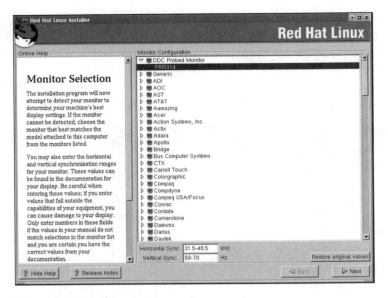

Figure 3-25 Choosing a monitor

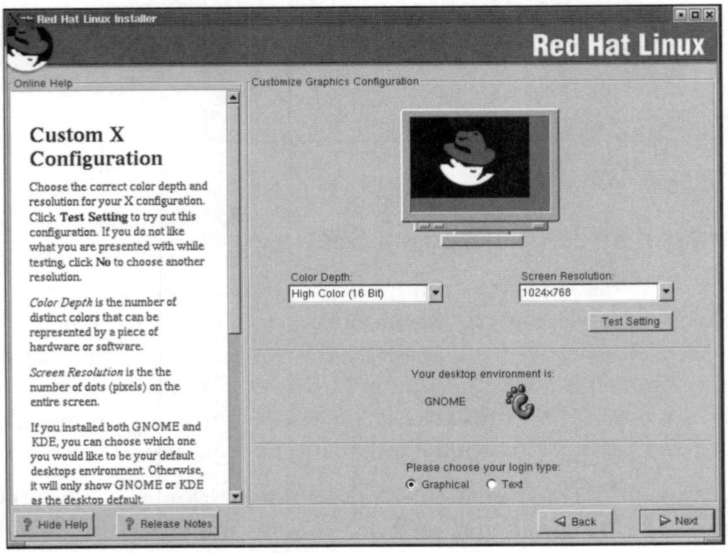

Figure 3-26 Configuring X Windows

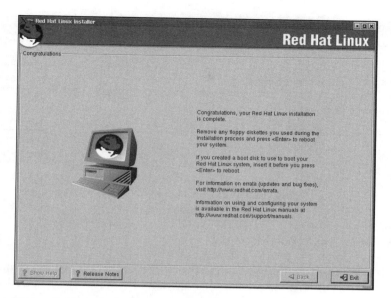

Figure 3-27   Completing the installation

Basic Linux Usage

Once the Linux operating system has been installed, you must log into the system with a valid username and password and interact with the user interface to perform useful tasks. To do this, it is essential to understand the different types of user interfaces that exist, as well as basic tasks such as executing commands, obtaining online help, and shutting down the Linux system.

Shells, Terminals, and the Kernel

Recall that an operating system is merely a collection of software that allows you to use your computer hardware in a meaningful fashion. Every operating system has a core component, which loads all other components and serves to control the activities of the computer centrally. This component is known as the kernel, and in Linux is simply a file, usually called "vmlinuz," which is located on the hard drive and loaded when you first turn your computer on.

When a user interacts with their computer, they are interacting with the kernel of the computer's operating system. However, this interaction cannot happen directly; there must exist a channel through which a user interface can access the kernel. The channel that allows a certain user to log in is called a **terminal**, and there can be many terminals in Linux that allow you to log in to the computer locally or across a network. Once a user logs into a terminal, they receive a user interface called a **shell**, which then accepts input from the user and passes this input to the kernel for processing. The shell that is used by default in Linux is the **BASH Shell (Bourne Again Shell)**, which is an improved version of the Bourne Shell from AT&T and the shell that we will be using throughout this textbook. The whole process looks similar to Figure 3-28.

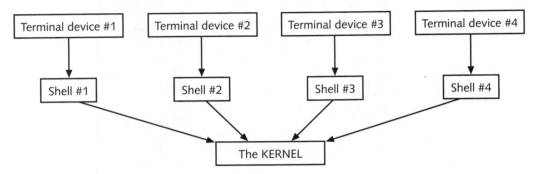

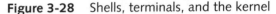

Figure 3-28   Shells, terminals, and the kernel

As mentioned earlier, Linux is a multi-user and multitasking operating system, and as such can allow for thousands of terminals. Each terminal could represent a separate logged-in user that has its own shell. The four different "channels" shown in Figure 3-28 could be different users logged into the same Linux computer. Two users could be logged locally to the server (seated at the server itself) and the other two could be logged in across a network, such as the Internet.

By default, when a user logs into a terminal, they receive a command-line shell (BASH Shell) in which they type commands to tell the Linux kernel what to do. However, in this computing age, most people prefer to use a graphical interface in which they may use a computer mouse to navigate and start tasks. In this case, you may simply choose to start a graphical user interface (GUI) environment on top of your BASH shell once logged in to a command-line terminal, or you may switch to a graphical terminal, which allows users to log in and immediately receive a GUI environment. A typical command-line terminal login prompt looks like the following:

```
Red Hat Linux release 7.2 (Enigma)
Kernel 2.4.7-10 on an i686

localhost login:
```

A typical graphical terminal login for Red Hat Linux (called the gdm or GNOME Display Manager) is depicted in Figure 3-29.

Figure 3-29 The gdm (GNOME Display Manager)

To access a terminal device at the local server, you can press a combination of keys such as Ctrl–Alt–F1 to change to a different terminal. If you are logging in across the network, you can use a variety of programs that connect to a terminal on the Linux computer. A list of local Linux terminals, and their names and types, can be seen in Table 3–2.

Table 3-2 Common Linux terminals

Terminal Name	Key Combination	Login Type
tty1	Ctrl-Alt-F1	command-line
tty2	Ctrl-Alt-F2	command-line
tty3	Ctrl-Alt-F3	command-line
tty4	Ctrl-Alt-F4	command-line
tty5	Ctrl-Alt-F5	command-line
tty6	Ctrl-Alt-F6	command-line
tty7 (:0)	Ctrl-Alt-F7	graphical

Once logged into a command-line terminal, one receives a prompt where one may enter in commands. If you log in as the root user (administrator), a # prompt will be used:

```
Red Hat Linux release 7.2 (Enigma)
Kernel 2.4.7-10 on an i686

localhost login: root
Password:
Last login: Mon Mar 25 09:45:42 on tty2
[root@localhost root]#_
```

However, if you log in as a regular user to a command-line terminal (for example, user1), then a $ prompt will be used:

```
Red Hat Linux release 7.2 (Enigma)
Kernel 2.4.7-10 on an i686

localhost login: user1
Password:
Last login: Mon Mar 25 09:49:31 on tty2
[root@localhost root]$_
```

When you log into a graphical terminal, the GUI environment of your choice is started; the default GUI environment in Red Hat Linux is GNOME. After the GUI environment starts, you may access a command-line terminal window by clicking the computer icon on the toolbar. An example of this is seen in Figure 3-30 and Figure 3-31.

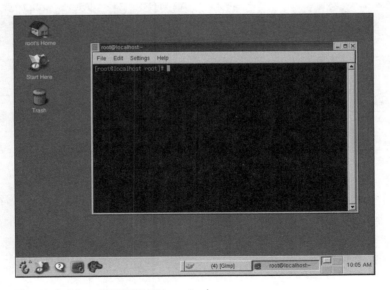

Figure 3-30   A GNOME terminal

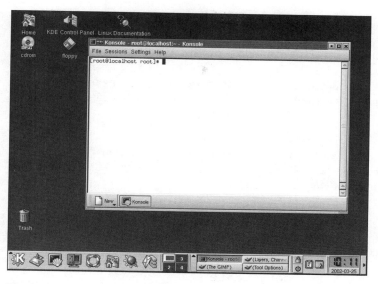

Figure 3-31   A KDE terminal

Basic Shell Commands

When using a command-line terminal, the shell ultimately interprets all information the user enters onto the command line. This information includes the command itself, as well as options and arguments. **Commands** indicate the name of the program to execute and are case sensitive. **Options** are specific letters that start with a dash "–" and appear after the command name to alter the way the command works. Options are specific to the command in question; the persons who developed the command determined which options to allow for that command.

> Some options start with 2 dashes "--"; these options are referred to as POSIX options and are usually comprised of a whole word, not just a letter.

Arguments also appear after the command name, yet do not start with a dash. They specify the parameters that the command works upon, which are not predetermined by the person who developed the command. Say, for example, that you wished to list all of the files in the /var/ftp/etc directory on the hard drive. You could use the *ls* command with the *-a* option (which tells the *ls* command to list all files) and the /var/ftp/etc argument (which tells *ls* to look in the /var/ftp/etc directory) as seen in the following example:

```
[root@localhost root]# ls -a /var/ftp/etc
.  ..  group ld.so.cache ld.so.conf passwd
[root@localhost root]#_
```

Once you typed the command and pressed Enter, the *ls* command showed you in the above output that there are four files in the /var/ftp/etc directory and returned your command prompt so that you may enter another command.

Commands, options, and arguments are case sensitive; an uppercase letter A, for instance, is treated differently than a lowercase letter a.

Always put a space between the command name, options, and arguments; otherwise the shell will not understand that they are separate and your command may not work as expected.

Although you may pass options and arguments to commands, not all commands need to have arguments or options supplied on the command line to work properly. The *date* command is one example that simply prints the current date and time:

```
[root@localhost root]# date
Tue Mar 26 08:58:36 EST 2002
[root@localhost root]#_
```

Some common commands that you may use without specifying any options or arguments are listed in Table 3-3.

Table 3-3   Some common Linux commands

Command	Description
clear	Clears the terminal screen
reset	Resets your terminal to use default terminal settings
finger	Displays information on system users
who	Displays currently logged in users
w	Displays currently logged in users and their tasks
whoami	Displays your login name
id	Displays the numbers associated with your user account name and group names. These are commonly referred to as User IDs (UIDs) and Group IDs (GIDs)
date	Displays the current date and time
cal	Displays the calendar for the current month
exit	Exits out of your current shell

If the output of a certain command is too large to fit on the terminal screen, simply use the Shift and Page Up keys simultaneously to view previous screens of information. Also, Shift and Page Down can be used to navigate in the opposite direction when pressed simultaneously.

One can recall commands previously entered in the BASH Shell using the keyboard cursor keys (the up, down, right, and left arrow keys). Thus, if you wish to enter the same command again, simply cycle through the list of available commands with the keyboard cursor keys and press Enter to re-execute that command.

Shell Metacharacters

Another important feature of the shell is shell **metacharacters**, which are keyboard characters that have special meaning. One of the most commonly used metacharacters is the $ character, which tells the shell that the following text refers to a variable. A variable is simply a piece of information that is stored in memory; variable names are typically uppercase words, and most variables are set by the Linux system automatically when you log in. An example of how one may use the $ metacharacter to refer to a variable is by using the *echo* command (which prints text to the terminal screen):

```
[root@localhost root]# echo Hi There!
Hi There!
[root@localhost root]# echo My shell is $SHELL
My Shell is /bin/bash
[root@localhost root]#_
```

Notice from the above output that $SHELL was translated into its appropriate value from memory (/bin/bash, the BASH Shell) because the shell recognized SHELL as a variable since it was prefixed by the $ metacharacter. A list of common BASH Shell metacharacters that will be discussed throughout this textbook are listed in Table 3-4.

Table 3-4   Common BASH Shell metacharacters

Metacharacter(s)	Description
$	Shell variable
~	Special home directory variable
&	Background command execution
;	Command termination
< << > >>	Input/output redirection
		Command piping
* ? [ ]	Shell wildcards
' " \	Metacharacter quotes
`	Command substitution
( ) { }	Command grouping

It is good practice to avoid metacharacters when typing commands unless you need to take advantage of their special functionality, as the shell will readily interpret them, which may lead to unexpected results.

If you accidentally use one of these characters and your shell does not return you to the normal prompt, simply press Ctrl and c simultaneously and your current command will be cancelled.

There are some circumstances where you may need to use a metacharacter in a command and prevent the shell from interpreting its special meaning. To do this, simply enclose the metacharacter in single quotes ' '. Single quotes will protect metacharacters from being interpreted specially by the shell (i.e., a $ will be interpreted as a $ character and not a variable identifier). You may also use double quotes " " to perform the same task; however, double quotes do not protect $, \, and ` characters. If only one character needs to be protected from shell interpretation, you may precede that character by a \ rather than enclosing it within quotes. An example of this type of quoting is:

```
[root@localhost root]# echo My Shell is $SHELL
My Shell is /bin/bash
[root@localhost root]# echo 'My Shell is $SHELL'
My Shell is $SHELL
[root@localhost root]# echo "My Shell is $SHELL"
My Shell is /bin/bash
[root@localhost root]# echo My Shell is \$SHELL
My Shell is $SHELL
[root@localhost root]#_
```

As seen in Table 3-4, not all quote characters protect characters from the shell. The back-quote characters ` ` may be used to perform command substitution; anything between backquotes is treated as another command by the shell and its output will be substituted in place of the backquotes. Take the expression `date` as an example:

```
[root@localhost root]# echo Today is `date`
Today is Tue Mar 26 09:28:11 EST 2002
[root@localhost root]#_
```

Getting Command Help

Most distributions of Linux contain more than 1000 different Linux commands in common configurations, and thus it would be impractical to memorize the syntax and use of each command. Fortunately, Linux stores documentation for each command in central locations so that they may be accessed easily. The most common form of documentation for Linux commands are **manual pages** (commonly referred to as man pages). One simply types the *man* command followed by a command name, and extensive information about that Linux command is displayed page-by-page on the terminal screen. This information includes a description of the command and its syntax, available options, and related files and commands. For example, to receive information on the format and usage of the *whoami* command, you could type the following:

```
[root@localhost root]# man whoami
```

The manual page is then displayed page-by-page on the terminal screen. You may use the cursor keys on the keyboard to scroll though the information or press q to quit. The manual page for *whoami* is similar to the following:

```
WHOAMI(1)                 FSF                 WHOAMI(1)

       whoami - print effective userid

SYNOPSIS
       whoami [OPTION]...

DESCRIPTION
       Print the user name associated with the current
       effective user id. Same as id -un.

       --help display this help and exit

       --version
           output version information and exit

AUTHOR
     Written by Richard Mlynarik.

REPORTING BUGS
       Report bugs to <bug-sh-utils@gnu.org>.

COPYRIGHT
       Copyright (c) 2000 Free Software Foundation, Inc.
       This is free software; see the source for copying
       conditions. There is NO warranty; not even for
       MERCHANTABILITY or FITNESS FOR A PARTICULAR
       PURPOSE.

SEE ALSO
       The full documentation for whoami is maintained as
       a Tex-info manual. If the info and who programs
       are properly installed at your site, the command

           info whoami

       should give you access to the complete manual.




GNU sh-utils 2.0.11       July 2001       WHOAMI(1)
[root@localhost root]#_
```

Notice that the *whoami* command is displayed as WHOAMI(1) in the manual page output above. The (1) denotes a section of the manual pages; section (1) means that whoami is a command that may be executed by any user. All manual pages contain certain section numbers, which describe the category of the command in the manual page database; a list of the different manual page section numbers can be found in Table 3-5.

Table 3-5   Manual page section numbers

Manual Page Section	Description
1	Commands that any user may execute
2	Linux system calls
3	Library routines
4	Special device files
5	File formats
6	Games
7	Macro packages
8	Commands that only the root user may execute
9	Linux kernel routines
n	New commands not categorized yet

Sometimes, there is more than one command, library routine, or file that has the same name. If you run the man command with that name as an argument, Linux will return the manual page with the lowest section number. For example, if there was a file called whoami as well as a command named whoami and you type *man whoami*, the manual page for the whoami command (section 1 of the manual pages) would be displayed. To display the manual page for the whoami file format instead, you would simply type *man 5 whoami* (section 5 of the manual pages).

Recall that there are many commands available to the Linux user; thus it may be cumbersome to find the command that you need to perform a certain task without using a Linux command dictionary. Fortunately, you have the ability to search the manual pages by keyword. To find all of the commands that have the word "who" in their name or description, type the following:

```
[root@localhost root] # man -k who
```

This command will produce the following output:

```
at.allow [at]        (5) - determine who can submit jobs via
at or batch
at.deny [at]         (5) - determine who can submit jobs via
at or batch
biff                 (1) - be notified if mail arrives and
who it is from
```

3

```
DLAED4 [dlaed4]     (l) - subroutine computes the I-th
updated eigenvalue of a symmetric rank-one modification
to a diagonal matrix whose elements are given in the
array d, and that D(i) < D(j) for i < j and that RHO > 0
DLASD4 [dlasd4]     (l) - subroutine computes the square
root of the I-th updated eigenvalue of a positive
symmetric rank-one modification to a positive diagonal
matrix whose entries are given as the squares of the
corresponding entries in the array d, and that 0 <= D(i)
< D(j) for i < j and that RHO > 0
ftpwho               (1) - show current process information
for each ftp user
fwhois [whois]       (1) - query a whois or nicname database
ICMAX1 [icmax1]      (l) - find the index of the element
whose real part has maximum absolute value
IZMAX1 [izmax1]      (l) - find the index of the element
whose real part has maximum absolute value
rusers               (1) - who is logged in to machines on
local network
rwho                 (1) - who is logged in on local
machines
rwhod                (8) - system status server
SLAED4 [slaed4]      (l) - subroutine computes the I-th
updated eigenvalue of a symmetric rank-one modification
to a diagonal matrix whose elements are given in the
array d, and that D(i) < D(j) for i < j and that RHO > 0
SLASD4 [slasd4]      (l) - subroutine computes the square
root of the I-th updated eigenvalue of a positive
symmetric rank-one modification to a positive diagonal
matrix whose entries are given as the squares of the
corresponding entries in the array d, and that 0 <= D(i)
< D(j) for i < j and that RHO > 0
w                    (1) - Show who is logged on and what
they are doing
who                  (1) - show who is logged on
whoami               (1) - print effective userid
whois                (1) - query a whois or nicname database
whom                 (1) - report to whom a message would go
[root@localhost root]#_
```

Once you find the command needed, you may simply run the man command on it without the –*k* option to find out detailed information about its syntax.

You may also use the *apropos who* command to perform the same function as the *man -k who* command. Both commands yield the exact same output on the terminal screen.

Another utility, originally intended to replace the man command in Linux, is the GNU **info pages**. You can access this utility by typing the *info* command followed by the name of the command in question. The info command returns an easy-to-read description of each command and also contains links to other information pages (called hyperlinks). Today, however, both the info pages and the manual pages are used to find documentation because manual pages have been utilized in Linux since its inception, and for over two decades in the UNIX operating system. An example of using the info utility to find information about the *whoami* command follows:

```
[root@localhost root]# info whoami
```

The info page is then displayed interactively:

```
File: sh-utils.info, Node: whoami invocation, Next: groups
invocation, Prev: logname invocation, Up: User information

`whoami': Print effective user id
===================================

   `whoami' prints the user name associated with the
current effective user id. It is equivalent to the
command   `id -un'.

   The only options are `—help' and `—version'. *Note
Common options::.



[root@localhost root]#_
```

While in the info utility, press the Ctrl and h keys together to display a help screen that describes the usage of info. As with the man command, you may use the q key to quit.

Some commands do not have manual pages or info pages. These commands are usually functions that are built into the BASH Shell itself. To find help on these commands, you must use the *help* command as follows:

```
[root@localhost root]# help echo
echo: echo [-neE] [arg ...]
    Output the ARGs. If -n is specified, the trailing
    newline is suppressed. If the -e option is given,
    interpretation of the following backslash-escaped
    characters is turned on:
      \a      alert (bell)
      \b      backspace
      \c      suppress trailing newline
```

3

```
\E         escape character
\f         form feed
\n         new line
\r         carriage return
\t         horizontal tab
\v         vertical tab
\\         backslash
\num       the character whose ASCII code is NUM (octal).
```

You can explicitly turn off the interpretation of the above characters with the -E option.

```
[root@localhost root]#_
```

Shutting Down the Linux System

Since the operating system handles the writing of data from computer memory to the disk drives in a computer, simply turning off the power to the computer may result in damaged user and system files. Thus it is important to prepare the operating system for shutdown before turning off the power to the hardware components of the computer. To do this you may issue the *shutdown* command, which can halt or reboot (restart) your computer after a certain period of time. To halt your system in 15 minutes, for example, you could type:

```
[root@localhost root] # shutdown -h +15m
```

This will produce the following output:

```
Broadcast message from root (tty2) at Tue Mar 26 04:08:18
2002 ..
The system is going DOWN for system halt in 15 minutes !!
```

Notice from the above output that you do not receive the command prompt back again once the shutdown command has started. Thus, to stop the shutdown, simply press the Ctrl and c keys in combination to cancel the command. Alternatively, you may log into another terminal and issue the command *shutdown –c* to cancel the shutdown.

To halt your system now, you could type:

```
[root@localhost root] # shutdown -h now
```

This command will produce the following output:

```
Broadcast message from root (tty2) at Tue Mar 26 04:08:18 20
02 ..
The system is going DOWN for system halt now !!
```

Other examples of the shutdown command and their descriptions can be seen in Table 3-6.

Table 3-6   Commands to halt and reboot the Linux operating system

Command	Description
shutdown –h +4m	Halts your system in 4 minutes
shutdown –r +4m	Reboots your system in 4 minutes
shutdown –h now	Halts your system immediately
shutdown –r now	Reboots your system immediately
shutdown –c	Cancels a scheduled shutdown
halt	Halts your system immediately
reboot	Reboots your system immediately

CHAPTER SUMMARY

❐ Most software information can be specified at the time of installation; however, the network configuration and package selection should be carefully planned before installation.

❐ Although there are many methods available for installing Linux, a CD-ROM-based installation is the easiest, most common method and seldom requires the creation of an installation boot disk.

❐ A typical Linux installation prompts the user for information such as language, boot loader, hard disk partitions, network configuration, firewall configuration, time zone, user accounts, authentication, and package selection. In addition, you should verify that any hardware detected during the installation was detected properly and make the appropriate changes if needed.

❐ Users must log into a terminal and receive a shell before they are able to interact with the Linux system and kernel. One user may log in several different times simultaneously to several different terminals locally or across a network.

❐ Regardless of the type of terminal that you use (graphical or command-line), you are able to enter commands, options, and arguments at a shell prompt to perform system tasks, obtain command help, or shut down the Linux system. The shell is case sensitive and understands a variety of special characters called shell metacharacters, that must be protected if their special meaning is not required.

KEY TERMS

arguments — Text that appears after a command name, does not start with a dash "–" character, and specifies information the command requires to work properly.

authentication — The process whereby each user must log in with a valid username and password before gaining access to the user interface of a system.

BASH Shell — The Bourne Again Shell; it is the default command line interface in Linux.

boot disk — A bootable floppy disk that can be used to start a Linux system or initiate a Linux installation.

boot loader — A small program started by BIOS ROM, which executes the Linux kernel in memory; LILO and GRUB are the two most common boot loaders for Linux.

command — A program that exists on the hard drive and is executed when typed on the command line.

Disk Druid — An easy-to-use graphic program used to partition or modify the partitions on an HDD.

ext2 — A non-journaling Linux filesystem.

ext3 — A journaling Linux filesystem.

framebuffer — An abstract representation of video hardware used by programs such that they do not need to communicate directly with the video hardware.

GRand Unified Bootloader (GRUB) — A common boot loader used in Linux.

info pages — A set of local, easy-to-read command syntax documentation available by typing the info command-line utility.

journaling — A filesystem function that keeps track of the information that needs to be written to the hard drive in a journal; common Linux journaling filesystems include ext3 and REISER.

Large Block Addressing 32-bit (LBA32) — A parameter that may be specified that enables Large Block Addressing in a boot loader; it is required only if a large hard disk that is not fully supported by the system BIOS is used.

LInux LOader (LILO) — A common boot loader used in Linux.

manual pages — The most common set of local command syntax documentation, available by typing the man command-line utility. Also known as man pages.

metacharacters — Key combinations that have special meaning in the Linux operating system.

options — Specific letters that start with a dash "-" or two and appear after the command name to alter the way the command works.

rawrite — A Windows utility that can be used to create installation boot disks.

Redundant Array of Inexpensive Disks (RAID) — A type of storage that can be used to combine hard disks together for fault-tolerance.

REISER — A journaling filesystem used in Linux.

shell — A user interface that accepts input from the user and passes the input to the kernel for processing.

swap memory — *See* virtual memory.

terminal — The channel that allows a certain user to log in and communicate with the kernel via a user interface.

vfat (virtual file allocation table) — A non-journaling filesystem that may be used in Linux.

virtual memory — An area on a hard disk (swap partition) that can be used to store information that normally resides in physical memory (RAM), if the physical memory is being used excessively.

REVIEW QUESTIONS

1. What is the default shell in Linux called?

    a. SH

    b. BSH

    c. CSH

    d. BASH

2. What equivalent to the man command generally provides an easier-to-read description of the queried command and also contains links to other related information?

    a. who

    b. man help

    c. man –descriptive

    d. info

3. What command can one use to safely shutdown the Linux system immediately?

    a. shutdown –c

    b. shutdown –r

    c. down

    d. halt

    e. crash stop

4. What command is equivalent to the man –k *keyword* command?

    a. find *keyword*

    b. man *keyword*

    c. apropos *keyword*

    d. appaloosa *keyword*

5. The Red Hat Linux 7.2 installation can be performed in which two of the following modes?

    a. text

    b. full

    c. subtext

    d. graphical

    e. administrator assisted

6. Linux commands entered via the command line are not case sensitive. True or False?

7. Which command blanks the terminal screen erasing previously displayed output?

   a. erase

   b. clean

   c. blank

   d. clear

8. When sitting at a computer running Linux what key combination is pressed to open the graphical terminal?

   a. Ctrl-Alt-F1

   b. Ctrl-Alt-7

   c. Ctrl-Alt-F7

   d. Ctrl-7

9. Once a user logs into a terminal, they receive a user interface called a
   _____ .

   a. GUID

   b. shell

   c. text box

   d. command screen

10. Users enter commands directly to the kernel of the Linux operating system. True or False?

11. How can one protect a metacharacter (such as the $ character) from shell interpretation?

    a. precede it with a /

    b. follow it with a \

    c. precede it with a $

    d. it cannot be done as metacharacters are essential

    e. precede it with a \

12. You know that there is a Linux command that will perform a desired function for you, but you cannot remember the full name of the command. You do remember it will flush a variable from your system. What command typed at a command prompt would display a list of commands that would likely contain the command you desire?

    a. man –k flush

    b. man –k find all

    c. man flush

    d. man –key flush

13. Which command displays the users who are currently logged into the Linux system?

    a. finger

    b. who

    c. id

    d. date

14. Which of the following packages can be used to standardize configuration files across Linux systems?

    a. Samba

    b. Apache

    c. NIS

    d. NFS

15. Which prompt does the root user receive when logged into the system?

    a. $

    b. @

    c. #

    d. !

16. Which prompt do regular users receive when logged into the system?

    a. $

    b. @

    c. #

    d. !

17. Which installation screen only appears if certain hardware was detected by the installation program?

    a. firewall configuration

    b. network configuration

    c. boot loader configuration

    d. X Windows customization

18. Which two partitions must one create at minimum during a Red Hat Linux 7.2 installation?

    a. /

    b. /boot

    c. swap

    d. /home

3

19. If you are planning to install 2.3GB of packages when installing your Linux server, how much free space should you have on your hard disk to create the necessary filesystems?

    a. 2.3GB

    b. 3GB

    c. 3.5GB

    d. 4.6GB

20. Which boot loaders are available to choose from during the installation of Red Hat Linux 7.2? (Choose all that apply.)

    a. LILO

    b. ABOOT

    c. GRUB

    d. TeX

HANDS-ON PROJECTS

These projects should be completed in the order given. All hands-on projects should take a total of three hours to complete. The requirements for this lab include:

❏ A Red Hat 7.2 CD-ROM installation set (Two CD-ROMs)

❏ An Intel architecture computer that meets the minimum Red Hat Linux installation requirements and contains Red Hat Linux-supported hardware components including a 4.5GB or greater IDE hard disk drive and a CD-ROM drive

❏ Access to a functional Web browser and an Internet connection

Project 3-1

In this hands-on project, you will install Red Hat Linux 7.2 on a computer.

1. Turn on the computer and place the first Red Hat Linux 7.2 CD-ROM in the CD-ROM tray. A "Welcome to Red Hat Linux 7.2!" screen should appear after a few seconds.

If the "Welcome to Red Hat Linux 7.2!" screen does not appear, ensure that your CD-ROM is listed in the boot order in your computer's BIOS settings. If the CD-ROM is listed and still fails to display the welcome screen, create a boot floppy using the instructions provided earlier in this chapter.

2. At the "Welcome to Red Hat Linux 7.2!" screen, read the available options and press **Enter** to start the installation.

3. At the "Language Selection" screen, ensure that **English** is selected and click **Next**.

4. At the "Keyboard Configuation" screen, verify that your keyboard model and layout are correct and click **Next**.

5. At the "Mouse Configuation" screen, verify that your mouse model and port are correct and click **Next**.

6. At the "Welcome to Red Hat Linux" screen, click **Next**.

7. At the "Install Options" screen, choose **Custom** and click **Next**.

8. At the "Choosing Your Partitioning Strategy" screen, choose **Manually partition with Disk Druid** and click **Next**.

9. At the "Partitions" screen, use your mouse to highlight any existing partitions on your hard drive device and press the **Delete** button. Click **YES** to confirm the action.

10. Use your mouse to highlight the **free** space on your hard drive device and click **New**. Enter the following information in the screen displayed:

    Mount Point =   /

    Type   =   ext3

    Size (Fixed) =   put in the value you obtained for "Space available for Filesystems" from the hands-on exercise in Chapter 2. This value should be greater than 3500Mb.

    Click **OK** when finished.

11. Use your mouse to highlight the **free** space on your hard drive device and click **New**. Enter the following information in the screen displayed:

    Type   =   swap

    Size (Fixed) =   put in the value you obtained for "Space required for swap partition" from the hands-on exercise in Chapter 2.

    Click **OK** when finished.

12. Observe the names of your partitions. Verify that you still have 50MB of free space on your hard disk device and click **Next**.

13. At the "Boot Loader Installation" screen, choose **Use LILO as the boot loader**. Ensure that the boot loader will be installed on the **Master Boot Record (MBR)** of the first hard disk device (usually /dev/hda) and click **Next**.

14. At the "Network Configuration" screen, ensure that **Activate on boot** is selected for the eth0 device and that the hostname is **localhost.localdomain**. Enter the appropriate IP address, netmask, and gateway information (unless you select DHCP) and click **Next**. (This step will not exist if your network card was not automatically detected.)

15. At the "Firewall Configuration" screen, select **No firewall** and click **Next**.

16. At the "Language Support Selection" screen, ensure that **English (USA)** is selected and click **Next**.

3

17. At the "Time Zone Selection" screen, choose your time zone and click **Next**.

18. At the "Account Configuration" screen, enter the password of **secret** in the Root Password and Confirm areas. Then click **Add** to add a new user and enter the following information in the areas provided:

    User Name: **user1**

    Full Name: **sample user one**

    Password: **secret**

    Confirm: **secret**

    When finished, click **OK** to close the dialog box and click **Next**.

19. At the "Authentication Configuration" screen, ensure that **Enable MD5 passwords** and **Enable shadow passwords** are enabled and click **Next**.

20. At the "Selecting Package Groups" screen, scroll down to the bottom of the list of available packages, choose **Everything** and click **Next**.

21. At the "Video Configuration" screen, ensure that your video card make and model are highlighted. Also ensure that the correct amount of video card RAM is displayed. Click **Next**.

22. At the "About to Install" screen, click **Next**. An "Installing Packages" screen will be displayed. This step usually takes between 30 and 60 minutes depending on your hardware and will require that you place the second CD-ROM in the CD-ROM tray when prompted.

23. At the "Boot Disk Creation" screen, insert a blank formatted floppy disk into your floppy disk drive and click **Next**.

24. At the "Monitor Selection" screen, ensure that your monitor is selected and that the correct values for Horizontal and Vertical Sync are displayed. Click **Next**.

25. At the "Custom X Configuration" screen, select a screen resolution of **800 × 600** and a color depth of **High Color (16 Bit)** or greater. Verify that the default desktop is **GNOME** and **Graphical** login is selected, then click **Next**.

26. At the congratulations screen, click **Exit**. Your system will now shutdown and boot into the Red Hat Linux operating system.

Project 3-2

In this hands-on project, you will explore some command-line terminals on a Linux system and enter in some basic commands to the BASH Shell.

1. Once your Linux system has been loaded, you will be placed at a graphical terminal (tty7). Switch to a command-line terminal (tty2) by pressing **Ctrl–Alt–F2** and log into the terminal using the username of **root** and the password of **secret**. Which prompt did you receive and why?

2. At the command prompt, type **date** and press **Enter** to view the current date and time. Now, type **Date** and press **Enter**. Why did you receive an error message? Can you tell which shell gave you the error message?

3. Switch to a different command-line terminal (tty5) by pressing **Ctrl–Alt–F5** and log into the terminal using the username of **user1** and the password of **secret**. Which prompt did you receive and why?

4. At the command prompt, type **who** and press **Enter** to view the users logged into the system. Who is logged in and on which terminal(s)?

5. Switch back to the terminal tty2 by pressing **Ctrl–Alt–F2**. Did you need to log in? Are the outputs from the date and Date commands still visible?

6. Try typing in each command listed in Table 3-3 in order (pressing **Enter** after each) and observe the output. What did the last command (exit) do?

7. Switch to the terminal tty5 by pressing **Ctrl–Alt–F5** and type **exit** and press **Enter** to log out of your shell.

Project 3-3

In this hands-on project, you will log into the graphical terminal in Red Hat Linux and interact with the GNOME and KDE desktops.

1. Switch to the graphical terminal (tty7) by pressing **Ctrl–Alt–F7** and log in using the username of **root** and the password of **secret**. Which desktop is started and why?

2. Observe the GNOME desktop. Move your mouse over the icons on the toolbar at the bottom of the screen and pause on each one. A dialog box should appear labeling what each icon does. When you reach the icon that is labeled "Terminal emulation program", click that icon to open up a BASH Shell prompt. What prompt do you receive and why?

3. At the command prompt, type **who** and press **Enter** to view the users logged into the system. Who is logged in and on which terminal(s)? Does the graphical desktop appear as tty7 or as :0?

4. Move your mouse over the icons on the toolbar and click on the one labeled **Main Menu**. From this menu, click on the option **Log out** and press **Yes** to confirm the action.

5. At the graphical login screen, use your mouse to select the **Session** menu and choose **KDE** from that menu. Log in as the user **user1** with the password **secret**. When you are prompted to make KDE the default desktop when logging in, choose **No**.

6. Observe the KDE desktop. Move your mouse over the icons on the toolbar at the bottom of the screen and pause on each one. A dialog box should appear labeling what each icon does. When you reach the icon that is labeled "Konsole", click that icon to open up a BASH Shell prompt. What prompt do you receive and why?

7. At the command prompt, type **echo $SHELL** and press **Enter** to view your current shell. Is this shell the same shell used for command-line terminals?

8. Move your mouse over the icons on the toolbar and click on the one labeled **Start Application**. From this menu, click on the option **Logout** and click **Logout** to confirm the action. When you are asked about changes to the KDE Personalizer, press **Cancel**.

Project 3-4

In this hands-on project, you will use and protect shell metacharacters.

1. Switch to a command-line terminal (tty2) by pressing **Ctrl-Alt-F2** and log into the terminal using the username of **root** and the password of **secret**.

2. At the command prompt, type **date;who** and press **Enter** to run the date command immediately followed by the who command. Use the information in Table 3-4 to describe the purpose of the **;** metacharacter.

3. At the command prompt, type **echo This is OK** and press **Enter** to display a message on the terminal screen.

4. At the command prompt, type **echo Don't do this** and press **Enter**. Which character needs to be protected in the previous command? Press the **Ctrl** and **c** keys together to cancel your command and return to a BASH Shell prompt.

5. At the command prompt, type **echo "Don't do this"** and press **Enter**. What was displayed on the terminal screen?

6. At the command prompt, type **echo Don\'t do this** and press **Enter**. What was displayed on the terminal screen?

7. At the command prompt, type **echo $SHELL** and press **Enter** to view the expansion of a variable using a shell metacharacter. What was displayed on the terminal screen? Next, type **echo $TEST** and press **Enter** to find out what happens when a variable that does not exist is used in a command. What was displayed?

8. At the command prompt, type **echo You have $4.50** and press **Enter**. What was displayed? Why? Which character needs to be protected in the previous command? What are two different ways that you can protect this character from interpretation by the shell?

9. At the command prompt, type **echo 'You have $4.50'** and press **Enter**. What was displayed on the terminal screen? Did the single quotes protect this metacharacter from shell interpretation?

10. At the command prompt, type **echo "You have $4.50"** and press **Enter**. What was displayed on the terminal screen? Did the double quotes protect this metacharacter from shell interpretation?

11. At the command prompt, type **echo You have \$4.50** and press **Enter**. What was displayed on the terminal screen? Did the backslash protect this metacharacter from shell interpretation?

12. At the command prompt, type **echo My name is `whoami`** and press **Enter**. What function do backquotes perform?

13. Type **exit** and press **Enter** to log out of your shell.

Project 3-5

In this hands-on project, you will find information about commands using online help utilities, and then properly shutdown your Linux system.

1. Switch to a command-line terminal (tty2) by pressing **Ctrl-Alt-F2** and log into the terminal using the username of **root** and the password of **secret**.

2. At the command prompt, type **man –k cron** and press **Enter** to view a list of manual pages that have the word **cron** in the name or description. Use Table 3-5 to determine what type of manual pages are displayed. How many manual pages are there for crontab? Are they different types of manual pages?

3. At the command prompt, type **man crontab** and press **Enter** to view the manual page for the crontab command. Observe the syntax of the crontab command, and press **q** when finished to quit out of the manual page and return to your command prompt.

4. At the command prompt, type **man 5 crontab** and press **Enter** to view the manual page for the crontab file format. Observe the syntax of the crontab file format, and press **q** when finished to quit out of the manual page and return to your command prompt.

5. At the command prompt, type **info** and press **Enter** to view a list of available GNU info pages. When finished, press **q** to quit out of the info utility.

6. At the command prompt, type **info date** and press **Enter** to view syntax information regarding the date command, and press **q** to quit out of the info utility when finished.

7. At the command prompt, type **help** to view a list of BASH Shell functions that have documentation. As the list is too long for your terminal, press the **Shift** and **Page Up** keys simultaneously to shift one page up to view the top of the list. Then press the **Shift** and **Page Down** keys simultaneously to shift one page down to view your command prompt again.

8. At the command prompt, type **help exit** to view information on the exit command, a function of your BASH Shell.

9. At the command prompt, type **shutdown –h now** to halt your system immediately. Which command from Table 3-6 performs the same function as **shutdown –h now**?

DISCOVERY EXERCISES

1. You are the network administrator for Slimjim, a peripheral device company. The network uses Linux and you need help information on some commands to perform your job. Open the manual pages and find all the commands that have the word "copy" in their name or description. What command did you use to accomplish this task? Are there any commands in this list that only a root user can execute? How are they indicated? Select any two of them and compare their *info* and *manual* pages. Access and read the manual pages on three other commands that interest you either by using the command name or by searching for them by related keyword (try using *apropos*).

2. Identify the errors with the following commands and indicate possible solutions. (*Hint:* Try typing them out at a shell prompt to view the error message.)

   Echo "This command does not work properly"

   date −z

   apropos man −k

   help date

   finger route

   shutdown −c now

   echo "I would like lots of $$$"

   man 8 date

EXPLORING LINUX FILESYSTEMS

**After completing this chapter,
you will be able to:**

- Understand and navigate the Linux directory structure using relative & absolute pathnames
- Describe the various types of Linux files
- View filenames & file types
- Use shell wildcards to specify multiple filenames
- Display the contents of text files and binary files
- Search text files for regular expressions using grep
- Identify common text editors used today
- Use the vi editor to manipulate text files

An understanding of the structure and commands surrounding the Linux filesystem is essential for effectively using Linux to manipulate data. In the first part of this chapter, you explore the Linux filesystem hierarchy by changing your position in the filesystem tree and listing filenames of various types. Next, you examine the shell wildcard metacharacters used to specify multiple filenames as well as view the contents of files using standard Linux commands. This is followed by a discussion of the regular expression metacharacters used when searching for text within files, and concluded with an introduction to the vi text editor and its equivalents.

THE LINUX DIRECTORY STRUCTURE

Fundamental to using the Linux operating system is an understanding of how Linux stores files on the hard drive. Typical Linux systems could have thousands of data and program files on the hard drive, thus a structure that organizes those files is necessary to make it easier to find and manipulate data and run programs. Recall from the previous chapter that Linux uses a logical directory tree to organize files into different directories (also known as folders). When a user stores files in a certain **directory**, they are physically stored in the filesystem of a certain partition on a hard disk inside the computer. Most people are familiar with the Windows operating system directory tree structure as depicted in Figure 4-1; each filesystem on a hard drive partition is referred to by a drive letter (such as C: or D:) and has a root directory (indicated by the \ character) containing subdirectories that together form a hierarchical tree.

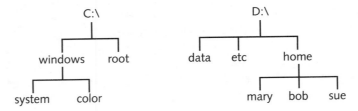

Figure 4-1   The Windows filesystem structure

It is important to describe directories in the directory tree properly; the **absolute pathname** to a file or directory is the full pathname of a certain file or directory starting from the root directory. From Figure 4-1, the absolute pathname for the color directory is C:\windows\color and the absolute pathname for the sue directory is D:\home\sue. In other words, we refer to C:\windows\color as the color directory below the windows directory below the root of C drive. Similarly, we refer to D:\home\sue as the sue directory below the home directory below the root of D drive.

Linux uses a similar directory structure. However, there are no drive letters; there is a single root (referred to using the / character), and different filesystems on hard drive partitions are mounted to different directories on this directory tree such that filesystems are transparent to the user. An example of a sample Linux directory tree equivalent to the Windows sample directory tree shown in Figure 4-1 is depicted in Figure 4-2.

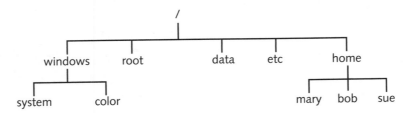

Figure 4-2   The Linux filesystem structure

From Figure 4-2, the absolute pathname for the color directory is /windows/color and the absolute pathname for the sue directory is /home/sue. In other words, we refer to the /windows/color directory as the color directory below the windows directory below the root of system (the / character). Similarly, we refer to the /home/sue directory as the sue directory below the home directory below the root of the system.

Changing Directories

When a user logs into their Linux system they are placed in their **home directory**, which is a place unique to each user to store their personal files. Regular users usually have a home directory named after their user account under the /home directory as in /home/sue. The root user, however has a home directory called root under the root directory of the system (/root) as seen in Figure 4-2. You can confirm the directory that you are currently in on the system by observing the name at the end of the shell prompt or by typing the **pwd command (print working directory)** at a command-line prompt and pressing Enter. If you are logged in as the root user, the following output will be displayed on the terminal screen:

```
[root@localhost root]# pwd
/root
[root@localhost root]#_
```

However, if logged in as the user sue, you will see the following output:

```
[sue@localhost sue]$ pwd
/home/sue
[sue@localhost sue]$_
```

To change directories, you can issue the **cd (change directory) command** with an argument specifying the destination directory. If you do not specify a destination directory, the **cd** command simply returns you to your home directory:

```
[root@localhost root]# cd /home/mary
[root@localhost mary]# pwd
/home/mary
[root@localhost mary]# cd /etc
[root@localhost etc]# pwd
/etc
[root@localhost etc]# cd
[root@localhost root]# pwd
/root
[root@localhost root]#_
```

The **~ metacharacter** can also be used to refer to the current user's home directory. Or you can use the ~ metacharacter to specify another user's home directory by appending a username at the end of the ~ metacharacter:

```
[root@localhost root]# cd ~mary
[root@localhost mary]# pwd
/home/mary
```

```
[root@localhost mary]# cd ~
[root@localhost root]# pwd
/root
[root@localhost root]#_
```

In many of the examples discussed earlier, the argument specified after the **cd** command is an absolute pathname to a directory, meaning that the system has all the information it needs to find the destination directory because the pathname starts from the root (/) of the system. However, in most Linux commands, you may also use a relative pathname in place of an absolute pathname to reduce typing. A **relative pathname** is the pathname of a target file or directory relative to your current directory in the tree. To specify a directory underneath your current directory simply refer to that directory by name (do not start the pathname with a / character). To refer to a directory one step closer to the root of the tree (also known as a parent directory), simply use two dots (**..**). An example of using relative pathnames to move around the directory tree is seen below:

```
[root@localhost root]# cd /home/mary
[root@localhost mary]# pwd
/home/mary
[root@localhost mary]# cd ..
[root@localhost home]# pwd
/home
[root@localhost home]# cd mary
[root@localhost mary]# pwd
/home/mary
[root@localhost mary]#_
```

In the above example, we used ".." to move up one parent directory and then used the word "mary" to specify the mary **subdirectory** relative to our current location in the tree. You may also move more than one level up or down the directory tree:

```
[root@localhost root]# cd /home/mary
[root@localhost mary]# pwd
/home/mary
[root@localhost mary]# cd ../..
[root@localhost /]# pwd
/
[root@localhost /]# cd home/mary
[root@localhost mary]# pwd
/home/mary
[root@localhost mary]#_
```

 You can also use one dot (.) to refer to the current directory. Although this is not useful when using the **cd** command, you will use it later in the book.

Although absolute pathnames are straightforward to use as arguments to commands when specifying the location of a certain file or directory, relative pathnames may save you a great deal of typing and reduce the potential for error if your current directory is far away from the root directory. Say, for example, that the current directory is /home/sue/ projects/acme/plans and you need to change this to the /home/sue/projects/acme directory. Using an absolute pathname, you would type `cd /home/sue/projects/ acme;` however, by using a relative pathname, you would only need to type `cd ..` to perform the same task, since the /home/sue/projects/acme directory is one parent directory above the current location in the directory tree.

An alternate method for saving time when typing pathnames as arguments to commands is to use the **Tab-completion** feature of the BASH Shell. To do this, type enough unique letters of a directory and press the Tab key to allow the BASH Shell to find the intended file or directory being specified and fill in the appropriate information. If there is more than one possible match, then the Tab-completion feature will alert the user with a beep sound; pressing the Tab key again after this beep sound will present the user with a list of possible files or directories.

Observe the directory structure in Figure 4-2. To use Tab completion to change the current directory to /home/sue, you would simply type `cd /h` and then press the Tab key. This will change the previous characters on the terminal screen to display cd /home/ (the BASH Shell was able to fill in the appropriate information since the /home directory is the only directory underneath the / directory that starts with the letter h). Then, you could add an s character to the command such that the command line displays cd /home/s and press the Tab key once again to allow the shell to fill in the remaining letters. This will result in the command `cd /home/sue/` being displayed on the terminal screen (the sue directory is the only directory that begins with the s character underneath the /home directory). At this point, you may press Enter to execute the command and change the current directory to /home/sue.

The Tab-completion feature of the BASH Shell can also be used to specify the pathname to files and executable programs as well as directories.

VIEWING FILES AND DIRECTORIES

Once a directory structure exists to organize files into an easy-to-use format, you may list directory contents to locate the file you need to execute, view, or edit. Before doing this, you should understand the various types of files and filenames that can be listed, as well as the different commands used to select filenames for viewing.

File Types

Fundamental to viewing files and directories is a solid understanding of the various types of files present on most Linux systems. There are several different types of files that may exist on a Linux system; the most common include:

- Text files
- Binary data files

- Executable program files
- Directory files
- Linked files
- Special device files
- Named pipes & sockets

Most files on a Linux system that contain configuration information are **text files**. Programs are also files that exist on the hard drive before they are executed in memory to become processes, and are usually associated with several supporting **binary data files** that store information such as common functions and graphics. In addition, directories themselves are just special files that serve as placeholders to organize other files. When one creates a directory, a file is placed on the hard drive to represent that directory.

Linked files are files that have an association with one another; they may represent the same data or they may point to another file (also known as a shortcut file). **Special device files** are less common than the other file types that have been mentioned, yet they are important for system administrators as they represent different devices on the system such as hard disks and serial ports. These device files are used in conjunction with commands that manipulate devices on the system; special device files are typically found only in the /dev directory and will be discussed in later chapters of this textbook. As with special device files, **named pipe files** are uncommon and used primarily by administrators. Named pipes identify a channel that passes information from one process in memory to another, and in some cases can be mediated by files on the hard drive. Writes to a file are processed while another process reads from the same file to achieve this passing of information. Another variant of a named pipe file is a **socket file**, which allows a process on another computer to write to a file on the local computer while another process reads from that file.

Filenames

Files are recognized by their **filenames**, which can include up to 255 characters, yet are rarely longer than 20 characters on most Linux systems. Filenames are typically comprised of alphanumeric characters, the underscore (_) character, the dash (-) character, and the period (.) character.

 It is important to avoid using the shell metacharacters discussed in the previous chapter when naming files. Using a filename that contains a shell metacharacter as an argument to a Linux command may produce unexpected results.

 Filenames that start with a period (.) are referred to as hidden files, and require a special command to be seen. This command will be discussed later in this chapter.

Although filenames used by the Windows operating system typically end with a period and three characters that describe the file type, as in document.txt (text) and server.exe (**executable program**), most files on the hard drive of a Linux system do not follow this pattern. However, some files on the Linux filesystem do contain characters at the end of the filename that indicate the file type. These characters are commonly referred to as **filename extensions**; common examples of filename extensions and their associated file types are shown in Table 4-1.

Table 4-1   Common filename extensions

Metacharacter	Description
.c	C programming language source code files
.cc .cpp	C++ programming language source code files
.html .htm	HTML (Hypertext Markup Language) files
.ps	Files formatted for printing with Postscript
.txt	Text files
.tar	Archived files (contain other files within)
.gz .bz2 .Z	Compressed files
.tar.gz .tgz .tar.bz2 .tar.Z	Compressed archived files
.conf .cfg	Configuration files (contain text)
.so	Shared object (programming library) files
.o	Compiled object files
.pl	PERL (Practical Extraction and Report Language) programs
.tcl	TCL (Tool Command Language) programs
.jpg .jpeg .png .tiff .xpm .gif	Binary files that contain graphical images
.sh	Shell scripts (contain text that is executed by the shell)

Listing Files

Linux hosts a variety of commands, which can be used to display files and their types in various directories on hard drive partitions. By far, the most common method for displaying files is by using the **ls command**. Following is an example of a file listing in the root user's home directory:

```
[root@localhost root]# pwd
/root
[root@localhost root]# ls
current  myprogram  project    project12  project2  project4
Desktop  myscript   project1   project13  project3  project5
[root@localhost root]#_
```

The files listed above and discussed throughout this chapter are for example purposes only. The hands-on projects will use different files.

The `ls` command displays all the files in the current directory in columnar format; however, you may also pass an argument to the `ls` command indicating the directory to be listed if different from current directory listing. In the following example, the files underneath the /home/bob directory are listed without changing the current directory:

```
[root@localhost root]# pwd
/root
[root@localhost root]# ls /home/bob
assignment1  file1  letter  letter2  project1
[root@localhost root]#_
```

When running the ls command you will notice that files of different types are often represented as different colors; however, the specific colors used to represent files of certain types may vary from terminal to terminal and distribution to distribution. As a result, do not use color alone to determine the file type.

Windows uses the dir command to list files and directories; to simplify the learning of Linux for Windows users, there is a `dir` command in Linux, which is simply a pointer or shortcut to the ls command.

Recall from the previous chapter that you may use switches to alter the behavior of commands. To view a list of files and their type, use the −F switch to the ls command:

```
[root@localhost root]# pwd
/root
[root@localhost root]# ls -F
current@  myprogram*  project    project12  project2  project4
Desktop/  myscript*   project1   project13  project3  project5
[root@localhost root]#_
```

The ls -F command appends a special character at the end of each filename displayed to indicate the type of file. In the above output, note that the filenames current, Desktop, myprogram, and myscript have special characters appended to their names. The @ symbol indicates a linked file, the * symbol indicates an executable file, and the / indicates a subdirectory. Two other special characters are not shown above: the = character indicates a socket, and the | character indicates a named pipe. All other file types do not have a special character appended to them and could be text files, binary data files, or special device files.

It is common convention to name directories starting with an uppercase letter, such as the D in the Desktop directory seen in the above output. This ensures that directories are listed at the beginning of the ls command output and allows you to determine quickly which names refer to directories when running the ls command without any options that specify file type.

Although the ls -F command is a quick way of getting file type information in an easy-to-read format, there are times when you will need to obtain more detailed information about each file. The ls -l command can be used to provide a long listing for each file in a certain directory:

```
[root@localhost root]# pwd
/root
[root@localhost root]# ls -l
total 548
lrwxrwxrwx  1 root root       9 Apr  7 09:56 current -> project12
drwx------  3 root root    4096 Mar 29 10:01 Desktop
-rwxr-xr-x  1 root root  519964 Apr  7 09:59 myprogram
-rwxr-xr-x  1 root root      20 Apr  7 09:58 myscript
-rw-r--r--  1 root root      71 Apr  7 09:58 project
-rw-r--r--  1 root root      71 Apr  7 09:59 project1
-rw-r--r--  1 root root      71 Apr  7 09:59 project12
-rw-r--r--  1 root root       0 Apr  7 09:56 project13
-rw-r--r--  1 root root      71 Apr  7 09:59 project2
-rw-r--r--  1 root root      90 Apr  7 10:01 project3
-rw-r--r--  1 root root      99 Apr  7 10:01 project4
-rw-r--r--  1 root root     108 Apr  7 10:01 project5
[root@localhost root]#_
```

Each file listed in the above example has eight components of information listed in columns from left to right:

1. A file type character

   - The d character represents a directory
   - The l character represents a symbolically linked file (discussed in Chapter 5)
   - The b or c characters represent special device files (discussed in Chapter 6)

- The n character represents a named pipe
- The s character represents a socket
- The − character represents all other file types (text files, binary data files)

2. A list of permissions on the file (the nine characters following the file type, also called the mode of the file)

3. A hard link count

4. The owner of the file

5. The group owner of the file

6. The file size

7. The most recent modification time of the file

8. The file name (some files are shortcuts or pointers to other files and indicated with an arrow -> as with the file called "current" in the above output; these are known as symbolic links and will be discussed in Chapter 5)

For the file named project in the previous example, you can see that this file is a regular file as the long listing of it begins with a - character, the permissions on the file are rw-r--r--, the hard link count is 1, the owner of the file is the root user, the group owner of the file is the root group, the size of the file is 71 bytes, and the file was modified last on April 7th at 9:58 AM.

 On most Linux systems there is a shortcut to the ls command that can be used to display the same columns of information as the ls -l command. Some users prefer to use this shortcut, commonly known as an alias, which is invoked when a user types ll at a command prompt. This is also known as the **ll command**.

The ls -F and ls -l commands are valuable to a user who wishes to display file types; however, neither of these commands can display all file types using special characters. To display the file type of any file, you can use the **file command**; simply give the file command an argument specifying what file to analyze. You may also pass multiple files as arguments or use the * metacharacter to refer to all files in the current directory. An example of using the file command in the root user's home directory is shown below:

```
[root@localhost root]# pwd
/root
[root@localhost root]# ls
current  myprogram  project   project12  project2  project4
Desktop  myscript   project1  project13  project3  project5
[root@localhost root]# file Desktop
Desktop:   directory
[root@localhost root]# file project Desktop
project:   ASCII text
Desktop:   directory
```

```
[root@localhost root]# file *
Desktop:    directory
current:    symbolic link to project12
myprogram:  ELF 32-bit LSB executable, Intel 80386, version 1,
dynamically linked (uses shared libs), stripped
myscript:   Bourne-Again shell script text executable
project:    ASCII text
project1:   ASCII text
project12:  ASCII text
project13:  empty
project2:   ASCII text
project3:   ASCII text
project4:   ASCII text
project5:   ASCII text
[root@localhost root]#_
```

As seen in the above example, the `file` command can also identify the differences between types of executable files. The myscript file is a **text file** that contains executable commands (also known as a shell script), whereas the myprogram file is a 32-bit executable compiled program. The file command also identifies empty files, such as project13 in the previous example.

Some filenames inside each user's home directory represent important configuration files or program directories. Since these files are rarely edited by the user and may clutter up the listing of files, they are normally hidden from view when using the `ls` and `file` commands. Recall from earlier that their filenames start with a period character (.). To view them, simply pass the `-a` option to the `ls` command. Some **hidden files** that are commonly seen in the root user's home directory are seen below:

```
[root@localhost root]# ls
current   myprogram  project    project12  project2   project4
Desktop   myscript   project1   project13  project3   project5
[root@localhost root]# ls -a
.                              .gimp-1.2         project
..                             .gnome            project1
.bash_history                  .gnome-desktop    project12
.bash_logout                   .gnome_private    project13
.bash_profile                  .gtkrc            project2
.bashrc                        .ICEauthority     project3
.cshrc                         .kde              project4
current                        .mcop             project5
.DCOPserver_localhost.localdomain  .MCOP-random-seed  .sane
Desktop                        .mcoprc           .sawfish
.first_start_kde               .mozilla          .tcshrc
.galeon                        myprogram         .Xauthority
.gconf                         myscript          .Xresources
.gconfd                        .nautilus
[root@localhost root]#_
```

As discussed earlier, the (.) character refers to the current working directory and the (..) character refers to the parent directory relative to your current location in the directory tree. Each of these pointers is seen as a special (or fictitious) file when using the ls -a command, as each starts with a period.

You may also specify several options simultaneously for most commands on the command line and receive the combined functionality of all the options. For example, to view all hidden files and their file types, you could type:

```
[root@localhost root]# ls -aF
./                                   .gimp-1.2/          project
../                                  .gnome/             project1
.bash_history                        .gnome-desktop/     project12
.bash_logout                         .gnome_private/     project13
.bash_profile                        .gtkrc              project2
.bashrc                              .ICEauthority       project3
.cshrc                               .kde/               project4
current@                             .mcop/              project5
.DCOPserver_localhost.localdomain@   .MCOP-random-seed   .sane/
Desktop/                             .mcoprc             .sawfish/
.first_start_kde                     .mozilla/           .tcshrc
.galeon/                             myprogram*          .Xauthority
.gconf/                              myscript            .Xresources
.gconfd/                             .nautilus/          .xsession-
errors
[root@localhost root]#_
```

The aforementioned options for the ls command (ls -l, ls -F, ls -a) are the most common options you would use when navigating the Linux directory tree; however, there are many options available in the ls command that alter the listing of files on the filesystem. These options and their descriptions are depicted in Table 4-2.

Table 4-2   Common options to the ls command

Option	Description
-a --all	Lists all filenames
-A --almost-all	Lists most filenames (excludes the . and .. special files)
-C	Lists filenames in column format
--color=n	Lists filenames without color
-f	Lists all filenames without sorting
-F --classify	Lists filenames classified by file type
--full-time	Lists filenames in long format and displays the full modification time
-l	Lists filenames in long format

Table 4-2　Common options to the ls command (continued)

Option	Description
-lh -l --human-readable	Lists filenames in long format with human-readable (easy-to-read) file sizes
-lG -l --no-group -o	Lists filenames in long format but omits the group information
-r --reverse	Lists filenames reverse sorted
-R --recursive	Lists filenames in the specified directory and all subdirectories
-s	Lists filenames and their associated size in kilobytes (K)
-S	Lists filenames sorted by file size
-t	Lists filenames sorted by modification time
-U	Lists filenames without sorting
-x	Lists filenames in rows rather than in columns

Wildcard Metacharacters

In the previous section you saw that the * metacharacter was used to indicate, or "match," all the files in the current directory, much like a wildcard matches certain cards in a card game. As a result, the * metacharacter is called a **wildcard metacharacter**. Wildcard metacharacters can simplify commands that specify more than one filename on the command line. These wildcard metacharacters are interpreted by the shell and can be used with most common Linux filesystem commands, including the few we have already mentioned (ls, file, and cd). These metacharacters match certain portions of filenames, or the entire filename itself. A list of wildcard metacharacters can be found in Table 4–3 alongside their descriptions.

Table 4-3　Wildcard metacharacters

Metacharacter	Description
*	Matches 0 or more characters in a filename
?	Matches 1 character in a filename
[aegh]	Matches 1 character in a filename—provided this character is either an a, e, g, or h
[a-e]	Matches 1 character in a filename—provided this character is either an a, b, c, d, or e
[!a-e]	Matches 1 character in a filename—provided this character is NOT an a, b, c, d, or e

Wildcards can be demonstrated using the ls command. Examples of using wildcard metacharacters to narrow down the listing produced by the ls command are seen below:

```
[root@localhost root]# ls
current  myprogram project   project12  project2  project4
Desktop  myscript  project1  project13  project3  project5
[root@localhost root]# ls project*
project project1 project12 project13 project2 project3
project4 project5
[root@localhost root]# ls project?
project1  project2  project3  project4  project5
[root@localhost root]# ls project??
project12  project13
[root@localhost root]# ls project[135]
project1  project3  project5
[root@localhost root]# ls project[!135]
project2  project4
```

DISPLAYING THE CONTENTS OF TEXT FILES

So far, this chapter has discussed commands that can be used to navigate the Linux directory structure and view filenames and file types; it is usual now to display the contents of these files. By far the most common file type that one displays is text files. These files are usually small and contain configuration information or instructions that the shell interprets (called a shell script), but can also contain other forms of text, as in e-mail letters. To view an entire text file on the terminal screen (also referred to as **concatenation**), you can use the **cat command**. Below is an example of using the cat command to display the contents of an e-mail message (in the fictitious example file project4):

```
[root@localhost root]# ls
current  myprogram project   project12  project2  project4
Desktop  myscript  project1  project13  project3  project5
[root@localhost root]# cat project4
Hi there, I hope this day finds you well.

Unfortunately we were not able to make it to your dining
room this year while vacationing in Algonquin Park - I
especially wished to see the model of the Highland Inn
and the train station in the dining room.

I have been reading on the history of Algonquin Park but
no where could I find a description of where the Highland
Inn was originally located on Cache lake.

If it is no trouble, could you kindly let me know such that
I need not wait until next year when I visit your lodge?
```

```
Regards,
Mackenzie Elizabeth
[root@localhost root]#_
```

You can also use the `cat` command to display the line number of each line in the file in addition to the contents by passing the –n option to the `cat` command. In the following example, the number of lines in the fictitious example project4 file are displayed:

```
[root@localhost root]# cat -n project4
     1  Hi there, I hope this day finds you well.
     2
     3  Unfortunately we were not able to make it to your dining
     4  room this year while vacationing in Algonquin Park - I
     5  especially wished to see the model of the Highland Inn
     6  and the train station in the dining room.
     7
     8  I have been reading on the history of Algonquin Park but
     9  no where could I find a description of where the Highland
    10  Inn was originally located on Cache lake.
    11
    12  If it is no trouble, could you kindly let me know such that
    13  I need not wait until next year when I visit your lodge?
    14
    15  Regards,
    16  Mackenzie Elizabeth
[root@localhost root]#_
```

In some cases, you may wish to display the contents of a certain text file in reverse order, which is useful when displaying files that have text appended to them continuously by system services. These files, also known as **log files**, contain the most recent entries at the bottom of the file. To display a file in reverse order, use the **tac command** ("cat" spelled backwards), as seen below with the fictitious example file project4:

```
[root@localhost root]# tac project4
Mackenzie Elizabeth
Regards,

I need not wait until next year when I visit your lodge?
If it is no trouble, could you kindly let me know such that

Inn was originally located on Cache lake.
no where could I find a description of where the Highland
I have been reading on the history of Algonquin Park but

and the train station in the dining room.
especially wished to see the model of the Highland Inn
room this year while vacationing in Algonquin Park - I
Unfortunately we were not able to make it to your dining

Hi there, I hope this day finds you well.
[root@localhost root]#_
```

If the file displayed is very large and you only wish to view the first few lines of it, you may use the head command. The **head command** displays by default the first 10 lines (including blank lines) of a text file to the terminal screen, but can also take a numeric option specifying a different number of lines to display. An example of using the head command to view the top of the project4 file is seen below:

```
[root@localhost root]# head project4
Hi there, I hope this day finds you well.

Unfortunately we were not able to make it to your dining
room this year while vacationing in Algonquin Park - I
especially wished to see the model of the Highland Inn
and the train station in the dining room.

I have been reading on the history of Algonquin Park but
no where could I find a description of where the Highland
Inn was originally located on Cache lake.
[root@localhost root]# head -3 project4
Hi there, I hope this day finds you well.

Unfortunately we were not able to make it to your dining
[root@localhost root]#_
```

Just as the head command displays the beginning of text files, the **tail command** can be used to display the end of text files. By default, the tail command displays the last 10 lines of a file, but can also take a numeric option specifying the number of lines to display to the terminal screen as seen below with the project4 file:

```
[root@localhost root]# tail project4

I have been reading on the history of Algonquin Park but
no where could I find a description of where the Highland
Inn was originally located on Cache lake.

If it is no trouble, could you kindly let me know such that
I need not wait until next year when I visit your lodge?

Regards,
Mackenzie Elizabeth
[root@localhost root]# tail -2 project4
Regards,
Mackenzie Elizabeth
[root@localhost root]#_
```

The tail command also accepts another option specifying the line number to start at when displaying text to the terminal screen. For example, to display the end of a text file starting from line 10 and continuing on until the end of the file, simply use the +10 option with the `tail` command, as seen below:

```
[root@localhost root]# tail +10 project4
Inn was originally located on Cache lake.

If it is no trouble, could you kindly let me know such that
I need not wait until next year when I visit your lodge?

Regards,
Mackenzie Elizabeth
[root@localhost root]#_
```

4

While some text files can be displayed completely on the terminal screen, you may encounter text files that are too large to be displayed. In this case the `cat` command will display the entire file contents in order to the terminal screen, and the top of the file will not be displayed as there is not enough screen area to do so. Thus, it is useful to display text files in a page-by-page fashion by using either the more or less commands.

The **more command** gets its name from the pg command once used on UNIX systems. The `pg` command displayed a text file page-by-page on the terminal screen starting at the beginning of the file; pressing the spacebar or Enter key would display the next page and so on. The `more` command does more than `pg` did, as it displays the next complete page of a text file if you press the spacebar, but displays only the next line of a text file if you press Enter. In that way, you can browse the contents of a text file page-by-page or line-by-line. The example file project5 is an excerpt from Shakespeare's tragedy Macbeth and is too large to be displayed fully on the terminal screen using the cat command. Using the more command to view its contents would result in the following output:

```
[root@localhost root]# more project5
Go bid thy mistress, when my drink is ready,
She strike upon the bell. Get thee to bed.
Is this a dagger which I see before me,
The handle toward my hand? Come, let me clutch thee.
I have thee not, and yet I see thee still.
Art thou not, fatal vision, sensible
To feeling as to sight? or art thou but
A dagger of the mind, a false creation,
Proceeding from the heat-oppressed brain?
I see thee yet, in form as palpable
As this which now I draw.
Thou marshall'st me the way that I was going;
And such an instrument I was to use.
Mine eyes are made the fools o' the other senses,
Or else worth all the rest; I see thee still,
And on thy blade and dudgeon gouts of blood,
Which was not so before. There's no such thing:
It is the bloody business which informs
```

```
Thus to mine eyes. Now o'er the one halfworld
Nature seems dead, and wicked dreams abuse
The curtain'd sleep; witchcraft celebrates
Pale Hecate's offerings, and wither'd murder,
Alarum'd by his sentinel, the wolf,
--More--(71%)
```

Note from the above output that the **more** command displays the first page without returning you to the shell prompt. Instead, the **more** command displays a prompt at the bottom of the terminal screen that indicates how much of the file is displayed on the screen as a percentage of the total file size. In the above example, 71% of the project5 file is displayed. At this prompt, you may press the spacebar to advance one whole page, or the Enter key to advance to the next line. In addition, the **more** command allows other user interaction at this prompt. Pressing the h character at the prompt displays a help screen as seen in the following output, and pressing the q character quits out of the **more** command completely without viewing the remainder of the file.

```
--More--(71%)
Most commands optionally preceded by integer argument k.
Defaults in brackets. Star (*) indicates argument becomes new
default.
-------------------------------------------------------------
<space>                 Display next k lines of text [current screen size]
z                       Display next k lines of text [current screen size]*
<return>                Display next k lines of text [1]*
d or ctrl-D             Scroll k lines [current scroll size, initially 11]*
q or Q or <interrupt>   Exit from more
s                       Skip forward k lines of text [1]
f                       Skip forward k screenfuls of text [1]
b or ctrl-B             Skip backwards k screenfuls of text [1]
'                       Go to place where previous search started
=                       Display current line number
/<regular expression>   Search for kth occurrence of regular expression[1]
n                       Search for kth occurrence of last r.e [1]
!<cmd> or :!<cmd>       Execute <cmd> in a subshell
v                       Start up /usr/bin/vi at current line
ctrl-L                  Redraw screen
:n                      Go to kth next file [1]
:p                      Go to kth previous file [1]
:f                      Display current file name and line number
.                       Repeat previous command
-------------------------------------------------------------
--More--(71%)
```

Just as the more command was named as a result of allowing more user functionality, the **less command** is named similarly, as it can do more than the more command (remember that "less is more," more or less). Like the more command, the less command can browse the contents of a text file page-by-page by pressing the spacebar and line-by-line by pressing the Enter key; however, you may also use the cursor keys on the keyboard to scroll up and down the contents of the file. The output of the less command when used to view the project5 file is seen below:

```
[root@localhost root]# less project5
Go bid thy mistress, when my drink is ready,
She strike upon the bell. Get thee to bed.
Is this a dagger which I see before me,
The handle toward my hand? Come, let me clutch thee.
I have thee not, and yet I see thee still.
Art thou not, fatal vision, sensible
To feeling as to sight? or art thou but
A dagger of the mind, a false creation,
Proceeding from the heat-oppressed brain?
I see thee yet, in form as palpable
As this which now I draw.
Thou marshall'st me the way that I was going;
And such an instrument I was to use.
Mine eyes are made the fools o' the other senses,
Or else worth all the rest; I see thee still,
And on thy blade and dudgeon gouts of blood,
Which was not so before. There's no such thing:
It is the bloody business which informs
Thus to mine eyes. Now o'er the one halfworld
Nature seems dead, and wicked dreams abuse
The curtain'd sleep; witchcraft celebrates
Pale Hecate's offerings, and wither'd murder,
Alarum'd by his sentinel, the wolf,
Whose howl's his watch, thus with his stealthy pace.
project5
```

Like the more command, the less command displays a prompt at the bottom of the file using the : character or the filename of the file being viewed (project5 in our example), yet the less command contains more keyboard shortcuts for searching out text within files. At the less prompt, you may press the h key to obtain a help screen or the q key to quit. The first help screen for the less command, which describes some of the keyboard shortcuts, is seen below:

```
               SUMMARY OF LESS COMMANDS

    Commands marked with * may be preceded by a number, N.
    Notes in parentheses indicate the behavior if N is given.

h  H                     Display this help.
q  :q  Q  :Q  ZZ         Exit.
 -----------------------------------------------------------
```

```
                              MOVING

   e  ^E  j  ^N  CR    *  Forward  one line    (or N lines).
   y  ^Y  k  ^K  ^P    *  Backward one line    (or N lines).
   f  ^F  ^V  SPACE    *  Forward  one window (or N lines).
   b  ^B  ESC-v        *  Backward one window (or N lines).
   z                   *  Forward  one window (and set window to N).
   w                   *  Backward one window (and set window to N).
   ESC-SPACE           *  Forward  one window, but don't stop at end-of-file
   d  ^D               *  Forward  one half-window(and set half-window to N)
   u  ^U               *  Backward one half-window(and set half-window to N)
   ESC-(  RightArrow   *  Left  8 character positions (or N positions).
   ESC-)  LeftArrow    *  Right 8 character positions (or N positions).
   F                      Forward forever; like "tail -f".

   HELP -- Press RETURN for more, or q when done
```

The more and less commands can also be used in conjunction with the output of other commands if that output is too large to fit on the terminal screen. To do this, simply use the | metacharacter after the command followed by either the more or less command, as seen below:

```
[root@localhost root]# cd /etc
[root@localhost etc]# ls -l | more
total 2388
-rw-r--r--    1 root      root      15223 Jun 25  2001 a2ps.cfg
-rw-r--r--    1 root      root       2561 Jun 25  2001
a2ps-site.cfg
-rw-r--r--    1 root      root         48 Apr  8 07:12 adjtime
drwxr-xr-x    4 root      root       4096 Mar 28 04:10 alchemist
-rw-r--r--    1 root      root       1109 Mar 28 05:03 aliases
-rw-r--r--    1 root      root      12288 Apr 11 20:42 aliases.db
drwxr-xr-x    3 amanda    disk       4096 Mar 28 04:59 amanda
-rw-r--r--    1 amanda    disk          0 Jul 13  2001 amandates
-rw-------    1 root      root        688 Jul 18  2001 amd.conf
-rw-r-----    1 root      root        105 Jul 18  2001 amd.net
-rw-r--r--    1 root      root        370 Jun 24  2001 anacrontab
-rw-------    1 root      root          1 Aug  2  2001 at.deny
-rw-r--r--    1 root      root        212 Aug 29  2001 auto.master
-rw-r--r--    1 root      root        575 Aug 29  2001 auto.misc
-rw-r--r--    1 root      root       1229 May 21  2001 bashrc
drwxr-xr-x    2 root      root       4096 Mar 28 04:17 cipe
drwxr-xr-x    3 root      root       4096 Sep  5  2001 CORBA
drwxr-xr-x    2 root      root       4096 Mar 28 04:19 cron.d
drwxr-xr-x    2 root      root       4096 Mar 28 05:06 cron.daily
--More--
```

In the previous example, the output of the `ls -l` command was redirected to the `more` command, which displays the first page of output on the terminal. You may then advance through the output page-by-page or line-by-line. This type of redirection will be discussed later, in Chapter 8.

DISPLAYING THE CONTENTS OF BINARY FILES

It is important to employ text file commands such as `cat`, `tac`, `head`, `tail`, `more`, and `less` only on files that contain text; otherwise you may find yourself with random output on the terminal screen, or even a dysfunctional terminal. To view the contents of binary files, you would typically use the program that was used to create the file; however, there are some commands that can be used to display safely the contents of most binary files. The **strings command** searches for text characters in a binary file and outputs them to the screen. In many cases these text characters may indicate what the binary file is used for. For example, to find the text characters inside the /bin/echo binary executable program, you could use the following command:

```
[root@localhost root]# strings /bin/echo
u∫x[ ]├U
σSRφ
]ⁿ𝔽├
memory exhausted
Try '%s --help' for more information.
Usage: %s [OPTION]... [STRING]...
Echo the STRING(s) to standard output.
  -n        do not output the trailing newline
  -e        enable interpretation of the backslash-escaped char-
acters
            listed below
  -E        disable interpretation of those sequences in STRINGs
      --help      display this help and exit (should be alone)
      --version   output version information and exit
(should be alone)
Without -E, the following sequences are recognized and
interpolated:
  \NNN    the character whose ASCII code is NNN (octal)
  \\      backslash
  \a      alert (BEL)
  \b      backspace
  \c      suppress trailing newline
  \f      form feed
  \n      new line
  \r      carriage return
  \t      horizontal tab
  \v      vertical tab
```

```
Report bugs to <bug-sh-utils@gnu.org>.
/usr/share/locale
POSIXLY_CORRECT
FIXME unknown
2.0.11
GNU sh-utils
echo
write error
%s: %s
version
help
clocale
escape
shell-always
shell
literal
Copyright (C) 2000 Free Software Foundation, Inc.
This is free software; see the source for copying
conditions.  There is
NO
warranty; not even for MERCHANTABILITY or FITNESS FOR A
PARTICULAR PURPOSE.
%s (%s) %s
%s %s
Written by %s.
[root@localhost root]#_
```

While this output may not be easy to read, it does contain portions of text that could point a user in the right direction to find out more about the /bin/echo command. Another command that is safe to use on binary files and text files is the **od command**, which displays the contents of the file in octal format (numeric base 8 format). An example of using the od command to display the contents of the file project4 is seen in the following example:

```
[root@localhost root]# od project4
0000000 064510 072040 062550 062562 020054 020111 067550 062560
0000020 072040 064550 020163 060544 020171 064546 062156 020163
0000040 067571 020165 062567 066154 006456 006412 052412 063156
0000060 071157 072564 060556 062564 074554 073440 020145 062567
0000100 062562 067040 072157 060440 066142 020145 067564 066440
0000120 065541 020145 072151 072040 020157 067571 071165 062040
0000140 067151 067151 020147 005015 067562 066557 072040 064550
0000160 020163 062571 071141 073440 064550 062554 073040 061541
0000200 072141 067551 064556 063556 064440 020156 066101 067547
0000220 070556 064565 020156 060520 065562 026440 044440 006440
0000240 062412 070163 061545 060551 066154 020171 064567 064163
0000260 062145 072040 020157 062563 020145 064164 020145 067555
0000300 062544 020154 063157 072040 062550 044040 063551 066150
0000320 067141 020144 067111 020156 005015 067141 020144 064164
0000340 020145 071164 064541 020156 072163 072141 067551 020156
```

```
0000360  067151  072040  062550  062040  067151  067151  020147  067562
0000400  066557  020056  005015  005015  020111  060550  062566  061040
0000420  062545  020156  062562  062141  067151  020147  067157  072040
0000440  062550  064040  071551  067564  074562  067440  020146  066101
0000460  067547  070556  064565  020156  060520  065562  061040  072165
0000500  006440  067012  020157  064167  071145  020145  067543  066165
0000520  020144  020111  064546  062156  060440  062040  071545  071143
0000540  070151  064564  067157  067440  020146  064167  071145  020145
0000560  064164  020145  064510  064147  060554  062156  006440  044412
0000600  067156  073440  071541  067440  064562  064547  060556  066154
0000620  020171  067554  060543  062564  020144  067157  041440  061541
0000640  062550  066040  065541  027145  005015  005015  063111  064440
0000660  020164  071551  067040  020157  071164  072557  066142  026145
0000700  061440  072557  062154  074440  072557  065440  067151  066144
0000720  020171  062554  020164  062555  065440  067556  020167  072563
0000740  064143  072040  060550  020164  005015  020111  062556  062145
0000760  067040  072157  073440  064541  020164  067165  064564  020154
0001000  062556  072170  074440  060545  020162  064167  067145  044440
0001020  073040  071551  072151  074440  072557  020162  067554  063544
0001040  037545  005015  005015  062522  060547  062162  026163  005015
0001060  060515  065543  067145  064572  020145  066105  075151  061141
0001100  072145  006550  006412  000012
0001107
[root@localhost root]#_
```

SEARCHING FOR TEXT WITHIN FILES

Recall that Linux was modeled after the UNIX operating system. The UNIX operating system is often referred to as the "grandfather" of all operating systems because it is over 30 years old and has formed the basis for most advances in computing technology. The major use of the UNIX operating system in the past 30 years involved simplifying business and scientific management through database applications; as a result, many commands (referred to as **text tools**) were developed for the UNIX operating system that could search for and manipulate text, such as database information, in many different and advantageous ways. A set of text wildcards was also developed to ease the searching of specific text information. These text wildcards are called **regular expressions (regexp)** and are recognized by several text tools and programming languages including, but not limited to:

- grep
- awk
- sed
- vi

- emacs

- ex

- ed

- C++

- PERL

- Tcl

Since Linux is a close relative of the UNIX operating system, these text tools and regular expressions are available to Linux as well. By combining text tools together (as we shall see later), a typical Linux system can search for and manipulate data in almost every way possible. As a result, regular expressions and the text tools that use them are commonly used in business today.

Regular Expressions

As mentioned earlier, regular expressions (also referred to by the word regexp) allow you to specify a certain pattern of text within a text document. They work similarly to wildcard metacharacters in that they are used to match characters, yet they have many differences:

- Wildcard metacharacters are interpreted by the shell, whereas regular expressions are interpreted by a text tool program.

- Wildcard metacharacters match characters in filenames (or directory names) on a Linux filesystem, whereas regular expressions match characters *within* text files on a Linux filesystem.

- Wildcard metacharacters typically have different definitions than regular expression metacharacters.

- There are more regular expression metacharacters available than wildcard metacharacters.

In addition, regular expression metacharacters are divided into two different categories: common regular expressions and extended regular expressions. Common regular expressions are available to most text tools; extended regular expressions are less common and available in only certain text tools. Definitions and examples of some common and extended regular expressions can be seen in Table 4-4.

Table 4-4   Regular expressions

Regular Expression	Description	Example	Type
*	Matches 0 or more occurrences of the previous character	**letter*** matches lette, letter, letterr, letterrrr, letterrrrr, etc.	Common
?	Matches 0 or 1 occurrences of the previous character	**letter?** matches lette, letter	Extended
+	Matches 1 or more occurrences of the previous character	**letter+** matches letter, letterr, letterrrr, letterrrrr, etc.	Extended
. (period)	Matches 1 character of any type	**letter.** matches lettera, letterb, letterc, letter1, letter2, letter3, etc.	Common
[...]	Matches one character from the range specified within the braces	**letter[1238]** matches letter1, letter2, letter3, and letter8 **letter[a-c]** matches lettera, letterb, and letterc	Common
[^...]	Matches one character NOT from the range specified within the braces	**letter[^1238]** matches letter4, letter5, letter6, lettera, letterb, etc. (any character except 1, 2, 3, or 8)	Common
{ }	Matches a specific number or range of the previous character	**letter{3}** matches letterrr **letter{2,4}** matches letterr, letterrr, and letterrrr	Extended
^	Matches the following characters if they are the first characters on the line	**^letter** matches letter if letter is the first set of characters in the line	Common
$	Matches the previous characters if they are the last characters on the line	**letter$** matches letter if letter is the last set of characters in the line	Common
(... | ...)	Matches either of two sets of characters	**(mother | father)** matches the word mother or father	Extended

The grep Command

The most common text tool that allows you the ability to search for information using regular expressions is the grep command. **Grep** stands for **Global Regular Expression Print** and is used to display lines in a text file that match a certain common regular expression. To display lines of text that match extended regular expressions, you must use the **egrep command** (or the –E option to the grep command) There also exists an **fgrep command** (or the –F option to the grep command) that does not interpret any regular expressions and consequently returns results much faster. Take, for example, the project4 file seen earlier:

```
[root@localhost root]# cat project4
Hi there, I hope this day finds you well.

Unfortunately we were not able to make it to your dining
room this year while vacationing in Algonquin Park - I
especially wished to see the model of the Highland Inn
and the train station in the dining room.

I have been reading on the history of Algonquin Park but
nowhere could I find a description of where the Highland
Inn was originally located on Cache Lake.

If it is no trouble, could you kindly let me know such that
I need not wait until next year when I visit your lodge?

Regards,
Mackenzie Elizabeth
[root@localhost root]#_
```

The grep command requires two arguments at minimum: the first argument specifies which text to search for, and the remaining arguments specify the files to search inside. If a pattern of text is matched, the grep command displays the entire line on the terminal screen. For example, to list only those lines in the file project4 that contain the words "Algonquin Park", you could enter the following grep command:

```
[root@localhost root]# grep "Algonquin Park" project4
room this year while vacationing in Algonquin Park - I
I have been reading on the history of Algonquin Park but
[root@localhost root]#_
```

To return the lines that do not contain the text "Algonquin Park", you may use the –v option of the grep command to reverse the meaning of the previous command:

```
[root@localhost root]# grep -v "Algonquin Park" project4
Hi there, I hope this day finds you well.

Unfortunately we were not able to make it to your dining
especially wished to see the model of the Highland Inn
and the train station in the dining room.

nowhere could I find a description of where the Highland
Inn was originally located on Cache Lake.

If it is no trouble, could you kindly let me know such that
I need not wait until next year when I visit your lodge?
```

```
        Regards,
        Mackenzie Elizabeth
        [root@localhost root]#_
```

Keep in mind that the text being searched is case sensitive; to perform a case-insensitive search, use the –i option to the grep command:

```
[root@localhost root]# grep "algonquin park" project4
[root@localhost root]#_
[root@localhost root]# grep -i "algonquin park" project4
room this year while vacationing in Algonquin Park - I
I have been reading on the history of Algonquin Park but
[root@localhost root]#_
```

Another important note to keep in mind regarding text tools such as grep is that they match only patterns of text; they are unable to discern words or phrases unless they are specified. Say, for example, that you want to search for the lines that contain the word "we"; the grep command used to perform this task is seen below:

```
[root@localhost root]# grep "we" project4
Hi there, I hope this day finds you well.
Unfortunately we were not able to make it to your dining
[root@localhost root]#_
```

Notice from the above output that the first line displayed does not contain the word "we"; the word "well" contains the text pattern "we" and is displayed as a result. To display only lines that contain the word "we", you could type the following to match the letters "we" surrounded by space characters:

```
[root@localhost root]# grep " we " project4
Unfortunately we were not able to make it to your dining
[root@localhost root]#_
```

None of the previous grep examples used regular expression metacharacters to search for text in the project4 file. Some examples of using regular expressions (Table 4-4) when searching this file are seen throughout the remainder of this section.

To view lines that contain the word "toe" or "two" or "the" or "tie", you can enter the following command:

```
[root@localhost root]# grep " t.e " project4
especially wished to see the model of the Highland Inn
and the train station in the dining room.
I have been reading on the history of Algonquin Park but
nowhere could I find a description of where the Highland
[root@localhost root]#_
```

To view lines that start with the word "I", you can enter the following command:

```
[root@localhost root]# grep "^I " project4
I have been reading on the history of Algonquin Park but
I need not wait until next year when I visit your lodge?
[root@localhost root]#_
```

To view lines that contain the text "lodge" or "lake", you need to use an extended regular expression and the egrep command, as seen below:

```
[root@localhost root]# egrep "(lodge|lake)" project4
Inn was originally located on Cache Lake.
I need not wait until next year when I visit your lodge?
[root@localhost root]#_
```

EDITING TEXT FILES

Recall that text files are the most common type of file that Linux users and administrators will modify. Most system configuration is stored in text files, as well as common information such as e-mail and program source code. Consequently, there are many text editors that are packaged with most Linux distributions and many more available for Linux systems via the Internet. Text editors come in two varieties: editors that can be used on the command-line, including vi (vim), pico, mcedit, and emacs; and editors that must be used in a GUI environment, including xemacs, xedit, nedit, gedit, and kedit.

The vi Editor

The vi editor (pronounced "vee eye") is one of the oldest and most popular visual text editors available for UNIX operating systems; its Linux equivalent (known as vim—"vi improved") is standard on almost every Linux distribution as a result. Although the vi editor is not the easiest of the editors to use when editing text files, it has the advantage of portability. A Red Hat Linux user who is proficient in using the vi editor will find editing files on all other UNIX and Linux systems easy, as the interface and features of the vi editor are nearly identical across Linux and UNIX systems. In addition to this, the vi editor supports regular expressions and can perform over 1000 different functions for the user.

To open an existing text file for editing, type vi filename (or vim filename) where filename specifies the file to be edited. To open a new file for editing, simply type vi or vim at the command line:

```
[root@localhost root]# vi
```

The vi editor will then run interactively and replace the command line interface with the following output:

```
~
~
~
~
~
~                          VIM - Vi IMproved
~
~                             version 5.8.7
~                         by Bram Moolenaar et al.
~
```

```
~                          Vim is freely distributable
~               type    :help uganda<Enter>          if you like Vim
~
~               type    :q<Enter>                    to exit
~               type    :help<Enter>  or   <F1>      for on-line help
~               type    :help version5<Enter>        for version info
~
~
~
~
~
~
~
```

The tilde (~) characters seen along the left indicate the end of the file; they will be pushed further down the screen as you enter text. The vi editor is called a bi-modal editor as it functions in one of two modes: **command mode** and **insert mode**. When you first open the vi editor, you are placed in command mode and may use the keys on the keyboard to perform useful functions such as deleting text, copying text, saving changes to a file, and exiting the vi editor. To insert text into the document, you must enter insert mode by typing one of the characters listed in Table 4-5. For example, if you type the i key on the keyboard while in command mode, the vi editor will then display --INSERT-- at the bottom of the screen and allow you to enter a sentence such as the one below:

```
This is a sample sentence.
~
~
~
~
~
~
~
~                              VIM - Vi IMproved
~
~                              version 5.8.7
~                          by Bram Moolenaar et al.
~
~                          Vim is freely distributable
~               type    :help uganda<Enter>          if you like Vim
~
~               type    :q<Enter>                    to exit
~               type    :help<Enter>  or   <F1>      for on-line help
~               type    :help version5<Enter>        for version info
~
~
~
~
~
~
~
-- INSERT --
```

Table 4-5   Common keyboard keys used to change to and from insert mode

Key	Description
I	Changes to insert mode and places the cursor before the current character for entering text
A	Changes to insert mode and places the cursor after the current character for entering text
O	Changes to insert mode and opens a new line underneath the current line for entering text
Shift-I	Changes to insert mode and places the cursor at the beginning of the current line for entering text
Shift-A	Changes to insert mode and places the cursor at the end of the current line for entering text
Shift-O	Changes to insert mode and opens a new line above the current line for entering text
[Esc]	Changes back to command mode while in insert mode

When in insert mode, you may use the keyboard to type text as required but must return to command mode by pressing the Esc key when finished to perform other functions via keys on the keyboard. A list of keys useful in command mode and their associated functions is seen in Table 4-6. Once in command mode, to save the text in a file called samplefile in the current directory, you first need to press the : character (by pressing the Shift and ; keys simultaneously) to reach a : prompt. Then you can enter a command to save the contents of the current document to a file, as seen below and in Table 4-7.

Table 4-6   Key combinations commonly used in command mode

Key	Description
w, W, e, E	Moves the cursor forward one word
b, B	Moves the cursor backward one word
53G	Moves the cursor to line 53
G	Moves the cursor to the last line in the document
0, ^	Moves the cursor to the beginning of the line
$	Moves the cursor to the end of the line
x	Deletes the character the cursor is on
3x	Deletes three characters starting from the character the cursor is on
dw	Deletes one word starting from the character the cursor is on
d3w, 3dw	Deletes three words starting from the character the cursor is on
dd	Deletes one whole line starting from the line the cursor is on
d3d, 3dd	Deletes three whole lines starting from the line the cursor is on
d$	Deletes from the cursor character to the end of the current line
d^, d0	Deletes from the cursor character to the beginning of the current line

Table 4-6   Key combinations commonly used in command mode (continued)

Key	Description
yw	Copies one word (starting from the character the cursor is on) into a temporary buffer in memory for later use
y3w, 3yw	Copies three words (starting from the character the cursor is on) into a temporary buffer in memory for later use
yy	Copies the current line into a temporary buffer in memory for later use
y3y, 3yy	Copies three lines (starting from the current line) into a temporary buffer in memory for later use
y$	Copies the current line from the cursor to the end of the line into a temporary buffer in memory for later use
y^, y0	Copies the current line from the cursor to the beginning of the line into a temporary buffer in memory for later use
p	Pastes the contents of the temporary memory buffer underneath the current line
P	Pastes the contents of the temporary memory buffer above the current line
J	Joins the line underneath the current line to the current line
[Ctrl]-g	Displays current line statistics
u	Undoes the last function (undo)
.	Repeats the last function (repeat)
/pattern	Searches for the first occurrence of pattern in the forward direction
?pattern	Searches for the first occurrence of pattern in the reverse direction
n	Repeats the previous search in the forward direction
N	Repeats the previous search in the reverse direction

Table 4-7   Key combinations commonly used at the command mode : prompt

Function	Description
:q	Quits from the vi editor if no changes were made
:q!	Quits from the vi editor and does not save any changes
:wq	Saves any changes to the file and quits from the vi editor
:w filename	Saves the current document to a file called filename
:!date	Executes the date command using a BASH Shell
:r !date	Reads the output of the date command into the document under the current line
:r filename	Reads the contents of the text file called filename into the document under the current line
:set all	Displays all vi environment settings
:set	<$>Sets a vi environment setting to a certain value
:s/the/THE/g	Searches for the regular expression "the" and replaces each occurrence globally throughout the current line with the word "THE"
:1,$ s/the/THE/g	Searches for the regular expression "the" and replaces each occurrence globally from line 1 to the end of the document with the word "THE"

```
         This is a sample sentence.
         ~
         ~
         ~
         ~
         ~
         ~                                 VIM - Vi IMproved
         ~
         ~                                  version 5.8.7
         ~                             by Bram Moolenaar et al.
         ~
         ~                             Vim is freely distributable
         ~               type  :help uganda<Enter>       if you like Vim
         ~
         ~               type  :q<Enter>                 to exit
         ~               type  :help<Enter>  or  <F1>  for on-line help
         ~               type  :help version5<Enter>    for version info
         ~
         ~
         ~
         ~
         ~
         ~
         :w samplefile
```

As you see from Table 4-7, you may quit the vi editor by pressing the : character and entering q, which then returns the user to the shell prompt:

```
         This is a sample sentence.
         ~
         ~
         ~
         ~
         ~
         ~                                 VIM - Vi IMproved
         ~
         ~                                  version 5.8.7
         ~                             by Bram Moolenaar et al.
         ~
         ~                             Vim is freely distributable
         ~               type  :help uganda<Enter>       if you like Vim
         ~
         ~               type  :q<Enter>                 to exit
         ~               type  :help<Enter>  or  <F1>  for on-line help
         ~               type  :help version5<Enter>    for version info
         ~
         ~
         ~
```

```
        ~
        ~
        ~
        ~
        :q
        [root@localhost root]# _
```

As depicted in Table 4-7, the vi editor also offers some advanced features to Linux users. Examples of some of these features will be discussed below using the project4 file seen earlier in this chapter. To edit the project4 file, simply type vi project4 and view the following screen:

```
        Hi there, I hope this day finds you well.

        Unfortunately we were not able to make it to your dining
        room this year while vacationing in Algonquin Park - I
        especially wished to see the model of the Highland Inn
        and the train station in the dining room.

        I have been reading on the history of Algonquin Park but
        nowhere could I find a description of where the Highland
        Inn was originally located on Cache Lake.

        If it is no trouble, could you kindly let me know such that
        I need not wait until next year when I visit your lodge?

        Regards,
        Mackenzie Elizabeth
        ~
        ~
        ~
        ~
        ~
        ~
        ~
        "project4" 17L, 583C
```

Note that the name of the file as well as the number of lines and characters in total are displayed at the bottom of the screen (project4 has 17 lines and 583 characters in this example). To insert the current date and time at the bottom of the file, you could simply move the cursor to the last line in the file and type the following at the : prompt while in command mode:

```
        Hi there, I hope this day finds you well.

        Unfortunately we were not able to make it to your dining
        room this year while vacationing in Algonquin Park - I
        especially wished to see the model of the Highland Inn
        and the train station in the dining room.
```

```
I have been reading on the history of Algonquin Park but
nowhere could I find a description of where the Highland
Inn was originally located on Cache Lake.

If it is no trouble, could you kindly let me know such that
I need not wait until next year when I visit your lodge?

Regards,
Mackenzie Elizabeth
~
~
~
~
~
~
~
~
:r !date
```

When you press Enter, the output of the `date` command is inserted below the current line:

```
Hi there, I hope this day finds you well.

Unfortunately we were not able to make it to your dining
room this year while vacationing in Algonquin Park - I
especially wished to see the model of the Highland Inn
and the train station in the dining room.

I have been reading on the history of Algonquin Park but
nowhere could I find a description of where the Highland
Inn was originally located on Cache Lake.

If it is no trouble, could you kindly let me know such that
I need not wait until next year when I visit your lodge?

Regards,
Mackenzie Elizabeth
Sat Apr 20 18:33:10 EDT 2002
~
~
~
~
~
~
```

To change all occurrences of the word "Algonquin" to "ALGONQUIN" you could simply type the following at the : prompt while in command mode:

```
Hi there, I hope this day finds you well.
```

Unfortunately we were not able to make it to your dining
room this year while vacationing in Algonquin Park - I
especially wished to see the model of the Highland Inn
and the train station in the dining room.

I have been reading on the history of Algonquin Park but
nowhere could I find a description of where the Highland
Inn was originally located on Cache Lake.

If it is no trouble, could you kindly let me know such that
I need not wait until next year when I visit your lodge?

Regards,
Mackenzie Elizabeth
Sat Apr 20 18:33:10 EDT 2002

```
~
~
~
~
~
~
:1,$ s/Algonquin/ALGONQUIN/g
```

Doing so would result in the following output:

Hi there, I hope this day finds you well.

Unfortunately we were not able to make it to your dining
room this year while vacationing in ALGONQUIN Park - I
especially wished to see the model of the Highland Inn
and the train station in the dining room.

I have been reading on the history of ALGONQUIN Park but
nowhere could I find a description of where the Highland
Inn was originally located on Cache Lake.

If it is no trouble, could you kindly let me know such that
I need not wait until next year when I visit your lodge?

Regards,
Mackenzie Elizabeth
Sat Apr 20 18:33:10 EDT 2002

```
~
~
~
~
~
~
~
```

Another attractive feature of the vi editor is its ability to customize the user environment through settings that can be altered at the : prompt while in command mode. Simply type the words "`set all`" at this prompt to observe the list of available settings and their current values:

```
:set all
-- Options --
noautoindent           isprint=@,161-255    scrolloff=0         textwidth=0
noautowrite            joinspaces           nosecure            notildeop
  background=light     keymodel=              selectmode=         timeout
  backspace=2          keywordprg=man         shell=/bin/bash     timeoutlen=1000
nobackup               laststatus=1           shellcmdflag=-c   nottimeout
  backupext=~          nolazyredraw           shellquote=         ttimeoutlen=-1
nobinary               lines=25               shellxquote=        ttybuiltin
  cmdheight=1          nolisp                 noshiftround      nottyfast
  columns=80           nolist                   shiftwidth=8      ttymouse=
nocompatible           listchars=eol:$      noshortname         ttyscroll=999
  cpoptions=aABceFs    magic                  noshowfulltag       ttytype=ansi
  display=             matchtime=5            noshowmatch         undolevels=1000
noedcompatible         maxmapdepth=1000       showmode          updatecount=200
  endofline            maxmem=5120              sidescroll=0        updatetime=4000
  equalalways          maxmemtot=10240        nosmartcase         verbose=0
  equalprg=            modeline               nosmarttab        novisualbell
noerrorbells           modelines=5            softtabstop=0     warn
  esckeys              modified               nosplitbelow      noweirdinvert
noexpandtab            more                   startofline       whichwrap=b,s
noexrc                 mouse=                 swapfile          wildchar=<Tab>
  fileformat=dos       mousemodel=extend        swapsync=fsync     wildcharm=^@
  formatoptions=tcq    mousetime=500            switchbuf=          wildmode=full
  formatprg=           nonumber                 tabstop=8          winheight=1
nogdefault             nopaste              tagbsearch          winminheight=1
-- More --
```

Note from the above output that most settings are set to either on or off; those that are turned off are prefixed with a "no." In the above example, line numbering is turned off (nonumber in the above output); however, one may turn it on by typing set number at the : prompt while in command mode. This will result in the following output in vi:

```
1 Hi there, I hope this day finds you well.
2
3 Unfortunately we were not able to make it to your dining
4 room this year while vacationing in ALGONQUIN Park - I
5 especially wished to see the model of the Highland Inn
```

```
 6 and the train station in the dining room.
 7
 8 I have been reading on the history of ALGONQUIN Park but
 9 nowhere could I find a description of where the Highland
10 Inn was originally located on Cache Lake.
11
12 If it is no trouble, could you kindly let me know such that
13 I need not wait until next year when I visit your lodge?
14
15 Regards,
16 Mackenzie Elizabeth
17 Sat Apr 20 18:33:10 EDT 2002
18
~
~
~
~
~
~
:set number
```

Conversely, to turn line numbering off again, you could simply type set nonumber at the : prompt while in command mode.

Other Common Text Editors

Although the vi editor is the most common text editor used on Linux and UNIX systems, other text editors that are easier to use exist. By far, the easiest alternative to the vi editor is **pico (PIne COmposer) editor**, which is commonly used to create and edit e-mails. To open the project4 file for editing with pico, simply type pico project4 at a command prompt and the following interactive screen is displayed:

```
UW PICO(tm) 4.0                              File: project4

Hi there, I hope this day finds you well.

Unfortunately we were not able to make it to your dining
room this year while vacationing in Algonquin Park - I
especially wished to see the model of the Highland Inn
and the train station in the dining room.

I have been reading on the history of Algonquin Park but
nowhere could I find a description of where the Highland
Inn was originally located on Cache Lake.
```

```
If it is no trouble, could you kindly let me know such that
I need not wait until next year when I visit your lodge?

Regards,
Mackenzie Elizabeth




                                  [ Read 17 lines ]
^G Get Help    ^O WriteOut  ^R Read File ^Y Prev Pg   ^K Cut Text
^C Cur Pos     ^X Exit       ^J Justify    ^W Where is ^V Next Pg
^U UnCut Text ^T To Spell
```

The caret symbol (^) used in pico indicates the Ctrl key; thus to exit the pico editor, simply press the Ctrl and X keys simultaneously.

The **mcedit editor (Midnight Commander Editor)** is another easy-to-use text editor, which resembles pico yet has more functionality, support for regular expressions, and ability to use the mouse for highlighting text. To edit the project4 file using mcedit, simply type mcedit project4 at a command prompt and the following will be displayed on the terminal screen:

```
project4          [----] 0 L:[  1+ 0  1/ 18] *(0  / 583b)
Hi there, I hope this day finds you well.

Unfortunately we were not able to make it to your dining
room this year while vacationing in Algonquin Park - I
especially wished to see the model of the Highland Inn
and the train station in the dining room.

I have been reading on the history of Algonquin Park but
nowhere could I find a description of where the Highland
Inn was originally located on Cache Lake.

If it is no trouble, could you kindly let me know such that
I need not wait until next year when I visit your lodge?

Regards,
Mackenzie Elizabeth




1Help   2Save  3Mark  4Replace  5Copy  6Move
7Search  8Delete  9PullDn  10Quit
```

Note that you may access much of the functionality of mcedit by using the function keys on the keyboard as described at the bottom of the screen (F1 = Help, F2 = Save, etc.).

Both pico and mcedit are simple and straightforward text editors to use, yet they lack the functionality seen in the vi editor. An alternative to the vi editor that offers an equal set of functionality is the GNU **emacs (Editor MACroS) editor**. Like pico, the emacs editor uses the Ctrl key in combination with certain letters to perform special functions, yet can be used with the LISP (LISt Processing) artificial intelligence programming language and supports hundreds of keyboard functions like the vi editor. A list of some common keyboard functions used in the emacs editor can be seen in Table 4-8.

Table 4-8   Keyboard functions commonly used in the GNU emacs editor

Key	Description
Ctrl-a	Moves the cursor to the beginning of the line
Ctrl-e	Moves the cursor to the end of the line
Ctrl-h	Displays emacs documentation
Ctrl-d	Deletes the current character
Ctrl-k	Deletes from the cursor position to the end of the line
Esc-d	Deletes the current word
Ctrl-x + Ctrl-c	Exits the emacs editor
Ctrl-x + Ctrl-s	Saves the current document
Ctrl-x + Ctrl-w	Saves the current document as a new filename
Ctrl-x + u	Undoes the last change

Unfortunately, the emacs editor is not an easy-to-use editor as the user must memorize several key combinations to work effectively. A version of emacs that runs in the KDE or GNOME GUI environments is called the **xemacs editor** and is much easier to use, as the key combinations are replaced by graphical icons for many features. To open the project4 file with the xemacs editor, simply open a command-line terminal in either the KDE or GNOME desktop and type xemacs project4, as seen in Figure 4-3.

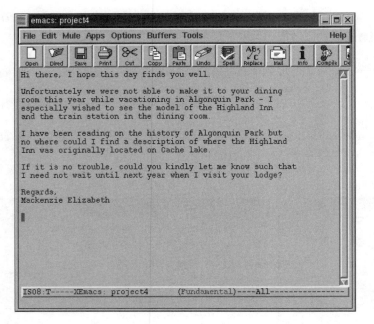

Figure 4-3 The xemacs text editor

Although the xemacs editor may not be available in every distribution that contains a GUI environment, there are two easy-to-use graphical editors derived from UNIX systems that are common on most Linux distributions: the older **xedit editor** and the popular **nedit editor**. An example of the displays seen when you type xedit project4 and nedit project4 on a command-line terminal in a GUI environment are seen in Figure 4-4 and Figure 4-5, respectively.

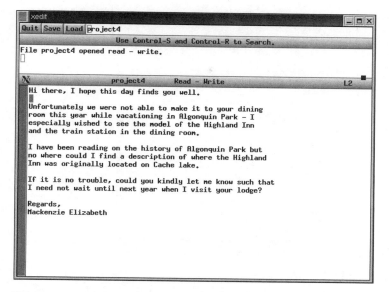

Figure 4-4   The xedit text editor

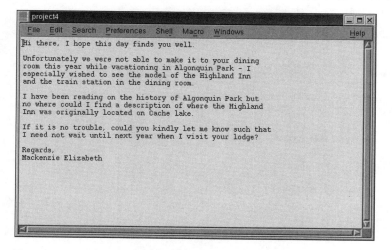

Figure 4-5   The nedit text editor

The GNOME and KDE GUI environments are now also distributed with their own text editors (**gedit editor** and **kedit editor**), which are similar to nedit yet offer more functionality. An example of the displays seen when you type gedit project4 and kedit project4 on a command-line terminal in a GUI environment are seen in Figure 4-6 and Figure 4-7, respectively.

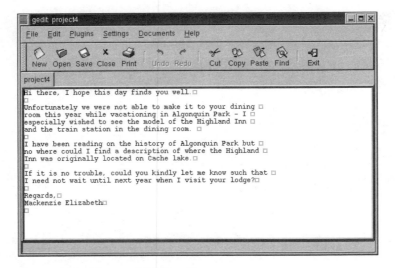

Figure 4-6   The gedit text editor

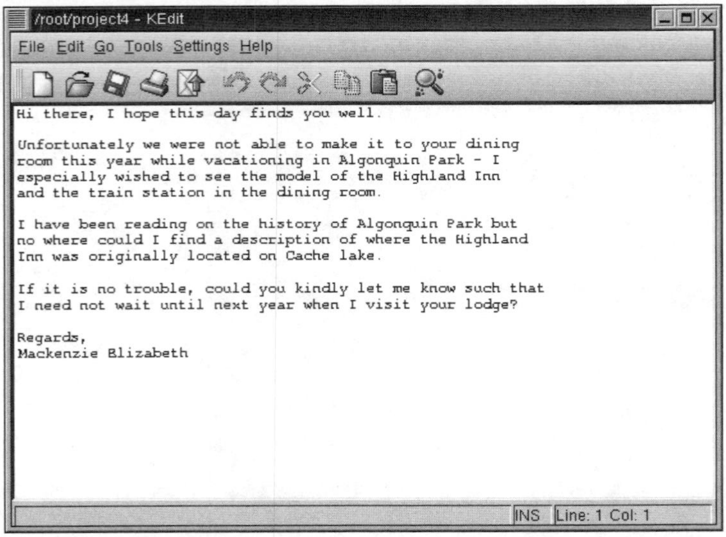

Figure 4-7   The kedit text editor

Chapter Summary

❏ The Linux filesystem is arranged hierarchically using a series of directories to store files, and the location of these directories and files can be described using absolute or relative pathnames.

❏ There are many types of files that may exist on the Linux filesystem, such as text files, binary data, executable programs, directories, linked files, and special device files.

❏ The `ls` command can be used to view filenames and offers a wide range of options to modify this view.

❏ Wildcard metacharacters can be used to simplify the selection of several files when using common Linux file commands.

❏ Text files are the most common file type whose contents may be viewed by several utilities such as `head`, `tail`, `cat`, `tac`, `more`, and `less`.

❏ Regular expression metacharacters can be used to specify certain patterns of text when used with certain programming languages and text tool utilities such as `grep`.

❏ Although there are many command-line and graphical text editors, vi (vim) is a powerful, bi-modal text editor that is standard on most UNIX and Linux systems.

Key Terms

. (metacharacter) — A special metacharacter used to indicate the user's current directory in the directory tree.

.. (metacharacter) — A special metacharacter used to represent the user's parent directory in the directory tree.

~ (metacharacter) — A metacharacter used to represent a user's home directory.

absolute pathname — The full pathname to a certain file or directory starting from the root directory.

binary data file — A file that contains machine language (binary 1s and 0s) and stores information (such as common functions and graphics) used by binary compiled programs.

cat command — A Linux command used to display (or concatenate) the entire contents of a text file to the screen.

cd command — A Linux command used to change the current directory in the directory tree.

command mode — One of the two input modes in the vi editor; it allows a user to perform any available text editing task that is not related to inserting text into the document.

concatenation — The joining of text together to make one larger whole; in Linux, words and strings of text are joined together to form a displayed file.

directory — A special file on the filesystem used to organize other files into a logical tree structure.

egrep command — A variant of the grep command used to search files for patterns using extended regular expressions.

emacs (Editor MACroS) editor — A popular and wide-spread text editor more conducive to word processing than vi; developed by Richard Stallman.

executable program — A file that can be executed by the Linux operating system to run in memory as a process and perform a useful function.

fgrep command — A variant of the grep command that does not allow the use of regular expressions.

file command — A Linux command that displays the file type of a specified filename.

filename — The user-friendly identifier given to a file.

filename extension — A series of identifiers following a dot (.) at the end of a filename used to denote the type of the file; the filename extention .txt denotes a text file.

gedit editor — A text editor for the GNOME desktop.

grep (Global Regular Expression Print) command — A Linux command that searches files for patterns of characters using regular expression metacharacters.

head command — A Linux command that displays the first set of lines of a text file; by default the head command displays the first 10 lines.

hidden files — Files that are not normally displayed to the user via common filesystem commands.

home directory — A directory on the file system set aside for users to store personal files and information.

insert mode — One of the two input modes in the vi editor; it allows the user to insert text into the document but does not allow any other functionality.

kedit editor — A text editor for the KDE desktop.

less command — A Linux command used to display a text file page-by-page on the terminal screen; users may then use the cursor keys to navigate the file.

linked file — A file that represents the same data as other files.

ll command — An alias for the ls –l command; it gives a long file listing.

log file — A file that contains past system events.

ls command — A Linux command used to list the files in a given directory.

mcedit editor (Midnight Commander Editor) — A user-friendly terminal text editor that supports regular expressions and the computer mouse.

more command — A Linux command used to display a text file page-by-page and line-by-line on the terminal screen.

4

named pipe file — A temporary connection that sends information from one command or process in memory to another; it can also be represented by a file on the filesystem.

nedit editor — A commonly used graphical text editor available in most Linux distributions.

od command — A Linux command used to display the contents of a file in octal format.

pico editor — A terminal text editor with shortcut keys for common commands; pico stands for PIne COmposer.

pwd (print working directory) command — A Linux command used to display the current directory in the directory tree.

regular expressions (regexp) — Special metacharacters used to match patterns of text within text files; they are commonly used by many text tool commands such as grep.

relative pathname — The pathname of a target directory relative to your current directory in the tree.

socket file — A named pipe connecting processes on two different computers; it can also be represented by a file on the filesystem.

special device file — A file used to identify hardware devices such as hard disks and serial ports.

strings command — A Linux command used to search for and display text characters in a binary file.

subdirectory — A directory that resides within another directory in the directory tree.

Tab-completion — A feature of the BASH Shell that fills in the remaining characters of a unique filename or directory name when the user presses the Tab key.

tac command — A Linux command that displays a file to the screen beginning with the last line of the file and ending with the first line of the file.

tail command — A Linux command used to display the last several lines of text in a text file; by default the tail command displays the last 10 lines of the file.

text file — A file that stores information in a readable text format.

text tools — Programs that allow for the creation, modification, and searching of text files.

vi editor — A powerful command line text editor available on most UNIX and Linux systems.

wildcard metacharacters — Metacharacters used to match certain characters in a file or directory name; they are often used to specify multiple files.

xedit editor — A commonly used graphical text editor available in most Linux distributions.

xemacs editor — A graphical version of the emacs text editor.

REVIEW QUESTIONS

1. A directory is a type of file. True or False?

2. What is at the beginning of every directory structure (or directory tree)?

    a. trunk directory

    b. main directory

    c. base directory

    d. root directory

3. Linux files can use filename extensions to indicate file types; however, these filename extensions are optional. True or False?

4. What command would a user type on the command line to find out what directory in the directory tree they are currently in?

    a. pd

    b. cd

    c. where

    d. pwd

5. Which of the following is/are an absolute path name? (Choose all that apply.)

    a. Home/resume

    b. C:\myfolder\resume

    c. resume

    d. /home/resume

    e. C:home/resume

6. A special device file is used to _____.

    a. enable proprietary custom built devices to work with Linux

    b. represent hardware devices such as hard disk drives and ports

    c. keep a list of device settings specific to each individual user

    d. do nothing in Linux

7. Which of the following are graphical text editors? (Choose all that apply.)

    a. vi

    b. xvi

    c. emacs

    d. xemacs

    e. xedit

    f. nedit

8. If a user's current directory was **/home/mary/project1**, which command could they use to move to the **etc** directory directly under the root?

   a. `cd ..`

   b. `cd /home/mary/etc`

   c. `cd etc`

   d. `cd /etc`

   e. `cd \etc`

9. A user types the `ll` command at a command prompt to see a long listing of files in their current directory. What other command performs the same function as `ll`?

   a. `ls -l`

   b. `file`

   c. `lf`

   d. `ls -F`

10. After typing the `ls -a` command, you notice that there is a file whose filename begins with a dot (.). What does this mean?

    a. It is a binary file.

    b. It is a system file.

    c. It is a file in the current directory.

    d. It is a hidden file.

11. After typing the `ls -F` command, you notice a filename that ends with an * asterisk character. What does this mean?

    a. It is a hidden file.

    b. It is a linked file.

    c. It is a special device file.

    d. It is an executable file.

12. The vi editor can function in which two of the following modes? (Choose both that apply.)

    a. text

    b. command

    c. input

    d. interactive

    e. insert

13. When using the Linux operating system, the root directory is represented by a
    _____ character. When using a Microsoft operating system, the root
    directory is represented by a _____ character.

    a. / , \

    b. \ , /

    c. / , /

    d. \ , /

14. The **less** command offers less functionality than the **more** command. True or False?

15. Which command searches for and displays any text contents of a binary file?

    a. **text**

    b. **strings**

    c. **od**

    d. **less**

16. How can a user switch from insert mode to command mode when using the
    vi editor?

    a. Press the Ctrl-Alt-Del keys simultaneously

    b. Press the Del key

    c. Type in a : character

    d. Press the Esc key

17. If *resume* is the name of a file in the *home* directory off the root of the file system
    and your present working directory is *home*, what is the relative name for the file
    named *resume*?

    a. /home/resume

    b. /resume

    c. resume

    d. \home\resume

18. Extended regular expressions are more powerful and recognized by more text
    tools and programming languages than common regular expressions. True or False?

19. What will the wildcard regular expression file[a–c] return?

    a. filea–c

    b. filea, filec

    c. filea, fileb, filec

    d. fileabc

20. What will typing q! at the : prompt in command mode do when using the vi editor?

    a. quit as no changes were made

    b. quit after saving any changes

c. nothing as the ! is a metacharacter

d. quit without saving any changes

21. A user types in the command head /poems/mary. What will be displayed to the terminal screen?

    a. the first line of the file mary

    b. the header for the file mary

    c. the first 20 lines of the file mary

    d. the last 10 lines of the file mary

    e. the first 10 lines of the file mary

22. What is used to send information from one process in memory to another process in memory?

    a. a socket

    b. an extension

    c. a named pipe

    d. a named socket

23. The `tac` command _____.

    a. is not a valid Linux command

    b. displays the contents of hidden files

    c. displays the contents of a file in reverse order, last word on the line first and first word on the line last

    d. displays the contents of a file in reverse order, last line first and first line last

24. How can one specify a text pattern that must be at the beginning of a line of text using a regular expression?

    a. precede the string with a /

    b. follow the string with a \

    c. precede the string with a $

    d. precede the string with a ^

25. Linux has only one root directory per directory tree. True or False?

26. Using wildcard metacharacters, how can one indicate a character that is NOT a or b or c or d?

    a. [^abcd]

    b. not [a-d]

    c. [!a-d]

    d. !a-d

27. Which command displays the contents of a file in Base 8 or octal format?

    a. `octal`

    b. `show base -8`

    c. `ls -8`

    d. `od`

28. A user typed in the command **pwd** and saw the output: /home/jim/sales/pending. How could that user navigate to the /home/jim directory?

    a. `cd ..`

    b. `cd /jim`

    c. `cd ../..`

    d. `cd ./.`

29. The current directory is /home and the contents of this directory include the following subdirectories: jobs, work, letters, last. What will be displayed if one types cd /home/la and then presses the Tab key?

    a. last

    b. directory not found

    c. cd /home/last/

    d. cd /last

30. Sue's current directory in the directory tree is /home/classmarks/linux-am. She then types the command **cd .** and presses Enter. What directory will be displayed if Sue types the **pwd** command?

    a. /

    b. /home/classmarks

    c. \home\classmarks\linux-am

    d. /home/classmarks/linux-am

HANDS-ON PROJECTS

These projects should be completed in the order given. All hands-on projects should take a total of three hours to complete. The requirements for this lab include

❑ A computer with Red Hat Linux 7.2 installed.

Project 4-1

In this hands-on project, you will log on to the computer and navigate the file structure.

1. Turn on your computer. Once your Linux system has been loaded, you will be placed at a graphical terminal (tty7). Switch to a command-line terminal (tty2) by

pressing **Ctrl–Alt–F2** and log into the terminal using the username of **root** and the password of **secret**.

2. At the command prompt, type **pwd** and press **Enter** to view the current working directory. What is your current working directory?

3. At the command prompt, type **cd** and press **Enter**. At the command prompt, type **pwd** and press **Enter** to view the current working directory. Did your current working directory change? Why or why not?

4. At the command prompt, type **cd .** and press **Enter**. At the command prompt, type **pwd** and press **Enter** to view the current working directory. Did your current working directory change? Why or why not?

5. At the command prompt, type **cd ..** and press **Enter**. At the command prompt, type **pwd** and press **Enter** to view the current working directory. Did your current working directory change? Why or why not?

6. At the command prompt, type **cd root** and press **Enter**. At the command prompt, type **pwd** and press **Enter** to view the current working directory. Did your current working directory change? Where are you now? Did you specify a relative or absolute pathname to your home directory when you used the **cd root** command?

7. At the command prompt, type **cd etc** and press **Enter**. What error message did you receive and why?

8. At the command prompt, type **cd /etc** and press **Enter**. At the command prompt, type **pwd** and press **Enter** to view the current working directory. Did your current working directory change? Did you specify a relative or absolute pathname when you used the **cd /etc** command?

9. At the command prompt, type **cd /** and press **Enter**. At the command prompt, type **pwd** and press **Enter** to view the current working directory. Did your current working directory change? Did you specify a relative or absolute pathname when you used the **cd /** command?

10. At the command prompt, type **cd ~** and then press **Enter**. At the command prompt, type **pwd** and press **Enter** to view the current working directory. Did your current working directory change? Which command discussed earlier performs the same function as the **cd ~** command?

11. At the command prompt, type **cd Desktop** and press **Enter** (make sure you use a capital D). At the command prompt, type **pwd** and press **Enter** to view the current working directory. Did your current working directory change? Where are you now? What kind of pathname did you use here (absolute or relative)?

12. Currently, you are in a subdirectory of your home folder and are two levels below the root. To go up two parent directories to the / directory, type **cd ../..** and press **Enter** at the command prompt. Next, type **pwd** and press **Enter** to ensure that you are in the / directory.

13. At the command prompt, type **cd /etc/samba** and press **Enter** to change the current working directory using an absolute pathname. Next, type **pwd** and press **Enter** at the command prompt to ensure that you have changed to the /etc/samba directory. Now type in the command **cd ../sysconfig** at the command prompt and press **Enter**. Type the **pwd** command and press **Enter** to view you current location. Explain how the relative pathname seen in the cd ../sysconfig command specified your current working directory.

14. At the command prompt, type **cd ../../root/Desktop** and press **Enter** to change your current working directory to the Desktop directory underneath your home directory. Verify that you are in the desired directory by typing the **pwd** command at a command prompt and pressing **Enter**. Would it have been more advantageous to use an absolute pathname to change to this directory instead of the relative pathname that we used?

15. Type **exit** and press **Enter** to log out of your shell.

Project 4-2

In this hands-on project, you will navigate the Linux filesystem using the Tab-completion feature of the BASH Shell.

1. Switch to a command-line terminal (tty2) by pressing **Ctrl–Alt–F2** and log into the terminal using the username of **root** and the password of **secret**. At the command prompt, type **cd /** and press **Enter**.

2. Next, type **cd r** at the command prompt and press **Tab**. What is displayed on the screen and why? How many subdirectories under the root begin with "r"?

3. Press the **Ctrl** and **c** keys simultaneously to cancel the command and return to an empty command prompt.

4. At the command prompt, type **cd b** and press **Tab**. Did the display change? Why did you hear a beep?

5. Press **Tab** again. How many subdirectories under the root begin with "b"?

6. Type the letter **i**. Notice that the command now reads "cd bi". Press **Tab** again. Which directory did it expand to? Why? Press the **Ctrl** and **c** keys simultaneously to cancel the command and return to an empty command prompt.

7. At the command prompt, type **cd m** and press **Tab**. Press **Tab** once again after hearing the beep. How many subdirectories under the root begin with "m"?

8. Type the letter **i**. Notice that the command now reads "cd mi". Press **Tab**.

9. Press **Enter** to execute the command at the command prompt. Next, type **pwd** and press **Enter** to verify that you are in the /**misc** directory.

10. Type **exit** and press **Enter** to log out of your shell.

Project 4-3

In this hands–on project, you will examine files and file types using the `ls` and `file` commands.

1. Switch to a command-line terminal (tty2) by pressing **Ctrl–Alt–F2** and log into the terminal using the username of **root** and the password of **secret**.

2. At the command prompt, type **cd /etc** and press **Enter**. Verify that you are in the `/etc` directory by typing **pwd** at the command prompt and press **Enter**.

3. At the command prompt, type **ls** and press **Enter**. What do you see listed in the four columns? Do any of the files have extensions? What is the most common extension you see and what does it indicate? Is the list you are viewing on the screen the entire contents of /etc?

4. At the command prompt, type **ls | more** and then press **Enter** (the | symbol is usually near the **Enter** key on the keyboard and is obtained by pressing the **Shift** and \ keys in combination). What does the display show? Notice the highlighted --More-- prompt at the bottom of the screen. Press **Enter**. Press **Enter** again. Press **Enter** once more. Notice that each time you press **Enter** you advance one line further into the file. Now press the spacebar. Press the spacebar again. Notice that with each press of the spacebar you advance one full page into the displayed directory contents. Press the **h** key to get a help screen. Examine the command options.

5. Press the **q** key to quit out of the **more** command and return to an empty command prompt.

6. At the command prompt, type **ls | less** and then press **Enter**. What does the display show? Notice the : at the bottom of the screen. Press **Enter**. Press **Enter** again. Press **Enter** once more. Notice that each time you press **Enter** you advance one line further into the file. Now press the spacebar. Press the spacebar again. Notice that with each press of the spacebar you advance one full page into the displayed directory contents. Press the **h** key to get a help screen. Examine the command options then press **q** to return to the command output.

7. Press the ↑ cursor key. Press ↑ again. Press ↑ once more. Notice that each time you press the up cursor you go back up one line into the file display toward the beginning of the file. Now press the ↓ cursor key. Press ↓ again. Press ↓ once more. Notice that each time you press the down cursor you move forward into the file display.

8. Press the **q** key to quit the **less** command and return to a shell command prompt.

9. At the command prompt, type **cd** and press **Enter**. At the command prompt, type **pwd** and press **Enter**. What is your current working directory? At the command prompt, type **ls** and press **Enter**.

10. At the command prompt, type **ls /etc** and press **Enter**. How does this output compare with what you saw in Step 9? Has your current directory changed? Verify your answer by typing **pwd** at the command prompt and pressing **Enter**. Notice that you were able to list the contents of another directory by giving the absolute name of it as an argument to the **ls** command without leaving the directory you are currently in.

11. At the command prompt, type **ls /etc/skel** and press **Enter**. Did you see a listing of any files? At the command prompt, type **ls -a /etc/skel** and press **Enter**. What is special about these files? What do the first two entries on the list (**.** and **..**) represent?

12. At the command prompt, type **ls -aF /etc/skel** and press **Enter**. Which file types are available in the /etc/skel directory?

13. At the command prompt, type **ls /bin** and press **Enter**. Did you see a listing of any files? At the command prompt, type **ls -F /bin** and press **Enter**. What file types are present in the /bin directory?

14. At the command prompt, type **ls /boot** and press **Enter**. Next, type **ls -l /boot** and press **Enter**. What additional information is available on the screen? What types of files are available in the /boot directory? At the command prompt, type **ll /boot** and press **Enter**. Is the output any different from that of the ls -l /boot command you just entered? Why or why not?

15. At the command prompt, type **file /etc** and press **Enter**. What kind of file is etc?

16. At the command prompt, type **file /etc/inittab** and press **Enter**. What type of file is /etc/inittab?

17. At the command prompt type **file /boot/*** to see the types of files in the /boot directory. Is this information more specific than the information you gathered in Step 14?

18. Type **exit** and press **Enter** to log out of your shell.

Project 4-4

In this hands-on project, you will display file contents using the cat, tac, head, tail, strings, and od commands.

1. Switch to a command-line terminal (tty2) by pressing **Ctrl-Alt-F2** and log into the terminal using the username of **root** and the password of **secret**.

2. At the command prompt, type **cat /etc/hosts** and press **Enter** to view the contents of the file hosts, which resides in the directory /etc. Next type **cat -n /etc/hosts** and press **Enter**. How many lines does the file have? At the command prompt, type **tac /etc/hosts** and press **Enter** to view the same file in reverse order. The output of both commands should be visible on the same screen. Compare them.

3. To see the contents of the same file in octal format instead of ASCII text, type **od /etc/hosts** at the command prompt and press **Enter**.

4. At the command prompt, type **cat /etc/inittab** and press **Enter**.

5. At the command prompt, type **head /etc/inittab** and press **Enter**. What is displayed to the screen? How many lines are displayed, which ones are they, and why?

6. At the command prompt, type **head –5 /etc/inittab** and press **Enter**. How many lines are displayed and why? Next, type **head –3 /etc/inittab** and press **Enter**. How many lines are displayed and why?

7. At the command prompt, type **tail /etc/inittab** and press **Enter**. What is displayed to the screen? How many lines are displayed, which ones are they, and why?

8. At the command prompt, type **tail –5 /etc/inittab** and press **Enter**. How many lines are displayed and why? Next, type **tail +40 /etc/inittab** and press **Enter**. How many lines are displayed and why? Type the **cat –n /etc/inittab** command at a command prompt and press **Enter** to justify your answer.

9. At the command prompt, type **file /bin/nice** and press **Enter**. What type of file is it? Should you use a text tool command on this file?

10. At the command prompt, type **strings /bin/nice** and press **Enter**. Notice that you are able to see some text within this binary file. Next, type **strings /bin/nice | more** to view the same content page-by-page. When finished, press **q** to quit out of the more command.

11. Type **exit** and press **Enter** to log out of your shell.

Project 4-5

In this hands-on project, you will create and edit text files using the vi editor.

1. Switch to a command-line terminal (tty2) by pressing **Ctrl-Alt-F2** and log into the terminal using the username of **root** and the password of **secret**.

2. At the command prompt, type **pwd** and press **Enter**, and ensure that /root is displayed showing that you are in the root user's home folder. At the command prompt, type **vi sample1** and press **Enter** to open the vi editor and create a new text file called sample1. Notice that this name appears at the bottom of the screen along with the indication that it is a new file.

3. At the command prompt, type **My letter** and press **Enter**. Why was nothing displayed to the screen? To switch from command mode to insert mode to allow the typing of text, press **i**. Notice that the word Insert appears at the bottom of the screen. Next, type **My letter** and notice that this text is displayed to the screen. What types of tasks can be accomplished in insert mode?

4. Press **Esc**. Did the cursor move? What mode are you in now? Press ← two times until the cursor is under the last "t" in letter. Press the **x** key. What happened? Next, press **i** to enter insert mode and type the letter **h**. Did the letter "h" get inserted before or after the cursor?

5. Press **Esc** to switch back to command mode and then move your cursor to the end of the line. Next, press the **o** key to open a line underneath the current line and enter insert mode.

6. Type the following:

   It might look like I am doing nothing, but at the cellular level I can assure you that I am quite busy.

   Notice that the line wraps to the next line part way through the sentence. Though displayed over two lines on the screen, this sentence is treated as one continuous line of text in vi. Press **Esc** to return to command mode, then press ↑. Where does the cursor move? Use the cursor keys to navigate to the letter "l" at the beginning of the word **level** and press the **i** key to enter insert mode. Press the **Enter** key while in insert mode. Next press **Esc** to return to command mode and press ↑. Where does the cursor move?

7. Type **dd** three times to delete all lines in the file.

8. Press **i** to enter insert mode, then type:

   Hi there, I hope this day finds you well.
   and press **Enter**. Press **Enter** again. Type:
   Unfortunately we were not able to make it to your dining
   and press **Enter**. Type:
   room this year while vacationing in Algonquin Park – I
   and press **Enter**. Type:
   especially wished to see the model of the Highland Inn
   and press **Enter**. Type:
   and the train station in the dining room.
   and press **Enter**. Press **Enter** again. Type:
   I have been reading on the history of Algonquin Park but
   and press **Enter**. Type:
   nowhere could I find a description of where the Highland
   and press **Enter**. Type:
   Inn was originally located on Cache lake.
   and press **Enter**. Press **Enter** again. Type:
   If it is no trouble, could you kindly let me know such that
   and press **Enter**. Type:
   I need not wait until next year when I visit your lodge?
   and press **Enter**. Press **Enter** again. Type:
   Regards,
   and press **Enter**. Type:
   Mackenzie Elizabeth
   and press **Enter**. You should now have the sample letter used in this chapter on your screen. It should resemble the letter in Figure 4-3.

9. Press **Esc** to switch to command mode. Next, press the **Shift** and **;** keys simultaneously to open the : prompt at the bottom of the screen. At this prompt, type **w** and press **Enter** to save the changes you have made to the file. What is displayed at the bottom of the file when you are finished?

10. Press the **Shift** and **;** keys simultaneously to open the : prompt at the bottom of the screen again, and type **q** and then press **Enter** to exit the vi editor.

11. At the command prompt, type **ls** and press **Enter** to view the contents of your current directory. Notice that there is now a file called **sample1** listed.

12. Next, type **file sample1** and press **Enter**. What type of file is **sample1**? At the command prompt, type **cat sample1** and press **Enter**.

13. At the command prompt, type **vi sample1** and press **Enter** to open the letter again in the vi editor. What is displayed at the bottom of the screen? How does this compare with Step 9?

14. Press **F1** to display a help file for vi and its commands. Use the **Page Down** and **Page Up** keys to navigate the help file. When finished, press the **Shift** and **;** keys simultaneously to open the : prompt at the bottom of the screen again, and type **q** and then press **Enter** to exit the help screen.

15. Use your cursor keys to navigate to the bottom of the document. Press the **Shift** and **;** keys simultaneously to open the : prompt at the bottom of the screen again, and type **!date** and press **Enter**. The current system date and time appears at the bottom of the screen. As indicated, press **Enter** to return to the document. Press the **Shift** and **;** keys simultaneously again to open the : prompt at the bottom of the screen again, and type **r !date** and press **Enter**. What happened and why?

16. Use the cursor keys to position your cursor on the line in the document that displays the current date and time, and type **yy** to copy it to the buffer in memory. Next, use your cursor keys to position your cursor on the first line in the document and type **P** (capitalized) to paste the contents of the memory buffer above your current line. Does the original line remain at the bottom of the document?

17. Use the cursor keys to position your cursor on the line at the end of the document that displays the current date and time and type **dd** to delete it.

18. Use the cursor keys to position your cursor on the "t" in the word "there" on the second line of the file that reads `Hi there, I hope this day finds you well.` and type **dw** to delete the word. Next, press **i** to enter insert mode, type the word **Bob**, and then press **Esc** to switch back to command mode.

19. Press the **Shift** and **;** keys simultaneously to open the : prompt at the bottom of the screen again, and type **w sample2** and press **Enter**. What happened and why?

20. Press **i** to enter insert mode and type the word **test**. Next, press **Esc** to switch to command mode. Press the **Shift** and **;** keys simultaneously to open the : prompt at the bottom of the screen again, and type **q** and press **Enter** to quit the vi editor. Were you able to quit? Why not?

21. Press the **Shift** and **;** keys simultaneously to open the : prompt at the bottom of the screen again, and type **q!** and press **Enter** to quit the vi editor and throw away any changes since the last save.

22. At the command prompt, type **ls** and press **Enter** to view the contents of your current directory. Notice that there is now a file called `sample2`, which was created in Step 19.

23. At the command prompt, type **vi sample2** and press **Enter** to open the letter again in the vi editor.

24. Use the cursor keys to position your cursor on the line that reads `Hi Bob, I hope this day finds you well.`

25. Press the **Shift** and **;** keys simultaneously to open the : prompt at the bottom of the screen, and type **s/Bob/Barb/g** and press **Enter** to change all occurrences of "Bob" to "Barb" on the current line.

26. Press the **Shift** and **;** keys simultaneously to open the : prompt at the bottom of the screen again and type **1,$ s/to/TO/g** and press **Enter** to change all occurrences of "to" to "TO" for the entire file.

27. Press the **u** key to undo the last function performed. What happened and why?

28. Press the **Shift** and **;** keys simultaneously to open the : prompt at the bottom of the screen again, and type **wq** and press **Enter** to save your document and quit the vi editor.

29. At the command prompt, type **vi sample3** and press **Enter** to open a new file called `sample3` in the vi editor. Press **i** to enter insert mode. Next, type **P.S. How were the flies this year?**

30. Press the **Esc** key, and then press the **Shift** and **;** keys simultaneously to open the : prompt at the bottom of the screen again, and type **wq** and press **Enter** to save your document and quit the vi editor.

31. At the command prompt, type **vi sample1** and press **Enter** to open the file `sample1` again, and use the cursor keys to position your cursor on the line that reads `Mackenzie Elizabeth.`

32. Press the **Shift** and **;** keys simultaneously to open the : prompt at the bottom of the screen again, then type **r sample3** and press **Enter** to insert the contents of the file `sample3` below your current line.

33. Press the **Shift** and **;** keys simultaneously to open the : prompt at the bottom of the screen, and type **s/flies/flies and bears/g** and press **Enter**. What happened and why?

34. Press the **Shift** and **;** keys simultaneously to open the : prompt at the bottom of the screen again, and type **set number** and press **Enter** to turn on line numbering.

35. Press the **Shift** and **;** keys simultaneously to open the : prompt at the bottom of the screen again, and type **set nonumber** and press **Enter** to turn off line numbering.

36. Press the **Shift** and **;** keys simultaneously to open the : prompt at the bottom of the screen again and type **set all** and press **Enter** to view all vi parameters. Press **Enter** to advance through the list, and press **q** when finished to return to the vi editor.

37. Press the **Shift** and **;** keys simultaneously to open the : prompt at the bottom of the screen again, and type **wq** and press **Enter** to save your document and quit the vi editor.

38. Type **exit** and press **Enter** to log out of your shell.

Project 4-6

In this hands-on project, you will use the ls command alongside wildcard metacharacters in your shell to explore the contents of your home directory.

1. Switch to a command-line terminal (tty2) by pressing **Ctrl–Alt–F2** and log into the terminal using the username of **root** and the password of **secret**.

2. At the command prompt, type **pwd** and press **Enter**, and ensure that /root is displayed showing that you are in the root user's home folder. At the command prompt, type **ls**. How many files with a name beginning with the word "sample" exist in /root?

3. At the command prompt, type **ls** * and press **Enter**. What is listed and why?

4. At the command prompt, type **ls sample*** and press **Enter**. What is listed and why?

5. At the command prompt, type **ls sample?** and press **Enter**. What is listed and why?

6. At the command prompt, type **ls sample??** and press **Enter**. What is listed and why?

7. At the command prompt, type **ls sample[13]** and press **Enter**. What is listed and why?

8. At the command prompt, type **ls sample[!13]** and press **Enter**. What is listed and why? How does this compare to the results from Step 7?

9. At the command prompt, type **ls sample[1–3]** and press **Enter**. What is listed and why?

10. At the command prompt, type **ls sample[!1–3]** and press **Enter**. What is listed and why? How does this compare to the results from Step 9?

11. Type **exit** and press **Enter** to log out of your shell.

Project 4-7

In this hands-on project, you will use the grep and egrep commands alongside regular expression metacharacters and to explore the contents of text files.

1. Switch to a command-line terminal (tty2) by pressing **Ctrl–Alt–F2** and log into the terminal using the username of **root** and the password of **secret**.

2. At the command prompt, type **grep "Inn" sample1** and press **Enter**. What is displayed and why?

3. At the command prompt, type **grep −v "Inn" sample1** and press **Enter**. What is displayed and why? How does this compare to the results from Step 3?

4. At the command prompt, type **grep "inn" sample1** and press **Enter**. What is displayed and why?

5. At the command prompt, type **grep −i "inn" sample1** and press **Enter**. What is displayed and why? How does this compare to the results from Steps 2 and 4?

6. At the command prompt, type **grep "I" sample1** and press **Enter**. What is displayed and why?

7. At the command prompt, type **grep " I " sample1** and press **Enter**. What is displayed and why? How does it differ from the results from Step 6 and why?

8. At the command prompt, type **grep "t.e" sample1** and press **Enter**. What is displayed and why?

9. At the command prompt, type **grep "w...e" sample1** and press **Enter**. What is displayed and why?

10. At the command prompt, type **grep "^I" sample1** and press **Enter**. What is displayed and why?

11. At the command prompt, type **grep "^I " sample1** and press **Enter**. What is displayed and why? How does this differ from the results in Step 10 and why?

12. At the command prompt, type **grep "(we|next)" sample1** and press **Enter**. Is anything displayed? Why?

13. At the command prompt, type **egrep "(we|next)" sample1** and press **Enter** What is displayed and why?

14. At the command prompt, type **grep "Inn$" sample1** and press **Enter**. What is displayed and why?

15. At the command prompt, type **grep "?$" sample1** and press **Enter**. What is displayed and why? Does the "?" metacharacter have special meaning here? Why?

16. At the command prompt, type **grep "^$" sample1** and press **Enter**. Is anything displayed? (*Hint*: be sure to look closely!) Can you explain the output?

17. Type **exit** and press **Enter** to log out of your shell.

Discovery Exercises

1. You are the system administrator for a scientific research company that employs over 100 scientists who write and run Linux programs to analyze their work. All of these programs are stored in each scientist's home directory on the Linux system. One scientist has left the company, and you are instructed to salvage any work from that scientist's home directory. When you enter the home directory for that user, you notice that there are very few files and only two directories (one named **Projects** and one named **Lab**). List the commands that you would use to navigate through this user's home directory and view filenames and file types. If there are any text files, what commands could you use to view their contents?

4

2. When you type the **pwd** command, you notice that your current location on the Linux filesystem is the **/usr/local** directory. Answer the following questions, assuming that your current directory is **/usr/local** for each question.

    a. Which command could you use to change to the **/usr** directory using an absolute pathname?

    b. Which command could you use to change to the **/usr** directory using a relative pathname?

    c. Which command could you use to change to the **/usr/local/share/info** directory using an absolute pathname?

    d. Which command could you use to change to the **/usr/local/share/info** directory using a relative pathname?

    e. Which command could you use to change to the **/etc** directory using an absolute pathname?

    f. Which command could you use to change to the **/etc** directory using a relative pathname?

3. Use wildcard metacharacters and options with the **ls** command to view:

    a. all the files that end with **.cfg** under the **/etc** directory

    b. all hidden files in the /home/user1 directory

    c. the directory names that exist under the **/var** directory

    d. all the files that start with the letter "a" underneath the **/bin** directory

    e. all the files that have exactly three letters in their filename in the **/bin** directory

    f. all the files that have exactly three letters in their filename and end with either the letter **t** or the letter **h** in the **/bin** directory

4. Explore the manual pages for the **ls, grep, cat, od, tac, head, tail, pwd, cd, strings,** and **vi** commands. Experiment with what you learn on the file **sample1** that you created earlier.

5. The famous quote from Shakespeare's Hamlet, "To be or not to be," can be represented by the following regular expression:

    `(2b|[^b]{2})`

    If you used this expression when searching a text file using the egrep command `(egrep "(2b|[^b]{2})" filename)`, what would be displayed? Try this command out on a file that you have created. Why does it display what it does? That is the question.

6. The vi editor comes with a short 30 minute tutorial on its usage. Start this tutorial by typing **vimtutor** at a command prompt and follow the directions. Provided you have a functional Web browser and an Internet connection, explore the resources available at *http://www.vim.org*.

7. Enter the following text into a new document called **question7** using the vi editor. Next, use the vi editor to fix the mistakes in the file using the information in Table 4-5, Table 4-6, and Table 4-7 as well as the examples provided in this chapter.

```
Hi there,
Unfortunately we were not able to make it to your dining room
Unfortunately we were not able to make it to your dining room
this year while vacationing in Algonquin Park - I especially wished
to see the model of the highland inn and the train station in the
dining rooms.

I have been readng on the history of Algonquin Park but
nowhere could I find a description of where the Highland Inn was
originally located on Cache Lake.

If it is not trouble, could you kindly let me that I need
not wait until next year when we visit Lodge?

I hope this day finds you well.
Regard
Elizabeth Mackenzie
```

8. The knowledge gained from using the vi editor may be transferred easily to the emacs editor. Perform Question 7 using the emacs editor instead of the vi editor.

9. When one uses the vi editor and changes environment settings at the : prompt such as **:set number** to enable line numbering, those changes are lost when the user exits the vi editor. To continuously apply the same environment settings, one may choose to put the **set** commands in a special hidden file in their home directory called **.exrc**—this **.exrc** file is then applied each time that user opens the vi editor. Enter the vi editor and find three environment settings that you would like to change in addition to line numbering. Then create a new file called **.exrc** in your home directory and enter the four lines changing these vi environment settings (do not start each line with a : character, just enter the set command—i.e., **set number**). When finished, test to see whether the settings were applied automatically by opening the vi editor to edit a new file.

5

LINUX FILESYSTEM MANAGEMENT

**After completing this chapter,
you will be able to:**

♦ Explain the function of the Filesystem Hierarchy Standard

♦ Use standard Linux commands to manage files and directories

♦ Find files and directories on the filesystem

♦ Understand and create linked files

♦ Modify file and directory ownership

♦ Define and change Linux file and directory permissions

♦ Identify the default permissions created on files and directories

♦ Apply special file and directory permissions

In the previous chapter, you learned about navigating the Linux filesystem as well as viewing and editing files. This chapter focuses on the organization of files on the Linux filesystem, as well their linking and security. First, you explore standard Linux directories using the Filesystem Hierarchy Standard. Next, you explore common commands used to manage files and directories, followed by a discussion on finding files and directories. Finally, you learn about describing file and directory linking, as well as common and special permissions available for files and directories.

THE FILESYSTEM HIERARCHY STANDARD

There are many thousands of files on a typical Linux system, which are logically organized into directories in the Linux directory tree. This complexity allows different Linux distributions to place files in different locations. As a result, a great deal of time can be spent searching for a common configuration file on a foreign Linux system. To solve this problem, the **Filesystem Hierarchy Standard (FHS)** was created.

FHS defines a standard set of directories for use by all Linux and UNIX systems, as well as the file and subdirectory contents of each directory. This ensures that, because the filename and location follow a standard convention, a Red Hat Linux user will find the correct configuration file on a Caldera Linux or Hewlett-Packard UNIX computer with little difficulty. FHS also gives Linux software developers the ability to locate files on a Linux system regardless of the distribution, allowing them to create software that is not distribution specific.

A comprehensive understanding of the standard types of directories found on Linux systems is valuable when locating and managing files and directories; some standard UNIX and Linux directories defined by FHS and their descriptions are found in Table 5-1. These directories will be discussed throughout this chapter and following chapters.

 To read the complete Filesystem Hierarchy Standard definition, visit the Internet at *http://www.pathname.com/fhs/*.

Table 5-1   Linux directories defined by the Filesystem Hierarchy Standard

Directory	Description
/bin	Contains binary commands for use by all users
/boot	Contains the Linux kernel and files used by the boot loader
/dev	Contains device files
/etc	Contains system-specific configuration files
/home	Default location for user home directories
/lib	Contains shared program libraries (used by the commands in /bin and /sbin) as well as kernel modules
/mnt	Empty directory used for accessing (mounting) disks such as floppy disks and CD-ROMs
/opt	Stores additional software programs
/proc	Contains process and kernel information
/root	The root user's home directory
/sbin	Contains system binary commands (used for administration)
/tmp	Holds temporary files created by programs

Table 5-1   Linux directories defined by the Filesystem Hierarchy Standard (continued)

Directory	Description
/usr	Contains most system commands and utilities—will contain the following directories: /usr/bin—user binary commands /usr/games—educational programs and games /usr/include—C program header files /usr/lib—libraries /usr/local—local programs /usr/sbin—system binary commands /usr/share—files that are architecture independent /usr/src—source code /usr/X11R6—the XWindow system
/usr/local	Location for most additional programs
/var	Contains log files and spools

MANAGING FILES AND DIRECTORIES

As mentioned earlier, using a Linux system involves navigating around several directories and manipulating the files inside them. Thus, an efficient Linux user must understand how to create directories as needed, copy or move files from one directory to another, and delete files and directories. These tasks are commonly referred to as file management tasks.

Following is an example of a directory listing while the user is logged in as the root user:

```
[root@localhost root]# pwd
/root
[root@localhost root]# ls -F
current@  myprogram*  project     project12  project2  project4
Desktop/  myscript*   project1    project13  project3
project5 [root@localhost root]#_
```

As seen in the above output there is only one directory (Desktop), two executable files (myprogram and myscript) and several project-related files (project*). Although this directory structure is not cluttered and appears in an easy-to-read format on the terminal screen, typical home directories on a Linux system contain many more files; a typical Linux user may have over 100 files in their home directory. As a result, it is good practice to organize these files into subdirectories based on file purpose. Since there are several project files in the root user's home directory in the above output, you could create a subdirectory called **proj_files** to contain the project-related files and decrease the size of the directory listing. To do this, you use the **mkdir command**, which takes arguments specifying the absolute or relative pathnames of the directories to create. To create a `proj_files` directory underneath the current directory, you can use the `mkdir` command with a relative pathname:

```
[root@localhost root]# mkdir proj_files
[root@localhost root]# ls -F
current@  myprogram*  project    project12  project2  project4
Desktop/  myscript*   project1   project13  project3  project5
proj_files/
[root@localhost root]#_
```

Now you can move the project files into the `proj_files` subdirectory by using the **mv (move) command**. The `mv` command requires two arguments at minimum: the **source file/directory** and the **target file/directory**. If several files are to be moved, simply specify several source arguments; the last argument then becomes the target directory. Both the source(s) and destination may be absolute or relative pathnames, and the source may contain wildcards if several files are to be moved. For example, to move all of the project files to the `proj_files` directory, you could type `mv` with the source argument `project*` (to match all files starting with the letters "project") and the target argument `proj_files` (relative pathname to the destination directory), as seen in the following output:

```
[root@localhost root]# mv project* proj_files
[root@localhost root]# ls -F
current@  Desktop/  myprogram*  myscript*  proj_files/
[root@localhost root]# ls -F proj_files
project  project1  project12  project13  project2  project3
project4  project5
[root@localhost root]#_
```

In the above output, the current directory listing does not show the project files anymore, yet the listing of the `proj_files` subdirectory indicates that they were moved successfully.

 If the target is the name of a directory, then the mv command will move those files to that directory. If the target is a filename of an existing file in a certain directory and there is one source file, then the mv command will overwrite the target with the source. If the target is a filename of a non-existent file in a certain directory, then the mv command will create a new file with that filename in the target directory and move the source file to that file.

Another important use of the mv command is to rename files, which is simply moving a file to the same directory but with a different filename. To rename the myscript file from earlier examples to myscript2 you can use the following mv command:

```
[root@localhost root]# ls -F
current@  Desktop/  myprogram*  myscript*  proj_files/
[root@localhost root]# mv myscript myscript2
[root@localhost root]# ls -F
```

```
current@  Desktop/  myprogram*  myscript2*  proj_files/
[root@localhost root]#_
```

Similarly, the **mv** command can rename directories. If the source is the name of an existing directory, it will be renamed to whatever directory name is specified as the target.

The **mv** command works similarly to a "cut and paste" operation in which the file is copied to a new directory and deleted from the source directory. There may be times, however, when the file in the source directory should be maintained; this is referred to as copying a file and can be accomplished using the **cp command**. Much like the **mv** command, the **cp** command takes two arguments at minimum. The first argument specifies the source file/directory to be copied and the second argument specifies the target file/directory. If several files need to be copied to a destination directory, simply specify several source arguments, and the last argument on the command line becomes the target directory. Each argument may be an absolute or relative pathname and may contain wildcards or the special metacharacters " . " (specifies the current directory) and " .. " (specifies the parent directory). For example, to make a copy of the file **/etc/hosts** in the current directory (/root), you can specify the absolute pathname to the **/etc/hosts** file (/etc/hosts) and the relative pathname indicating the current directory (.):

```
[root@localhost root]# cp /etc/hosts .
[root@localhost root]# ls -F
current@  Desktop/  hosts  myprogram*  myscript2*  proj_files/
[root@localhost root]#_
```

You may also make copies of files in the same directory. To make a copy of the **hosts** file called **hosts2** in the current directory, type the following command:

```
[root@localhost root]# cp hosts hosts2
[root@localhost root]# ls -F
current@  Desktop/  hosts  hosts2  myprogram*  myscript2*
proj_files/ [root@localhost root]#_
```

One notable difference between the **mv** and **cp** commands, aside from their purpose, is that they work on directories differently. The **mv** command simply renames a directory, while the **cp** command creates a whole new copy of the directory and its contents. To copy a directory full of files in Linux, you must tell the **cp** command that the copy will be **recursive** (involve files and subdirectories too) by using the **-r** option. The following example demonstrates copying the **proj_files** directory and all of its contents to the /home/user1 directory without and with the **-r** option:

```
[root@localhost root]# ls -F
current@  Desktop/  hosts  myprogram*  myscript2*  proj_files/
[root@localhost root]# ls -F /home/user1
Desktop/
[root@localhost root]# cp proj_files /home/user1
cp: omitting directory 'proj_files'
```

```
[root@localhost root]# ls -F /home/user1
Desktop/
[root@localhost root]# cp -r proj_files /home/user1
[root@localhost root]# ls -F /home/user1
Desktop/  proj_files/
[root@localhost root]#_
```

When copying or moving files, if the target is a file that exists, the **mv** and **cp** commands will warn the user that the target file will be overwritten and ask whether to continue. This is not a feature of the command as normally invoked, but a feature of the default configuration in Red Hat Linux since the BASH Shell in Red Hat Linux contains aliases to the **cp** and **mv** commands. Aliases are special variables in memory that point to commands; they will be discussed fully in Chapter 8. When you type **mv**, you are really running the **mv** command with the **-i** option, which interactively prompts the user to choose whether to overwrite the existing file if the target file already exists when the command is executed. Similarly, when you type the **cp** command, the **cp -i** command is run to perform the same function. To see the aliases present in your current shell, simply type alias, as seen in the output below:

```
[root@localhost root]# alias
alias cp='cp -i'
alias l.='ls -d .[a-zA-Z]* --color=tty'
alias ll='ls -l --color=tty'
alias ls='ls --color=tty'
alias mv='mv -i'
alias rm='rm -i'
alias which='alias | /usr/bin/which --tty-only --read-alias
--show-dot --show-tilde'
[root@localhost root]#_
```

If you wish to override this interactive option, use the **-f** (force) option to override the choice, as seen in the following example in which the root user tries to rename the **hosts** file to the **hosts2** file that already exists without and with the **-f** option to the **mv** command:

```
[root@localhost root]# ls -F
current@ Desktop/ hosts  hosts2  myprogram*  myscript2*
proj_files/ [root@localhost root]# mv hosts hosts2
mv: overwrite 'hosts2'? n
[root@localhost root]# mv -f hosts hosts2
[root@localhost root]# ls -F
current@ Desktop/ hosts2  myprogram*  myscript2*
proj_files/ [root@localhost root]#_
```

Creating directories, copying files and moving files are file management tasks that preserve or create data on the hard disk. To remove files or directories, you must use either the **rm** command or the **rmdir** command.

The **rm command** takes a list of arguments specifying the absolute or relative pathnames of files to remove. As with most commands, wildcards may be used to simplify specifying multiple files to remove. Once a file has been removed from the filesystem, it cannot be recovered. As a result, the rm command is aliased in Red Hat Linux to the rm command with the –i option, which interactively prompts the user to choose whether or not to continue with the deletion. Like the cp and mv commands, the rm command also accepts the –f option to override this choice and immediately delete the file. An example demonstrating the use of the rm and rm –f commands to remove the current and hosts2 files is seen below:

```
[root@localhost root]# ls -F
current@  Desktop/  hosts2  myprogram*  myscript2*
proj_files/
[root@localhost root]# rm current
rm: remove 'current'? y
[root@localhost root]# rm -f hosts2
[root@localhost root]# ls -F
Desktop/  myprogram*  myscript2*  proj_files/
[root@localhost root]# _
```

To remove a directory, you can use the rmdir command; however the **rmdir command** will only remove a directory if there are no files within it. To remove a directory and the files inside, you must use the rm command and specify that a directory full of files should be removed. Recall from earlier that you needed to use the recursive option –r with the cp command to copy directories; to remove a directory full of files, you can also use the recursive option –r with the rm command. Say, for example, that the root user wished to remove the proj_files subdirectory and all of the files within it without being prompted to confirm each file deletion; the command that must be used to do this is rm –rf proj_files as seen below:

```
[root@localhost root]# ls -F
Desktop/  myprogram*  myscript2*  proj_files/
[root@localhost root]# rmdir proj_files
rmdir: 'proj_files': Directory not empty
[root@localhost root]# rm -rf proj_files
[root@localhost root]# ls -F
Desktop/  myprogram*  myscript2*
[root@localhost root]# _
```

In most commands, such as rm and cp, both the –r and the –R options have the same meaning (recursive).

The –r option to the rm command is dangerous if you are not sure which files exist in the directory to be deleted recursively. As a result, the –r option to the rm command is commonly referred to as the -résumé option; if you use it incorrectly, you may need to prepare your résumé.

It is important to note that the aforementioned file management commands are commonly used by Linux users, developers, and administrators alike. A summary of these common file management commands can be found in Table 5-2.

Table 5-2 Common Linux file management commands

Command	Description
mkdir	Creates directories
rmdir	Removes empty directories
mv	Moves / renames files and directories
cp	Copies files and directories full of files (with the –r option)
alias	Displays BASH Shell aliases
rm	Removes files and directories full of files (with the –r option)

FINDING FILES

Before using the file management commands mentioned in the last section, you must know the locations of the files involved. The fastest method to search for files in the Linux directory tree is to use the **locate command**, which is a shortcut to the `slocate` (or secure locate) command. To view all of the files underneath the root directory that have the word `inittab` as all or part of the filename, you can simply type `locate inittab` at a command prompt, which produces the following output:

```
[root@localhost root]# locate inittab
/etc/inittab
/usr/lib/linuxconf/descriptions/eng/inittab
/usr/lib/linuxconf/descriptions/es/inittab
/usr/lib/linuxconf/descriptions/fr/inittab
/usr/lib/linuxconf/descriptions/hu/inittab
/usr/lib/linuxconf/descriptions/ko/inittab
/usr/lib/linuxconf/descriptions/se/inittab
/usr/lib/linuxconf/descriptions/sk/inittab
/usr/lib/linuxconf/help.bg5/inittab-msg-1.25r7.bg5
/usr/lib/linuxconf/help.cn/inittab-msg-1.25r7.cn
/usr/lib/linuxconf/help.cs/inittab-msg-1.25r7.cs
/usr/lib/linuxconf/help.de/inittab-msg-1.25r7.de
/usr/lib/linuxconf/help.eng/inittab-msg-1.25r7.eng
/usr/lib/linuxconf/help.es/inittab-msg-1.25r7.es
/usr/lib/linuxconf/help.fi/inittab-msg-1.25r7.fi
/usr/lib/linuxconf/help.fr/inittab-msg-1.25r7.fr
/usr/lib/linuxconf/help.hu/inittab-msg-1.25r7.hu
/usr/lib/linuxconf/help.it/inittab-msg-1.25r7.it
/usr/lib/linuxconf/help.ko/inittab-msg-1.25r7.ko
/usr/lib/linuxconf/help.no/inittab-msg-1.25r7.no
/usr/lib/linuxconf/help.pt/inittab-msg-1.25r7.pt
```

```
/usr/lib/linuxconf/help.ro/inittab-msg-1.25r7.ro
/usr/lib/linuxconf/help.ru_SU/inittab-msg-1.25r7.ru_SU
/usr/lib/linuxconf/help.se/inittab-msg-1.25r7.se
/usr/lib/linuxconf/help.sk/inittab-msg-1.25r7.sk
/usr/lib/linuxconf/images/inittab.xpm
/usr/lib/linuxconf/images/mini-inittab.xpm
/usr/lib/linuxconf/install/inittab.redhat-4.0
/usr/lib/linuxconf/install/inittab.debian
/usr/lib/linuxconf/install/inittab.redhat
/usr/lib/linuxconf/modules/inittab.so.1.25.7
/usr/share/doc/vim-common-5.8/syntax/inittab.vim
/usr/share/man/man5/inittab.5.gz
/usr/share/terminfo/a/ansi+inittabs
/usr/share/vim/vim58/syntax/inittab.vim
/usr/include/linuxconf/module_apis/inittab_apidef.h
/usr/include/linuxconf/module_apis/inittab_api.h
[root@localhost root]# _
```

5

Quite often, the `locate` command returns too much information to display on the screen, as it searches all files on the filesystem. You can use the `more` (or `less`) command to pause the output, as in `locate inittab | more`, or else you must ensure that the word being searched is very specific.

The `locate` command looks in a pre-made database, which contains a list of all the files on the system. This database is indexed much like a textbook for fast searching, yet can become outdated as files are added to and removed from the system, which happens on a regular basis. As a result, the database used for the locate command (/var/lib/slocate/slocate.db) is updated each day automatically and can be updated manually by running either the `updatedb` or `slocate -u` commands at a command prompt.

A slower, yet more versatile method for locating files on the filesystem is to use the **find command**. The find command does not use a pre-made index of files, but instead searches the directory tree recursively, starting from a certain directory, for files that meet certain criteria. The format of the find command is:

```
find  <start directory>  -criteria  <what to find>
```

For example, to find any files named `inittab` underneath the `/etc` directory, you can use the command `find /etc -name inittab` to receive the following output:

```
[root@localhost root]# find /etc -name inittab
/etc/inittab
[root@localhost root]# _
```

You may also use wildcard metacharacters with the `find` command; however, these wildcards must be protected from shell interpretation, as they must only be interpreted by the `find` command. To do this, ensure that any wildcard metacharacters are enclosed within quote characters. An example of using the `find` command with wildcard metacharacters to find all files that start with the letters `host` underneath the `/etc` directory is seen in the following output:

```
[root@localhost root]# find /etc -name "host*"
/etc/host.conf
/etc/hosts.allow
/etc/hosts.deny
/etc/ups/hosts.conf
/etc/hosts
[root@localhost root]# _
```

Although searching by name is the most common criterion used with the `find` command, there are many other criteria that may be used as well. To find all files starting from the `/var` directory that have a size greater than 1024K (Kilobytes), you could use the following command:

```
[root@localhost root]# find /var -size +1024k
/var/lib/rpm/Packages
/var/lib/rpm/Basenames
/var/lib/slocate/slocate.db
/var/log/lastlog
/var/log/cron
/var/cache/man/whatis
/var/ftp/lib/libc-2.2.4.so
[root@localhost root]# _
```

In addition, if you wished to find all the directories only underneath the `/dev` directory, you could type the following command:

```
[root@localhost dev]# find /dev -type d
/dev
/dev/pts
/dev/ataraid
/dev/cciss
/dev/compaq
/dev/dri
/dev/i2o
/dev/ida
/dev/inet
/dev/input
/dev/logicalco
/dev/logicalco/bci
/dev/logicalco/dci1300
/dev/raw
/dev/rd
/dev/shm
/dev/usb
/dev/video
[root@localhost root]# _
```

A list of some common criteria used with the `find` command can be found in Table 5-3.

Table 5-3 Common criteria used with the `find` command

Criteria	Description
-amin -x	Searches for files that were accessed less than x minutes ago
-amin +x	Searches for files that were accessed more than x minutes ago
-atime -x	Searches for files that were accessed less than x days ago
-atime +x	Searches for files that were accessed more than x days ago
-empty	Searches for empty files or directories
-fstype x	Searches for files if they are on a certain filesystem x (where x could be ext2, ext3, etc.)
-group x	Searches for files that are owned by a certain group or GID (x)
-inum x	Searches for files that have an inode number of x
-mmin -x	Searches for files that were modified less than x minutes ago
-mmin +x	Searches for files that were modified more than x minutes ago
-mtime -x	Searches for files that were modified less than x days ago
-mtime +x	Searches for files that were modified more than x days ago
-name x	Searches for a certain filename x (x may contain wildcards)
-regexp x	Searches for certain filenames using regular expressions instead of wildcard metacharacters
-size -x	Searches for files with a size less than x
-size x	Searches for files with a size of x
-size +x	Searches for files with a size greater than x
-type x	Searches for files of type x where x is: • b for block files • c for character files • d for directory files • p for named pipes • f for regular files • l for symbolic links (shortcuts) • s for sockets
-user x	Searches for files owned by a certain user or UID (x)

Although the `find` command can be used to search for files based on many criteria, it may take several minutes to complete the search if the number of directories and files being searched is large. To reduce the time needed to search, narrow down the directories searched by specifying a subdirectory when possible. It takes less time to search the `/usr/local/bin` directory and its subdirectories as compared to searching the `/usr` directory and all of its subdirectories. In addition, if the filename that you are searching for is an executable file, then that file can likely be found in less time using the **which command**. The which command only searches directories that are listed in a special variable called **PATH** in the current BASH Shell. Before exploring the `which` command, you must understand the usage of PATH.

Executable files may be stored in directories scattered around the directory tree. Recall from FHS that most executable files are stored in directories named **bin** or **sbin**, yet there are over 20 **bin** and **sbin** directories scattered around the directory tree after a typical Red Hat Linux installation. To ensure that users do not need to specify the full pathname to commands such as **ls** (which is the executable file **/bin/ls**), there exists a special variable that is placed into memory each time a user logs into the Linux system called PATH. Recall that you may see the contents of a certain variable in memory by using the **$** metacharacter with the **echo** command:

```
[root@localhost root]# echo $PATH
/usr/kerberos/sbin:/usr/kerberos/bin:/usr/local/sbin:
/usr/local/bin:/sbin:/bin:/usr/sbin:/usr/bin:/usr/X11R6/
bin:/root/bin
[root@localhost root]# _
```

The PATH variable lists directories that are searched for executable files if a relative or absolute pathname was not specified when executing a command on the command-line. In the scenario presented above, when a user types the **ls** command on the command-line and presses [Enter], the system recognizes that the command was not an absolute pathname (i.e., /bin/ls) or relative pathname (i.e., ../../bin/ls) and then proceeds to look for the **ls** executable file in the **/usr/kerberos/sbin** directory, then the **/usr/kerberos/bin** directory, then the **/usr/local/sbin** directory, and so on. If all the directories in the PATH variable are searched and no **ls** command was found, then the shell gives an error message to the user stating that the command was not found. In the above output, the **/bin** directory is in the PATH variable and thus the **ls** command will be found and executed, but not until the previous directories in the PATH variable are searched first.

To search the directories in the PATH variable for the file called **grep** you could use the word **grep** as an argument for the **which** command and receive the following output:

```
[root@localhost sbin]# which grep
/bin/grep
[root@localhost root]# _
```

If the file being searched does not exist in the PATH variable directories, then the **which** command lets you know which directories it was not found in, as seen below:

```
[root@localhost sbin]# which grepper
/usr/bin/which: no grepper in (/usr/kerberos/sbin:/usr/
kerberos/bin:/usr/local/sbin:/usr/local/bin:/sbin:/bin:
/usr/sbin:/usr/bin:/
usr/X11R6/bin:/root/bin)
[root@localhost root]# _
```

LINKING FILES

Recall that files may be linked to one another. This linking can happen in one of two ways: one file may simply be a pointer or shortcut to another file (known as a **symbolic link** or symlink), or two files may share the same data (known as a **hard link**).

To understand better how files are linked, you must understand how files are stored on a filesystem. On a structural level, a filesystem has three main sections:

- The superblock
- The inode table
- Data blocks

The **superblock** is the section that contains information about the filesystem in general, such as the number of inodes and data blocks, as well as how much data a data block stores in Kilobytes. The **inode table** consists of several **inodes** (information nodes); each inode describes one file or directory on the filesystem, and contains a unique inode number for identification. More importantly, the inode stores information such as the file size, data block locations, last date modified, permissions, and ownership. When a file is deleted, only its inode (which serves as a pointer to the actual data) is deleted. The data that makes up the contents of the file as well as the filename are stored in **data blocks**, which are referenced by the inode. In filesystem neutral terminology, blocks are known as allocation units because they are the unit by which disk space is allocated for storage.

 Each file and directory must have an inode. All files except for special device files also have data blocks associated with the inode. Special device files will be discussed in the next chapter.

 Recall that directories are simply files that are used to organize other files; they too have an inode and data blocks, but their data blocks contain a list of filenames that are located within the directory.

Hard-linked files are direct copies of one another, as they share the same inode and inode number. All hard-linked files have the same size, and when one file is modified, the other hard-linked files are updated as well. This relationship between hard-linked files can be seen in Figure 5-1. You can hard-link a file an unlimited number of times; however, the hard-linked files must reside on the same filesystem. This is because inode numbers are unique only on the same filesystem and hard links are recognized by ignoring this rule.

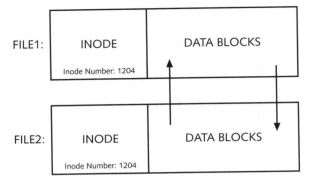

Figure 5-1   The structure of hard linked files

To create a hard link, you must use the **ln (link) command** and specify two arguments: the existing file to hard-link, and the target file that will be created as a hard link to the existing file. Each argument may be the absolute or relative pathname to a file. Take, for example, the following contents of the root user's home directory:

```
[root@localhost root]# ls -l
total 520
drwx------   3 root   root      4096 Apr  8 07:12 Desktop
-rwxr-xr-x   1 root   root    519964 Apr  7 09:59 file1
-rwxr-xr-x   1 root   root      1244 Apr 27 18:17 file3
[root@localhost root]# _
```

If you wished to make a hard link to `file1` called `file2`, as in Figure 5-1, you could issue the command `ln file1 file2` at the command prompt; a file called `file2` will be created and hard-linked to `file1`. To view the hard-linked filenames after creation, you could use the `ls -l` command:

```
[root@localhost root]# ln file1 file2
[root@localhost root]# ls -l
total 1032
drwx------   3 root   root      4096 Apr  8 07:12 Desktop
-rwxr-xr-x   2 root   root    519964 Apr  7 09:59 file1
-rwxr-xr-x   2 root   root    519964 Apr  7 09:59 file2
-rwxr-xr-x   1 root   root      1244 Apr 27 18:17 file3
[root@localhost root]# _
```

Notice from the long listing above that `file1` and `file2` share the same inode, as they have the same size, permissions, ownership, modification date, etc. Also note that the link count (the number after the permission set) for `file1` has increased from the number 1 to the number 2 in the above output. A link count of one indicates that there is only one inode that is shared by the file. A file that is hard-linked to another file shares two inodes and thus has a link count of two. Similarly, a file that is hard-linked to three other files shares four inodes and thus has a link count of four.

Although hard links share the same inode, deleting a hard–linked file does not delete all the other hard–linked files as well. Removing a hard link can be achieved by removing one of the files, which will then lower the link count.

To view the inode number of hard-linked files to verify that they are identical, you can use the **-i** option to the **ls** command in addition to any other options. The inode number is placed on the left of the directory listing on each line, as seen in the following output:

```
[root@localhost root]# ls -li
total 1032
   37595 drwx------  3 root   root      4096   Apr  8 07:12 Desktop
    1204 -rwxr-xr-x  2 root   root    519964   Apr  7 09:59 file1
    1204 -rwxr-xr-x  2 root   root    519964   Apr  7 09:59 file2
   17440 -rwxr-xr-x  1 root   root      1244   Apr 27 18:17 file3
[root@localhost root]# _
```

Directory files are not normally hard-linked, as the result would consist of two directories that contain the same contents. However, the root user has the ability to hard-link directories in some cases using the **-F** or **-d** option to the **ln** command.

Symbolic links (shown in Figure 5-2) are different than hard links because they do not share the same inode and inode number with their target file; one is merely a pointer to the other and thus both files have different sizes. The data blocks in a symbolically linked file contain only the pathname to the target file. When you edit a symbolically linked file, you are actually editing the target file. Thus, if the target file is deleted, then the symbolic link serves no function, as it points to a non–existent file.

Symbolic links are sometimes referred to as soft links.

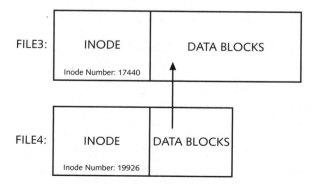

Figure 5-2   The structure of symbolically linked files

To create a symbolic link, you would use the **-s** option to the **ln** command. To create a symbolic link to **file3** called **file4**, as in Figure 5-2, you could type **ln -s file3 file4** at the command prompt. As with hard links, the arguments specified may be absolute or relative pathnames. To view the symbolically linked filenames after creation, you can use the **ls -l** command, as seen below:

```
[root@localhost root]# ln -s file3 file4
[root@localhost root]# ls -l
total 1032
drwx------   3 root   root     4096 Apr  8 07:12 Desktop
-rwxr-xr-x   2 root   root   519964 Apr  7 09:59 file1
-rwxr-xr-x   2 root   root   519964 Apr  7 09:59 file2
-rwxr-xr-x   1 root   root     1244 Apr 27 18:17 file3
lrwxrwxrwx   1 root   root        5 Apr 27 19:05 file4 -> file3
[root@localhost root]# _
```

Notice from the above output that **file4** does not share the same inode, as the permissions, size, and modification date are different from **file3**. Symbolic links are easier to identify than hard links; the file type character (before the permissions) is l, which indicates a symbolic link, and the filename points to the target using an arrow. The **ls -F** command also indicates symbolic links by appending an @ symbol, as seen in the following output:

```
[root@localhost root]# ls -F
Desktop/  file1*  file2*  file3*  file4@
[root@localhost root]# _
```

Another difference between hard links and symbolic links is that symbolic links need not reside on the same filesystem as their target since they do not share the same inode. Instead, they point to the target filename and do not require the same inode, as seen in the following output:

```
[root@localhost root]# ls -li
total 1032
37595 drwx------   3 root   root     4096 Apr  8 07:12 Desktop
 1204 -rwxr-xr-x   2 root   root   519964 Apr  7 09:59 file1
 1204 -rwxr-xr-x   2 root   root   519964 Apr  7 09:59 file2
17440 -rwxr-xr-x   1 root   root     1244 Apr 27 18:17 file3
19926 lrwxrwxrwx   1 root   root        5 Apr 27 19:05 file4 -> file3
[root@localhost root]# _
```

Unlike hard links, symbolic links are commonly made to directories to simplify navigating the filesystem tree. Also, symbolic links made to directories are typically used to maintain compatibility with other UNIX and Linux systems. On Red Hat Linux, for example, the /usr/tmp directory is symbolically linked to the /var/tmp directory, and the /etc/init.d directory is symbolically linked to the /etc/rc.d/init.d directory for this reason.

FILE AND DIRECTORY PERMISSIONS

Recall that all users must successfully log in with a username and password to gain access to a Linux system. Once logged in, users are identified by their username and group memberships; all access to resources depends on whether their username and group memberships have the required **permission**. Thus, a firm understanding of ownership and permissions is necessary to operate a Linux system in a secure manner and deny unauthorized users access to sensitive files, directories, and commands.

File and Directory Ownership

When a user creates a file or directory, that user's name and **primary group** become the owner and group owner of the file, respectively. This affects the permission structure as you will see in the next section; however, it also determines who has the ability to modify file and directory permissions and ownership. The owner of the file or directory and the root user are the only two users on a Linux system who can modify permissions on a file or directory or change its ownership.

To view your current username, you can use the `whoami` command. To view your group memberships and primary group, you can use the `groups` command. An example of these two commands when logged in as the root user is seen below:

```
[root@localhost root]# whoami
root
[root@localhost root]# groups
root bin daemon sys adm disk wheel
[root@localhost root]# _
```

Notice from the above output that the root user is a member of seven groups, yet the root user's primary group is also called root, as it is the first group mentioned in the output of the groups command. If this user was to create a file, then the owner will be root and the group owner will also be root. To create an empty file quickly, you can use the **touch command**:

```
[root@localhost root]# touch file1
[root@localhost root]# ls -l
total 4
drwx------   3 root   root   4096 Apr  8 07:12 Desktop
-rw-r--r--   1 root   root      0 Apr 29 15:40 file1
[root@localhost root]# _
```

Notice from the above output that the owner of `file1` is root and the group owner of `file1` is the root group. To change the ownership of a file or directory, you can use the **chown (change owner) command**, which takes two arguments at minimum: the new owner and the files or directories to change. Both arguments may be absolute or relative pathnames, and you may also change permissions recursively throughout the directory tree using the `-R` option to the **chown** command. To change the ownership of file1 to the user user1 and the ownership of the directory `Desktop` and all of its contents to user1 as well, you can enter the following commands:

```
[root@localhost root]# chown user1 file1
[root@localhost root]# chown -R user1 Desktop
[root@localhost root]# ls -l
total 4
drwx------   3 user1   root   4096 Apr  8 07:12 Desktop
-rw-r--r--   1 user1   root      0 Apr 29 15:40 file1
[root@localhost root]# ls -l Desktop
total 28
-rw-------   1 user1   root   1117 Mar 29 09:58 cdrom
-rw-------   1 user1   root    151 Mar 29 09:58 floppy
-rw-r--r--   1 user1   root   2588 Mar 29 09:58 Home
-rw-r--r--   1 user1   root    149 Mar 29 09:58 KDE Control Panel
-rw-r--r--   1 user1   root     80 Mar 29 09:58 Linux Documentation
drwx------   2 user1   root   4096 Mar 29 09:58 Trash
-rw-r--r--   1 user1   root    107 Mar 29 09:58 www.redhat.com
[root@localhost root]# _
```

Recall that only the owner of a particular file or directory and the root user have the ability to change ownership of that file or directory. If a regular user changed the ownership of a file or directory that they owned, that user cannot gain the ownership back. Instead, the new owner of that file or directory must change it back to the original user. However, the above examples involve the root user, who always has the ability to gain the ownership back:

```
[root@localhost root]# chown root file1
[root@localhost root]# chown -R root Desktop
[root@localhost root]# ls -l
total 4
drwx------   3 root   root   4096 Apr  8 07:12 Desktop
-rw-r--r--   1 root   root      0 Apr 29 15:40 file1
[root@localhost root]# ls -l Desktop
total 28
-rw-------   1 root   root   1117 Mar 29 09:58 cdrom
-rw-------   1 root   root    151 Mar 29 09:58 floppy
-rw-r--r--   1 root   root   2588 Mar 29 09:58 Home
-rw-r--r--   1 root   root    149 Mar 29 09:58 KDE Control Panel
-rw-r--r--   1 root   root     80 Mar 29 09:58 Linux Documentation
drwx------   2 root   root   4096 Mar 29 09:58 Trash
-rw-r--r--   1 root   root    107 Mar 29 09:58 www.redhat.com
[root@localhost root]# _
```

Just as the **chown** command can be used to change the owner of a file or directory, you may use the **chgrp (change group) command** to change the group owner of a file or directory. The chgrp command takes two arguments at minimum: the new group owner and the files or directories to change. As with the **chown** command, the **chgrp** command also accepts the **-R** option to change group ownership recursively throughout the directory tree. To change the group owner of `file1` and the `Desktop` directory recursively throughout the directory tree, you can execute the following commands:

```
[root@localhost root]# chgrp sys file1
[root@localhost root]# chgrp -R sys Desktop
[root@localhost root]# ls -l
total 4
drwx------   3 root   sys   4096 Apr  8 07:12 Desktop
-rw-r--r--   1 root   sys      0 Apr 29 15:40 file1
[root@localhost root]# ls -l Desktop
total 28
-rw-------   1 root   sys   1117 Mar 29 09:58 cdrom
-rw-------   1 root   sys    151 Mar 29 09:58 floppy
-rw-r--r--   1 root   sys   2588 Mar 29 09:58 Home
-rw-r--r--   1 root   sys    149 Mar 29 09:58 KDE Control Panel
-rw-r--r--   1 root   sys     80 Mar 29 09:58 Linux Documentation
drwx------   2 root   sys   4096 Mar 29 09:58 Trash
-rw-r--r--   1 root   sys    107 Mar 29 09:58 www.redhat.com
[root@localhost root]# _
```

Regular users may change the group of a file or directory only to a group of which they are a member.

Normally, you change both the ownership and group ownership on a file when that file needs to be maintained by someone else. To simplify this, you may change both the owner and the group owner at the same time using the **chown** command. To change the owner to user1 and the group to root for `file1` and the directory `Desktop` recursively, you can enter the following commands:

```
[root@localhost root]# chown user1.root file1
[root@localhost root]# chown -R user1.root Desktop
[root@localhost root]# ls -l
total 4
drwx------   3 user1   root   4096 Apr  8 07:12 Desktop
-rw-r--r--   1 user1   root      0 Apr 29 15:40 file1
[root@localhost root]# ls -l Desktop
total 28
-rw-------   1 user1   root   1117 Mar 29 09:58 cdrom
-rw-------   1 user1   root    151 Mar 29 09:58 floppy
-rw-r--r--   1 user1   root   2588 Mar 29 09:58 Home
-rw-r--r--   1 user1   root    149 Mar 29 09:58 KDE Control Panel
-rw-r--r--   1 user1   root     80 Mar 29 09:58 Linux Documentation
drwx------   2 user1   root   4096 Mar 29 09:58 Trash
-rw-r--r--   1 user1   root    107 Mar 29 09:58 www.redhat.com
[root@localhost root]# _
```

Note that there must be no spaces before and after the **.** character in the **chown** commands seen in the above output.

 You may also use the : character instead of the . character in the chown command to change both the owner and group ownership (i.e., chown -R user1:root Desktop)

Most files that reside in a user's home directory should be owned by that user for good security; some files in a user's home directory (especially the hidden files and directories) require this to function properly. To change the ownership back to the root user for **file1** and the **Desktop** directory to avoid future problems, you could type the following:

```
[root@localhost root]# chown root.root file1
[root@localhost root]# chown -R root.root Desktop
[root@localhost root]# ls -l
total 4
drwx------   3 root   root   4096 Apr  8 07:12 Desktop
-rw-r--r--   1 root   root      0 Apr 29 15:40 file1
[root@localhost root]# ls -l Desktop
total 28
-rw-------   1 root   root   1117 Mar 29 09:58 cdrom
-rw-------   1 root   root    151 Mar 29 09:58 floppy
-rw-r--r--   1 root   root   2588 Mar 29 09:58 Home
-rw-r--r--   1 root   root    149 Mar 29 09:58 KDE Control Panel
-rw-r--r--   1 root   root     80 Mar 29 09:58 Linux Documentation
drwx------   2 root   root   4096 Mar 29 09:58 Trash
-rw-r--r--   1 root   root    107 Mar 29 09:58 www.redhat.com
[root@localhost root]# _
```

Managing File and Directory Permissions

Every file and directory file on a Linux filesystem contains information regarding permissions in its inode. The section of the inode that stores permissions is called the **mode** of the file and is divided into three sections based on the user(s) that receive(s) the permissions to that file or directory:

- User (owner) permissions
- Group (group owner) permissions
- Other (everyone on the Linux system) permissions

Furthermore, there are three regular permissions that you may assign to each of these user(s):

- Read
- Write
- Execute

Interpreting the Mode

Recall that the three sections of the mode and the permissions that you may assign to each section are viewed when you perform an `ls -l` command; a detailed depiction of this can be seen in Figure 5-3. It is important to note that the root user supercedes all file and directory permissions; in other words, the root user has all permissions to every file and directory regardless of what the mode of the file or directory indicates.

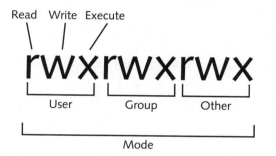

Figure 5-3   The structure of a mode

Take the root user's home directory listing seen below as an example:

```
[root@localhost root]# ls -l
total 28
drwx------   3 root   root   4096 Apr  8 07:12 Desktop
-r---w---x   1 root   root    282 Apr 29 22:06 file1
-------rwx   1 root   root    282 Apr 29 22:06 file2
-rwxrwxrwx   1 root   root    282 Apr 29 22:06 file3
----------   1 root   root    282 Apr 29 22:06 file4
-rw-r--r--   1 root   root    282 Apr 29 22:06 file5
-rw-r--r--   1 user1  sys     282 Apr 29 22:06 file6
[root@localhost root]# _
```

Note from the above output that all permissions (as seen in Figure 5-3) need not be on a file or directory; if the permission is unavailable, a dash character (-) will replace its position in the mode. Be sure not to confuse the character to the left of the mode (which determines the file type) with the mode, as it is unrelated to the permissions on the file or directory. From the above output, the `Desktop` directory gives the **user** or **owner** of the directory (the root user) read, write, and execute permission, yet members of the **group** (the root group) will not receive any permissions to the directory. Note that **other** (everyone on the system) does not receive permissions to this directory either.

Permissions are additive; the root user is also a member of the root group and always a part of the other category, thus the root user receives the permissions that are available to all three categories of users. In the example above, this means that the root user will have read, write, and execute permissions to the `Desktop` directory.

Along the same lines, the file called `file1` in the above output gives the user or owner of the file (the root user) read permission, and gives members of the group (the root group) write permission, and finally gives other (everyone on the system) execute permission. Since permissions are additive and the root user is matched by all three categories of users, the root user shall receive read, write, and execute permissions to `file1`.

Since permissions are additive in Linux, the other category seldom contains entries on sensitive files, as it will apply to all users. Although `file2` in our example does not give the user or group any specific permissions, all users will receive read, write, and execute permission via the other category. Thus `file2` should not contain sensitive data, since all users have full access to it. For the same reason, it is bad form to assign all permissions to a file that contains sensitive data, as seen with `file3` in the above example.

On the contrary, it is also possible to have a file that has no permissions assigned to it, as seen in `file4` above. In this case, the only user that has permissions to the file is the root user. (Also remember that the owner of the file can change these permissions if needed.)

The permission structure that you choose for a file or directory may result in too few or too many permissions. You can follow some general guidelines to avoid these situations. The owner of a file or directory is typically the person who maintains it; members of the group are typically users in the same company department and will likely need some form of limited access to the file or directory. As a result, most files and directories that you find on a Linux filesystem will have more permissions assigned to the user of the file/directory than the group of the file/directory, and the other category will have either the same permissions or less than the group of the file/directory, depending on how private that file or directory is. The file `file5` in the previous output depicts this common permission structure. In addition, files in a user's home directory are typically owned by that user; however, one may occasionally find files that are not. For these files, their permission definition changes as seen in `file6` above. The user or owner of `file6` is user1, who has read and write permissions to the file. The group owner of `file6` is the sys group, thus any members of the sys group have read permission to the file. Finally, everyone on the system receives read permission to the file via the other category. Remember, regardless of the mode, the root user receives all permissions to this file.

Interpreting Permissions

Once you understand how to identify the permissions that are applied to user, group, and other on a certain file or directory, you may then interpret the function of those permissions. Permissions for files are interpreted differently than those for directories. Also, if a user has a certain permission on a directory, that user does not automatically have the same permission for all files or subdirectories within that directory; file and directory permissions are treated separately by the Linux system. A summary of the different permissions and their definitions can be seen in Table 5-4.

Table 5-4   Linux permissions

Permission	Definition for Files	Definition for Directories
Read	Allows a user to open and read the contents of a file	Allows a user to list the contents of the directory (if they've also been given execute permission)
Write	Allows a user to open, read, and edit the contents of a file	Allows a user to add to or remove files from the directory (if they've also been given execute permission)
Execute	Allows a user to execute the file in memory (if it is a program file) and shell scripts	Allows a user to enter the directory and work with directory contents

The implications of the permission definitions described in Table 5-4 are important to understand. If a user has the read permission to a text file, then that user can use, among others, the `cat`, `more`, `head`, `tail`, `less`, `strings`, and `od` commands to view its contents. That same user can also open that file with a text editor such as vi; however, the user will not have the ability to save any changes to the document unless that user has the write permission to the file as well.

Recall from earlier that some text files contain instructions for the shell to execute and are called shell scripts. Shell scripts are executed in much the same way that binary compiled programs are; the user who attempts to execute the shell script must have execute permission to that file to execute it as a program.

 It is important to avoid giving execute permission to files that are not programs or shell scripts. This ensures that these files will not be executed accidentally, causing the shell to try to interpret the contents.

Remember that directories are simply special files that have an inode and a data section, yet the contents of the data section is a list of that directory's contents. If you wish to read that list, using the `ls` command for example, then you require the read permission to the directory. To modify that list, by adding or removing files, you require the write permission to the directory. Thus, if you wish to create a new file in a directory with a text editor such as vi, you must have the write permission to that directory. Similarly, when a source file is copied to a target directory with the `cp` command, a new file is created in the target directory and you must have the write permission to the target directory for the copy to be successful. Conversely, to delete a certain file, you must have the write permission to the directory that contains that file. It is also important to note that a user who has the write permission to a directory has the ability to delete all files and subdirectories within it.

The execute permission on a directory is sometimes referred to as the search permission, and works similar to a light switch. When a light switch is turned on, you may navigate through a room and use the objects within it. However, when a light switch is turned off, you cannot see the objects in the room, nor can you walk around and view them.

5

A user who does not have the execute permission to a directory is prevented from listing the directory's contents, adding and removing files, and working with files and subdirectories inside that directory, regardless of what permissions the user has to those files. In short, a quick way to deny a user from accessing a directory and all of its contents in Linux is to take away the execute permission on that directory. Since the execute permission on a directory is crucial for user access, it is commonly given to all users via the other category, unless the directory must be private.

Changing Permissions

To change the permissions for a certain file or directory, you may use the **chmod (change mode) command**. The chmod command takes two arguments at minimum; the first argument specifies the criteria used to change the permissions (see Table 5-5), and the remaining arguments indicate the filenames to change.

Table 5-5   Criteria used within the chmod command

Category	Operation	Permission
u (user)	+ (adds a permission)	r (read)
g (group)	- (removes a permission)	w (write)
o (other)	= (makes a permission equal to)	x (execute)
a (all categories)		

Take, for example, the directory list used earlier:

```
[root@localhost root]# ls -l
total 28
drwx------   3 root    root    4096 Apr  8 07:12 Desktop
-r---w---x   1 root    root     282 Apr 29 22:06 file1
-------rwx   1 root    root     282 Apr 29 22:06 file2
-rwxrwxrwx   1 root    root     282 Apr 29 22:06 file3
----------   1 root    root     282 Apr 29 22:06 file4
-rw-r--r--   1 root    root     282 Apr 29 22:06 file5
-rw-r--r--   1 user1   sys      282 Apr 29 22:06 file6
[root@localhost root]# _
```

To change the mode of file1 to rw-r--r--, you must add the write permission to the user of the file, add the read permission and take away the write permission for the group of the file, and add the read permission and take away the execute permission for other.

From the information listed in Table 5-5, you can use the following command:

```
[root@localhost root]# chmod u+w,g+r-w,o+r-x file1
[root@localhost root]# ls -l
total 28
drwx------    3 root    root    4096 Apr  8 07:12 Desktop
-rw-r--r--    1 root    root     282 Apr 29 22:06 file1
----r--rwx    1 root    root     282 Apr 29 22:06 file2
-rwxrwxrwx    1 root    root     282 Apr 29 22:06 file3
----------    1 root    root     282 Apr 29 22:06 file4
-rw-r--r--    1 root    root     282 Apr 29 22:06 file5
-rw-r--r--    1 user1   sys      282 Apr 29 22:06 file6
[root@localhost root]# _
```

 You should ensure that there are no spaces between any criteria used in the chmod command since all criteria make up the first argument only.

You may also use the = criteria from Table 5-5 to specify the exact permissions to change. To change the mode on file2 in the above output to the same as file1 (rw-r--r--), you can use the following chmod command:

```
[root@localhost root]# chmod u=rw,g=r,o=r file2
[root@localhost root]# ls -l
total 28
drwx------    3 root    root    4096 Apr  8 07:12 Desktop
-rw-r--r--    1 root    root     282 Apr 29 22:06 file1
-rw-r--r--    1 root    root     282 Apr 29 22:06 file2
-rwxrwxrwx    1 root    root     282 Apr 29 22:06 file3
----------    1 root    root     282 Apr 29 22:06 file4
-rw-r--r--    1 root    root     282 Apr 29 22:06 file5
-rw-r--r--    1 user1   sys      282 Apr 29 22:06 file6
[root@localhost root]# _
```

If the permissions to be changed are identical for the user, group, and other categories, you can use the a character to refer to all categories, as seen in Table 5-5 and below when adding the execute permission to user, group, and other for file1:

```
[root@localhost root]# chmod a+x file1
[root@localhost root]# ls -l
total 28
drwx------    3 root    root    4096 Apr  8 07:12 Desktop
-rwxr-xr-x    1 root    root     282 Apr 29 22:06 file1
-rw-r--r--    1 root    root     282 Apr 29 22:06 file2
-rwxrwxrwx    1 root    root     282 Apr 29 22:06 file3
----------    1 root    root     282 Apr 29 22:06 file4
-rw-r--r--    1 root    root     282 Apr 29 22:06 file5
-rw-r--r--    1 user1   sys      282 Apr 29 22:06 file6
[root@localhost root]# _
```

However, if there is no character specifying the category of user to affect, all users are assumed, as seen below when adding the execute permission to user, group, and other for file2:

```
[root@localhost root]# chmod +x file2
[root@localhost root]# ls -l
total 28
drwx------   3 root   root   4096 Apr  8 07:12 Desktop
-rwxr-xr-x   1 root   root    282 Apr 29 22:06 file1
-rwxr-xr-x   1 root   root    282 Apr 29 22:06 file2
-rwxrwxrwx   1 root   root    282 Apr 29 22:06 file3
----------   1 root   root    282 Apr 29 22:06 file4
-rw-r--r--   1 root   root    282 Apr 29 22:06 file5
-rw-r--r--   1 user1  sys     282 Apr 29 22:06 file6
[root@localhost root]# _
```

All of the aforementioned **chmod** examples use the symbols listed in Table 5-5 as the criteria for changing the permissions on a file or directory. You may instead choose to use numeric criteria with the **chmod** command to change permissions. All permissions are stored in the inode of a file or directory as binary powers of two:

- read $= 2^{2} = 4$
- write $= 2^{1} = 2$
- execute $= 2^{0} = 1$

Thus, the mode of a file or directory may be represented using the numbers 421421421 instead of rwxrwxrwx. Since permissions are grouped into the categories user, group, and other, you can then simplify this further by using only three numbers, one for each category that represents the sum of the permissions, as depicted in Figure 5-4.

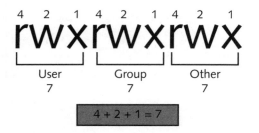

Figure 5-4   Numeric representation of the mode

Similarly, to represent the mode **rw-r--r--**, you can use the numbers 644, since user has read and write (4+2=6), group has read (4), and other has read (4). The mode **rwxr-x---** can also be represented by the numbers 750 since user has read, write, and execute (4+2+1=7), group has read and execute (4+1=5), and other has nothing (0). A list of the different permissions and their corresponding numbers can be seen in Table 5-6.

Table 5-6   Numeric representations of the permissions in a mode

Mode (One Section Only)	Corresponding Number
rwx	4 + 2 + 1 = 7
rw-	4 + 2 = 6
r-x	4 + 1 = 5
r--	4
-wx	2 + 1 = 3
-w-	2
--x	1
---	0

To change to `r-xr-----`, the mode of the `file1` file used earlier, you can use the command `chmod 540 file1`, as seen below:

```
[root@localhost root]# chmod 540 file1
[root@localhost root]# ls -l
total 28
drwx------  3 root   root   4096 Apr  8 07:12 Desktop
-r-xr-----  1 root   root    282 Apr 29 22:06 file1
-rwxr-xr-x  1 root   root    282 Apr 29 22:06 file2
-rwxrwxrwx  1 root   root    282 Apr 29 22:06 file3
----------  1 root   root    282 Apr 29 22:06 file4
-rw-r--r--  1 root   root    282 Apr 29 22:06 file5
-rw-r--r--  1 user1  sys     282 Apr 29 22:06 file6
[root@localhost root]# _
```

Similarly, to change the mode of all files in the directory that start with the word `file` to 644 (which are common permissions for files), you can use the following command:

```
[root@localhost root]# chmod 644 file*
[root@localhost root]# ls -l
total 28
drwx------  3 root   root   4096 Apr  8 07:12 Desktop
-rw-r--r--  1 root   root    282 Apr 29 22:06 file1
-rw-r--r--  1 root   root    282 Apr 29 22:06 file2
-rw-r--r--  1 root   root    282 Apr 29 22:06 file3
-rw-r--r--  1 root   root    282 Apr 29 22:06 file4
-rw-r--r--  1 root   root    282 Apr 29 22:06 file5
-rw-r--r--  1 user1  sys     282 Apr 29 22:06 file6
[root@localhost root]# _
```

As with the `chown` and `chgrp` commands, the `chmod` command can also be used to change the permission on a directory and all of its contents recursively by using the **–R** option, as seen below when changing the mode of the `Desktop` directory:

```
[root@localhost root]# chmod -R 755 Desktop
[root@localhost root]# ls -l
total 28
drwxr-xr-x  3 root   root   4096 Apr  8 07:12 Desktop
-rw-r--r--  1 root   root    282 Apr 29 22:06 file1
-rw-r--r--  1 root   root    282 Apr 29 22:06 file2
-rw-r--r--  1 root   root    282 Apr 29 22:06 file3
-rw-r--r--  1 root   root    282 Apr 29 22:06 file4
-rw-r--r--  1 root   root    282 Apr 29 22:06 file5
-rw-r--r--  1 user1  sys     282 Apr 29 22:06 file6
[root@localhost root]# ls -l Desktop
total 28
-rwxr-xr-x  1 root   root   1117 Mar 29 09:58 cdrom
-rwxr-xr-x  1 root   root    151 Mar 29 09:58 floppy
-rwxr-xr-x  1 root   root   2588 Mar 29 09:58 Home
-rwxr-xr-x  1 root   root    149 Mar 29 09:58 KDE Control Panel
-rwxr-xr-x  1 root   root     80 Mar 29 09:58 Linux Documentation
drwxr-xr-x  2 root   root   4096 Mar 29 09:58 Trash
-rwxr-xr-x  1 root   root    107 Mar 29 09:58 www.redhat.com
[root@localhost root]# _
```

Default Permissions

Recall that permissions provide security for files and directories by allowing only certain users access, and that there are common guidelines for setting permissions on files and directories, so that permissions are neither too strict nor too permissive. Also important to maintaining security are the permissions that are given to new files and directories once they are created. New files are given rw-rw-rw- by the system when they are created (since execute should not be given unless necessary) and new directories are given rwxrwxrwx by the system when they are created. These default permissions are too permissive for most files, as they allow other full access to directories and nearly full access to files. Hence, there is a special variable on the system called the **umask** (user mask), which takes away permissions on new files and directories immediately after they are created. The most common umask that one will find is 022, which specifies that nothing (0) will be taken away from the user, write permission (2) will be taken away from members of the group, and write permission (2) will be taken away from other on new files and directories when they are first created and given permissions by the system.

Keep in mind that the umask only applies to newly created files and directories; it will never be used to modify the permissions of existing files and directories. You must use the `chmod` command to modify existing permissions.

An example of how a umask of 022 can be used to alter the permissions of a new file or directory after creation is seen in Figure 5-5.

	New Files	New Directories
Permissions assigned by system	rw-rw-rw-	rwxrwxrwx
- umask	0 2 2	0 2 2
= resulting permissions	rw-r--r--	rwxr-xr-x

Figure 5-5 Performing a umask 007 calculation

To verify the umask used, you may use the **umask** command. To ensure that the umask functions as seen in Figure 5-5, simply create a new file using the **touch** command and a new directory using the **mkdir** command as seen in the following output:

```
[root@localhost root]# ls -l
total 28
drwx------  3 root   root  4096 Apr  8 07:12 Desktop
[root@localhost root]# umask
022
[root@localhost root]# mkdir dir1
[root@localhost root]# touch file1
[root@localhost root]# ls -l
total 8
drwx------  3 root   root  4096 Apr  8 07:12 Desktop
drwxr-xr-x  2 root   root  4096 May  3 21:39 dir1
-rw-r--r--  1 root   root     0 May  3 21:40 file1
[root@localhost root]# _
```

Since the umask is a variable stored in memory, it may be changed. To change the current umask you may specify the new umask as an argument to the **umask** command. Say, for example, you wished to change the umask to 007; the resulting permissions on new files and directories is calculated in Figure 5-6.

	New Files	New Directories
Permissions assigned by system	rw-rw-rw-	rwxrwxrwx
- umask	0 0 7	0 0 7
= resulting permissions	rw-rw----	rwxrwx---

Figure 5-6 Performing a umask 007 calculation

To change the umask to 007 and view its effect, you can type in the following commands on the command line:

```
[root@localhost root]# ls -l
total 8
drwx------   3 root   root   4096 Apr   8 07:12 Desktop
drwxr-xr-x   2 root   root   4096 May   3 21:39 dir1
-rw-r--r--   1 root   root      0 May   3 21:40 file1
[root@localhost root]# umask 007
[root@localhost root]# umask
007
[root@localhost root]# mkdir dir2
[root@localhost root]# touch file2
[root@localhost root]# ls -l
total 12
drwx------   3 root   root   4096 Apr   8 07:12 Desktop
drwxr-xr-x   2 root   root   4096 May   3 21:39 dir1
drwxrwx---   2 root   root   4096 May   3 21:41 dir2
-rw-r--r--   1 root   root      0 May   3 21:40 file1
-rw-rw----   1 root   root      0 May   3 21:41 file2
[root@localhost root]# _
```

Special Permissions

Read, write, and execute are the regular file permissions that you would use to assign security to files; however, there are three more special permissions that you may optionally use on files and directories:

- SUID (Set User ID)
- SGID (Set Group ID)
- Sticky bit

Defining Special Permissions

The SUID has no special function when set on a directory; however, if the SUID is set on a file and that file is executed, then the person who executed the file temporarily becomes the owner of the file while it is executing. There are many commands on a typical Linux system that have this special permission set; the **ping** command (**/bin/ping**), which is used to test network connectivity, is one such file. Since this file is owned by the root user, when a regular user executes the **ping** command, that user temporarily becomes the root user while the **ping** command is executing in memory. This ensures that any user will be able to test network connectivity as the person who has all rights to do so on the system. The SUID can only be applied to binary compiled programs. The Linux kernel will not let you apply the SUID to a shell script, since shell scripts are easy to edit and thus pose a security hazard to the system.

Contrary to the SUID, the SGID has a function when applied to both files and directories. Just as the SUID allows regular users to execute a binary compiled program and become the owner of the file for the duration of execution, the SGID allows regular users to execute a binary compiled program and become a member of the group that is attached to the file during execution of the program. Thus, if a file is owned by the group sys and also has the SGID permission, then any user who executes that file will be a member of the group sys during execution. If a command or file required the user executing it to have the same permissions applied to the sys group, then setting the SGID on the file would simplify assigning rights to the file for user execution.

The SGID also has a special function when placed on a directory. When a user creates a file, recall that that user's name and primary group become the owner and group of the file, respectively. However, if a user creates a file in a directory that has the SGID permission set, then that user's name will still become the owner of the file, but the directory's group will become the group of the file.

Finally, the sticky bit was used on files in the past to lock them in memory; however, today the sticky bit performs a useful function only on directories. Recall from earlier that the write permission applied to a directory allows one to add and remove any file to or from that directory. Thus, if one had the write permission to a certain directory but no permission to files within it, one could still delete all of those files. Consider a company that requires a common directory that gives all employees the ability to add files; this directory must give everyone the write permission.

Unfortunately, the write permission also gives all employees the ability to delete all files and directories within, including the ones that others have added to the directory. If the sticky bit were applied to this common directory in addition to the write permission, then employees may add files to the directory but only delete those files that they have added and not others.

 Note that all special permissions also require the execute permission in order to work properly; the SUID and SGID work on executable files, and the SGID and sticky bit work on directories (which must have execute permission for access).

Setting Special Permissions

The mode of a file that is displayed using the `ls -l` command does not have a section for special permissions. However, since special permissions require execute, they mask the execute permission when displayed using the `ls -l` command as seen in Figure 5-7.

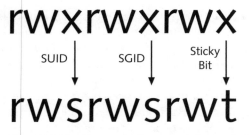

Figure 5-7 Representing special permissions in the mode

Note that the system will allow you to set special permissions even if the file or directory you choose does not have execute permission. This will prevent the special permissions from performing their function. If special permissions are set on a file or directory without execute permission, the special permissions masking the execute permission in a long listing are capitalized as seen in Figure 5-8, letting you know that they won't be operational.

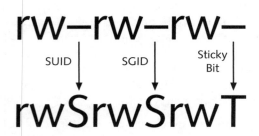

Figure 5-8 Representing special permission in the absence of the execute permission

To set the special permissions, you can visualize them to the left of the mode as seen in Figure 5-9.

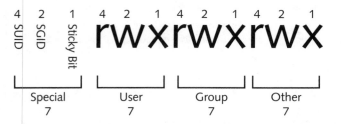

Figure 5-9 Numeric representation of regular and special permissions

Thus, to set all of the special permissions on a certain file or directory, you could use the command `chmod 7777 <name>` as indicated from Figure 5-9. However, the SUID and SGID bits are typically set on files. To change the permissions on the `file1` file used earlier such that other has the ability to view and execute the file as the owner and a member of the group, you could use the command `chmod 6755 file1` as seen below:

```
[root@localhost root]# ls -l
total 12
drwx------   3 root   root   4096 Apr  8 07:12 Desktop
drwxr-xr-x   2 root   root   4096 May  3 21:39 dir1
drwx------   2 root   root   4096 May  3 21:41 dir2
-rw-r--r--   1 root   root      0 May  3 21:40 file1
-rw-------   1 root   root      0 May  3 21:41 file2
[root@localhost root]# chmod 6755 file1
[root@localhost root]# ls -l
total 12
drwx------   3 root   root   4096 Apr  8 07:12 Desktop
drwxr-xr-x   2 root   root   4096 May  3 21:39 dir1
drwx------   2 root   root   4096 May  3 21:41 dir2
-rwsr-sr-x   1 root   root      0 May  3 21:40 file1
-rw-------   1 root   root      0 May  3 21:41 file2
[root@localhost root]# _
```

Similarly, to set the sticky bit permission on the directory `dir1` used earlier, you could use the command `chmod 1777 dir1`, which would allow all users (including other) to add files to the `dir1` directory since we gave the write permission, yet only delete the files that they own in `dir1` since we set the sticky bit. An example of this is seen below:

```
[root@localhost root]# ls -l
total 12
drwx------   3 root   root   4096 Apr  8 07:12 Desktop
drwxr-xr-x   2 root   root   4096 May  3 21:39 dir1
drwx------   2 root   root   4096 May  3 21:41 dir2
-rwsr-sr-x   1 root   root      0 May  3 21:40 file1
-rw-------   1 root   root      0 May  3 21:41 file2
[root@localhost root]# chmod 1777 dir1
[root@localhost root]# ls -l
total 12
drwx------   3 root   root   4096 Apr  8 07:12 Desktop
drwxrwxrwt   2 root   root   4096 May  3 21:39 dir1
drwx------   2 root   root   4096 May  3 21:41 dir2
-rwsr-sr-x   1 root   root      0 May  3 21:40 file1
-rw-------   1 root   root      0 May  3 21:41 file2
[root@localhost root]# _
```

Also, remember that assigning special permissions without execute renders those permissions useless. If you forget to give execute permission to either user, group, or other and the long listing covers the execute permission with a special permission, then the special permission will be capitalized, as seen below when `dir2` is not given execute underneath the position in the mode that indicates the sticky bit (t):

```
[root@localhost root]# ls -l
total 12
drwx------   3 root    root    4096 Apr  8 07:12 Desktop
drwxrwxrwt   2 root    root    4096 May  3 21:39 dir1
drwx------   2 root    root    4096 May  3 21:41 dir2
-rwsr-sr-x   1 root    root       0 May  3 21:40 file1
-rw-------   1 root    root       0 May  3 21:41 file2
[root@localhost root]# chmod 1770 dir2
[root@localhost root]# ls -l
total 12
drwx------   3 root    root    4096 Apr  8 07:12 Desktop
drwxrwxrwt   2 root    root    4096 May  3 21:39 dir1
drwxrwx--T   2 root    root    4096 May  3 21:41 dir2
-rwsr-sr-x   1 root    root       0 May  3 21:40 file1
-rw-------   1 root    root       0 May  3 21:41 file2
[root@localhost root]# _
```

CHAPTER SUMMARY

❑ The Linux directory tree obeys the Filesystem Hierarchy Standard, which allows Linux users and developers to locate system files in standard directories.

❑ There are many file management commands that exist to create, change the location of, or remove files and directories. The most common of these include `cp`, `mv`, `rm`, `rmdir`, and `mkdir`.

❑ You may find files on the filesystem using a pre-indexed database (the `locate` command), or by searching the directories listed in the PATH variable (the `which` command). However, the most versatile command used to find files is the `find` command, which searches for files based on a wide range of criteria.

❑ Files may be created as a pointer to another file or as a linked duplicate of another file. These are called symbolic and hard links, respectively.

❑ Each file and directory has an owner and a group owner. The owner of the file or directory has the ability to change permissions and give ownership to others.

❑ Permissions can be set on the user or owner of a file, members of the group of the file, as well as everyone on the system (other).

❑ There are three regular file and directory permissions (read, write, execute) and three special file and directory permissions (SUID, SGID, sticky bit). The definitions of these permissions are separate between files and directories.

❑ Permissions may be changed using the `chmod` command by specifying symbols or numbers to represent the changed permissions.

□ To ensure security, new files and directories receive default permissions from the system less the value of the umask variable.

□ The root user has all permissions to all files and directories on the Linux filesystem. Similarly, the root user may change the ownership of any file or directory on the Linux filesystem.

KEY TERMS

/bin directory — Contains binary commands for use by all users.

/boot directory — Contains the Linux kernel and files used by the boot loader data block.

chgrp (change group) command — The command used to change the group owner of a file or directory.

chmod (change mode) command — The command used to change the mode (permissions) of a file or directory.

chown (change owner) command — The command used to change the owner and group owner of a file or directory.

cp command — The command used to create copies of files and directories.

data blocks — Store the information of a certain file as well as the filename.

/dev directory — Contains device files.

/etc directory — Contains system-specific configuration files.

Filesystem Hierarchy Standard (FHS) — A standard outlining the location of set files and directories on a Linux system.

find command — The command used to find files on the filesystem using various criteria.

group — When used in the mode of a certain file or directory, it refers to group ownership of that file or directory.

hard link — A file joined to other files on the same file system that share the same inode.

/home directory — Default location for user home directories.

inode — That portion of a file that stores information on the file's attributes, access permissions, location, ownership, and file type.

inode table — The collection of inodes for all files and directories on a filesystem.

interactive mode — Refers to the mode that file management commands use when a file may be overwritten; the system interacts with a user asking for the user to confirm the action.

/lib directory — Contains shared program libraries (used by the commands in /bin and /sbin) as well as kernel modules.

ln (link) command — The command used to create hard and symbolic links.

locate command — The command used to locate files from a file database.

mkdir command — The command used to create directories.

/mnt directory — Empty directory used for accessing (mounting) disks such as floppy disks and CD-ROMs.

mode — That part of the inode that stores information on access permissions.

mv (move) command — The command used to move/rename files and directories.

/opt directory — Stores additional software programs.

other — When used in the mode of a certain file or directory, it refers to all users on the Linux system.

owner — The user whose name appears in a long listing of a file or directory and who has the ability to change permissions on that file or directory.

PATH variable — A variable that stores a list of directories that will be searched in order when commands are executed without an absolute or relative pathname.

permissions — A list of who can access a file or folder, and their level of access.

primary group — The default group to which a user belongs.

/proc directory — Contains process and kernel information.

recursive — Referring to itself and its own contents; a recursive search includes all subdirectories in a directory and their contents.

rm command — The command used to remove files and directories.

rmdir command — The command used to remove empty directories.

/root directory — The root user's home directory.

/sbin directory — Contains system binary commands (used for administration).

source file/directory — The portion of a command that refers to the file or directory from which information is taken.

superblock — That portion of a file system that stores critical information such as the inode table and block size.

symbolic link — A pointer to another file on the same or another filesystem; commonly referred to as a shortcut.

target file/directory — The portion of a command that refers to the file or directory to which information is directed.

/tmp directory — Holds temporary files created by programs.

touch command — The command used to create new files. It was originally used to update the timestamp on a file.

umask — Used to alter the permissions on all new files and directories by taking select default file and directory permissions away.

umask command — The command used to view and change the umask variable.

user — When used in the mode of a certain file or directory, it refers to the owner of that file or directory.

/usr directory — Contains most system commands and utilities.

/usr/local directory — Location for most additional programs.

/var directory — Contains log files and spools.

which command — The command used to locate files that exist within directories listed in the PATH variable.

REVIEW QUESTIONS

5

1. A symbolic link is also known as a soft link and depicted by an @ appearing at the beginning of the file name when viewed using the `ls -l` command. True or False?

2. What was created to define a standard directory structure and common file location for Linux?

   a FSH

   b. X.500

   c. FHS

   d. root directory

3. There is no real difference between the "S" and "s" special permissions when displayed using the `ls -l` command. One just means it is on a file and the other that it is on a directory. True or False?

4. The default permissions given by the system prior to analyzing the umask are _____ for directories, and _____ for files.

   a. rw-rw-rw-, and rw-rw-rw-

   b. rw-rw-rw-, r--r--r--

   c. rw-rw-rw-, rwxrwxrwx

   d. rwxrwxrwx, rw-rw-rw-

   e. rwxrw-rw-, rwx-rw-rw-

5. Which of the following is the folder where administrative commands would be found?

   a. /bin

   b. \sbin

   c. /root

   d. /superuser

   e. /sbin

6. All files have a _____.

   a. superblock

   b. inode

   c. PATH

   d. home directory

7. What must a user do to run **cp** or **mv** interactively and be asked if they wish to overwrite an existing file?

   a. There is no choice as the new file will overwrite the old one by default.

   b. Type *interactive cp* or *interactive mv*.

   c. Type *cp -i* or *mv-i*.

   d. Type *cp -interactive* or *mv - interactive*.

   e. Just type *cp* or *mv* as they run in interactive mode by default.

8. A users enters the command to copy the file *project1* to the folder */user1*; however, when they subsequently enter the command **ls –F /user1** they notice that the file was not copied over. Why was the file not copied over?

   a. The user is not the root user.

   b. The command syntax is wrong for the **ls** command.

   c. The user does not have the write permission to the directory /user1.

   d. The user does not have the write permission to the file project1.

   e. The was copied, but the **ls –F** command will not show copied files, only originals.

9. A user utilizes the **chgrp** command to give ownership of a file to another user. What must they do to regain ownership of the file?

   a. run **chgrp** again listing themselves as the new owner

   b. nothing, as the this is a one way one time action

   c. have the new owner run **chgrp** and list the original owner as the new owner

   d. run **chown** and list themselves as the new owner

10. After typing the **ls –F** command, you see the following line in the output:

    -rw-r-xr--   1 user1   root   0 Apr 29 15:40 file1

    What does this mean?

    a. user1 has read and write, members of the root group have read and execute, and all others have read permissions to the file

    b. members of the root group have read and write, user1 has read and execute, and all others have read permissions to the file

    c. all users have read and write, members of the root group have read and execute, and user1 has read permissions to the file

    d. user1 has read and write, all others have read and execute, and members of the root group have read permissions to the file

11. After typing the command `umask 731` the permissions on all subsequently created files and directories will be affected. In this case what will the permissions on all new files be?

    a. rw–rw–rw–

    b. rwxrw–r––

    c. –––r––rw–

    d. ––––wx––x

12. What will be the result of the `cp /etc/hosts .` command?

    a. the same as the `cp /etc/hosts ..` command

    b. copy the /etc/hosts file to the clipboard

    c. create a copy of the file hosts in the /etc directory

    d. create a copy of the hosts file from /etc to the current directory

13. Under which directory would one find commands and supporting files needed by users on a regular basis? (Choose all that apply.)

    a. /bin

    b. /sbin

    c. /lib

    d. /root

    e. /usr

14. As hard-linked files share the same inode and data, when one of the files hard-linked together is deleted they are all deleted. True or False?

15. When one changes the data in a file that is hard-linked to three others, _____.

    a. only the data in the file you modified is affected

    b. only the data in the file you modified and any hard-linked files in the same directory are affected

    c. the data in the file you modified and the data in all hard-linked files are modified as they have different inodes

    d. the data in the file you modified as well as the data in all hard-linked files are modified as they share the same data and all have the same inode and file size

5

16. Jim has rw-rw-rw- to the file *resume* which resides in the directory *jobs*. He modifies and prints off a copy and then wants to delete the file *resume* but cannot. Why can he not delete the file?

    a. Jim needs execute permission to the file *resume*.

    b. Jim needs write permission to the directory *jobs*.

    c. Jim must save the modified file before he can delete it.

    d. Only root users can delete files.

17. The command `chmod 317 file1` would produce which of the following lines in the `ls` command?

    a. --w-r--rwx   1 user1   root   0 Apr 29 15:40 file1

    b. --wx--xrwx   1 user1   root   0 Apr 29 15:40 file1

    c. -rwxrw-r-x   1 user1   root   0 Apr 29 15:40 file1

    d. --w-rw-r-e   1 user1   root   0 Apr 29 15:40 file1

18. In order to see a directory's contents a user only needs to have execute permission to that directory. True or False?

19. What command is used to create a new file?

    a. `mkfile filename`

    b. `make file filename`

    c. `touch filename`

    d. `take file filename`

20. Which of the following commands will change the user ownership and group ownership of *file1* to user1 and root respectively?

    a. `chown user1:root file1`

    b. `chown user1 : root file1`

    c. cannot be done as user and group ownership properties of a file must be modified separately

    d. `chown root:user1file1`

    e. `chown root : user1file1`

21. What does the `/var` directory contain?

    a. various additional programs

    b. spools and log files

    c. temporary files

    d. files that are architecture independent

    e. local variance devices

22. What does the **mv** command do? (Choose all that apply.)

    a. makes a volume

    b. makes a directory

    c. moves a directory

    d. moves a file

23. A file has the following permissions *r----x-w-*. The command **chmod 143** would have the same effect as the command _____. (Choose all that apply.)

    a. chmod u+x-r,g+r-x,o+w file1

    b. chmod u=w,g=rw,o=rx file1

    c. chmod u-r-w,g+r-w,o+r-x file1

    d. chmod u=x,g=r,o=wx file1

    e. chmod u+w,g+r-w,o+r-x file1

    f. chmod u=rw,g=r,o=r file1

24. The **which** command _____.

    a. can only be used to search for executables

    b. searches for a file in all directories starting from the root

    c. is not a valid Linux command

    d. searches for a file only in directories that are in the PATH variable

25. Hard links need to reside on the same filesystem as the target, whereas symbolic links need not be on the same filesystem as the target. True or False?

26. When applied to a directory the SGID special permission _____.

    a. causes all new files created in the directory to have the same group membership as the directory and not the entity that created them

    b. cannot be done as it is only applied to files

    c. allows users to use more than 2 groups for files that they create within the directory

    d. causes users to have their permissions checked before they are allowed to access files in the directory

27. Which command do you use to rename files and directories?

    a. cp

    b. mv

    c. rn

    d. rename

28. What command would be used to remove *Jobs*, a directory that contains several files and subfolders?

    a. `rm jobs`

    b. `remdir jobs`

    c. it cannot be done; the directory must be empty so you have to delete the contents first

    d. `rm -r jobs`

29. What command is used to create a new directory or subdirectory?

    a. none; the FHS is a set standardized directory structure that cannot be modified

    b. `/mnt/dir directory name`

    c. `mkdir directory name`

    d. `make dir directory name`

30. What are the three standard Linux permissions?

    a. Full control, read–execute, write

    b. Read, write, modify

    c. Execute, read, write

    d. Read, write, examine

31. Given the following output from the `ls` command how many files are linked with file1?

```
drwxr-xr-x    3 root     root         4096 Apr  8 07:12 Desktop
-rw-r--r--    3 root     root          282 Apr 29 22:06 file1
-rw-r--r--    1 root     root          282 Apr 29 22:06 file2
-rw-r--r--    4 root     root          282 Apr 29 22:06 file3
-rw-r--r--    2 root     root          282 Apr 29 22:06 file4
-rw-r--r--    1 root     root          282 Apr 29 22:06 file5
-rw-r--r--    1 user1    sys           282 Apr 29 22:06 file6
```

    a. one

    b. two

    c. three

    d. four

HANDS-ON PROJECTS

These projects should be completed in the order given. All hands-on projects should take a total of three hours to complete. The requirements for this lab include:

❑ A computer with Red Hat Linux 7.2 installed according to Hands-on Project 2-2

❑ Completion of all hands-on projects in Chapter 3

Project 5-1

In this hands-on project, you will log in to the computer and create new directories.

1. Turn on your computer. Once your Linux system has been loaded, you will be placed at a graphical terminal (tty7). Switch to a command-line terminal (tty2) by pressing **Ctrl–Alt–F2** and log into the terminal using the username of **root** and the password of **secret**.

2. At the command prompt, type **ls –F** and press **Enter**. What are the contents of your home folder? How many files and subdirectories are there?

3. At the command prompt, type **mkdir mysamples** and press **Enter**. Next, type **ls –F** at the command prompt and press **Enter**. How many files and subdirectories are there? Why?

4. At the command prompt, type **cd mysamples** and press **Enter**. Next, type **ls –F** at the command prompt and press **Enter**. What are the contents of the subdirectory `mysamples`?

5. At the command prompt, type **mkdir undermysamples** and press **Enter**. Next, type **ls –F** at the command prompt and press **Enter**. What are the contents of the subdirectory `mysamples`?

6. At the command prompt, type **mkdir todelete** and press **Enter**. Next, type **ls –F** at the command prompt and press **Enter**. Does the subdirectory **todelete** you just created appear listed in the display?

7. At the command prompt, type **cd ..** and press **Enter**. Next, type **ls –R** and press **Enter**. Notice that the subdirectory `mysamples` and its subdirectory `undermysamples` are both displayed. You have used the recursive option with the `ls` command.

8. At the command prompt, type **cd ..** and press **Enter**. At the command prompt, type **pwd** and press **Enter**. What is your current directory?

9. At the command prompt, type **mkdir foruser1** and press **Enter**. At the command prompt, type **ls –F** and press **Enter**. Does the subdirectory you just created appear listed in the display?

10. Type **exit** and press **Enter** to log out of your shell.

Project 5-2

In this hands-on project, you will copy files using the **cp** command.

1. Switch to a command-line terminal (tty2) by pressing **Ctrl–Alt–F2** and log into the terminal using the username of **root** and the password of **secret**.

2. Next, type **ls –F** at the command prompt and press **Enter**. How many files are listed and what are their names?

3. At the command prompt, type **cp sample1** and press **Enter**. What error message was displayed and why?

4. At the command prompt, type **cp sample1 sample1A** and press **Enter**. Next, type **ls –F** at the command prompt and press **Enter**. How many files are there and what are their names? Why?

5. At the command prompt, type **cp sample1 mysamples/sample1B** and press **Enter**. Next, type **ls –F** at the command prompt and press **Enter**. How many files are there and what are their names? Why?

6. At the command prompt, type **cd mysamples** and press **Enter**. Next, type **ls –F** at the command prompt and press **Enter**. Was sample1B copied successfully?

7. At the command prompt, type **cp /root/sample2 .** and press **Enter**. Next, type **ls –F** at the command prompt and press **Enter**. How many files are there and what are their names? Why?

8. At the command prompt, type **cp sample1B ..** and press **Enter**. Next, type **cd ..** at the command prompt and press **Enter**. At the command prompt, type **ls –F** and press **Enter**. Was the sample1B file copied successfully?

9. At the command prompt, type **cp sample1 sample2 sample3 mysamples** and press **Enter**. What message do you get and why? Choose **y** and press **Enter**. Next, type **cd mysamples** at the command prompt and press **Enter**. At the command prompt, type **ls –F** and press **Enter**. How many files are there and what are their names? Why?

10. At the command prompt, type **cd ..** and press **Enter**. Next, type **cp mysamples mysamples2** at the command prompt and press **Enter**. What error message did you receive? Why?

11. At the command prompt, type **cp –r mysamples mysamples2** and press **Enter**. Next, type **ls –F** at the command prompt and press **Enter**. Was the directory copied successfully? Type **ls –F mysamples2** at the command prompt and press **Enter**. Were the contents of mysamples copied to mysamples2 successfully?

12. Type **exit** and press **Enter** to log out of your shell.

Project 5-3

In this hands-on project, you will use the mv command to rename files and directories.

1. Switch to a command-line terminal (tty2) by pressing **Ctrl-Alt-F2** and log into the terminal using the username of **root** and the password of **secret**.

2. Next, type **ls –F** at the command prompt and press **Enter**. How many files are listed and what are their names?

3. At the command prompt, type **mv sample1** and press **Enter**. What error message was displayed and why?

4. At the command prompt, type **mv sample1 sample4** and press **Enter**. Next, type **ls –F** at the command prompt and press **Enter**. How many files are listed and what are their names? What happened to sample1?

5. At the command prompt, type **mv sample4 mysamples** and press **Enter**. Next, type **ls –F** at the command prompt and press **Enter**. How many files are there and what are their names? Where did `sample4` go?

6. At the command prompt, type **cd mysamples** and press **Enter**. Next, type **ls –F** at the command prompt and press **Enter**. Notice that the `sample4` file you moved in Step 5 above was moved here.

7. At the command prompt, type **mv sample4 ..** and press **Enter**. Next, type **ls –F** at the command prompt and press **Enter**. How many files are there and what are their names? Where did the `sample4` file go?

8. At the command prompt, type **cd ..** and press **Enter**. Next, type **ls –F** at the command prompt and press **Enter** to view the new location of `sample4`.

9. At the command prompt, type **mv sample4 mysamples/sample2** and press **Enter**. What message appeared on the screen and why?

10. Type **y** and press **Enter** to confirm you wish to overwrite the file in the destination folder.

11. At the command prompt, type **mv sample? mysamples** and press **Enter**. Type **y** and press **Enter** to confirm you wish to overwrite the file **sample2** in the destination folder. If necessary, confirm the override for `sample3`, as well.

12. At the command prompt, type **ls –F** and press **Enter**. How many files are there and why?

13. At the command prompt, type **mv sample1* mysamples** and press **Enter**. Type **y** and press **Enter** to confirm you wish to overwrite the file **sample1B** in the destination directory.

14. At the command prompt, type **ls –F** and press **Enter**. Notice that there are no sample files in the **/root** directory.

15. At the command prompt, type **cd mysamples** and press **Enter**. Next, type **ls –F** at the command prompt and press **Enter**. Notice that all files originally in **/root** have been moved to this directory.

16. At the command prompt, type **cd ..** and press **Enter**. Next, type **ls –F** at the command prompt and press **Enter**. Type **mv mysamples samples** and press **Enter**. Next, type **ls –F** at the command prompt and press **Enter**. Why did you not need to specify the recursive option to the `mv` command to rename the `mysamples` directory to `samples`?

17. Type **exit** and press **Enter** to log out of your shell.

Project 5-4

In this hands-on project, you will make and view links to files and directories.

1. Switch to a command-line terminal (tty2) by pressing **Ctrl–Alt–F2** and log into the terminal using the username of **root** and the password of **secret**.

2. At the command prompt, type **cd samples** and press **Enter**. Next, type **ls –F** at the command prompt and press **Enter**. What files do you see? Now, type **ls –l** at the command prompt and press **Enter**. What is the link count for the `sample1` file?

3. At the command prompt, type **ln sample1 hardlinksample** and press **Enter**. Next, type **ls –F** at the command prompt and press **Enter**. Does anything in the terminal output indicate that `sample1` and `hardlinksample` are hard-linked? Next, type **ls –l** at the command prompt and press **Enter**. Does anything in the terminal output indicate that `sample1` and `hardlinksample` are hard-linked? What is the link count for `sample1` and `hardlinksample`? Next, type **ls –li** at the command prompt and press **Enter** to view the inode numbers of each file. Do the two hard-linked files have the same inode number?

4. At the command prompt, type **ln sample1 hardlinksample2** and press **Enter**. Next, type **ls –l** at the command prompt and press **Enter**. What is the link count for the files `sample1`, `hardlinksample`, and `hardlinksample2`? Why?

5. At the command prompt, type **vi sample1** and press **Enter**. Enter a sentence of your choice into the **vi** editor, then save your document and quit the **vi** editor.

6. At the command prompt, type **cat sample1** and press **Enter**. Next, type **cat hardlinksample** at the command prompt and press **Enter**. Now type **cat hardlinksample2** at the command prompt and press **Enter**. Are the contents of each file the same? Why?

7. At the command prompt, type **ln –s sample2 symlinksample** and press **Enter**. Next, type **ls –F** at the command prompt and press **Enter**. Does anything in the terminal output indicate that `sample2` and `symlinksample` are symbolically linked? Which file is the target file? Next, type **ls –l** at the command prompt and press **Enter**. Does anything in the terminal output indicate that `sample1` and `hardlinksample` are hard-linked? Next, type **ls –li** at the command prompt and press **Enter** to view the inode numbers of each file. Do the two symbolically linked files have the same inode number?

8. At the command prompt, type **vi symlinksample** and press **Enter**. Enter a sentence of your choice into the **vi** editor, then save your document and quit the **vi** editor.

9. At the command prompt, type **ls –l** and press **Enter**. What is the size of the `symlinksample` file compared to `sample2`? Why? Next, type **cat sample2** at the command prompt and press **Enter**. What are the contents and why?

10. At the command prompt, type **ln –s /etc/sysconfig/network-scripts netscripts** and press **Enter**. Next, type **ls –F** at the command prompt and press **Enter**. What file type is indicated for `netscripts`? Now, type **cd netscripts** at the command prompt and press **Enter**. Type **pwd** at the command prompt and view your current directory? What is your current directory? Next, type **ls –F** at the command prompt and press **Enter**. What files are listed? Next, type **ls –F /etc/sysconfig/network-scripts** at the command prompt and press

Enter. Note that your `netscripts` directory is merely a pointer to the `/etc/sysconfig/network-scripts` directory. How can this type of linking be useful?

11. Type **exit** and press **Enter** to log out of your shell.

Project 5-5

In this hands-on project, you will find files on the filesystem using the `find`, `locate`, and `which` commands.

1. Switch to a command-line terminal (tty2) by pressing **Ctrl-Alt-F2** and log into the terminal using the username of **root** and the password of **secret**.

2. At the command prompt, type **touch newfile** and press **Enter**. Next, type **locate newfile** at the command prompt and press **Enter**. Did the `locate` command find the file? Why?

3. At the command prompt, type **updatedb** and press **Enter**. When the command is finished, type **locate newfile** at the command prompt and press **Enter**. Did the `locate` command find the file? How quickly did it find it? Why?

4. At the command prompt, type **find / -name "newfile"** and press **Enter**. Did the `find` command find the file? How quickly did it find it? Why?

5. At the command prompt, type **find /root -name "newfile"** and press **Enter**. Did the `find` command find the file? How quickly did it find it? Why?

6. At the command prompt, type **which newfile** and press **Enter**. Did the `which` command find the file? Why? Type **echo $PATH** at the command prompt and press **Enter**. Is the `/root` directory listed in the PATH variable? Is the `/bin` directory listed in the PATH variable?

7. At the command prompt, type **which grep** and press **Enter**. Did the `which` command find the file? Why?

8. At the command prompt, type **find /root –name "sample*"** and press **Enter**. What files are listed? Why?

9. At the command prompt, type **find /root –type l** and press **Enter**. What files are listed? Why?

10 At the command prompt, type **find /root –size 0** and press **Enter**. What files are listed? Type **find /root –size 0 | more** to see all of the files listed.

11. Type **exit** and press **Enter** to log out of your shell.

Project 5-6

In this hands-on project, you will delete files and directories using the `rmdir` and `rm` commands.

1. Switch to a command-line terminal (tty2) by pressing **Ctrl-Alt-F2** and log into the terminal using the username of **root** and the password of **secret**.

5

2. At the command prompt, type **cd samples** and press **Enter**. At the command prompt, type **ls -R** and press **Enter**. Note the two empty directories todelete and undermysamples.

3. At the command prompt, type **rmdir undermysamples todelete** and press **Enter**. Did the command work? Why? Next, type **ls -F** at the command prompt and press **Enter**. Were both directories deleted successfully?

4. At the command prompt, type **rm sample1*** and press **Enter**. What message is displayed? Answer **n** to all 3 questions.

5. At the command prompt, type **rm -f sample1*** and press **Enter**. Why were you not prompted to continue? Next, type **ls -F** at the command prompt and press **Enter**. Were all 3 files deleted successfully?

6. At the command prompt, type **cd ..** and press **Enter**. Next, type **rmdir samples** at the command prompt and press **Enter**. What error message do you receive and why?

7. At the command prompt, type **rm -rf samples** at the command prompt and press **Enter**. Next, type **ls -F** at the command prompt and press **Enter**. Were the samples directory and all files within deleted successfully?

8. Type **exit** and press **Enter** to log out of your shell.

Project 5-7

In this hands-on project, you will apply and modify access permissions on files and directories and test their effects.

1. Switch to a command-line terminal (tty2) by pressing **Ctrl-Alt-F2** and log into the terminal using the username of **root** and the password of **secret**.

2. At the command prompt, type **touch permsample** and press **Enter**. Next, type **chmod 777 permsample** at the command prompt and press **Enter**.

3. At the command prompt, type **ls -l** and press **Enter**. Who has permissions to this file?

4. At the command prompt, type **chmod 000 permsample** and press **Enter**. Next, type **ls -l** at the command prompt and press **Enter**. Who has permissions to this file?

5. At the command prompt, type **rm -f permsample** and press **Enter**. Were you able to delete this file? Why?

6. At the command prompt, type **cd /** and press **Enter**. Next, type **pwd** at the command prompt and press **Enter**. What directory are you in? Type **ls -F** at the command prompt and press **Enter**. What directories do you see?

7. At the command prompt, type **ls -l** and press **Enter** to view the owner, group owner and permissions on the foruser1 directory created in Hands-on Project 5-1. Who are the owner and group owner? If you were logged in as the user

user1, which category would you be placed in (user, group, other)? What permissions do you have as this category (read, write, execute)?

8. At the command prompt, type **cd /foruser1** and press **Enter** to enter the foruser1 directory. Next, type **ls –F** at the command prompt and press **Enter**. Are there any files in this directory? Type **cp /etc/hosts .** at the command prompt and press **Enter**. Next, type **ls –F** at the command prompt and press **Enter** to ensure that a copy of the hosts file was made in your current directory.

9. Switch to a different command-line terminal (tty3) by pressing **Ctrl-Alt-F3** and log into the terminal using the username of **user1** and the password of **secret**.

10. At the command prompt, type **cd /foruser1** and press **Enter**. Were you successful? Why? Next, type **ls –F** at the command prompt and press **Enter**. Were you able to see the contents of the directory? Why? Now, type **rm –f hosts** at the command prompt and press **Enter**. What error message did you see? Why?

11. Switch back to your previous command-line terminal (tty2) by pressing **Ctrl-Alt-F2**. Note that you are logged in as the **root** user on this terminal.

12. At the command prompt, type **chmod o+w /foruser1** and press **Enter**. Were you able to change the permissions on the /foruser1 directory successfully? Why?

13. Switch back to your previous command-line terminal (tty3) by pressing **Ctrl-Alt-F3**. Note that you are logged in as the **user1** user on this terminal.

14. At the command prompt, type **cd /foruser1** and press **Enter**. Next, type **rm –f hosts** at the command prompt and press **Enter**. Were you successful now? Why?

15. Switch back to your previous command-line terminal (tty2) by pressing **Ctrl-Alt-F2**. Note that you are logged in as the **root** user on this terminal.

16. At the command prompt, type **cd /foruser1** and press **Enter** to enter the foruser1 directory. Type **cp /etc/hosts .** at the command prompt and press **Enter** to place another copy of the hosts file in your current directory.

17. At the command prompt, type **ls –l** and press **Enter**. Who is the owner and group owner of this file? If you were logged in as the user **user1**, which category would you be placed in (user, group, other)? What permissions do you have as this category (read, write, execute)?

18. Switch back to your previous command-line terminal (tty3) by pressing **Ctrl-Alt-F3**. Note that you are logged in as the **user1** user on this terminal.

19. At the command prompt, type **cd /foruser1** and press **Enter** to enter the foruser1 directory. Type **cat hosts** at the command prompt and press **Enter**. Were you successful? Why? Next, type **vi hosts** at the command prompt to open the hosts file in the **vi** editor. Delete the first line of this file and save your changes. Were you successful? Why? Exit the **vi** editor and discard your changes.

20. Switch back to your previous command-line terminal (tty2) by pressing **Ctrl-Alt-F2**. Note that you are logged in as the **root** user on this terminal.

21. At the command prompt, type **chmod o+w /foruser1/hosts** and press **Enter**.

5

22. Switch back to your previous command-line terminal (tty3) by pressing **Ctrl-Alt-F3**. Note that you are logged in as the `user1` user on this terminal.

23. Type **vi hosts** at the command prompt to open the `hosts` file in the `vi` editor. Delete the first line of this file and save your changes. Why were you successful this time? Exit the `vi` editor.

24. At the command prompt, type **ls –l** and press **Enter**. Do you have permission to execute the `hosts` file? Should you make this file executable? Why? Next, type **ls –l /bin** at the command prompt and press **Enter** and note how many of these files you have execute permission to. Type **file /bin/*** at the command prompt and press **Enter** to view the file types of the files in the `/bin` directory. Should these files have the execute permission?

25. Type **exit** and press **Enter** to log out of your shell.

26. Switch back to your previous command-line terminal (tty2) by pressing **Ctrl-Alt-F2**. Note that you are logged in as the `root` user on this terminal.

27. Type **exit** and press **Enter** to log out of your shell.

Project 5-8

In this hands-on project, you will view and manipulate the default file and directory permissions using the umask variable.

1. Switch to a command-line terminal (tty3) by pressing **Ctrl-Alt-F3** and log into the terminal using the username of **user1** and the password of **secret**.

2. At the command prompt, type **ls –l** and press **Enter**. What files do you see?

3. At the command prompt, type **umask** and press **Enter**. What is the default umask variable?

4. At the command prompt, type **touch utest1** and press **Enter**. Next, type **ls –l** at the command prompt and press **Enter**. What are the permissions on the `utest1` file? Do these agree with the calculation in Figure 5-5? Create a new directory by typing the command **mkdir udir1** at the command prompt and press **Enter**. Next, type **ls –l** at the command prompt and press **Enter**. What are the permissions on the `udir1` directory? Do these agree with the calculation in Figure 5-5?

5. At the command prompt, type **umask 007** and press **Enter**. Next, type **umask** at the command prompt and press **Enter** to verify that your umask variable has been changed to `007`.

6. At the command prompt, type **touch utest2** and press **Enter**. Next, type **ls –l** at the command prompt and press **Enter**. What are the permissions on the `utest2` file? Do these agree with the calculation in Figure 5-6? Create a new directory by typing the command **mkdir udir2** at the command prompt and press **Enter**. Next, type **ls –l** at the command prompt and press **Enter**. What are the permissions on the `udir2` directory? Do these agree with the calculation in Figure 5-6?

7. Type **exit** and press **Enter** to log out of your shell.

Project 5-9

In this hands-on project, you view and change file and directory ownership using the `chown` and `chgrp` commands.

1. Switch to a command-line terminal (tty3) by pressing **Ctrl–Alt–F3** and log into the terminal using the username of **user1** and the password of **secret**.

2. At the command prompt, type **touch ownersample** and press **Enter**. Next, type **mkdir ownerdir** at the command prompt and press **Enter**. Now, type **ls –l** at the command prompt and press **Enter** to verify that the file `ownersample` and directory `ownerdir` were created and that `user1` is the owner and group owner of each.

3. At the command prompt, type **mv ownersample ownerdir** and press **Enter**. Next, type **ls –lR** at the command prompt and press **Enter** to note that the `ownersample` file now exists within the `ownerdir` directory and that both are owned by `user1`.

4. At the command prompt, type **chgrp –R sys ownerdir** and press **Enter** to change the group ownership to the `sys` group recursively for `ownerdir`. What error message do you receive and why?

5. Switch to a command-line terminal (tty2) by pressing **Ctrl–Alt–F2** and log into the terminal using the username of **root** and the password of **secret**.

6. At the command prompt, type **cd /home/user1** and press **Enter** to change the current directory to `/home/user1`. Next, type **ls –l** at the command prompt and press **Enter**. Who owns the directory `ownerdir`?

7. At the command prompt, type **chgrp –R sys ownerdir** and press **Enter** to change the group ownership to the `sys` group recursively for `ownerdir`. Were you successful? Why? Next, type **ls –lR** at the command prompt and press **Enter** to verify that the group owner has been changed recursively.

8. At the command prompt, type **chown –R nobody ownerdir** and press **Enter** to change the ownership to the `nobody` user recursively for the directory `ownerdir`. Next, type **ls –lR** at the command prompt and press **Enter** to verify that the owner has been changed recursively.

9. At the command prompt, type **chown –R root.bin ownerdir** and press **Enter**. What does this command do? Next, type **ls –lR** at the command prompt and press **Enter**. Who is the owner and group owner for `ownerdir` and `ownersample`?

10. Switch back to the command-line terminal (tty3) by pressing **Ctrl–Alt–F3**. Note that you are logged in as `user1` in this terminal.

11. At the command prompt, type **rm -rf ownerdir** and press **Enter**. Why were you unable to delete this directory? What permissions does `user1` have to this directory?

12. Switch back to the command-line terminal (tty2) by pressing **Ctrl–Alt–F2**. Note that you are logged in as `root` in this terminal.

13. At the command prompt, type **chown user1 ownerdir** and press **Enter** to change the ownership to user1 for the ownerdir directory. What permissions does user1 have to this directory?

14. Switch back to the command-line terminal (tty3) by pressing **Ctrl-Alt-F3**. Note that you are logged in as user1 in this terminal.

15. Next, type **ls –lR** at the command prompt and press **Enter**. Who owns the ownersample file? Who owns the ownerdir directory?

16. At the command prompt, type **rm –rf ownerdir** and press **Enter**. Why were you able to delete this directory and the ownersample file within if you were not the owner of ownersample?

17. Type **exit** and press **Enter** to log out of your shell.

18. Switch back to the command-line terminal (tty2) by pressing **Ctrl-Alt-F2**.

19. Type **exit** and press **Enter** to log out of your shell.

Project 5-10

In this hands-on project, you view and set special permissions on files and directories.

1. Switch to a command-line terminal (tty3) by pressing **Ctrl-Alt-F3** and log into the terminal using the username of **user1** and the password of **secret**.

2. At the command prompt, type **touch specialfile** and press **Enter**. Next, type **ls-l** at the command prompt and press **Enter** to verify that specialfile was created successfully. Who is the owner and group owner of specialfile?

3. At the command prompt, type **chmod 4777 specialfile** and press **Enter**. Next, type **ls –l** at the command prompt and press **Enter**. Which special permission is set on this file? If this file were executed by another user, who would that user be during execution?

4. At the command prompt, type **chmod 6777 specialfile** and press **Enter**. Next, type **ls –l** at the command prompt and press **Enter**. Which special permission is set on this file? If this file were executed by another user, who would that user be during execution and which group would that user be a member of?

5. At the command prompt, type **chmod 6444 specialfile** and press **Enter**. Next, type **ls –l** at the command prompt and press **Enter**. Can you tell if execute is not given underneath the special permission listings? Would the special permissions retain their meaning in this case?

6. Switch to a command-line terminal (tty2) by pressing **Ctrl-Alt-F2** and log into the terminal using the username of **root** and the password of **secret**.

7. At the command prompt, type **mkdir /public** and press **Enter**. Next, type **chmod 1777 /public** at the command prompt and press **Enter**. Which special permission is set on this directory? Who can add or remove files to and from this directory?

8. At the command prompt, type **touch /public/rootfile** and press **Enter**.

9. At the command prompt, type **cd /home/user1** and press **Enter**. Next, type **touch rootfile** at the command prompt and press **Enter**.

10. Type **exit** and press **Enter** to log out of your shell.

11. Switch back to your previous command-line terminal (tty3) by pressing **Ctrl–Alt–F3**. Note that you are logged in as the user1 user on this terminal.

12. At the command prompt, type **touch /public/user1file** and press **Enter**. Next, type **ls –l /public** at the command prompt and press **Enter**. What files exist in this directory and who are the owners?

13. At the command prompt, type **rm /public/user1file** and press **Enter**. Were you prompted to confirm the deletion of the file?

14. At the command prompt, type **rm /public/rootfile** and press **Enter**. What message did you receive? Why?

15. Type **exit** and press **Enter** to log out of your shell.

DISCOVERY EXERCISES

1. Use the `ls` command with the **–F** option to explore directories described in the Filesystem Hierarchy Standard starting with **/bin**. Do you recognize any of the commands in **/bin**? Explore several other FHS directories and note their contents. Refer to table 5-1 for a list of directories to explore. Further to this, visit *http://www.pathname.com/fhs/* and read about the Filesystem Hierarchy Standard. What benefits does it offer Linux?

2. Write the commands required for the following tasks. Try out each command on your system to ensure that it is correct:

   a. Make a hierachical directory structure under **/root** that consists of one directory containing three subdirectories.

   b. Copy two files into each of the subdirectories.

   c. Create one more directory with three subdirectories beneath it and mv files from the subdirectories containing them to the counterparts you just created.

   d. Hard-link three of the files. Examine their inodes.

   e. Symbolically link two of the files and examine their link count and inode information.

   f. Make symbolic links from your home directory to two directories in this structure and examine the results.

   g. Delete the symbolic links in your home directory and the directory structure you created under **/root**.

3. Write the command below that can be used to answer the following questions: (*Hint*: Try each out on the system to check your results.)

   a. Find all files on the system that have the word "test" as part of their filename.

   b. Search the PATH variable for the pathname to the **awk** command.

   c. Find all files in the /usr directory and subdirectories that are larger than 50 Kilobytes in size.

   d. Find all files in the /usr directory and subdirectories that are less than 70 Kilobytes in size.

   e. Find all files in the / directory and subdirectories that are symbolic links.

   f. Find all files in the /var directory and subdirectories that were accessed less than 60 minutes ago.

   g. Find all files in the /var directory and subdirectories that were accessed less than 6 days ago.

   h. Find all files in the /home directory and subdirectories that are empty.

   i. Find all files in the /etc directory and subdirectories that are owned by the group bin.

4. For each of the following modes, write the numeric equivalent (i.e., 777):

   a. rw-r--r--

   b. r--r--r--

   c. ---rwxrw-

   d. -wxr-xrw-

   e. rw-rw-rwx

   f. -w-r-----

5. Fill in the following permission table with check marks assuming that all four files are in the directory **/public**, which has a mode of **rwxr-xr-x**.

Filename	Mode		Read	Edit	Execute	List	Delete
sample1	rw-rw-rw-	User Group Other					
sample2	r--r----	User Group Other					
sample3	rwxr-x---	User Group Other					
sample4	r-x------	User Group Other					

6. Fill in the following permission table with check marks assuming that all four files are in the directory **/public**, which has a mode of **rwx--x---**.

Filename	Mode		Read	Edit	Execute	List	Delete
sample1	rwxr--r--	*User*					
		Group					
		Other					
sample2	r-xr--rw-	*User*					
		Group					
		Other					
sample3	--xr-x---	*User*					
		Group					
		Other					
sample4	r-xr--r--	*User*					
		Group					
		Other					

7. For each of the following umasks, calculate the default permissions given to new files and new directories:

   a. 017

   b. 272

   c. 777

   d. 000

   e. 077

   f. 027

8. From the list of the umasks in Question 7, list the umasks that are reasonable to use to increase security on your Linux system and explain why.

9. Starting from the Linux default permissions for files and directories, what umask would you use to ensure that for all new:

   a. Directories, the owner would have read, write, and execute; members of the group would have read and execute; and other would have read?

   b. Files, the owner would have read and execute; the group would have read, write, and execute; and other would have execute?

   c. Files, the owner would have write; the group would have read, write, and execute; and other would have read and write?

   d. Directories, the owner would have read, write, and execute; the group would have read, write, and execute; and other would have read, write, and execute?

   e. Directories, the owner would have execute; the group would have read, write, and execute; and other would have no permissions?

    f. Files, the owner would have read and write, the group would have no permissions, and other would have write?

    g. Directories, the owner would have read, write, and execute; the group would have read; and other would have read and execute?

    h. Directories, the owner would have write; the group would have read, write, and execute; and other would have read, write, and execute?

    i. Files, the owner would have no permissions, the group would have no permissions, and other would have no permissions?

10. What `chmod` command would you use to impose the following permissions:

    a. On a directory such that the owner would have read, write, and execute; the group would have read and execute; and other would have read?

    b. On a file such that the owner would have read and write, the group would have no permissions, and other would have write?

    c. On a file such that the owner would have write; the group would have read, write, and execute; and other would have read and write?

    d. On a file such that the owner would have read and execute; the group would have read, write, and execute; and other would have execute?

    e. On a directory such that the owner would have execute; the group would have read, write, and execute; and other would have no permissions?

    f. On a directory such that the owner would have write; the group would have read, write, and execute; and other would have read, write, and execute?

    g. On a directory such that the owner would have read, write, and execute; the group would have read; and other would have read and execute?

    h. On a directory such that the owner would have read, write, and execute; the group would have read, write, and execute; and other would have read, write, and execute?

    i. On a file such that the owner would have no permissions, the group would have no permissions, and other would have no permissions?

LINUX FILESYSTEM
ADMINISTRATION

**After completing this chapter,
you will be able to:**

♦ Identify the structure and types of device files in the /dev directory

♦ Understand common filesystem types and their features

♦ Mount and unmount floppy disks to and from the Linux directory tree

♦ Mount and unmount CD-ROMs to and from the Linux directory tree

♦ Create hard disk partitions

♦ Mount and unmount hard disk partitions to and from the Linux directory tree

♦ Monitor free space on mounted filesystems

♦ Check filesystems for errors

♦ Use hard disk quotas to limit user space usage

Navigating the Linux directory tree and manipulating files are common tasks that are performed on a daily basis by all users. However, administrators must provide this directory tree for users as well as manage and fix the disk devices that support it. In this chapter, you learn about the various device files that represent disk devices and the different filesystems that may be placed on those devices. Next, you learn how to create and manage filesystems on floppy disks and CD-ROMs, followed by a discussion of hard disk partitioning and filesystem management. Finally, this chapter concludes with a discussion of disk usage, filesystem errors, and restricting the ability of users to store files.

THE /DEV DIRECTORY

Fundamental to administrating the disks used to store information is an understanding of how these disks are specified by the Linux operating system. Most devices on a Linux system (such as disks, terminals, and serial ports) are represented by a file on the hard disk called a **device file**. There is one file per device, and these files are typically found in the /dev directory. This allows you to specify devices on the system by using the pathname to the file that represents it in the /dev directory. To specify the first floppy disk in the Linux system, you can type the pathname /dev/fd0 (floppy disk 0) in the appropriate section of a command. To represent the second floppy disk in the Linux system, you can specify the pathname to the file /dev/fd1 (floppy disk 1).

Furthermore, each device file specifies how data should be transferred to and from the device. There are two methods for transferring data to and from a device. The first method involves transferring information character-by-character to and from the device. Devices that transfer data in this fashion are referred to as **character devices**. The second method transfers chunks, or blocks, of information at a time by using physical memory to buffer the transfer; devices that use this method of transfer are called **block devices**, and can transfer information much faster than character devices. Device files that represent disks such as floppy disks, CD-ROMs, and hard disks are typically block device files since a fast data transfer rate is preferred. Tape drives and most other devices, however, are typically represented by character device files.

To see whether a particular device transfers data character-by-character or block-by-block, recall that the ls −l command displays a c or b character in the type column indicating the type of device file. To view the type of the file /dev/fd0, you could use the following command:

```
[root@localhost root]# ls −l /dev/fd0
brw-rw----    1 root       floppy    2,   0 Aug 30   2001 /dev/fd0
[root@localhost root]#_
```

From the leftmost character in the above output, you can see that /dev/fd0 is a block device file. A list of some common device files and their types can be seen in Table 6-1.

Table 6-1   Common device files

Device File	Description	Block or Character
/dev/fd0	First floppy disk on the system	Block
/dev/fd1	Second floppy disk on the system	Block
/dev/hda1	First primary partition on the first IDE hard disk drive (primary master)	Block
/dev/hdb1	First primary partition on the second IDE hard disk drive (primary slave)	Block
/dev/hdc1	First primary partition on the third IDE hard disk drive (secondary master)	Block

Table 6-1   Common device files (continued)

Device File	Description	Block or Character
/dev/hdd1	First primary partition on the fourth IDE hard disk drive (secondary slave)	Block
/dev/sda1	First primary partition on the first SCSI hard disk drive	Block
/dev/sdb1	First primary partition on the second SCSI hard disk drive	Block
/dev/tty1	First local terminal on the system ([Ctrl]-[Alt]-F1)	Character
/dev/tty2	Second local terminal on the system ([Ctrl]-[Alt]-F2)	Character
/dev/ttyS0	First serial port on the system (COM1)	Character
/dev/ttyS1	Second serial port on the system (COM2)	Character
/dev/psaux	PS/2 mouse port	Character
/dev/lp0	First parallel port on the system (LPT1)	Character
/dev/null	A device file that represents nothing; any data sent to this device is discarded	Character
/dev/st0	The first SCSI tape device in the system	Character
/dev/usb/*	USB device files	Character

After a typical Red Hat 7.2 Linux installation, there are over 13,000 different device files in the /dev directory; most of these device files represent devices that may not exist on your particular Linux system and hence are never used. Providing this large number of redundant device files on a Linux system does not require much disk space, since all device files consist of inodes and no data blocks; as a result, the entire contents of the /dev directory is usually less than 300 Kilobytes in size, which could fit easily on a floppy disk. When using the ls –l command to view device files, the portion of the listing describing the file size in Kilobytes is replaced by two numbers: the major number and the minor number. The **major number** of a device file points to the device driver for the device in the Linux kernel; several different devices may share the same major number if they are of the same general type (i.e., two different floppy disk drives may share the same major number). The **minor number** indicates the particular device itself, and the first floppy disk drive in the computer will have a different minor number than the second floppy disk drive in the computer. In the following output, you can see that both /dev/fd0 and /dev/fd1 share the same major number of 2, yet the minor number for /dev/fd0 is 0 and the minor number for /dev/fd1 is 1, which differentiates them from one another.

```
[root@localhost root]# ls –l /dev/fd0 /dev/fd1
brw-rw----   1 root      floppy    2,   0 Aug 30   2001 /dev/fd0
brw-rw----   1 root      floppy    2,   1 Aug 30   2001 /dev/fd1
[root@localhost root]#
```

Together, the device file type (block or character), the major number (device driver), and the minor number (specific device) make up the unique characteristics of each device file. To create a device file, you simply need to know these three pieces of information.

If a device file becomes corrupted, it will usually be listed as a regular file instead of a block or character special file. Recall from Chapter 5 that the find /dev —type f command could be used to search for regular files underneath the /dev directory to identify whether corruption has taken place. If you find a corrupted device file, or accidentally delete a device file, the mknod command can be used to recreate the device file if you know the type, major, and minor numbers. An example of recreating the /dev/fd0 block device file used earlier with a major number of 2 and a minor number of 0 is seen below:

```
[root@localhost root]# ls —l /dev/fd0
brw-rw----   1 root      floppy    2,   0 Aug 30  2001 /dev/fd0
[root@localhost root]# rm -f /dev/fd0
[root@localhost root]# ls —l /dev/fd0
[root@localhost root]# mknod /dev/fd0 b 2 0
[root@localhost root]# ls —l /dev/fd0
brw-r--r--   1 root      root      2,   0 May  8 13:26 /dev/fd0
[root@localhost root]#_
```

However, if you do not know the type or the major or minor number of the device, you may use the /dev/MAKEDEV program to recreate the device, based on the common name:

```
[root@localhost root]# ls —l /dev/fd0
brw-r--r--   1 root      root      2,   0 May  8 13:26 /dev/fd0
[root@localhost root]# rm -f /dev/fd0
[root@localhost root]# ls —l /dev/fd0
[root@localhost root]# /dev/MAKEDEV fd0
[root@localhost root]# ls —l /dev/fd0
brw-rw----   1 root      floppy    2,   0 May  8 13:30 /dev/fd0
[root@localhost root]#_
```

Recall from earlier that most device files present in the /dev directory are never used. To see a list of devices currently used on the system and their major numbers, you can view the contents of the /proc/devices file, as seen below:

```
[root@localhost root]# cat /proc/devices
Character devices:
  1 mem
  2 pty
  3 ttyp
  4 ttyS
  5 cua
  7 vcs
 10 misc
 29 fb
 36 netlink
128 ptm
129 ptm
130 ptm
131 ptm
132 ptm
```

```
133 ptm
134 ptm
135 ptm
136 pts
137 pts
138 pts
139 pts
140 pts
141 pts
142 pts
143 pts
162 raw
180 usb
226 drm
254 iscsictl

Block devices:
  1 ramdisk
  2 fd
  3 ide0
  9 md
 22 ide1
[root@localhost root]#_
```

FILESYSTEMS

Recall from Chapter 2 that files need to be stored on the hard disk in a defined format called a **filesystem**, so that the operating system may work with them. The type of filesystem used determines how files are managed on the physical hard disk. Each filesystem may have different methods for storing files and features, which make the filesystem robust against errors. Although there are many different types of filesystems available, all filesystems share three common components, as discussed in Chapter 5: the superblock, the inode table, and data blocks. On a structural level, these three components work together to organize files and allow rapid access to and retrieval of data. All storage mediums, such as floppy disks, hard disks, and CD-ROMs, need to be formatted with a filesystem before they can be used.

 Creating a filesystem on a device is commonly referred to as **formatting**.

Filesystem Types

As mentioned, there are many filesystems available for use in the Linux operating system. Each has its own strengths and weaknesses, thus some filesystems are better suited to certain tasks and not as well-suited to others. One benefit of Linux is that you need not use only one type of filesystem on the system; you may use several different devices formatted with different filesystems under the same directory tree. In addition, files and directories appear the same throughout the directory tree regardless of whether there is one filesystem or twenty different filesystems in use by the Linux system. Some common filesystems available for use in Linux are listed in Table 6-2.

 For a full listing of filesystem types and their features, you may refer to the Filesystem HOWTO on the Internet at *http://www.tldp.org/HOWTO/ Filesystems-HOWTO.html*.

Table 6-2   Common Linux filesystems

Filesystem	Description
bfs	Boot File System—a small bootable filesystem used to hold the files necessary for system startup; it is commonly used on UNIX systems
cdfs	Compact disc filesystem—used to view all tracks and data on a CD-ROM as normal files
ext2	Second extended filesystem—currently the most common filesystem used on Linux, it supports Access Control Lists (individual user permissions). It retains its name from being the new version of the original extended filesystem, based on the Minix filesystem
ext3	Third extended filesystem; a variation on ext2 that allows for journaling and thus has a faster startup and recovery time
hfs	Hierarchical File System—a filesystem native to Apple Macintosh computers
hpfs	High Performance File System—an IBM-proprietary OS/2 filesystem that provides long file name support and is optimized to manipulate data on large disk volumes
iso9660	The CD-ROM filesystem—originated from the International Standards Organization recommendation 9660 and used to access data stored on CD-ROMs
minix	The MINIX filesystem—the filesystem used by Linus Torvalds in the early days of Linux development
msdos	The DOS FAT filesystem
ntfs	New Technology File System—a Microsoft-proprietary filesystem developed for its NT4 and Windows 2000 operating systems, currently available as a read-only filesystem under Linux
reiserfs	The REISERFS filesystem—a journaling filesystem similar to ext3 more suited for use with databases
vfat	The DOS FAT filesystem with long file name support
vxfs	The Veritas filesystem—a journaling filesystem that offers large file support, supports Access Control Lists (individual user permissions), and is commonly used by major versions of UNIX

Mounting

The term **mounting** originated in the 1960s, when information was stored on large tape reels that had to be mounted on computers to make the data available. Today, mounting still refers to making data available. More specifically, it refers to the process whereby a device is made accessible to users via the logical directory tree. This device is attached to a certain directory on the directory tree called a **mount point**. Users may then create files and subdirectories in this mount point directory, which will then be stored on the filesystem that was mounted to that particular directory.

Remember that directories are files that do not contain data; they are a list of files and subdirectories contained within them. Thus, it is easy for the Linux system to cover up directories to prevent user access to that data. This is essentially what happens when a device is mounted to a certain directory; the mount point directory is temporarily covered up by that device while the device remains mounted. Any file contents that were present in the mount point directory prior to mounting are not lost. When the device is unmounted, the mount point directory is uncovered, and the previous file contents are revealed. Say, for example, that you mount a floppy device containing a filesystem to the /mnt directory. The /mnt directory is a directory that contains two subdirectories and is a commonly used and convenient mount point for mounting removable media devices. Before mounting, the directory structure would resemble that depicted in Figure 6-1. After the floppy was mounted to the /mnt directory, the contents of the /mnt directory would be covered up by the floppy filesystem, as illustrated in Figure 6-2.

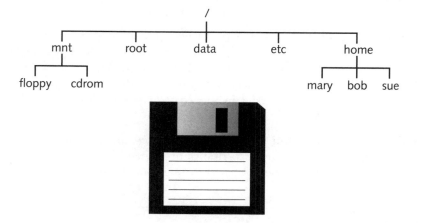

Figure 6-1   The directory structure prior to mounting

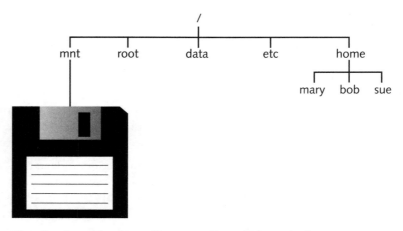

Figure 6-2   The directory structure after mounting a floppy device

If a user then stores a file in the **/mnt** directory as shown in Figure 6-2, that file will be stored on the floppy disk device. Similarly, if a user creates a subdirectory under the **/mnt** directory depicted in Figure 6-2, that subdirectory will be made on the floppy disk.

It is important to note that any existing directory may be used as a mount point. If a user mounted a floppy device to the **/bin** directory, then all files in the **/bin** directory would be covered up for the duration that floppy disk was mounted, including the command used to unmount the floppy. Thus, it is safe practice to create empty directories used specifically for mounting devices to avoid making existing files inaccessible to users.

When the Linux system is first turned on, a filesystem present on the hard drive is mounted to the **/** directory. This is referred to as the **root filesystem** and contains most of the operating system files. Other filesystems present on hard disks inside the computer may also be mounted to various mount point directories underneath the **/** directory at boot time as well via entries in the **/etc/fstab** (filesystem table) file discussed in the following sections.

The **mount** command is used to mount devices to mount point directories, and the **umount** command is used to unmount devices from mount point directories; both of these commands will be discussed throughout the remainder of this chapter.

WORKING WITH FLOPPY DISKS

When transferring small amounts of information from computer to computer, it is commonplace to use floppy disk removable media to store the files. However, floppy disks must be prepared before they are used in Linux.

Recall that each disk device must be formatted with a filesystem prior to being used to store files. To do this, you may use the **mkfs** (make filesystem) command and specify the filesystem type using the **−t** switch and the device file representing the floppy disk device. To format the floppy disk inside the first floppy disk drive in the computer with the ext2 filesystem, you must place a floppy disk in the floppy disk drive and type the following command:

```
[root@localhost root]# mkfs —t ext2 /dev/fd0
mke2fs 1.23, 15-Aug-2001 for EXT2 FS 0.5b, 95/08/09
Filesystem label=
OS type: Linux
Block size=1024 (log=0)
Fragment size=1024 (log=0)
184 inodes, 1440 blocks
72 blocks (5.00%) reserved for the super user
First data block=1
1 block group
8192 blocks per group, 8192 fragments per group
184 inodes per group

Writing inode tables: done
Writing superblocks and filesystem accounting information: done

This filesystem will be automatically checked every 34 mounts or
180 days, whichever comes first.  Use tune2fs -c or -i to override.
[root@localhost root]#_
```

Alternatively, you may specify a different filesystem after the —t option, such as the DOS FAT filesystem. This may result in a different output from the mkfs command, as seen below:

```
[root@localhost root]# mkfs —t msdos /dev/fd0
  mkfs.msdos 2.7 (14 Feb 2001)
  [root@localhost root]#_
```

If you do not specify the filesystem using the mkfs command, the default filesystem assumed is the ext2 filesystem, as seen below:

```
[root@localhost root]# mkfs /dev/fd0
mke2fs 1.23, 15-Aug-2001 for EXT2 FS 0.5b, 95/08/09
Filesystem label=
OS type: Linux
Block size=1024 (log=0)
Fragment size=1024 (log=0)
184 inodes, 1440 blocks
72 blocks (5.00%) reserved for the super user
First data block=1
1 block group
8192 blocks per group, 8192 fragments per group
184 inodes per group

Writing inode tables: done
Writing superblocks and filesystem accounting information: done
```

6

```
This filesystem will be automatically checked every 34 mounts or
180 days, whichever comes first.  Use tune2fs -c or -i to override.
[root@localhost root]#_
```

Although the most common command to create filesystems is the **mkfs** command, other variants and shortcuts to the **mkfs** command exist. To create an ext2 filesystem, you may simply type **mke2fs /dev/fd0** on the command line. Other alternatives to the **mkfs** command are listed in Table 6-3.

Table 6-3   Commands used to create filesystems

Command	Description
mkfs	Used to create filesystems of most types
mkfs.msdos	Used to create a DOS FAT filesystem
mkfs.bfs	Used to create a SCO UNIX bfs filesystem
mkfs.minix	Used to create a MINIX filesystem
mkdosfs	Used to create a DOS FAT filesystem
mke2fs	Used to create an ext2 filesystem
mke2fs −j	Used to create an ext3 filesystem (j = journaling)
mkisofs	Used to create a CD-ROM filesystem
mkreiserfs	Used to create a REISERFS filesystem

Once a floppy disk has been formatted with a filesystem, it must be mounted on the directory tree before it can be used. A list of currently mounted filesystems can be obtained by using the mount command with no options or arguments, which reads the information listed in the /etc/mtab (mount table) file, as seen in the output below:

```
[root@localhost root]# mount
/dev/hda1 on / type ext3 (rw)
none on /proc type proc (rw)
usbdevfs on /proc/bus/usb type usbdevfs (rw)
none on /dev/pts type devpts (rw,gid=5,mode=620)
none on /dev/shm type tmpfs (rw)
none on /proc/sys/fs/binfmt_misc type binfmt_misc (rw)
[root@localhost root]# cat /etc/mtab
/dev/hda1 / ext3 rw 0 0
none /proc proc rw 0 0
usbdevfs /proc/bus/usb usbdevfs rw 0 0
none /dev/pts devpts rw,gid=5,mode=620 0 0
none /dev/shm tmpfs rw 0 0
none /proc/sys/fs/binfmt_misc binfmt_misc rw 0 0
[root@localhost root]#_
```

From the above output, you can see that the device /dev/hda1 is mounted on the / directory and contains an ext3 filesystem. The other filesystems listed above are special filesystems that are used by the system and will be discussed later in this textbook.

To mount a device on the directory tree, you can use the **mount** command with options and arguments to specify the filesystem type, the device to mount, and the directory to mount the device to (mount point). It is important to ensure that no user is currently using the mount point directory; otherwise the system will give you an error message and the disk will not be mounted. To check whether the /mnt/floppy directory is being used, you can use the **fuser** command with the −u option as seen below:

```
[root@localhost root]# fuser -u /mnt/floppy
/mnt/floppy:
No process references; use -v for the complete list
[root@localhost root]#_
```

The above output indicates that the /mnt/floppy directory is not being used by any user processes. To mount the first floppy device formatted with the ext2 filesystem to the /mnt/floppy directory, you could simply type the following command:

```
[root@localhost root]# mount —t ext2  /dev/fd0  /mnt/floppy
[root@localhost root]# mount
/dev/hda1 on / type ext3 (rw)
none on /proc type proc (rw)
usbdevfs on /proc/bus/usb type usbdevfs (rw)
none on /dev/pts type devpts (rw,gid=5,mode=620)
none on /dev/shm type tmpfs (rw)
none on /proc/sys/fs/binfmt_misc type binfmt_misc (rw)
/dev/fd0 on /mnt/floppy type ext2 (rw)
[root@localhost root]#_
```

Notice that /dev/fd0 appears mounted to the /mnt/floppy directory in the output of the **mount** command above. To access and store files on the floppy device, you may now treat the /mnt/floppy directory as the root of the floppy disk.

When an ext2 filesystem is created on a disk device, one directory is created by default called **lost+found**, which is used by the **fsck** command discussed later in this chapter. To explore the recently mounted floppy filesystem, you can use the following commands:

```
[root@localhost root]# cd /mnt/floppy
[root@localhost floppy]# pwd
/mnt/floppy
[root@localhost floppy]# ls -F
lost+found/
[root@localhost floppy]#_
```

To copy files to the floppy device, simply specify the /mnt/floppy directory as the target for the **cp** command as seen below:

```
[root@localhost floppy]# cd /etc
[root@localhost etc]# cat hosts
# Do not remove the following line, or various programs
# that require network functionality will fail.
127.0.0.1               localhost.localdomain localhost
```

6

```
[root@localhost etc]# cp hosts /mnt/floppy
[root@localhost etc]# cd /mnt/floppy
[root@localhost floppy]# ls -F
hosts  lost+found/
[root@localhost floppy]# cat hosts
# Do not remove the following line, or various programs
# that require network functionality will fail.
127.0.0.1              localhost.localdomain localhost
[root@localhost floppy]#_
```

Similarly, you may also create subdirectories underneath the floppy device to store files; these subdirectories are referenced underneath the mount point directory. To make a directory called workfiles on the floppy mounted in the previous example and copy the /etc/inittab file to it, you could use the following commands:

```
[root@localhost floppy]# pwd
/mnt/floppy
[root@localhost floppy]# ls -F
hosts  lost+found/
[root@localhost floppy]# mkdir workfiles
[root@localhost floppy]# ls -F
hosts  lost+found/  workfiles/
[root@localhost floppy]# cd workfiles
[root@localhost workfiles]# pwd
/mnt/floppy/workfiles
[root@localhost workfiles]# cp /etc/inittab .
[root@localhost workfiles]# ls -F
inittab
[root@localhost workfiles]#_
```

Even though you may eject the floppy disk from the floppy disk drive without permission from the system, doing so is likely to cause error messages to appear on the terminal screen. Before a floppy is ejected, it must be unmounted properly using the umount command. The umount command can take the name of the device to unmount or the mount point directory as an argument. Similar to mounting a floppy disk, unmounting a floppy disk also requires that the mount point directory has no users using it. If you try to unmount the floppy disk mounted to the /dev/floppy directory while it is being used, the following output will be produced:

```
[root@localhost floppy]# pwd
/mnt/floppy
[root@localhost floppy]# umount /mnt/floppy
umount: /mnt/floppy: device is busy
[root@localhost floppy]# fuser -u /mnt/floppy
/mnt/floppy:        17368c(root)
[root@localhost floppy]# cd /root
[root@localhost root]# umount /mnt/floppy
[root@localhost root]# mount
/dev/hdc1 on / type ext3 (rw)
```

```
none on /proc type proc (rw)
usbdevfs on /proc/bus/usb type usbdevfs (rw)
none on /dev/pts type devpts (rw,gid=5,mode=620)
none on /dev/shm type tmpfs (rw)
none on /proc/sys/fs/binfmt_misc type binfmt_misc (rw)
[root@localhost root]#_
```

Notice from the above output that you were still using the /mnt/floppy directory since it was the current working directory. The **fuser** command also indicated that you had a process using the directory. Once the current working directory was changed, the **umount** command was able to unmount the floppy from the /mnt/floppy directory and the output of the **mount** command indicated that the floppy disk was no longer mounted.

Recall that mounting simply attaches a disk device to the Linux directory tree so that you may treat the device like a directory full of files and subdirectories; a device may be mounted to any existing directory. However, if the directory already contains files, those files are inaccessible until the device is unmounted. Say, for example, that you create a directory called /flopper for mounting floppy disks and a file inside called **samplefile** as seen in the output below:

```
[root@localhost root]# mkdir /flopper
[root@localhost root]# touch /flopper/samplefile
[root@localhost root]# ls -F /flopper
samplefile
[root@localhost root]#_
```

If the floppy disk used earlier is mounted to the /flopper directory, then a user who uses the /flopper directory shall be using the floppy disk. However, when nothing is mounted to the /flopper directory, the previous contents will be available for use:

```
[root@localhost root]# mount -t ext2 /dev/fd0 /flopper
[root@localhost root]# mount
/dev/hda1 on / type ext3 (rw)
none on /proc type proc (rw)
usbdevfs on /proc/bus/usb type usbdevfs (rw)
none on /dev/pts type devpts (rw,gid=5,mode=620)
none on /dev/shm type tmpfs (rw)
none on /proc/sys/fs/binfmt_misc type binfmt_misc (rw)
/dev/fd0 on /flopper type ext2 (rw)
[root@localhost root]# ls -F /flopper
hosts   lost+found/   workfiles/
[root@localhost root]# umount /flopper
[root@localhost root]# ls -F /flopper
samplefile
[root@localhost root]#_
```

The **mount** command used in the above output specifies the filesystem type, the device to mount, and the mount point directory; to save time typing on the command line, you may alternatively specify one argument and allow the system to look up the remaining information in the /etc/fstab (filesystem table) file. The /etc/fstab file has a dual purpose; it is used to mount devices at boot time, and is consulted when a user does not specify enough arguments on the command line when using the **mount** command. There are six fields present in the /etc/fstab file:

\<device to mount\> **\<mount point\>** **\<type\>** **\<mount options\>**
\<dump#\> **\<fsck#\>**

The device to mount may be the path to a device file or the label that describes the volume in the superblock. The mount point specifies where to mount the device. The type can be a specific value (such as ext2) or may be automatically detected. The mount options are additional options that the command accepts when mounting the volume (such as read only, or "ro"). Any filesystems with the mount option "noauto" are not automatically mounted at boot time. (A complete list of options that the **mount** command accepts can be found by viewing the manual page for the command.)

The dump# is used by the **dump** command, discussed later in this textbook, when backing up filesystems. A "1" in this field indicates that the filesystem should be backed up, whereas a "0" indicates that no back-up is necessary. The fsck# is used by the **fsck** command, discussed later in this chapter, when checking filesystems at boot time for errors. Any filesystems with a "1" in this field are checked first before any filesystems with a number "2," and filesystems with a number "0" are not checked.

To mount all filesystems in the /etc/fstab file that are intended to mount at boot time, you may simply type the mount —a command.

The following output displays the contents of the /etc/fstab file:

```
[root@localhost root]# cat /etc/fstab
LABEL=/              /              ext3       defaults                    1 1
none            /dev/pts          devpts     gid=5,mode=620              0 0
none            /proc             proc       defaults                    0 0
none            /dev/shm          tmpfs      defaults                    0 0
/dev/hdc2       swap              swap       defaults                    0 0
/dev/cdrom      /mnt/cdrom        iso9660    noauto,owner,kudzu,ro 0 0
/dev/fd0        /mnt/floppy       auto       noauto,owner,kudzu    0 0
  [root@localhost root]#
  [root@localhost root]# _
```

Thus, to mount the first floppy device (/dev/fd0) to the /mnt/floppy directory and detect the type of filesystem on the device automatically, you specify enough information for the **mount** command to find the appropriate line in the /etc/fstab file:

```
    [root@localhost root]# mount /dev/fd0
    [root@localhost root]# mount
    /dev/hda1 on / type ext3 (rw)
    none on /proc type proc (rw)
    usbdevfs on /proc/bus/usb type usbdevfs (rw)
```

```
none on /dev/pts type devpts (rw,gid=5,mode=620)
none on /dev/shm type tmpfs (rw)
none on /proc/sys/fs/binfmt_misc type binfmt_misc (rw)
/dev/fd0 on /mnt/floppy type ext2 (rw)
[root@localhost root]# umount /dev/fd0
[root@localhost root]#_
```

The `mount` command in the above output succeeded because there existed a line in `/etc/fstab` that described the mounting of the `/dev/fd0` device. Alternatively, you can specify the mount point as an argument to the `mount` command to mount the same device via the correct entry in `/etc/fstab`:

```
[root@localhost root]# mount /mnt/floppy
[root@localhost root]# mount
/dev/hda1 on / type ext3 (rw)
none on /proc type proc (rw)
usbdevfs on /proc/bus/usb type usbdevfs (rw)
none on /dev/pts type devpts (rw,gid=5,mode=620)
none on /dev/shm type tmpfs (rw)
none on /proc/sys/fs/binfmt_misc type binfmt_misc (rw)
/dev/fd0 on /mnt/floppy type ext2 (rw)
[root@localhost root]# umount /mnt/floppy
[root@localhost root]#_
```

Commands that are useful when mounting and unmounting floppy disks can be seen in Table 6-4.

Table 6-4   Commands useful when mounting and unmounting filesystems

Command	Description
mount	Displays mounted filesystems
mount –t <type> <device> <mount point>	Mounts a <device> of a certain <type> to a <mount point> directory
fuser –u <directory>	Displays the users using a particular directory
umount <mount point> or umount <device>	Unmounts a <device> from a certain <mount point> directory

Although the commands listed in Table 6-4 allow complete control over the mounting process, you may also mount floppy devices using icons in a GUI environment. However, these floppy devices are mounted to the `/mnt/floppy` directory from the entry listed in `/etc/fstab`. To mount a floppy disk in a GUI environment, use the right mouse button to click on the desktop background, then select Disks and Floppy from the menu, as seen in Figure 6-3.

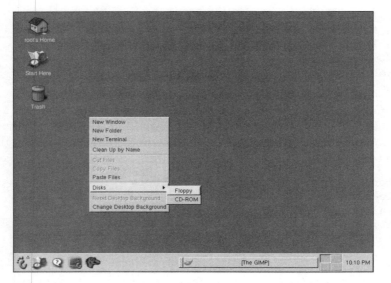

Figure 6-3   Mounting a floppy device using a GUI environment

Choosing this option in the GUI environment places an icon representing the floppy on the desktop; you may then double-click the left mouse button on the icon to open a listing of the files on the floppy, as seen in Figure 6-4, or use the right mouse button to obtain a menu from which you user may unmount the floppy, as depicted in Figure 6-5.

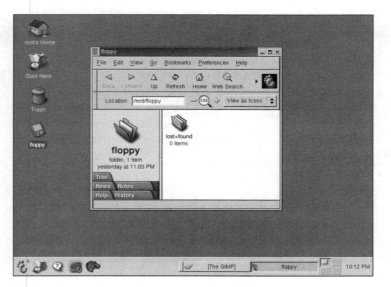

Figure 6-4   Viewing the contents of a floppy device in a GUI environment

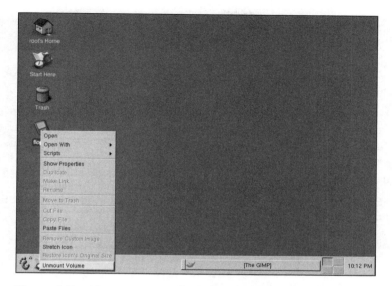

Figure 6-5   Unmounting a floppy device in a GUI environment

WORKING WITH CD-ROMs

Most software that is not downloaded from the Internet is packaged on CD-ROMs, as they have a much larger storage capacity than floppy disks. In fact, one CD-ROM can store more than 500 times the data a floppy disk can store. Like floppies, CD-ROMs can be mounted with the **mount** command and unmounted with the **umount** command, as seen in Table 6-4; however, the device file used with these commands is different. Most Linux systems have an ATAPI compliant IDE CD-ROM drive that attaches to the mainboard via an IDE ribbon cable. These CD-ROMs act as a normal IDE hard disk, and must be configured in one of the four configurations discussed in Chapter 2. These configurations and their associated device files are seen below:

- Primary master (/dev/hda)
- Primary slave (/dev/hdb)
- Secondary master (/dev/hdc)
- Secondary slave (/dev/hdd)

Thus, you may specify your CD-ROM device file if the configuration is known. At installation, however, Red Hat Linux creates a symbolic link called **/dev/cdrom** to the appropriate device. If a system's CD-ROM is configured as a secondary slave, a long listing of **/dev/cdrom** will show the following:

```
[root@localhost root]# ls -l /dev/cdrom
lrwxrwxrwx    1 root    root    8 Mar 28 10:19 /dev/cdrom -> /dev/hdd
[root@localhost root]#_
```

Similarly, if the Linux system has a SCSI CD-ROM device, then the long listing will point to the appropriate SCSI device, as seen below:

```
[root@localhost root]# ls -l /dev/cdrom
lrwxrwxrwx    1 root    root    8 Mar 29 12:52 /dev/cdrom -> /dev/sdb
[root@localhost root]#_
```

In addition, CD-ROMs typically use the iso9660 filesystem type and are not writable. Thus, to mount a CD-ROM to the /mnt/cdrom directory, you should use the filesystem type of iso9660 and add the −r (read-only) option to the **mount** command. To mount a sample CD-ROM to /mnt/cdrom and view its contents, you could use the following commands:

```
[root@localhost root]# mount -r -t iso9660 /dev/cdrom /mnt/cdrom
[root@localhost root]# mount
/dev/hda1 on / type ext3 (rw)
none on /proc type proc (rw)
usbdevfs on /proc/bus/usb type usbdevfs (rw)
none on /dev/pts type devpts (rw,gid=5,mode=620)
none on /dev/shm type tmpfs (rw)
none on /proc/sys/fs/binfmt_misc type binfmt_misc (rw)
/dev/cdrom on /mnt/cdrom type iso9660 (ro)
[root@localhost root]# ls -l /mnt/cdrom
autorun.inf*  install*  graphics/  jungle/  jungle.txt*  joystick/
[root@localhost root]# umount /mnt/cdrom
[root@localhost root]#_
```

As with floppies, you may specify only a single argument to the mount command to mount a CD-ROM via an entry in the /etc/fstab file, and use the **umount** command to unmount the CD-ROM from the directory tree. Also remember that the mount point directory must not be in use to mount or unmount CD-ROM discs successfully; the **fuser** command can be used to verify this.

Unlike floppy disks, CD-ROMs cannot be ejected from the CD-ROM drive until the CD-ROM is properly unmounted, since the **mount** command locks the CD-ROM device as a precaution. Like floppy disks, you may also mount CD-ROMs to the /mnt/cdrom directory from a GUI environment using the entry from /etc/fstab as seen in Figure 6-3 earlier. However, this is rarely needed, as CD-ROMs are mounted and viewed automatically when inserted for the first time into the CD-ROM drive. This is seen in Figure 6-6, using the CD-ROM from the example above.

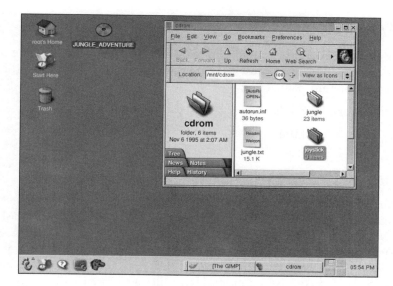

Figure 6-6   Viewing the contents of a CD-ROM in a GUI environment

Note from Figure 6-6 that an icon is also placed on the desktop, which can be used to manipulate or unmount the device when the user highlights the icon and presses the right mouse button, as seen in Figure 6-7.

Figure 6-7   Unmounting a CD-ROM device in a GUI environment

WORKING WITH HARD DISKS

Hard disk drives come in two flavors, IDE and SCSI. IDE hard disk drives attach to the mainboard with an IDE cable and must be configured in one of four configurations, each of which has a different device file:

- Primary master (/dev/hda)

- Primary slave (/dev/hdb)

- Secondary master (/dev/hdc)

- Secondary slave (/dev/hdd)

SCSI hard disk drives typically have faster data transfer speeds, and usually connect to the mainboard via a controller card inserted into an expansion slot. Not only do SCSI drives offer faster access speed, but depending on the type, there may be 15 or more SCSI hard disks attached to a single controller. As a result of these benefits, SCSI hard disks are well-suited to Linux servers that require a great deal of storage space for programs and user files. However, SCSI hard disks have different device files associated with them:

- First SCSI hard disk drive (/dev/sda)

- Second SCSI hard disk drive (/dev/sdb)

- Third SCSI hard disk drive (/dev/sdc)

- Fourth SCSI hard disk drive (/dev/sdd)

- Fifth SCSI hard disk drive (/dev/sde)

- Sixth SCSI hard disk drive (/dev/sdf)

- And so on

Hard Disk Partitioning

Recall that hard disks have the largest storage capacity of any device that you would use to store information on a regular basis. This also poses some problems, because as the size of a disk increases, organization becomes more difficult and the chance of error increases. To solve these problems, you typically divide a hard disk into smaller, more usable sections called **partitions**. Each partition may contain a separate filesystem and may be mounted to different mount point directories. Recall from Chapter 2 that Linux requires two partitions at minimum: a partition that is mounted to the root directory (the root partition) and a partition used to hold virtual memory (the swap partition). The swap partition does not require a filesystem, as it is written to and maintained by the operating system alone. It is good practice, however, to use more than just two partitions on a Linux system. This division can be useful to:

- Segregate different types of data—i.e., home directory data is stored on a separate partition mounted to /home

- Allow for the use of more than one type of filesystem on one hard disk drive—i.e., some filesystems are tuned for database use

- Reduce the chance that filesystem corruption will render a system unusable; if the partition that is mounted to the /home directory becomes corrupted, it does not affect the system as operating system files are stored on a separate partition mounted to the / directory

- Speed up access to stored data by keeping filesystems as small as possible

Segregation of data into physically separate areas of the hard disk drive can be exceptionally useful from an organizational standpoint. Keeping different types of data on different partitions gives you the ability to manipulate one type of data without affecting the rest of the system. This also reduces the likelihood that filesystem corruption will affect all files in the directory tree, and access speed is improved because a smaller area needs to be searched by the magnetic heads in a hard disk drive to locate data. This process is similar to searching a warehouse; if a penny is placed in a 20,000 square foot warehouse, it will take much less time to find it if that warehouse is divided into four separate departments of 5,000 square feet each and you know which department the penny is located in. Searching and maneuvering around is much quicker and easier in a smaller defined space than in a larger one.

On a physical level, hard disks are circular metal platters that spin at a fast speed. Data is read off of these disks in concentric circles called **tracks**. Each track is divided into **sectors** of information, and sectors are combined into more usable **blocks** of data, as seen in Figure 6-8. Most hard disk drives have several platters inside them organized on top of each other such that they may be written to simultaneously to speed up data transfer. A series consisting of the same concentric tracks on all of the metal platters inside a hard disk drive is known as a **cylinder**.

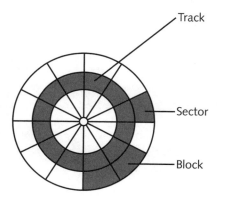

Figure 6-8   The physical areas of a hard disk

Partition definitions are stored in the first readable sector of the hard disk, known as the master boot record (MBR) or master boot block (MBB). If this area of the hard disk becomes corrupted, the entire contents of the hard disk may be lost.

It is common for Linux servers to have several hard disks. In these situations, it is also common to configure one partition on each hard disk and mount each partition to different directories on the directory tree. Thus, if one partition fails, an entire hard disk may be replaced with a new one and the data retrieved from a back-up source.

Recall from Chapter 2 that hard disks may contain up to four primary partitions; to overcome this limitation, you may use an extended partition in place of one of these primary partitions. An extended partition may then contain many more sub-partitions called logical drives. Since it is on these partitions that you place a filesystem, there exist device files that refer to the various types of partitions that you may have on a hard disk. These device files start with the name of the hard disk (/dev/hda, /dev/hdb, /dev/sda, /dev/sdb, etc.) and append a number indicating the partition on that hard disk. The first primary partition is given the number one, the second primary partition is given the number two, the third primary partition is given the number three, and the fourth primary partition is given the number four. If any one of these primary partitions is labeled as an extended partition, then the logical drives within are named starting with the number five. Some common hard disk partition names are listed in Table 6-5.

Table 6-5   Common hard disk partition device files for /dev/hda and /dev/sda

Partition	IDE Device Name (assuming /dev/hda)	SCSI Device Name (assuming /dev/sda)
1st primary partition	/dev/hda1	/dev/sda1
2nd primary partition	/dev/hda2	/dev/sda2
3rd primary partition	/dev/hda3	/dev/sda3
4th primary partition	/dev/hda4	/dev/sda4
1st logical drive in the extended partition	/dev/hda5	/dev/sda5
2nd logical drive in the extended partition	/dev/hda6	/dev/sda6
3rd logical drive in the extended partition	/dev/hda7	/dev/sda7
4th logical drive in the extended partition	/dev/hda8	/dev/sda8
5th logical drive in the extended partition	/dev/hda9	/dev/sda9
nth logical drive in the extended partition	/dev/hdan	/dev/sdan

Note that any one of the primary partitions may be labeled as an extended partition. Also, for different disk drives than those listed in Table 6-5 (i.e., /dev/hdc), the partition numbers remain the same (i.e., /dev/hdc1, /dev/hdc2, etc.).

Hard disk partitions may be created specific to a certain filesystem. To create a partition that will later be formatted with an ext2 or ext3 filesystem, you should create a Linux partition (also known as type 83). Similarly, you should create a Linux swap partition (also known as type 82) if that partition is intended for use as a virtual memory partition. This explicit choice of partition type allows for partitions that better suit the needs of a filesystem.

A typical Linux hard disk structure for the primary master IDE hard disk (/dev/hda) may contain a partition for the / filesystem (/dev/hda1) and an extended partition (/dev/hda2) that further contains a swap partition (/dev/hda5) and some free space, as seen in Figure 6-9.

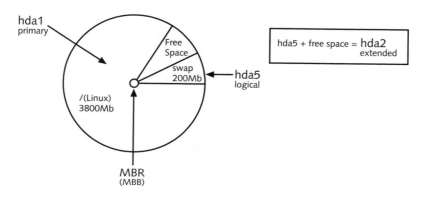

Figure 6-9   A sample Linux partitioning strategy

A more complicated Linux hard disk structure for the primary master IDE hard disk may involve preserving the Windows operating system partition, allowing a user to boot into and use the Linux operating system or boot into and use the Windows operating system. This is known as dual-booting and will be discussed in the next chapter.

In Figure 6-10, the Windows partition was created as a primary partition (/dev/hda1) and the Linux partitions are contained within the extended partition (/dev/hda2). Figure 6-10 also creates a separate filesystem for users' home directories mounted to /home (/dev/hda6).

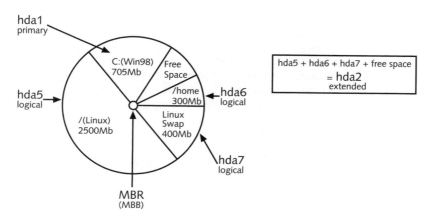

Figure 6-10   A sample dual-boot Linux partitioning strategy

Working with Hard Disk Partitions

Recall that the creation of partitions may be accomplished at installation using either the fdisk utility or the Disk Druid utility. Disk Druid is an easy-to-use partitioning tool used with Red Hat Linux, specifically designed for installation only. To create partitions after installation, you use the **fdisk** command. To use the **fdisk** command, you simply specify the hard disk to partition as an argument. An example of using **fdisk** with the secondary master IDE hard disk (/dev/hdc) is seen in the output below:

```
[root@localhost root]# fdisk /dev/hdc

The number of cylinders for this disk is set to 1247.
There is nothing wrong with that, but this is larger than 1024,
and could in certain setups cause problems with:
1) software that runs at boot time (e.g., old versions of LILO)
2) booting and partitioning software from other OSs
   (e.g., DOS FDISK, OS/2 FDISK)

Command (m for help):_
```

Note from the above output that the **fdisk** command displays a prompt for you to accept **fdisk** commands. A list of possible **fdisk** commands may be seen if you press the **m** key at this prompt, as seen below:

```
Command (m for help): m
Command action
   a   toggle a bootable flag
   b   edit bsd disklabel
   c   toggle the dos compatibility flag
   d   delete a partition
   l   list known partition types
   m   print this menu
   n   add a new partition
   o   create a new empty DOS partition table
   p   print the partition table
   q   quit without saving changes
   s   create a new empty Sun disklabel
   t   change a partition's system id
   u   change display/entry units
   v   verify the partition table
   w   write table to disk and exit
   x   extra functionality (experts only)

Command (m for help):_
```

To print a list of the partitions currently set on /dev/hdc, you could press the p key at the **fdisk** prompt:

```
Command (m for help): p

Disk /dev/hdc: 255 heads, 63 sectors, 1247 cylinders
Units = cylinders of 16065 * 512 bytes

   Device Boot      Start        End     Blocks   Id  System
/dev/hdc1    *          1        510    4096543+  83  Linux
/dev/hdc2             511        561     409657+  82  Linux swap
/dev/hdc3             562       1247    5510295   83  Linux

Command (m for help):_
```

Notice that the device names appear on the left-hand side of the above output, including the partition that is booted to (/dev/hdc1), the start and end location of partitions on the physical hard disk (start and end cylinders), the number of total blocks for storing information in the partition (typically, 1 block = 1 kilobyte), and the partition type and description (83 is a Linux partition, 82 is a Linux swap partition). A Linux partition may contain a Linux filesystem such as ext2 or ext3.

To remove the **/dev/hdc3** partition and all the data contained on the filesystem within, you could use the **d** key noted earlier:

```
Command (m for help): d
Partition number (1-4): 3

Command (m for help): p

Disk /dev/hdc: 255 heads, 63 sectors, 1247 cylinders
Units = cylinders of 16065 * 512 bytes

   Device Boot      Start        End     Blocks   Id  System
/dev/hdc1    *          1        510    4096543+  83  Linux
/dev/hdc2             511        561     409657+  82  Linux swap

Command (m for help):_
```

To create an extended partition using the fourth primary partition (/dev/hdc4) with 2 logical drives (/dev/hdc5 and /dev/hdc6), you could use the n key noted earlier and specify the partition to create, the starting cylinder on the hard disk, and the size (+1000M makes a 1000Mb partition):

```
Command (m for help): n
Command action
   e   extended
   p   primary partition (1-4)
e
Partition number (1-4): 4
```

```
First cylinder (562-1247, default 562): 562
Last cylinder or +size or +sizeM or +sizeK (562-1247, default 1247):
1247

Command (m for help): p

Disk /dev/hdc: 255 heads, 63 sectors, 1247 cylinders
Units = cylinders of 16065 * 512 bytes

    Device Boot     Start       End     Blocks    Id  System
/dev/hdc1     *         1       510   4096543+    83  Linux
/dev/hdc2             511       561    409657+    82  Linux swap
/dev/hdc4             562      1247   5510295      5  Extended

Command (m for help): n
Command action
   l   logical (5 or over)
   p   primary partition (1-4)
l
First cylinder (562-1247, default 562): 562
Last cylinder or +size or +sizeM or +sizeK (562-1247, default 1247):
+1000M

Command (m for help): p

Disk /dev/hdc: 255 heads, 63 sectors, 1247 cylinders
Units = cylinders of 16065 * 512 bytes

    Device Boot     Start       End     Blocks    Id  System
/dev/hdc1     *         1       510   4096543+    83  Linux
/dev/hdc2             511       561    409657+    82  Linux swap
/dev/hdc4             562      1247   5510295      5  Extended
/dev/hdc5             562       689   1028128+    83  Linux

Command (m for help): n
Command action
   l   logical (5 or over)
   p   primary partition (1-4)
l
First cylinder (690-1247, default 690): 690
Last cylinder or +size or +sizeM or +sizeK (690-1247, default 1247):
+2000M

Command (m for help): p

Disk /dev/hdc: 255 heads, 63 sectors, 1247 cylinders
Units = cylinders of 16065 * 512 bytes
```

```
   Device Boot     Start       End     Blocks    Id  System
/dev/hdc1    *         1       510    4096543+   83  Linux
/dev/hdc2            511       561     409657+   82  Linux swap
/dev/hdc4            562      1247    5510295     5  Extended
/dev/hdc5            562       689    1028128+   83  Linux
/dev/hdc6            690       944    2048256    83  Linux

Command (m for help):_
```

Notice from above output that the default type for new partitions created with **fdisk** is 83 (Linux). To change this, you may press the **t** key at the **fdisk** prompt. To change the **/dev/hdc6** partition to type 82 (Linux swap), you could do the following at the **fdisk** prompt:

```
Command (m for help): t
Partition number (1-6): 6
Hex code (type L to list codes): L
```

```
 0   Empty            1b   Hidden Win95 FA 64   Novell Netware    bb   Boot Wizard hid
 1   FAT12            1c   Hidden Win95 FA 65   Novell Netware    c1   DRDOS/sec (FAT-
 2   XENIX root       1e   Hidden Win95 FA 70   DiskSecure Mult   c4   DRDOS/sec (FAT-
 3   XENIX usr        24   NEC DOS         75   PC/IX             c6   DRDOS/sec (FAT-
 4   FAT16 <32M       39   Plan 9          80   Old Minix         c7   Syrinx
 5   Extended         3c   PartitionMagic  81   Minix / old Lin   da   Non-FS data
 6   FAT16            40   Venix 80286     82   Linux swap        db   CP/M / CTOS / .
 7   HPFS/NTFS        41   PPC PReP Boot   83   Linux             de   Dell Utility
 8   AIX              42   SFS             84   OS/2 hidden C:    df   BootIt
 9   AIX bootable     4d   QNX4.x          85   Linux extended    e1   DOS access
 a   OS/2 Boot Manag  4e   QNX4.x 2nd part 86   NTFS volume set   e3   DOS R/O
 b   Win95 FAT32      4f   QNX4.x 3rd part 87   NTFS volume set   e4   SpeedStor
 c   Win95 FAT32 (LB  50   OnTrack DM      8e   Linux LVM         eb   BeOS fs
 e   Win95 FAT16 (LB  51   OnTrack DM6 Aux 93   Amoeba            ee   EFI GPT
 f   Win95 Ext'd (LB  52   CP/M            94   Amoeba BBT        ef   EFI (FAT-12/16/
10   OPUS             53   OnTrack DM6 Aux 9f   BSD/OS            f1   SpeedStor
11   Hidden FAT12     54   OnTrackDM6      a0   IBM Thinkpad hi   f4   SpeedStor
12   Compaq diagnost  55   EZ-Drive        a5   BSD/386           f2   DOS secondary
14   Hidden FAT16 <3  56   Golden Bow      a6   OpenBSD           fd   Linux raid auto
16   Hidden FAT16     5c   Priam Edisk     a7   NeXTSTEP          fe   LANstep
17   Hidden HPFS/NTF  61   SpeedStor       b7   BSDI fs           ff   BBT
18   AST SmartSleep   63   GNU HURD or Sys b8   BSDI swap
```

```
Hex code (type L to list codes): 82
Changed system type of partition 6 to 82 (Linux swap)

Command (m for help): p

Disk /dev/hdc: 255 heads, 63 sectors, 1247 cylinders
Units = cylinders of 16065 * 512 bytes
```

6

```
    Device Boot      Start         End      Blocks   Id  System
/dev/hdc1     *          1         510     4096543+  83  Linux
/dev/hdc2              511         561      409657+  82  Linux swap
/dev/hdc4              562        1247     5510295    5  Extended
/dev/hdc5              562         689     1028128+  83  Linux
/dev/hdc6              690         944     2048256   82  Linux swap

Command (m for help):_
```

Finally, to save partition changes to the hard disk and attempt to reload the new partition information back into memory, you may use the w key at the **fdisk** prompt:

```
Command (m for help): w
The partition table has been altered!

Calling ioctl() to re-read partition table.
Re-read table failed with error 16: Device or resource busy.
Reboot your system to ensure the partition table is updated.

WARNING: If you have created or modified any DOS 6.x
partitions, please see the fdisk manual page for additional
information.
Syncing disks.
[root@localhost root]#_
```

If the **fdisk** command indicates that the new partition information must be reloaded manually (as in the above example), simply reboot your machine. For this reason, it is good form to always reboot your machine after running **fdisk**.

Once the machine has rebooted, you may then use the **mkfs**, **mount**, and **umount** commands discussed earlier specifying the partition device file as an argument. To create an ext2 filesystem on the **/dev/hdc5** partition created earlier, you could use the following command:

```
[root@localhost root]# mkfs -t ext2 /dev/hdc5
mke2fs 1.23, 15-Aug-2001 for EXT2 FS 0.5b, 95/08/09
Filesystem label=
OS type: Linux
Block size=4096 (log=2)
Fragment size=4096 (log=2)
128768 inodes, 257032 blocks
12851 blocks (5.00%) reserved for the super user
First data block=0
8 block groups
32768 blocks per group, 32768 fragments per group
16096 inodes per group
Superblock backups stored on blocks:
        32768, 98304, 163840, 229376

Writing inode tables: done
Writing superblocks and filesystem accounting information: done
```

```
This filesystem will be automatically checked every 35 mounts or
180 days, whichever comes first.  Use tune2fs -c or -i to override.
[root@localhost root]#_
```

In addition, you may choose to convert this filesystem to ext3 by using the `tune2fs` command to create a journal file on the filesystem:

```
[root@localhost root]# tune2fs -j /dev/hdc5
tune2fs 1.23, 15-Aug-2001 for EXT2 FS 0.5b, 95/08/09
Creating journal inode: done
This filesystem will be automatically checked every 35 mounts or
180 days, whichever comes first.  Use tune2fs -c or -i to override.
[root@localhost root]#_
```

Alternatively, you could have used the `mke2fs —j /dev/hdc5` command to create an ext3 filesystem. To mount this ext3 filesystem to a new mount point directory called `/data` and view the contents, you could use the following commands:

```
[root@localhost root]# mkdir /data
[root@localhost root]# mount -t ext3 /dev/hdc5 /data
[root@localhost root]# mount
/dev/hdc1 on / type ext3 (rw)
none on /proc type proc (rw)
usbdevfs on /proc/bus/usb type usbdevfs (rw)
none on /dev/pts type devpts (rw,gid=5,mode=620)
none on /dev/shm type tmpfs (rw)
none on /proc/sys/fs/binfmt_misc type binfmt_misc (rw)
/dev/hdc5 on /data type ext3 (rw)
[root@localhost root]# ls —F /data
lost+found/
[root@localhost root]#_
```

To allow the system to mount this filesystem automatically at every boot, you could edit the `/etc/fstab` file such that it has the following entry for `/dev/hdc5`:

```
[root@localhost root]# cat /etc/fstab
LABEL=/        /              ext3      defaults              1 1
none           /dev/pts       devpts    gid=5,mode=620        0 0
none           /proc          proc      defaults              0 0
none           /dev/shm       tmpfs     defaults              0 0
/dev/hdc2      swap           swap      defaults              0 0
/dev/cdrom     /mnt/cdrom     iso9660   noauto,owner,kudzu,ro 0 0
/dev/fd0       /mnt/floppy    auto      noauto,owner,kudzu    0 0
/dev/hdc5      /data          ext3      defaults              0 0
 [root@localhost root]#_
```

6

Monitoring Filesystems

Once filesystems are created on disk devices and those disk devices are mounted to the directory tree, they should be checked periodically for errors, disk space usage, and inode usage. This minimizes the problems that can occur as a result of a damaged filesystem and reduces the likelihood that a file cannot be saved due to insufficient disk space.

Disk Usage

There may be several filesystems mounted to the directory tree. As mentioned earlier, the more filesystems that are used, the less likely it is that a corrupted filesystem may interfere with normal system operations. Conversely, more filesystems typically results in less hard disk space per filesystem and may result in system errors if certain filesystems fill up with data. Many users create filesystems for the /, /usr, and /var directories during installation. The /usr directory contains most utilities and installed programs on a Linux system, and should have enough space for future software installations. The /var directory grows in size continuously as it stores log files. Old log files should be removed periodically to leave room for new ones. The / filesystem is the most vital of these, and should always contain a great deal of free space used as working space for the operating system. As a result, the / filesystem should be monitored frequently. If free space on the / filesystem falls below 10%, the system may suffer from poorer performance.

The easiest method for monitoring free space by mounted filesystem is to use the **df** (disk free space) command as seen below:

```
[root@localhost root]# df
Filesystem           1k-blocks      Used Available Use% Mounted on
/dev/hdc1              4032092   2848744    978524  75% /
none                   192232         0    192232   0% /dev/shm
[root@localhost root]#_
```

From the above output, the only filesystem used is the / filesystem; the /usr and /var directories are simply directories on the / filesystem, which increases the importance of monitoring the / filesystem. Since the / filesystem is 75% used in the above output, there is no immediate concern. However, log files and software installed in the future will increase this number and may warrant the purchase of an additional hard disk for data to reside on.

Alternatively, you may view the output of the **df** command in a more user-friendly (or human-readable) format by using the **−h** option, which prints sizes in the most convenient format (G = gigabyte, M = megabyte), as seen below:

```
[root@localhost root]# df -h
Filesystem            Size  Used Avail Use% Mounted on
/dev/hdc1             3.8G  2.8G  955M  75% /
none                  188M     0  187M   0% /dev/shm
[root@localhost root]#_
```

It is important to remember that the df command only views mounted filesystems, thus to get disk free space statistics for a floppy filesystem, you should mount it prior to viewing the output of the df command:

```
[root@localhost root]# mount /dev/fd0
[root@localhost root]# df
Filesystem            1k-blocks       Used Available Use% Mounted on
/dev/hdc1              4032092     2848756    978512  75% /
none                   192232           0    192232   0% /dev/shm
/dev/fd0                  1412          17      1323   2% /mnt/flopp
y
[root@localhost root]# umount /dev/fd0
[root@localhost root]# df
Filesystem            1k-blocks       Used Available Use% Mounted on
/dev/hdc1              4032092     2848756    978512  75% /
none                   192232           0    192232   0% /dev/shm
[root@localhost root]#_
```

If a filesystem is approaching full capacity, it may be useful to examine which directories on that filesystem are taking up the most disk space, so that you may remove or move files from that directory to another filesystem that has sufficient space. To view the size of a directory and its contents in Kilobytes, you may use the du (directory usage) command. If the directory is large, you should use either the more or less commands to view the output page by page, as seen with the /usr directory below:

```
[root@localhost root]# du /usr |more
100        /usr/bin/filter
56         /usr/bin/auth/passwd
20         /usr/bin/auth/resolv
80         /usr/bin/auth
76         /usr/bin/control
20         /usr/bin/rnews.libexec
196028     /usr/bin
8          /usr/lib/locale/af_ZA/LC_MESSAGES
248        /usr/lib/locale/af_ZA
8          /usr/lib/locale/ar_AE/LC_MESSAGES
248        /usr/lib/locale/ar_AE
8          /usr/lib/locale/ar_AE.utf8/LC_MESSAGES
552        /usr/lib/locale/ar_AE.utf8
4          /usr/lib/locale/ar_BH/LC_MESSAGES
24         /usr/lib/locale/ar_BH
4          /usr/lib/locale/ar_BH.utf8/LC_MESSAGES
24         /usr/lib/locale/ar_BH.utf8
4          /usr/lib/locale/ar_DZ/LC_MESSAGES
20         /usr/lib/locale/ar_DZ
4          /usr/lib/locale/ar_DZ.utf8/LC_MESSAGES
20         /usr/lib/locale/ar_DZ.utf8
4          /usr/lib/locale/ar_EG/LC_MESSAGES
20         /usr/lib/locale/ar_EG
--More--
```

6

To view only a summary of the total size of a directory, simply use the —s— switch to the du command, as seen below with the /usr directory:

```
[root@localhost root]# du —s /usr
2633772 /usr
[root@localhost root]# _
```

As with the df command, the du command also accepts the —h option to make the view more human-readable. The following indicates that the total size of the /usr directory is 2.6 Gigabytes:

```
[root@localhost root]# du —hs /usr
2.6G    /usr
[root@localhost root]# _
```

Recall that every filesystem has an inode table that contains the inodes for the files and directories on the filesystem. This inode table is made during filesystem creation and is usually proportionate to the size of the filesystem. Each file and directory uses one inode, thus a filesystem with several small files may use up all of the inodes in the inode table and prevent new files from being created on the filesystem. To view the total number of inodes and free inodes for an ext2 or ext3 filesystem, you may use the dumpe2fs command with the —h switch, as seen below:

```
[root@localhost root]# df
Filesystem          1k-blocks       Used Available Use% Mounted on
/dev/hdc1            4032092     2848756    978512   75% /
none                  192232           0    192232    0% /dev/shm
[root@localhost root]# dumpe2fs -h /dev/hdc1
dumpe2fs 1.23, 15-Aug-2001 for EXT2 FS 0.5b, 95/08/09
Filesystem volume name:     /
Last mounted on:            <not available>
Filesystem UUID:            6379283e-422a-11d6-9d53-f6a7b697142f
Filesystem magic number:    0xEF53
Filesystem revision #:      1 (dynamic)
Filesystem features:        has_journal filetype needs_recovery sparse
_super
Filesystem state:           clean
Errors behavior:            Continue
Filesystem OS type:         Linux
Inode count:                513024
Block count:                1024135
Reserved block count:       51206
Free blocks:                295830
Free inodes:                334993
First block:                0
Block size:                 4096
Fragment size:              4096
Blocks per group:           32768
Fragments per group:        32768
Inodes per group:           16032
```

```
Inode blocks per group:   501
Last mount time:          Sun May 12 21:33:00 2002
Last write time:          Sun May 12 21:33:00 2002
Mount count:              25
Maximum mount count:      -1
Last checked:             Thu Mar 28 04:01:27 2002
Check interval:           0 (<none>)
Reserved blocks uid:      0 (user root)
Reserved blocks gid:      0 (group root)
First inode:              11
Inode size:               128
Journal UUID:             <none>
Journal inode:            8
Journal device:           0x0000
First orphan inode:       02.6G      /usr
[root@localhost root]# _
```

In the above output, you can see that there are 513024 inodes in the inode table and that 334993 of them are free to use when creating new files and directories.

Checking Filesystems for Errors

Filesystems themselves may accumulate errors over time. These errors are often referred to as **filesystem corruption** and are common on most filesystems. Those filesystems that are accessed frequently are more prone to corruption than those that are not. As a result, such filesystems should be checked regularly for errors. The most common filesystem corruption occurs because a system was not shut down properly using the **shutdown**, **halt**, or **reboot** commands. Data is stored in memory for a short period of time before it is written to a file on the hard disk. This process of saving data to the hard disk is called **syncing**. If the power is turned off on the computer, data in memory may not be synced properly to the hard disk and corruption may occur. Filesystem corruption may also occur if the hard disks are used frequently for time-intensive tasks such as database access. As the usage of any system increases, so does the possibility for operating system errors when writing to the hard disks. Along the same lines, the physical hard disks themselves are mechanical in nature and can wear over time. Some areas of the disk may become unusable if they can no longer hold a magnetic charge; these areas are known as **bad blocks**. When the operating system finds a bad block, it puts a reference to that bad block in the bad blocks table on the filesystem. Any entries in the bad blocks table are not used for any future disk storage.

To check a filesystem for errors, you may use the **fsck** (filesystem check) command, which can check filesystems of many different types. The **fsck** command takes an option specifying the filesystem type and an argument specifying the device to check; if the filesystem type is not specified, the ext2 filesystem is assumed. It is also important to note that the filesystem being checked must be unmounted beforehand for the `fsck` command to work properly, as seen below:

```
[root@localhost root]# fsck -t ext2 /dev/fd0
Parallelizing fsck version 1.23 (15-Aug-2001)
e2fsck 1.23, 15-Aug-2001 for EXT2 FS 0.5b, 95/08/09
/dev/fd0 is mounted.

WARNING!!!  Running e2fsck on a mounted filesystem may cause
SEVERE filesystem damage.

Do you really want to continue (y/n)? n

check aborted.
[root@localhost root]# umount /dev/fd0
[root@localhost root]# fsck -t ext2 /dev/fd0
Parallelizing fsck version 1.23 (15-Aug-2001)
e2fsck 1.23, 15-Aug-2001 for EXT2 FS 0.5b, 95/08/09
/dev/fd0: clean, 14/184 files, 45/1440 blocks
[root@localhost root]# _
```

 Since the / filesystem cannot be unmounted, you should only run the `fsck` command on the / filesystem in single-user mode, which is discussed later in this book.

Notice from the above output that the `fsck` command does not give lengthy output on the terminal screen when checking the filesystem. This is because the `fsck` command only performs a quick check for errors unless the –f option is used to perform a full check, as seen below:

```
[root@localhost root]# fsck -f -t ext2 /dev/fd0
Parallelizing fsck version 1.23 (15-Aug-2001)
e2fsck 1.23, 15-Aug-2001 for EXT2 FS 0.5b, 95/08/09
Pass 1: Checking inodes, blocks, and sizes
Pass 2: Checking directory structure
Pass 3: Checking directory connectivity
Pass 4: Checking reference counts
Pass 5: Checking group summary information
/dev/fd0: 14/184 files (0.0% non-contiguous), 45/1440 blocks
[root@localhost root]# _
```

A list of common options used with the `fsck` command is displayed in Table 6-6.

If the `fsck` command finds a corrupted file, it displays a message to the user asking whether to fix the error or not; to avoid these messages, one may use the –a option listed in Table 6-6 to specify that the `fsck` command should repair any corruption automatically. If there are files that the `fsck` command cannot repair, it will place them in the `lost+found` directory on that filesystem and rename the file to the inode number.

Table 6-6   Common options to the `fsck` command

Option	Description
-f	Performs a full filesystem check
-a	Allows `fsck` to repair any errors automatically
-A	Checks all filesystems in `/etc/fstab` that have a 1 or 2 in the sixth field
-Cf	Performs a full filesystem check and displays a progress line
-AR	Checks all filesystems in `/etc/fstab` that have a 1 or 2 in the sixth field but skips the / filesystem
-V	Displays verbose output

6

To view the contents of the **lost+found** directory, simply mount the device and view the contents of the lost+found directory immediately underneath the mount point. Since it is difficult to identify lost files by their inode number, most users simply delete the contents of this directory periodically. Recall that the **lost+found** directory is created automatically when an ext2 or ext3 filesystem is created by the **mkfs** command.

Just as you may use the **mke2fs** command to make an ext2 filesystem, you may use the **e2fsck** command to check an ext2 or ext3 filesystem. The **e2fsck** command accepts more options and can check a filesytem more thoroughly than **fsck**, but only works with an ext2 or ext3 filesystem. By using the **-c** option to the **e2fsck** command, you may check for bad blocks on the hard disk and add them to a bad block table on the filesystem so that they are not used in the future, as seen below:

```
[root@localhost root]# e2fsck -c /dev/fd0
e2fsck 1.23, 15-Aug-2001 for EXT2 FS 0.5b, 95/08/09
Checking for bad blocks (read-only test): done
Pass 1: Checking inodes, blocks, and sizes
Pass 2: Checking directory structure
Pass 3: Checking directory connectivity
Pass 4: Checking reference counts
Pass 5: Checking group summary information

/dev/fd0: ***** FILE SYSTEM WAS MODIFIED *****
/dev/fd0: 14/184 files (0.0% non-contiguous), 45/1440 blocks
[root@localhost root]# _
```

 The badblocks command can be used to perform the same function as e2fsck -c.

Recall from earlier that the **fsck** command is run at boot time when filesystems are mounted from entries in the `/etc/fstab` file. Any entries in `/etc/fstab` that have a 1 in the sixth field are checked first, followed by entries that have a 2 in the sixth field. However, typically every 20–40 times an ext2 or ext3 filesystem is mounted (or every

180 days alternatively), a full filesystem check is forced. This may delay booting for several minutes, or even hours, depending on the size of the filesystems being checked. To change this interval, you may use the −i option to the tune2fs command, as seen below:

```
[root@localhost root]# tune2fs -i 0 /dev/fd0
tune2fs 1.23, 15-Aug-2001 for EXT2 FS 0.5b, 95/08/09
Setting interval between check 0 seconds
[root@localhost root]# _
```

The tune2fs command can be used to change or tune filesystem parameters after a filesystem has been created. Changing the interval between checks to 0 seconds, as seen in the above example, disables filesystem checks.

HARD DISK QUOTAS

If there are several users on a Linux system, there must be enough hard disk space to support the files that each user is expected to store on the hard disk. However, if hard disk space is limited or company policy limits disk usage, you should impose limits on filesystem usage. These restrictions are called hard disk quotas, and may be applied to users or groups of users. Furthermore, quotas may restrict how many files and directories a user may create (i.e., restrict the number of inodes created) on a particular filesystem, or the total size of all files that a user may own on a filesystem. There are two types of quota limits: soft limits and hard limits. **Soft limits** allow the user to extend them for a certain period of time (seven days by default), whereas **hard limits** are rigid and will prevent the user from going past them. Quotas are typically enabled at boot time if there are quota entries in /etc/fstab, but can also be turned on and off afterwards by using the quotaon and quotaoff commands, respectively.

To set up quotas for the / filesystem and restrict the user "user1," you may carry out the following steps:

1. Edit the /etc/fstab file to add the usrquota and grpquota mount options for the / filesystem. The resulting /etc/fstab file should look like the following:

```
[root@localhost root]# cat /etc/fstab
LABEL=/       /              ext3     defaults,usrquota,grpquota    1 1
none          /dev/pts       devpts   gid=5,mode=620                0 0
none          /proc          proc     defaults                      0 0
none          /dev/shm       tmpfs    defaults                      0 0
/dev/hdc2     swap           swap     defaults                      0 0
/dev/cdrom    /mnt/cdrom     iso9660  noauto,owner,kudzu,ro         0 0
/dev/fd0      /mnt/floppy    auto     noauto,owner,kudzu            0 0
 [root@localhost root]# _
```

2. Remount the root filesystem as read-write to update the system with the new options from /etc/fstab. The command to do this is:

```
[root@localhost root]# mount / -o remount,rw
[root@localhost root]# _
```

3. Run the quotacheck —mavug command which looks on the system for file ownership and updates the quota database for all filesystems with quota options listed in /etc/fstab (-a), giving verbose output (-v) for all users and groups (-u and -g) even if the filesystem is used by other processes (-m). This creates two files in the root of the filesystem: /aquota.user and /aquota.group. See the following:

```
[root@localhost root]# quotacheck -mavug
quotacheck: Scanning /dev/hdc1 [/] done
quotacheck: Checked 9929 directories and 168094 files
[root@localhost root]# ls —F /aquota*
/aquota.group  /aquota.user
[root@localhost root]# _
```

4. Turn quotas on for the / filesystem using the quotaon / command:

```
[root@localhost root]# quotaon /
[root@localhost root]# _
```

Alternatively, you may use the quotaoff / command to turn them off.

5. Edit the quotas for certain users by using the edquota —u <username> command. This will bring up the vi editor and allow the user to set soft and hard quotas for the number of blocks a user may own on the filesystem (typically, 1 block = 1 Kilobyte) and the total number of inodes (files and directories) that a user may own on the filesystem. A soft limit and hard limit of zero (0) indicates that there is no limit. To set a hard limit of 20Mb (=20480Kb) and 1000 inodes, as well as a soft limit of 18Mb (=18432Kb) and 900 inodes, you could do the following:

```
[root@localhost root]# edquota —u user1
Disk quotas for user user1 (uid 500):
 Filesystem      blocks      soft      hard       inodes      soft      hard
 /dev/hda1        1188         0         0          326         0         0
~
~
~
~
~
~
~
~
~
~
~
~
```

```
~
~
"/tmp//EdP.aclpslv" 3L, 216C
```

Next, place the appropriate values in the columns provided, then save and quit the vi editor:

```
Disk quotas for user user1 (uid 500):
  Filesystem        blocks       soft       hard     inodes       soft       hard
  /dev/hda1           1188      18432      20480        326        900       1000

~
~
~
~
~
~
~
~
~
~
~
~
~
:wq
"/tmp/EdP.aclpslv" 3L, 216C written
[root@localhost root]# _
```

6. Edit the time limit for which users may go beyond soft quotas by using the edquota —u —t command. The default time limit for soft quotas is seven days, but may be changed as seen below:

```
[root@localhost root]# edquota —u -t
Grace period before enforcing soft limits for users:
Time units may be: days, hours, minutes, or seconds
  Filesystem               Block grace period      Inode grace period
  /dev/hda1                       7days                   7days
~
~
~
~
~
~
~
~
~
~
~
~
"/tmp//EdP.alvzfSy" 4L, 233C
```

7. Ensure that quotas were updated properly by gathering a report for quotas by user on the / filesystem using the `repquota` command, as seen below:

```
[root@localhost root]# repquota /
*** Report for user quotas on device /dev/hdc1
Block grace time: 7days; Inode grace time: 7days
                         Block limits            File limits
User              used    soft   hard  grace    used  soft  hard  grace
-----------------------------------------------------------------------
root        -- 2790996       0      0          175022     0     0
amanda      --     744       0      0              56     0     0
nobody      --       4       0      0               1     0     0
bin         --   14884       0      0            2176     0     0
daemon      --       8       0      0               3     0     0
lp          --    1976       0      0               5     0     0
rpm         --   33680       0      0              89     0     0
ntp         --       4       0      0               2     0     0
user1       --    1188   18432  20480             326   900  1000
junkbust    --      80       0      0               2     0     0
sue         --      48       0      0              13     0     0
mailman     --       0       0      0               1     0     0
news        --    5336       0      0             196     0     0
gdm         --       4       0      0               1     0     0
radvd       --       4       0      0               1     0     0
uucp        --    1028       0      0              18     0     0
xfs         --       4       0      0               2     0     0
pcap        --      72       0      0              13     0     0
games       --       0       0      0              59     0     0
apache      --       8       0      0               2     0     0
ldap        --       8       0      0               2     0     0
squid       --       8       0      0               2     0     0
pvm         --       4       0      0               1     0     0
named       --      20       0      0               5     0     0
postgres    --      20       0      0               6     0     0
mysql       --       8       0      0               7     0     0
rpcuser     --      16       0      0               4     0     0
nfsnobody   --      32       0      0               9     0     0
[root@localhost root]#
```

Note that most users in the above output are system users and do not have quotas applied to them. These users will be discussed later in this book.

The aforementioned commands must be performed by the root user; however, regular users may view their own quota using the `quota` command. The root user may also use the `quota` command to view quotas for himself or for other users:

```
[root@localhost root]# quota
Disk quotas for user root (uid 0): none
[root@localhost root]# quota -u user1
```

```
Disk quotas for user user1 (uid 500):
Filesystem blocks quota limit grace  files quota limit grace
/dev/hdc1   1188  18432 20480         326   900  1000
[root@localhost root]# _
```

CHAPTER SUMMARY

❑ Disk devices are represented by device files that reside in the /dev directory. These device files specify the type of data transfer, the major number of the device driver in the Linux kernel, and the minor number of the specific device.

❑ Each disk device must contain a filesystem, which is then mounted to the Linux directory tree for usage using the **mount** command. This filesystem can later be unmounted using the **umount** command. The directory used to mount the device must not be used by any logged in users for mounting and unmounting to take place.

❑ Hard disks must be partitioned into distinct sections before filesystems are created on those partitions. The **fdisk** command can be used to partition a hard disk.

❑ There are many different filesystems available to Linux; each filesystem is specialized for a certain purpose and several different filesystems may be mounted to different mount points on the directory tree. You can create a filesystem on a device using the **mkfs** command and its variants.

❑ It is important to monitor disk usage using the **df**, **du**, and **dumpe2fs** commands to avoid running out of storage space. Similarly, it is important to check disks for errors using the **fsck** command and its variants.

❑ If hard disk space is limited, you can use hard disk quotas to limit the space that each user has on filesystems.

KEY TERMS

/dev directory — The directory off the root where device files are typically stored.

/dev/MAKEDEV — The command used to recreate a device file if one or more of the following pieces of device information is unknown: major number, minor number, or type (character or block).

/etc/fstab — A file used to specify which filesystems to mount automatically at boot time and queried by the mount command if an insufficient number of arguments are specified.

/etc/mtab — A file that stores a list of currently mounted filesystems.

/proc/devices — A file that contains currently used device information.

bad blocks — Those areas of a storage medium unable to store data properly.

block — The unit of data commonly used by filesystem commands; a block may contain several sectors.

6

block devices — Storage devices that transfer data to and from the system in chunks of many data bits by caching the information in RAM; they are represented by block device files.

character devices — Storage devices that transfer data to and from the system one data bit at a time; they are represented by character device files.

cylinder — A series of tracks on a hard disk that are written to simultaneously by the magnetic heads in a hard disk drive.

device file — A file used by Linux commands that represents a specific device on the system; these files do not have a data section and use major and minor numbers to reference the proper driver and specific device on the system, respectively.

df command — A command that displays disk free space by filesystem.

du command — A command that displays directory usage.

edquota command — A command used to specify quota limits for users and groups.

fdisk command — A command used to create, delete, and manipulate partitions on hard disks.

filesystem — The organization imposed on a physical storage medium that is used to manage the storage and retrieval of data.

filesystem corruption — Errors in a filesystem structure that prevent the retrieval of stored data.

formatting — The process where a filesystem is placed on a disk device.

fsck command — A command used to check the integrity of a filesystem and repair damaged files.

fuser command — A command used to identify any users or processes using a particular file or directory.

hard disk quotas — Limits on the number of files, or total storage space on a hard disk drive, available to a user.

hard limit — A limit imposed that cannot be exceeded.

major number — Used by the kernel to identify what device driver to call to interact properly with a given category of hardware; hard disk drives, CD-ROMs, and video cards are all categories of hardware; similar devices share a common major number.

minor number — Used by the kernel to identify which specific hardware device, within a given category, to use a driver to communicate with; *see* **major number**.

mkfs command — A command used to format or create filesystems.

mknod command — A command used to recreate a device file provided the major number, minor number, and type (character or bock) are known.

mount command — A command used to mount filesystems on devices to mount point directories.

mount point — The directory in a file structure to which something is mounted.

mounting — A process used to associate a device with a directory in the logical directory tree such that users may store data on that device.

partition — A physical division of a hard disk drive.

quota command — A command used to view disk quotas imposed on a user.

quotaoff command — A command used to deactivate disk quotas.

quotaon command — A command used to activate disk quotas.

quotas — Limits that may be imposed upon users and groups for filesystem usage.

repquota command — A command used to produce a report on quotas for a particular filesystem.

root filesystem — The filesystem that contains most files that make up the operating system; it should have enough free space to prevent errors and slow performance.

sector — The smallest unit of data storage on a hard disk; sectors are arranged into concentric circles called tracks and may be grouped into blocks for use by the system.

soft limit — A limit imposed that can be exceeded for a certain period of time.

syncing — The process of writing data to the hard disk drive that was stored in RAM.

track — The area on a hard disk that forms a concentric circle of sectors.

tune2fs command — A command used to modify ext2 and ext3 filesystem parameters.

umount command — A command used to break the association between a device and a directory in the logical directory tree.

REVIEW QUESTIONS

1. You can only mount and unmount CD-ROM and floppy disk drives from the command-line. True or False?

2. You find that a device file in the /dev directory has become corrupted. You know that this device is /dev/tty3 and that it is a character device file. What should you do?

   a. Use the fsck command to repair the file.

   b. Use the mknod command to recreate the file.

   c. Use the /dev/MAKEDEV command to recreate the file.

   d. Without the minor number you cannot recreate the file.

3. Once a partition on a hard disk drive is formatted with a filesystem all partitions on that hard disk drive must use the same filesystem. True or False?

4. You wish to see the filesystems that are presently in use on the system. What command could you use?

   a. cat /etc/fstab

   b. type /etc/fstab

   c. ls /etc/fstab

   d. cat /etc/mtab

   e. ls /etc/fstab

5. Entities such as terminals, serial ports, floppy disk drives, and hard disk drives are _____.

   a. things that need to be formatted

   b. represented by a peripheral file in `/dev`

   c. represented by a device file in `/`

   d. represented by a peripheral file in `/root`

   e. represented by a device file in `/dev`

6. All filesystems have a _____.

   a. bad block table that records areas of the physical media that are defective and should not be used to store data

   b. bad block table that records files in the filesystem that have become corrupt and whose data cannot be read

   c. bad block table that is used by `fsck` to record the names of corrupted files it could not repair

   d. bad block table that is used by `fsck` to see what portions of the physical medium it must repair so that it can again be used for file storage

7. Jim has just purchased two new SCSI hard disk drives and a controller card for them. He installs the hardware in his machine properly. Before he can use them for data storage and retrieval what must he do?

   a. Mount the two hard drives so they are accessible by the operating system.

   b. Use Disk Druid to create one or more partitions on each of the hard disk drives.

   c. Mount a filesystem to each of the hard disk drives.

   d. Use the `fdisk` command to create one or more partitions on each of the hard disk drives.

   e. Use the vi editor to edit `/etc/mtab` and create an entry for the controller card and the hard disk drives.

   f. Mount any partitions created on the two hard drives such that they are accessible by the operating system.

   g. Format any partitions created with a valid filesystem recognized by Linux.

6

8. Given the following output from /etc/fstab, which filesystems will be checked automatically on boot by the fsck command?

```
LABEL=/         /              ext3     defaults                 1 1
none            /dev/pts       devpts   gid=5,mode=620           1 0
none            /proc          proc     defaults                 0 1
none            /dev/shm       tmpfs    defaults                 1 0
/dev/hdc2       swap           swap     defaults                 0 1
/dev/cdrom      /mnt/cdrom     iso9660  noauto,owner,kudzu,ro    0 0
/dev/fd0        /mnt/floppy    auto     noauto,owner,kudzu       0 0
```

   a. none; fsck must be run manually

   b. /, /dev/pts, and /dev/shm

   c. /, /proc, and swap

   d. all of them as fsck is run automatically at boot

9. A user mounts a device to a mount point directory and realizes afterwards there are files previously found within the mount point directory that are needed. What should this user do?

   a. The files are lost and cannot ever be accessed.

   b. The files could not have been there as you can only mount to empty directories.

   c. Unmount the device from the directory.

   d. Run the fsck command to recover the files.

   e. Look in the lost+found directory for the file.

10. What command is used to display how much free space exists on a filesystem?

   a. fsck

   b. quota

   c. disk free

   d. diskfree

   e. du

   f. df

11. Character devices transfer data _____.

   a. sector by sector

   b. always in an error-free manner

   c. only between floppy disk drives and hard disk drives

   d. character by character

12. What must you do to run the **fsck** command on a filesystem successfully?

    a. Run the **fsck** command with the **-u** switch to unmount the filesystem automatically first.

    b. When warned that running **fsck** on a mounted filesystem may cause damage and asked if you wish to continue, answer yes.

    c. Unmount the file system.

    d. Ensure that the file system is mounted.

13. Character devices typically transfer data more quickly than block devices. True or False?

14. Jim wants to know the major number for the first floppy disk drive he has attached to his machine. How does he find it?

    a. Display the contents of the file **/dev/fd0** and read the major number from it.

    b. Go to the manufacturer's Web site to locate the driver used for that floppy disk drive.

    c. Use the **ls -l /dev/fd0** command and read the first number in what would normally be the file size column.

    d. Use the **ls -l /dev/fd0** command and read the second number in what would normally be the file size column.

15. What does the **du /var** command do?

    a. shows what users are connected to the **/var** directory

    b. shows the size and contents of the **/var** directory

    c. dumps the **/var** directory

    d. shows the amount of free space in the **/var** directory

16. What does the command **dumpe2fs -h** do?

    a. backs up an ext2 filesystem

    b. displays the number of inodes used and available in an ext2 filesystem

    c. dumps an ext2 filesystem

    d. is not a valid command name

17. In a device file, the minor number points to a specific device on the system and the major number indicates the device driver to be used. True or False?

6

18. The first floppy drive on the system is not responding. You enter the `file` `/dev/fd0` command and receive the output listed below. What is the problem?

    ```
    [root@localhost root]# file /dev/fd0
    /dev/fd0:  ASCII text
    [root@localhost root]#
    ```

    a. The floppy drive cable has come loose.

    b. There is no floppy disk in the drive.

    c. The device file has become corrupted.

    d. The floppy drive is seen as a character device.

19. Which of the following statements is true? (Choose all that apply.)

    a. Quotas may only limit user space.

    b. Quotas may only limit the number of files a user may own.

    c. Quotas may limit both user space and the number of files a user may own.

    d. Hard limits can never be exceeded.

    e. Hard limits allow a user to exceed them for a certain period of time.

    f. Soft limits can never be exceeded.

    g. Soft limits allow a user to exceed them for a certain period of time.

    h. Either a hard limit or a soft limit may be set, but not both concurrently.

20. You attempt to mount a floppy disk drive to the `/home/jim` directory and receive a warning stating the operation cannot be completed. Why?

    a. You can only mount floppy disk drives to `/mnt/floppy`.

    b. The directory `/home/jim` is not empty.

    c. A file in the directory `/home/jim` is being accessed by a user.

    d. The directory `/home/jim` is not formatted with the mnt filesystem.

    e. The directory `/home/jim` must be partitioned.

21. What does the `quota` command do?

    a. when run by a user it shows any quotas applied to them

    b. is used to set and modify quotas

    c. when run by the root user can be used to set and modify quotas

    d. is not a valid Linux command

22. A device file _____. (Choose all that apply.)

    a. has no inode section

    b. has no data section

    c. has no size

    d. displays a major and minor number in place of a file size

    e. has a fixed size of 300 kilobytes

23. If the filesystem type is not specified with the `mkfs` command it
_____.

   a. prompts the user for the file system to use

   b. is not a valid Linux command

   c. uses the ext3 filesystem by default

   d. uses the ext2 filesystem by default

24. Hard disk drives need to be partitioned even if all space on the entire hard drive will be used and configured with one filesystem. True or False?

25. What will be the result if at the command prompt Jim types `mount /mnt/floppy`?

   a. The system will respond with a message prompting for more information.

   b. The system will respond with a message that the command failed due to missing parameters.

   c. The command will succeed because a line with the necessary parameters exists in `/etc/fstab`.

   d. The command will succeed because a line with the necessary parameters exists in `/etc/mtab`.

   e. The command will succeed because a line with the necessary parameters exists in `/dev`.

26. What command will mount all existing filesystems in `/etc/fstab`?

   a. `mount -all`

   b. `mount -a`

   c. `mount /etc/fstab`

   d. `mount /etc/mtab`

27. A user runs the `fsck` command with the `-a` switch on a filesystem that is showing signs of corruption. How would that user locate any files the system was unable to repair?

   a. They would not as the switch used is wrong; it is the `-r` switch not `-a` that is used to repair files automatically with `fsck`.

   b. The system would prompt the user for direction when it comes across a file it cannot repair.

   c. Mount the filesystem and check the `lost+found` directory underneath the mount point.

   d. View the contents of the directory `/lost+found`.

6

28. What command is used to format a partition on a hard disk drive?

   a. `format`

   b. none, since the hard disk drive and not the partition must be formatted

   c. `mkfs  -t type device`

   d. `make FS — type device`

29. You find a floppy disk and wonder what is on it. You mount the device `/dev/fd0` to `/home/jim`. What must you do now?

   a. type `ls fd0`

   b. type `ls mountpoint fd0`

   c. type `ls /home/jim`

   d. type `ls flopper`

30. Given the following output from the `ls` command, what kind of device is fd0?

```
[root@localhost root]# ls -l /dev/fd0 /dev/fd1
crw-rw----    1 root       floppy      2,   0 Aug 30  2001 /dev/fd0
brw-rw----    1 root       floppy      2,   1 Aug 30  2001 /dev/fd1
[root@localhost root]#_
```

   a. fixed

   b. block

   c. character

   d. superblock

31. Which of the following statements is true?

   a. CD-ROM and floppy disk drives can only be mounted from the command-line.

   b. Hard disk drives can only be mounted from the command-line.

   c. When mounting filesystems, the command-line and GUI are equivalent.

   d. Partitions on hard disk drives can only be mounted from the command-line.

HANDS-ON PROJECTS

These projects should be completed in the order given. All hands-on projects should take a total of three hours to complete. The requirements for this lab include:

- ❏ A computer with Red Hat 7.2 installed according to Hands-on Project 3-1
- ❏ A 3 ½ inch floppy disk

Project 6-1

In this hands-on project, you will view and create device files.

1. Turn on your computer. Once your Linux system has been loaded, you will be placed at a graphical terminal (tty7). Switch to a command-line terminal (tty2) by pressing **Ctrl-Alt-F2** and log into the terminal using the username of **root** and the password of **secret**.

2. At the command prompt, type **ls –l /dev/tty6** and press **Enter**. What device does **/dev/tty6** represent? Is this file a block or character device file? Why? What are the major and minor numbers for this file?

3. At the command prompt, type **rm –f /dev/tty6** and press **Enter**. Next, type **ls –l /dev/tty6** at the command prompt and press **Enter**. Was the file removed successfully?

4. Switch to the command-line terminal (tty6) by pressing **Ctrl-Alt-F6** and attempt to log into the terminal using the username of **root** and the password of **secret**. What error message did you receive and why?

5. Switch back to the command-line terminal (tty2) by pressing **Ctrl-Alt-F2**, type the command **mknod /dev/tty6 c 4 6** at the command prompt, and press **Enter**. What did this command do? What other command can be used to do the same function? Next, type **ls –l /dev/tty6** at the command prompt and press **Enter**. Was the file recreated successfully?

6. At the command prompt, type **reboot** and press **Enter**. Once your Linux system has been loaded, switch to a command-line terminal (tty6) by pressing **Ctrl-Alt-F6** and log into the terminal using the username of **root** and the password of **secret**. Why were you successful?

7. At the command prompt, type **ls –l /dev/tty?** and press **Enter**. What is similar between all of these files? Is the major number different for each file? Is the minor number different for each file? Why?

8. At the command prompt, type **find /dev** and press **Enter** to list all of the filenames underneath the **/dev** directory. Are there many files? Next, type **du –s /dev** at the command prompt and press **Enter**. How large in Kilobytes are all files within the **/dev** directory? Why?

9. At the command prompt, type **cat /proc/devices | more** and press **Enter**. Which devices and major numbers are present on your system? What character device has a major number of 4? How does this compare with what you observed in Step 2?

10. Type **exit** and press **Enter** to log out of your shell.

Project 6-2

In this hands-on project, you will create filesystems on floppy disks, mount them to the directory tree, and view their contents.

1. Switch to a command-line terminal (tty2) by pressing **Ctrl-Alt-F2** and log into the terminal using the username of **root** and the password of **secret**.

2. At the command prompt, type **mkdir /mymount** and press **Enter** to create a new mount point directory. Next, type **ls –F /mymount** at the command prompt and press **Enter**. Are there any files in the /mymount directory? Now, type **cp /etc/hosts /mymount** at the command prompt and press **Enter**. Next, type **ls –F /mymount** at the command prompt and press **Enter** to verify that the hosts file was copied successfully.

3. At the command prompt, type **mkfs –t ext2 /dev/fd0** and press **Enter**. What error message did you receive and why? Next, place a floppy disk into the floppy disk drive of your computer, type **mkfs –t ext2 /dev/fd0** at the command prompt and press **Enter**. Was it successful?

4. At the command prompt, type **mount –t ext2 /dev/fd0 /mymount** and press **Enter**. Next, type **mount** at the command prompt and press **Enter**. Was the floppy disk successfully mounted to the /mymount directory?

5. At the command prompt, type **ls -F /mymount** and press **Enter**. What files do you see? Why? What happened to the hosts file? Next, type **cp /etc/ inittab /mymount** at the command prompt and press **Enter**. Did the light on the floppy disk drive of your computer turn on? At the command prompt, type **ls -F /mymount** and press **Enter** to verify that the file was copied to the floppy successfully.

6. At the command prompt, type **umount /mymount** and press **Enter**. Next, type **mount** at the command prompt and press **Enter**. Was the floppy disk successfully unmounted from the /mymount directory?

7. At the command prompt, type **ls -F /mymount** and press **Enter**. What files do you see? Why? What happened to the inittab file and lost+found directory? Is the hosts file present?

8. At the command prompt, type **mount /dev/fd0** and press **Enter**. Next, type **mount** at the command prompt and press **Enter**. To which directory was the floppy disk mounted? Why? At the command prompt, type **cat /etc/fstab** and press **Enter** to justify your answer.

9. At the command prompt, type **cd /mnt/floppy** and press **Enter**. Next, type **pwd** at the command prompt and press **Enter** to verify that the current directory is /mnt/floppy.

10. At the command prompt, type **ls -F** and press **Enter**. What files do you see and why? Next, type **umount /mnt/floppy** at the command prompt and press **Enter**. What error message do you receive and why?

11. At the command prompt, type **fuser –u /mnt/floppy** and press **Enter**. Who is using the /mnt/floppy directory? Next, type **cd** at the command prompt and press **Enter** to return to your home directory. Now, type **umount /mnt/floppy** at the command prompt and press **Enter**. Did you receive an error message? Type **mount** at the command prompt and press **Enter** to verify that the floppy was successfully unmounted from the /mnt/floppy directory.

12. Remove the floppy disk from your computer's floppy disk drive. Keep this floppy disk in a safe place as it will be used in an exercise in a later chapter.

13. Type **exit** and press **Enter** to log out of your shell.

Project 6-3

In this hands–on project, you will mount CD-ROM disks to the directory tree and view their contents.

1. Switch to a command-line terminal (tty2) by pressing **Ctrl–Alt–F2** and log into the terminal using the username of **root** and the password of **secret**.

2. At the command prompt, type **ls –l /dev/cdrom** and press **Enter**. What device file does the /dev/cdrom symbolic link point to?

3. Next, insert the first RedHat 7.2 installation CD-ROM into your computer's CD-ROM drive. At the command prompt, type **mount –r –t iso9660 /dev/cdrom /mymount** and press **Enter**. Next, type **mount** at the command prompt and press **Enter**. Was the CD-ROM disc successfully mounted to the /mymount directory?

4. At the command prompt, type **ls -F /mymount** and press **Enter**. What files do you see? Why? Next, type **cd /mymount/RedHat/RPMS** at the command prompt and press **Enter**. At the command prompt, type **ls -F** and press **Enter** to view some of the software packages used to install your Linux operating system.

5. At the command prompt, type **cd** and press **Enter** to return to your home directory. Next, type **umount /mymount** at the command prompt and press **Enter**. Was the CD-ROM disc successfully unmounted from the /mymount directory? Type the **mount** command at a command prompt and press **Enter** to verify this.

6. At the command prompt, type **mount /dev/cdrom** and press **Enter**. Next, type **mount** at the command prompt and press **Enter**. To which directory was the CD-ROM disc mounted? Why? At the command prompt, type **cat /etc/fstab** and press **Enter** to justify your answer.

7. At the command prompt, type **umount /dev/cdrom** and press **Enter**. Next, type **mount** at the command prompt and press **Enter** to verify that the CD-ROM was unmounted successfully.

8. Eject the CD-ROM disc from the CD-ROM disc drive.

9. Type **exit** and press **Enter** to log out of your shell.

10. Switch to the graphical terminal (tty7) by pressing **Ctrl–Alt–F7** and log into the terminal using the username of **root** and the password of **secret**. What desktop are you using?

11. Next, insert the first Red Hat 7.2 installation CD-ROM in your computer's CD-ROM drive and wait for a few seconds. What happened? Is there a link placed on the desktop for your CD-ROM device?

12. Close the Nautilus file browser. Highlight the icon that represents your CD-ROM device and press the right mouse button. Next, select **Unmount Volume** from the menu. Remove the disk from the disk drive.

13. Press the GNOME button and choose **logout**. When asked to confirm the logout, choose **yes** to log out of your terminal.

Project 6-4

In this hands-on project, you will create a hard disk partition using the `fdisk` utility. Next, you will create an ext2 filesystem on the partition and mount it to the directory tree. Finally, you will convert the filesystem to ext3 and use the `/etc/fstab` file to mount the partition automatically.

1. Switch to a command-line terminal (tty2) by pressing **Ctrl–Alt–F2** and log into the terminal using the username of **root** and the password of **secret**.

2. At the command prompt, type **fdisk /dev/hda** and press **Enter**. At the `fdisk` prompt, type **m** and press **Enter** to view the various fdisk commands.

3. At the `fdisk` prompt, type **p** and press **Enter** to view the partition table on `/dev/hda`. Which two partitions are present? When were they created? What are their types?

4. At the `fdisk` prompt, type **n** and press **Enter** to create a new partition. Next, type **p** to select a primary partition and press **Enter**. When prompted for the partition number, type **3** and press **Enter**. When prompted for the start cylinder, observe the valid range within the brackets and press **Enter** to select the default (the first available cylinder). When prompted for the end cylinder, observe the valid range within the brackets and press **Enter** to select the default (the last available cylinder).

5. At the `fdisk` prompt, type **p** and press **Enter** to view the partition table on `/dev/hda`. How many partitions are present? What is the type of partition `/dev/hda3`?

6. At the `fdisk` prompt, type **l** and press **Enter** to view the different partition types. Which character would one type at the **fdisk** prompt to change the type of partition?

7. At the `fdisk` prompt, type **w** and press **Enter** to save the changes to the hard disk and exit the `fdisk` utility.

8. At the command prompt, type **reboot** and press **Enter** to reboot your machine and ensure that the partition table was read into memory correctly. Once your Linux system has been loaded, switch to a command-line terminal (tty2) by pressing **Ctrl-Alt-F2** and log into the terminal using the username of **root** and the password of **secret**.

9. At the command prompt, type **mkfs –t ext2 /dev/hda3** and press **Enter** to create an ext2 filesystem on the partition created earlier.

10. At the command prompt, type **mkdir /newmount** and press **Enter** to create a mount point directory underneath the / directory for mounting the `/dev/hda3` partition.

11. At the command prompt, type **mount –t ext2 /dev/hda3 /newmount** and press **Enter** to mount `/dev/hda3` to the `/newmount` directory. Next, type the **mount** command and press **Enter** to verify that the filesystem was mounted correctly.

12. At the command prompt, type **ls –F /newmount** and press **Enter**. Is the `lost+found` directory present? Next, type **cp /etc/hosts /newmount** at the command prompt and press **Enter** to copy the `hosts` file to the new partition. Verify that the copy was successful by typing the **ls –F /newmount** command at the command prompt again and pressing **Enter**.

13. At the command prompt, type **umount /newmount** and press **Enter**. Next, type the **mount** command and press **Enter** to verify that the filesystem was unmounted correctly.

14. At the command prompt, type **tune2fs –j /dev/hda3** and press **Enter** to convert the filesystem on `/dev/hda3` to ext3.

15. At the command prompt, type **mount –t ext3 /dev/hda3 /newmount** and press **Enter** to mount `/dev/hda3` to the `/newmount` directory. Next, type the **mount** command and press **Enter** to verify that the filesystem was mounted correctly. Is the type of filesystem recognized as ext3 by the **mount** command?

16. At the command prompt, type **ls –F /newmount** and press **Enter**. Was the `hosts` file copied to the ext2 filesystem earlier preserved? Why?

17. At the command prompt, type **vi /etc/fstab** and press **Enter**. Observe the contents of the file. Add a line to the bottom of the file as follows:

```
/dev/hda3      /newmount     ext3        defaults      0   0
```

18. Save your changes and quit the `vi` editor.

19. At the command prompt, type **reboot** and press **Enter**. Once your Linux system has been loaded, switch to a command-line terminal (tty2) by pressing

Ctrl–Alt–F2 and log into the terminal using the username of **root** and the password of **secret**.

20. At the command prompt, type **mount** and press **Enter**. Is the /dev/hda3 partition mounted? Why?

21. At the command prompt, type **umount /newmount** and press **Enter**. Next, type the **mount** command to verify that the filesystem was unmounted correctly.

22. At the command prompt, type **mount -a** and press **Enter**. Next, type the **mount** command and press **Enter**. Is the /dev/hda3 partition mounted? Why?

23. Type **exit** and press **Enter** to log out of your shell.

Project 6-5

In this hands-on project, you will view disk usage and check filesystems for errors.

1. Switch to a command-line terminal (tty2) by pressing **Ctrl-Alt-F2** and log into the terminal using the username of **root** and the password of **secret**.

2. At the command prompt, type **df** and press **Enter**. What filesystems are displayed? Can you see the swap partition? Why?

3. At the command prompt, type **dumpe2fs –h /dev/hda3** and press **Enter**. How many inodes are available to this filesystem? How many inodes are free to be used? Why?

4. At the command prompt, type **fsck –t ext3 /dev/hda3** and press **Enter**. What error message do you receive and why? Press **n** at the prompt to quit the fsck command.

5. At the command prompt, type **umount /newmount** and press **Enter**. Next, type the **mount** command and press **Enter** to verify that the filesystem was unmounted correctly.

6. At the command prompt, type **fsck –t ext3 /dev/hda3** and press **Enter**. How long did the filesystem check take and why?

7. At the command prompt, type **fsck –f –t ext3 /dev/hda3** and press **Enter**. How long did the filesystem check take and why?

8. At the command prompt, type **fsck –Cf –t ext3 /dev/hda3** and press **Enter**. What does the –C option do when displaying the results to the terminal screen?

9. At the command prompt, type **e2fsck –c /dev/hda3** and press **Enter**. What does this command do?

10. At the command prompt, type **tune2fs –i 0 /dev/hda3** and press **Enter** to change the interval for forced checks such that they are avoided. Is this a good idea for the ext3 filesystem? Why?

11. At the command prompt, type **mount /dev/hda3** and press **Enter**. Next, type the **mount** command and press **Enter** to verify that the filesystem was mounted correctly.

12. Insert the floppy disk used earlier in these hands-on projects into the floppy disk drive of your computer. At the command prompt, type **debugfs –w /dev/fd0** and press **Enter** to enter the filesystem debugger in edit mode.

13. At the **debugfs** prompt, type **mi inittab** to edit the inode of the inittab file on the floppy, and then press **Enter**. When prompted to change the mode of the file, press **Enter**. Repeat this for the User ID, Group ID, and so on until you are prompted to change the Link Count. When prompted to change the Link Count, type **0** and press **Enter** to give an invalid Link Count of **0** to the `hosts` file. Press **Enter** for all remaining choices.

14. Type **q** to quit the `debugfs` command.

15. At the command prompt, type **fsck –f –t ext2 /dev/fd0** and press **Enter**. At each error message, press **y** to allow `fsck` to fix the error. How many errors occurred as a result of one invalid inode?

16. Type **exit** and press **Enter** to log out of your shell.

Project 6-6

In this hands-on project, you will enable, set, and view disk quotas for the `/dev/hda3` filesystem created earlier.

1. Switch to a command-line terminal (tty2) by pressing **Ctrl-Alt-F2** and log into the terminal using the username of **root** and the password of **secret**.

2. At the command prompt, type **chmod 777 /newmount** to give all users the ability to create files within the **/newmount** directory.

3. Switch to a command-line terminal (tty3) by pressing **Ctrl-Alt-F3** and log into the terminal using the username of **user1** and the password of **secret**.

4. At the command prompt, type **touch /newmount/samplefile** to create a file in /newmount that is owned by the user "user1."

5. Type **exit** and press **Enter** to log out of your shell.

6. Switch back to the command-line terminal (tty2) by pressing **Ctrl-Alt-F2**.

7. At the command prompt, type **vi /etc/fstab** and press **Enter**. Observe the options for the /dev/hda3 filesystem. Change the line that mounts /dev/hda3 to the following:

```
/dev/hda3     /newmount     ext3     defaults,usrquota,grpquota     0   0
```

8. Save your changes and quit the **vi** editor.

9. Remount the filesystem as read-write by typing the command **mount /newmount –o remount,rw** and press **Enter**.

10. At the command prompt, type **quotacheck -mavug** and press **Enter**. What does this command do? Next, type **ls –F /newmount** and press **Enter**. What new files exist and why? What are these files used for?

6

11. At the command prompt, type **quotaon /newmount** and press **Enter** to activate quotas on this partition.

12. At the command prompt, type **edquota –u user1** and press **Enter**. Are there any quota limits applied to the user "user1" by default? Change the value of the soft quota for blocks to **50000** and the value of the hard quota for blocks to **60000**. Similarly, change the value of the soft quota for inodes to **300** and the value of the hard quota for inodes to **400**. How many files and directories can "user1" create on this partition? How much space can "user1" use in total on this partition?

13. Save your changes and quit the **vi** editor.

14. At the command prompt, type **edquota –u -t** and press **Enter**. Change the time limit for users who extend the soft limit to **5 days** for both inodes and blocks.

15. Save your changes and quit the **vi** editor.

16. At the command prompt, type **repquota /newmount** and press **Enter**. Are the quota changes you made for the user "user1" visible? How many files has "user1" stored on this volume so far?

17. At the command prompt, type **quota –u user1** and press **Enter**. How do the values compare with those from the previous step?

18. Type **exit** and press **Enter** to log out of your shell.

Discovery Exercises

1. Answer the following questions regarding your system by using the commands listed in this chapter. For each question write the command you used to obtain the answer.

   a. What are the total number of inodes in the root filesystem? How many are currently utilized? How many are available for use?

   b. What filesystems are currently mounted on your system?

   c. What filesystems are available to be mounted on your system?

   d. What filesystems will be mounted automatically at boot time?

2. List the major numbers for the following devices:

   a. fd0
   b. fd1
   c. fd3
   d. hda1
   e. hda2
   f. hda3

g. sda1

h. sda2

i. sda3

How do they compare? Is there a pattern? Why or why not?

3. Provided you have access to a functional Web browser and Internet connection, gather information on four filesystems compatible with Linux. For each filesystem, list the situations for which the filesytem was designed and the key features that the filesystem provides.

4. You have a Linux system that has a 10Gb hard disk drive, which has a 9Gb partition containing an ext3 filesystem mounted to the / directory and a 1Gb swap partition. Currently, this Linux system is only used by a few users for storing small files; however, the department manager wishes to upgrade this system and use it to run a database application that will be used by 100 users. The database application and the associated data will take up over 5Gb of hard disk space. In addition, these 100 users will store their personal files on the hard disk of the system. Each user must have a maximum of 5Gb of storage space. The department manager has made it very clear that this system must not exhibit any downtime as a result of hard disk errors. How much hard disk space will you require and what partitions would you need to ensure that the system will perform as needed? Where would these partitions be mounted? What quotas would you implement? What commands would you need to run and what entries to /etc/fstab would you need to create? Justify your answers.

5. You have several filesystems on your hard disk, which are mounted to separate directories on the Linux directory tree. The /dev/hdc6 filesystem was unable to be mounted at boot time. What could have caused this? What commands could you use to find more information about the nature of the problem?

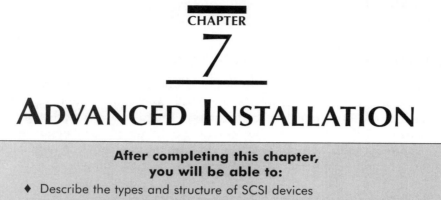

CHAPTER

7

ADVANCED INSTALLATION

**After completing this chapter,
you will be able to:**

♦ Describe the types and structure of SCSI devices

♦ Identify default IRQs, I/O addresses, and DMAs

♦ Explain how Plug-and-Play can be used to assign configuration to
peripheral devices

♦ Install Linux using a text interface

♦ Outline the steps used to install Linux from source files on a hard
disk or network server

♦ Summarize the precautions necessary when installing Linux on
different architectures

♦ Troubleshoot the installation process

A Linux installation is a large and complicated task; it requires a great deal of hardware and software knowledge. In Chapter 3 you examined the installation process using common hardware components and practices. This chapter examines hardware further and emphasizes hardware that is less common and more difficult to configure. In addition, you explore various methods of installing Linux and common installation problems.

ADVANCED HARDWARE CONFIGURATION

Some of the hardware peripherals utilized on your system may require specialized setup and configuration. In Chapter 3, the IDE hard disk drive configuration was emphasized, as it is the most common configuration found in home and office computers today. Chapter 2 also introduced the configuration of peripheral components using IRQs, I/O Addresses, and DMAs. This section explores the configuration of SCSI hard disks, as well as common peripheral configurations seen in most computers.

SCSI Hard Disk Drive Configuration

The Small Computer Systems Interface (SCSI) was designed as a way of connecting multiple peripherals to the system in a scalable, high-speed manner. Recall that a SCSI device is not usually connected directly to the mainboard, but rather to a controller card, which in turn connects all devices attached to it to the mainboard. Disk devices attach to the SCSI controller card via one cable with several connectors for them to plug in to. Information is then sent from device to device along this cable in a daisy-chain fashion. To prevent signals from bouncing back and forth on the cable, each end of the cable must be terminated with a device that stops signals from being perpetuated. This device is called a **terminator**. Typically, one terminator is on the controller card itself, as seen in the top half of Figure 7-1. Systems that have several hard drives attached to one controller, however, typically place the controller in the middle of the daisy-chain, as seen in the bottom half of Figure 7-1.

SCSI disk drives must be configured such that each hard disk drive can be uniquely identified by the system; this is accomplished by assigning a unique ID number known as a **SCSI ID** or **target ID** to each device. Most SCSI controllers today support up to 15 devices and identify these devices with the numbers 0–15 (one number must be reserved for the controller card itself). This SCSI ID also gives priority to the device. The highest priority device is given the number 7, followed by 6, 5, 4, 3, 2, 1, 0, 15, 14, 13, 12, 11, 10, 9, and 8.

Much like IDE hard disks, the SCSI ID of a SCSI hard disk is typically configured using jumper switches on the physical hard drive itself.

Some SCSI devices act as a gateway to other devices; if this is the case, then each device will be associated with a unique **Logical Unit Number (LUN)**.

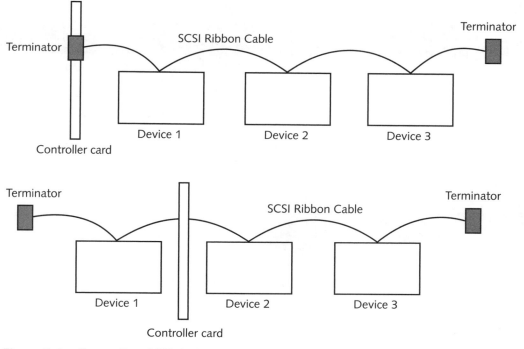

Figure 7-1 Connecting SCSI devices

SCSI technology has evolved over time; it was initially adopted as an industry-defined standard in 1986. At that time, SCSI used an 8-bit wide data path on a controller card that held up to seven devices and had a data transfer speed of 5MB per second. This was commonly referred to as SCSI-1 (SCSI Standard 1). By 1994 it had evolved to a standard that used a 16-bit wide data path on a controller card that could hold up to 15 devices and had a transfer speed of 20MB per second. This advent was referred to as SCSI-2 (SCSI Standard 2). SCSI-3 was introduced a short time later and provided speeds of over 160MB per second. Newer technology today, such as Firewire (IEEE 1394), can transfer data to and from SCSI devices at speeds over 400MB per second. A description of various SCSI technologies can be seen in Table 7-1.

Table 7-1 Common SCSI standards

SCSI TYPE	Speed (MB/s)	Bus Width (bits)	Connector	Number of Devices Supported
SCSI-1 (narrow, slow)	5	8	50-pin Centronics or 50-pin LPT (Line Port Terminal) type	7
SCSI-2 (fast) SCSI-2 (wide)	10 20	8 16	50-pin LPT type 68-pin LPT type	7 15

Table 7-1   Common SCSI standards (continued)

SCSI TYPE	Speed (MB/s)	Bus Width (bits)	Connector	Number of Devices Supported
SCSI-3 (ultra) (ultra2 wide) (ultra3 wide)	40 80 160	16	68-pin LPT type	15

You can identify the type of SCSI device by observing the connector. To identify a SCSI-1 50-pin Centronics or LPT connector, you may compare them to Figures 7-2 and 7-3, respectively.

50 pin Centronics connector used with older 8-bit wide data path devices.
Normally held in place via spring clips

Figure 7-2   A 50-pin Centronics SCSI connector

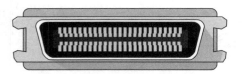

50-pin LPT type connector used
for 8-bit wide data paths

Figure 7-3   A 50 pin LPT SCSI connector

SCSI-2 devices used a 50-pin LPT connector as seen in Figure 7-3; however, later versions of SCSI-2 and SCSI-3 used a 68-pin LPT connector, depicted in Figure 7-4.

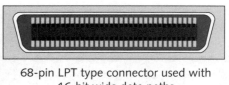

68-pin LPT type connector used with
16-bit wide data paths

Figure 7-4   A 68 pin LPT SCSI connector

Mainboard Flow Control: IRQs, DMAs, and I/O Addresses

Recall from the last section that multiple SCSI devices attached to a single controller card need to be uniquely identified and their requests for service prioritized. The same is true of multiple devices attached to the mainboard via expansion slots. Recall that the unique identifier used with peripheral components is the IRQ.

The processor of a computer executes processes in physical memory for devices. Its time and capacity must be shared among all devices in the computer, which can be accomplished in one of two ways: **polling** or interruption. In the first method, the processor polls system devices to see if there are tasks to be run. Not all devices may have processes to run, and thus the processor wastes time and resources polling them. There is also no efficient way of prioritizing tasks using processor polling. The second method is a more effective way to share processor time; the processor is interrupted by devices only when resources are needed. **Interrupt Requests (IRQs)** are so named because they are used to identify devices and give priorities that are considered when a device needs to access the processor. If two devices require access to the processor at the same time, the one with the lowest IRQ (highest priority) will be attended to first.

Initially, eight IRQs were created to identify and prioritize devices attached to the original ISA slots, which used an 8-bit wide data path and were numbered 0 through 7. The highest priority was given the lowest number, thus a device with an IRQ of 0 would have a higher priority than a device assigned an IRQ of 4. With the evolution of the 16-bit wide ISA expansion slot came the need for eight more IRQs, numerically identified as 8 through 15. Unlike SCSI however, these additional IRQs were not appended to the priority list, but rather squeezed into the middle of the priority sequence between IRQ 2 and IRQ 3. This means that IRQs do not follow a straightforward priority order; while IRQ 10 has higher priority than IRQ 13, IRQ 10 also has a higher priority than IRQ 4. The IRQ priority scheme today is illustrated in Figure 7-5.

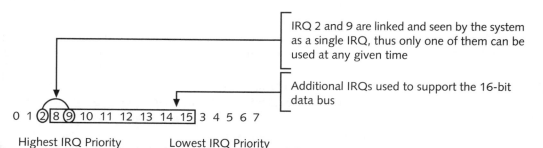

IRQ 2 and 9 are linked and seen by the system as a single IRQ, thus only one of them can be used at any given time

Additional IRQs used to support the 16-bit data bus

0 1 ② 8 ⑨ 10 11 12 13 14 15 3 4 5 6 7

Highest IRQ Priority   Lowest IRQ Priority

Figure 7-5   IRQ Priorities

One consequence of adding the eight additional IRQs is that IRQ 2 and IRQ 9 are linked such that they are seen by the system as a single IRQ; only one or the other may be used at any given time. This means that, though numbered 0 through 15, there are only 15 available IRQs on the system.

While IRQs are used to identify and assign priority sequence to devices, not all 15 IRQs are available, because the system reserves some for certain devices. Before utilizing an IRQ and assigning it to a device it is important to ensure that it is free to use. Assigning the same IRQ to two devices will cause system problems, and neither device may function properly. Table 7-2 outlines common IRQ assignments used on systems today.

Table 7-2   Default IRQ assignments

IRQ	Description
0	System timer
1	Keyboard
2	Linked to IRQ 9—available if 9 not used
3	COM2, COM4
4	COM1, COM3
5	Available (usually for sound card or LPT2)
6	Floppy disk controller
7	Parallel port (LPT1)
8	Real-time clock
9	Linked to IRQ2—available if 2 not used
10	Available
11	Available
12	Available
13	Math co-processor
14	Primary IDE hard disk drive controller
15	Secondary IDE hard disk drive controller

In addition to identification and priority control, each peripheral device needs its own working space in physical memory where it can communicate with other devices. This working space is identified by a hexadecimal number range representing a certain area of RAM and is referred to as an Input/Output (I/O) address. There are many I/O addresses commonly reserved for certain devices on a system; a list of these can be found in Table 7-3. As with IRQs, it is important to ensure that the I/O address of a device has not been assigned to another device or both devices will not function properly.

Table 7-3   Default I/O address assignments

I/O Address	Device
3F8-3FF	COM1
2F8-2FF	COM2
3E8-3EF	COM3
2E8-2EF	COM4

Table 7-3 Default I/O address assignments (continued)

I/O Address	Device
378-37F	LPT1
278-27F	LPT2
000-01F	DMA controller
020-03F	Primary interrupt controller
040-05F	Timer
060-06F	Keyboard
070-07F	Real-time clock
0A0-0BF	Secondary interrupt controller
0F0-0F7	Math co-processor
1F0-1F7	Hard disk
3D0-3DF	VGA
3F0-3F7	Floppy disk controller

7

At minimum, each device must have a unique IRQ and I/O address.

DMA improves efficiency and performance on the system by allowing a device direct access to physical memory via one of a limited number of unique channels. Normally only the processor is allowed direct access to physical memory, and devices must pass all calls to it through the processor. If a device makes great use of physical memory, such as a sound card, the constant load on the processor can impact system performance. Granting such devices direct access to physical memory improves overall system performance; sound cards, network cards, and SCSI disk controllers benefit greatly from DMA channels as they read and write a great deal of data to physical memory.

Again, there is a development history with DMA channels. 8-bit data buses used four DMA channels, which was expanded to eight channels with the introduction of the 16-bit data bus. The fourth DMA channel is unavailable due to the expansion. As with IRQs and I/O addresses, only one device at a time can use a DMA channel, and so DMA assignments should be unique. Table 7-4 details the default DMA channel assignments.

Table 7-4 Default DMA assignments

DMA	Device	Data Path Width
0	Available	8 bits
1	Available	8 bits
2	Floppy disk drive controller	8 bits
3	Available	8 bits

Table 7-4 Default DMA assignments (continued)

DMA	Device	Data Path Width
4	Unavailable—used by DMA itself	16 bits
5	Available	16 bits
6	Available	16 bits
7	Available	16 bits

Plug-and-Play

Assigning each device a unique IRQ and I/O address is a time-consuming and error-prone task to perform manually; for this reason, **Plug-and-Play (PnP)** technology has been introduced. A Plug-and-Play BIOS automatically assigns the necessary configuration information (IRQs, I/O addresses, and DMAs) to devices and avoids conflicts. For Plug-and-Play to work properly, the device and operating system must support it, as well as the computer BIOS.

Plug-and-Play assigns configuration information in a set manner described as follows:

1. A table containing all IRQs, I/O addresses, and DMA channels that are available by default and not used by the system is generated.

2. The system probes all devices connected to it to see if they are PnP capable or not.

3. The system then retrieves a table it stored on a **Complimentary Metal Oxide Semiconductor (CMOS)** memory chip prior to shutdown. This table contains the devices connected to it during the last boot and the IRQ, I/O address, and DMA assignments made. If the list has not changed, the boot process skips the following steps (4–7); if a change is detected, the system continues to Step 4.

4. The system marks any assignments made to non-PnP devices as unavailable in the table created in Step 1.

5. The system checks the BIOS settings to see if any IRQ, I/O address, or DMA settings have been marked as reserved or unavailable and marks them as unavailable in the table created in Step 1.

6. The BIOS then assigns any PnP-capable devices with the necessary configuration information known available from the table updated in Steps 4 and 5.

7. The table of currently connected devices and their settings is stored for use in Step 3 on future start-ups.

RAID Configuration

Recall that you typically create several partitions during installation to decrease the likelihood that the failure of a filesystem on one partition will affect the rest of the system. These partitions should be spread across several different hard disks to minimize the impact of a hard disk failure; if one hard disk fails, then the data on the other hard disks is unaffected.

If a hard disk failure occurs, you must power down the computer, replace the failed hard disk drive, power on the computer, and restore the data that was originally on the hard disk drive from a back-up source such as a tape device. The whole process may take several hours. For systems that must experience little or no downtime, such as a database server, there exist hard disk configurations that reduce the time it takes to recover from a hard disk failure. These configurations are called **fault-tolerant** and are typically implemented by a **Redundant Array of Inexpensive Disks (RAID)**. RAID configurations may be handled by software running on an operating system, but are more commonly handled by the hardware contained within a SCSI hard disk controller.

There are currently seven basic RAID configurations, labeled level 0 through 6. RAID level 0 refers to RAID configurations that are not fault-tolerant. One type of RAID level 0 is referred to as **spanning**, and consists of two hard disks that are seen as one large volume. Thus, if you had two 2GB hard disks, you could create one partition 4GB in size. Another type of RAID level 0 is called **disk striping**. If there are three hard disks in this RAID configuration, then a file that is saved to the hard drive would be divided into three sections, with each section written to each hard disk concurrently; this allows the file to be saved in one third the amount of time. This same file can be read in one third the amount of time for the same reason. Unfortunately, if a hard disk fails in a RAID level 0 configuration, all data is lost.

RAID level 1 is often referred to as **disk mirroring**, and provides fault tolerance in the case of a hard disk failure. In this RAID configuration, the same data is written to two separate hard disks at the same time. This results in two hard disks that have identical information. If one fails, then there is another copy that can replace the failed hard disk in a short period of time. The only drawback to RAID level 1 is the cost involved, as you need to purchase twice the hard disk space needed for a certain computer.

RAID level 2 is no longer used and was a variant of RAID 0 that allowed for error and integrity checking on hard disk drives. Modern hard disk drives do this intrinsically.

RAID level 3 is disk striping with a parity bit, or marker, that indicates what data is where. It requires a minimum of three hard disk drives to function, and one of these hard disks is used to store the parity information. Should one of the hard disks containing data fail, you can replace the hard disk drive and regenerate the data using the parity information stored on the parity disk. If the parity disk fails, then the system must be restored from a back-up device.

RAID level 4 is only a slight variant on RAID level 3. RAID level 4 offers greater access speed than RAID level 3, as it is able to store data in blocks and thus does not need to access all disks in the array at once to read data.

RAID level 5 replaces RAID levels 3 and 4, and is the most common RAID configuration used today. It is commonly referred to as **Disk Striping with Parity**. As with RAID levels 3 and 4, it requires a minimum of three hard disk drives for implementation; however, the parity information is not stored on a separate drive, but intermixed with data on the drives comprising the set. This offers better performance and fault-tolerance; if any drive in the RAID configuration fails, then the information on the other drives may be used to regenerate the lost information once the failed hard disk has been replaced. If two hard disks fail, then the system must be restored from a back-up device. An example of how a RAID level 5 configuration can be restored using parity information is shown in Figure 7-6. The parity bits shown in Figure 7-6 are a sum of the information on the other two disks (22 + 12 = 34). If the third hard disk fails, then the information can be regenerated since only one element is missing from each equation:

$$22 + 12 = 34$$
$$68 - 65 = 3$$
$$13 - 9 = 4$$

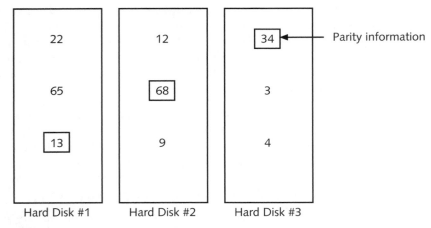

Figure 7-6   Organization of data on RAID Level 5

RAID level 6 is basically the same as RAID level 5, but adds a second set of parity bits for added fault tolerance and allows up to two simultaneous hard disk drive failures while remaining fault tolerant.

RAID levels are often combined; RAID level 15 refers to a Stripe Set with Parity (RAID level 5) that is mirrored (RAID level 1) to another Stripe Set with Parity.

ADVANCED INSTALLATION METHODS

Recall that installing Red Hat Linux graphically using a CD-ROM containing the correct installation files is the most common and easiest method for installing Linux. However, there are other methods for installing Linux, which you will learn about in the following sections. These methods do not use a graphical interface for the installation, and may use a different source for the installation files, such as a **network server** or local hard disk. You may also choose to install Linux on a non–Intel architecture; these installations require different installation media than those used for installation on Intel architectures and involve extra steps.

Text-Based CD-ROM Installation

While it is easy to navigate, the graphical Red Hat Linux installation program is not a full-fledged GUI with the support that X Windows and GUI environments have for hardware. As a result, it may not automatically detect the video card used (especially newer embedded video cards) or may not support certain hardware configurations (such as certain USB mice).

In these situations, you may choose to perform a **text–based installation**, which does not rely on the hardware configuration. This type of installation is much faster, because the **graphical installation** program is not loaded, and the processor does not need to spend time drawing graphics on the screen. Many Linux administrators perform text-based installations for this reason alone.

Recall from Chapter 3 that you may start a CD-ROM installation of Red Hat Linux by booting from the first Red Hat Linux installation CD-ROM or by creating a boot disk, if the CD-ROM is not bootable in your computer configuration. Once the CD–ROM is booted to, you will see the welcome screen depicted in Figure 7-7.

An alternate method for starting the Red Hat Linux installation is to run the `autoboot.bat` file in the `dosutils` folder on the first Red Hat Linux 7.2 installation CD-ROM from the DOS operating system.

As seen in Figure 7-7, you need only to type the word "text" and press Enter at the boot: prompt to start a text-based installation. This will start the installation program in text mode and prompt you for language, keyboard, and mouse settings, as seen in Figures 7-8, 7-9, and 7-10.

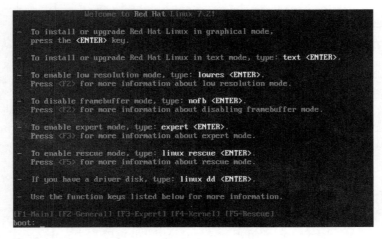

Figure 7-7   Installation welcome screen

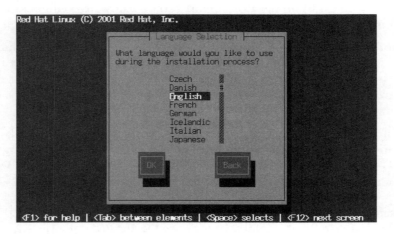

Figure 7-8   Language Selection screen during a text installation

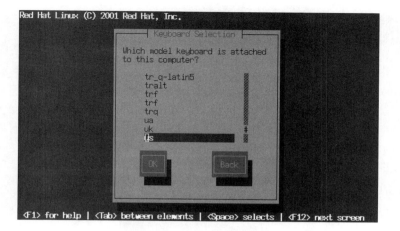

Figure 7-9 Keyboard selection screen during a text installation

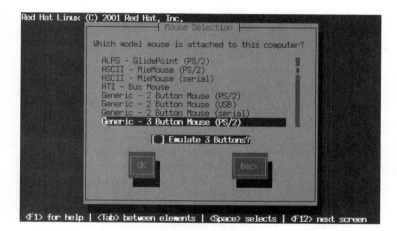

Figure 7-10 Mouse Selection screen during a text installation

The text-based installation does not allow the use of a mouse to maneuver the choices. Instead, you must use the Tab key to change the current position on the screen in order to make choices and use the spacebar to select options. Also, there is no description of the different options on the left-hand side of the screen as with a graphical installation. You must press the F1 function key on the keyboard to obtain help. For all of these reasons, the text-based installation is more difficult to navigate, yet it does prompt you for the same information as the graphical installation. This can be seen when comparing the partition configuration screens from a graphical installation and a text-based installation, as shown in Figures 7-11 and 7-12.

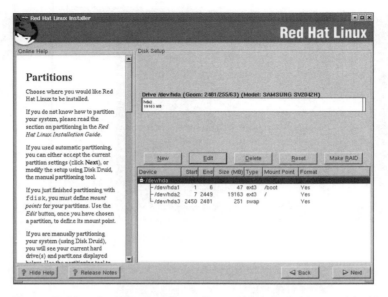

Figure 7-11   Partition configuration screen during a graphical installation

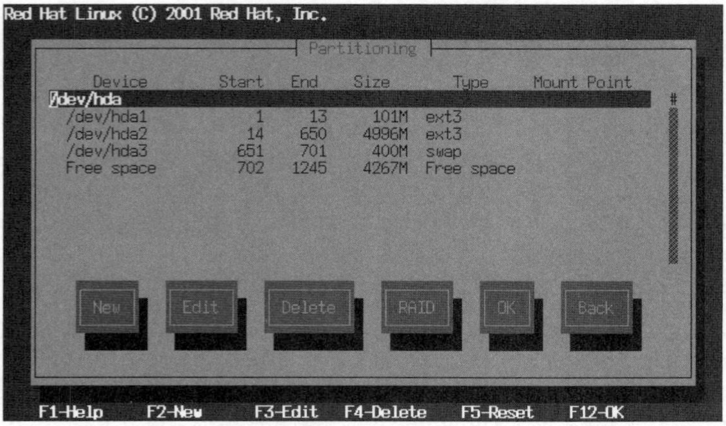

Figure 7-12   Partition configuration screen during a text installation

As seen in Figure 7-12, there are often keyboard function keys listed at the bottom of the screen, which can be used to select certain options. This allows the text-based installation to be navigated easier. (Using only the Tab key to navigate around choices when creating the partitions in Figure 7-12 may take several minutes.) To make navigation even easier, the text-based installation divides the information normally seen on one screen into several smaller screens if there are many choices to navigate. Take, for example, the boot loader configuration during a graphical installation, as shown in Figure 7-13. There are many selections that are well suited to several smaller screens in the absence of precise graphics and a mouse, shown in Figures 7-14, 7-15, 7-16, and 7-17.

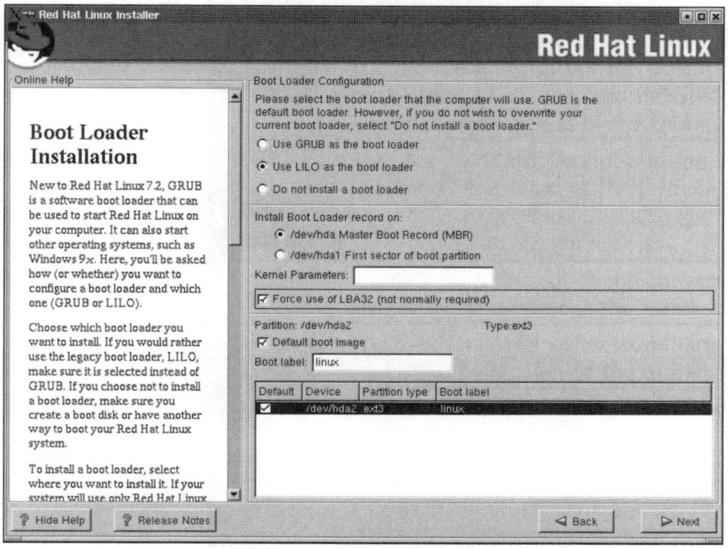

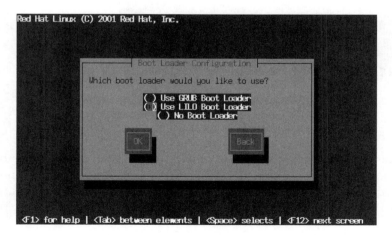

Figure 7-13   Boot loader configuration screen during a graphical installation

Figure 7-14   Choosing a boot loader during a text installation

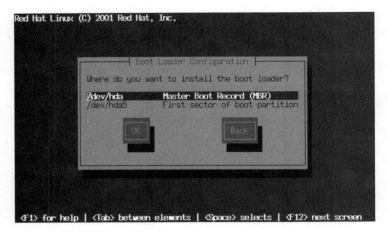

Figure 7-15   Choosing a boot loader location during a text installation

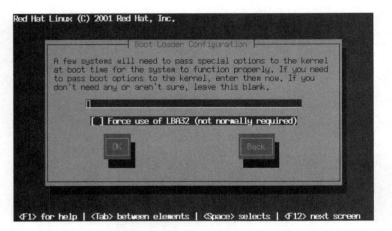

Figure 7-16   Configuring boot kernel parameters during a text installation

Hard Disk Installation

Not everyone installs Linux from CD-ROMs. It is common today to download the Red Hat Linux 7.2 ISO installation images from the Internet. You may use these images in conjunction with a writeable CD drive to create the installation CD-ROMs, yet you may also install directly from the downloaded **ISO images** on the hard disk.

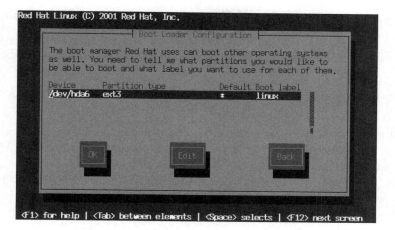

```
Red Hat Linux (C) 2001 Red Hat, Inc.

                        ┤ Boot Loader Configuration ├

     The boot manager Red Hat uses can boot other operating systems
     as well. You need to tell me what partitions you would like to
     be able to boot and what label you want to use for each of them.

     Device    Partition type            Default Boot label
     /dev/hda6  ext3                         *      linux



          ┌─────────┐      ┌─────────┐      ┌─────────┐
          │   OK    │      │  Edit   │      │  Back   │
          └─────────┘      └─────────┘      └─────────┘



  <F1> for help | <Tab> between elements | <Space> selects | <F12> next screen
```

Figure 7-17 Configuring boot labels during a text installation

To obtain the ISO images from the Internet for a Red Hat Linux 7.2 installation, you may visit either *http://www.redhat.com* or *http://www.linuxiso.org*.

Once the ISO images have been copied to the hard disk on a partition that is formatted with either the FAT, ext2, or ext3 filesystem, you may start a text-based installation and specify the target image. Since starting a text-based installation by booting from the first Red Hat Linux installation CD-ROM assumes that the source of files will be from the CD-ROM, you should create an installation floppy boot disk. To create this disk from within the Windows operating system, you may perform the following steps:

1. Insert the first Red Hat 7.2 installation CD-ROM disc into your CD-ROM drive.

2. Double-click **My Computer** and choose your CD-ROM drive (D: for example).

3. Double-click the **dosutils** directory on your first Red Hat 7.2 installation CD-ROM.

4. Double-click the **rawrite** program to execute it. When prompted for the source image file, type **D:\images\boot.img** (if D: is your CD-ROM drive in Windows) and press **Enter**. When prompted for the destination drive, place a blank, formatted floppy disk in your floppy drive, type **A:** and press **Enter**.

Alternatively, you may create this boot disk from within Linux using the following steps:

1. Insert the first Red Hat 7.2 installation CD-ROM disc into your CD-ROM drive.

2. Type **mount −r −t iso9660 /dev/cdrom /mnt/cdrom** at the command prompt to mount the CD-ROM and press **Enter**.

3. Type **cd /mnt/cdrom/images** at the command prompt and press **Enter**.

4. Insert a blank, formatted floppy disk in your floppy drive, type **dd if=boot.img of=/dev/fd0 bs=1440K** at the command prompt, and press **Enter** to image the **boot.img** file to the floppy disk.

Next, you boot from the installation boot floppy. When presented with the screen seen in Figure 7-7, press Enter. Without a Red Hat 7.2 installation CD-ROM in the CD-ROM drive of the computer, a text-based installation will begin and prompt you for the language and keyboard information seen in Figures 7-18 and Figure 7-19, respectively. Next, the installation program will prompt for whether to install from a local CD-ROM or partition on the hard disk, as seen in Figure 7-20.

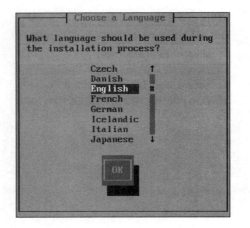

Figure 7-18   Language Selection during a text installation from an installation boot floppy disk

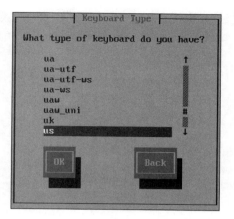

Figure 7-19   Keyboard Selection during a text installation using an installation boot floppy

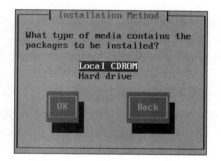

Figure 7-20   Selecting a method of installation during a text installation using an installation boot floppy disk

After choosing to install from the hard disk, the installation prompts you for the partition and directory that contains the ISO images of the Red Hat Linux installation media. Once the correct information has been specified, the text-based installation proceeds normally and you are prompted for the information required to complete the installation.

Network-Based Installations

Although less common than CD-ROM or hard disk installations, you may also choose to use installation media that is stored on another machine and accessible across a network via a Network Interface Card (NIC) in the computer. For this method of installation, you must create a **network installation** boot floppy and use it to start the installation program. The network installation boot floppy contains common NIC drivers and allows you to connect to a server with the appropriate installation files via one of the following protocols:

- NFS
- FTP
- HTTP

Linux may also be installed across the network from a Windows server hosting the installation files. This method uses the Server Message Blocks (SMB) protocol and must be set up manually in Red Hat Linux; as a result, we will not discuss this method here.

Network Installations Using NFS

Network File System (NFS) allows UNIX and Linux computers to share files transparently. In NFS one computer shares a certain directory in the directory tree (a process called exporting) by placing the name of that directory in the `/etc/exports` file, and the other computer may access that directory across the network by using the mount command to mount the remote directory on the local computer. An example of the syntax for the mount command to do this is:

```
mount -t nfs remotecomputename:/exporteddirectoryname /localmountpoint
```

Thus, you may export a directory that contains the installation files for Red Hat Linux 7.2 and use the network installation boot floppy disk to access those files in the same manner. When using the network installation boot floppy disk to gain access to the installation files, you must specify the remote computer name (or IP address), as well as the name of the directory on the machine that contains the installation files. The installation program will perform the aforementioned `mount` command in the background to complete the installation. Installation using an NFS exported directory from a remote computer is the fastest type of network installation of Linux and is relatively easy to configure. To configure the NFS server that will host the installation files for other computers to install from using Red Hat 7.2, you may perform the following steps:

1. Create a directory that will host the installation files by typing **mkdir /source** at the command prompt and pressing **Enter**. (*Note*: The name of the directory is arbitrary, but you should write it down, as it will need to be specified during the installation.)

2. Insert the first Red Hat Linux 7.2 installation CD-ROM disc into the CD-ROM drive of the NFS server.

3. Mount the CD-ROM by typing **mount -r -t iso9660 /dev/cdrom /mnt/cdrom** at the command prompt and pressing **Enter**.

4. Type **cp —r /mnt/cdrom/RedHat /source** at the command prompt and press **Enter**. This will copy the Red Hat directory and its contents to the /source directory.

5. Next, type **umount /mnt/cdrom** to unmount the first Red Hat Linux 7.2 installation CD-ROM from the /mnt/cdrom directory.

6. Insert the second Red Hat 7.2 installation CD-ROM disc into the CD-ROM drive of the NFS server.

7. Mount the CD-ROM by typing **mount —r —t iso9660 /dev/cdrom /mnt/cdrom** at the command prompt and pressing **Enter**.

8. Type **cp —r /mnt/cdrom/RedHat /source** at the command prompt and press **Enter**. This will copy the Red Hat directory and its contents to the /source directory.

9. Next, type **umount /mnt/cdrom** to unmount the second Red Hat Linux 7.2 installation CD-ROM from the /mnt/cdrom directory.

10. Next, edit the **/etc/exports** file and add a single line:

    /source

    Save your changes to the file and return to the command prompt.

11. Restart the NFS processes by typing the following commands at the command prompt and pressing **Enter**:

    /etc/rc.d/init.d/nfs restart
    /etc/rc.d/init.d/nfslock restart

 There may be additional steps to perform if packet filtering, firewalls, or other network security processes have been enabled on the NFS server.

Network Installations Using FTP

The most common protocol used to transfer files on networks today is the **File Transfer Protocol (FTP)**. Most operating systems come with an FTP client program, which can connect to an FTP server that hosts directories of files for users to download to their computers. FTP hosts files differently than NFS does; a special directory may be made available to any user who wishes to connect (called anonymous access), or users may be connected to their home directory on the FTP server, provided they enter a valid username and password in the FTP client program. You may use either method during a Red Hat Linux 7.2 installation to connect to an FTP server. Simply specify the name or IP address of the FTP server as well as the subdirectory underneath the anonymous directory or home directory that contains the appropriate installation files.

To configure the FTP server that will host the installation files for other computers to install from using Red Hat 7.2 (provided they log in as the user "user1" with a valid password), you may perform the following steps:

1. Create a directory underneath a sample user's home directory that will host the installation files by typing **mkdir /home/user1/source** at the command prompt and pressing **Enter**. (*Note*: As with the NFS installation, the name of the directory is arbitrary and will need to be specified during the installation.)

2. Insert the first Red Hat 7.2 installation CD-ROM into the CD-ROM drive of the FTP server.

3. Mount the CD-ROM by typing **mount −r −t iso9660 /dev/cdrom /mnt/cdrom** at the command prompt and pressing **Enter**.

4. Type **cp −r /mnt/cdrom/RedHat /home/user1/source** at the command prompt and press **Enter**. This will copy the Red Hat directory and its contents to the **/home/user1/source** directory.

5. Next, type **umount /mnt/cdrom** to unmount the first Red Hat Linux 7.2 installation CD-ROM from the **/mnt/cdrom** directory.

6. Insert the second Red Hat 7.2 installation CD-ROM into the CD-ROM drive of the FTP server.

7. Mount the CD-ROM by typing **mount −r −t iso9660 /dev/cdrom /mnt/cdrom** at the command prompt and pressing **Enter**.

8. Type **cp −r /mnt/cdrom/RedHat /home/user1/source** at the command prompt and press **Enter**. This will copy the Red Hat directory and its contents to the **/home/user1/source** directory.

9. Next, type **umount /mnt/cdrom** to unmount the second Red Hat Linux 7.2 installation CD-ROM from the **/mnt/cdrom** directory.

10. Change the ownership of the **/home/user1/source** directory to "user1" recursively by typing the command **chown −R user1 /home/user1/source** at the command prompt and pressing **Enter**.

11. Next, edit the **/etc/xinetd.d/wu-ftpd** file and change the line:

    disable = yes

    such that it reads:

    disable = no

    Save your changes to the file and return to the command prompt.

12. Restart the xinetd process, which allows for FTP sessions, by typing the following command at the command prompt and pressing **Enter**:

    /etc/rc.d/init.d/xinetd restart

Network Installations Using HTTP

If NFS and FTP are not available on the network, then installation from a Web server on the network using the **Hyper Text Transfer Protocol (HTTP)** is an alternative. Recall that Web servers hand out HTML files and other Web content from a specific directory in the directory tree. If you create a subdirectory under this directory that contains the Red Hat Linux 7.2 installation files, you may specify this directory along with the IP address or name of the Web server during installation.

To configure the Apache Web server to host the installation files for other computers to install from using Red Hat 7.2, you may perform the following steps:

1. Create a directory underneath the Web content directory that will host the installation files by typing **mkdir /var/www/html/source** at the command prompt and pressing **Enter**. (*Note*: As with the NFS and FTP installations, the name of the directory is arbitrary and will need to be specified during the installation.)

2. Insert the first Red Hat 7.2 installation CD-ROM into the CD-ROM drive of the Web server.

3. Mount the CD-ROM by typing **mount -r -t iso9660 /dev/cdrom /mnt/cdrom** at the command prompt and pressing **Enter**.

4. Type **cp -r /mnt/cdrom/RedHat /var/www/html/source** at the command prompt and press **Enter**. This will copy the Red Hat directory and its contents to the **/var/www/html/source** directory.

5. Next, type **umount /mnt/cdrom** to unmount the first Red Hat Linux 7.2 installation CD-ROM from the **/mnt/cdrom** directory.

6. Insert the second Red Hat 7.2 installation CD-ROM into the CD-ROM drive of the Web server.

7. Mount the CD-ROM by typing **mount -r -t iso9660 /dev/cdrom /mnt/cdrom** at the command prompt and pressing **Enter**.

8. Type **cp -r /mnt/cdrom/RedHat /var/www/html/source** at the command prompt and press **Enter**. This will copy the Red Hat directory and its contents to the **/var/www/html/source** directory.

9. Next, type **umount /mnt/cdrom** to unmount the second Red Hat Linux 7.2 installation CD-ROM from the **/mnt/cdrom** directory.

10. Start the Apache Web server by typing the following command at the command prompt and pressing **Enter**:

    ```
    /etc/rc.d/init.d/httpd start
    ```

Installations from Network Clients

To start any of these network-based installations from a client computer, you must create a network installation boot floppy disk. To create this disk from a Windows operating system you may perform the following steps:

1. Insert the first Red Hat 7.2 installation CD-ROM into your CD-ROM drive.

2. Double-click **My Computer** and choose your CD-ROM drive (D: for example).

3. Double-click the **dosutils** directory on your first Red Hat 7.2 installation CD-ROM.

4. Double-click the **rawrite** program to execute it. When prompted for the source image file, type **D:\images\bootnet.img** (if D: is your CD-ROM drive in Windows) and press **Enter**. When prompted for the destination drive, place a blank, formatted floppy disk in your floppy drive, type **A:** and press **Enter**.

As discussed previously, you may also use Linux to create this boot disk using the following steps:

1. Insert the first Red Hat 7.2 installation CD-ROM into your CD-ROM drive.

2. Mount the CD-ROM by typing **mount −r −t iso9660 /dev/cdrom /mnt/cdrom** at the command prompt and pressing **Enter**.

3. Type **cd /mnt/cdrom/images** at the command prompt and press **Enter**.

4. Insert a blank, formatted floppy disk in your floppy drive, type **dd if=bootnet.img of=/dev/fd0 bs=1440K** at the command prompt, and press **Enter** to image the **bootnet.img** file to the floppy disk.

Once the floppy has been created, you may simply boot the client computer using it and press Enter at the screen shown previously in Figure 7-7. After the text-based installation program has loaded, you are then prompted to choose the language and keyboard type as with the hard disk installation discussed earlier and depicted in Figure 7-18 and Figure 7-19. Next, you are prompted to choose the type of network installation, as seen in Figure 7-21.

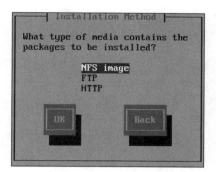

Figure 7-21   Choosing a network installation type during a text installation using a network installation boot floppy

Regardless of the installation type chosen in Figure 7–21, you are then prompted to configure the network settings, as seen in Figure 7–22.

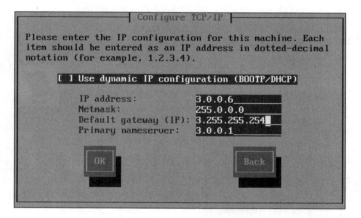

Figure 7-22   Configuring network settings during a text installation using a network installation boot floppy disk

The values for the IP address and subnet mask are typically assigned by the Internet Service Provider (ISP) or the network administrator, so that the computer using the IP address can communicate with the correct set of machines on the network. You may, however, choose to receive the configuration from a DHCP or BOOTP server on the network automatically. The default gateway and the Primary DNS name server are optional if configuring manually, but should be used if the values are known.

If you chose an NFS installation, then the installation will prompt for the DNS name or IP address of the NFS server on the network and the exported directory. These selections are depicted in Figure 7–23 using the exported /source directory from the steps discussed earlier to set up an NFS server.

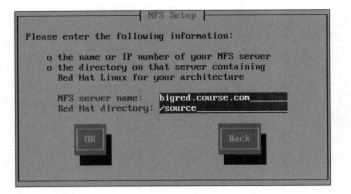

Figure 7-23   Entering NFS configuration during a text installation from a network installation boot floppy disk

Alternatively, if you chose to perform an FTP installation, then you will be prompted to enter the type of FTP installation (anonymous or user) as well as the DNS name or IP address of the FTP server. Figure 7-24 displays the choices that you would choose given the FTP configuration discussed earlier; you will be prompted to log in as the user "user1" with a valid password. The directory specified must be the directory underneath the /home/user1 directory and contain the Red Hat directory from the installation CD-ROMs.

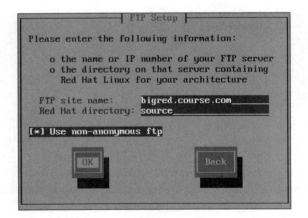

Figure 7-24   Entering FTP configuration during a text installation from a network installation boot floppy disk

Like an FTP installation, an HTTP installation requires the DNS name or IP address of the Web server as well as the name the directory underneath the Web server content directory (/var/www/html by default) that contains the Red Hat directory from the installation CD-ROMs, as seen in Figure 7-25.

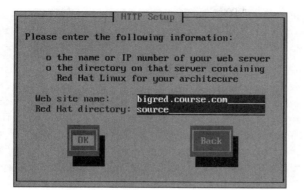

Figure 7-25   Enter HTTP configuration during a text installation from a network
installation boot floppy disk

Once the source has been chosen, the installation proceeds in the same fashion as a text-
based installation and the user is prompted for the information necessary to complete
the process.

Installing Linux on Non-Intel Architectures

Although Linux is commonly installed on the 32-bit Intel architecture, recall that an
advantage of Linux over other operating systems is its support for a multitude of different hardware architectures. Most large companies purchase expensive and powerful non-
Intel servers for hosting databases and custom software; once this equipment has
depreciated, it is typically replaced by newer servers since the reliability of any hardware
decreases with age. This may result in a large number of unused servers. For these servers,
installing Linux will be a cost-effective way of putting them back into production to
serve a useful, yet non-mission-critical, purpose. Some common roles for older hardware
that can be achieved by installing Linux include but are not limited to:

- DHCP servers
- DNS servers
- File & print servers
- E-mail servers
- Web servers
- Routers
- Firewalls
- News servers

Although Linux may allow the re-use of older hardware, most companies place Linux on new, non-Intel hardware to perform large, mission-critical, and calculation-intensive tasks; many companies have replaced their UNIX servers with Linux servers as a result.

To install Linux on a non-Intel architecture, you must obtain the correct installation media for the architecture as well as understand the structure of the architecture and the specifics of the hardware inside the computer. In addition to this, you should thoroughly research the Linux installation method for the architecture and any problems that others have encountered. This information is available on the Internet; often there are Web sites and newsgroups geared specifically towards using Linux on a particular hardware architecture. A list of some architectures and Web sites that host installation information is seen in Table 7-5.

Table 7-5   Internet installation resources for different architectures

Architecture	Web Sites
SPARC/UltraSPARC	*http://www.ultralinux.org* *http://www.sun.com/software/linux*
Alpha	*http://www.linuxalpha.org* *http://www.compaq.com* *http://www.unix-ag.org/Linux-Alpha/*
Power PC	*http://www.yellowdoglinux.com* *http://penguinppc.org*
s390 (Mainframe)	*http://linux.s390.org* *http://www.s390.ibm.com/linux/*
Itanium (Intel 64-bit)	*http://www.linuxia64.org*

Once started, the Red Hat Linux installation program for different architectures involves many of the same steps. Differences are typically minor, for example, the boot loader used for SPARC architectures is called **SILO** and the boot loader used for Alpha architectures is called **ABOOT**, which will be reflected during the "Boot Loader Configuration" screen of the installation.

By far, the largest difference encountered when installing Linux on different architectures is the method used to start the installation itself. Take, for example, the Alpha architecture that boots to a blue SRM (System Reference Manual) console from which you may choose to boot an operating system or perform maintenance tasks on the hardware. The Alpha SRM console provides you with a prompt, such as P00>>> (indicating that the current processor is the first one), and allows you to enter in commands. To start the Linux installation, you must understand the devices in the computer and their respective names inside the SRM console, as well as the commands used at the SRM console to start the Red Hat Linux installation. This information may be found by visiting the Web sites listed in Table 7-5.

Some common Alpha device names are seen in Table 7-6.

Table 7-6 Common Alpha device labels

Device Label	Type of Device
dr	RAID device
dv	Floppy device
ew or ei	Ethernet device
pk	SCSI controller
dk	SCSI disk
mk	SCSI tape

In addition to the device labels seen in Table 7-6, each device name has the number of the controller it is attached to (a = first controller, b = second controller, c = third controller, etc.) and the device number (0 = first device on the controller, 1 = second device on the controller, etc.) appended to the label. Thus, to represent the first floppy device on the first floppy controller on an Alpha SRM console, you could use the name **dva0**; Linux refers to the same device in a comparable fashion as **/dev/fd0**. Similarly, to represent the first SCSI hard disk on the first SCSI controller on an Alpha SRM console, you would use the name **dka0**, which is analogous to **/dev/sda** in Linux.

To view the devices present on the Alpha system, you may enter the **show dev** command at the SRM console prompt, as seen below:

```
P00>>>
P00>>> show dev
polling ncr0 (NCR 53C810) slot 1, bus 0 PCI, hose 1 SCSI
Bus ID 7
dka500.5.0.1.1  DKA500    RRD46 1337
polling isp0 (Qlogic ISP10X0) slot 2, bus 0 PCI, hose 1
SCSI Bus ID 7
dkb0.0.0.2.1    DKB0      RZ1CB-CA  LYJ0
polling floppy0 (FLOPPY) PCEB-XBUS hose 0
dva0.0.0.1000.0 DVA0      RX23
polling tulip0 (DE500-BA) slot 3, bus 0 PCI, hose 0
ewa0.0.0.3.0    00-00-F8-08-F4-60 Twisted-Pair
P00>>>
```

Notice in the above output that there are two SCSI devices (**dka500** and **dkb0**), which are attached to different controllers. If the **dka500** device (attached to the NCR controller) represents the SCSI CD-ROM in the computer, you may start a Red Hat Linux installation by inserting the first Red Hat Linux installation CD-ROM for the Alpha architecture into the CD-ROM drive of the computer and entering the following command at the SRM prompt to boot from the **dka500** device:

```
P00>>> boot dka500 -fl 0
```

The previous command will allow the Alpha computer to boot the installation program from the first Red Hat Linux installation CD-ROM, resulting in the output seen in Figure 7–26.

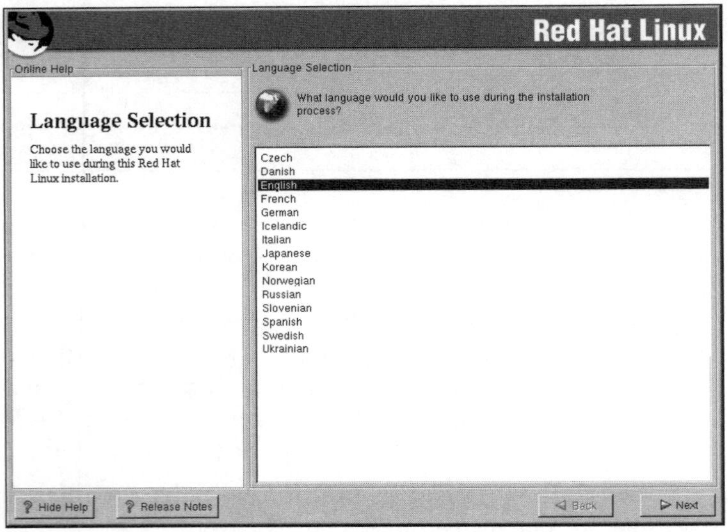

Figure 7-26 Language Selection screen after starting an installation of Linux on the Alpha architecture

Once the installation program has finished, the computer will be automatically set to boot to Linux, and the device names used at the SRM console will no longer be necessary as they are replaced with the associated Linux device names while the Linux operating system is running.

TROUBLESHOOTING INSTALLATION

Computers today typically have different hardware BIOS configurations, and installation on different computers is almost never the same. As a result, you may encounter problems while installing Linux on one computer but not another. These problems are almost entirely related to hardware support or configuration, and are typically fixed with a change to the hardware configuration of the system. Furthermore, you may divide these problems into three categories, based on when they occur:

- Problems starting the installation
- Problems during installation
- Problems after installation

Problems Starting the Installation

You will typically start a Linux installation by booting from a CD-ROM that contains the appropriate installation files, or a floppy, which may then connect to a CD-ROM, hard disk, or network server to get the installation files. For this to occur, you must ensure that the boot order located in the BIOS is set to look for an operating system on the floppy or CD-ROM before it looks to the hard disk. The BIOSes on different computers may be radically different; some BIOSes have sections labeled First Boot Device, Second Boot Device, and Third Boot Device, while others have a section labeled Boot Order. To ensure that you are changing the correct setting, consult the user's manual for your mainboard.

Recall that BIOS settings are stored in a CMOS memory chip on the computer, which is given a continuous supply of power via a small lithium battery attached to the mainboard. If this battery dies, then any changes to the BIOS settings will be lost and default values will be loaded. When this occurs, the system will warn you upon system startup with a message similar to "BIOS Error – Defaults Loaded – Press F1 to continue." In this case, the battery will need to be replaced before the boot order is changed; otherwise the setting will be lost once the computer is powered off.

Even if the boot order in the BIOS specifies booting from the CD-ROM before the hard disk, there are some older CD-ROM devices that will not boot the installation program. In this case, you will need to create a floppy boot disk from the **boot.img** file discussed earlier.

While checking the BIOS for the boot order, it is good practice also to check the BIOS for any reserved peripheral configuration (IRQ, I/O address, DMA). Recall that most devices on systems today are Plug-and-Play and receive their configuration from the BIOS of the system. Some older ISA devices must have this information configured statically, thus there exists the possibility that Plug-and-Play will assign a configuration that is already in use by an older ISA device. If there are ISA devices in the computer that are statically configured in this manner, you must ensure that their configuration is reserved in the BIOS such that it is not available to be assigned by Plug-and-Play.

Problems During Installation

Once the installation program has loaded, you are prompted for the method of installation. For those who install Linux graphically, the installation program must first detect the video card and mouse in the computer and load the appropriate drivers into memory. If, after the initial welcome screen, the graphical installation screens do not appear or appear as scrambled lines across the computer screen, then the video card is likely not supported by the mode and resolution of the graphical installation. To solve this, you should restart the installation, and at the initial welcome screen either type **nofb** and press Enter to start the installation without framebuffer support, or type **lowres** and press Enter to start the installation with a resolution of 640×480.

7

If the graphical installation does start successfully but the mouse does not work, then an alternative is to start a text-based installation; simply restart the installation, type `text`, and press Enter at the initial welcome screen.

On some older systems, the computer may freeze randomly during the installation; this is a result of improper device communication. To fix this, simply restart the computer and disable Plug-and-Play support in the BIOS of the computer prior to installation. Once the installation has completed, Plug-and-Play support may be enabled again in the BIOS.

Sometimes an installation ends abnormally and the screen displays a "fatal signal 11" error message. This indicates an error known as a segmentation fault; it means that a program accessed a certain area of RAM that was not assigned. While this may be a problem with software, during installation it is likely a hardware problem. Unfortunately, this hardware problem could be almost anywhere in the computer, but is likely an error with the RAM memory itself. Often, this error may be fixed by turning off the CPU cache memory or increasing the number of wait states in the BIOS. If the memory is too slow for the mainboard (i.e., the memory is 70ns RAM and the mainboard requires 60ns RAM), then the RAM in the computer should be replaced. Some BIOSes allow the user to change the voltage for the RAM and CPU; incorrect values may cause a "fatal signal 11" error, as well. Other causes include bad memory chips, an AMD K6 processor, laptop power management conflicts, and overclocked CPUs.

An **overclocked** CPU is a CPU that has a speed greater than the speed originally intended for the processor. Although this may lead to increased performance, it also produces more heat on the processor and may result in intermittent computer crashes.

If the installation fails with an error other than fatal signal 11, you should consult the support documentation on the Internet at *http://www.redhat.com*. Also, certain hardware, such as Winmodems, are not compatible with Linux; ensure that all hardware is listed on the Hardware Compatibility List prior to installation.

Some installations fail to place a boot loader on the hard disk properly; this is often the case with large hard disk drives that have over 1024 cylinders. To avoid this problem, ensure that the / partition starts before the 1024th cylinder (usually the 8GB mark on most hard disks) or create a partition for the `/boot` directory that starts before the 1024th cylinder.

Problems After Installation

Although a Red Hat Linux installation may finish successfully, you may still have problems if the installation program did not detect the hardware in the computer properly or certain programs failed to be installed. As a result, it is good form to check the **installation log file** `/tmp/install.log` after installation to see whether any applications failed to install, as well as to verify settings on the system after installation to ensure that all hardware was detected with the correct values. You may verify hardware settings by examining the content of the /proc directory or bootup log files.

The /proc directory is mounted to a special filesystem contained within RAM, which lists system information made available by the Linux kernel. Since this is an administrative filesystem, all files within it are readable only by the "root" user. A listing of the /proc directory will show the following file and subdirectory contents:

```
[root@localhost root]# ls -F /proc
1/     1184/ 184/   647/ 924/   driver/      irq/      misc        slabinfo
1012/  1185/ 185/   667/ 965/   execdomains  isapnp    modules     stat
1030/  1186/ 2/     695/ 993/   fb           kcore     mounts      swaps
1114/  1193/ 23195/ 7/   apm    filesystems  kmsg      mtrr        sys/
1150/  1194/ 3/     8/   bus/   fs/          ksyms     net/        sysvipc/
1180/  1199/ 4/     807/ cmdline ide/        loadavg   partitions  tty/
1181/  1200/ 5/     88/  cpuinfo interrupts  locks     pci         uptime
1182/  1201/ 6/     891/ devices iomem       mdstat    scsi        version
1183/  13/   642/   9/   dma    ioports      meminfo   self@
[root@localhost root]#_
```

The subdirectories that start with a number in the above output are used to display process information; other directories may contain kernel parameters. The files listed in the above output are text representations of various parts of the Linux system; they are updated regularly by the Linux kernel and can be viewed using standard text commands such as **cat** or **more**.

To view the information that Linux has detected regarding the CPU in the computer, simply view the contents of the cpuinfo file in the /proc directory:

```
[root@localhost root]# cat /proc/cpuinfo
processor       : 0
vendor_id       : GenuineIntel
cpu family      : 6
model           : 6
model name      : Celeron (Mendocino)
stepping        : 0
cpu MHz         : 367.507
cache size      : 128 KB
fdiv_bug        : no
hlt_bug         : no
f00f_bug        : no
coma_bug        : no
fpu             : yes
fpu_exception   : yes
cpuid level     : 2
wp              : yes
flags           : fpu vme de pse tsc msr pae mce cx8 sep
                  mtrr pge mca cmov pat pse36 mmx fxsr
```

```
bogomips        : 734.00
[root@localhost root]#_
```

The above output indicates that there is only one processor, which runs at 366MHz (approximately) and has 128Kb of processor cache. If, for example, the computer in actuality has two processors instead of one, then Linux has failed to detect the second processor. In this case, you may need to change a setting in BIOS or research a solution to the problem on the mainboard or processor manufacturer's Web site.

It is also important to ensure that Linux has detected the correct amount of RAM in the system after installation. To do this, you may view the contents of the /proc/meminfo file, as seen below:

```
[root@localhost root]# cat /proc/meminfo
total:      used:      free:   shared: buffers:   cached:
Mem:   393695232 85921792 307773440    196608 12222464 35864576
Swap: 419479552         0 419479552
MemTotal:      384468 kB
MemFree:       300560 kB
MemShared:        192 kB
Buffers:        11936 kB
Cached:         35024 kB
SwapCached:         0 kB
Active:         14764 kB
Inact_dirty:    32388 kB
Inact_clean:        0 kB
Inact_target:    1548 kB
HighTotal:          0 kB
HighFree:           0 kB
LowTotal:      384468 kB
LowFree:       300560 kB
SwapTotal:     409648 kB
SwapFree:      409648 kB
NrSwapPages:   102412 pages
[root@localhost root]# _
```

In the above output the total amount of memory detected by the Linux operating system (MemTotal) is 384468KB or 384MB. If this value is incorrect, you may also specify the correct values to the kernel by adding the line append"mem=512M" to the file /etc/lilo.conf file if the boot loader used is **LInux LOader (LILO)**, or the /boot/grub/grub.conf file if the boot loader used is **Grand Unified Bootloader (GRUB)**. Boot loaders and the append keyword will be discussed further in Chapter 8.

Likewise, to ensure that the IRQs, DMAs, and I/O ports are recognized at the correct values, you could view the dma, interrupts, and ioports files in the /proc directory, as seen below:

```
[root@localhost root]# cat /proc/dma
 1: SoundBlaster8
 2: floppy
```

```
    4: cascade
    5: SoundBlaster16
[root@localhost root]# cat /proc/interrupts
CPU0
    0:       20421          XT-PIC   timer
    1:         393          XT-PIC   keyboard
    2:           0          XT-PIC   cascade
    5:           2          XT-PIC   soundblaster
    6:          35          XT-PIC   floppy
    8:           1          XT-PIC   rtc
   10:           0          XT-PIC   usb-uhci
   11:          10          XT-PIC   NE2000
   12:         711          XT-PIC   PS/2 Mouse
   14:          13          XT-PIC   ide0
   15:        4852          XT-PIC   ide1
NMI:            0
ERR:            0
[root@localhost root]# cat /proc/ioports
0000-001f : dma1
0020-003f : pic1
0040-005f : timer
0060-006f : keyboard
0070-007f : rtc
0080-008f : dma page reg
00a0-00bf : pic2
00c0-00df : dma2
00f0-00ff : fpu
0170-0177 : ide1
01f0-01f7 : ide0
0213-0213 : isapnp read
0220-022f : soundblaster
0240-025f : eth0
02f8-02ff : serial(auto)
0330-0333 : MPU-401 UART
0376-0376 : ide1
03c0-03df : vga+
03f0-03f5 : floppy
03f6-03f6 : ide0
03f7-03f7 : floppy DIR
03f8-03ff : serial(auto)
0a79-0a79 : isapnp write
0cf8-0cff : PCI conf1
d400-d41f : Intel Corporation 82371AB PIIX4 USB
d400-d41f : usb-uhci
d800-d80f : Intel Corporation 82371AB PIIX4 IDE
d800-d807 : ide0
d808-d80f : ide1
```

7

```
    e400-e43f : Intel Corporation 82371AB PIIX4 ACPI
    e800-e81f : Intel Corporation 82371AB PIIX4 ACPI
    [root@localhost root]#_
```

Like memory, if the values are incorrect for any of the hardware devices listed above, you may also add the append keyword with the correct parameters to the /etc/lilo.conf or /etc/grub/grub.conf file (depending upon the boot loader used). This will send the correct device information to the Linux kernel during system startup.

There are several devices that require that their driver be inserted into the Linux kernel as a module. Sound cards, Network Interface Cards, and USB devices typically have modules inserted into the kernel. To see a list of modules currently inserted into the Linux kernel, you could view the /proc/modules file, as seen below:

```
[root@localhost root]# cat /proc/modules
nls_iso8859-1        2832   1 (autoclean)
nls_cp437            4352   1 (autoclean)
vfat                 9584   1 (autoclean)
fat                 32384   0 (autoclean) [vfat]
binfmt_misc          6416   1
iscsi               21984   0 (unused)
scsi_mod            95696   1 [iscsi]
autofs              11520   0 (autoclean) (unused)
ne                   7456   1
8390                 6752   0 [ne]
appletalk           20912   0 (autoclean)
ipx                 16448   0 (autoclean)
sb                   7888   0 (unused)
sb_lib              34704   0 [sb]
uart401              6576   0 [sb_lib]
sound               59680   0 [sb_lib uart401]
soundcore            4464   5 [sb_lib sound]
usb-uhci            21536   0 (unused)
usbcore             51712   1 [usb-uhci]
ext3                64624   2
jbd                 40992   2 [ext3]
[root@localhost root]#_
```

From the above output, you see that the module for the SoundBlaster sound card (sb), as well as the sound support modules (sound and soundcore), are inserted into the kernel. If they were not inserted, you would need to run the command init3 to boot into runlevel 3 and sndconfig to configure the sound card manually. Runlevels and the init command are discussed in Chapter 9.

There are many more files in the /proc directory than those discussed above that may be useful when examining a system after installation. A description of these files can be seen in Table 7-7.

Table 7-7   Files commonly found in the `/proc` directory

Filename	Description
apm	Contains information about Advanced Power Management
cmdline	Contains the current location of the Linux kernel
cpuinfo	Contains information regarding the processors in the computer
devices	Contains a list of the character and block devices that are currently in use by the Linux kernel
execdomains	Contains a list of execution domains for processes on the system; execution domains allow a process to execute in a specific manner
fb	Contains a list of framebuffer devices in use on the Linux system; typically these include video adapter card devices
filesystems	Contains a list of filesystems supported by the Linux kernel
interrupts	Contains a list of IRQs in use on the system
iomem	Contains a list of memory addresses currently used
ioports	Contains a list of memory address ranges reserved for device use
isapnp	Contains a list of Plug-and-Play devices in ISA slots on the Linux system
kcore	Represents the physical memory inside the computer; this file should not be viewed
kmsg	Is a temporary storage location for messages from the kernel
ksyms	Contains exported kernel symbols used to load modules
loadavg	Contains statistics on the performance of the processor
locks	Contains a list of files currently locked by the kernel
mdstat	Contains the configuration of multiple-disk RAID hardware
meminfo	Contains information regarding physical and virtual memory on the Linux system
misc	Contains a list of miscellaneous devices (major number = 10)
modules	Contains a list of currently loaded modules in the Linux kernel
mounts	Contains a list of currently mounted filesystems
partitions	Contains information regarding partition tables loaded in memory on the system
pci	Contains a list of the PCI devices on the system and their configurations
swap	Contains information on virtual memory utilization
scsi	Contains information on SCSI devices on the Linux system
version	Contain the version information for the Linux kernel and libraries

7

Hardware is detected by the Linux kernel at system startup (see Figure 7-27); thus observing the boot process is a valuable source for hardware information.

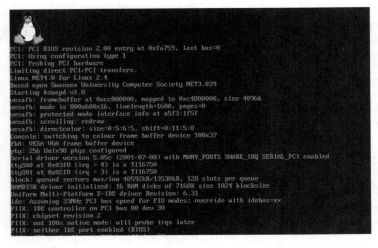

Figure 7-27 Information displayed by Linux at boot time

Unfortunately, the information available at system startup is displayed too fast to read; however, the system logs all information regarding hardware detection and the startup of system processes in log files, which can be viewed at a later time.

To view the hardware detected during the most recent boot time, you may use the **dmesg** command seen in the output below. Much of this information is also stored in the /var/log/dmesg logfile:

```
[root@localhost root]# dmesg
Linux version 2.4.7-
10 (bhcompile@stripples.devel.redhat.com) (gcc
version 2.96 20000731 (Red Hat Linux 7.1 2.96-98)) #1 Thu Sep 6
17:27:27 EDT 2001
BIOS-provided physical RAM map:
 BIOS-e820: 0000000000000000 - 000000000009fc00 (usable)
 BIOS-e820: 000000000009fc00 - 00000000000a0000 (reserved)
 BIOS-e820: 00000000000f0000 - 0000000000100000 (reserved)
 BIOS-e820: 0000000000100000 - 0000000017ffd000 (usable)
 BIOS-e820: 0000000017ffd000 - 0000000017fff000 (ACPI data)
 BIOS-e820: 0000000017fff000 - 0000000018000000 (ACPI NVS)
 BIOS-e820: 00000000ffff0000 - 0000000100000000 (reserved)
Scanning bios EBDA for MXT signature
On node 0 totalpages: 98301
zone(0): 4096 pages.
zone(1): 94205 pages.
zone(2): 0 pages.
Kernel command line: auto BOOT_IMAGE=linux ro root=1602
BOOT_FILE=/boot/vmlinuz-2.4.7-10
Initializing CPU#0
Detected 367.508 MHz processor.
Console: colour VGA+ 80x25
```

```
Calibrating delay loop... 734.00 BogoMIPS
Memory: 381868k/393204k available (1269k kernel code,
8888k reserved, 90k data, 220k init, 0k highmem)
Dentry-cache hash table entries: 65536 (order: 7, 524288 bytes)
Inode-cache hash table entries: 32768 (order: 6, 262144 bytes)
Mount-cache hash table entries: 8192 (order: 4, 65536 bytes)
Buffer-cache hash table entries: 32768 (order: 5, 131072 bytes)
Page-cache hash table entries: 131072 (order: 8, 1048576 bytes)
CPU: Before vendor init, caps: 0183f9ff 00000000 00000000,
vendor = 0
CPU: L1 I cache: 16K, L1 D cache: 16K
CPU: L2 cache: 128K
Intel machine check architecture supported.
Intel machine check reporting enabled on CPU#0.
CPU: After vendor init, caps: 0183f9ff 00000000 00000000 00000000
CPU:      After generic, caps: 0183f9ff 00000000 00000000 00000000
CPU:            Common caps: 0183f9ff 00000000 00000000 00000000
CPU: Intel Celeron (Mendocino) stepping 00
Enabling fast FPU save and restore... done.
Checking 'hlt' instruction... OK.
POSIX conformance testing by UNIFIX
mtrr: v1.40 (20010327) Richard Gooch (rgooch@atnf.csiro.au)
mtrr: detected mtrr type: Intel
PCI: PCI BIOS revision 2.10 entry at 0xf06d0, last bus=1
PCI: Using configuration type 1
PCI: Probing PCI hardware
Unknown bridge resource 0: assuming transparent
Unknown bridge resource 1: assuming transparent
Unknown bridge resource 2: assuming transparent
PCI: Using IRQ router PIIX [8086/7110] at 00:04.0
Limiting direct PCI/PCI transfers.
isapnp: Scanning for PnP cards...
isapnp: Calling quirk for 02:00
isapnp: SB audio device quirk - increasing port range
isapnp: Calling quirk for 02:02
isapnp: AWE32 quirk - adding two ports
isapnp: Card 'D-Link DE-220P PnP ISA Card'
isapnp: Card 'Creative SB AWE64 PnP'
isapnp: 2 Plug & Play cards detected total
Linux NET4.0 for Linux 2.4
Based upon Swansea University Computer Society NET3.039
Initializing RT netlink socket
Simple Boot Flag extension found and enabled.
apm: BIOS version 1.2 Flags 0x03 (Driver version 1.14)
mxt_scan_bios: enter
Starting kswapd v1.8
VFS: Diskquotas version dquot_6.5.0 initialized
pty: 2048 Unix98 ptys configured
Serial driver version 5.05c (2001-07-08) with MANY_PORTS
MULTIPORT SHARE_IRQ SERIAL_PCI ISAPNP enabled
```

```
ttyS00 at 0x03f8 (irq = 4) is a 16550A
ttyS01 at 0x02f8 (irq = 3) is a 16550A
Real Time Clock Driver v1.10d
block: queued sectors max/low 253208kB/122136kB, 768 slots
per queue
RAMDISK driver initialized: 16 RAM disks of 4096K size 1024
blocksize
Uniform Multi-Platform E-IDE driver Revision: 6.31
ide: Assuming 33MHz PCI bus speed for PIO modes; override with
idebus=xx
PIIX4: IDE controller on PCI bus 00 dev 21
PIIX4: chipset revision 1
PIIX4: not 100% native mode: will probe irqs later
    ide0: BM-DMA at 0xd800-0xd807, BIOS settings: hda:DMA, hdb:pio
    ide1: BM-DMA at 0xd808-0xd80f, BIOS settings: hdc:DMA, hdd:DMA
hda: QUANTUM FIREBALL CX6.4A, ATA DISK drive
hdc: QUANTUM FIREBALLlct10 10, ATA DISK drive
hdd: ATAPI CDROM, ATAPI CD/DVD-ROM drive
ide0 at 0x1f0-0x1f7,0x3f6 on irq 14
ide1 at 0x170-0x177,0x376 on irq 15
hda: 12594960 sectors (6449 MB) w/418KiB Cache, CHS=784/255/63,
UDMA(33)
hdc: 20044080 sectors (10263 MB) w/418KiB Cache, CHS=19885/16/63,
UDMA(33)
ide-floppy driver 0.97
Partition check:
 hda: hda1
 hdc: [PTBL] [1247/255/63] hdc1 hdc2 hdc3 hdc4 < hdc5 >
Floppy drive(s): fd0 is 1.44M
FDC 0 is a post-1991 82077
ide-floppy driver 0.97
md: md driver 0.90.0 MAX_MD_DEVS=256, MD_SB_DISKS=27
md: Autodetecting RAID arrays.
md: autorun ...
md: ... autorun DONE.
NET4: Linux TCP/IP 1.0 for NET4.0
IP Protocols: ICMP, UDP, TCP, IGMP
IP: routing cache hash table of 4096 buckets, 32Kbytes
TCP: Hash tables configured (established 32768 bind 32768)
Linux IP multicast router 0.06 plus PIM-SM
NET4: Unix domain sockets 1.0/SMP for Linux NET4.0.
RAMDISK: Compressed image found at block 0
Freeing initrd memory: 319k freed
VFS: Mounted root (ext2 filesystem).
Journalled Block Device driver loaded
kjournald starting.  Commit interval 5 seconds
EXT3-fs: mounted filesystem with ordered data mode.
Freeing unused kernel memory: 220k freed
Adding Swap: 514072k swap-space (priority -1)
usb.c: registered new driver usbdevfs
```

```
usb.c: registered new driver hub
usb-uhci.c: $Revision: 1.259 $ time 17:36:49 Sep  6 2001
usb-uhci.c: High bandwidth mode enabled
PCI: Found IRQ 10 for device 00:04.2
usb-uhci.c: USB UHCI at I/O 0xd400, IRQ 10
usb-uhci.c: Detected 2 ports
usb.c: new USB bus registered, assigned bus number 1
hub.c: USB hub found
hub.c: 2 ports detected
usb-uhci.c: v1.251:USB Universal Host Controller Interface driver
EXT3 FS 2.4-0.9.8, 25 Aug 2001 on ide1(22,2), internal journal
kjournald starting.  Commit interval 5 seconds
EXT3 FS 2.4-0.9.8, 25 Aug 2001 on ide1(22,1), internal journal
EXT3-fs: mounted filesystem with ordered data mode.
kjournald starting.  Commit interval 5 seconds
EXT3 FS 2.4-0.9.8, 25 Aug 2001 on ide1(22,5), internal journal
EXT3-fs: mounted filesystem with ordered data mode.
0x378: FIFO is 16 bytes
0x378: writeIntrThreshold is 9
0x378: readIntrThreshold is 9
0x378: PWord is 8 bits
0x378: Interrupts are ISA-Pulses
0x378: ECP port cfgA=0x10 cfgB=0x48
0x378: ECP settings irq=7 dma=<none or set by other means>
parport0: PC-style at 0x378 (0x778) [PCSPP,TRISTATE,COMPAT,
EPP,ECP]
parport0: irq 7 detected
parport0: cpp_daisy: aa5500ff(38)
parport0: assign_addrs: aa5500ff(38)
parport0: cpp_daisy: aa5500ff(38)
parport0: assign_addrs: aa5500ff(38)
NET4: Linux IPX 0.47 for NET4.0
IPX Portions Copyright (c) 1995 Caldera, Inc.
IPX Portions Copyright (c) 2000, 2001 Conectiva, Inc.
NET4: AppleTalk 0.18a for Linux NET4.0
ne.c: ISAPnP reports Generic PNP at i/o 0x240, irq 5.
ne.c:v1.10 9/23/94 Donald Becker (becker@scyld.com)
Last modified Nov 1, 2000 by Paul Gortmaker
NE*000 ethercard probe at 0x240: 00 80 c8 d6 74 43
eth0: NE2000 found at 0x240, using IRQ 5.
SCSI subsystem driver Revision: 1.00
iSCSI version 2.0.1.8 ( 8-Aug-2001)
iSCSI control device major number 254
iSCSI: detected HBA d76d58fc, host #0
scsi0 : iSCSI (2.0.1.8)
[root@localhost root]#_
```

You may also view the system processes that started successfully or unsuccessfully during boot time by viewing the contents of the /var/log/boot.log or /var/log/ messages log files. Both of these files are appended to on each system startup and thus may be very large; these files contain much of the same information; however, `boot.log` contains only boot information whereas `messages` contains boot information as well as other messages from the system after boot time. A sample `boot.log` is seen in the output below:

```
[root@localhost root]# cat /var/log/boot.log
May 27 07:56:47 localhost syslog: syslogd startup succeeded
May 27 07:56:47 localhost syslog: klogd startup succeeded
May 27 07:56:47 localhost portmap: portmap startup succeeded
May 27 07:56:47 localhost nfslock: rpc.statd startup succeeded
May 27 07:56:48 localhost keytable: Loading keymap: succeeded
May 27 07:56:48 localhost keytable: Loading system font: succeeded
May 27 07:56:48 localhost random: Initializing random number generator: succeeded
May 27 07:56:08 localhost rc.sysinit: Mounting proc filesystem: succeeded
May 27 07:56:08 localhost rc.sysinit: Unmounting initrd: succeeded
May 27 07:56:08 localhost sysctl: net.ipv4.ip_forward = 0
May 27 07:56:08 localhost sysctl: net.ipv4.conf.default.rp_filter = 1
May 27 07:56:08 localhost sysctl: kernel.sysrq = 0
May 27 07:56:08 localhost rc.sysinit: Configuring kernel parameters: succeeded
May 27 07:56:08 localhost date: Mon May 27 07:56:02 EDT 2002
May 27 07:56:08 localhost rc.sysinit: Setting clock (localtime): Mon May 27 07:56:02
EDT 2002 succeeded
May 27 07:56:08 localhost rc.sysinit: Loading default keymap succeeded
May 27 07:56:08 localhost rc.sysinit: Setting default font (lat0-sun16): succeeded
May 27 07:56:08 localhost rc.sysinit: Activating swap partitions: succeeded
May 27 07:56:08 localhost rc.sysinit: Setting hostname localhost.localdomain:
succeeded
May 27 07:56:08 localhost rc.sysinit: Mounting USB filesystem: succeeded
May 27 07:56:08 localhost rc.sysinit: Initializing USB controller (usb-uhci):
succeeded
May 27 07:56:08 localhost fsck: /: clean, 176676/640000 files, 726451/1279175 blocks
May 27 07:56:08 localhost rc.sysinit: Checking root filesystem succeeded
May 27 07:56:08 localhost rc.sysinit: Remounting root filesystem in read-write mode:
succeeded
May 27 07:56:15 localhost rc.sysinit: Finding module dependencies: succeeded
May 27 07:56:16 localhost fsck: /boot: clean, 36/26104 files, 13665/104391 blocks
May 27 07:56:16 localhost fsck: /home: clean, 22/26104 files, 7443/104391 blocks
May 27 07:56:16 localhost rc.sysinit: Checking filesystems succeeded
May 27 07:56:17 localhost rc.sysinit: Mounting local filesystems: succeeded
May 27 07:56:17 localhost rc.sysinit: Enabling local filesystem quotas: succeeded
May 27 07:56:17 localhost rc.sysinit: Turning on process accounting succeeded
May 27 07:56:18 localhost rc.sysinit: Enabling swap space: succeeded
May 27 07:56:21 localhost kudzu: Updating /etc/fstab succeeded
May 27 07:56:50 localhost netfs: Mounting other filesystems: succeeded
May 27 07:56:32 localhost kudzu: succeeded
May 27 07:56:33 localhost sysctl: net.ipv4.ip_forward = 0
May 27 07:56:33 localhost sysctl: net.ipv4.conf.default.rp_filter = 1
May 27 07:56:33 localhost sysctl: kernel.sysrq = 0
May 27 07:56:33 localhost network: Setting network parameters: succeeded
```

```
May 27 07:56:33 localhost network: Bringing up interface lo: succeeded
May 27 07:56:46 localhost network: Bringing up interface eth0: succeeded
May 27 07:56:50 localhost apmd: apmd startup succeeded
May 27 07:56:51 localhost autofs: automount startup succeeded
May 27 07:56:51 localhost rc: Starting pcmcia: succeeded
May 27 07:56:51 localhost sshd: Starting sshd:
May 27 07:56:52 localhost sshd: succeeded
May 27 07:56:52 localhost sshd:
May 27 07:56:52 localhost rc: Starting sshd: succeeded
May 27 07:56:55 localhost xinetd: xinetd startup succeeded
May 27 07:56:58 localhost sendmail: sendmail startup succeeded
May 27 07:56:58 localhost iscsi: iscsilun startup succeeded
May 27 07:56:58 localhost gpm: gpm startup succeeded
May 27 07:56:59 localhost crond: crond startup succeeded
May 27 07:57:01 localhost xfs: xfs startup succeeded
May 27 07:57:01 localhost anacron: anacron startup succeeded
May 27 07:57:02 localhost atd: atd startup succeeded
May 27 07:57:04 localhost linuxconf: Running Linuxconf hooks: succeeded
May 27 07:57:04 localhost rc: Starting wine: succeededext3
[root@localhost root]#_
```

CHAPTER SUMMARY

❒ There are many different SCSI standards, which have been developed since 1986. SCSI hard disk drives are uniquely identified by a SCSI ID and attach to a controller via a terminated cable.

❒ Each peripheral device must be configured with an IRQ and I/O address prior to use, and may optionally use a DMA channel. This configuration may be given to devices automatically if they are Plug-and-Play compliant.

❒ Computers that require fault-tolerance typically employ SCSI hard disks configured using RAID.

❒ Although Linux is typically installed from CD-ROM media, it may also be installed using files located on hard disks, or NFS, FTP, and HTTP servers. You need to create a boot disk to perform these types of installation.

❒ Text installations of Linux present the same choices to the user as graphical installations of Linux.

❒ Installing Linux on non-Intel architectures requires a solid understanding of the hardware and characteristics of the architecture, which can be obtained from sources on the Internet.

❒ Unsupported video cards, overclocked CPUs, PnP support, and improper RAM settings may cause an installation to fail.

❒ The /proc directory contains information regarding detected hardware on the system and is useful when verifying whether an installation was successful.

KEY TERMS

/proc/cpuinfo — The directory that contains information on current CPU setup on the system.

/proc/dma — The directory that contains information on current Direct Memory Access assignments on the system.

/proc/interrupts — The directory that contains information on current Interrupt Request assignments on the system.

/proc/ioports — The directory that contains information on current Input/Output address assignments on the system.

/proc/meminfo — The directory that contains information on the current memory usage situation, both physical and virtual, on the system.

/proc/modules — The directory that contains information on what modules are current incorporated into the kernel.

ABOOT — The boot loader for Alpha architecture platforms.

Alpha — A 64-bit processor platform from Compaq.

Complimentary Metal Oxide Semiconductor (CMOS) — A memory store on the mainboard used to store configuration information for use during the boot process; not a true ROM chip, it requires a low level flow of electricity from an onboard battery to maintain the memory store.

disk mirroring — Also known as RAID 1, it consists of two identical hard disks, which are written to in parallel with the same information to ensure fault tolerance.

disk striping — A type of RAID 0, which is used to write separate information to different hard disks to speed up access time.

Disk Striping with Parity — Also known as RAID 5, it is used to write separate information to hard disks to speed up access time, and also contains parity information to ensure fault-tolerance.

fault-tolerance — The measure of downtime a device exhibits in the event of a failure.

File Transfer Protocol (FTP) — The most common protocol used to transfer files across the Internet.

Grand Unified Bootloader (GRUB) — A program used to boot the Linux operating system.

graphical installation — An installation method that presents interactive material in a GUI-based format, rather than a command-line text-based interface.

Hexadecimal — A numerical system that represents information in base-16 format.

Hyper Text Transfer Protocol (HTTP) — The underlying protocol used to transfer information over the Internet.

installation log file — A log file created at installation to record actions that occurred or failed during the installation process.

Interrupt Request (IRQ) — Used by the processor to prioritize simultaneous requests for service from peripheral devices.

ISO images — Large single files that are exact copies of the information contained on a CD-ROM.

Itanium (Intel 64-bit) — A 64-bit processor architecture proprietary to Intel.

LInux LOader (LILO) — A program used to boot the Linux operating system.

Logical Unit Number (LUN) — Uniquely identifies each device attached to any given node in a SCSI chain.

Network File System (NFS) — A distributed file system developed by Sun Microsystems that allows computers of differing types to access files shared on the network.

network installation — An installation where the installation source files are accessed across the network from a network share.

network server — A computer with files shared out on the network for other computers to access.

overclocked — Running a processor at a higher clock speed than it has been rated for.

Plug-and-Play (PnP) — The process allowing devices automatically to be assigned required IRQ, I/O address, and DMA information by the system BIOS.

polling — The act of querying devices to see if they have services that need to be run.

PowerPC — A processor architecture developed by Motorola.

Redundant Array of Inexpensive Disks (RAID) — The process of combining the storage space of several hard disk drives into one larger logical storage unit.

s390 (Mainframe) — An IBM-developed Mainframe architecture.

Scalable Processor Architecture (SPARC) — A RISC processor architecture developed by Sun Microsystems; UltraSPARC is a form of this architecture.

SCSI ID — Uniquely identifies and prioritizes devices attached to a SCSI controller.

SILO — A program used to boot Linux on SPARC processor architecture computers.

spanning — A type of RAID level 0 that allows two or more devices to be represented as a single large volume.

target ID — *See* SCSI ID.

terminator — A device used to terminate an electrical conduction medium to absorb the transmitted signal and prevent signal bounce.

text-based installation — An installation method that presents interactive material in a command-line text-based format rather than a GUI-based interface.

REVIEW QUESTIONS

1. Two peripheral devices can share and use the same Interrupt Request setting at the same time. True or False?

2. What is used to give each device a separate unique portion of physical memory to utilize?

   a. SCSI

   b. IDE

   c. DMA

   d. IRQ

   e. RIQ

   f. I/O address

   g. O/I address

3. Interrupt Requests can only be used on 8-bit wide data paths. True or False?

4. You wish to view log files to get information about a problem you are having. In what directory will you likely find the log files?

   a. /rav/log

   b. /root/log

   c. /sys/log

   d. /var/log

   e. /etc/log

5. Which of the following RAID levels is not fault tolerant?

   a. RAID 0

   b. RAID 1

   c. RAID 4

   d. RAID 5

   e. They all are; that is what RAID is, an array of redundant disks for fault tolerance

6. Which of the following do DMAs and IRQs have in common? (Choose all that apply.)

   a. They both have assignments that function to serve two different data path widths, 16-bit and 8-bit.

   b. They have nothing in common.

   c. They both have one assignment that is lost to normal user usage.

   d. They are both lists of prioritized assignments.

7. In order to take advantage of Plug-and-Play, which of the following must be met? (Choose all that apply.)

   a. The user must be the root user.

   b. The operating system must support Plug-and-Play.

   c. The system must have used up all available IRQs.

   d. The system must have used up all available I/O addresses.

   e. The device to be configured must support Plug-and-Play.

   f. The BIOS must support Plug-and-Play.

8. Observe Figure 7-28, which follows. Which of the following would utilize connector B?

 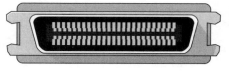

        A   B

   a. SCSI-1 devices

   b. SCSI-2 devices

   c. SCSI-3 devices

   d. None of them, as it is a printer connector not a SCSI connector

9. What is the default IRQ setting for the keyboard?

   a. IRQ0

   b. IRQ8

   c. IRQ7

   d. IRQ2

   e. IRQ1

10. In order to install Linux on an Alpha processor architecture platform, which of the following must be obtained?

   a. nothing; it cannot be done—Linux only runs on an Intel architecture processor

   b. a SCSI-3 hard disk drive set arranged in a RAID 5 setup

   c. a distribution designed to run on the Alpha processor architecture

   d. the GRUB boot loader program

   e. a network server utilizing the NFS filesystem

11. A SCSI-1 controller card can accommodate how many peripheral devices at each node?

    a. seven

    b. eight

    c. fourteen

    d. fifteen

12. Where is the /proc file stored?

    a. in RAM

    b. on the hard disk drive in the / directory

    c. on the hard disk drive in the /etc directory

    d. on the hard disk drive in the /var directory

    e. on the hard disk drive in the /root directroy

13. What is the default IRQ for COM 1?

    a. 2

    b. 4

    c. 1

    d. 0

14. Each device must have a unique IRQ, DMA, and I/O address assignment. True or False?

15. SCSI devices that use an 8-bit wide data path use _____.

    a. an 8-pin connector

    b. a 15-pin connector

    c. a 50-pin connector

    d. a 68-pin connector

16. How many Direct Memory Access channels are there?

    a. 2

    b. 5

    c. 8

    d. 7

17. Where are the BIOS configuration settings stored?

    a. on the BIOS chip, maintained by a small flow of electricity from a battery

    b. on the CMOS chip, maintained by a small flow of electricity from a battery

    c. in LILO

    d. in the appropriate file in the /proc directory

18. The Linux operating system can only be installed on an Intel 32-bit processor platform. True or False?

19. List the following SCSI ID's in proper priority order.

    a. 5

    b. 7

    c. 15

    d. 8

    e. 2

    f. 11

    g. 13

    h. 1

    i. 0

20. How does one begin a text-based installation?

    a. Click the text box option when asked during install if you want text based or GUI.

    b. Type "text" at the initial welcome screen right after you start the install.

    c. You do not have a choice; the default install is GUI and only if the video is not supported will it automatically switch to text mode.

    d. Use the second of the two Linux install disks, which will begin the install in text mode.

21. Which DMA channels are not available for assignment by default?

    a. 0 & 2

    b. 0 & 4

    c. 1 & 2

    d. 2 & 4

    e. 5 & 2

    f. 5 & 6

    g. 6 & 4

22. Which RAID level is also referred to as mirroring?

    a. RAID 0

    b. RAID 1

    c. RAID 4

    d. RAID 5

23. A SCSI-3 controller card can always accommodate more devices than a SCSI-2 controller card. True or False?

24. What is the default IRQ and I/O setting for LPT1?

    a. IRQ 7 and I/O address 378–37F

    b. IRQ 5 and I/O address 378–37F

    c. IRQ 7 and I/O address 3F8–3FF

    d. IRQ 5 and I/O address 3F8–3FF

    e. IRQ 7 and I/O address 278–27F

25. SCSI–1 is also referred to as _____

    a. fast and wide

    b. slow and wide

    c. slow and narrow

    d. fast and narrow

26. You need to find out the IRQ, DMA, and I/O address assignments currently made on your computer. What do you do?

    a. Open a command prompt and type "IRQ ?", "DMA ?", or "I/O address ?" as appropriate.

    b. Open the GUI and go to system information.

    c. Cat the appropriate files in the `/etc` directory.

    d. View the contents of the appropriate files in the `/settings` directory.

    e. View the contents of the appropriate files in the `/proc` directory.

27. Immediately after installation you want to view the installation log file. What file should you view?

    a. `/tmp/install.log`

    b. `/var/install.log`

    c. `/etc/install.log`

    d. `/proc/install.log`

28. List the following Interrupt Requests in proper priority order.

    a. 15

    b. 0

    c. 2

    d. 11

    e. 4

    f. 8

    g. 6

    h. 12

29. How many usable or assignable IRQs are there?

    a. 7

    b. 15

    c. 8

    d. 16

30. In order to accommodate five hard disk drive units you must purchase a SCSI controller card that _____.

    a. meets the SCSI-2 specifications

    b. has five device plug-in slots to accommodate the desired number of devices

    c. meets the SCSI-1 specifications as they have seven device plug-in slots

    d. has a single device plug-in slot

HANDS-ON PROJECTS

These projects should be completed in the order given. All hands-on projects should take a total of three hours to complete. The requirements for this lab include:

- ❏ A pre-installation checklist completed in Hands-on Project 2-1

- ❏ A computer with Red Hat 7.2 installed according to Hands-on Project 3-1

- ❏ A Red Hat 7.2 CD-ROM installation set (two CD-ROMs)

- ❏ An Intel architecture computer that meets the minimum Red Hat Linux installation requirements and contains Red Hat Linux-supported hardware components, including a 4.5GB or greater IDE hard disk drive and a CD-ROM drive

- ❏ A blank floppy diskette

Project 7-1

In this hands-on project, you will create an installation boot floppy.

1. Turn on your computer. Once your Linux system has been loaded, you will be placed at a graphical terminal (tty7). Switch to a command-line terminal (tty2) by pressing **Ctrl–Alt–F2** and log into the terminal using the username of **root** and the password of **secret**.

2. Place the first Red Hat 7.2 installation CD-ROM in your CD-ROM drive.

3. At the command prompt, type **mount –r –t iso9660 /dev/cdrom /mnt/cdrom** and press **Enter**. Next, type the **mount** command at the command prompt and press **Enter** to verify that the CD-ROM was mounted successfully.

4. At the command prompt, type **cd /mnt/cdrom/images** and press **Enter**. Next, type **ls –F** at the command prompt and press **Enter**. What image files do you see? What are each used for? Is there a help file in this directory that one can view?

5. Place a blank 3.5–inch floppy disk in the floppy disk drive of your computer. At the command prompt, type **dd if=boot.img of=/dev/fd0** and press **Enter**.

6. When the copy is completed, type **exit** and press **Enter** to log out of your shell.

Project 7-2

In this hands–on project, you will install Red Hat Linux 7.2 on a computer using a text-based interface.

1. Turn on the computer and place the installation boot floppy created in Hands-on Project 7–1 into the floppy disk drive of the computer. A "Welcome to Red Hat Linux 7.2!" screen should appear after a few seconds.

If the "Welcome to Red Hat Linux 7.2!" screen does not appear, ensure that your floppy disk is listed first in the boot order in your computer's BIOS settings.

2. At the "Welcome to Red Hat Linux 7.2!" screen read the available options. Next, type **text** and press the **Enter** key to start the installation.

3. At the "Language Selection" screen, ensure that **English** is selected and press **Enter**.

4. At the "Keyboard Selection" screen, verify that your keyboard model and layout are correct and press **Enter**.

5. At the "Mouse Selection" screen, verify that your mouse model and port are correct, use the **Tab** key to navigate to the OK button, and press **Enter**.

6. At the "Welcome to Red Hat Linux" screen, press **Enter**.

7. At the "Installation Type" screen, select **Custom**, use the **Tab** key to navigate to the OK button, and press **Enter**.

8. At the "Disk Partitioning Setup" screen, choose **Disk Druid**, use the **Tab** key to navigate to the Disk Druid button, and press **Enter**.

9. At the "Partitioning" screen, use the cursor keys to highlight any existing partitions on your hard drive device and press the **F4** key to delete them. For each deletion, press **Enter** to confirm the action.

10. Place your cursor over the **free** space on your hard drive device and press the **F2** key to create a new partition. Enter the following information in the screen displayed, and press **OK** when finished:

Mount Point = /boot

Type = ext3

Size (Fixed) = 100Mb

Why is it a good idea to give the **/boot** directory its own partition?

11. Place your cursor over the **Free space** on your hard drive device and press the **F2** key to create a new partition. Enter the following information in the screen displayed:

Mount Point   =   **/home**

Type   =   **ext3**

Size (Fixed)   =   **100Mb**

Press the **OK** button when finished.

Why is it a good idea to give the **/home** directory its own partition?

12. Place your cursor over the **Free space** on your hard drive device and press the **F2** key to create a new partition. Enter the following information in the screen displayed, and press **OK** when finished:

Mount Point   =   **/**

Type   =   **ext3**

Size (Fixed)   =   **This value should be equal to the value in the "Space available for filesystems" section of the pre-installation checklist from Hands-on Project 2-1 less 200Mb.**

13. Place your cursor over the **Free space** on your hard drive device and press the **F2** key to create a new partition. Enter the following information in the screen displayed, and press **OK** when finished:

Type   =   **swap**

Size (Fixed)   =   **This value should be equal to the value in the "Space required for swap partition" section of the pre-installation checklist from Hands-on Project 2-1.**

14. Observe the names of your partitions. Were all primary partitions used? Are there any logical drives? Which of the filesystems was made a logical drive? Press **OK**.

15. At the "Boot Loader Configuration" screen, choose to use **LILO** as the boot loader (use the **spacebar** to select), use the **Tab** key to navigate to the OK button, and press **Enter**.

16. At the "Boot Loader Configuration" screen, ensure that the boot loader will be installed on the **Master Boot Record (MBR)** of the first hard disk device (usually /dev/hda), use the **Tab** key to navigate to the OK button, and press **Enter**.

17. At the "Boot Loader Configuration" screen, note that LBA is not selected and that there are no options listed which need to be passed to the kernel, use the **Tab** key to navigate to the OK button, and press **Enter**.

18. At the "Boot Loader Configuration" screen, observe the label given to this Linux installation; use the **Tab** key to navigate to the OK button and press **Enter**.

19. If a network configuration screen appears because your network card was detected automatically, configure this using the values in Hands-on Project 2-1.

20. At the "Firewall Configuration" screen, select **No firewall** using the **spacebar**, use the **Tab** key to navigate to the OK button, and press **Enter**.

21. At the "Language Support" screen, ensure that **English (USA)** is selected, use the **Tab** key to navigate to the OK button, and press **Enter**.

22. At the "Time Zone Selection" screen, select your time zone, use the **Tab** key to navigate to the OK button, and press **Enter**.

23. At the "Root Password" screen, enter the password of **secret** in the Root Password and Confirm areas, use the **Tab** key to navigate to the OK button, and press **Enter**.

24. At the "Add User" screen, fill in the following information, use the **Tab** key to navigate to the OK button, and press **Enter**.

    User Name: **user1**

    Password: **secret**

    Confirm: **secret**

    Full Name: **sample user one**

25. At the "User Account Setup" screen, observe the user that you created in the previous step, use the **Tab** key to navigate to the OK button, and press **Enter**.

26. At the "Authentication Configuration" screen, ensure that **Enable MD5 passwords** and **Enable shadow passwords** are enabled, use the **Tab** key to navigate to the OK button, and press **Enter**.

27. At the "Package Group Selection" screen, scroll down to the bottom of the list of available packages, use the **spacebar** to select **Everything**, use the **Tab** key to navigate to the OK button, and press **Enter**.

28. At the "Video Card Configuration" screen, ensure that your video card make and model are displayed. Also ensure that the correct amount of video card RAM is displayed. Use the **Tab** key to navigate to the OK button and press **Enter**.

29. At the "Installation to Begin" screen, view the pathname to the installation log file and press **Enter**. An "Installing Packages" screen will be displayed. This step usually takes between 30 and 60 minutes depending on your hardware and will require that you place the second CD-ROM in the CD-ROM tray when prompted.

30. At the "Boot Disk" screen, use the **Tab** key to navigate to the NO button and press **Enter**.

31. At the "Monitor Configuration" screen, ensure that your monitor and the correct values for Horizontal and Vertical Sync are displayed. Use the **Tab** key to navigate to the OK button and press **Enter**.

32. At the "X Customization" screen, select a screen resolution of **800 × 600** and a color depth of **High Color (16bit)** or greater. Verify that the default desktop **GNOME** and **Graphical** login is selected, use the **Tab** key to navigate to the OK button, and press **Enter**.

33. At the "complete" screen, press **Enter**.

Project 7-3

In this hands-on project, you will view system information after installation.

1. Turn on your computer. Once your Linux system has been loaded, you will be placed at a graphical terminal (tty7). Switch to a command-line terminal (tty2) by pressing **Ctrl–Alt–F2** and log into the terminal using the username of **root** and the password of **secret**.

2. At the command prompt, type **cp /tmp/install.log ~** and press **Enter** to make a copy of the installation log file in your home directory. Next, type **less install.log** command at the command prompt and press **Enter** to view the entries in this file. Were there any errors during package installation?

3. At the command prompt, type **ls –F /proc** and press **Enter** to view the file and directory contents of the proc filesystem.

4. At the command prompt, type **less /proc/cpuinfo** and press **Enter**. Did the installation detect your CPU correctly? When finished, quit the less utility by pressing the **q** key.

5. At the command prompt, type **less /proc/dma** and press **Enter**. What DMA channels are in use on the system? How could you fix any discrepancies? When finished, quit the less utility by pressing the **q** key.

6. At the command prompt, type **less /proc/interrupts** and press **Enter**. What IRQs are in use on the system and by what devices? How could you fix any discrepancies? When finished, quit the less utility by pressing the **q** key.

7. At the command prompt, type **less /proc/ioports** and press **Enter**. What I/O addresses are reserved on the system and by what devices? How could you fix any discrepancies? When finished, quit the less utility by pressing the **q** key.

8. At the command prompt, type **less /proc/modules** and press **Enter**. What is displayed? What does each entry represent? How does this correspond to the information from Steps 5, 6, and 7? When finished, quit the less utility by pressing the **q** key.

9. At the command prompt, type **less /proc/meminfo** and press **Enter**. Does your Linux system recognize all the memory in your computer? If not, what could you do? When finished, quit the less utility by pressing the **q** key.

10. At the command prompt, type **less /proc/pci** and press **Enter**. What information is displayed regarding each PCI device in your computer? When finished, quit the less utility by pressing the **q** key.

11. At the command prompt, type **dmesg | less** and press **Enter**. Observe the entries. How do they correspond with the hardware information that you have seen in Steps 4 through 10? When finished, quit the **less** utility by pressing the **q** key.

12. At the command prompt, type **less /var/log/messages** and press **Enter**. What does each entry represent? How do these entries correspond with the information seen in Step 2? When finished, quit the **less** utility by pressing the **q** key.

13. Type **exit** and press **Enter** to log out of your shell.

7

DISCOVERY EXERCISES

1. Determine the following about your system:
   - What IRQs are in use
   - What DMA channels are in use
   - What I/O addresses are in use
   - Where the Linux kernel is located
   - If there are any PCI devices in use on the system
   - What modules are loaded into the kernel
   - Information about the physical memory on your system

2. Based on the information from Question 1 above, if you wished to add an additional hardware device:
   - What IRQs would be available for you to use?
   - What DMA channels would be available for you to use?

3. Provided you have an Internet connection and functional Web browser, gather information on three different commercial RAID controllers that perform RAID level 5 and write a short report, which compares and contrasts their features and cost. In which situations would you use each one?

4. You work in the IT department of a large company, which employs large RISC computers (SUN, HP, IBM, and Compaq). Your boss asks you to install Linux on these machines and put them to use in various departments around the company. What pieces of information would you need to find before you begin?

5. Provided you have an Internet connection and functional Web browser, search the Internet for five problems that people have had in the past during a Linux installation that are different than those described in this chapter. What were the solutions? If you had similar difficulties during installation, how could you get help?

8

WORKING WITH THE BASH SHELL

After completing this chapter, you will be able to:

♦ Redirect the input and output of a command
♦ Identify and manipulate common shell environment variables
♦ Create and export new shell variables
♦ Edit environment files to create variables upon shell startup
♦ Describe the purpose and nature of shell scripts
♦ Create and execute basic shell scripts
♦ Effectively use common decision constructs in shell scripts

A solid understanding of shell features is vital to both administrators and users, as they interact with the shell on a daily basis. The first part of this chapter describes how the shell can manipulate command input and output using redirection and pipe shell metacharacters. Next, you explore the different types of variables present in a BASH shell after login as well as their purpose and usage. Finally, this chapter ends with an introduction to creating and executing BASH shell scripts.

COMMAND INPUT AND OUTPUT

The BASH shell is responsible for providing a user interface and interpreting commands entered on the command line. In addition to this, the BASH shell can manipulate command input and output, provided the user specifies certain shell metacharacters on the command line alongside the command. Command input and output are represented by labels known as **file descriptors**. There are three file descriptors available to each command that can be manipulated by the BASH shell:

- Standard Input (stdin)
- Standard Output (stdout)
- Standard Error (stderr)

Standard Input (stdin) refers to the information that is processed by the command during execution, and is often in the form of user input typed on the keyboard. **Standard Output (stdout)** refers to the normal output of a command, whereas **Standard Error (stderr)** refers to any error messages generated by the command. Both Standard Output and Standard Error are displayed on the terminal screen by default. All three components are depicted in Figure 8-1.

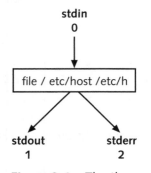

Figure 8-1 The three common file descriptors

Figure 8-1 also shows that each file descriptor is represented by a number; stdin is represented by the number 0, stdout is represented by the number 1, and stderr is represented by the number 2.

Although all three components are available to any command, not all commands use every component. The `ls /etc/hosts /etc/h` command used in Figure 8-1 gives Standard Output (the listing of the `/etc/hosts` file) and Standard Error (an error message indicating that the `/etc/h` file does not exist) to the terminal screen, as seen in the output below:

```
[root@localhost root]# ls /etc/hosts /etc/h
ls: /etc/h: No such file or directory
/etc/hosts
[root@localhost root]# _
```

Redirection

You can use the BASH shell to redirect Standard Output and Standard Error from the terminal screen to a file on the filesystem using the ">" shell metacharacter followed by the absolute or relative pathname of the file. To redirect only the Standard Output to a file called `goodoutput` for the command used in Figure 8-1, you simply append the number of the file descriptor (1) followed by the redirection symbol > and the file to redirect the Standard Output to (`goodoutput`) as seen below:

```
[root@localhost root]# ls /etc/hosts /etc/h  1>goodoutput
ls: /etc/h: No such file or directory
[root@localhost root]# _
```

You can include a space character after the ">" metacharacter, but it is not necessary.

Notice from the above output that the Standard Error was still displayed to the terminal screen as it was not redirected to a file. The listing of `/etc/hosts` was not displayed, as it was redirected to a file called `goodoutput` in the current directory. If the `goodoutput` file did not exist prior to running the command in the above output, then it would be created automatically. However, if the `goodoutput` file did exist prior to the redirection, then the BASH shell would clear its contents before executing the command. To see that the Standard Output was redirected to the `goodoutput` file, you may run the following commands:

```
[root@localhost root]# ls -F
Desktop/   goodoutput
[root@localhost root]# cat goodoutput
/etc/hosts
[root@localhost root]# _
```

Similarly, you may redirect the Standard Error of a command to a file; simply specify file descriptor number 2, as seen in the following output:

```
[root@localhost root]# ls /etc/hosts /etc/h  2>badoutput
/etc/hosts
[root@localhost root]# cat badoutput
ls: /etc/h: No such file or directory
[root@localhost root]# _
```

In the above output, only the Standard Error was redirected to a file called `badoutput`, thus the Standard Output (a listing of `/etc/hosts`) was displayed on the terminal screen.

Since redirecting the Standard Output to a file for later use is more common than redirecting the Standard Error to a file, the BASH shell assumes Standard Output in the absence of a numeric file descriptor:

```
[root@localhost root]# ls /etc/hosts /etc/h  >goodoutput
ls: /etc/h: No such file or directory
[root@localhost root]# cat goodoutput
/etc/hosts
[root@localhost root]# _
```

In addition, you may redirect both Standard Output and Standard Error to separate files at the same time, as seen in the following output:

```
[root@localhost root]# ls /etc/hosts /etc/h  >goodoutput  2>badoutput
[root@localhost root]# cat goodoutput
/etc/hosts
[root@localhost root]# cat badoutput
ls: /etc/h: No such file or directory
[root@localhost root]# _
```

The order of redirection on the command line does not matter; the command ls /etc/hosts /etc/h   >goodoutput   2>badoutput is the same as ls /etc/hosts /etc/h   2>badoutput   >goodoutput.

It is important to use separate filenames to hold the contents of Standard Output and Standard Error; using the same filename for both would result in a loss of data since the system attempts to write both contents to the file at the same time:

```
[root@localhost root]# ls /etc/hosts /etc/h  >goodoutput  2>goodoutput
[root@localhost root]# cat goodoutput
/etc/hosts
: No such file or directory
[root@localhost root]# _
```

To redirect both Standard Output and Standard Error to the same file without any loss of data, you must use special notation. To specify that Standard Output be sent to the file **goodoutput** and Standard Error be sent to the same place as Standard Output, you could do the following:

```
[root@localhost root]# ls /etc/hosts /etc/h  >goodoutput  2>&1
[root@localhost root]# cat goodoutput
ls: /etc/h: No such file or directory
/etc/hosts
[root@localhost root]# _
```

Alternatively, you could specify that the Standard Error be sent to the file `badoutput` and Standard Output be sent to the same place as Standard Error:

```
[root@localhost root]# ls /etc/hosts /etc/h  2>badoutput  >&2
[root@localhost root]# cat badoutput
ls: /etc/h: No such file or directory
/etc/hosts
[root@localhost root]# _
```

In all of the examples used earlier, the contents of the files used to store the output from commands were cleared prior to use by the BASH shell. Another example of this is seen below when redirecting the Standard Output of the `date` command to the file `dateoutput`:

```
[root@localhost root]# date >dateoutput
[root@localhost root]# cat dateoutput
Wed May 29 10:55:18 EDT 2003
[root@localhost root]# date >dateoutput
[root@localhost root]# cat dateoutput
Wed May 29 10:56:27 EDT 2003
[root@localhost root]# _
```

To prevent the file from being cleared by the BASH shell and append output to the existing output, you may specify two ">" metacharacters alongside the file descriptor, as seen below:

```
[root@localhost root]# date >dateoutput
[root@localhost root]# cat dateoutput
Wed May 29 10:58:17 EDT 2003
[root@localhost root]# date >>dateoutput
[root@localhost root]# cat dateoutput
Wed May 29 10:58:17 EDT 2003
Wed May 29 10:59:26 EDT 2003
[root@localhost root]# _
```

You may also redirect a file to the Standard Input of a command using the "<" metacharacter. Since there is only one file descriptor for input, there is no need to specify the number 0 before "<" metacharacter to indicate Standard Input, as seen below:

```
[root@localhost root]# cat </etc/hosts
# Do not remove the following line, or various programs
# that require network functionality will fail.
127.0.0.1               localhost.localdomain localhost
[root@localhost root]# _
```

In the above output, the BASH shell located and sent the `/etc/hosts` file to the `cat` command as Standard Input. Since the `cat` command normally takes the filename to be displayed as an argument on the command line (i.e., `cat /etc/hosts`), there is no need to use Standard Input redirection with the `cat` command as we did in the above

8

example; however, there are some commands on the Linux system that only accept files when they are passed by the shell through Standard Input. The `tr` command is one such command that can be used to replace characters in a file sent via Standard Input. To translate all of the lowercase "l" characters in the `/etc/hosts` file to uppercase "L" characters, you may run the following command:

```
[root@localhost root]# tr l L </etc/hosts
# Do not remove the foLLowing Line, or various programs
# that require network functionaLity wiLL faiL.
127.0.0.1     LocaLhost.LocaLdomain LocaLhost
[root@localhost root]# _
```

The command above does not modify the `/etc/hosts` file; it simply takes a copy of the `/etc/hosts` file, manipulates it, then sends the Standard Output to the terminal screen. To save a copy of the Standard Output for later use, you may use both Standard Input and Standard Output redirection together:

```
[root@localhost root]# tr l L </etc/hosts >newhosts
[root@localhost root]# cat newhosts
# Do not remove the foLLowing Line, or various programs
# that require network functionaLity wiLL faiL.
127.0.0.2     LocaLhost.LocaLdomain LocaLhost
[root@localhost root]# _
```

As with redirecting Standard Output and Standard Error in the same command, you should use different filenames when redirecting Standard Input and Standard Output. However, the reason for this is that the BASH shell clears a file that already exists before performing the redirection. An example of this is seen below:

```
[root@localhost root]# sort <newhosts  >newhosts
[root@localhost root]# cat newhosts
[root@localhost root]# _
```

The `newhosts` file has no contents when displayed in the above output. Since the BASH shell saw that output redirection was indicated on the command line, it cleared the contents of the file `newhosts`, then sorted the blank file and saved the output (nothing in our example) into the file `newhosts`. Because of this feature of shell redirection, Linux administrators commonly use the command `>filename` at the command prompt to clear the contents of a file.

 The contents of logfiles are typically cleared periodically using the command `>/path/to/logfile`.

A summary of the different types of redirection seen in this section can be found in Table 8-1.

Table 8-1 Common redirection examples

Command	Description
command 1>file command >file	The Standard Output of the command is sent to a file instead of the terminal screen.
command 2>file	The Standard Error of the command is sent to a file instead of the terminal screen.
command 1>fileA 2>fileB command >fileA 2>fileB	The Standard Output of the command is sent to fileA instead of the terminal screen, and the Standard Error of the command is sent to fileB instead of the terminal screen.
command 1>file 2>&1 command >file 2>&1 command 1>&2 2>file command >&2 2>file	Both the Standard Output and the Standard Error are sent to the same file instead of the terminal screen.
command 1>>file command >>file	The Standard Output of the command is appended to a file instead of being sent to the terminal screen.
command 2>>file	The Standard Error of the command is appended to a file instead of being sent to the terminal screen.
command 0<file command <file	The Standard Input of a command is taken from a file.

Pipes

Note from Table 8-1 that redirection only occurs from a command to a file and vice versa. You may also send the Standard Output of one command to another command as Standard Input. To do this, you must use the pipe " | " shell metacharacter and specify commands on either side. The shell will then send the Standard Output of the command on the left to the command on the right, which then interprets the information as Standard Input. This process is depicted in Figure 8-2.

 The whole command that includes the pipe " | " metacharacter is commonly referred to as a **pipe**.

Figure 8-2 Piping information from one command to another

 The pipe symbol can be created on most keyboards by pressing Shift+\.

For example, the Standard Output of the `ls -l /etc` command is too large to fit on one terminal screen. To send the Standard Output of this command to the `less` command, which views Standard Input page-by-page, you could use the following command:

```
[root@localhost root]# ls -l /etc | less
total 2384
-rw-r--r--   1 root       root       15223 Jun 25   2001 a2ps.cfg
-rw-r--r--   1 root       root        2561 Jun 25   2001 a2ps-site.cfg
-rw-r--r--   1 root       root          47 May 29 12:03 adjtime
drwxr-xr-x   4 root       root        4096 May 26 07:33 alchemist
-rw-r--r--   1 root       root        1109 May 26 10:33 aliases
-rw-r--r--   1 root       root        2288 May 30 00:21 aliases.db
drwxr-xr-x   3 amanda     disk        4096 May 26 10:30 amanda
-rw-r--r--   1 amanda     disk           0 Jul 13   2001 amandates
-rw-------   1 root       root         688 Jul 18   2001 amd.conf
-rw-r-----   1 root       root         105 Jul 18   2001 amd.net
-rw-r--r--   1 root       root         370 Jun 24   2001 anacrontab
-rw-------   1 root       root           1 Aug  2   2001 at.deny
-rw-r--r--   1 root       root         212 Aug 29   2001 auto.master
-rw-r--r--   1 root       root         575 Aug 29   2001 auto.misc
-rw-r--r--   1 root       root        1229 May 21   2001 bashrc
-rw-r--r--   1 root       root         756 Aug  8   2001 cdrecord.conf
drwxr-xr-x   2 root       root        4096 May 27 23:11 cipe
-rw-------   1 root       root          94 May 26 10:33 conf.linuxconf
-rw-------   1 root       root          71 May 26 10:33 conf.linuxconf.OLD
drwxr-xr-x   3 root       root        4096 Sep  5   2001 CORBA
drwxr-xr-x   2 root       root        4096 Jun 24   2001 cron.d
drwxr-xr-x   2 root       root        4096 May 27 23:12 cron.daily
drwxr-xr-x   2 root       root        4096 Jul 19   2001 cron.hourly
:
```

You need not have spaces around the "|" metacharacter; the command `ls -l /etc|less` and `ls -l /etc    |    less` are equivalent.

A common use of piping is to reduce the amount of information displayed on the terminal screen from commands that display too much information. Recall the `mount` command used earlier:

```
[root@localhost root]# mount
/dev/hdc2 on / type ext3 (rw)
none on /proc type proc (rw)
/dev/hdc1 on /boot type ext3 (rw)
none on /dev/pts type devpts (rw,gid=5,mode=620)
none on /dev/shm type tmpfs (rw)
none on /proc/sys/fs/binfmt_misc type binfmt_misc (rw)
[root@localhost root]# _
```

To view only those lines that contain the information regarding filesystems mounted from the secondary master IDE hard disk (/dev/hdc), you could send the Standard Output of the mount command to the grep command as Standard Input, as seen below:

```
[root@localhost root]# mount | grep /dev/hdc
/dev/hdc2 on / type ext3 (rw)
/dev/hdc1 on /boot type ext3 (rw)
[root@localhost root]# _
```

The grep command in the above output receives the full output from the mount command and then displays only those lines that have /dev/hdc in them. The grep command normally takes two arguments; the first specifies the text to search for and the second specifies the filename(s) to search within. The grep command used above requires no second argument since the material to search comes from Standard Input (the mount command) instead of a file.

Furthermore, you may use more than one pipe "|" metacharacter on the command line to pipe information from one command to another command in much the same fashion as an assembly line in a factory. A manufacturing factory usually contains several departments that each do a specialized task very well. For example, one department may assemble the product, another may paint the product, and yet another one may package the product. Every product must pass through each department in order to be complete.

Similarly, Linux has several commands that can manipulate data in some manner. The piping of each of these commands may be compared to the flow of a manufacturing factory; information is manipulated by one command and then that manipulated information is sent to another command, which manipulates it further. After being manipulated by several commands in this fashion, the information is in a form that the user desires. This process is depicted in Figure 8-3.

command1 | command2 | command3 | command4

Figure 8-3   Piping several commands

Any command that can take from Standard Input and give to Standard Output is called a filter command. It is important to note that commands such as ls and mount are not filter commands, since they do not accept Standard Input from other commands, but instead find information from the system and display it to the user. As a result these commands must be at the beginning of a pipe. Other programs such as the vi editor are interactive and thus cannot exist within a pipe, since they cannot take from Standard Input and give to Standard Output.

There are several hundred filter commands available to Linux users; some common ones useful throughout this textbook are listed in Table 8-2.

Table 8-2   Common filter commands

Command	Description
sort sort -r	Sorts lines in a file alphanumerically Reverse sorts lines in a file alphanumerically
wc wc -l wc -w wc -c	Counts the number of lines, words, and characters in a file Counts the number of lines in a file Counts the number of words in a file Counts the number of characters in a file
pr pr -d	Formats a file for printing (has several options available); places a date and page number at the top of each page Formats a file double-spaced
tr	Replaces characters in the text of a file
grep	Displays lines in a file that match a regular expression
nl	Numbers lines in a file

Take, for example, the prologue from Shakespeare's "Romeo and Juliet:"

```
[root@localhost root]# cat prologue
Two households, both alike in dignity,
In fair Verona, where we lay our scene,
From ancient grudge break to new mutiny,
Where civil blood makes civil hands unclean.
From forth the fatal loins of these two foes
A pair of star-cross'd lovers take their life;
Whole misadventured piteous overthrows
Do with their death bury their parents' strife.
The fearful passage of their death-mark'd love,
And the continuance of their parents' rage,
Which, but their children's end, nought could remove,
Is now the two hours' traffic of our stage;
The which if you with patient ears attend,
What here shall miss, our toil shall strive to mend.
[root@localhost root]# _
```

If you wish to replace all lowercase "a" characters with uppercase "A" characters in the file above, then sort the contents by the first character on each line, then double space the output and view the results page-by-page, you could use the following pipe:

```
[root@localhost root]# cat prologue | tr a A | sort | pr -d | less

2003-05-30 09:32                                    Page 1

And the continuAnce of their pArents' rAge,
```

```
A pAir of stAr-cross'd lovers tAke their life;

Do with their deAth bury their pArents' strife.

From Ancient grudge breAk to new mutiny,

From forth the fAtAl loins of these two foes

In fAir VeronA, where we lAy our scene,

Is now the two hours' trAffic of our stAge;

The feArful pAssAge of their deAth-mArk'd love,

The which if you with pAtient eArs Attend,

Two households, both Alike in dignity,
:
```

8

The command used in the above example displays the final Standard Output to the terminal screen via the **less** command. In many cases, you may wish to display the results of the pipe as well as have a saved copy in a file on the hard disk. As a result, there exists a **tee** filter command that takes information from Standard Input and sends that information to a file, as well as to Standard Output.

To save a copy of the manipulated prologue above before displaying it to the terminal screen with the **less** command, you could use the following command:

```
[root@localhost root]# cat prologue | tr a A | sort | pr -d | tee newfile | less

2003-05-30 09:32        Page 1

And the continuAnce of their pArents' rAge,

A pAir of stAr-cross'd lovers tAke their life;

Do with their deAth bury their pArents' strife.

From Ancient grudge breAk to new mutiny,

From forth the fAtAl loins of these two foes

In fAir VeronA, where we lAy our scene,

Is now the two hours' trAffic of our stAge;

The feArful pAssAge of their deAth-mArk'd love,

The which if you with pAtient eArs Attend,
```

```
Two households, both Alike in dignity,
:q
[root@localhost root]# _
[root@localhost root]# cat newfile

2003-05-30 09:58                                    Page 1

And the continuAnce of their pArents' rAge,

A pAir of stAr-cross'd lovers tAke their life;

Do with their deAth bury their pArents' strife.

From Ancient grudge breAk to new mutiny,

From forth the fAtAl loins of these two foes

In fAir VeronA, where we lAy our scene,

Is now the two hours' trAffic of our stAge;

The feArful pAssAge of their deAth-mArk'd love,

The which if you with pAtient eArs Attend,

Two households, both Alike in dignity,

WhAt here shAll miss, our toil shAll strive to mend.

Where civil blood mAkes civil hAnds uncleAn.

Which, but their children's end, nought could remove,

Whole misAdventured piteous overthrows

[root@localhost root]# _
```

In addition, you may combine redirection and piping together; however, input redirection must occur at the beginning of the pipe and output redirection must occur at the end of the pipe. An example of this is seen in the following output, which replaces all lowercase "a" characters with uppercase "A" characters in the prologue file used in previous example, then sorts the file, numbers each line and saves the output to a file called `newprologue` instead of sending the output to the terminal screen:

```
[root@localhost root]# tr a A <prologue | sort |
nl >newprologue
[root@localhost root]# cat newprologue
     1  And the continuAnce of their pArents' rAge,
     2  A pAir of stAr-cross'd lovers tAke their life;
```

```
     3  Do with their deAth bury their pArents' strife.
     4  From Ancient grudge breAk to new mutiny,
     5  From forth the fAtAl loins of these two foes
     6  In fAir VeronA, where we lAy our scene,
     7  Is now the two hours' trAffic of our stAge;
     8  The feArful pAssAge of their deAth-mArk'd love,
     9  The which if you with pAtient eArs Attend,
    10  Two households, both Alike in dignity,
    11  WhAt here shAll miss, our toil shAll strive
        to mend.
    12  Where civil blood mAkes civil hAnds uncleAn.
    13  Which, but their children's end, nought could
        remove,
    14  Whole misAdventured piteous overthrows
[root@localhost root]# _
```

SHELL VARIABLES

8

A BASH shell has several variables in memory at any one time. Recall that a variable is simply a reserved portion of memory containing information that may be accessed. Most variables in the shell are referred to as **environment variables** since they are typically set by the system and contain information that the system and programs access regularly. You may also create your own custom variables. These variables are called **user–defined** variables. In addition to these two types of variables, there are special variables that are useful when executing commands and creating new files and directories.

Environment Variables

There are many environment variables, which are set by default in the BASH shell. To see a list of these variables and their current values, you may use the **set** command, as seen below:

```
[root@localhost root]# set
BASH=/bin/bash
BASH_ENV=/root/.bashrc
BASH_VERSINFO=([0]="2" [1]="05" [2]="8" [3]="1" [4]=
"release" [5]="i386-redhat-l
inux-gnu")
BASH_VERSION=$'2.05.8(1)-release'
COLORS=/etc/DIR_COLORS
COLUMNS=80
DIRSTACK=()
EUID=0
GROUPS=()
HISTFILE=/root/.bash_history
HISTFILESIZE=1000
HISTSIZE=1000
```

```
HOME=/root
HOSTNAME=localhost.localdomain
HOSTTYPE=i386
IFS=$' \t\n'
INPUTRC=/etc/inputrc
KDEDIR=/usr
LAMHELPFILE=/etc/lam/lam-helpfile
LANG=en_US
LESSOPEN=$'|/usr/bin/lesspipe.sh %s'
LINES=25
LOGNAME=root
LS_COLORS=
MACHTYPE=i386-redhat-linux-gnu
MAIL=/var/spool/mail/root
MAILCHECK=60
OPTERR=1
OPTIND=1
OSTYPE=linux-gnu
PATH=/usr/kerberos/sbin:/usr/kerberos/bin:/usr/local/sbin:
/usr/local/bin:/sbin:/
bin:/usr/sbin:/usr/bin:/usr/X11R6/bin:/root/bin
PIPESTATUS=([0]="0")
PPID=3986
PS1=$'[\\u@\\h \\W]\\$ '
PS2=$'> '
PS4=$'+ '
PVM_ROOT=/usr/share/pvm3
PVM_RSH=/usr/bin/rsh
PWD=/root
QTDIR=/usr/lib/qt-2.3.1
REMOTEHOST=3.0.0.2
SHELL=/bin/bash
SHELLOPTS=braceexpand:hashall:histexpand:monitor:history:
interactive-comments:em
acs
SHLVL=1
SSH_ASKPASS=/usr/libexec/openssh/gnome-ssh-askpass
SUPPORTED=en_US:en
TERM=ansi
UID=0
USER=root
USERNAME=root
XPVM_ROOT=/usr/share/pvm3/xpvm
_=newprologue
langfile=/root/.i18n
sourced=1
mc ()
```

```
{
    mkdir -p ~/.mc/tmp 2>/dev/null;
    chmod 700 ~/.mc/tmp;
    MC=~/.mc/tmp/mc-$$;
    /usr/bin/mc -P "$@" >"$MC";
    cd "`cat $MC`";
    /bin/rm "$MC";
    unset MC
}
[root@localhost root]# _
```

Some environment variables seen in the above output are used by programs that require information about the system; the OSTYPE (Operating System TYPE) and SHELL (Pathname to shell) variables are two examples. Other variables are used to set the user's working environment; the most common of these include:

- PS1 (the default shell prompt)
- HOME (the absolute pathname to the user's home directory)
- PWD (the present working directory in the directory tree)
- PATH (a list of directories to search for executable programs)

The PS1 variable represents the BASH shell prompt. To view the contents of this variable only, you may use the **echo** command and specify the variable name prefixed by the "$" shell metacharacter, as seen in the output below:

```
[root@localhost root]# echo $PS1
[\u@\h \W]\$
[root@localhost root]# _
```

Note that there is special notation used to define the prompt in the above output: "\u" indicates the username, "\h" indicates the hostname, and "\W" indicates the name of the current directory. A list of BASH notation can be found by navigating through the manual page for the **bash** shell as seen in the following output:

```
[root@localhost root]# man bash
    \a    an ASCII bell character (07)
    \d    the date  in  "Weekday  Month  Date"  format
          (e.g., "Tue May 26")
```

8

```
    \e    an ASCII escape character (033)
    \h    the hostname up to the first `.'
    \H    the hostname
    \j    the  number of jobs currently managed by the shell
    \l    the basename of the shell's terminal  device
          name
    \n    newline
    \r    carriage return
    \s    the  name   of  the shell, the basename of $0
          (the portion following the final slash)
    \t    the current time in 24-hour HH:MM:SS format
    \T    the current time in 12-hour HH:MM:SS format
    \@    the current time in 12-hour am/pm format
    \u    the username of the current user
    \v    the version of bash (e.g., 2.00)
    \V    the release of bash, version + patchlevel
          (e.g., 2.00.0)
    \w    the current working directory
    \W    the  basename  of the current working direc¡
          tory
    \!    the history number of this command
    \#    the command number of this command
    \$    if the effective UID is 0, a #, otherwise  a
          $
  \nnn the  character  corresponding  to  the octal
          number nnn
    \\    a backslash
    \[    begin a sequence of non-printing  characters,
          which could be used to embed a terminal con¡
          trol sequence into the prompt
    \]    end a sequence of non-printing characters
lines 2421-2444 byte 139123  code ASCII  (press RETURN)
:q
[root@localhost root]# _
```

To change the value of a variable, you simply need to specify the variable name followed immediately by an equal sign "=" and the new value. The following output demonstrates how you may change the value of the PS1 variable. The new prompt will take effect immediately and allow the user to type commands.

```
[root@localhost root]# PS1="This is the new prompt: #"
This is the new prompt: # _
This is the new prompt: # date
Fri May 31 10:15:56 EDT 2003
This is the new prompt: # _
This is the new prompt: # who
root       pts/0     May 30 09:58 (3.0.0.2)
This is the new prompt: # _
This is the new prompt: # PS1="[\u@\h \W]#"
[root@localhost root]# _
```

The HOME variable is used by programs that require the pathname to the current user's home directory to store or search for files, and therefore it should not be changed. If the "root" user logs into the system, then the HOME variable is set to /root; alternatively, the HOME variable is set to /home/user1 if the user named "user1" logs into the system. Recall that the tilde "~" metacharacter represents the current user's home directory; this metacharacter is a pointer to the HOME variable as seen below:

```
[root@localhost root]# echo $HOME
/root
[root@localhost root]# echo ~
/root
[root@localhost root]# HOME=/etc
[root@localhost root]# echo $HOME
/etc
[root@localhost root]# echo ~
/etc
[root@localhost root]# _
```

Like the HOME variable, the PWD (Print Working Directory) variable is vital to your environment and should not be changed. PWD stores the current user's location in the directory tree. It is affected by the **cd** command and used by other commands such as **pwd** when the current directory needs to be identified. The output below demonstrates how this variable works:

```
[root@localhost root]# pwd
/root
[root@localhost root]# echo $PWD
/root
[root@localhost root]# cd /etc
[root@localhost etc]# pwd
/etc
[root@localhost root]# echo $PWD
/etc
[root@localhost root]# _
```

The PATH variable is one of the most important variables in the BASH shell, as it allows users to execute commands by typing the command name alone. Recall that most commands are represented by an executable file on the hard drive typically located in one of several directories named **bin** or **sbin** throughout the Linux directory tree. To execute the **ls** command, you could either type the absolute or relative pathname to the file (i.e., **/bin/ls** or **../../bin/ls**), or simply type the letters **ls** and allow the system to search the directories listed in the PATH variable for a command named **ls**. Sample contents of the PATH variable are shown below:

```
[root@localhost root]# echo $PATH
/usr/kerberos/sbin:/usr/kerberos/bin:/usr/local/sbin:/usr/
local/bin:/sbin:/bin:/usr/sbin:/usr/bin:/usr/X11R6/bin:/root/bin
[root@localhost root]# _
```

From the above output, if you simply type the command **ls** at the command prompt and press Enter, the shell will notice that there is no "/" character in the pathname and proceed to search for the file **ls** in the **/usr/kerberos/sbin** directory, then the **/usr/kerberos/bin** directory, the **/usr/local/sbin** directory, the **/usr/local/bin** directory, the **/sbin** directory, and then the **/bin** directory before finding the **ls** executable file. If there was no **ls** file found in any directory in the PATH variable, then the shell would return an error message, as seen below with a misspelled command:

```
[root@localhost root]# lss
bash: lss: command not found
[root@localhost root]# _
```

Thus, if a command is located within a directory that is listed in the PATH variable, then you may simply type the name of the command on the command line to execute it, as the shell will be able to find the appropriate executable file on the filesystem. All of the commands used in this textbook up until this section have been located in directories listed in the PATH variable. However, if the executable file is not in a directory listed in the PATH variable, then you must specify either the absolute or relative pathname to the executable file. An example of this is seen below using the **myprogram** file in the **/root** directory (a directory not listed in the PATH variable):

```
[root@localhost root]# pwd
/root
[root@localhost root]# ls -F
Desktop/  myprogram*
[root@localhost root]# myprogram
bash: myprogram: command not found
[root@localhost root]# /root/myprogram
This is a sample program.
[root@localhost root]# ./myprogram
This is a sample program.
[root@localhost root]# cp myprogram /bin
[root@localhost root]# myprogram
```

```
This is a sample program.
[root@localhost root]# _
```

Once the `myprogram` executable file was copied to the `/bin` directory in the above output, the user was able to execute it simply by typing its name, since the `/bin` directory is listed in the PATH variable.

A list of environment variables used in most BASH shells can be seen in Table 8-3.

Table 8-3   Common BASH environment variables

Variable	Description
BASH	Full path to the BASH shell
BASH_VERSION	The version of the current BASH shell
DISPLAY	Used to redirect the output of X Windows to another computer or device
ENV	Location of the BASH runtime configuration file (usually ~/.bashrc)
EUID	Effective UID (User ID) of the current user
HISTFILE	The filename used to store previously entered commands in the BASH shell (usually ~/.bash_history)
HISTFILESIZE	The number of previously entered commands that can be stored in the HISTFILE upon logout for use during the next login—it is typically 1000 commands
HISTSIZE	The number of previously entered commands that will be stored in memory during the current login session—it is typically 1000 commands
HOME	The absolute pathname of the current user's home directory
HOSTNAME	The hostname of the Linux system
LOGNAME	The username of the current user when logging into the shell
MAIL	The location of the mailbox file (where e-mail is stored)
OLDPWD	The most recent previous working directory
OSTYPE	Identifies the current operating system
PATH	The directories to search for executable program files in the absence of an absolute or relative pathname containing a / character
PS1	The current shell prompt
PWD	The current working directory
RANDOM	Creates a random number when accessed
SHELL	The absolute pathname of the current shell
TERM	Used to determine the terminal settings—it is typically set to "linux" on newer Linux systems and "console" on older Linux systems

User-Defined Variables

You may set your own variables using the same method discussed earlier to change the contents of existing environment variables. To do so, you simply specify the name of the

variable (known as the **variable identifier**) followed immediately by the equal sign "="
and the new contents. When creating new variables, it is important to note the following features of variable identifiers:

- They can contain alphanumeric characters (0–9, A–Z, a–z), the dash "–" character, or the underscore "_" character.

- They must not start with a number.

- They are typically capitalized to follow convention (i.e., HOME, PATH, etc.).

To create a variable called MYVAR with the contents "This is a sample variable" and
display its contents, you could use the following commands:

```
[root@localhost root]# MYVAR="This is a sample variable"
[root@localhost root]# echo $MYVAR
This is a sample variable
[root@localhost root]# _
```

The above command created a variable that is available to the current shell. Most commands that are run by the shell are run in a separate **subshell**, which is created by the
current shell. Variables created in the current shell are not available to those subshells and
the commands running within them. Thus, if you create a variable to be used within a
certain program such as a database editor, then that variable should be exported to all
subshells using the **export** command to ensure that all programs started by the current
shell have the ability to access the variable.

Recall from earlier that all environment variables in the BASH shell may be listed using
the **set** command; user-defined variables are also indicated in this list. Similarly, to see
a list of all exported environment and user-defined variables in the shell, you may use
the **env** command. Since the outputs of **set** and **env** are typically large, you would
commonly redirect the Standard Output of these commands to the **grep** command to
display certain lines only.

To see the difference between the **set** and **env** commands as well as export the
MYVAR variable created earlier, you may perform the following commands:

```
[root@localhost root]# set | grep MYVAR
MYVAR=$'This is a sample variable.'
[root@localhost root]# env | grep MYVAR
[root@localhost root]# _
[root@localhost root]# export MYVAR
[root@localhost root]# env | grep MYVAR
MYVAR=This is a sample variable.
[root@localhost root]# _
```

Not all environment variables are exported; the PS1 variable is an example of a variable
that does not need to be available to subshells and is not exported as a result. However,
it is good form to export user-defined variables since they will likely be used by

processes that run in subshells. As a result, to create and export a user-defined variable called MYVAR2, you may use the export command alone, as seen below:

```
[root@localhost root]# export MYVAR2="This is another sample variable"
[root@localhost root]# set | grep MYVAR2
MYVAR2=$'This is another sample variable.'
_=MYVAR2
[root@localhost root]# env | grep MYVAR2
MYVAR2=This is another sample variable.
[root@localhost root]# _
```

Other Variables

There are other variables that are not displayed by the set or env commands; these variables perform specialized functions in the shell.

The UMASK variable used earlier in this textbook is an example of a special variable that performs a special function in the BASH shell and must be set by the umask command. Also recall that when you type the cp command, you are actually running an alias to the cp -i command. Aliases are shortcuts to commands stored in special variables, which may be created and viewed using the alias command. To create an alias to the command mount -t ext2 /dev/fd0 /mnt/floppy called mf and view it, you could use the following commands:

```
[root@localhost root]# alias mf="mount -t ext2 /dev/fd0 /mnt/floppy"
[root@localhost root]# alias
alias cp='cp -i'
alias l.='ls -d .[a-zA-Z]* --color=tty'
alias ll='ls -l --color=tty'
alias ls='ls --color=tty'
alias mf='mount -t ext2 /dev/fd0 /mnt/floppy'
alias mv='mv -i'
alias rm='rm -i'
alias which='alias | /usr/bin/which --tty-only
--read-alias --show-dot --show-tilde'
[root@localhost root]# _
```

Now, you simply need to run the mf command to mount a floppy device that contains an ext2 filesystem to the /mnt/floppy directory, as seen below:

```
[root@localhost root]# mf
[root@localhost root]# mount
/dev/hdc2 on / type ext3 (rw)
none on /proc type proc (rw)
/dev/hdc1 on /boot type ext3 (rw)
none on /dev/pts type devpts (rw,gid=5,mode=620)
none on /dev/shm type tmpfs (rw)
none on /proc/sys/fs/binfmt_misc type binfmt_misc (rw)
/dev/fd0 on /mnt/floppy type ext2 (rw)
[root@localhost root]# _
```

You may also create aliases to multiple commands provided they are separated by the ";" metacharacter. To create and test an alias called **dw** that runs the **date** command followed by the **who** command, you could do the following:

```
[root@localhost root]# alias dw="date;who"
[root@localhost root]# alias
alias cp='cp -i'
alias dw='date;who'
alias l.='ls -d .[a-zA-Z]* --color=tty'
alias ll='ls -l --color=tty'
alias ls='ls --color=tty'
alias mf='mount -t ext2 /dev/fd0 /mnt/floppy'
alias mv='mv -i'
alias rm='rm -i'
alias which='alias | /usr/bin/which --tty-only --read-
alias --show-dot --show-tilde'
[root@localhost root]# dw
Sun Jun  2 10:25:45 EDT 2003
root      pts/0   Jun  1 08:44 (3.0.0.2)
root      pts/1   Jun  1 11:54 (:0)
[root@localhost root]# _
```

 It is important to use unique alias names since the shell searches for them before it searches for executable files; if you create an alias called who, then that alias would be used instead of the who command on the filesystem.

Environment Files

Recall that variables are stored in memory. When you exit your BASH shell, all variables stored in memory are destroyed along with the shell itself. Thus, to ensure that variables are accessible to a shell at all times, you must place variables in a file that is executed each time you log in and start a BASH shell. These files are called **environment files**. Some common BASH shell environment files and the order they are executed in are listed below:

- /etc/profile
- ~/.bash_profile
- ~/.bash_login
- ~/.profile

The /etc/profile file is always executed immediately after login for all users on the system and sets most environment variables such as HOME and PATH. After /etc/profile finishes executing, the home directory of the user is searched for the hidden environment files .bash_profile, .bash_login, and .profile. If these files exist, the first one found will be executed; as a result, only one of these files is typically used. These hidden environment files allow you to set your own customized variables independent of BASH shells used by other users on the system; any values assigned to variables in these files override those set in /etc/profile due to the order of execution.

To add a variable to any of these files, you simply add a line that has the same format as the command used on the command line. To add the MYVAR2 variable used above to the .bash_profile file, you would edit the file using a text editor such as **vi** and add the line export MYVAR2="This is another sample variable" to the file.

Variables are not the only type of information that may be entered into an environment file; any command that can be executed on the command line may also be placed inside any environment file. If you wished to set the UMASK to 077, display the date after each login, and create an alias, then you could add the following lines to one of the hidden environment files in your home directory:

```
umask 077
date
alias dw="date;who"
```

There also exists a special environment file that is always executed before the other hidden environment files are searched and when you start any new BASH shell after login. This file is located in your home directory and is called .bashrc (BASH runtime configuration).

You may wish to execute cleanup tasks upon exiting the shell; to do this, you may simply add those cleanup commands to the .bash_logout file in your home directory.

SHELL SCRIPTS

We saw in the previous section that the BASH shell can execute commands that exist within environment files. The BASH shell also has the ability to execute other text files containing commands and special constructs. These files are referred to as **shell scripts** and are typically used to create custom programs that perform administrative tasks on Linux systems. Any command that can be entered on the command line in Linux may be entered into a shell script, since it is a BASH shell that interprets the contents of the shell script itself. The most basic shell script is one that contains a list of commands, one per line, for the shell to execute in order, as seen below in the text file called **myscript**:

```
[root@localhost root]# cat myscript
#!/bin/bash
#this is a comment
date
who
ls -F /
[root@localhost root]#
```

The first line in the shell script above (#!/bin/bash) is called a **hashpling**; it specifies the pathname to the shell that will interpret the contents of the shell script. Different shells may use different constructs in their shell scripts, thus it is important to identify which shell was used to create a particular shell script. The hashpling gives a user who uses the C shell (for example) the ability to use a BASH shell when executing the `myscript` shell script seen above. The second line of the shell script is referred to as a comment since it begins with a # character and is ignored by the shell; the only exception to this is the hashpling on the first line of a shell script. The remainder of the shell script seen in the above output consists of three commands that will be executed by the shell in order: `date`, `who`, and `ls`.

If you have read permission to a shell script, then you may execute the shell script by starting another BASH shell and specifying the shell script as an argument. To execute the `myscript` shell script seen earlier, you may use the following command:

```
[root@localhost root]# bash myscript
Sat Jun  1 08:46:43 EDT 2003
root     pts/0    Jun  1 08:44 (3.0.0.2)
bin/   dev/  home/   lib/       misc/  opt/   root/   tftpboot/  usr/
boot/  etc/  initrd/ lost+found/ mnt/  proc/  sbin/   tmp/ var/
[root@localhost root]# _
```

Alternatively, if you have read and execute permission to a shell script, then you may execute the shell script like any other executable program on the system as seen below using the `myscript` shell script:

```
[root@localhost root]# chmod a+x myscript
[root@localhost root]# ./myscript
Sat Jun  1 08:48:56 EDT 2003
root      pts/0    Jun  1 08:44 (3.0.0.2)
bin/   dev/  home/    lib/       misc/  opt/   root/
tftpboot/  usr/
boot/  etc/  initrd/ lost+found/  mnt/   proc/  sbin/
tmp/        var/ [root@localhost root]# _
```

The above output is difficult to read as the output from each command is not separated by blank lines or identified by a label. Utilizing the `echo` command results in a more user-friendly `myscript` as seen below:

```
[root@localhost root]# cat myscript
#!/bin/bash
echo "Today's date is:"
date
echo ""
echo "The people logged into the system include:"
who
echo ""
echo "The contents of the / directory are:"
ls -F /
[root@localhost root]# ./myscript
Today's date is:
Sat Jun  1 08:55:52 EDT 2003
```

```
The people logged into the system include:
root      pts/0    Jun  1 08:44 (3.0.0.2)

The contents of the / directory are:
bin/    dev/    home/     lib/          misc/   opt/    root/   tftpboot/   usr/
boot/   etc/    initrd/   lost+found/   mnt/    proc/   sbin/   tmp/        var/
[root@localhost root]# _
```

Escape Sequences

In the previous example, we used the echo command to manipulate data that appeared on the screen. The echo command also supports several special notations called **escape sequences** that you may use to manipulate the way text is displayed to the terminal screen further, provided the −e option is specified to the echo command. A list of these echo escape sequences is found in Table 8-4.

Table 8-4 Common echo escape sequences

Escape Sequence	Description
\???	Inserts an ASCII character represented by a three-digit octal number (???)
\\	Backslash
\a	ASCII beep
\b	Backspace
\c	Prevents a new line following the command
\f	Form feed
\n	Starts a new line
\r	Carriage return
\t	Horizontal tab
\v	Vertical tab

The escape sequences listed in Table 8-4 may be used to manipulate further the output of the myscript shell script used earlier, as seen below:

```
[root@localhost root]# cat myscript
#!/bin/bash
echo -e "Today's date is: \c"
date
echo -e "\nThe people logged into the system include:"
who
echo -e "\nThe contents of the / directory are:"
ls -F /
[root@localhost root]# ./myscript
Today's date is: Sat Jun  1 09:13:31 EDT 2003
```

```
The people logged into the system include:
root     pts/0    Jun  1 08:44 (3.0.0.2)

The contents of the / directory are:
bin/    dev/  home/   lib/         misc/  opt/   root/  tftpboot/  usr/
boot/   etc/  initrd/ lost+found/  mnt/   proc/  sbin/  tmp/       var/
[root@localhost root]# _
```

Notice from above that the \c escape sequence prevented the newline character at the end of the output **Today's date is:** when myscript was executed. Similarly, newline characters (\n) were inserted prior to displaying **The people logged into the system include:** and **The contents of the / directory are:** to create blank lines between command outputs. This eliminated the need for using the echo "" command seen earlier.

Reading Standard Input

There may also be times where a shell script may need input from the user executing the program; this input may then be stored in a variable for later use. The read command takes user input from Standard Input and places it in a variable specified by an argument to the read command. After the input has been read into a variable, the contents of that variable may then be used, as seen in the following shell script:

```
[root@localhost root]# cat newscript
#!/bin/bash
echo "What is your name? -->\c"
read USERNAME
echo "Hello $USERNAME"
[root@localhost root]# chmod a+x newscript
[root@localhost root]# ./newscript
What is your name? --> Fred
Hello Fred
[root@localhost root]# _
```

Note from the above output that the echo command used to pose a question to the user ends with - - > to simulate an arrow prompt on the screen and the \c escape sequence to place the cursor after the arrow prompt. This is common practice among Linux administrators when writing shell scripts.

Decision Constructs

Decision constructs are the most common type of construct used in shell scripts; they alter the flow of a program based on whether a command in the program completed successfully, or based on a decision that the user makes given a question posed by the program. This is reflected in Figures 8-4 and 8-5.

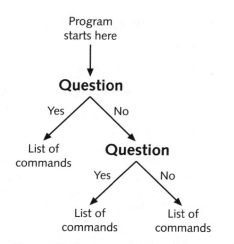

Figure 8-4   A sample decision construct

Figure 8-5   A sample decision construct

The if Construct

The most common type of decision construct is known as the **if** construct. The syntax of the **if** construct is seen below:

```
if       this is true
then
  do these commands
elif     this is true
then
  do these commands
else
  do these commands
fi
```

There are some common rules that govern `if` constructs:

- `elif` (else if) and `else` statements are optional.
- You may have an unlimited number of `elif` statements.
- The *do these commands* section may consist of multiple commands, one per line.
- The *do these commands* section is typically indented from the left hand side of the text file for readability, but does not need to be.
- The end of the statement must be a backwards "if" (`fi`).
- The *this is true* part of the `if` syntax seen earlier may be a command or a test statement: commands return true if they perform their function properly, and test statements are enclosed within square brackets or prefixed by the word "test" and used to test certain conditions on the system.

An example of using a basic `if` construct to ensure that the `etc/sample` directory is created successfully, and that the `/etc/hosts` file is copied to it, is seen in the following output:

```
[root@localhost root]# cat testmkdir
#!/bin/bash
if mkdir /etc/sample
then
    cp /etc/hosts /etc/sample
    echo "The hosts file was successfully copied to
/etc/sample"
else
    echo "The /etc/sample directory could not be created."
fi
[root@localhost root]# chmod a+x testmkdir
[root@localhost root]# ./testmkdir
The hosts file was successfully copied to /etc/sample
[root@localhost root]# _
```

In the above output, the `mkdir /etc/sample` command is always run; if it runs successfully, then the shell script will proceed to the `cp /etc/hosts /etc/sample` and `echo "The hosts file was successfully copied to /etc/sample"` commands. If the `mkdir /etc/sample` command was unsuccessful, then the shell script will skip ahead and execute the `echo "The /etc/sample directory could not be created."` command. If there were more lines of text following the `fi` in the above shell script, they would be executed after the `if` construct, regardless of its outcome.

Often, it is useful to use the `if` construct to alter the flow of the program given input from the user. Recall the `myscript` shell script used earlier:

```
[root@localhost root]# cat myscript
#!/bin/bash
echo -e "Today's date is: \c"
date
```

```
echo -e "\nThe people logged into the system include:"
who
echo -e "\nThe contents of the / directory are:"
ls -F /
[root@localhost root]# _
```

To ask the user whether or not to display the contents of the / directory, you could use the following if construct in the myscript file:

```
[root@localhost root]# cat myscript
#!/bin/bash
echo -e "Today's date is: \c"
date
echo -e "\nThe people logged into the system include:"
who
echo -e "\nWould you like to see the contents of /?(y/n)-->\c"
read ANSWER
if [ $ANSWER = "y" ]
then
      echo -e "\nThe contents of the / directory are:"
      ls -F /
fi
[root@localhost root]# ./myscript
Today's date is: Sat Jun  1 09:13:31 EDT 2003

The people logged into the system include:
root        pts/0     Jun  1 08:44 (3.0.0.2)

Would you like to see the contents of /?(y/n)--> y

The contents of the / directory are:
bin/    dev/   home/    lib/          misc/   opt/    root/    tftpboot/   usr/
boot/   etc/   initrd/  lost+found/   mnt/    proc/   sbin/    tmp/        var/
[root@localhost root]# _
```

Notice from the above output that the test statement [$ANSWER = "y"] is used to test to see whether the contents of the ANSWER variable are equal to the letter y. Any other character in this variable will cause this test statement to return false and the directory listing would then be skipped altogether. The type of comparison used above is called a string comparison, as two values are compared for strings of characters. It is indicated by the operator of the test statement, which is the equal sign "=" in the example. A list of common operators used in test statements and their definitions are seen in Table 8-5.

The test statement [$ANSWER = "y"] is equivalent to the test statement test $ANSWER = "y".

It is important to ensure that there is a space character after the beginning square bracket and before the ending square bracket; otherwise the test statement will produce an error.

Table 8-5   Common test statements

Test Statement	Returns true if
[A = B]	String A is equal to string B
[A != B]	String A is not equal to string B
[A -eq B]	A is numerically equal to B
[A -ne B]	A is numerically not equal to B
[A -lt B]	A is numerically less than B
[A -gt B]	A is numerically greater than B
[A -le B]	A is numerically less than or equal to B
[A -ge B]	A is numerically greater than or equal to B
[-r A]	A is a file/directory that exists and is readable (r permission)
[-w A]	A is a file/directory that exists and is writeable (w permission)
[-x A]	A is a file/directory that exists and is executable (x permission)
[-f A]	A is a file that exists
[-d A]	A is a directory that exists

You may also combine any test statement together with another test statement using the special comparison operators −o (OR) and −a (AND) or reverse the meaning of a test statement with the ! (NOT) operator. Examples of using these operators in test statements are listed in Table 8-6.

There may be several −o, −a, and ! operators in one test statement.

Table 8-6   Special operators in test statements

Test Statement	Returns true if
[A = B -o C = D]	String A is equal to string B **OR** string C is equal to string D
[A = B -a C = D]	String A is equal to string B **AND** string C is equal to string D
[! A = B]	String A is **NOT** equal to string B

Considering the **myscript** shell script, you may proceed with the directory listing if you enter "y" or "Y" in the following example:

```
[root@localhost root]# cat myscript
#!/bin/bash
echo -e "Today's date is: \c"
```

```
date
echo -e "\nThe people logged into the system include:"
who
echo -e "\nWould you like to see the contents of /?(y/n)-->\c"
read ANSWER
if [ $ANSWER = "y" -o $ANSWER = "Y" ]
then
      echo -e "\nThe contents of the / directory are:"
      ls -F /
fi
[root@localhost root]# ./myscript
Today's date is: Sat Jun  1 09:13:31 EDT 2003

The people logged into the system include:
root      pts/0     Jun  1 08:44 (3.0.0.2)

Would you like to see the contents of /?(y/n)--> Y

The contents of the / directory are:
bin/    dev/   home/    lib/         misc/  opt/   root/   tftpboot/   usr/
boot/   etc/   initrd/  lost+found/  mnt/   proc/  sbin/   tmp/        var/
[root@localhost root]# _
```

The case Construct

The **if** construct used earlier is well-suited for offering a small number of choices. But consider the **myscript** example used earlier, this time with several **elif** statements to perform different tasks based on the user input:

```
[root@localhost root]# cat myscript
#!/bin/bash
echo -e "What would you like to see?
Todays date (d)
Currently logged in users (u)
The contents of the / directory (r)

Enter your choice(d/u/r)-->\c"
read ANSWER
if [ $ANSWER = "d" -o $ANSWER = "D" ]
then
      echo -e "Today's date is: \c"
      date
elif [ $ANSWER = "u" -o $ANSWER = "U" ]
then
      echo -
e "\nThe people logged into the system include:"
      who
elif [ $ANSWER = "r" -o $ANSWER3 = "R" ]
```

8

```
then
        echo -e "\nThe contents of the / directory are:"
        ls -F /
fi
[root@localhost root]# _
[root@localhost root]# ./myscript
What would you like to see?
Todays date (d)
Currently logged in users (u)
The contents of the / directory (r)

Enter your choice(d/u/r)--> d
Today's date is: Sat Jun  1 11:10:03 EDT 2003
[root@localhost root]# _
```

The above shell script becomes increasingly difficult to read as the number of choices available increase. Thus, when presenting several choices, it is commonplace to use a **case** construct. The syntax of the **case** construct is seen below:

```
case variable in
        pattern1  )  do this
                         ;;
        pattern2  )  do this
                         ;;
        pattern3  )  do this
                         ;;
esac
```

The **case** statement compares the value of a variable with several different patterns of text or numbers. If there is a match, then the commands to the right of the pattern will be executed (*do this* in the above syntax). As with the **if** construct, the **case** construct must be ended by a backwards "case" (**esac**).

An example that simplifies the **myscript** example above by using the **case** construct is seen in the following output:

```
[root@localhost root]# cat myscript
#!/bin/bash
echo -e "What would you like to see?
Todays date (d)
Currently logged in users (u)
The contents of the / directory (r)

Enter your choice(d/u/r)-->\c"
read ANSWER
```

```
case $ANSWER in
   d | D ) echo -e "\nToday's date is: \c"
           date
           ;;
   u | U ) echo -
e "\nThe people logged into the system include:"
           who
           ;;
   r | R ) echo -
e "\nThe contents of the / directory are:"
           ls -F /
           ;;
       *) echo -e "Invalid choice! \a"
           ;;
esac
[root@localhost root]# ./myscript
What would you like to see?
Todays date (d)
Currently logged in users (u)
The contents of the / directory (r)

Enter your choice(d/u/r)--> d
Today's date is: Sat Jun  1 11:33:23 EDT 2003
[root@localhost root]# _
```

The example above prompts you with a menu and allows you to select an item that is then placed into the ANSWER variable. If the ANSWER variable is equal to the letter d or D, then the **date** command is executed. However, if the ANSWER variable is equal to the letter u or U, then the who command is executed, and if the ANSWER variable is equal to the letter r or R, then the ls command is executed. If the ANSWER variable contains something other than the aforementioned letters, then the * wildcard metacharacter will match it and print an error message to the screen. As with **if** constructs, any statements present in the shell script following the **case** construct would be executed after the **case** construct.

The && and || Constructs

Although the **if** and **case** constructs are versatile, there are some shortcut constructs that take less time when only one decision needs to be made during the execution of a program; these constructs are && and ||. The syntax of these constructs is listed below:

```
command  &&  command

command  ||  command
```

For the && syntax above, the command on the right of the && construct is only executed if the command on the left of the && construct completed successfully. The opposite is true for the || syntax above; the command on the right of the || construct will only be executed if the command on the left of the || construct did not complete successfully.

Consider the `testmkdir` example used earlier:

```
[root@localhost root]# cat testmkdir
#!/bin/bash
if mkdir /etc/sample
then
    cp /etc/hosts /etc/sample
    echo "The hosts file was successfully copied to /etc/sample"
else
    echo "The /etc/sample directory could not be created."
fi
[root@localhost root]# _
```

You may consider rewriting the above shell script utilizing the `&&` construct as follows:

```
[root@localhost root]# cat testmkdir
#!/bin/bash
mkdir /etc/sample && cp /etc/hosts /etc/sample
[root@localhost root]# _
```

The above shell script will create the directory `/etc/sample` and only copy the `/etc/hosts` file to it if the `mkdir /etc/sample` command was successful. You may then use the `||` construct to generate error messages if one of the commands fails to execute properly:

```
[root@localhost root]# cat testmkdir
#!/bin/bash
mkdir /etc/sample || echo "Could not create /etc/sample"
cp /etc/hosts /etc/sample || echo "Could not copy /etc/hosts"
[root@localhost root]# _
```

CHAPTER SUMMARY

- There are three components available to commands: Standard Input, Standard Output, and Standard Error. Not all commands use every component.

- Standard Input is typically user input taken from the keyboard, whereas Standard Output and Standard Error are sent to the terminal screen by default.

- You may redirect the Standard Output and Standard Error of a command to a file using redirection symbols. Similarly, you may use redirection symbols to redirect a file to the Standard Input of a command.

- To redirect the Standard Output from one command to the Standard Input of another, you must use the pipe symbol.

- Most variables available to the BASH shell are environment variables, which are loaded into memory after login from environment files.

❑ You may create your own variables in the BASH shell and export them such that they are available to programs started by the shell. These variables may also be placed in environment files such that they are loaded into memory on every shell login.

❑ The UMASK variable and command aliases are special variables that must be set using a certain command.

❑ Shell scripts can be used to execute several Linux commands.

❑ Decision constructs may be used within shell scripts to execute certain Linux commands based on user input or the results of a certain command.

KEY TERMS

| — A shell metacharacter used to pipe Standard Output from one command to the Standard Input of another command.

< — A shell metacharacter used to obtain Standard Input from a file.

> — A shell metacharacter used to redirect Standard Output and Standard Error to a file.

alias command — A command used to create special variables that are shortcuts to longer command strings.

decision construct — A special construct used in a shell script to alter the flow of the program based on the outcome of a command or contents of a variable—common decision constructs include if, case, && and ||.

echo command — A command used to display or echo output to the terminal screen—it may utilize escape sequences.

env command — A command used to display a list of exported variables present in the current shell except special variables.

environment files — Files used immediately after login to execute commands—they are typically used to load variables into memory.

environment variables — Variables that store information commonly accessed by the system or programs executing on the system—together these variables form the user environment.

escape sequences — Character sequences that have special meaning inside the echo command—they are prefixed by the \ character.

export command — A command used to send variables to subshells.

file descriptors — Numeric labels used to define command input and command output.

filter — A command that can take from Standard Input and send to Standard Output—in other words, a filter is a command that can exist in the middle of a pipe.

grep command (Global Regular Expression Print) — A program used to search one or more text files for a desired string of characters.

hashpling — The first line in a shell script, which defines the shell that will be used to interpret the commands in the script file.

pipe — A string of commands connected by "|" metacharacters.

8

read command — A command used to read Standard Input from a user into a variable.

redirection — The process of changing the default locations of Standard Input, Standard Output, and Standard Error.

set command — A command used to view all variables in the shell except special variables.

shell scripts — Text files that contain a list of commands or constructs for the shell to execute in order.

sort command — A command used to sort lines in a file.

Standard Error — Represents any error messages generated by a command.

Standard Input — Represents information inputed to a command during execution.

Standard Output — Represents the desired output from a command.

subshell — A shell started by the current shell.

tee command — A command used to take from Standard Input and send to both Standard Output and a specified file.

test statement — A statement used to test a certain condition and generate a True/False value.

tr command — A command used to transform or change characters received from Standard Input.

user-defined variables — Variables that are created by the user and are not used by the system—these variables are typically exported to subshells.

variable — An area of memory used to store information—variables are created from entries in environment files when the shell is first created after login and are destroyed when the shell is destroyed upon logout.

variable identifier — The name of a variable.

REVIEW QUESTIONS

1. Since Standard Error and Standard Output represent the results of a command and Standard Input represent the input required for a command, only Standard Error and Standard Output can be redirected to a file. True or False?

2. Before a user-defined variable can be used by processes that run in subshells, that variable must be _____.

   a. imported

   b. validated by running the env command

   c. It cannot be used outside the user's own subshell; it is only for that user.

   d. exported

   e. redirected to the BASH shell

3. The **alias** command can be used to make a shortcut to a single command. True or False?

4. What command can be used to display the current value for the environment variable called PWD?

   a. `echo PWD`

   b. `ls PWD`

   c. `display PWD`

   d. `echo $PWD`

   e. `ls $PWD`

   f. `display $PWD`

5. What environment variable is used to define where to look for executable commands when the absolute or relative pathname is not listed on the command line?

   a. COM

   b. PATH

   c. TERM

   d. WHERE

   e. WHO

6. Which of the following files is always executed immediately after a user logs into a Linux system and receives a BASH shell?

   a. `/etc/profile`

   b. `~/.bash_profile`

   c. `~/.bash_login`

   d. `~/.profile`

7. Which of the following is a file descriptor? (Choose all that apply.)

   a. Standard Output

   b. Standard deviation

   c. Standard settings

   d. Standard Error

   e. User input

   f. Variable input

8. In order to use escape sequences with the `echo` command what option must be used with the `echo` command?

   a. `-e`

   b. `-esc`

   c. `-a`

   d. `-t`

9. Which command could you use to see a list of all environment and user–defined shell variables as well as their current values?

   a. `ls /var`

   b. `env`

   c. `set`

   d. `grep`

   e. `echo`

10. Every `if` construct begins with `if` and must be terminated with?

   a. `end`

   b. `endif`

   c. `stop`

   d. `fi`

   e. `term`

11. What variable can be used to redirect the X Windows display to another computer?

   a. It cannot be done.

   b. DISPLAY

   c. RANDOM

   d. REDIRECT

12. Which of the following will display the message **welcome home** if the `cd /home/user1` command is successfully executed?

   a. `cd /home/user1 && echo "welcome home"`

   b. `cat "welcome home" || cd /home/user1`

   c. `cd /home/user1 || echo welcome home`

   d. `cd /home/user1 || cat "welcome home"`

   e. `echo "welcome home"  && cd /home/user1`

13. The current value for the HOME variable is displayed by which of the following commands? (Choose all that apply.)

   a. `echo HOME=`

   b. `echo ~`

   c. `echo $HOME`

   d. `echo ls HOME`

14. A pipe is a temporary software connection between two commands that takes the stdout of the first command and uses it as the stdin of the second. True or False?

15. What does 2>&1 accomplish when entered on the command line after a command?
    a. appends Standard Output to the existing contents of the specified file
    b. redirects both Standard Error and Standard Output to the same file
    c. redirects both Standard Error and Standard Input to the same file
    d. sends Standard Error to the same location as Standard Output
    e. redirects both Standard Input and Standard Output to the same file

16. Which of the following file descriptors represents stdout?
    a. 2
    b. 0
    c. 1
    d. 3

17. Which of the following operators reverses the meaning of a test statement?
    a. #!
    b. -o
    c. -a
    d. !
    e. #

18. Due to their contradictory nature, Standard Output and Standard Error can never be redirected to the same file. True or False?

19. Environment variables _____.
    a. are always set by the user
    b. are set by the system and not modifiable
    c. are set by the system and are not viewable by any user but root
    d. are normally set by the system but can be modified if desired

20. Which of the following result in a command prompt of [:{) ?
    a. PS1 [:{)
    b. PS1=[:{)
    c. PS1="[:{)"
    d. PS1 "[:{)"

8

21. You desire to redirect all Standard Errors to a central file called `/var/Errors` for review at a later time instead of viewing the errors on the terminal screen. To accomplish this you generate the following command: `"ls /home/user1 2>/var/Errors"`. What will happen if you run the command for the first time and the `Errors` file does not exist?

    a. The operation will fail as the file to which the information is to be stored does not exist, and you will be informed of this by an error message to the screen.

    b. The operation will fail as the file to which the information is to be stored does not exist, but you will not know this as you have prevented Standard Error from being displayed to the screen.

    c. The system will prompt you to create the file `Errors` and then will place the error messages, if any, into it.

    d. The system will automatically create the necessary file without user intervention and place any error messages generated into it.

22. What would be the effect of using the `alias` command to make an alias for the `date` command named `cat` in honor of your favorite pet?

    a. It cannot be done, as there already is an environment variable `cat` associated with the `cat` command.

    b. It cannot be done, as there already is a command `cat` on the system.

    c. When you use the `cat` command at the command prompt with the intention of viewing a text file, the date will appear instead.

    d. There will be no effect until the alias is imported as it is a user-declared variable.

23. How do you indicate a comment line in a shell script?

    a. There are no comment lines; a shell script is a list of commands to be executed in order.

    b. begin the line with #!

    c. begin the line with !

    d. begin the line with #

24. You have redirected Standard Error to a file called `Errors`. You view the contents of this file afterwards and notice that there are six error messages. After repeating the procedure, you notice that there are only two error messages in this file. Why?

    a. Once you open the file and view the contents, the contents are lost.

    b. The system generated different Standard Output.

    c. You did not append the Standard Error to the `Error` file and as a result, it was overwritten when the command was run a second time.

    d. You must specify a new file each and every time you redirect as the system creates the specified file by default.

25. The `grep` command requires two arguments; the first is the file to be searched and the second is the text string to search for. True or False?

26. What is wrong with the following command string:
    `ls /etc/hosts     >listofhostfile`?

    a. nothing

    b. The file descriptor was not declared and unless 1 for Standard Output or 2 for Standard Error is indicated the command will fail.

    c. The `ls` command is one of the commands that cannot be used with redirection; you must use | to pipe instead.

    d. The file `listofhostfile` will always only contain Standard Error, as a file descriptor was not declared.

27. Which of the following is not necessarily generated by every command on the system? (Choose all that apply.)

    a. Standard Input

    b. Standard deviation

    c. Standard Output

    d. Standard Error

28. What construct can be used in a shell script to read Standard Input and place it in a variable?

    a. `read`

    b. `sum`

    c. `verify`

    d. `test`

29. A variable identifier must _____.

    a. not begin with a number

    b. not begin with a capital letter

    c. start with a number

    d. start with an underscore "_"

30. What does >> accomplish when entered on the command line after a command?

    a. It is a double redirect and redirects both Standard Error and Standard Output to the same location.

    b. Nothing, it is a typo; you just hit the same key twice in error.

    c. It is a double redirect and redirects Standard Error and Standard Input to the same location.

    d. It appends Standard Output to a file.

8

31. Examine the following shell script.

```
echo -e "What is your favorite colour?--> \c"
read REPLY
if [ "$REPLY" = "red"  -o  "$REPLY" = "blue" ]
then
    echo "The answer is red or blue."
else
    echo "The answer is neither red nor blue."
fi
```

What would be displayed if a user executes this program and answered *Blue* when prompted?

a. "The answer is red or blue."

b. "The answer is neither red nor blue."

c. The code would cause an error.

d. "The answer is red or blue. The answer is neither red nor blue."

HANDS-ON PROJECTS

These projects should be completed in the order given. All hands-on projects should take a total of three hours to complete. The requirements for this lab include:

❏ A computer with Red Hat 7.2 installed according to Hands-on Project 7-2

Project 8-1

In this hands-on project, you use the shell to redirect the Standard Output and Standard Error to a file and take Standard Input from a file.

1. Switch to a command-line terminal (tty2) by pressing **Ctrl-Alt-F2** and log into the terminal using the username of **root** and the password of **secret**.

2. At the command prompt, type **touch sample1 sample2** and press **Enter** to create two new files named **sample1** and **sample2** in your home directory. Verify their creation by typing **ls -F** at the command prompt and press **Enter**.

3. At the command prompt, type **ls -l sample1 sample2 sample3** and press **Enter**. Is there any Standard Output displayed on the terminal screen? Is there any Standard Error displayed on the terminal screen? Why?

4. At the command prompt, type **ls -l sample1 sample2 sample3 > file** and press **Enter**. Is there any Standard Output displayed on the terminal screen? Is there any Standard Error displayed on the terminal screen? Why?

5. At the command prompt, type **cat file** and press **Enter**. What are the contents of **file** and why?

6. At the command prompt, type **ls –l sample1 sample2 sample3   2> file** and press **Enter**. Is there any Standard Output displayed on the terminal screen? Is there any Standard Error displayed on the terminal screen? Why?

7. At the command prompt, type **cat file** and press **Enter**. What are the contents of `file` and why? Were the previous contents retained? Why?

8. At the command prompt, type **ls –l sample1 sample2 sample3   > file 2>file2** and press **Enter**. Is there any Standard Output displayed on the terminal screen? Is there any Standard Error displayed on the terminal screen? Why?

9. At the command prompt, type **cat file** and press **Enter**. What are the contents of `file` and why?

10. At the command prompt, type **cat file2** and press **Enter**. What are the contents of `file2` and why?

11. At the command prompt, type **ls –l sample1 sample2 sample3   > file 2>&1** and press **Enter**. Is there any Standard Output displayed on the terminal screen? Is there any Standard Error displayed on the terminal screen? Why?

12. At the command prompt, type **cat file** and press **Enter**. What are the contents of `file` and why?

13. At the command prompt, type **ls –l sample1 sample2 sample3 > &2 2>file2** and press **Enter**. Is there any Standard Output displayed on the terminal screen? Is there any Standard Error displayed on the terminal screen? Why?

14. At the command prompt, type **cat file2** and press **Enter**. What are the contents of `file2` and why?

15. At the command prompt, type **date   > file** and press **Enter**.

16. At the command prompt, type **cat file** and press **Enter**. What are the contents of `file` and why?

17. At the command prompt, type **date   >> file** and press **Enter**.

18. At the command prompt, type **cat file** and press **Enter**. What are the contents of `file` and why? Can you tell when each `date` command was run?

19. At the command prompt, type **tr o O /etc/hosts** and press **Enter**. What error message do you receive and why?

20. At the command prompt, type **tr o O </etc/hosts** and press **Enter**. What happened and why?

21. Type **exit** and press **Enter** to log out of your shell.

Project 8-2

In this project, you redirect Standard Output and Standard Input using pipe metacharacters.

1. Switch to a command-line terminal (tty2) by pressing **Ctrl-Alt-F2** and log into the terminal using the username of **root** and the password of **secret**.

2. At the command prompt, type **cat /etc/inittab** and press **Enter** to view the /etc/inittab file. Next, type **cat /etc/inittab | less** at the command prompt and press **Enter** to perform the same task page-by-page. Explain what the | metacharacter does in the previous command. How is this different from the `less /etc/inittab` command?

3. At the command prompt, type **cat /etc/inittab | grep tty** and press **Enter**. How many lines are displayed? Why did we not need to specify a filename with the `grep` command?

4. At the command prompt, type **cat /etc/inittab | grep tty | tr t T** and press **Enter**. Explain the output on the terminal screen.

5. At the command prompt, type **cat /etc/inittab | grep tty | tr t T | sort –r** and press **Enter**. Explain the output on the terminal screen.

6. At the command prompt, type **cat /etc/inittab | grep tty | tr t T | sort –r | tee file** and press **Enter**. Explain the output on the terminal screen. Next, type **cat file** at the command prompt and press **Enter**. What are the contents? Why? What does the `tee` command do in the pipe above?

7. At the command prompt, type **cat /etc/inittab | grep tty | tr t T | sort –r | tee file | wc –l** and press **Enter**. Explain the output on the terminal screen. Next, type **cat file** at the command prompt and press **Enter**. What are the contents? Why?

8. Type **exit** and press **Enter** to log out of your shell.

Project 8-3

In this project, you will create and use an alias, as well as view and change existing shell variables. In addition to this, you will export user-defined variables and load variables automatically upon shell startup.

1. Switch to a command-line terminal (tty2) by pressing **Ctrl–Alt–F2** and log into the terminal using the username of **root** and the password of **secret**.

2. At the command prompt, type **set | less** and press **Enter** to view the BASH shell environment variables currently loaded into memory. Scroll through this list using the cursor keys on the keyboard. When finished, press **q** to quit the `less` utility.

3. At the command prompt, type **env | less** and press **Enter** to view the exported BASH shell environment variables currently loaded into memory. Scroll through this list using the cursor keys on the keyboard. Is this list larger or smaller than the list generated in Step 2? Why? When finished, press **q** to quit the `less` utility.

4. At the command prompt, type **PS1="Hello There:"** and press **Enter**. What happened and why? Next, type **echo $PS1** at the command prompt and press **Enter** to verify the new value of the PS1 variable.

5. At the command prompt, type **exit** and press **Enter** to log out of the shell. Next, log into the terminal using the username of **root** and the password of **secret**. What prompt did you receive and why? How could you ensure that the "Hello There:" prompt occurs at every login?

6. At the command prompt, type **vi .bash_profile** and press **Enter**. At the bottom of the file, add the following lines. When finished, save and quit the vi editor.

```
echo -e "Would you like a hello prompt? (y/n) -->\c"
read ANSWER
if [ $ANSWER = "y" ]
then
    PS1="Hello There: "
fi
```

Explain what the above lines will perform after each login.

7. At the command prompt, type **exit** and press **Enter** to log out of the shell. Next, log into the terminal using the username of **root** and the password of **secret**. When prompted for a hello prompt, type **y** and press **Enter**. What prompt did you receive and why?

8. At the command prompt, type **exit** and press **Enter** to log out of the shell. Next, log into the terminal using the username of **root** and the password of **secret**. When prompted for a hello prompt, type **n** and press **Enter** to receive the default prompt.

9. At the command prompt, type **vi .bash_profile** and remove the lines that were added in Step 6. When finished, save your changes and quit the vi editor.

10. At the command prompt, type **MYVAR="My sample variable"** and press **Enter** to create a variable called MYVAR. Verify its creation by typing **echo $MYVAR** at the command prompt and press **Enter**.

11. At the command prompt, type **set | grep MYVAR** and press **Enter**. Is the MYVAR variable listed? Why?

12. At the command prompt, type **env | grep MYVAR** and press **Enter**. Is the MYVAR variable listed? Why?

13. At the command prompt, type **export MYVAR** and press **Enter**. Next, type **env | grep MYVAR** at the command prompt and press **Enter**. Is the MYVAR variable listed now? Why?

14. At the command prompt, type **exit** and press **Enter** to log out of the shell. Next, log into the terminal using the username of **root** and the password of **secret**.

15. At the command prompt, type **echo $MYVAR** and press **Enter** to view the contents of the MYVAR variable. What is listed and why?

16. At the command prompt, type **vi .bash_profile** and press **Enter**. At the bottom of the file, add the following line. When finished, save and quit the **vi** editor.

```
export MYVAR="My sample variable"
```

17. At the command prompt, type **exit** and press **Enter** to log out of the shell. Next, log into the terminal using the username of **root** and the password of **secret**.

18. At the command prompt, type **echo $MYVAR** and press **Enter** to list the contents of the MYVAR variable. What is listed and why?

19. At the command prompt, type **alias** and press **Enter**. What aliases are present in your shell?

20. At the command prompt, type **alias asample="cd /etc ; cat hosts ; cd ~ ; ls –F"** and press **Enter**. What does this command do?

21. At the command prompt, type **asample** and press **Enter**. What happened and why?

22. Type **exit** and press **Enter** to log out of your shell.

Project 8-4

In this project, you will create a basic shell script and execute it on the system.

1. Switch to a command-line terminal (tty2) by pressing **Ctrl-Alt-F2** and log into the terminal using the username of **root** and the password of **secret**.

2. At the command prompt, type **vi myscript** and press **Enter** to open a new file for editing called `myscript` in your home directory.

3. Enter the following text into the **myscript** file. When finished, save and quit the **vi** editor.

```
#!/bin/bash
echo -e "This is a sample shell script. \t It displays
mounted filesystems \a"
mount
```

4. At the command prompt, type **ll myscript** and press **Enter**. What permissions does the `myscript` file have? Next, type **bash myscript** at the command prompt and press **Enter**. Did the shell script execute? What do the \t and \a escape sequences do?

5. Next, type **./myscript** at the command prompt and press **Enter**. What error message did you receive and why?

6. At the command prompt, type **chmod u+x myscript** and press **Enter**. Next, type **./myscript** at the command prompt and press **Enter**. Did the script execute? Why?

7. Type **exit** and press **Enter** to log out of your shell.

Project 8-5

In this project, you will create a shell script which uses decision constructs to analyze user input.

1. Switch to a command-line terminal (tty2) by pressing **Ctrl-Alt-F2** and log into the terminal using the username of **root** and the password of **secret**.

2. At the command prompt, type **vi myscript2** and press **Enter** to open a new file for editing called **myscript2** in your home directory.

3. Enter the following text into the **myscript** file. When finished, save and quit the vi editor.

```
#!/bin/bash

echo -e "This program adds entries to a family database
file.\n"

echo -e "Please enter the name of the family member
 --> \c"

read NAME

echo -e "Please enter the family member's relation to you
(i.e., mother) --> \c"

read RELATION

echo -e "Please enter the family member's telephone
number --> \c"

read PHONE

echo "$NAME\t$RELATION\t$PHONE" >> database
```

4. At the command prompt, type **chmod u+x myscript2** and press **Enter**. Next, type **./myscript2** at the command prompt and press **Enter**. Answer the questions with information regarding one of your family members.

5. At the command prompt, type **cat database** and press **Enter**. Was the entry from Step 4 present? Why?

6. Perform Step 4 several times to populate the database file with entries.

7. At the command prompt, type **vi myscript2** and press **Enter**. Edit the text inside the **myscript2** shell script such that it reads:

```
#!/bin/bash
echo -e "Would you like to add an entry to the family database file?\n"
read ANSWER1
if [ $ANSWER1 = "y" -o $ANSWER1 = "Y" ]
then
  echo -e "Please enter the name of the family member --> \c"
  read NAME
  echo -e "Please enter the family member's relation to you  (i.e., mother)-->\c"
  read RELATION
  echo -e "Please enter the family member's telephone number   --> \c"
  read PHONE
  echo "$NAME\t$RELATION\t$PHONE" >> database
fi
echo -e "Would you like to search an entry in the family database file?\n"
```

```
read ANSWER2
if [ $ANSWER2 = "y" -o $ANSWER2 = "Y" ]
then
  echo -e "What word would you like to look for? --> \c"
  read WORD
  grep "$WORD" database
fi
```

8. At the command prompt, type **./myscript2** and press **Enter**. When prompted to enter an entry into the database, choose **y** and press **Enter**. Answer the questions with information regarding one of your family members. Next, when prompted to search the database, answer **y** and press **Enter**. Search for the name that you just entered a few seconds ago. Was it there?

9. At the command prompt, type **./myscript2** and press **Enter**. When prompted to enter an entry into the database, choose **n** and press **Enter**. Next, when prompted to search the database, answer **y** and press **Enter**. Search for a name that you entered earlier in Step 6. Was it there? Why?

10. At the command prompt, type **vi myscript2** and press **Enter**. Edit the text inside the **myscript2** shell script such that it reads:

```
#!/bin/bash
echo -e "What would you like to do?
Add an entry (a)
Search an entry (s)
Enter your choice (a/s)-->\c"
read ANSWER
case $ANSWER in
a|A) echo -e "Please enter the name of the family member --> \c"
    read NAME
    echo -e "Please enter the family member's relation to you (i.e,. mother)-->\c"
    read RELATION
    echo -e "Please enter the family member's telephone number --> \c"
    read PHONE
    echo "$NAME\t$RELATION\t$PHONE" >> database;;
s|S) echo "What word would you like to look for? --> \c"
    read WORD
    grep "$WORD" database;;
  *) echo "You must enter either the letter a or s.";;
esac
```

11. At the command prompt, type **./myscript2** and press **Enter**. Choose **y** and press **Enter**. What error message do you receive and why?

12. At the command prompt, type **./myscript2** and press **Enter**. Choose **a** and press **Enter**. Enter information about another family member. Does it matter whether you entered **a** or **A** at the prompt earlier? Why?

13. At the command prompt, type **./myscript2** and press **Enter**. Choose **s** and press **Enter**. Search for the family member entered in Step 12. Does it matter whether you entered **s** or **S** at the prompt earlier? Why?

14. At the command prompt, type **vi myscript3** and press **Enter** to edit a new file called **myscript3** in your home directory.

15. Enter the following text into the **myscript3** file. When finished, save and quit the vi editor.

```
#!/bin/bash
echo -e "This program copies a file to the /stuff directory.\n"
echo -e "Which file would you like to copy? --> \c"
read FILENAME
mkdir /stuff || echo "The /stuff directory could not be created."
cp -f $FILENAME /stuff && echo "$FILENAME was successfully copied to /stuff"
```

16. At the command prompt, type **chmod u+x myscript3** and press **Enter**. Next, type **./myscript3** at the command prompt and press **Enter**. When prompted for a filename, type **/etc/hosts** and press **Enter**. Was the /stuff directory created successfully? Why or why not? Was the /etc/hosts file copied successfully to the /stuff directory? Why or why not?

17. Type **./myscript3** at the command prompt and press **Enter**. When prompted for a filename, type **/etc/inittab** and press **Enter**. Was the /stuff directory created successfully? Why or why not? Was the /etc/inittab file copied successfully to the /stuff directory? Why or why not?

18. Type **exit** and press **Enter** to log out of your shell.

DISCOVERY EXERCISES

1. Which command can be used to:

   a) create an alias called **mm** that displays only those filesystems that are mounted and contain an ext2 filesystem?

   b) create and export a variable called NEWHOME, which is equivalent to the value contained in the HOME variable?

   c) find all files that start with the word "host" beginning at the /etc directory, and save the Standard Output to a file called **file1** and the Standard Error to the same file?

   d) display only the lines from the output of the **set** command that have the word **bash** in them? (The output on the terminal screen should be sorted alphabetically.)

2. What would happen if you executed the following command?

   tr a A </etc/hosts | sort -r | pr -d >/etc/hosts

   Explain the output.

3. Recall that only Standard Output may be sent across a pipe to another command. Using the information presented in this chapter, how could you send Standard Error across the pipe in the following command?

   ls /etc/hosts /etc/h | tr h H

4. Which test statement can be used to test whether:

   a) you have read permission to the **/etc/hosts** file?

   b) you have read and execute permission to the **/etc** directory?

   c) the contents of the variable $TEST are equal to the string "success"?

   d) the contents of the variable $TEST are numerically equal to the contents of the variable $RESULT?

   e) the contents of the variable $TEST are equal to the string "success" and the file **/etc/hosts** exists?

   f) the contents of the variable $TEST are equal to the string "success", or the number 5, or the contents of the variable $RESULT?

5. Examine the **/root/.bash_profile** file seen below. Using the information presented in this chapter, describe what each line of this file does.

   ```
   # .bash_profile

   # Get the aliases and functions
   if [ -f ~/.bashrc ]; then
           . ~/.bashrc
   fi

   # User specific environment and startup programs

   PATH=$PATH:$HOME/bin
   BASH_ENV=$HOME/.bashrc
   USERNAME="root"

   export USERNAME BASH_ENV PATH
   ```

6. Write a shell script that contains a hashpling and comments. It should perform the following tasks:

   —displays a list of currently logged in users

   —displays the system's hostname

   —displays the time and date

   —displays the disk usage

   —displays the current working directory

   —displays the pathname to the BASH shell

7. Write a shell script that prompts the user for a grade between 0 and 100. The shell script should calculate the corresponding letter for this grade based on the following criteria:

    0–49 = F

    50–59 = D

    60–69 = C

    70–79 = B

    80–100 = A

8

9

SYSTEM INITIALIZATION

**After completing this chapter,
you will be able to:**

♦ Summarize the major steps necessary to boot a Linux system

♦ Configure the LILO boot loader

♦ Configure the GRUB boot loader

♦ Dual boot Linux with the Windows operating system using LILO, GRUB, and NTLOADER

♦ Understand how the init daemon initializes the system at boot time

Earlier in this text, you chose a boot loader for the Linux kernel during the Red Hat installation program. In this chapter you investigate the boot process in greater detail. You explore the different types and configurations of boot loaders, as well as the process of dual booting the Linux operating system with the Windows operating system. Later in this chapter, you learn the procedure used to start daemons after the kernel has loaded and how to manipulate this procedure to start and stop new daemons.

THE BOOT PROCESS

When a computer first initializes, the BIOS on the mainboard performs a **Power On Self Test (POST)**. Following the POST, the BIOS checks its configuration in the CMOS chip on the mainboard for boot devices to search for and operating systems to execute. Typically, computers first check for an operating system on floppy disk and CD-ROM devices if they are present in the computer and have a disk inside them. This ensures that installation of an operating system from CD-ROM or floppy disk may occur at boot time. After these two devices are checked for an operating system, the computer then usually checks the **Master Boot Record (MBR)** on the first hard disk inside the computer.

Recall that you may alter the order that boot devices are checked in the computer BIOS.

The MBR may have a **boot loader** on it that can then locate and execute the kernel of the operating system. Alternatively, the MBR may contain a pointer to a partition on the system that contains a boot loader on the first sector; the partition that the MBR points to is referred to as the **active partition**. There can only be one active partition per hard disk.

Regardless of whether the boot loader is loaded from the Master Boot Record or the first sector of the active partition, the remainder of the boot process is the same. The boot loader then executes the Linux kernel from the partition that contains it.

The Linux kernel is stored in the **/boot** directory and is named **vmlinuz-<kernel version>**.

Once the Linux kernel is loaded into memory, the boot loader is no longer active; instead the Linux kernel continues to initialize the system by loading daemons into memory. A **daemon** is simply a system process that performs useful tasks such as printing, scheduling, and operating system maintenance. The first daemon process on the system is called **init (initialize daemon)**; it is responsible for loading all other daemons on the system required to bring the system to a useable state where users may log in and interact with services. The whole process is depicted in Figure 9-1.

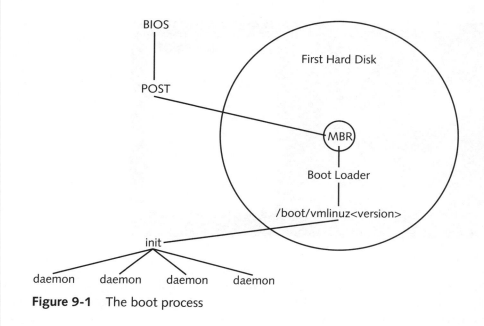

Figure 9-1   The boot process

BOOT LOADERS

As discussed in the previous section, the primary function of boot loaders during the boot process is to load the Linux kernel into memory. However, boot loaders may perform other functions as well including passing information to the kernel during system startup and booting other operating systems that are present on the hard disk. Using one boot loader to boot one of several operating systems is known as dual booting; the boot loader simply loads a different operating system kernel based on user input.

 Only one operating system may be active at any one time.

Although there are many different boot loaders that you may use to boot Linux, the two most common boot loaders used on Linux systems today are LILO and GRUB.

LILO

LInux LOader (LILO) is the traditional Linux boot loader. Although it may reside on the first sector of an active Linux partition, it is typically located on the Master Boot Record of the hard disk. When the computer completes the POST and locates the LILO boot loader, a screen similar to the one depicted in Figure 9-2 will be displayed.

Figure 9-2   LILO boot loader screen

From Figure 9-2, you may press Enter to boot the highlighted operating system kernel (linux) or wait 5 seconds for the system to boot it by default. Alternatively, you may press the Ctrl-x key combination to obtain a LILO boot prompt where commands may be entered to boot the system.

After the operating system is fully loaded, you may configure the LILO boot loader by editing the **/etc/lilo.conf** file; an example of this file is seen below:

```
[root@localhost root]# cat /etc/lilo.conf
prompt
timeout=50
default=linux
boot=/dev/hda
map=/boot/map
install=/boot/boot.b
message=/boot/message
lba32

image=/boot/vmlinuz-2.4.7-10
        label=linux
        initrd=/boot/initrd-2.4.7-10.img
        read-only
        root=/dev/hda3
[root@localhost root]# _
```

The /etc/lilo.conf file shown above indicates that LILO boots the Linux kernel /boot/vmlinuz-2.4.7-10 provided you choose the default boot label (label=linux) from the graphical boot loader screen (/boot/message) seen earlier in Figure 9-2. Furthermore, the system will continue to boot the default operating system (default=linux) if you do not enter any input for 5 seconds (timeout=50). Once the kernel is loaded, it will mount the root filesystem onto the /dev/hda3 partition.

Some keywords commonly used in `/etc/lilo.conf` and their definitions are seen in Table 9-1.

Table 9-1   Common /etc/lilo.conf keywords

Keyword	Description
image=	Specifies the absolute pathname to the Linux kernel
root=	Specifies the device that contains the Linux root filesystem
prompt	Displays a LILO boot prompt provided there is no `message=` keyword specified
message=	Specifies the absolute pathname to the file that contains the graphical LILO screen
timeout=	The number of 1/10th seconds to wait for user input before loading the default operating system kernel
default=	Specifies the label for the default operating system kernel
label=	The friendly name given to an operating system kernel
boot=	Specifies where LILO should be installed to (if the device specified is a partition on a hard disk, then LILO is installed at the beginning of the partition; if the device specified is a disk, then LILO is installed to the MBR on that device)
linear	Specifies that LILO uses linear sector addressing
read-only	Initially mounts the Linux root filesystem as read-only to reduce any errors with running `fsck` during system startup
initrd=	The pathname to a ramdisk image used to load modules into memory needed for the Linux kernel at boot time
password=	Specifies a password required to boot the Linux kernel
append=	Specifies parameters that are passed to the Linux kernel when loaded
map=	Specifies the file that contains the exact location of the Linux kernel on the hard disk
install=	Specifies the file that contains the physical layout of the disk drive
lba32	Used to specify large block addressing (32-bit) for hard disks that have more than 1024 cylinders

Lines may be commented out of `/etc/lilo.conf` by preceding those lines with a # symbol.

If the `message=` keyword is not used to specify a graphical LILO screen or if you press the Ctrl-x key combination depicted in Figure 9-2, you will be presented with a LILO boot prompt, as seen below:

```
boot:
```

You may then press the Tab key at this prompt to see any operating system labels and type the name of the label to load the operating system:

```
boot:
linux
boot: linux
Loading Linux .....................
Uncompressing Linux... Ok, booting the kernel.
```

Alternatively, you may wait for the time period specified by the `timeout=` keyword in `/etc/lilo.conf` for the default operating system to load or simply press Enter to load the default operating system kernel specified by `default=` in `/etc/lilo.conf`.

The `append=` keyword in `/etc/lilo.conf` is useful for passing information to the Linux kernel manually at boot time if the kernel does not detect the correct system information. Recall that the system exports detected hardware information to the `/proc` directory; viewing the contents of files in the `/proc` directory will indicate whether hardware was detected correctly by the Linux kernel or not. If the Linux kernel does not recognize all the physical memory in the `/proc/meminfo` file, you may simply add the line `append="mem=xxxM"` to `/etc/lilo.conf` where xxx is the correct amount of memory in Megabytes. In addition, if the hard disk used is not detected properly by the system, you may send the correct number of cylinders, heads, and sectors for the hard disk to the kernel at boot time; to do this you should add the line `append="hd=C,H,S"` to `/etc/lilo.conf` where C= # of cylinders, H= # of heads, and S= # of sectors.

Almost any hardware information may be passed to the kernel via the `append=` keyword. The format of the information depends on the type of hardware involved.

If you change the `/etc/lilo.conf` file, LILO must be reinstalled using the new information in `/etc/lilo.conf` for those changes to take effect. To do this, you may simply use the `lilo` command by typing `lilo` at the command prompt:

```
[root@localhost root]# lilo
Added linux *
[root@localhost root]# _
```

To uninstall LILO from an active partition or the MBR, you may use the `lilo -u` command.

Although LILO is a robust boot loader, it may encounter errors and fail to load properly; if this occurs, you are given an error code that indicates the nature of the problem. Common LILO error codes and possible solutions are listed in Table 9-2.

Table 9-2   LILO error codes

Error Code	Description
L	The first part of the LILO boot loader failed to load, usually as a result of incorrect hard disk parameters. Simply rebooting the machine sometimes fixes this problem; however, you may also need to add the word linear to /etc/lilo.conf.
LI	The second part of the LILO boot loader failed to load or the /boot/boot.b file is missing. Adding the word linear to /etc/lilo.conf may fix the problem.
LIL LIL- LIL?	LILO has loaded properly but cannot find certain files required to operate such as the /boot/map and /boot/boot.b files. Adding the word linear to /etc/lilo.conf may fix the problem.

GRUB

GRand Unified Bootloader (GRUB) resembles common UNIX boot loaders and is more recent than the LILO boot loader. The first major part of the GRUB boot loader (called Stage1) typically resides on the Master Boot Record, the remaining parts of the boot loader (called Stage1.5 and Stage2) reside in the /boot/grub directory. GRUB Stage1 simply points to GRUB Stage1.5, which loads filesystem support and proceeds to load GRUB Stage2. GRUB Stage2 performs the actual boot loader functions and displays a graphical boot loader screen similar to that seen in Figure 9-3.

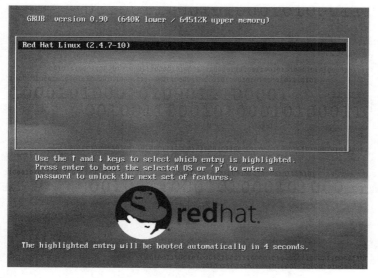

Figure 9-3   GRUB boot loader screen

Much like LILO, the configuration of GRUB is accomplished by editing a configuration file. However, GRUB does not need to be reinstalled after editing this configuration file as LILO does; this is due to the fact that the configuration file (**/boot/grub/grub.conf**) is read directly by the Stage2 boot loader. An example `/boot/grub/grub.conf` file is seen below:

```
[root@localhost root]# cat /boot/grub/grub.conf
# grub.conf generated by anaconda
#
# Note that you do not have to rerun grub after making
# changes to this file
# NOTICE:  You have a /boot partition.  This means that
#          all kernel and initrd paths are relative to
#          /boot/, eg.
#          root (hd0,0)
#          kernel /vmlinuz-version ro root=/dev/hda2
#          initrd /initrd-version.img
#boot=/dev/hda
default=0
timeout=10
splashimage=(hd0,0)/grub/splash.xpm.gz
password --md5 $1$·˜A_†Õ.R$W.uLzTHpvhCchfS0iTTSO0
title Red Hat Linux (2.4.7-10)
        root (hd0,0)
        kernel /vmlinuz-2.4.7-10 ro root=/dev/hda2
        initrd /initrd-2.4.7-10.img
[root@localhost root]# _
```

 Alternatively, you may view and edit the `/etc/grub.conf` file, which is simply a symbolic link to `/boot/grub/grub.conf`.

To understand the entries in the `/boot/grub/grub.conf` file, you must first understand how GRUB refers to partitions on hard disks. Hard disks and partitions on those hard disks are identified by numbers in the following format: (hd<drive#>,<partition#>). Thus the (`hd0,0`) notation in the above `/boot/grub/grub.conf` file refers to the first hard disk on the system (regardless of whether it is SCSI or IDE) and the first partition on that hard disk respectively. Similarly, the second partition on the first hard disk would be referred to as (`hd0,1`), and the fourth partition on the third hard disk would be referred to as (`hd2,3`).

In addition, GRUB calls the partition that contains Stage2 of the GRUB boot loader the **GRUB root partition**. Normally, the GRUB root partition is the filesystem that contains the `/boot` directory and should not be confused with the Linux root filesystem.

Thus, the example `/boot/grub/grub.conf` file seen earlier displays a graphical boot screen (`splashimage=(hd0,0)/grub/splash.xpm.gz`) and boots the default operating system kernel on the first hard drive (`default=0`) in 10 seconds (`timeout=10`). The default operating system kernel is located on the GRUB root filesystem (`root (hd0,0)`) and called `vmlinuz-2.4.7-10`.

The kernel then mounts the root filesystem on /dev/hda2 initially as read-only to avoid problems with the fsck command and uses a ramdisk image to load modules needed at boot time (initrd /initrd-2.4.7-10.img).

 To pass information to the kernel from the GRUB boot loader, the append= keyword can also be used in /boot/grub/grub.conf using the same syntax as the append= keyword in /etc/lilo.conf.

Normally, GRUB allows users to manipulate the boot loader during system startup; to prevent this, you may optionally password protect GRUB modifications during boot time. The line password --md5 1•˜AŠ†Ǒ.R$W.uLzTHpvhCchfS0iTTSO0 in the /boot/grub/grub.conf file above will prompt a user for a password if they wish to modify the boot loader during system startup. Furthermore, the password specified in this file is encrypted to prevent users from viewing the password when viewing the file.

 To create an encrypted password for use in /boot/grub/grub.conf, you may use the **grub-md5-crypt command**.

9

If passwords are enabled, you will see a screen at boot time similar to Figure 9-3; at this screen, you may press Enter to boot the default Linux kernel or wait for 10 seconds for it to boot by itself. However, if you wish to manipulate the boot process using the GRUB boot loader, that you must press p and enter the correct password at Figure 9-3. This will result in a screen similar to Figure 9-4, in which you may press e to edit the configuration used in /boot/grub/grub.conf or press c to obtain a grub> prompt.

Figure 9-4   GRUB configuration boot loader screen

If you choose to open a **grub>** prompt as seen in Figure 9-5, you may enter a variety of commands to view system hardware configuration, find and display files, alter the configuration of GRUB, or boot an operating system kernel. To view all available commands when at the **grub>** prompt, you may type **help** as seen in Figure 9-6.

Figure 9-5 GRUB prompt boot loader screen

```
grub> help
background RRGGBB                  blocklist FILE
boot                              border RRGGBB
cat FILE                          chainloader [--force] FILE
cmp FILE1 FILE2                   color NORMAL [HIGHLIGHT]
configfile FILE                   debug
display MODEL                     displayapm
displaymem                        embed STAGE1_5 DEVICE
find FILENAME                     foreground RRGGBB
fstest                            geometry DRIVE [CYLINDER HEAD SECTOR [
halt [--no-apm]                   help [PATTERN ...]
hide PARTITION                    impsprobe
initrd FILE [ARG ...]             install [--stage2=STAGE2_FILE] [--forc
ioprobe DRIVE                     kernel [--no-mem-option] [--type=TYPE]
lock                              makeactive
map TO_DRIVE FROM_DRIVE           md5crypt
module FILE [ARG ...]             modulenounzip FILE [ARG ...]
partnew PART TYPE START LEN       parttype PART TYPE
password [--md5] PASSWD [FILE]    pause [MESSAGE ...]
read ADDR                         reboot
root [DEVICE [HDBIAS]]            rootnoverify [DEVICE [HDBIAS]]
savedefault                       serial [--unit=UNIT] [--port=PORT] [--
setkey [TO_KEY FROM_KEY]          setup [--prefix=DIR] [--stage2=STAGE2_
shade INTEGER                     splashimage FILE
terminal [--dumb] [--timeout=SECS] [co testload FILE
testvbe MODE                      unhide PARTITION
uppermem KBYTES                   vbeprobe [MODE]
viewport x y width height
grub>
```

Figure 9-6 GRUB boot loader help screen

The `grub>` prompt may also be used to boot the system in the same manner as seen in `/boot/grub/grub.conf`; to boot the Linux operating system used in the previous examples, you would simply type `kernel /vmlinuz ro root=/dev/hda2` at the `grub>` prompt and press Enter to specify the kernel to boot, followed by the word "boot" and Enter again to continue the boot process.

Recall that you are required to choose a boot loader during installation. Regardless of which boot loader is chosen, you may switch from LILO to GRUB and vice versa at any time after installation. To install LILO, we saw from the last section that you simply must type `lilo` at the command prompt; the LILO boot loader will then be installed based on the configuration of the `/etc/lilo.conf` file. However, to install the GRUB boot loader, you must use the **grub-install command**. To install GRUB Stage1 on the Master Boot Record of the first IDE hard disk, you could type the following command:

```
[root@localhost root]# grub-install /dev/hda
Installation finished. No error reported.
This is the contents of the device map /boot/grub/
device.map. Check if this is correct or not.
If any of the lines is incorrect, fix it and re-
run the script `grub-install'.

# this device map was generated by anaconda
(fd0)    /dev/fd0
(hd0)    /dev/hda
[root@localhost root]# _
```

Alternatively, to install GRUB Stage1 at the beginning of the first primary partition of the same hard disk, you could type the following at the command prompt:

```
[root@localhost root]# grub-install /dev/hda1
Installation finished. No error reported.
This is the contents of the device map /boot/grub/
device.map. Check if this is correct or not.
If any of the lines is incorrect, fix it and re-
run the script `grub-install'.

# this device map was generated by anaconda
(fd0)    /dev/fd0
(hd0)    /dev/hda
[root@localhost root]# _
```

Dual Booting Linux

Linux servers are usually dedicated to their role all day long. However, those who use Linux as a workstation may wish to use the Linux operating system at certain times only; at other times, the same computer could be used with a different operating system. Since you may use only one operating system at a time, there must exist a mechanism that allows you to choose which operating system to load at boot time; this mechanism is typically handled by the boot loader.

Using LILO or GRUB to Dual Boot other Operating Systems

If you are using LILO or GRUB to **dual boot** another operating system in addition to Linux, then it is easiest if Linux is installed after the other operating system has been installed; this allows the installation program to detect the other operating system on the disk and place the appropriate entries in `/etc/lilo.conf` and `/boot/grub/grub.conf`.

Take, for example, an installation of Linux that creates Linux partitions on the free space of a hard disk containing a partition (`/dev/hda1`) with the Windows operating system installed on it as seen in Figure 9-7.

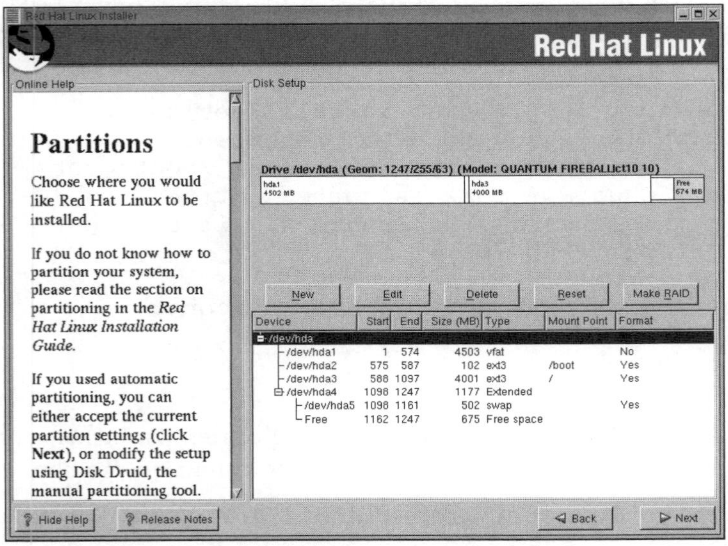

Figure 9-7 Partitioning for a dual boot system

If the Windows partition is preserved during partitioning, then the boot loader configuration options will include a section that allows you to choose to dual boot Linux with the Windows operating system using LILO or GRUB as seen in Figure 9-8.

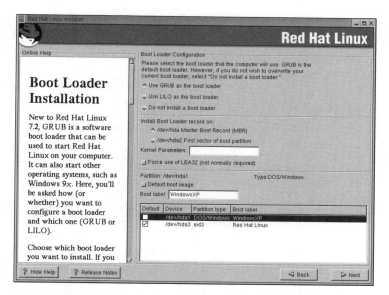

Figure 9-8 Choosing a boot loader for a dual boot system

9

 Regardless of the boot loader chosen during installation, the installation program configures entries for /etc/lilo.conf and /boot/grub/grub.conf such that you may choose to use either boot loader in the future without further configuration.

The /etc/lilo.conf file generated by the installation program depicted in Figures 9-7 and 9-8 is seen below:

```
[root@localhost root]# cat /etc/lilo.conf
prompt
timeout=50
default=Red Hat Linux
boot=/dev/hda
map=/boot/map
install=/boot/boot.b
message=/boot/message
lba32

image=/boot/vmlinuz-2.4.7-10
        label=Red Hat Linux
        initrd=/boot/initrd-2.4.7-10.img
        read-only
        root=/dev/hda3

other=/dev/hda1
        optional
        label=WindowsXP
[root@localhost root]# _
```

Since LILO cannot boot a Windows kernel directly, there is an **other=** keyword in the above /etc/lilo.conf file that loads the boot loader that is present on the /dev/hda1 partition. The **optional** keyword allows this operating system to be ignored if it becomes unavailable, and the **label** keyword identifies this operating system using a name that will be displayed at the LILO graphical screen for you to choose from. This name is also defined at the LILO **boot:** prompt if a graphical screen is not used.

The /boot/grub/grub.conf file created by the installation program shown in Figures 9-7 and 9-8 is seen in the following output:

```
[root@localhost root]# cat /boot/grub/grub.conf
# grub.conf generated by anaconda
#
# Note that you do not have to rerun grub after making
# changes to this file
# NOTICE:  You have a /boot partition.  This means that
#          all kernel and initrd paths are relative to
# /boot/, eg.
#          root (hd0,1)
#          kernel /vmlinuz-version ro root=/dev/hda3
#          initrd /initrd-version.img
#boot=/dev/hda
default=1
timeout=10
splashimage=(hd0,1)/grub/splash.xpm.gz
title Red Hat Linux (2.4.7-10)
        root (hd0,1)
        kernel /vmlinuz-2.4.7-10 ro root=/dev/hda3
        initrd /initrd-2.4.7-10.img
title WindowsXP
        rootnoverify (hd0,0)
        chainloader +1
[root@localhost root]# _
```

The **title** keyword in the above output identifies the new operating system and will be displayed at the GRUB graphical screen during boot time. The **rootnoverify (hd0,0)** line indicates that the operating system lies on the first partition on the first hard disk and that it should not automatically be mounted by GRUB (since it may contain a foreign filesystem). Because GRUB cannot load a Windows kernel directly, GRUB must load the Windows boot loader from the Windows partition; this boot loader typically starts on the first block of the Windows partition. The **chainloader +1** line allows GRUB to load another boot loader starting from the first block of the partition (hd0,0).

Using FIPS

It is common to use all the space on a hard disk drive in a workstation computer for a Windows partition when installing Windows; however, this leaves no free space to install Linux afterwards. One solution to this problem is to repartition the hard disk with a smaller Windows partition and reinstall the Windows operating system on it. Linux may then be installed on the free space outside the Windows partition afterwards. Another solution is to resize the Windows partition using a utility called **First non–destructive Interactive Partition Splitter (FIPS)**; this will preserve the Windows operating system on the Windows partition yet allow for free space to install Linux.

There are some guidelines to using FIPS, which should be met prior to using it; these limitations are:

- Version 2.0 of FIPS supports the FAT 16 and FAT 32 filesystems only. The NTFS file system is not supported by FIPS.

- FIPS will only work with primary Windows partitions and will not resize logical drives within extended partitions.

- FIPS works by splitting the Windows partition into two primary partitions; the first will contain the original Windows filesystem and the second may be used for Linux or safely removed and replaced with Linux partitions during a Linux installation. Recall that there can be only 4 primary partitions per hard disk; ensure that there is a free primary partition for FIPS to use.

- There must be sufficient free space within the existing Windows partition to allow for the installation of Linux once the partition has been resized.

FIPS can be found in the *dosutils* folder on the first Red Hat 7.2 installation CD-ROM, or downloaded from the Internet at the Red Hat FTP site *ftp://ftp.redhat.com/pub/redhat/dos/fips11.zip* or the FIPS home page *http://www.igd.fhg.de/~aschaefe/fips/*.

You should also read the `FIPS.doc` file that comes with the program and meet the requirements outlined inside. The following is a sample list of steps to follow to resize a Windows partition using FIPS:

1. Remove any old, unwanted, unused, or unnecessary files from the Windows partition to be resized to free up the greatest amount of space for Linux.

2. Defragment the Windows partition to be resized using a defragmentation program such as DEFRAG.

3. Ensure there is sufficient free space on the Windows partition to install Linux.

4. Run programs to check the integrity of the hard disk drive and identify any bad sectors with a program such as CHKDSK or SCANDISK.

5. Back up all data on the Windows partition in case of failure during the FIPS process.

6. Obtain or create a DOS or Windows boot disk.

7. Copy the files FIPS.exe, ERRORS.txt, and RESTORRB.exe to the boot disk from the *dosutils/fips20/* directory on the first Red Hat 7.2 Installation CD-ROM.

8. Boot the system using the boot disk created in the previous step. FIPS will not work while the Windows operating system is active.

9. At the DOS prompt type fips to invoke the FIPS program.

10. FIPS then checks the current hard disk drive and the partition structure for free space. If there is more than one hard disk drive present it will ask which drive it should check.

11. Once it has determined what free space there is FIPS displays the suggested partition split. CAUTION: Do not accept the default presented as it severs off all free space from the existing partition leaving it with none; the Windows operating system should contain some free space to function properly.

12. Adjust the partition division to the desired split of hard disk drive space.

13. Once you indicate that FIPS can split the partition it will offer to create a back-up copy of the MBR on the hard disk drive with an extension of .000. You may restore this back-up copy of the MBR using RESTORRB.exe in the future.

14. FIPS resizes the original Windows partition to a smaller size and creates a new partition from free space previously on the original Windows partition.

15. Run SCANDISK on the original Windows partition to ensure there are no errors.

16. Run the Linux installation program; when prompted to partition, you may safely remove the second partition created by FIPS and replace it with Linux partitions.

Provided the FIPS procedure completed successfully, there is only one difference that may be present while using the Windows operating system: drive letters assigned by the Windows operating system to drives such as CD-ROMs may be changed since there is now a different partition structure on the hard disk drive.

Using a Windows Boot Loader to Dual Boot Linux

You may choose to use a Windows boot loader to load the Linux operating system; simply specify the location of GRUB or LILO in the Windows boot loader configuration. Similar to LILO and GRUB, the **NTLOADER** boot loader that is available with Windows NT/2000/XP can be used to display a screen at boot time that prompts you to choose an operating system to boot. Thus, if the operating system that is dual booted with Linux is Windows NT/2000/XP, then you may use the Windows NTLOADER boot loader to load LILO or GRUB.

You must ensure that Windows NT/2000/XP is installed on the system first and located on the first primary partition of the system; the NTLOADER boot loader will be placed on the MBR of the hard disk by default. Next, you may install Linux and specify that LILO or GRUB is installed on the first sector of the **/boot** partition as seen in Figure 9-9; otherwise, LILO or GRUB will overwrite NTLOADER on the MBR of the hard disk.

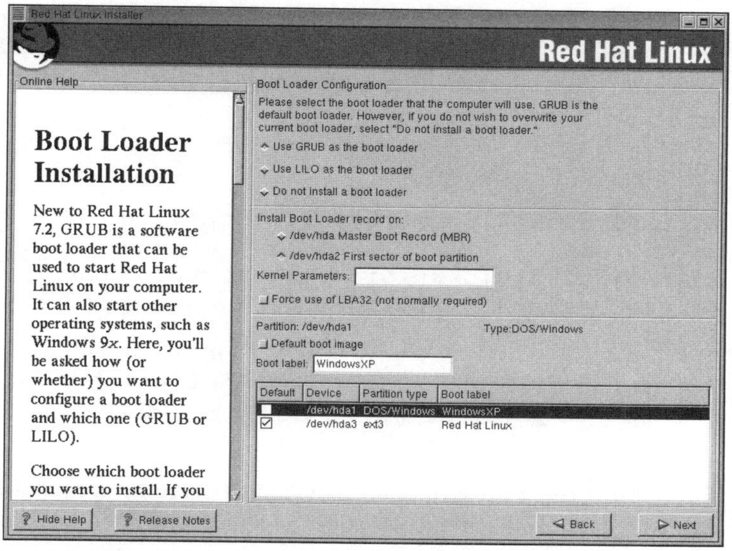

Figure 9-9 Configuration screen to put GRUB or LILO to the boot partition

It is important to create a boot disk when prompted to do so during the installation; this will ensure that you may boot into Linux immediately following the installation and prior to configuring the Windows NTLOADER boot loader.

Once Linux has been installed successfully, you may then boot into Linux by placing the boot floppy into the floppy disk drive. Once the system has loaded successfully from the boot loader on the floppy boot disk, you may create a bootable image file of LILO or GRUB. Say that LILO or GRUB was installed to the first sector of the /boot partition /dev/hda2; to create an image of the first sector of /dev/hda2 called linboot.bin, you could execute the following command at the command prompt:

```
[root@localhost root]# dd if=/dev/hda2 bs=512 count=1 of=linboot.bin
1+0 records in
1+0 records out
[root@localhost root]# _
```

Next, you must copy this image to a DOS floppy disk such that it may be used later in the Windows operating system:

```
[root@localhost root]# mkfs —t msdos /dev/fd0
mkfs.msdos 2.7 (14 Feb 2001)
[root@localhost root]# mount -t msdos /dev/fd0 /mnt/floppy
[root@localhost root]# cp linboot.bin /mnt/floppy
[root@localhost root]# umount /mnt/floppy
[root@localhost root]# _
```

Once the image has been created successfully, you may boot into the Windows operating system, copy the `linboot.bin` file to C:\, and configure the NTLOADER configuration file (C:\boot.ini) to include a section that may be used to boot it. A sample **boot.ini** file is seen below:

```
[boot loader]
timeout=30
default=multi(0)disk(0)rdisk(0)partition(1)\WINDOWS
[operating systems]
multi(0)disk(0)rdisk(0)partition(1)\WINDOWS="Microsoft
Windows XP Professional" /fastdetect
```

The above boot.ini file boots the default Windows operating system labeled "Microsoft Windows XP Professional" from the first partition (`partition(1)`) on the first hard disk (`rdisk(0)`) on the first IDE hard disk controller (`multi(0)`) in 30 seconds (`timeout=30`).

To have NTLOADER boot the Linux operating system, you must specify the path to the `linboot.bin` file created earlier and specify a label to be displayed at the NTLOADER boot screen:

```
[boot loader]
timeout=30
default=multi(0)disk(0)rdisk(0)partition(1)\WINDOWS
[operating systems]
multi(0)disk(0)rdisk(0)partition(1)\WINDOWS="Microsoft
Windows XP
Professional" /fastdetect
C:\linboot.bin="Red Hat Linux 7.2"
```

When the system is rebooted, the NTLOADER boot loader will load and present a list of operating systems to choose from including Linux as portrayed in Figure 9-10.

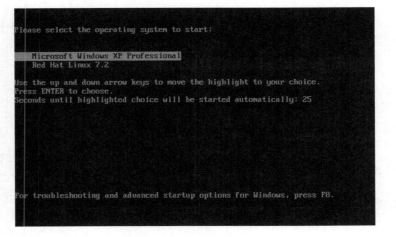

Figure 9-10   Dual boot operating system choice screen at start up

LINUX INITIALIZATION

Recall that once a boot loader loads the Linux operating system kernel into memory, the kernel resumes control and executes the first daemon process on the system called init. The init daemon then uses its configuration file **/etc/inittab** (init table) to load other daemons on the system that provide system services and ultimately allow users to log in and use the system. Furthermore, the init daemon is responsible for unloading daemons that are loaded in memory when the system is halted or rebooted.

Runlevels

Since there may be several daemons that need to be managed by the init daemon on a typical Linux system, the init daemon categorizes the system into runlevels. A **runlevel** defines the number and type of daemons that are loaded into memory and executed by the kernel on a particular system. There are seven standard runlevels that a Linux system may be in at any one time; these runlevels are defined in Table 9–3.

Table 9-3 Linux runlevels

Runlevel	Common Name	Description
0	Halt	A system that has no daemons active in memory and is ready to be powered off.
1 s S single	Single User Mode	A system that has only enough daemons to allow one user to log in and perform system maintenance tasks. A user is automatically logged into the system as the root user when entering Single User Mode.
2	Multi-User Mode	A system that has most daemons started and allows multiple users to log in and use system services. Most common network services other than the Network File System are available in this runlevel as well.
3	Extended Multi User Mode	A system that has the same abilities as Multi-User Mode, yet with all extra networking services started (i.e., NFS).
4	Not used	Not normally used, but may be defined manually if needed.
5	Graphical Mode	A system that has the same abilities as Extended Multi-User Mode, yet with a graphical login program called **X Display Manager (xdm)** or **GNOME Display Manager (gdm)** started on tty7 that allows for graphical logins.
6	Reboot	A special runlevel used to reboot the system.

Since the init daemon is responsible for starting and stopping daemons and hence changing runlevels, runlevels are often called **initstates** as well.

To see the current runlevel of the system and the previous runlevel (if runlevels have been changed since system startup), you may use the **runlevel command**, as seen in the output below:

```
[root@localhost root]# runlevel
N 5
[root@localhost root]# _
```

The above `runlevel` command indicates that the system is in runlevel 5 and that the most recent runlevel prior to entering this runlevel is non-existent (N).

To change the runlevel on a running system, you simply need to specify the **init command** followed by the new runlevel; to change from runlevel 5 to runlevel 1 to perform system maintenance tasks, you could use the following commands:

```
[root@localhost root]# runlevel
N 5
[root@localhost root]# init 1
INIT: Switching to runlevel: 1
INIT: Sending processes the TERM signal
Stopping atd:                                           [  OK  ]
Shutting down xfs:                                      [  OK  ]
Shutting down console mouse services:                   [  OK  ]
Shutting down sendmail:                                 [  OK  ]
Stopping xinetd:                                        [  OK  ]
Stopping crond:                                         [  OK  ]
Shutting down APM daemon:                               [  OK  ]
Saving random seed:                                     [  OK  ]
Shutting down NFS file locking services:
Shutting down NFS statd:                                [  OK  ]
Stopping portmapper:                                    [  OK  ]
Shutting down kernel logger:                            [  OK  ]
Shutting down system logger:                            [  OK  ]
Loading keymap:                                         [  OK  ]
Loading system font:                                    [  OK  ]
Telling INIT to go to single user mode.
INIT: Going single user
INIT: Sending processes the TERM signal
INIT Sending processes the KILL signal
sh-2.05# _
sh-2.05# runlevel
1 S
sh-2.05# _
```

The **telinit command** is a shortcut to the `init` command, thus the command `telinit 1` may instead be used to switch to Single User Mode.

When in single user mode, the `runlevel` command displays S (Single User Mode) for the current runlevel and 1 (Single User Mode) for the most recent runlevel; however, when the runlevel is changed back to runlevel 5, the `runlevel` command displays the current and most recent runlevels properly, as seen in the output below:

```
sh-2.05# init 5
INIT: Switching to runlevel: 5
INIT: Sending processes the TERM signal
INIT: Sending processes the KILL signal
Updating /etc/fstab                                    [  OK  ]
Checking for new hardware                              [  OK  ]
Setting network parameters:                            [  OK  ]
Bringing up interface lo:                              [  OK  ]
Starting system logger:                                [  OK  ]
Starting kernel logger:                                [  OK  ]
Starting portmapper:                                   [  OK  ]
Starting NFS file locking services:
Starting NFS statd:                                    [  OK  ]
Initializing random number generator:                  [  OK  ]
Mounting other filesystems:                            [  OK  ]
Starting up APM daemon:                                [  OK  ]
Starting automount: No Mountpoints Defined             [  OK  ]
Starting xinetd:                                       [  OK  ]
Starting lpd: No Printers Defined                      [  OK  ]
Starting sendmail:                                     [  OK  ]
Starting console mouse services:                       [  OK  ]
Starting crond:                                        [  OK  ]
Starting xfs:                                          [  OK  ]
Starting anacron:                                      [  OK  ]
Starting atd:                                          [  OK  ]
[root@localhost root]# _
[root@localhost root]# runlevel
S 5
[root@localhost root]# _
```

 You may also boot to a certain runlevel when the system is at the LILO `boot:` prompt; simply type the name of the Linux image followed by 1, S, s, or single.

The /etc/inittab File

When the init daemon needs to change the runlevel of the system by starting or stopping daemons, it consults the `/etc/inittab` file. This file is also consulted when bringing the system to a certain runlevel at boot time. An example of `/etc/inittab` is seen below:

```
[root@localhost root]# cat /etc/inittab
#
# inittab        This file describes how the INIT process should set up
```

```
#               the system in a certain run-level.
#
# Author:       Miquel van Smoorenburg, <miquels@drinkel.nl.mugnet.org>
#               Modified for RHS Linux by Marc Ewing and Donnie Barnes
#

# Default runlevel. The runlevels used by RHS are:
#   0 - halt (Do NOT set initdefault to this)
#   1 - Single user mode
#   2 - Multiuser, without NFS (The same as 3, if you do not have networking)
#   3 - Full multiuser mode
#   4 - unused
#   5 - X11
#   6 - reboot (Do NOT set initdefault to this)
    #
    id:5:initdefault:

    # System initialization.
    si::sysinit:/etc/rc.d/rc.sysinit

    l0:0:wait:/etc/rc.d/rc 0
    l1:1:wait:/etc/rc.d/rc 1
    l2:2:wait:/etc/rc.d/rc 2
    l3:3:wait:/etc/rc.d/rc 3
    l4:4:wait:/etc/rc.d/rc 4
    l5:5:wait:/etc/rc.d/rc 5
    l6:6:wait:/etc/rc.d/rc 6

    # Things to run in every runlevel.
    ud::once:/sbin/update

    # Trap CTRL-ALT-DELETE
    ca::ctrlaltdel:/sbin/shutdown -t3 -r now

    # When our UPS tells us power has failed, assume we have
    a few minutes of power left.
    # Schedule a shutdown for 2 minutes from now.
    # This does, of course, assume you have powerd installed
    # and your UPS connected and working correctly.
    pf::powerfail:/sbin/shutdown -f -
    h +2 "Power Failure; System Shutting Down"

    # If power was restored before the shutdown kicked in,
    # cancel it.
    pr:12345:powerokwait:/sbin/shutdown -c "Power Restored;
    Shutdown Cancelled"
```

```
# Run gettys in standard runlevels
1:2345:respawn:/sbin/mingetty tty1
2:2345:respawn:/sbin/mingetty tty2
3:2345:respawn:/sbin/mingetty tty3
4:2345:respawn:/sbin/mingetty tty4
5:2345:respawn:/sbin/mingetty tty5
6:2345:respawn:/sbin/mingetty tty6

# Run xdm in runlevel 5
# xdm is now a separate service
x:5:respawn:/etc/X11/prefdm -nodaemon
[root@localhost root]# _
```

The format of entries in the `/etc/inittab` file is as follows:

```
label : runlevel(s) : action : command
```

The `label` is just an identifier that allows the init daemon to examine this file in alphabetical order; the `runlevel` specifies which runlevel the line in `/etc/inittab` corresponds to; the `command` tells the init daemon what to execute when entering the runlevel; and the `action` tells the init daemon how to execute the command.

Thus, the line `id:5:initdefault:` in the `/etc/inittab` file shown above tells the init daemon that runlevel 5 is the default runlevel to boot to when initializing the Linux system at system startup. In addition, the `si::sysinit:/etc/rc.d/rc.sysinit` line tells the init daemon to run the program **/etc/rc.d/rc.sysinit** before entering a runlevel at system initialization. This program initializes the hardware components of the system, sets environment variables such as PATH and HOSTNAME, checks filesystems and performs system tasks required for daemon loading. The output from the `/etc/rc.d/rc.sysinit` program is indicated on the terminal screen during system startup depicted in Figure 9-11.

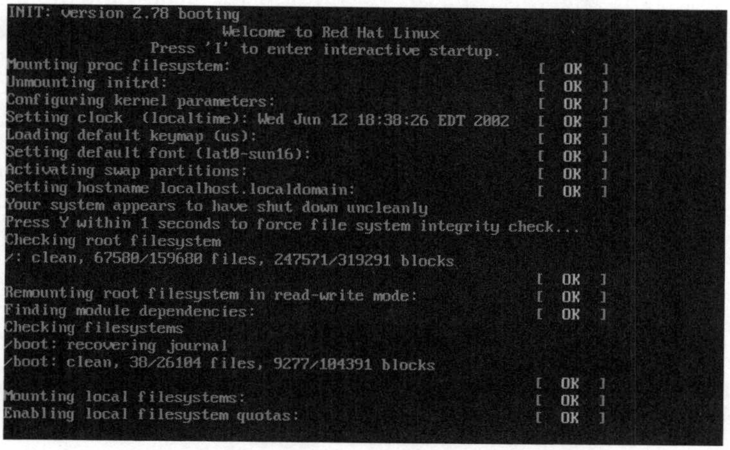

Figure 9-11   System startup as a result of /etc/rc.d/rc.sysinit

Since the default runlevel is 5, only the line `l5:5:wait:/etc/rc.d/rc 5` will be executed in the next section of the `/etc/inittab` file seen earlier. This line executes the `/etc/rc.d/rc 5` command and waits for it to finish before proceeding to the rest of the `/etc/inittab` file. The `/etc/rc.d/rc 5` command executes all files that start with S or K in the `/etc/rc.d/rc5.d/` directory. Each file in this directory is a symbolic link to a script that starts a certain daemon, and each of these files is executed in alphabetical order; the S or the K indicates whether to Start or Kill the daemon upon entering this runlevel respectively. Some sample contents of the `/etc/rc.d/rc5.d` directory are seen below:

```
[root@localhost root]# ls /etc/rc.d/rc5.d
K03rhnsd        K34yppasswdd    K65krb524       S06reconfig     S56xinetd
K05innd         K35dhcpd        K65krb5kdc      S08ipchains     S60lpd
K09junkbuster   K35smb          K74ntpd         S08iptables     S80sendmail
K12mysqld       K35vncserver    K74ups          S09isdn         S83iscsi
K15httpd        K40mars-nwe     K74ypserv       S10network      S85gpm
K15postgresql   K45arpwatch     K74ypxfrd       S12syslog       S90crond
K16rarpd        K45named        K75gated        S13portmap      S90xfs
K20bootparamd   K46radvd        K84bgpd         S14nfslock      S95anacron
K20nfs          K50snmpd        K84ospf6d       S17keytable     S95atd
K20rstatd       K50tux          K84ospfd        S20random       S99linuxconf
K20rusersd      K54pxe          K84ripd         S25netfs        S99local
K20rwalld       K55routed       K84ripngd       S26apmd         S99wine
K20rwhod        K61ldap         K85zebra        S28autofs
K25squid        K65identd       K89bcm5820      S45pcmcia
K28amd          K65kadmin       K96irda         S55sshd
K30mcserv       K65kprop        S05kudzu        S56rawdevices
[root@localhost root]# _
```

From the above output, we can see that the init daemon will start the **cron** daemon (**S90crond**) upon entering this runlevel and kill the **ldap** daemon (**K61ldap**) if it exists in memory upon entering this runlevel. In addition, the files in the directory above are executed in alphabetical order; the file **K65identd** will be executed before the file **K65kadmin**.

Recall that runlevel 1 (Single User Mode) contains only enough daemons for a single user to log in and perform system tasks; if you tell the init daemon to change to this runlevel using the **init 1** command, the init daemon will find the appropriate entry in `/etc/inittab` (`l1:1:wait:/etc/rc.d/rc 1`) and proceed to execute every file that starts with S or K in the `/etc/rc.d/rc1.d` directory. Since few daemons are started in Single User Mode, most files in this directory start with a K:

```
[root@localhost root]# ls /etc/rc.d/rc1.d
K00linuxconf    K20rstatd       K45named        K74apmd         K88syslog
K03rhnsd        K20rusersd      K46radvd        K74ntpd         K89bcm5820
K05anacron      K20rwalld       K50snmpd        K74ups          K90network
K05atd          K20rwhod        K50tux          K74ypserv       K91isdn
K05innd         K25squid        K50xinetd       K74ypxfrd       K92ipchains
K09junkbuster   K25sshd         K54pxe          K75gated        K92iptables
```

```
K10wine          K28amd           K55routed        K75netfs         K95kudzu
K10xfs           K30mcserv        K60crond         K80random        K95reconfig
K12mysqld        K30sendmail      K60lpd           K84bgpd          K96irda
K15gpm           K34yppasswdd     K61ldap          K84ospf6d        K96pcmcia
K15httpd         K35dhcpd         K65identd        K84ospfd         S00single
K15postgresql    K35smb           K65kadmin        K84ripd          S17keytable
K16rarpd         K35vncserver     K65kprop         K84ripngd
K20bootparamd    K40mars-nwe      K65krb524        K85zebra
K20iscsi         K44rawdevices    K65krb5kdc       K86nfslock
K20nfs           K45arpwatch      K72autofs        K87portmap
[root@localhost root]# _
```

Most daemons that are loaded upon system startup are executed from entries in /etc/inittab that run the /etc/rc.d/rc command at system startup to load daemons from files that start with an S in the appropriate /etc/rc.d/rc*.d directory (where * refers to the default runlevel). As with the /etc/rc.d/rc.sysinit program, there is a message during boot time to indicate whether each file in the /etc/rc.d/rc*.d directory has loaded successfully or unsuccessfully; this is depicted in Figure 9-12.

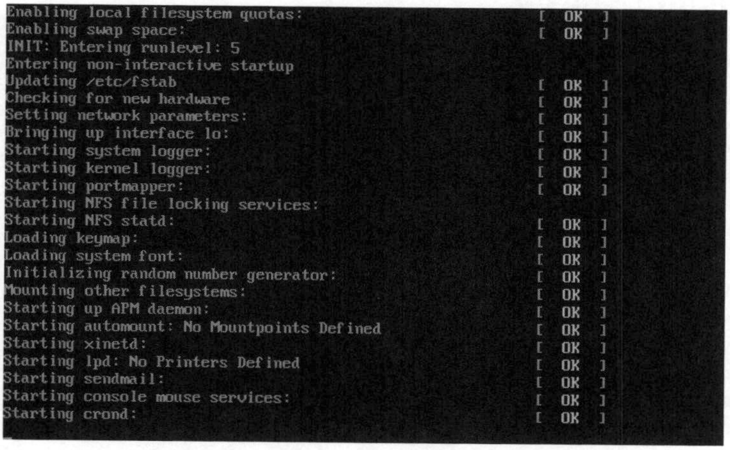

Figure 9-12   System startup as a result of /etc/rc.d/rc*.d

The remainder of the /etc/inittab file loads optional components and allows for login programs to run on terminals. For terminal logins, the **mingetty** program is started on tty1 through tty6 and restarted (respawn) continuously to allow for login after login. In addition, **gdm** is started only upon entering runlevel 5 from the last entry in /etc/inittab.

Once the entries in /etc/inittab have been executed, the **/etc/rc.d/rc.local** file is executed to perform tasks that must occur after system startup. The entire Linux initialization process is summarized in Figure 9-13.

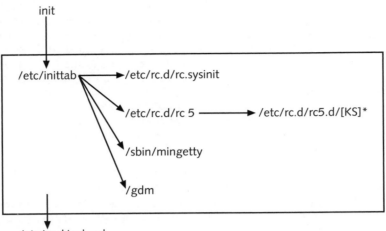

Figure 9-13   The Linux initialization process

Configuring Daemon Startup

Recall from the previous section that most daemons are started by the init daemon from symbolic links in the **/etc/rc.d/rc*.d** directories depending on the runlevel entered. Most of these links point to the appropriate daemon executable file in the **/etc/rc.d/init.d** directory. A partial listing of the /etc/rc.d/rc5.d directory demonstrates this:

```
[root@localhost root]# ls —l /etc/rc.d/rc5.d | head
total 0
lrwxrwxrwx 1 root   root    15 Jun 11 15:48 K03rhnsd -> ../init.d/rhnsd
lrwxrwxrwx 1 root   root    14 Jun 11 15:50 K05innd -> ../init.d/innd
lrwxrwxrwx 1 root   root    16 Jun 11 16:08 K12mysqld -> ../init.d/mysqld
lrwxrwxrwx 1 root   root    15 Jun 11 15:50 K15httpd -> ../init.d/httpd
lrwxrwxrwx 1 root   root    15 Jun 11 15:51 K16rarpd -> ../init.d/rarpd
lrwxrwxrwx 1 root   root    13 Jun 11 15:47 K20nfs -> ../init.d/nfs
lrwxrwxrwx 1 root   root    16 Jun 11 15:49 K20rstatd -> ../init.d/rstatd
lrwxrwxrwx 1 root   root    17 Jun 11 15:49 K20rusersd -> ../init.d/rusersd
lrwxrwxrwx 1 root   root    16 Jun 11 15:49 K20rwalld -> ../init.d/rwalld
[root@localhost root]# _
```

In addition, most daemons accept the arguments start, stop, and restart. Thus, to manipulate daemons after system startup, you may execute them directly from the /etc/rc.d/init.d directory as seen below with the **xinetd** daemon:

```
[root@localhost root]# /etc/rc.d/init.d/xinetd restart
Stopping xinetd:
[  OK  ]
```

```
Starting xinetd:
[   OK   ]
[root@localhost root]# _
```

 The /etc/init.d directory is symbolically linked to the /etc/rc.d/init.d directory; thus the /etc/init.d/xinetd restart command would perform the same function as the command used in the previous example.

Since most daemon executable files are stored centrally in the /etc/rc.d/init.d directory, if you wished to add a daemon that will be started automatically by the init daemon upon entering a certain runlevel at system startup, you could add the executable file for the daemon to this directory and create the appropriate links in each of the /etc/rc.d/rc*.d directories to start and kill the daemon upon entering certain runlevels.

Thus, to configure the init daemon to start an executable daemon file called **testdaemon** automatically when entering runlevels 2, 3, and 5 only, you could perform the following commands:

```
[root@localhost root]# cp testdaemon /etc/rc.d/init.d
[root@localhost root]# cd /etc/rc.d/init.d
[root@localhost root]# ln -s testdaemon /etc/rc.d/rc2.d/S99testdaemon
[root@localhost root]# ln -s testdaemon /etc/rc.d/rc3.d/S99testdaemon
[root@localhost root]# ln -s testdaemon /etc/rc.d/rc5.d/S99testdaemon
[root@localhost root]# _
```

Similarly, to configure the init daemon to kill **testdaemon** automatically when entering runlevel 0, 1, and 6, you could execute the following commands:

```
[root@localhost root]# cd /etc/rc.d/init.d
[root@localhost root]# ln -s testdaemon /etc/rc.d/rc0.d/K01testdaemon
[root@localhost root]# ln -s testdaemon /etc/rc.d/rc1.d/K01testdaemon
[root@localhost root]# ln -s testdaemon /etc/rc.d/rc6.d/K01testdaemon
[root@localhost root]# _
```

To see whether the daemon loaded successfully at boot time, recall that you may view the contents of the /var/log/messages file after the system has fully initialized as seen below:

```
[root@localhost root]# grep testdaemon /var/log/messages
Jun 15 12:44:34 localhost testdaemon: testdaemon startup
succeeded
[root@localhost root]# _
```

For ease of administration, Red Hat places a large number of files that start with K in most /etc/rc.d/rc*.d directories even though the daemons represented by those files are not likely started. This allows you to rename the file such that it starts with S to start the daemon upon entering that runlevel. Alternatively, you may use the **ntsysv** utility to modify the file entries in the /etc/rc.d/rc*.d directories.

If you type `ntsysv --level 5` to modify the daemons that will be started in runlevel 5, the screen depicted in Figure 9-14 will be displayed.

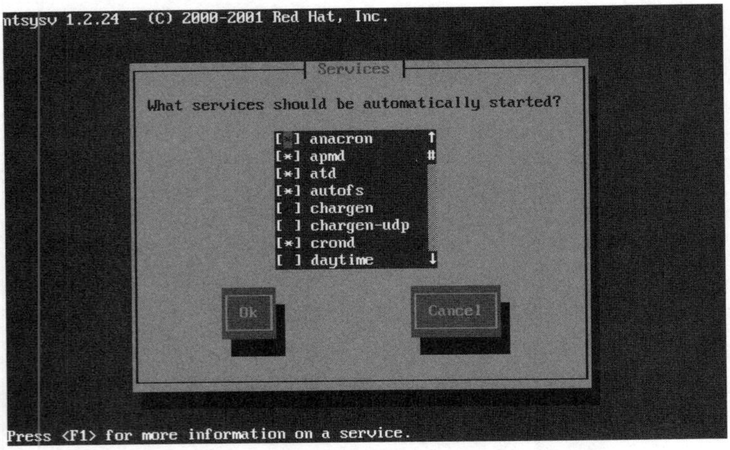

Figure 9-14   Results of ntsysv --level 5 command

CHAPTER SUMMARY

- Boot loaders are typically loaded by the system BIOS from the MBR or the first sector of the active partition of a hard disk.

- The boot loader is responsible for loading the Linux kernel.

- The LILO boot loader uses the `/etc/lilo.conf` configuration file, whereas the GRUB boot loader uses the `/boot/grub/grub.conf` configuration file.

- You may use the LILO or GRUB boot loader to dual boot Linux and the Windows operating system. Alternatively, the Windows NTLOADER boot loader may be used to do the same.

- The FIPS utility may be used to split a FAT16 or FAT32 partition in order to create enough space to install Linux.

- There are seven standard runlevels used to categorize a Linux system based on the number and type of daemons loaded in memory.

- The `init` daemon is responsible for loading and unloading daemons using its configuration file `/etc/inittab`.

- Daemons are typically stored in the `/etc/rc.d/init.d` directory and loaded at system startup from entries in the `/etc/rc.d/rc*.d` directories.

KEY TERMS

/boot — The directory that contains the kernel and boot-related files.

/boot/grub/grub.conf — The GRUB configuration file.

/etc/inittab — The configuration file for the init daemon.

/etc/lilo.conf — The LILO configuration file.

/etc/rc.d/init.d — The directory in which most daemons are located.

/etc/rc.d/rc — The script that executes files in the /etc/rc.d/rc*.d directories.

/etc/rc.d/rc*.d — The directories used to start and kill daemons in each runlevel.

/etc/rc.d/rc.local — The final script executed during system startup.

/etc/rc.d/rc.sysinit — The first script executed during system startup.

active partition — The partition searched for an operating system after the MBR.

boot loader — A program used to load an operating system.

boot.ini — The file used to configure NTLOADER.

daemon — A Linux system process that provides a certain service.

dual boot — A configuration where two or more operating systems exist on the hard disk of a computer; a boot loader allows the user to choose which operating system to load at boot time.

Extended Multi-User Mode — Also called runlevel 3; it provides most daemons and a full set of networking daemons.

First non-destructive Interactive Partition Splitter (FIPS) — A program used to create a new partition out of the free space on an existing FAT16 or FAT32 partition.

GNOME Display Manager (gdm) — Provides a graphical login screen.

Grand Unified Bootloader (GRUB) — A common boot loader used on Linux systems.

grub-install command — The command used to install the GRUB boot loader.

grub-md5-crypt command — The command used to generate an encrypted password for use in the /etc/grub/grub.conf file.

GRUB root partition — The partition containing the second stage of the GRUB boot loader and the /boot/grub/grub.conf file.

init command — The command used to change the operating system from one runlevel to another.

initialize (init) daemon — The first process started by the Linux kernel; it is responsible for starting and stopping other daemons.

initstate — *See* runlevel.

LInux LOader (LILO) — A common boot loader used on Linux systems.

lilo command — The command used to reinstall the LILO boot loader based on the configuration information in /etc/lilo.conf.

Master Boot Record (MBR) — A small program normally located on the first sector of the first hard disk drive used to define partitions and a boot loader.

mingetty — A program used to display a login prompt on a character based terminal.

9

Multi User–Mode — Also called runlevel 2; it provides most daemons and a partial set of networking daemons.

NTLOADER — The boot loader used to boot Windows NT/2000/XP operating system kernels.

Power On Self Test (POST) — An initial series of tests run when a computer is powered on to ensure that hardware components are functional.

runlevel — A term that defines a certain type and number of daemons on a Linux system.

runlevel command — The command used to display the current and most recent previous runlevel.

Single User Mode — Also called runlevel 1; it provides a single terminal and a limited set of services.

telinit command — An alias to the init command.

vmlinuz–<kernel version> — The Linux kernel file.

X Display Manager (xdm) — A graphical login screen.

REVIEW QUESTIONS

1. You can interact with boot loaders and pass them commands to alter the boot process. True or False?

2. Which of the following statements is true?

   a. GRUB needs to be reinstalled after it has been modified.

   b. LILO need not be reinstalled after it has been modified.

   c. GRUB points to LILO.

   d. GRUB need not be reinstalled after it has been modified.

3. When a computer first powers on what does it typically perform?

   a. POST

   b. PAST

   c. CMOS

   d. BIOS

   e. GRUB

   f. LILO

4. If GRUB has been password protected what must one type to enter the password when at the graphical GRUB screen?

   a. the password

   b. pass

   c. pwd

   d. passwd

   e. p

5. Which runlevel halts the system?

   a. 1

   b. 6

   c. 0

   d. 5

6. What file does init reference on startup to determine what to configure for a given run level?

   a. `/etc/initstate`

   b. `/root/inittab`

   c. `/inittab`

   d. `/etc/init`

   e. `/etc/inittab`

7. What does the action "respawn" do to a process when specified in the `/etc/inittab` file?

   a. create it

   b. kill it

   c. cause it to regenerate should it be killed

   d. There is no such value in `/etc/inittab`.

8. Which of the following statements is true?

   a. The operating system is first loaded by the MBR and then the boot loader.

   b. The boot loader points to the MBR.

   c. Either the MBR or the active partition may contain the boot loader.

   d. Both the MBR and the active partition point to the boot loader.

   e. The boot loader points to the active partition.

9. What command is used to reinstall LILO after its configuration has been altered?

   a. `lilo`

   b. `refresh`

   c. `set lilo`

   d. `reset lilo`

   e. It does not have to be reinstalled as it will do this automatically on the next boot.

10. What keyword in the LILO configuration file specifies the absolute pathname to the Linux kernel?

    a. default

    b. prompt

    c. root

    d. image

9

11. In order to make dual booting as easy as possible Linux should be the second operating system installed. True or False?

12. What file do you modify to reconfigure LILO?

    a. `/etc/lilo.conf`

    b. `/etc/lilo/conf`

    c. `config/lilo`

    d. `/root/lilo`

13. The Linux kernel is stored in a partition and named linux-<kernel number>. True or False?

14. How many active partitions can there be per hard disk drive?

    a. 4

    b. 16

    c. 1

    d. 2

15. Which of the following would indicate the second partition on the third hard disk drive to GRUB?

    a. (hdc,2)

    b. (hd2,3)

    c. (hd2,1)

    d. GRUB does not label hard disk drives and partitions; the operating system does once it is loaded.

16. Neither GRUB nor LILO can directly load a Windows operating system. True or False?

17. You power up a system and walk away only to return and find the Linux operating system is loaded. How did LILO know what to load?

    a. There is a line in `/etc/lilo.conf` that lists a default operating system to load should a user not specify one after a set time.

    b. This cannot happen; the user must specify what kernel to load from the graphical interface.

    c. There is a line in `/root/lilo.conf` that lists a default operating system to load should a user not specify one after a set time.

    d. There is a line in `/etc/lilo/conf` that lists a default operating system to load should a user not specify one after a set time.

18. Which runlevel will make the GUI login screen available?

    a. 1

    b. 6

    c. 0

    d. 5

19. What is the name of the directory that contains the configuration information for runlevel 2?

    a. `/etc/rc.d/rc2.d`

    b. `/rc.d/rc2.d`

    c. `/etc/rc.d/l2.d`

    d. `/etc/init/l2`

    e. `/etc/inittab/rc2/d`

20. In what directory is the Linux kernel stored?

    a. `/boot`

    b. `/root`

    c. `/bin`

    d. `/`

21. If a user enters Single User Mode who are they automatically logged in as?

    a. whatever user name they provided

    b. root

    c. admin

    d. There is no user available in Single User Mode.

22. The order in which devices are checked for boot information on a computer is fixed and not changeable. True or False?

23. The first process generated on a Linux system is _____.

    a. `initstate`

    b. `genesis`

    c. `inittab`

    d. `init`

    e. `linux`

24. Which runlevel reboots the system?

    a. 1

    b. 6

    c. 0

    d. 5

25. What command will cause the system to enter Single User Mode?

    a. `init 0`

    b. `init 1`

    c. `init 6`

    d. `initstate 5`

26. The timeout value in the GRUB configuration file is measured in
   _____.

   a. seconds
   b. 1/10 of minutes
   c. 1/10 of seconds
   d. 1/100 of seconds

27. What key combination do you press to obtain a LILO boot prompt when at the graphical LILO screen at boot time?
   a. Ctrl-Alt-Del
   b. Ctrl-F1
   c. Ctrl-x
   d. Shift-x

28. The timeout value in the LILO configuration file is measured in
   _____.

   a. seconds
   b. 1/10 of minutes
   c. 1/10 of seconds
   d. 1/100 of seconds

HANDS-ON PROJECTS

These projects should be completed in the order given. All hands-on projects should take a total of three hours to complete. The requirements for this lab include:

❑ A computer with Red Hat Linux 7.2 installed according to Hands-on Project 7-2

Project 9-1

In this hands-on project, you configure the LILO boot loader installed during Hands-on Project 7-2.

1. Switch to a command-line terminal (tty2) by pressing **Ctrl-Alt-F2** and log into the terminal using the username of **root** and the password of **secret**.

2. Reboot your system by typing **reboot** and pressing **Enter**. When the system reboots, observe the graphical LILO screen. Next, press the **Ctrl** and **x** keys simultaneously to obtain a LILO boot: prompt. At this prompt, press the **Tab** key. What is displayed?

3. At the LILO boot: prompt, type **linux single** and press the **Enter** key to boot the default operating system into Single User Mode. What other commands could you have typed at the LILO boot: prompt instead of `linux single` to accomplish the same task?

4. Once the system has reached Single User Mode, type **whoami** at the command prompt and press **Enter**. Who are you logged in as? Were you required to log in as this user in Single User Mode?

5. At the command prompt, type **vi /etc/lilo.conf** and press **Enter** to edit the LILO configuration file. Describe the purpose of each line of this file.

6. Comment out the line that reads `message=/boot/message` by placing a # character before it:

    #message=/boot/message

    What will this do?

7. Change the value of `timeout` from **50** to **600**. How long must you now wait before the default operating system is booted?

8. Open a new line underneath the line that reads `image=/boot/vmlinuz-2.4.7-10` and enter the following text:

    password = secret

    What will this entry do?

9. Save your changes and quit the **vi** editor.

10. At the command prompt, type **lilo** and press **Enter**. Why must you enter the `lilo` command after editing the `/etc/lilo.conf` file? *(Note: If there are any syntax errors in the `/etc/lilo.conf` file this command will not work. Simply edit the `/etc/lilo.conf` file again, fix any syntax errors, and rerun the `lilo` command.)*

11. Reboot your system by typing **reboot** and pressing **Enter**. When the system reboots, observe the LILO boot: prompt. At this prompt, press the **Tab** key. What is displayed? How long will you need to wait before the default operating system is booted? Why?

12. At the LILO boot: prompt, type **linux single** and press the **Enter** key to boot the system to Single User Mode. Were you prompted for a password? Why?

13. At the password prompt, type in **secret** and press **Enter**.

14. When the system has reached Single User Mode, type **ls –l /etc/lilo.conf** to view the permissions on the LILO configuration file. Who are the owner and group? What permissions does the *other* category have to this file? Is this a good or bad security procedure? Who will be able to view the line **password = secret** in the /etc/lilo.conf file?

15. At the command prompt, type **chmod 660 /etc/lilo.conf** and press **Enter** to prevent all users from viewing the boot password.

16. Reboot your system by typing **reboot** and pressing **Enter**. When the system reboots, observe the LILO boot: prompt.

9

17. At the LILO boot: prompt, press the **Enter** key to boot the default operating system specified in `/etc/lilo.conf`. When prompted, enter the password of **secret** and press **Enter** to boot the Linux operating system normally.

Project 9-2

In this hands-on project, you install and configure the GRUB boot loader.

1. Switch to a command-line terminal (tty2) by pressing **Ctrl-Alt-F2** and log into the terminal using the username of **root** and the password of **secret**.

2. At the command prompt, type **cat /boot/grub/grub.conf** and press **Enter** to view the GRUB configuration file. Can you tell where the boot loader is installed? What does each entry indicate?

3. At the command prompt, type **vi /boot/grub/grub.conf** and press **Enter** to edit the GRUB configuration file. Change the value of `timeout` from **10** to **100**. How long must you now wait before the default operating system is booted? Save your changes and quit the **vi** editor.

4. Next, type **grub-install /dev/hda** at the command prompt and press **Enter** to install GRUB on the MBR of the first IDE hard disk. If you were to edit the `/boot/grub/grub.conf` file again, would you need to rerun the `grub-install` command? Why?

5. Reboot your system by typing **reboot** and pressing **Enter**. When the system reboots, observe the graphical GRUB screen. At this screen, press **e** to edit the configuration of GRUB. Do you recognize the entries listed?

6. Next, type **c** at the GRUB screen to open a `grub>` prompt.

7. At the `grub>` prompt, type **help** and press **Enter** to view a list of commands you may use at the `grub>` prompt. Next, type **displaymem** at the `grub>` prompt and press **Enter**. Does GRUB recognize all the memory in your computer correctly?

8. At the `grub>` prompt, type **cat /grub/grub.conf** and press **Enter** to view the `/boot/grub/grub.conf` file. Why did you need to use an absolute pathname that started from the `/boot` directory in the `cat /grub/grub.conf` command?

9. At the `grub>` prompt, type **kernel /vmlinuz ro --root=/dev/hda2** and press **Enter** to load the Linux kernel (`/boot/vmlinuz`) into memory. *(Note: /boot/vmlinuz is a symbolic link to the current kernel.)*

10. At the `grub>` prompt, type **boot** and press **Enter** to continue the boot process using the Linux kernel loaded into memory during the previous step. Allow the system to boot normally.

11. Once the system has loaded successfully, switch to a command-line terminal (tty2) by pressing **Ctrl-Alt-F2** and log into the terminal using the username of **root** and the password of **secret**.

12. At the command prompt, type **grub-md5-crypt >passfile** and press **Enter**. This will result in a blank line; at this blank line, type **secret** and press **Enter**.

13. At the command prompt, type **cat passfile** and press **Enter**. Is the encrypted password there?

14. At the command prompt, type **vi /boot/grub/grub.conf** and press **Enter** to edit the GRUB configuration file. While in the **vi** editor, position the cursor on the line that says `splashimage=(hd0,0)/grub/splash.xpm.gz`.

15. Next, type **:** to obtain the interactive prompt at the bottom of the screen and then type **r !tail −1 passfile** to read the last line of the file `passfile` underneath the current line in the document. Your cursor shall now be on the first character of the encrypted password.

16. Type **i** to enter insert mode and type the following:

    ```
    password --md5
    ```

    The entire line should look similar to:

    ```
    password --md5  <encrypted password>
    ```

17. Save your changes and quit the **vi** editor.

18. Examine the permissions on the /boot/grub/grub.conf file by typing **ls −l /boot/grub/grub.conf** and pressing **Enter**. Are these permissions a security hazard? Even if the file allowed everyone the read permission, would they be able to see the boot password?

19. Reboot your system by typing **reboot** and pressing **Enter**. When the system reboots, observe the graphical GRUB screen. At this screen, press **p** to edit the configuration of GRUB. Enter the password of **secret** and press **Enter**. Do you recognize the screen displayed? What does the message on the screen read?

20. Press **Enter** to boot the default operating system.

Project 9-3

In this hands-on project, you will explore runlevels and the /etc/inittab file used to change runlevels at system startup and afterwards.

1. Switch to a command-line terminal (tty2) by pressing **Ctrl-Alt-F2** and log into the terminal using the username of **root** and the password of **secret**.

2. At the command prompt, type **runlevel** and press **Enter**. What is your current runlevel? Was this chosen during installation? If not, when? What is the most recent runlevel?

3. At the command prompt, type **less /etc/inittab** and press **Enter**. Which line in this file determines the default runlevel at boot time? Can this be changed?

4. At the command prompt, type **init 2** and press **Enter**. What is displayed on your terminal screen? Are any daemons started? Are any daemons stopped? Why? Are you required to log in? Why?

5. Log into the current terminal with the username of **root** and the password **secret**. Next, type **runlevel** at the command prompt and press **Enter**. What is your current runlevel? What is the most recent runlevel?

6. At the command prompt, type **init 1** and press **Enter**. What is displayed on your terminal screen? Are any daemons started? Are any daemons stopped? Why? Are you required to log in? Why?

7. Next, type **runlevel** at the command prompt and press **Enter**. What is your current runlevel? What is the most recent runlevel?

8. At the command prompt, type **init 5** and press **Enter**. What is displayed on your terminal screen? Are any daemons started? Are any daemons stopped? Why? What is displayed after switching to runlevel 5?

9. Switch to a command-line terminal (tty2) by pressing **Ctrl-Alt-F2** and log into the terminal using the username of **root** and the password of **secret**.

10. Next, type **runlevel** at the command prompt and press **Enter**. What is your current runlevel? What is the most recent runlevel?

11. At the command prompt, type **less /etc/inittab** and press **Enter**. Explain which lines in this file were read by the `init` daemon during Steps 4, 6, and 8.

12. Type **exit** and press **Enter** to log out of your shell.

Project 9-4

In this hands-on project, you will examine the system runlevel directories as well as start a fake daemon process upon system startup.

1. Switch to a command-line terminal (tty2) by pressing **Ctrl-Alt-F2** and log into the terminal using the username of **root** and the password of **secret**.

2. At the command prompt, type **ls /etc/rc.d** and press **Enter**. What directories are listed? What is contained within each directory?

3. At the command prompt, type **ls –F /etc/rc.d/rc0.d** and press **Enter**. What type of files is listed? In which order will these files be executed by the `init` daemon? How many of these start with K compared to S? Why?

4. At the command prompt, type **ls –F /etc/rc.d/rc5.d** and press **Enter**. What type of files is listed? How many of these start with K compared to S? Why?

5. At the command prompt, type **ls –F /etc/rc.d/init.d** and press **Enter**. What type of files is listed? What happens when you execute a file from this directory?

6. At the command prompt, type **/etc/rc.d/init.d/atd stop** and press **Enter**. What happened?

7. At the command prompt, type **/etc/rc.d/init.d/atd start** and press **Enter**. What happened?

8. At the command prompt, type **/etc/rc.d/init.d/atd restart** and press **Enter**. What happened?

9. At the command prompt, type **vi /etc/rc.d/init.d/sample** and press **Enter** to create a fake daemon in the `/etc/rc.d/init.d` directory.

10. Enter the following information in the **vi** editor. When finished, save your changes and quit the **vi** editor. (*Note: The variable $1 refers to the first argument given when executing the shell script on the command line.*)

```
#!/bin/bash
if [ $1 = "start" ]
then
        echo "The sample daemon has started"
        sleep 2
elif [ $1 = "stop" ]
then
        echo "The sample daemon has been stopped"
        sleep 2
elif [ $1 = "restart" ]
then
        echo "The sample daemon has been restarted"
        sleep 2
fi
```

11. At the command prompt, type **ls –l /etc/rc.d/init.d/sample** and press **Enter**. What are the permissions on the file?

12. At the command prompt, type **chmod 755 /etc/rc.d/init.d/sample** and press **Enter** to allow the **sample** file to be executed.

13. At the command prompt, type **ln –s /etc/rc.d/init.d/sample /etc/rc.d/rc5.d/S50sample** and press **Enter**. What does this command do? What will happen at system startup?

14. At the command prompt, type **reboot** and press **Enter** to reboot the system. Pay close attention to the startup screen as daemons are started. Does the sample daemon start? Why? Allow the system to boot normally.

15. When the system has booted successfully, switch to a command-line terminal (tty2) by pressing **Ctrl–Alt–F2** and log into the terminal using the username of **root** and the password of **secret**.

16. At the command prompt, type **/etc/rc.d/init.d/sample stop** and press **Enter**. What happened?

17. At the command prompt, type **/etc/rc.d/init.d/sample start** and press **Enter**. What happened?

18. At the command prompt, type **/etc/rc.d/init.d/sample restart** and press **Enter**. What happened?

19. Type **exit** and press **Enter** to log out of your shell.

9

DISCOVERY EXERCISES

1. Describe what would happen if you edited the /etc/inittab file and changed the line that read: **id:5:initdefault:**

   to read: **d:6:initdefault:**

2. You have created a daemon called **mydaemon** that performs database management tasks on the system; however, you wish to have this daemon start only in runlevel 5. This daemon should not exist in memory when the system is in any other runlevel. What directory should you place this daemon in? What links should you create to this daemon? Write the commands you would use to have this daemon start and stop automatically on the system.

3. Provided you have a functional Web browser and Internet access, research two boot loaders used for Linux other than LILO and GRUB. What configuration file do they use? What are their benefits and disadvantages compared to LILO and GRUB?

4. Provided you have a copy of the Windows operating system, install it on a hard disk drive leaving adequate free space outside the Windows partition for the installation of Linux. Next, install Linux and choose to dual boot Linux with the Windows operating system using LILO. Examine the /etc/lilo.conf file once the installation has completed. Following this, examine the /boot/grub/grub.conf file and switch your system to use the GRUB boot loader.

5. Runlevel number 4 is typically not used on most Linux systems. What file defines this runlevel? How could you start daemons in this runlevel if you needed to? Outline the steps required to utilize runlevel 4; it should load all daemons from runlevel 3 plus some special database daemons as well.

6. Examine the /etc/rc.d/rc.sysinit shell script. What does each section do? Why must this file be run before the files in the /etc/rc.d/rc*.d directories?

7. There are many different programs available that can be used to resize partitions or create partitions for dual booting. Through a resource book, Web site, or other resource, locate and describe the features of a program other than FIPS, which can be used to modify existing partitions without losing their contents.

CHAPTER

10

THE X WINDOW SYSTEM

**After completing this chapter,
you will be able to:**

♦ Explain the purpose of the major Linux GUI components: X Windows, window manager, and desktop environment

♦ List common window managers and desktop environments used in Linux

♦ Gather the hardware information necessary to configure X Windows

♦ Configure X Windows settings using various Linux utilities

In previous chapters, focus has been placed on performing tasks using a BASH shell command-line interface obtained after logging into a character terminal. Although the command-line interface is the most common among administrators, graphical user interfaces (GUIs) may be used to simplify some administrative tasks. In addition, Linux users typically use graphical interfaces for running user programs; thus it is important to possess a good understanding of the Linux GUI structure and its configuration. In the first part of this chapter you examine the various components that comprise the Linux GUI and the methods used to start and stop them. Later in this chapter you learn how to configure the Linux GUI using common Linux utilities.

LINUX GUI COMPONENTS

The Linux graphical user interface (GUI) was designed to function in the same manner regardless of the video hardware on the computer system. As a result, it is comprised of many components, which work separately from the video hardware (video adapter card & monitor). These components are illustrated in Figure 10-1.

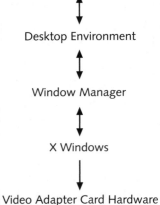

Figure 10-1   Components of the Linux GUI

Together the components listed in Figure 10-1 comprise a large part of a typical Linux installation. A typical installation of Red Hat Linux usually uses 400–600MB of data on the hard disk for the GUI and related programs.

X Windows

The core component of the GUI in Linux is **X Windows**. X Windows provides the ability to draw graphical images in windows that are displayed on a terminal screen. The programs that tell X Windows how to draw the graphics and display the results are known as **X clients**. X clients need not run on the same computer as X Windows; you may use X Windows on one computer to send graphical images to an X client on an entirely different computer by changing the DISPLAY environment variable discussed in Chapter 8. Because of this, X Windows is sometimes referred to as the server component of X Windows, or simply the **X server**.

X Windows was jointly developed by Digital Equipment Corporation (DEC) and the Massachusetts Institute of Technology (MIT) in 1984. Then, it was code-named Project Athena and was released in 1985 as X Windows in hopes that a new name would be found to replace the X. Shortly thereafter, X Windows was sought by many UNIX vendors, and by 1988 MIT released version 11 release 2 of X Windows (X11R2). Since

1988, X Windows has been maintained by The Open Group, which released version 11 release 6 of X Windows (X11R6) in 1995.

To find out more about X Windows, visit The Open Group on the Internet at *http://www.x.org*.

X Windows is governed by a separate license from the GPL, which restricts the usage of X Windows and its source code. As a result, Open Source developers created an Open Source version of X Windows. This freely available version of X Windows is used in Linux and is called **XFree86**, since it was originally intended for the Intel x86 platform.

To find out more about XFree86, visit The XFree86 Project on the Internet at *http://www.xfree86.org*.

Window Managers and Desktop Environments

Although X Windows performs most of the graphical functions in a GUI, there also exists a **window manager** that modifies the look and feel of X Windows. Thus, to change the appearance and behavior of X Windows, you can simply change the window manager used with X Windows. Optionally, you may use a **desktop environment** in addition to a window manager. Desktop environments come with a full set of GUI tools designed to be packaged together including Web browsers, file managers, and drawing programs. In addition to this, desktop environments provide development "toolkits" that allow software to be created more rapidly in much the same way a toolkit allows a carpenter or other artisan to complete a project faster. As discussed earlier in this book, the two most common desktop environments that are used on Linux are the Kommon Desktop Environment (KDE) and the GNU Object Model Environment (GNOME).

KDE is the traditional desktop environment used on Linux systems; it was created by Matthias Ettrich in 1996 and uses the **K Window Manager (kwm)** and the **Qt toolkit** for the C++ programming language. A typical KDE desktop screen is depicted in Figure 10-2.

To learn more about the KDE desktop, visit the Internet at *http://www.kde.org*.

The Qt toolkit was created by a company called Trolltech in Norway and unfortunately was not released as Open Source Software until 1998. In the mid-1990s, most Open Source developers preferred to develop in the C programming language instead of C++. They also did not like that the Qt toolkit source code was not freely modifiable at the time. As a result, the **GNOME Desktop Environment** was created in 1997. GNOME typically uses the **Sawfish Window Manager** and the **GTK+ toolkit** for the C programming language. The GTK+ toolkit was originally developed for the **GNU Image Manipulation Program (GIMP)**, and like the GIMP, is Open Source. The GNOME desktop is the default desktop in Red Hat Linux and can be seen in Figure 10-3.

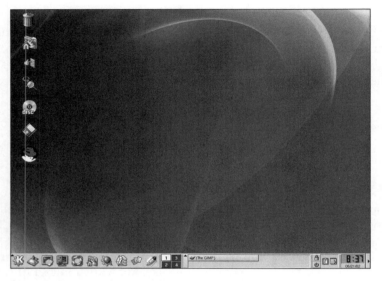

Figure 10-2   The KDE Desktop Environment

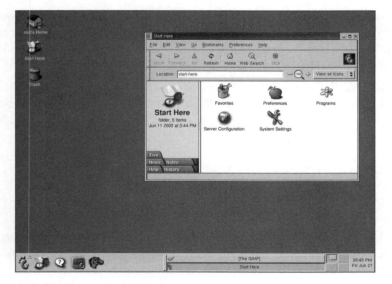

Figure 10-3   The GNOME Desktop Environment

To learn more about the GNOME desktop, you may visit the Internet at *http://www.gnome.org*.

Although desktop environments are commonplace for Linux users today, you may choose to use a window manager only. There are many different window managers available for Linux; some common ones are listed in Table 10-1 and depicted in Figures 10-4, 10-5, 10-6, and 10-7.

Table 10-1   Common window managers

Window Manager	Description
Enlightenment	A highly configurable window manager that allows for multiple desktops with different settings. It was used by the GNOME desktop prior to the Sawfish Window Manager.
fvwm	The Feeble Virtual Window Manager. It was based on the Tab Window Manager yet intended to use less computer memory and give the desktop a 3-D look.
kwm	The window manager used for the KDE desktop
Sawfish	The window manager used for the GNOME desktop. It allows you to configure most of its settings via tools or scripts.
twm	The Tab Window Manager. It is one of the oldest and most basic window managers.
Window Maker	A window manager that provides drag-and-drop mouse movement and imitates the NeXTSTEP operating system interface made by Apple Computer, Inc.

10

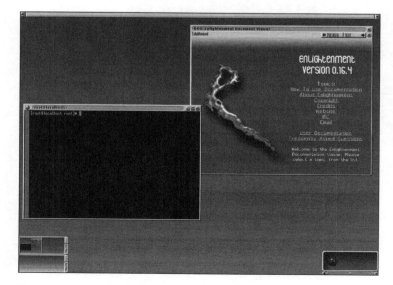

Figure 10-4   The Enlightenment Window Manager

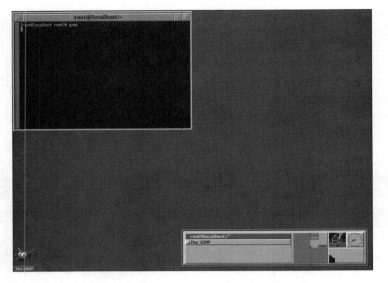

Figure 10-5   The Feeble Virtual Window Manager

Figure 10-6   The Tab Window Manager

Figure 10-7   The Window Maker Window Manager

STARTING AND STOPPING X WINDOWS

There must exist some method of starting X Windows, the window manager and the desktop environment (if used). Recall from the previous chapter that runlevel 5 starts the GNOME Display Manager (gdm) to display the graphical login screen depicted in Figure 10-8.

Figure 10-8   The GNOME Display Manager

This login screen allows you to choose the desktop environment or window manager to be used from the session menu prior to logging into the system and starting X Windows.

 You may configure the appearance and behavior of gdm by using the **GDM Configurator** tool in a desktop environment, or by editing the **/etc/X11/gdm/gdm.conf** file.

 The gdm is a variant of the **X Display Manager (xdm)**, which displays a basic graphical login for users. In addition, other Linux distributions may use the **KDE Display Manager (kdm)** to display a KDE-style graphical login for users.

If, however, you use runlevel 3 instead of runlevel 5, then you may type gdm at a character terminal to start the GNOME Display Manager manually, or use the **startx** command to start X Windows and the window manager or desktop environment specified in the .Xclients file in your home directory. If this file does not exist, the GNOME Desktop Environment is started by default. If this file exists, it simply points to the .Xclients-default file in your home directory, as seen below:

```
[root@localhost root]# cat .Xclients
#!/bin/bash

# Created by Red Hat Desktop Switcher

if [ -e "$HOME/.Xclients-$HOSTNAME$DISPLAY" ]; then
    exec $HOME/.Xclients-$HOSTNAME$DISPLAY
else
    exec $HOME/.Xclients-default
fi
[root@localhost root]# cat .Xclients-default
#!/bin/bash
# (c) 2000 Red Hat, Inc.

exec gnome-session
[root@localhost root]# _
```

Notice from the above output that the .Xclients-default file contains a line that executes the **gnome-session** command, which in turn starts the Sawfish Window Manager and the GNOME desktop on top of X Windows. Similarly, to start the KDE desktop on X Windows, you could edit the .Xclients-default file to include the following line:

```
[root@localhost root]# cat .Xclients-default
#!/bin/bash
# (c) 2000 Red Hat, Inc.

exec startkde
[root@localhost root]# _
```

You may also use the .Xclients-default file to start a window manager instead of a desktop environment. To accomplish this, simply change the line in this file to read exec /usr/bin/enlightenment to start the **Enlightenment Window Manager**; exec /usr/X11R6/bin/twm to start the **Tab Window Manager (twm)**; exec /usr/bin/wmaker to start the **Window Maker Window Manager**; or exec /usr/X11R6/bin/fvwm2 to start the **Feeble Virtual Window Manager (fvmm)**.

The settings used in the .Xclients-default file may also be set using the graphical **Desktop Switching Tool** in the GNOME or KDE desktop environments. An example of this tool in the GNOME desktop is depicted in Figure 10-9.

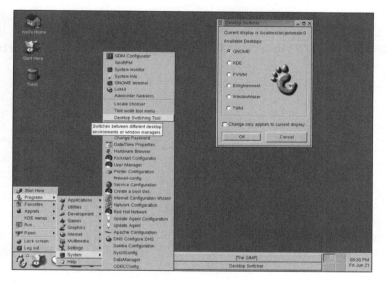

Figure 10-9   The Desktop Switching Tool

CONFIGURING X WINDOWS

X Windows is the component of the GUI that interfaces with the video hardware in the computer. In order for X Windows to perform its function, it needs information regarding the keyboard, mouse, monitor, and video adapter card. For the video adapter card, X Windows requires:

- the video adapter card model

- the amount of RAM on the video adapter card

- the **chipset** on the video adapter card (which may be the same as the model)

Although not normally required, X Windows may also need information about the RAMDAC and clockchip on the video card. The **RAM Digital Analog Converter**

(RAMDAC) chip is used to convert the digital signals used in a computer to analog signals understood by the computer monitor, and the **clockchip** coordinates the processing of information on the video card itself.

X Windows also requires the following information about the computer monitor that is attached to the video adapter card:

- **maximum resolution** supported
- horizontal sync (hsync) range
- vertical sync (vsync) range

To get this information, you may consult your computer manual. Alternatively, you may find monitor information by viewing the rear of the monitor itself, and probe the video adapter card for its information using the /usr/X11R6/bin/SuperProbe command, as seen below:

```
[root@localhost root]# SuperProbe


SuperProbe Version 2.23 (2000 November 28)
        (c) Copyright 1993,1994 by David Wexelblat
        <dwex@xfree86.org>
        (c) Copyright 1994-1998 by The XFree86 Project, Inc

        This work is derived from the 'vgadoc2.zip' and
        'vgadoc3.zip' documentation packages produced by
        Finn Thoegersen, and released with all appropriate
        permissions having been obtained. Additional information
        obtained from 'Programmer's Guide to the EGA and VGA,
        2nd ed',by Richard Ferraro, and from manufacturer's
        data books

Bug reports are welcome, and should be sent to XFree86@XFree86.org.
In particular, reports of chipsets that this program fails to
correctly detect are appreciated.

Before submitting a report, please make sure that you have the
latest version of SuperProbe (see http://www.xfree86.org/FAQ).

WARNING - THIS SOFTWARE COULD HANG YOUR MACHINE.
          READ THE SuperProbe.1 MANUAL PAGE BEFORE
          RUNNING THIS PROGRAM.

          INTERRUPT WITHIN FIVE SECONDS TO ABORT!
```

```
First video: Super-VGA
        Chipset: Cirrus CL-GD5446 (PCI Probed)
        Memory:  2048 Kbytes
        RAMDAC:  Cirrus Logic Built-in 8-bit
                 pseudo-color DAC
                 (with 6-bit wide lookup tables (or in 6-bit mode))
root@localhost root]# _
```

The **SuperProbe** command detects only a limited number of video cards. To see a list of video cards that are detected by SuperProbe, you can use the −info option to the command, as seen below:

```
[root@localhost root]# SuperProbe -info

SuperProbe Version 2.23 (2000 November 28)

SuperProbe can detect the following standard video
hardware:
        MDA, Hercules, CGA, MCGA, EGA, VGA
SuperProbe can detect the following SVGA chipsets/vendors:
        WD, Video7, MX, Genoa, UMC, Trident, SiS, Matrox,
        ATI, Ahead, NCR,
        S3, AL, Cirrus54, Cirrus64, Epson, Tseng, RealTek,
        Rendition, Primus,
        Yamaha, Oak, Cirrus, Compaq, HMC, Weitek,
        ARK Logic, Alliance,
        SigmaDesigns, Intergraphics, Silicon Motion, CT,
SuperProbe can detect the following graphics coprocessors/
vendors:
        ATI_Mach, 8514/A, I128, GLINT,
SuperProbe can detect the following RAMDACs:
        Generic, ALG1101, SS2410, Sierra15, Sierra16,
        Sierra24, MU9C4870,
        MU9C4910, ADAC1, 68830, 68860, 68875, ATIMisc,
        Cirrus8, Cirrus24B,
        Cirrus24, 20C490, 20C491, 20C492, 20C493, 20C497,
        Bt485, 20C504,
        20C505, TVP3020, TVP3025, EDSUN, 20C498, 22C498,
        STG1700, S3_GENDAC,
        S3_SDAC, TVP3026, RGB524, RGB514/525, RGB528,
        STG1703, 20C409,
        20C499, TKD8001, TGUIDAC, Integrated, MU9C1880,
        IMSG174, STG1702,
        CH8398, 20C408, TVP3030, ET6000, w30C516, PM642x,
        ICS5341, ICS5301,b
        MGA1064SG, MGAG100, MGAG200, SiS, SMI,
[root@localhost root]# _
```

10

The mouse, keyboard, monitor, and video adapter card information used by X Windows is stored in the **/etc/X11/XF86Config** file in text format. You may edit this file manually or use a program to edit it indirectly.

 You may instead edit the /usr/X11R6/lib/X11/XF86Config file, which is merely a symbolic link to /etc/X11/XF86Config. If you are planning to edit the /etc/X11/XF86Config file manually, ensure that you read the /usr/X11R6/lib/X11/doc/README.Config file first.

Since one mistake in the /etc/X11/XF86Config file could prevent the GUI from running, it is good practice to use a configuration program to edit it. To configure the mouse in Red Hat Linux, you may use the **mouseconfig** command, which displays a screen similar to the one depicted in Figure 10-10.

Figure 10-10   Mouse configuration using mouseconfig

Once the type of mouse has been selected from the menu in Figure 10-10, a screen similar to Figure 10-11 appears, confirming that the XF86Config file has been changed and that the changes will be effective when X Windows is restarted.

 To restart X Windows, you simply need to log out of X Windows and restart it by logging into the gdm or typing startx at the command prompt. Another method used to log out of X Windows is the Ctrl-Alt-Backspace key combination.

To configure the video adapter card and monitor information, you could use the **Xconfigurator** command, which results in a screen similar to that depicted in Figure 10-12.

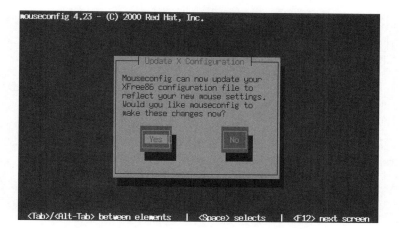

Figure 10-11   Updating the XF86Config file using mouseconfig

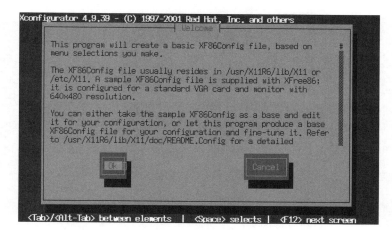

Figure 10-12   Starting the Xconfigurator utility

Xconfigurator tries automatically to detect the video adapter card and displays the results in the next screen, as seen in Figure 10-13.

Next, Xconfigurator prompts you for information about the monitor's hsync and vsync. You may choose from a list of known monitors, as depicted in Figure 10-14, or choose Custom to enter the hsync and vsync values manually.

Entries that specify the hsync and vsync ranges for the monitors listed in Figure 10-14 can be found in the **/usr/X11R6/share/Xconfigurator/MonitorsDB** file; if your monitor is listed in this file, then you do not need to specify the hsync and vsync values in Xconfigurator.

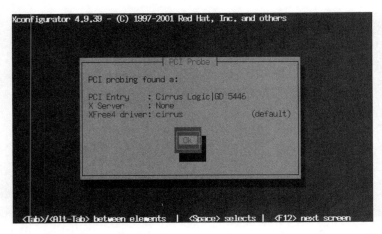

Figure 10-13   Detecting the video adapter card model using Xconfigurator

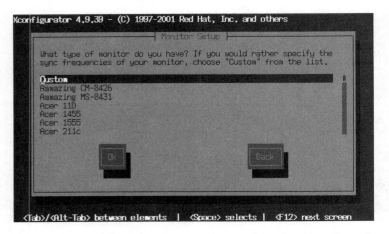

Figure 10-14   Choosing the monitor model using Xconfigurator

If you choose Custom from Figure 10-14 to configure the monitor's hsync and vsync manually, then Figures 10-15, 10-16, and 10-17 will appear to accept the information.

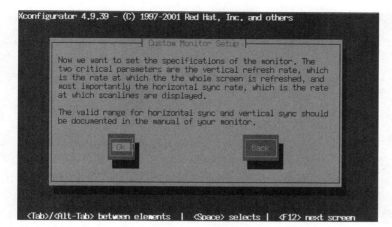

Figure 10-15 Choosing custom monitor settings using Xconfigurator

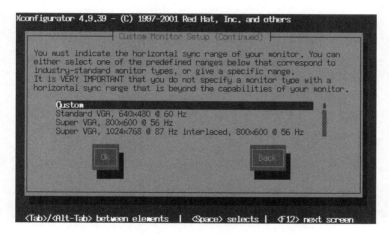

Figure 10-16 Choosing the hsync range using Xconfigurator

 If you choose Custom from Figure 10-16, then you will be prompted to enter the hsync and vsync ranges in manually.

Next, Xconfigurator will try automatically to detect the amount of memory on the video card, as well as the clockchip and RAMDAC, as seen in Figure 10-18. These values are used to compute the maximum color depth and resolution of your system.

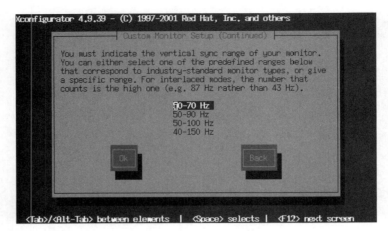

Figure 10-17   Choosing the vsync range using Xconfigurator

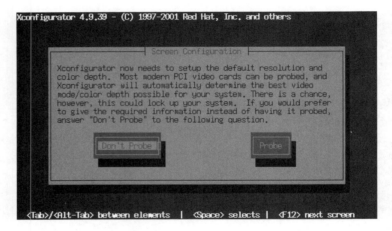

Figure 10-18   Probing for video adapter card information using Xconfigurator

If you choose not to probe for these values, you will need to enter the appropriate memory of your video card, as seen in Figure 10-19, and clockchip setting, as seen in Figure 10-20.

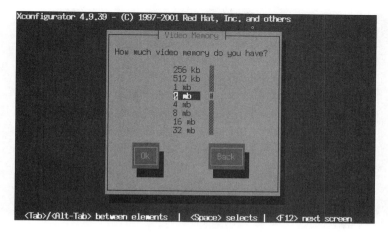

Figure 10-19 Manually selecting the video adapter card memory using Xconfigurator

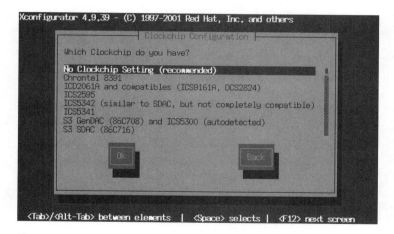

Figure 10-20 Manually choosing a clockchip setting using Xconfigurator

Once the memory and clockchip setting have been chosen, Red Hat runs the **X —probeonly** command to attempt to detect the chipset and verify any settings made previously, as seen in Figure 10-21.

Once this is completed, a list of possible color depths and resolutions is generated given the information entered in Figures 10-19, 10-20, and 10-21. You may then select which resolutions to support for each color depth, as seen in Figure 10-22. Later, you may cycle through these resolutions while in the GUI by pressing the Ctrl–Alt–+ key combination.

 Recall that 8-bit color gives 256 colors, while 16-bit and 24-bit color give 65,536 and 16,777,216 colors respectively.

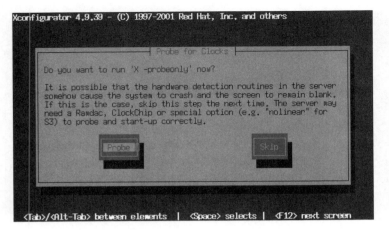

Figure 10-21   Probing for clockchips and RAMDACs using Xconfigurator

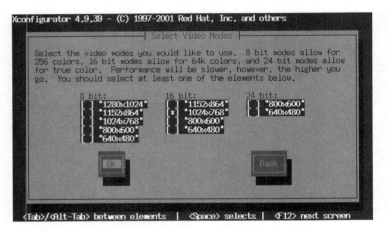

Figure 10-22   Choosing resolutions and color depths using Xconfigurator

Finally, Xconfigurator will let you start X Windows, as seen in Figure 10–23, to ensure the settings chosen will work, and will give you a completion screen similar to Figure 10–24.

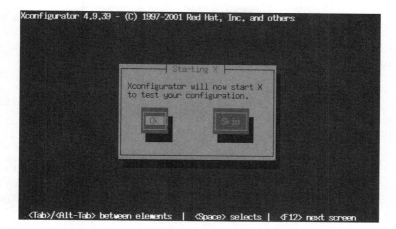

Figure 10-23   Starting X Windows to test configuration using Xconfigurator

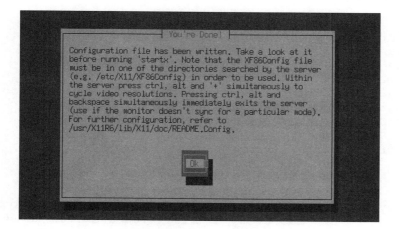

Figure 10-24   Completing the Xconfigurator utility

Xconfigurator and mouseconfig are utilities that are included in the Red Hat Linux distribution and may not be available in other distributions. The X Windows configuration program that ships with X Windows and is available on all distributions is **xf86config**, which displays a text interface when executed on the command line:

```
[root@localhost root]# xf86config
This program will create a basic XF86Config file, based on
menu selections you make.

The XF86Config file usually resides in /usr/X11R6/etc/X11
or /etc/X11. A sample XF86Config file is supplied with
XFree86; it is configured for a standard VGA card and
monitor with 640x480 resolution. This program will ask
for a pathname when it is ready to write the file.
```

> You can either take the sample XF86Config as a base and
> edit it for your configuration, or let this program
> produce a base XF86Config file for your configuration and
> fine-tune it.
>
> Before continuing with this program, make sure you know
> what video card you have, and preferably also the chipset
> it uses and the amount of video memory on your video card.
> SuperProbe may be able to help with this.
>
> Press enter to continue, or ctrl-c to abort.

Following this screen, you are prompted for the mouse information, including the type
and whether to enable ChordMiddle (required to activate the third mouse button on
some mice) or emulate the third mouse button:

> First specify a mouse protocol type. Choose one from the
> following list:
>
> 1. Microsoft compatible (2-button protocol)
> 2. Mouse Systems (3-button protocol)
> 3. Bus Mouse
> 4. PS/2 Mouse
> 5. Logitech Mouse (serial, old type, Logitech protocol)
> 6. Logitech MouseMan (Microsoft compatible)
> 7. MM Series
> 8. MM HitTablet
> 9. Microsoft IntelliMouse
>
> If you have a two-button mouse, it is most likely of
> type 1, and if you have a three-button mouse, it can
> probably support both protocol 1 and 2. There are two main
> varieties of the latter type: mice with a switch to select
> the protocol, and mice that default to 1 and require a
> button to be held at boot-time to select protocol 2. Some
> mice can be convinced to do 2 by sending a special sequence
> to the serial port (see the ClearDTR/ClearRTS options).
>
> Enter a protocol number: 1
>
> You have selected a Microsoft protocol mouse. If your mouse
> was made by Logitech, you might want to enable ChordMiddle
> which could cause the third button to work.
>
> Please answer the following question with either 'y' or
> 'n'.
> Do you want to enable ChordMiddle? n

```
You have selected a two-button mouse protocol. It is
recommended that you enable Emulate3Buttons.

Please answer the following question with either 'y' or
'n'.
Do you want to enable Emulate3Buttons? n

Now give the full device name that the mouse is connected
to, for example /dev/tty00. Just pressing enter will use
the default, /dev/mouse.

Mouse device: /dev/mouse
```

The mouse device **/dev/mouse** is actually a symbolic link to the correct mouse device file (PS/2, COM1, etc.) and is created during installation.

Next, you are prompted for the make and language of the keyboard, as well as a name for the keyboard layout (optional) and whether to enable special keyboard options (optional):

```
Please select one of the following keyboard types that is
the better description of your keyboard. If nothing really
matches, choose 1 (Generic 101-key PC)

 1   Generic 101-key PC
 2   Generic 102-key (Intl) PC
 3   Generic 104-key PC
 4   Generic 105-key (Intl) PC
 5   Dell 101-key PC
 6   Everex STEPnote
 7   Keytronic FlexPro
 8   Microsoft Natural
 9   Northgate OmniKey 101
10   Winbook Model XP5
11   Japanese 106-key
12   PC-98xx Series
13   Brazilian ABNT2
14   HP Internet
15   Logitech iTouch
16   Logitech Cordless Desktop Pro
17   Logitech Internet Keyboard
18   Compaq Internet
19   Microsoft Natural Pro
20   Genius Comfy KB-16M
21   IBM Rapid Access
22   IBM Rapid Access II
23   Chicony Internet Keyboard
```

10

```
Enter a number to choose the keyboard.
1

 1  U.S. English
 2  U.S. English w/ISO9995-3
 3  U.S. English w/ deadkeys
 4  Armenian
 5  Azerbaidjani
 6  Belarusian
 7  Belgian
 8  Brazilian
 9  Bulgarian
10  Canadian
11  Czech
12  Czech (qwerty)
13  Danish
14  Dvorak
15  Estonian
16  Finnish
17  French
18  Swiss French

Enter a number to choose the country.
Press enter for the next page
1

Please enter a variant name for 'us' layout. Or just press
enter for default variant


Please answer the following question with either 'y' or
'n'.
Do you want to select additional XKB options (group
switcher, group indicator, etc.)? n
```

Once the keyboard and mouse have been configured, xf86config prompts you for information regarding the monitor, including the hsync, vsync, and optional name for the monitor configuration:

```
Now we want to set the specifications of the monitor. The
two critical parameters are the vertical refresh rate,
which is the rate at which the the whole screen is
refreshed, and most importantly the horizontal sync rate,
which is the rate at which scanlines are displayed.


The valid range for horizontal sync and vertical sync
should be documented in the manual of your monitor. If in
doubt, check the monitor database /usr/X11R6/lib/X11/doc/
Monitors to see if your monitor is there.
```

Press enter to continue, or ctrl-c to abort.

You must indicate the horizontal sync range of your
monitor. You can either select one of the predefined
ranges below that correspond to industry-standard
monitor types, or give a specific range.

It is VERY IMPORTANT that you do not specify a monitor typ
e with a horizontal sync range that is beyond the
capabilities of your monitor. If in doubt, choose a
conservative setting.

```
       hsync in kHz; monitor type with characteristic modes
  1   31.5; Standard VGA, 640x480 @ 60 Hz
  2   31.5 - 35.1; Super VGA, 800x600 @ 56 Hz
  3   31.5, 35.5; 8514 Compatible, 1024x768 @ 87 Hz
      interlaced (no 800x600)
  4   31.5, 35.15, 35.5; Super VGA, 1024x768 @ 87 Hz
      interlaced, 800x600 @ 56 Hz
  5   31.5 - 37.9; Extended Super VGA, 800x600 @ 60 Hz,
      640x480 @ 72 Hz
  6   31.5 - 48.5; Non-Interlaced SVGA, 1024x768 @ 60 Hz,
      800x600 @ 72 Hz
  7   31.5 - 57.0; High Frequency SVGA, 1024x768 @ 70 Hz
  8   31.5 - 64.3; Monitor that can do 1280x1024 @ 60 Hz
  9   31.5 - 79.0; Monitor that can do 1280x1024 @ 74 Hz
 10   31.5 - 82.0; Monitor that can do 1280x1024 @ 76 Hz
 11   Enter your own horizontal sync range

Enter your choice (1-11): 3
```

10

You must indicate the vertical sync range of your
monitor. You can either select one of the predefined
ranges below that correspond to industry-standard
monitor types, or give a specific range. For interlaced
modes, the number that counts is the high one (e.g. 87 Hz
rather than 43 Hz).

```
  1   50-70
  2   50-90
  3   50-100
  4   40-150
  5   Enter your own vertical sync range

Enter your choice: 2
```

You must now enter a few identification/description
strings, namely an identifier, a vendor name, and a model
name. Just pressing enter will fill in default names.

The strings are free-form, spaces are allowed.
Enter an identifier for your monitor definition:

Finally, the xf86config utility prompts you for the video card model and memory. Then
it calculates the resolutions at certain color depths, confirms these resolutions with you,
and writes the changes to the /etc/X11/XF86Config file:

Now we must configure video card specific settings. At this
point you can choose to make a selection out of a database
of video card definitions. Because there can be variation in
Ramdacs and clock generators even between cards of the same
model, it is not sensible to blindly copy the settings
(e.g. a Device section). For this reason, after you make a
selection, you will still be asked about the components of
the card, with the settings from the chosen database entry
presented as a strong hint.

The database entries include information about the chipset,
what driver to run, the Ramdac and ClockChip, and comments
that will be included in the Device section. However, a lot
of definitions only hint about what driver to run (based on
the chipset the card uses) and are untested.

If you can't find your card in the database, there's
nothing to worry about. You should only choose a database
entry that is exactly the same model as your card;
choosing one that looks similar is just a bad idea
(e.g. a GemStone Snail 64 may be as different from a
GemStone Snail 64+ in terms of hardware as can be).

Do you want to look at the card database? **y**

0	2 the Max MAXColor S3 Trio64V+	S3 Trio64V+
1	2-the-Max MAXColor 6000	ET6000
2	3DLabs Oxygen GMX	PERMEDIA 2
3	3DVision-i740 AGP	Intel 740
4	3Dlabs Permedia2 (generic)	PERMEDIA 2
5	928Movie	S3 928
6	ABIT G740 8MB SDRAM	Intel 740
7	AGP 2D/3D V. 1N, AGP-740D	Intel 740
8	AGX (generic)	AGX-014/15/16
9	ALG-5434(E)	CL-GD5434
10	AOpen AGP 2X 3D Navigator PA740	Intel 740
11	AOpen PA2010	Voodoo Banshee
12	AOpen PA45	SiS6326

```
13   AOpen PA50D                    SiS6326
14   AOpen PA50E                    SiS6326
15   AOpen PA50V                    SiS6326
16   AOpen PA80/DVD                 SiS6326
17   AOpen PG128                    S3 Trio3D
```

Enter a number to choose the corresponding card
definition.
Press enter for the next page, q to continue
configuration.
157

Your selected card definition:

Identifier: Cirrus Logic GD544x
Chipset: CL-GD544x
Driver: cirrus

Press enter to continue, or ctrl-c to abort.

Now you must give information about your video card. This
will be used for the "Device" section of your video card
in XF86Config.

You must indicate how much video memory you have. It is
probably a good idea to use the same approximate amount as
that detected by the server you intend to use. If you
encounter problems that are due to the used server not
supporting the amount memory you have (e.g. ATI Mach64 is
limited to 1024K with the SVGA server), specify the
maximum amount supported by the server.

How much video memory do you have on your video card:

```
1   256K
2   512K
3   1024K
4   2048K
5   4096K
6   Other
```

Enter your choice: 4

You must now enter a few identification/description
strings, namely an identifier, a vendor name, and a model
name. Just pressing enter will fill in default names
(possibly from a card definition).

Your card definition is Cirrus Logic GD544x.

The strings are free-form, spaces are allowed.
Enter an identifier for your video card definition:

For each depth, a list of modes (resolutions) is defined.
The default resolution that the server will start-up with
will be the first listed mode that can be supported by the
monitor and card.

Currently it is set to:

"640x480" "800x600" "1024x768" "1280x1024" for 8-bit
"640x480" "800x600" "1024x768" for 16-bit
"640x480" "800x600" for 24-bit

Modes that cannot be supported due to monitor or clock
constraints will be automatically skipped by the server.

1   Change the modes for 8-bit (256 colors)
2   Change the modes for 16-bit (32K/64K colors)
3   Change the modes for 24-bit (24-bit color)
4   The modes are OK, continue.

Enter your choice: **4**

Please specify which color depth you want to use by
default:

1   1 bit (monochrome)
2   4 bits (16 colors)
3   8 bits (256 colors)
4   16 bits (65536 colors)
5   24 bits (16 million colors)

Enter a number to choose the default depth.
5

I am going to write the XF86Config file now. Make sure you
don't accidentally overwrite a previously configured one.

Shall I write it to /etc/X11/XF86Config? **y**
[root@localhost root]# _

The xf86config utility may also prompt for the chipset and RAMDAC of the
video card if needed.

Older versions of X Windows used the XF86Setup utility to configure the same settings that Xconfigurator, mouseadmin, and xf86config can configure.

Although most monitors today support a wide range of hsync and vsync values, choosing too high a value for either may damage the monitor. In addition, choosing an hsync or vsync value that is too low may result in headaches over time, since the human eye can see the flicker associated with lower refresh rates. After using the utilities discussed earlier to configure X Windows, you may fine-tune the vsync and hsync of the video card using the **xvidtune** utility once X Windows has started. Simply open a BASH shell in the GUI and type xvidtune to start the utility, as seen in Figure 10-25.

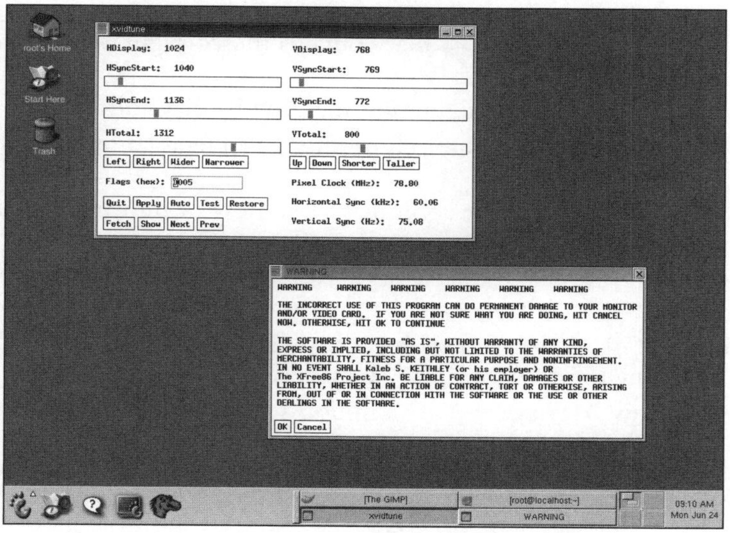

Figure 10-25 The xvidtune utility

CHAPTER SUMMARY

- ❐ The Linux GUI has several interchangeable components, including the X server, X client, window manager, and optional desktop environment.

- ❐ X Windows is the core component of the Linux GUI that draws graphics to the terminal screen and uses a text configuration file: /etc/X11/XF86Config.

- ❐ Window managers modify the look and feel of X Windows; they may be used with or without a desktop environment.

- ❐ Desktop environments include a window manager as well as a set of standard programs and development libraries; the two most common desktop environments for Linux are KDE and GNOME.

- ❏ You may start the Linux GUI from runlevel 3 by typing **startx** at a command prompt, or from runlevel 3 or 5 by using the **gdm**.

- ❏ Configuring X Windows requires a thorough knowledge of the video hardware used by the computer.

- ❏ The Xconfigurator, mouseconfig, xf86config, and xvidtune utilities may be used to configure the hardware settings of X Windows for such things as the mouse, keyboard, and video adapter card.

KEY TERMS

/dev/mouse — A symbolic link to the device file used for the mouse configured at installation.

/etc/X11/gdm/gdm.conf — The file that contains the configuration of the GNOME Desktop Manager.

/etc/X11/XF86Config — The configuration file used by X Windows.

chipset — The common set of computer chips on a peripheral component such as a video adapter card.

clockchip — The computer chip that coordinates the flow of information on a peripheral component such as a video adapter card.

desktop environment — Software that works with a window manager to provide a standard GUI environment that uses standard programs and development tools.

Desktop Switching Tool — A graphical tool that allows Red Hat Linux users to set the default desktop environment or window manager.

Enlightenment Window Manager — A common window manager used on Linux systems.

Feeble Virtual Window Manager (fvwm) — A common window manager used on Linux systems.

GDM Configurator — A graphical tool used to configure the appearance and behavior of the GNOME Display Manager.

GNOME Desktop Environment — The default desktop environment in Red Hat Linux; it was created in 1997.

GNU Image Manipulation Program (GIMP) — An Open Source graphics manipulation program that uses the GTK+ toolkit.

GTK+ toolkit — A development toolkit for C programming; it is used in the GNOME desktop and the GNU Image Manipulation Program (GIMP).

K Window Manager (kwm) — The window manager that works under the KDE Desktop Environment.

KDE Desktop Environment — A desktop environment created by Matthias Ettrich in 1996.

KDE Display Manager (kdm) — A graphical login screen for users that resembles the KDE desktop.

maximum resolution — The best clarity of an image displayed to the screen; it is determined by the number of pixels making up the image (i.e. 640 × 480 pixels).

mouseconfig — A command used to configure a mouse for use by X Windows.

Qt toolkit — The software toolkit used with the KDE Desktop Environment.

RAM Digital Analog Converter (RAMDAC) chip — Used to convert the digital video images used by the computer to the analog format needed for the monitor.

Sawfish Window Manager — The window manager that works under the GNOME Desktop Environment.

startx — A command used to start X Windows and the associated window manager and desktop environment.

SuperProbe — A program used to determine the computer's video adapter card properties.

Tab Window Manager (twm) — One of the oldest window managers used on Linux systems,

Window Maker Window Manager — A common window manager used on Linux systems.

window manager — The GUI component that is responsible for determining the appearance of the windows drawn on the screen by X Windows.

X client — The component of X Windows that requests graphics to be drawn from the X server and displays them on the terminal screen.

X server — The component of X Windows that draws graphics to windows on the terminal screen.

X Windows — The component of the Linux GUI that displays graphics to windows on the terminal screen.

X Display Manager (xdm) — Presents a graphical login screen to users.

Xconfigurator — A program that is used to configure video adapter card and monitor information for use by X Windows.

xf86config — A text-based X Windows configuration program that ships with X Windows; it allows the configuration of keyboard, mouse, video adapter card, and monitor information for use by X Windows.

XFree86 — The Open Source licensed version of X Windows version 11.

xvidtune — A program used to fine-tune the vsync and hsync video card settings for use in X Windows.

10

REVIEW QUESTIONS

1. The X server tells X clients how to draw graphics and display results to the screen. True or False?

2. Which of the following is a component of the GUI in Linux? (Choose all that apply.)

   a. Xconfigurator

   b. X Windows

   c. X server

   d. X client

   e. Sawfish

   f. gpm

   g. window manager

   h. vidtune

   i. desktop environment

3. The GUI in Linux was designed with many different components able to function independently from one another and the video hardware used. True or False?

4. Which of the following is a symbolic link to the actual device file for the mouse configured during installation?

   a. `/dev/term/mouse`

   b. `/dev/serial/mouse`

   c. `/dev/ps2/mouse`

   d. `/dev/mouse`

5. Because X Windows is not fully licensed under the GPL, what Open Source alternative was developed to provide the same functionality?

   a. Freewindow

   b. GNOME

   c. k manager

   d. gplwindow

   e. Xfree86

6. What is used to provide a more user-friendly environment offering additional GUI tools and a development tool kit?

   a. window manager

   b. desktop environment

   c. X client

   d. gmd

7. What command is used to fine-tune the vsync and hsync of a video card for use in X Windows?

    a. Vidtune

    b. synctune

    c. xvidtune

    d. vhtune

8. What three pieces of information about the display monitor attached to the system do you need to configure X Windows properly to use it?

    a. maximum resolution, vertical hold, horizontal hold

    b. minimum resolution, vertical sync, horizontal sync

    c. maximum resolution, vsync, hsync

    d. resolution, color depth, and hvsync

9. What is the component of the GUI that interfaces with the computer hardware?

    a. X client

    b. window manager

    c. X Windows

    d. desktop environment

10. X Windows was jointly developed by which two organizations?

    a. AT&T Laboratories and MIT

    b. DEC & GNU Foundation

    c. UCLA at Berkley & Bell Laboratories

    d. DEC & MIT

11. What text configuration file does X Windows use to store hardware settings about the mouse, keyboard, monitor, and video card?

    a. `/etc/X11/xconfigurator`

    b. `/etc/Xwindows/XF86config`

    c. `/etc/Xwindows/xconfigurator`

    d. `/etc/X11/XF86config`

12. What is used to provide a graphical login for Red Hat Linux?

    a. gdm

    b. kdm

    c. startx

    d. Sawfish

10

13. The Linux GUI consists of two portions: the X server and the X client. In order to function properly the X server and the X client must be on the same computer. True or False?

14. What key combination is used to exit the GUI?

    a. Ctrl-Q

    b. Ctrl-Esc

    c. Ctrl-Alt-Del

    d. Ctrl-Alt-Backspace

15. KDE and GNOME are examples of what?

    a. X Windows

    b. X clients

    c. window managers

    d. desktop environments

16. What is the X Windows configuration program that ships with all copies of X Windows and presents the user with a text-based series of choices?

    a. xf86config

    b. Xconfigurator

    c. Xf86configurator

    d. X-Windowconfig

17. You do not need a desktop environment to run a Linux GUI. True or False?

18. What command entered at a command prompt will start X Windows, the window manager, and the desktop environment?

    a. `startgui`

    b. `gdm`

    c. `startx`

    d. `winstart`

19. XFree86 is so named because _____.

    a. it is a free Open Source version of X Windows originally designed for the Intel x86 platform

    b. it is a free Open Source version of X Windows first released in 1986

    c. it is a free evaluation version of X Windows that runs for 86 days before expiring

    d. it is a free Open Source version of X Windows that offers an 86-color palette

20. What is used to convert the digital information of the computer to the analog format used by the display monitor?

    a. UART chip

    b. RAMDAC chip

    c. modem

    d. xconfig

21. What command is used to gain information regarding the video adapter card present in your computer?

    a. Probe

    b. Videoprobe

    c. Probevideo

    d. SuperProbe

22. What runlevel automatically starts a display manager to provide a graphical login screen?

    a. 1

    b. 3

    c. 4

    d. 5

23. What file does X Windows read to know the window manager or desktop environment to load without user intervention?

    a. `.kde-default`

    b. `.gnome-default`

    c. `.xwindows-default`

    d. `.Xclients-default`

    e. `.Xclients`

24. The Linux GUI was designed to be hardware specific and thus works only with selected video hardware. True or False?

25. What file could you configure to alter the appearance and behavior of the gdm?

    a. `/etc/X11/gdm/gdm.conf`

    b. `/etc/X11/gdm/gdm`

    c. `/etc/X11/gdm/gdm.configuration`

    d. `/etc/X-Windows/gdm/gdm.conf`

10

26. What window manager does the KDE Desktop Environment use?

    a. X Window Manager

    b. K Window Manager

    c. Starfish Window Manager

    d. Tab Window Manager

27. What three pieces of information do you need about your video card to configure X Windows properly?

    a. IRQ, DMA, I/O address

    b. slot type, speed, and clockchip

    c. Model, type of RAM, and chipset

    d. Model, amount of RAM, and chipset

28. What switch to SuperProbe will display a list of detectable video adapter card hardware?

    a. none; it will probe any video card attached to the system

    b. `-l`

    c. `-info`

    d. `-help`

29. What window manager does the GNOME Desktop Environment use?

    a. K Window Manager

    b. Starfish Window Manager

    c. Sawfish Window Manager

    d. Swordfish Window Manager

30. What command will allow you to configure the mouse used with the computer?

    a. `mouseadmin`

    b. `mouseconfig`

    c. `mouseconfigurator`

    d. `configmouse`

31. Which command below can be used to configure the video adapter card and monitor information?

    a. `vidconfig`

    b. `vidconfigurator`

    c. `Xconfigurator`

    d. `SuperProbe`

HANDS-ON PROJECTS

These projects should be completed in the order given. All hands-on projects should take a total of three hours to complete. The requirements for this lab include:

❑ A computer with Red Hat 7.2 installed according to Hands-on Project 7-2

Project 10-1

In this hands-on project, you will start and stop X Windows and the GNOME Desktop Environment from runlevel 3.

1. Turn on your computer. When fully booted, log into the gdm using the username of **root** and the password of **secret**.
2. When the GNOME desktop has loaded, press the **Ctrl-Alt-Bkspce** key combination. What happened? Why?
3. Switch to a command-line terminal (tty2) by pressing **Ctrl-Alt-F2** and log into the terminal using the username of **root** and the password of **secret**.
4. At the command prompt, type **runlevel** and press **Enter**. What is displayed? Why?
5. At the command prompt, type **init 3** and press **Enter**.
6. When runlevel 3 is reached, log in as the user **root** with a password of **secret**.
7. Type **startx** and press **Enter** to load the GNOME desktop.
8. When the GNOME desktop has loaded, press the **Ctrl-Alt-Bkspce** key combination. What happened? Why?
9. Type **exit** and press **Enter** to log out of your shell.

Project 10-2

In this hands-on project, you will start and stop X Windows and various window managers and desktop environments from runlevel 3.

1. Switch to a command-line terminal (tty2) by pressing **Ctrl-Alt-F2** and log into the terminal using the username of **root** and the password of **secret**.
2. At the command prompt, type **runlevel** and press **Enter**. If you are not in runlevel 3, type **init 3** at the command prompt and press **Enter**. When runlevel 3 is reached, log in as the user **root** with a password of **secret**.
3. Type **startx** and press **Enter** to load the GNOME desktop.
4. When the GNOME desktop has loaded, use the mouse to navigate to Toolbar → GNOME button (leftmost button) → Programs → System → Desktop Switching Tool.
5. Use the mouse to select **KDE** and click the **OK** button.
6. Press the **Ctrl-Alt-Bkspce** key combination to return to your shell.

10

7. At the command prompt, type **cat .Xclients-default** and press **Enter**. What is displayed?

8. At the command prompt, type **startx** and press **Enter**. Which desktop is loaded? Why?

9. Once the KDE desktop has loaded, use the mouse to navigate to Toolbar → K button (leftmost button) → System → Desktop Switching Tool.

10. Use the mouse to select **FVWM** and click **OK**.

11. Press the **Ctrl-Alt-Bkspce** key combination to return to your shell.

12. At the command prompt, type **cat .Xclients-default** and press **Enter**. What is displayed?

13. At the command prompt, type **startx** and press **Enter**. Which window manager is loaded? Why?

14. Use the left mouse button to click on the desktop background and choose **Exit Fvwn** → **Yes, Really Quit**.

15. At the command prompt, type **vi .Xclients-default** and press **Enter**. Change the line that reads:

    ```
    exec /usr/X11R6/bin/fvwm2
    ```

    To read:

    ```
    exec /usr/bin/enlightenment
    ```

    When finished, save your changes and quit the vi editor.

16. At the command prompt, type **startx** and press **Enter**. Which window manager is loaded? Why?

17. While holding down the **Ctrl** key, use the left mouse button to click on the desktop background and choose **Log Out** → **Yes, Log Out**.

18. At the command prompt, type **vi .Xclients-default** and press **Enter**. Change the line that reads:

    ```
    exec /usr/bin/enlightenment
    ```

    To read:

    ```
    exec /usr/bin/wmaker
    ```

    When finished, save your changes and quit the vi editor.

19. At the command prompt, type **startx** and press **Enter**. Which window manager is loaded? Why?

20. Use the right mouse button to click on the desktop background and choose **Exit** → **Exit**, then click **Exit** when prompted.

21. At the command prompt, type **vi .Xclients-default** and press **Enter**. Change the line that reads:

        exec /usr/bin/wmaker

    To read:

        exec /usr/X11R6/bin/twm

    When finished, save your changes and quit the vi editor.

22. At the command prompt, type **startx** and press **Enter**. Which window manager is loaded? Why?

23. Use the left mouse button to click on the desktop background and choose **Exit**.

24. At the command prompt, type **rm .Xclients*** and press **Enter**. Confirm the deletion of each file. Which 2 files were removed?

25. At the command prompt, type **startx** and press **Enter**. Which desktop is loaded? Why?

26. Press the **Ctrl–Alt–Bkspce** key combination to return to your shell.

27. Type **init 5** and press **Enter** to return to runlevel 5. What is displayed and why?

Project 10-3

10

In this hands-on project, you will configure the gdm using the GDM Configuration tool.

1. Switch to a graphical terminal by pressing **Ctrl–Alt–F7** and log into the GNOME desktop using the username of **root** and the password of **secret**.

2. Use your mouse to navigate to Toolbar → GNOME button (leftmost button) → Programs → System → GDM Configurator.

3. At the **Login appearance** tab, use your mouse to click on the top **Browse** button beside the **Logo:** section.

4. When the file browser dialog box is displayed, note that you are placed in the **/usr/share/pixmaps** directory by default. Select the **Ant.xpm** file and click the **OK** button.

5. Use your mouse to click on the **Login Behaviour** tab. Next, use your mouse to place a checkmark in the checkbox beside **Allow users to run the configurator from the system menu**.

6. Use your mouse to click on the **Face browser** tab. Next, use your mouse to place a checkmark in the checkbox beside **Show choosable user images**.

7. Use your mouse to click on the top **Browse** button beside the **Default face image:** section.

8. When the file browser dialog box is displayed, select **apple-red.png** from the **/usr/share/pixmaps** directory and click the **OK** button.

9. Use your mouse to click on the **Background** tab. Next, use your mouse to select **Color** beside the **Background type:** section.

10. Use your mouse to click on the button beside the **Background color** section. When the Pick a Color dialog box is displayed, choose a shade of **green** and click the **OK** button.

11. Next, clear the contents of the box beside the **Background program:** section.

12. Use your mouse to select the **Apply** button at the bottom of the window.

13. Click on the **Restart now** button. Confirm this action by clicking on the **Yes** button when prompted.

14. Observe the gdm. What color is the background? Is there a logo beside the login box? Are there logos to represent each valid user on the system?

15. Use your mouse to click on the **System** menu. Is there a link to the GDM Configurator on the menu?

16. Double-click on the **apple** icon that represents the **root** user. Enter the password of **secret** and press **Enter** to log into the system.

17. Press the **Ctrl-Alt-Bkspce** key combination to return to the gdm screen.

Project 10-4

In this hands-on project, you will record information regarding the video hardware in your system.

1. Switch to a command-line terminal (tty2) by pressing **Ctrl–Alt–F2** and log into the terminal using the username of **root** and the password of **secret**.

2. At the command prompt, type **SuperProbe** and press **Enter**. Use the information displayed about your video card adapter to fill in the following table:

Model	
Chipset (may be the same as the model)	
Amount of RAM	
RAMDAC (optional)	
Clockchip (optional)	

3. Use your computer manual to supply any missing video adapter card information in the table from the previous step.

4. Use your computer manual or information at the rear of your monitor to fill in the following table:

Monitor model	
Vsync range	
Hsync range	
Maximum resolution supported	

5. Use your computer manual or observe the rear of your computer to determine the type of mouse device that you have:

Model	
Port (PS/2, COM1, etc.)	

6. Type **exit** and press **Enter** to log out of your shell.

Project 10-5

In this hands-on project, you will configure X Windows using the **mouseconfig** and **Xconfigurator** utilities.

1. Switch to a command-line terminal (tty2) by pressing **Ctrl-Alt-F2** and log into the terminal using the username of **root** and the password of **secret**.

2. At the command prompt, type **mouseconfig** and press **Enter**. What is displayed? Is the correct mouse highlighted? Why?

3. If your mouse is not highlighted, use the cursor keys to scroll to the correct mouse in the list, use the **Tab** key to navigate to the **OK** button, and press **Enter**.

4. At the information screen, press **Enter**. When will your new mouse settings take effect?

5. At the command prompt, type **Xconfigurator** and press **Enter**. Read the information displayed and press **Enter**.

6. Was the correct video card probed by the system? Verify your answer by comparing it to the information you obtained in the previous hands-on project. Press **Enter** to advance to the next screen.

7. Try to locate your monitor from the list using the information from the previous hands-on project. Is it listed? If it is listed, use the **Tab** key to navigate to the **OK** button, press **Enter**, and proceed to Step 11 of this exercise. If it is not listed, choose **Custom** and use the **Tab** key to navigate to the **OK** button, press **Enter**, and proceed to the next step.

8. At the Custom Monitor Setup screen, read the information displayed and press **Enter**.

9. At the next Custom Monitor Setup screen, choose **Custom**, use the **Tab** key to navigate to the **OK** button, and press **Enter**.

10. Enter the correct hsync and vsync ranges for your monitor. These values can be found in the monitor table completed in the previous hands-on project. When finished use the **Tab** key to navigate to the **OK** button, and then press **Enter**.

10

11. At the screen configuration, use the **Tab** key to select the **Don't Probe** button and press **Enter**.

12. At the Video Memory screen, select the amount of memory on your video adapter card using the information from the previous hands-on project, then use the **Tab** key to select the **OK** button, and press **Enter**.

13. At the Clockchip Configuration screen, choose a clockchip setting using the information in the previous hands-on project. If your video adapter card does not use a clockchip, select **No Clockchip Setting**, use the **Tab** key to select the **OK** button, and press **Enter**.

14. At the Probe for Clocks screen (optional), use the **Tab** key to select **Probe** and press **Enter**.

    NOTE: if probing for the clockchip and RAMDAC settings causes your system to crash, turn the power off and on and repeat this exercise; when at this step in the future, choose **Skip** and press **Enter**.

15. At the Select Video Modes screen, observe the output. Does any mode exceed the maximum resolution listed in the previous hands-on project? Use the cursor keys and spacebar to select the resolutions that you desire from X Windows. When finished, use the **Tab** key to select the **OK** button and press **Enter**.

16. At the Starting X screen, press **Enter** to test the configuration that you have chosen. When finished, press **Enter** twice to complete the configuration.

17. Type **exit** and press **Enter** to log out of your shell.

Project 10-6

In this hands-on project, you will configure X Windows using the **xf86config** utility.

1. Switch to a command-line terminal (tty2) by pressing **Ctrl–Alt–F2** and log into the terminal using the username of **root** and the password of **secret**.

2. At the command prompt, type **xf86config** and press **Enter**. Read the screen output and press **Enter** when finished.

3. From the listing, choose your mouse type by typing the appropriate number at the prompt, and press **Enter**.

4. If prompted to enable ChordMiddle, choose **n** and press **Enter**.

5. If prompted to Emulate 3 Buttons, choose **n** and press **Enter**.

6. When prompted for the mouse device, press **Enter** to select the one configured during installation (`/dev/mouse`).

7. Type the number that corresponds to your keyboard type and press **Enter**.

8. When prompted for the keyboard language, type **1** and press **Enter** for U.S. English.

9. When prompted to enter an identifier for your keyboard layout, press **Enter**.

10. When prompted to use XKB options, type **n** and press **Enter**.

11. Read the information regarding monitor configuration and press **Enter** when finished.

12. At the hsync configuration prompt, choose **11** and press **Enter**. Next, enter the appropriate hsync range for your monitor and press **Enter**.

13. At the vsync configuration configuration prompt, choose **5** and press **Enter**. Next, enter the appropriate vsync range for your monitor and press **Enter**.

14. When prompted to specify an identifier for your monitor definition, press **Enter**.

15. When prompted to look at the video card database, type **y** and press **Enter**.

16. Use the **Tab** key to navigate through the list of video cards until you find your video card. Type in the number that corresponds to your video card and press **Enter**. Press **Enter** again. What is displayed? Is it correct?

17. Next, type in the number that corresponds to the correct amount of video memory on your video card and press **Enter**. If you are prompted for other information such as RAMDAC or clockchip, enter the appropriate information.

18. When prompted to choose an identifier for your video card definition, press **Enter**.

19. When the supported video modes are displayed, choose **4** and press **Enter**.

20. When prompted for the default video mode, choose **4** for 16-bit color and press **Enter**.

21. When prompted to overwrite the XF86Config file, choose **y** and press **Enter**.

22. Type **exit** and press **Enter** to log out of your shell.

10

DISCOVERY EXERCISES

1. Use the Internet, books, or another resource to learn more about three Linux window managers that were not discussed in this chapter. For each, describe its common usage and benefits over other window managers. In addition, list how each was developed.

2. Provided you have a functional Web browser and Internet access, visit the X Windows website on the Internet at *http://www.x.org* and explore the site. Can you find any links to information on the GNOME or the KDE Desktop Environments? Is there any information on year 2000 compliance? Are there any links to information on XFree86? Explore the site and its links.

   Next, visit *http://www.xfree86.org* to learn more about the XFree86 project. Describe the XFree86 project and its history. Are there any plans for future releases or updates? Is there a copy of XFree86 available for download?

   Next, visit *http://www.kde.org* to gain more information on the KDE Desktop Environment. Explore the site. What is KDE and what is its history? Visit the FAQ section of the site. Explore the documentation and look at some screenshots from the KDE desktop. Are there any KDE Desktop Environment applications available for download? What are some of them and what are they designed to do?

Next, visit *http://www.gnome.org* to gain more information on the GNOME Desktop Environment. Explore the site. Visit the FAQ section of the site. Describe GNOME and its history. Research the documentation available on the site. Are there any tutorials available? If so, use them. Are there any GNOME desktop applications available for download? If so, what are some of them and for what purpose were they designed?

3. View the **/usr/X11R6/lib/X11/doc/README.Config** file on how to configure X Windows manually. Briefly describe the main sections of this file and their purpose. Are there any other files in the **/usr/X11R6/lib/X11/doc** directory that may be useful for configuring X Windows? When would you need to edit the **/etc/X11/XF86Config** file manually? Provided you have a functional Web browser and Internet access, support your answer by viewing newsgroup postings that require a user to edit this file manually to allow X Windows to support it.

11

MANAGING LINUX PROCESSES

**After completing this chapter,
you will be able to:**

- ◆ Categorize the different types of processes on a Linux system
- ◆ View processes using standard Linux utilities
- ◆ Illustrate the difference between common kill signals
- ◆ Describe how binary programs and shell scripts are executed
- ◆ Create and manipulate background processes
- ◆ Use standard Linux utilities to modify the priority of a process
- ◆ Schedule commands to execute in the future using the at daemon
- ◆ Schedule commands to execute repetitively using the cron daemon

A typical Linux system may run thousands of processes simultaneously, including those that you have explored in previous chapters. In this chapter you focus on viewing and managing processes. In the first part of the chapter you examine the different types of processes on a Linux system and how to view them and terminate them. You then discover how processes are executed on a system, run in the background, and prioritized. Finally, you are introduced to the various methods used to schedule commands to execute in the future.

LINUX PROCESSES

Throughout previous chapters of this textbook as well as in the workplace, the terms "program" and "process" have been and will be used interchangeably; however, there is a definite, yet fine, difference between these two terms. A **program** is an executable file on the hard disk that may be run when you execute it. A **process** refers to a program that is running in memory and on the CPU; in other words, a process is a program in action.

If you start a process while logged into a terminal, then that process runs in that terminal and is labeled a **user process**. Examples of user processes include ls, grep, find, and most other commands that you have executed throughout this textbook. Recall that a system process that is not associated with a terminal is called a **daemon process**; these processes are typically started on system startup, but you may also start them manually. Most daemon processes provide system services such as printing, scheduling, and system maintenance, as well as network server services such as Web servers, database servers, file servers, and print servers.

Every process has a unique **Process ID (PID)** that allows the kernel to identify it uniquely. Each process may additionally start an unlimited number of other processes called **child processes**. Conversely, each process must have been started by an existing process called a **parent process**. As a result, each process has a **Parent Process ID (PPID)**, which identifies the process that started it. An example of the relationship between parent and child processes is depicted in Figure 11-1.

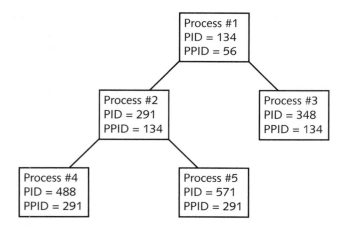

Figure 11-1   Parent and child processes

 PIDs are not given to new processes in sequential order; each PID is randomly generated from free entries in a process table used by the Linux kernel.

Remember that while each process may have an unlimited number of child processes, it may only have one parent process.

Recall that the first process started by the Linux kernel is the init daemon, which has a PID of 1 and a PPID of 0 referring to the kernel itself. The init daemon then starts most other daemons including those that allow for user logins. Once you log into the system, the login program starts a BASH shell. The BASH shell then interprets user commands and starts all user processes. Thus, each process on the Linux system may be traced back to the init daemon by examining the series of PPIDs, as seen in Figure 11-2.

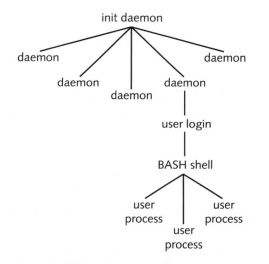

Figure 11-2   Process genealogy

The init daemon is often referred to as the "grandfather of all user processes."

VIEWING PROCESSES

Although there are several Linux utilities that can view processes, the most versatile and common is the **ps command**. Without arguments, the **ps** command simply displays a list of processes that are running in the current shell. An example of this, while logged into tty2, is seen in the following output:

```
[root@localhost root]# ps
  PID TTY          TIME CMD
 1232 tty2     00:00:00 login
```

11

```
        1281 tty2      00:00:00 bash
        1622 tty2      00:00:00 ps
     [root@localhost root]# _
```

The above output shows that there were three processes running in the terminal tty2 when the **ps** command executed. The command that started each process (CMD) is listed next to the time it has taken on the CPU (TIME), its PID, and its terminal (TTY). In this case, the process took less than one second to run, and so the time elapsed reads nothing. To find out more about these processes, you could instead use the **–f**, or full, option to the **ps** command, as seen below:

```
[root@localhost root]# ps –f
UID         PID   PPID  C STIME TTY           TIME CMD
root        1232  1011  0 08:45 tty2      00:00:00 login -- root
root        1281  1232  0 08:45 tty2      00:00:00 –bash
root        1622  1281  0 08:54 tty2      00:00:00 ps –f
[root@localhost root]# _
```

This listing provides more information about each process; it displays the user who started the process (UID), the PPID, the time it was started (STIME), as well as the CPU utilization (C), which starts at zero and is incremented each processor cycle the process runs on the CPU.

The most valuable information provided by the **ps –f** command is each process's PPID and lineage. The login process (PID = 1232) displays the login prompt on a terminal and accepts a username and password; it started the BASH shell (PID = 1281), since the bash process had a PPID of 1232. Similarly, the bash process started the **ps** command (PID = 1622), since the **ps** command had a PPID of 1281.

Since daemon processes are not associated with a terminal, they are not displayed by the **ps –f** command. To display an entire list of processes across all terminals and including daemons, you may add the **–e** option to any ps command, as seen in the output below:

```
[root@localhost root]# ps –ef
UID         PID   PPID  C STIME TTY           TIME CMD
root           1     0  0 08:40 ?         00:00:04 init [5]
root           2     1  0 08:40 ?         00:00:00 [keventd]
root           3     1  0 08:40 ?         00:00:00 [kapm-idled]
root           4     0  0 08:40 ?         00:00:00 [ksoftirqd_CPU0]
root           5     0  0 08:40 ?         00:00:00 [kswapd]
root           6     0  0 08:40 ?         00:00:00 [kreclaimd]
root           7     0  0 08:40 ?         00:00:00 [bdflush]
root           8     0  0 08:40 ?         00:00:00 [kupdated]
root           9     1  0 08:40 ?         00:00:00 [mdrecoveryd]
root          13     1  0 08:40 ?         00:00:00 [kjournald]
root          88     1  0 08:40 ?         00:00:00 [khubd]
root         202     1  0 08:40 ?         00:00:00 [kjournald]
root         660     1  0 08:40 ?         00:00:00 syslogd –m 0
root         665     1  0 08:40 ?         00:00:00 klogd –2
rpc          685     1  0 08:40 ?         00:00:00 portmap
rpcuser      713     1  0 08:40 ?         00:00:00 rpc.statd
root         825     1  0 08:40 ?         00:00:00 /usr/sbin/apmd –p 10 –w 5 –W –P
```

```
root           900       1    0  08:40  ?          00:00:00  /usr/sbin/sshd
root           933       1    0  08:40  ?          00:00:00  xinetd —stayalive —reuse
root           973       1    0  08:41  ?          00:00:00  sendmail: accepting connections
root          1001       1    0  08:41  ?          00:00:00  [scsi_eh_0]
root          1020       1    0  08:41  ?          00:00:00  gpm —t ps/2 —m /dev/mouse
root          1038       1    0  08:41  ?          00:00:00  crond
xfs           1108       1    0  08:41  ?          00:00:00  xfs —droppriv —daemon
root          1126       1    0  08:41  ?          00:00:00  smbd —D
root          1131       1    0  08:41  ?          00:00:00  nmbd —D
daemon        1167       1    0  08:41  ?          00:00:00  /usr/sbin/atd
root          1197       1    0  08:41  tty1       00:00:00  /sbin/mingetty tty1
root          1198       1    0  08:41  tty2       00:00:00  login -- root
root          1199       1    0  08:41  tty3       00:00:00  /sbin/mingetty tty3
root          1200       1    0  08:41  tty4       00:00:00  /sbin/mingetty tty4
root          1201       1    0  08:41  tty5       00:00:00  /sbin/mingetty tty5
root          1202       1    0  08:41  tty6       00:00:00  /sbin/mingetty tty6
root          1203       1    0  08:41  ?          00:00:00  /usr/bin/gdm —nodaemon
root          1211    1203    0  08:41  ?          00:00:00  /usr/bin/gdm —nodaemon
root          1212    1211    0  08:41  ?          00:00:01  /etc/X11/X :0
gdm           1218    1211    0  08:41  ?          00:00:00  /usr/bin/gdmlogin
root          1231     933    0  08:45  ?          00:00:00  in.telnetd: 3.0.0.2
root          1232    1011    0  08:45  tty2       00:00:00  login -- root
root          1281    1232    0  08:45  tty2       00:00:00  —bash
root          1594    1198    0  08:46  tty2       00:00:00  —bash
root         12183    1281    0  09:14  tty2       00:00:00  ps —ef
[root@localhost root]# _
```

As seen in the above output, the init daemon (PID = 1) starts most other daemons since those daemons have a PPID of 1. Additionally, there is a ? in the TTY column for daemons since they do not run on a terminal.

Since the output of the **ps —ef** command may be several hundred lines long on a Linux server, you usually pipe its output to the **less** command to send the output to the terminal screen page-by-page, or to the **grep** command, which can be used to display lines containing only certain information. For example, to display only the BASH shells in the above output, you could use the following command:

```
[root@localhost root]# ps —ef | grep bash
root          1281    1232    0  08:45  tty2       00:00:00  —bash
root          1594    1198    0  08:46  tty2       00:00:00  —bash
root         12263    1281    0  09:32  tty2       00:00:00  grep bash
[root@localhost root]# _
```

Notice that the **grep bash** command is also displayed alongside the BASH shells in the above output since it was running in memory at the time the **ps** command was executed. This may not always be the case, since the Linux kernel schedules commands to run based on a variety of different factors.

The **—e** and **—f** options are the most common options used with the **ps** command; however, there are many other options available. The **—l** option to the **ps** command lists

11

even more information about each process than the **−f** option. An example of using this option to view the processes in the terminal tty2 is seen in the following output:

```
[root@localhost root]# ps -l
  F S   UID   PID  PPID  C PRI  NI ADDR    SZ WCHAN  TTY          TIME CMD
100 S     0 13151 13150  0  70   0   -    580 wait4  tty2     00:00:00 login
100 S     0 13152 13151  3  72   0   -    612 wait4  tty2     00:00:00 bash
100 R     0 13201 13152  0  75   0   -    767 -      tty2     00:00:00 ps
[root@localhost root]# _
```

The process flag (F) indicates particular features of the process; the flag of 100 in the above output indicates that the root user ran the process. The **process state** (S) column is the most valuable to systems administrators as it indicates what the process is currently doing. If a process is not being run on the processor at the current time, then you will see an S (sleeping) in the process state column; processes are in this state most of the time, as seen with bash and login in the output above. You will see an R in this column if the process is currently running on the processor, or a T if it has stopped or is being traced by another process. In addition to these, you may also see a Z in this column indicating a **zombie process**. When a process finishes executing, the parent process must check to see if it executed successfully and then release the child process's PID so that it may be used again. While a process is waiting for its parent process to release the PID, the process is said to be in a zombie state, as it has finished but still retains a PID. On a busy Linux server, zombie processes may accumulate and prevent new processes from being created; if this occurs, you may simply kill the parent process of the zombies as discussed in the next section.

Zombie processes are also known as defunct processes.

Process priority (PRI) is the priority used by the kernel for the process; it is measured between 0 (high priority) and 127 (low priority). The **nice value (NI)** can be used to affect the process priority indirectly; it is measured between −20 (a greater chance of a high priority) and 19 (a greater chance of a lower priority). The ADDR in the output above indicates the memory address of the process, whereas the WCHAN indicates what the process is waiting for while sleeping. In addition, the size of the process in memory (SZ) is also listed and measured in kilobytes; it is roughly equivalent to the size of the executable file on the filesystem.

Some options to the **ps** command are not prefixed by a dash character; these are referred to as Berkeley style options. The two most common of these are the **a** option, which lists all processes across terminals, and the **x** option, which lists processes that do not run on a terminal, as seen in the following output:

```
[root@localhost root]# ps ax
  PID TTY        STAT     TIME COMMAND
    1 ?          S        0:04 init [5]
    2 ?          SW       0:00 [keventd]
    3 ?          SW       0:00 [kapm-idled]
```

```
   4 ?        SWN     0:00 [ksoftirqd_CPU0]
   5 ?        SW      0:00 [kswapd]
   6 ?        SW      0:00 [kreclaimd]
   7 ?        SW      0:00 [bdflush]
   8 ?        SW      0:00 [kupdated]
   9 ?        SW<     0:00 [mdrecoveryd]
  13 ?        SW      0:00 [kjournald]
  88 ?        SW      0:00 [khubd]
 202 ?        SW      0:00 [kjournald]
 660 ?        S       0:00 syslogd —m 0
 665 ?        S       0:00 klogd —2
 685 ?        S       0:00 portmap
 713 ?        S       0:00 rpc.statd
 825 ?        S       0:00 /usr/sbin/apmd —p 10 —w 5 —W —P /
 900 ?        S       0:00 /usr/sbin/sshd
 933 ?        S       0:00 xinetd —stayalive —reuse —pidfile
 973 ?        S       0:00 sendmail: accepting connections
1001 ?        SW      0:00 [scsi_eh_0]
1020 ?        S       0:00 gpm —t ps/2 —m /dev/mouse
1038 ?        S       0:00 crond
1108 ?        S       0:00 xfs —droppriv —daemon
1126 ?        S       0:00 smbd —D
1131 ?        S       0:00 nmbd —D
1167 ?        S       0:00 /usr/sbin/atd
1197 tty1     S       0:00 /sbin/mingetty tty1
1198 tty2     S       0:00 login -- root
1199 tty3     S       0:00 /sbin/mingetty tty3
1200 tty4     S       0:00 /sbin/mingetty tty4
1201 tty5     S       0:00 /sbin/mingetty tty5
1202 tty6     S       0:00 /sbin/mingetty tty6
1203 ?        S       0:00 /usr/bin/gdm —nodaemon
1211 ?        S       0:00 /usr/bin/gdm —nodaemon
1212 ?        S       0:01 /etc/X11/X :0 —auth
1218 ?        S       0:00 /usr/bin/gdmlogin —disable—sound
1594 tty2     S       0:00 —bash
14884 ?       SW      0:00 [usb-storage—0]
14885 ?       SW      0:00 [scsi_eh_1]
17513 ?       S       0:00 in.telnetd: 3.0.0.2
17514 tty2    S       0:00 login -- root
17515 tty2    S       0:00 —bash
17740 tty2    R       0:00 ps ax
[root@localhost root]# _
```

The columns listed above are equivalent to those discussed earlier; however, the process state column is identified with STAT and may contain a W to indicate that the process has no contents in memory, a < symbol to indicate a high priority process, or an N to indicate a low priority process.

There are several dozen options to the **ps** command that can be used to display processes and their attributes; the options we have listed in this section are the most common and are summarized in Table 11-1.

Table 11-1   Common options to the ps command

Option	Description
-e	Displays all processes running on terminals as well as processes that do not run on a terminal (daemons)
-f	Displays a full list of information about each process including the UID, PID, PPID, CPU utilization, start time, terminal, processor time, and command name
-l	Displays a long list of information about each process including the flag, state, UID, PID, PPID, CPU utilization, priority, nice value, address, size, WCHAN, terminal, and command name
a	Displays all processes running on terminals
x	Displays all processes that do not run on terminals

The **ps** command is not the only command that can view process information. The kernel exports all process information subdirectories under the **/proc** directory; each subdirectory is named the appropriate PID of the process it contains information about, as seen below:

```
[root@localhost root]# ls —F /proc
1/      1200/   17513/  665/   apm            ide/         mdstat       slabinfo
1001/   1201/   17514/  685/   bus/           interrupts   meminfo      stat
1020/   1202/   17515/  7/     cmdline        iomem        misc         swaps
1038/   1203/   17841/  713/   cpuinfo        ioports      modules      sys/
1108/   1211/   2/      8/     devices        irq/         mounts       sysvipc/
1126/   1212/   202/    825/   dma            isapnp       mtrr         tty/
1131/   1218/   3/      88/    driver/        kcore        net/         uptime
1167/   13/     4/      9/     execdomains    kmsg         partitions   version
1197/   14884/  5/      900/   fb             ksyms        pci
1198/   14885/  6/      933/   filesystems    loadavg      scsi/
1199/   1594/   660/    973/   fs/            locks        self@
[root@localhost root]# _
```

Thus, any program that can read from the **/proc** directory can display process information. The most common program used to display processes aside from **ps** is the **top command** and its variants. The **top** command displays an interactive screen listing processes organized by processor time. Processes that use the most processor time are listed at the top of the screen. An example of the screen that appears when you type the **top** command is seen below:

```
  6:53pm  up 1 day, 10:13,  2 users,  load average: 0.01, 0.03, 0.00
44 processes: 43 sleeping, 1 running, 0 zombie, 0 stopped
CPU states:  1.1% user,  0.2% system,  0.0% nice, 28.9% idle
Mem:   384468K av,  337004K used,   47464K free,       0K shrd,    93244K buff
Swap:  514040K av,       0K used,  514040K free                  111340K cached
```

```
   PID USER        PRI  NI  SIZE  RSS SHARE STAT %CPU %MEM   TIME COMMAND
 19706 root         19   0  1028 1024   832 R     0.9  0.2  0:00 top
     1 root          8   0   520  520   452 S     0.0  0.1  0:04 init
     2 root          8   0     0    0     0 SW    0.0  0.0  0:00 keventd
     3 root          9   0     0    0     0 SW    0.0  0.0  0:00 kapm-idled
     4 root         19  19     0    0     0 SWN   0.0  0.0  0:00 ksoftirqd_CPU0
     5 root          9   0     0    0     0 SW    0.0  0.0  0:00 kswapd
     6 root          9   0     0    0     0 SW    0.0  0.0  0:00 kreclaimd
     7 root          9   0     0    0     0 SW    0.0  0.0  0:00 bdflush
     8 root          9   0     0    0     0 SW    0.0  0.0  0:00 kupdated
     9 root         -1 -20     0    0     0 SW<   0.0  0.0  0:00 mdrecoveryd
    13 root          9   0     0    0     0 SW    0.0  0.0  0:00 kjournald
    88 root          9   0     0    0     0 SW    0.0  0.0  0:00 khubd
   202 root          9   0     0    0     0 SW    0.0  0.0  0:00 kjournald
   660 root          9   0   592  592   496 S     0.0  0.1  0:00 syslogd
   665 root          9   0  1100 1100   448 S     0.0  0.2  0:00 klogd
   685 rpc           9   0   588  588   504 S     0.0  0.1  0:00 portmap
   713 rpcuser       9   0   764  764   664 S     0.0  0.1  0:00 rpc.statd
   825 root          8   0   524  524   464 S     0.0  0.1  0:00 apmd
```

Note that the `top` command displays many of the same columns that the `ps` command does, yet contains a summary paragraph at the top of the screen and a cursor between the summary paragraph and the process list. From the output above, you can see that the `top` command itself uses the most processor time, followed by the init daemon.

You may come across a process that has encountered an error during execution and continuously uses up system resources. These processes are referred to as **rogue processes**, and will appear at the top of the listing produced by the `top` command. The `top` command can also be used to change the priority of processes or kill them; thus you may stop rogue processes from the `top` command immediately after they are identified. Process priority and killing processing will be discussed later in this chapter.

To get a full listing of the different commands that you can use while in the top utility, simply press h to get a help screen. An example of this help screen is seen below:

```
Proc-Top Revision 1.2
Secure mode off; cumulative mode off; noidle mode off

Interactive commands are:

space      Update display
^L         Redraw the screen
fF         add and remove fields
oO         Change order of displayed fields
h or ?     Print this list
S          Toggle cumulative mode
i          Toggle display of idle processes
I          Toggle between Irix and Solaris views (SMP-only)
c          Toggle display of command name/line
l          Toggle display of load average
m          Toggle display of memory information
t          Toggle display of summary information
```

11

```
k           Kill a task (with any signal)
r           Renice a task
N           Sort by pid (Numerically)
A           Sort by age
P           Sort by CPU usage
M           Sort by resident memory usage
T           Sort by time / cumulative time
u           Show only a specific user
n or #      Set the number of process to show
s           Set the delay in seconds between updates
W           Write configuration file ~/.toprc
q           Quit

Press any key to continue
```

KILLING PROCESSES

As indicated earlier, a large number of rogue and zombie processes will use up system resources and should be sent a **kill signal** to terminate them and increase overall system performance. The most common command used to send kill signals is the **kill command**. There are 63 different kill signals that the `kill` command may send to a certain process, and each of them operates in a different manner. To view the different kill signal names and associated numbers, you may use the -1 option to the `kill` command, as seen below:

```
[root@localhost root]# kill -1
 1) SIGHUP        2) SIGINT        3) SIGQUIT       4) SIGILL
 5) SIGTRAP       6) SIGABRT       7) SIGBUS        8) SIGFPE
 9) SIGKILL      10) SIGUSR1      11) SIGSEGV      12) SIGUSR2
13) SIGPIPE      14) SIGALRM      15) SIGTERM      17) SIGCHLD
18) SIGCONT      19) SIGSTOP      20) SIGTSTP      21) SIGTTIN
22) SIGTTOU      23) SIGURG       24) SIGXCPU      25) SIGXFSZ
26) SIGVTALRM    27) SIGPROF      28) SIGWINCH     29) SIGIO
30) SIGPWR       31) SIGSYS       32) SIGRTMIN     33) SIGRTMIN+1
34) SIGRTMIN+2   35) SIGRTMIN+3   36) SIGRTMIN+4   37) SIGRTMIN+5
38) SIGRTMIN+6   39) SIGRTMIN+7   40) SIGRTMIN+8   41) SIGRTMIN+9
42) SIGRTMIN+10  43) SIGRTMIN+11  44) SIGRTMIN+12  45) SIGRTMIN+13
46) SIGRTMIN+14  47) SIGRTMIN+15  48) SIGRTMAX-15  49) SIGRTMAX-14
50) SIGRTMAX-13  51) SIGRTMAX-12  52) SIGRTMAX-11  53) SIGRTMAX-10
54) SIGRTMAX-9   55) SIGRTMAX-8   56) SIGRTMAX-7   57) SIGRTMAX-6
58) SIGRTMAX-5   59) SIGRTMAX-4   60) SIGRTMAX-3   61) SIGRTMAX-2
62) SIGRTMAX-1   63) SIGRTMAX
[root@localhost root]# _
```

Most of the kill signals listed in the above output are not useful for systems administrators; the five most common kill signals used for administration are listed in Table 11-2.

Table 11-2 Common administrative kill signals

Name	Number	Description
SIGHUP	1	Also known as the hangup signal, it stops a process and then restarts it with the same PID. If you edit the configuration file used by a running daemon, that daemon may be sent a SIGHUP to restart it; when the daemon starts again, it will read the new configuration file.
SIGINT	2	This signal sends an interrupt signal to a process. Although this signal is one of the weakest kill signals, it works most of the time. When you use the Ctrl-c key combination to kill a currently running process, a SIGINT is actually being sent to the process.
SIGQUIT	3	Also known as a core dump, the quit signal terminates a process by taking the process information in memory and saving it to a file called core on the hard disk in the current working directory. You may use the Ctrl-\ key combination to send a SIGQUIT to a process that is currently running.
SIGTERM	15	The software termination signal is the most common kill signal used by processes to kill other processes. It is the default kill signal used by the kill command.
SIGKILL	9	Also known as the absolute kill signal, it forces the Linux kernel to stop executing the process by sending the process's resources to a special device file called /dev/null.

To send a kill signal to a process, you specify the kill signal to send as an option to the kill command, followed by the appropriate PID of the process. For example, to send a SIGQUIT to a process called sample, you could use the commands below to locate and terminate the process:

```
[root@localhost root]# ps —ef | grep sample
root        1199     1  0 Jun30 tty3      00:00:00 /sbin/sample
[root@localhost root]# kill —3 1199
[root@localhost root]# _
[root@localhost root]# ps —ef | grep sample
[root@localhost root]# _
```

Alternatively, you could have used the command kill —SIGQUIT 1199 to do the same as the kill —3 1199 command used in the above output.

If you do not specify the kill signal when using the kill command, the kill command will use a SIGTERM signal, as it is the default kill signal.

Some processes have the ability to ignore certain kill signals that are sent to them. This is known as **trapping** a signal. The only kill signal that cannot be trapped by any process is the SIGKILL. Thus, if a SIGINT, SIGQUIT, and SIGTERM do not terminate a stubborn process, then you may use a SIGKILL to terminate it. However, you should only use SIGKILL as a last resort since it prevents a process from closing temporary files and other resources properly.

If you send a kill signal to a process that has children, then that parent process will terminate all of its child processes before terminating itself. Thus, to kill several related processes, you may simply send a kill signal to their parent process. In addition, to kill zombie processes, it is often necessary to send a kill signal to its parent process.

Another command that can be used to send kill signals to processes is the **killall command**. The `killall` command works similarly to the `kill` command in that it takes the kill signal as an option; however, it uses the process name to kill instead of the PID. This allows multiple processes of the same name to be killed in one command. An example of using the `killall` command to send a SIGQUIT to multiple `sample` processes is seen in the following output:

```
[root@localhost root]# ps -ef | grep sample
root       1729    1    0 Jun30 tty3     00:00:00 /sbin/sample
root      20198    1    0 Jun30 tty4     00:00:00 /sbin/sample
[root@localhost root]# killall -3 sample
[root@localhost root]# _
[root@localhost root]# ps -ef | grep sample
[root@localhost root]# _
```

Alternatively, you could use the command `killall -SIGQUIT sample` to do the same as the `killall -3 sample` command used in the above output.

As with the `kill` command, if you do not specify the kill signal when using the `killall` command, it will assume a SIGTERM signal.

In addition to the `kill` and `killall` commands, the `top` command can be used to kill processes. While in the `top` utility, simply press the **k** key and supply the appropriate PID and kill signal when prompted.

PROCESS EXECUTION

There are three main types of Linux commands that you may execute:

- binary programs
- shell scripts
- shell functions

Most commands such as `ls`, `find`, and `grep` are binary programs that exist on the filesystem until executed. They were written in a certain programming language and compiled into a binary format that only the computer can understand. Other commands such as `cd` and `exit` are built into the BASH shell running in memory; these are called shell functions. Shell scripts may also contain a list of binary programs, shell functions, and special constructs for the shell to execute in order.

When executing compiled programs or shell scripts, the BASH shell that interprets the command you typed in creates a new BASH shell. This process is known as **forking** and is carried out by the fork function in the BASH shell. This new subshell then executes the binary program or shell script using its exec function. Once the binary program or shell script has completed, the new BASH shell uses its exit function to kill itself and return control to the original BASH shell. The original BASH shell uses its wait function to wait for the new BASH shell to carry out the aforementioned tasks before returning a prompt to the user. Figure 11-3 depicts this process when a user types the `date` command at the command-line.

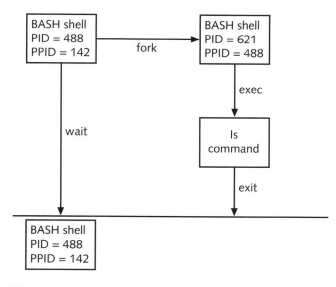

Figure 11-3   Process forking

RUNNING PROCESSES IN THE BACKGROUND

As discussed in the previous section, the BASH shell forks a subshell to execute most commands on the Linux system. Unfortunately, the original BASH shell must wait for the command in the subshell to finish before displaying a shell prompt to accept new commands; commands run in this fashion are known as **foreground processes**.

Alternatively, you may omit the wait function seen in Figure 11-3 by appending an ampersand (&) character to the command. Commands run in this fashion are known as **background processes**. When a command is run in the background, the shell immediately returns the shell prompt for the user to enter another command. To run a sample command in the background, you could enter the following command:

```
[root@localhost root]# sample &
[1] 2583
[root@localhost root]# _
```

Space characters between the command and the ampersand (&) are optional; the command `sample&` is equivalent to the command `sample &`, used above.

The shell returns the PID (2583 in the above example) and the background job ID (1 in the above example) so that you may manipulate the background job after it has been run. After the process has been started, you may use the ps command to view the PID or the **jobs command** to view the background job ID, as seen in the following output:

```
[root@localhost root]# jobs
[1]+  Running                     sample &
[root@localhost root]# ps | grep sample
2583 tty2     00:00:00 sample
[root@localhost root]# _
```

To terminate the background process, you may send a kill signal to the PID as seen earlier in this chapter, or to the background job ID. Background job IDs must be prefixed by a % character. To send the sample background process created earlier a SIGINT, you could use the following `kill` command:

```
[root@localhost root]# jobs
[1]+  Running                     sample &
[root@localhost root]# kill —2 %1
[root@localhost root]# jobs
[root@localhost root]# _
```

You may also use the `killall —2 sample` command or the top utility to terminate the sample background process used in the example above.

Once a background process has been started, it may be moved to the foreground by using the **foreground (fg) command** followed by the background job ID. Similarly, a foreground process may be paused using the Ctrl-z key combination and sent to the background with the **background (bg) command**. The Ctrl-z key combination assigns the foreground process a background job ID that is then used as an argument to the `bg` command. To start a sample process and move it to the foreground, then pause it and move it to the background again, you could use the following commands:

```
[root@localhost root]# sample &
[1] 7519
[root@localhost root]# fg %1
sample


[Ctrl]-z
[1]+  Stopped                 sample
[root@localhost root]# bg %1
[1]+ sample &
[root@localhost root]# jobs
[1]+  Running                 sample &
[root@localhost root]# _
```

When there are multiple background processes executing in the shell, the `jobs` command will indicate the most recent one with a + symbol, and the second most recent one with a − symbol. If you place the % notation in a command without specifying the background job ID, then the command will operate on the most recent background process. An example of this is seen in the following output, in which four sample processes are started and sent SIGQUIT kill signals using the % notation:

```
[root@localhost root]# sample &
[1] 7605
[root@localhost root]# sample2 &
[2] 7613
[root@localhost root]# sample3 &
[3] 7621
[root@localhost root]# sample4 &
[4] 7629
[root@localhost root]# jobs
[1]   Running                 sample &
[2]   Running                 sample2 &
[3]-  Running                 sample3 &
[4]+  Running                 sample4 &
[root@localhost root]# kill -3 %
/sbin/sample4: 7629 Quit
[4]+  Exit 131                sample4
[root@localhost root]# jobs
[1]   Running                 sample &
[2]-  Running                 sample2 &
[3]+  Running                 sample3 &
[root@localhost root]# kill -3 %
/sbin/sample3: 7621 Quit
[3]+  Exit 131                sample3
[root@localhost root]# jobs
[1]-  Running                 sample &
```

11

```
[2]+  Running                   sample2 &
[root@localhost root]# kill -3 %
/sbin/sample2: 7613 Quit
[2]+  Exit 131                  sample2
[root@localhost root]# jobs
[1]+  Running                   sample &
[root@localhost root]# kill -3 %
/sbin/sample: 7605 Quit

[1]+  Exit 131                  sample
[root@localhost root]# jobs
[root@localhost root]# _
```

PROCESS PRIORITIES

Recall that Linux is a multitasking operating system; it can perform several different tasks at the same time. Since most computers contain only a single CPU, Linux executes small amounts of each process on the processor in series; this allows processes to seem to the user as if they are executing simultaneously. The amount of time a process has to use the CPU is called a **time slice**; the more time slices a process has, the more time it has to execute on the CPU and the faster it will execute. Time slices are typically measured in milliseconds; thus several hundred processes may be executing on the processor in a single second.

The `ps -l` command lists the Linux kernel priority (PRI) of a process; this value is directly related to the amount of time slices a process has on the CPU. A PRI of 0 is the most likely to get time slices on the CPU, and a PRI of 127 is the least likely to receive time slices on the CPU. An example of this command is seen below:

```
[root@localhost root]# ps -l
  F S   UID   PID  PPID  C PRI  NI ADDR    SZ WCHAN  TTY          TIME CMD
100 S     0  1228  1227  0  69   0    -   578 wait4  pts/0    00:00:00 login
100 S     0  1229  1228  0  72   0    -   614 wait4  pts/0    00:00:00 bash
100 R     0  1802  1229  0  74   0    -   767 -      pts/0    00:00:00 ps
[root@localhost root]# _
```

The login, bash, and ps processes all have different PRI values since the kernel automatically assigns time slices based on several factors. You cannot change the PRI directly, but may influence it indirectly by assigning a certain nice value to a process. A negative nice value will increase the likelihood that the process will receive more time slices, whereas a positive nice value will do the opposite. The range of nice values is depicted in Figure 11-4.

−20	0	+19
Most likely to receive time slices; the PRI will be closer to zero	The default nice value for new processes	Least likely to receive time slices; the PRI will be closer to 127

Figure 11-4   The nice value scale

All users can be "nice" to other users of the same computer by lowering the priority of their own processes by increasing their nice value. However, only the root user has the ability to increase the priority of a process by lowering its nice value.

Processes are started with a nice value of 0 by default, as seen in the NI column of the ps −l output above. To start a process with a nice value of +19 (low priority), you may use the **nice command** and specify the nice value using the −n option and the command to start. If the −n option is omitted, a nice value of +10 will be assumed. To start the ps −l command with a nice value of +19, you could issue the following command:

```
[root@localhost root]# nice -n 19 ps -l
  F S   UID   PID  PPID  C PRI  NI ADDR    SZ WCHAN   TTY         TIME CMD
100 S     0  1228  1227  0  69   0    -   578 wait4   pts/0   00:00:00 login
100 S     0  1229  1228  0  70   0    -   614 wait4   pts/0   00:00:00 bash
100 R     0  1799  1229  0  79  19    -   767 -       pts/0   00:00:00 ps
[root@localhost root]# _
```

Notice from the above output that NI is 19 for the ps command as compared to 0 for the login and bash commands. Furthermore, the PRI of 79 for the ps command will result in fewer time slices than the PRI of 69 for the login command and the PRI of 70 for the bash shell.

Conversely, to increase the priority of the ps −l command, you could use the following command:

```
[root@localhost root]# nice -n -20 ps -l
 F S   UID   PID  PPID  C PRI  NI ADDR    SZ WCHAN   TTY         TIME CMD
00 S     0  1228  1227  0  69   0    -   578 wait4   pts/0   00:00:00 login
00 S     0  1229  1228  0  72   0    -   615 wait4   pts/0   00:00:00 bash
00 R     0  1970  1229  0  64 -20    -   767 -       pts/0   00:00:00 ps
[root@localhost root]# _
```

Note from the above output that the nice value of −20 for the ps command resulted in a PRI of 64, making it more likely to receive time slices than the login and bash processes, which have PRI values of 69 and 70 respectively.

 On some Linux systems, background processes are given a nice value of 4 by default to lower the chance they will receive time slices.

After a process has been started, you may change its priority by using the **renice command** and specifying the change to the nice value, as well as the PID of the processes to change. Say, for example, three sample processes are currently executing on a terminal:

```
[root@localhost root]# ps -l
  F S   UID   PID  PPID  C PRI  NI ADDR    SZ WCHAN   TTY          TIME CMD
100 S     0  1228  1227  0  69   0  -      578 wait4  pts/0    00:00:00 login
100 S     0  1229  1228  0  71   0  -      617 wait4  pts/0    00:00:00 bash
000 S     0  1990  1229  0  69   0  -      483 nanosl pts/0    00:00:00 /bin/sample
000 S     0  2180  1229  0  70   0  -      483 nanosl pts/0    00:00:00 /bin/sample
000 S     0  2181  1229  0  71   0  -      483 nanosl pts/0    00:00:00 /bin/sample
100 R     0  2196  1229  0  75   0  -      768 -      pts/0    00:00:00 ps
[root@localhost root]# _
```

To lower the priority of the first two sample processes by changing the nice value from 0 to +15 and view the new values, you could execute the following commands:

```
[root@localhost root]# renice +15 1990 2180
1990: old priority 0, new priority 15
2180: old priority 0, new priority 15
[root@localhost root]# ps -l
  F S   UID   PID  PPID  C PRI  NI ADDR    SZ WCHAN   TTY          TIME CMD
100 S     0  1228  1227  0  69   0  -      578 wait4  pts/0    00:00:00 login
100 S     0  1229  1228  0  71   0  -      617 wait4  pts/0    00:00:00 bash
000 S     0  1990  1229  0  73  15  -      483 nanosl pts/0    00:00:00 /bin/sample
000 S     0  2180  1229  0  76  15  -      483 nanosl pts/0    00:00:00 /bin/sample
000 S     0  2181  1229  0  71   0  -      483 nanosl pts/0    00:00:00 /bin/sample
100 R     0  2196  1229  0  75   0  -      768 -      pts/0    00:00:00 ps
[root@localhost root]# _
```

You may also use the top utility to change the nice value of a running process; simply press the r key and supply the PID and the nice value when prompted.

As with the nice command, only the root user may change the nice value to a negative value using the renice command.

The root user can use the **renice** command to change the priority of all processes that are owned by a certain user or group. To change the nice value to +15 for all processes owned by the users mary and bob, you could execute the command **renice +15 −u mary bob** at the command prompt. Similarly, to change the nice value to +15 for all processes started by members of the group sys, you could execute the command **renice +15 −g sys** at the command prompt.

SCHEDULING COMMANDS

Although most processes are begun by users executing commands while logged into a terminal, there are times when you may wish to schedule a command to execute at some point in the future. Scheduling system maintenance commands to run during non-working hours is good practice, as it will not disrupt normal business activities.

There are two different daemons that can be used to schedule commands: the **at daemon (atd)** and the **cron daemon (crond)**. The at daemon is used to schedule a command to execute once in the future, whereas the cron daemon is used to schedule a command to execute repeatedly in the future.

Scheduling Commands with atd

To schedule a command or set of commands for execution at a later time by the at daemon, you may specify the time as an argument to the **at command**; some common time formats used with the **at** command are listed in Table 11-3.

Table 11-3   Common at commands

Command	Description
at 10:15PM	Will schedule commands to run at 10:15PM on the current date
at 10:15PM July 15	Will schedule commands to run at 10:15PM on July 15
at midnight	Will schedule commands to run at midnight on the current date
at noon July 15	Will schedule commands to run at noon on July 15
at teatime	Will schedule commands to run at 4:00PM on the current date
at tomorrow	Will schedule commands to run at the current time the next day
at now + 5 minutes	Will schedule commands to run in 5 minutes
at now + 10 hours	Will schedule commands to run in 10 hours
at now + 4 days	Will schedule commands to run in 4 days
at now + 2 weeks	Will schedule commands to run in 2 weeks
at now or batch	Will schedule commands to run immediately
at 9:00AM 01/03/2004 or at 9:00AM 01032004 or at 9:00AM 03.01.2004	Will schedule commands to run at 9:00AM on January 3rd 2004

Once invoked, the `at` command will display an `at>` prompt allowing you to type in commands to be executed, one per line. Once the commands have been entered, use the Crtl-d key combination to schedule the commands using atd.

Note   The at daemon will use the current shell's environment when executing scheduled commands; the shell environment and scheduled commands are stored in the `/var/spool/at` directory.

If the standard output of any command scheduled using atd has not been redirected to a file, it will be mailed to the user. You may check your local mail by typing `mail` at a command prompt. More information about the mail utility can be found in its man page or info page.

To schedule the commands **date** and **who** to run at 10:15PM on July 15th, you may use the following commands:

```
[root@localhost root]# at 10:15pm July 15
warning: commands will be executed using (in order) a) $SHELL b) login
shell c) /bin/sh
at> date > /root/atfile
at> who >> /root/atfile
at> [Ctrl]–d
job 1 at 2003–07–15 22:15
[root@localhost root]# _
```

As seen in the above output, the **at** command returns an at Job ID so that you may subsequently query or remove the scheduled command. To display a list of at Job IDs, you may specify the **–l** option to the **at** command:

```
[root@localhost root]# at –l
1          2003–07–15 22:15 a root
[root@localhost root]# _
```

Alternatively, you may use the atq command to see scheduled at jobs; the atq command is simply a shortcut to the at –l command.

When running the at –l command, a regular user will only see their own scheduled at jobs; however, the root user will see all scheduled at jobs.

To see the contents of the at job listed in the previous output alongside the shell environment at the time the at job was scheduled, you may use the **–c** option to the **at** command and specify the appropriate at Job ID:

```
[root@localhost root]# at –c 1
#!/bin/sh
# atrun uid=0 gid=0
# mail     root 0
umask 22
PWD=/root; export PWD
REMOTEHOST=3.0.0.2; export REMOTEHOST
HOSTNAME=localhost.localdomain; export HOSTNAME
PVM_RSH=/usr/bin/rsh; export PVM_RSH
QTDIR=/usr/lib/qt–2.3.1; export QTDIR
LESSOPEN=\|/usr/bin/lesspipe.sh\ %s; export LESSOPEN
XPVM_ROOT=/usr/share/pvm3/xpvm; export XPVM_ROOT
KDEDIR=/usr; export KDEDIR
```

```
USER=root; export USER
LS_COLORS=; export LS_COLORS
MACHTYPE=i386-redhat-linux-gnu; export MACHTYPE
MAIL=/var/spool/mail/root; export MAIL
INPUTRC=/etc/inputrc; export INPUTRC
BASH_ENV=/root/.bashrc; export BASH_ENV
LANG=en_US; export LANG
LOGNAME=root; export LOGNAME
SHLVL=1; export SHLVL
USERNAME=root; export USERNAME
HOSTTYPE=i386; export HOSTTYPE
OSTYPE=linux-gnu; export OSTYPE
HISTSIZE=1000; export HISTSIZE
LAMHELPFILE=/etc/lam/lam-helpfile; export LAMHELPFILE
PVM_ROOT=/usr/share/pvm3; export PVM_ROOT
HOME=/root; export HOME
SSH_ASKPASS=/usr/libexec/openssh/gnome-ssh-askpass; export SSH_ASKPASS
PATH=/usr/kerberos/sbin:/usr/kerberos/bin:/usr/local/sbin:/usr/local/bi
n:/sbin:/bin:/usr/sbin:/usr/bin:/usr/X11R6/bin:/root/bin; export PATH
cd /root || {
        echo 'Execution directory inaccessible' >&2
        exit 1
}
date > /root/atfile
who >> /root/atfile
[root@localhost root]# _
```

To remove the at job used in the above example, simply specify the −d option to the at command followed by the appropriate at Job ID, as seen in the following output:

```
[root@localhost root]# at -d 1
[root@localhost root]# at -l
[root@localhost root]# _
```

Alternatively, you may use the atrm 1 command to remove the first at job; the atrm command is simply a shortcut to the at −d command.

If there are many commands to be scheduled using the at daemon, you may choose to place these commands in a shell script and schedule the shell script to execute at a later time using the −f option to the at command. An example of scheduling a shell script called myscript using the at command is seen below:

```
[root@localhost root]# cat myscript
#this is a sample shell script
date > /root/atfile
who >> /root/atfile
[root@localhost root]# at 10:15pm July 16 -f myscript
warning: commands will be executed using (in order) a) $SHELL b) login
shell c)/bin/sh
job 2 at 2003-07-16 22:15
[root@localhost root]# _
```

If the **/etc/at.allow** and **/etc/at.deny** files do not exist, only the root user is allowed to schedule tasks using the at daemon. To give this ability to other users, simply create an /etc/at.allow file and add the names of users allowed to use the at daemon, one per line. Conversely, you can use the /etc/at.deny file to deny certain users access to the at daemon; any user not listed in this file is then allowed to use the at daemon. If both files exist, then the system checks the /etc/at.allow file and does not process the entries in the /etc/at.deny file.

On Red Hat Linux systems, there exists only an /etc/at.deny file by default. Since this file is initially left blank, all users are allowed to use the at daemon after a Red Hat Linux installation.

Scheduling Commands with crond

The at daemon is useful for scheduling tasks that occur on a certain date in the future, yet is ill-suited for scheduling repetitive tasks, since each task will require its own at job ID. The cron daemon is better suited for repetitive tasks as it uses configuration files called **cron tables** to specify when a command should be executed.

Cron tables have six fields separated by space or tab characters. The first five fields specify the times to run the command and the sixth field is the absolute pathname to the command to be executed. As with the **at** command, you may place commands in a shell script and schedule the shell script to run repetitively; in this case, the sixth field will be the absolute pathname to the shell script. Each of the fields in a cron table is depicted in Figure 11-5.

```
1        2        3        4        5        command

        ┌──────────────────────────────────────────┐
        │ 1 = minute past the hour (0-59)           │
        │ 2 = hour (0-23)                           │
        │ 3 = day of month (1-31)                   │
        │ 4 = month of year (1-12)                  │
        │ 5 = day of week                           │
        │         0=Sun (or 7=Sun)                  │
        │         1=Mon                             │
        │         2=Tues                            │
        │         3=Wed                             │
        │         4=Thurs                           │
        │         5=Fri                             │
        │         6=Sat                             │
        └──────────────────────────────────────────┘
```

Figure 11-5   User cron table format

Thus, to execute the **/root/myscript** shell script at 5:20PM and 5:40PM Monday to Friday regardless of the day of the month or month of the year, you could use the cron table depicted in Figure 11-6.

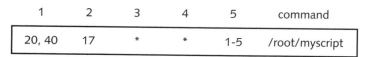

1	2	3	4	5	command
20, 40	17	*	*	1-5	/root/myscript

Figure 11-6   Sample user cron table entry

The first field in Figure 11-6 specifies the minute past the hour. Since the command must be run at 20 minutes and 40 minutes past the hour, there are two values in this field, separated by a comma. The second field specifies the time in 24-hour format, 5PM being the 17th hour. The third and fourth fields specify the day of the month and month of the year to run the command, respectively. Since the command may run during any month regardless of the day of the month, both of these fields use the * wildcard metacharacter to match all values. The final field indicates the day of the week to run the command; as with the first field, the command must be run on multiple days, but a range of days was specified (day 1 to day 5).

There are two different types of cron tables used by the cron daemon. User cron tables exist in **/var/spool/cron** and represent tasks that individual users schedule, whereas the system cron tables contain system tasks and exist in the **/etc/cron.d** directory as well as the **/etc/crontab** file.

User Cron Tables

On a newly installed Red Hat Linux system, all users have the ability to schedule tasks using the cron daemon. However, you may create an **/etc/cron.allow** file to list users that have the ability to schedule tasks using the cron daemon. All other users will be denied. Conversely, you may create an **/etc/cron.deny** file to list those users who are denied the ability to schedule tasks. Thus, only users not listed in this file are allowed to schedule tasks only. If both files exist, then only the /etc/cron.allow file will be processed.

To create or edit a user cron table, you may use the −e option to the **crontab command**, which will open the vi editor. You may then enter the appropriate cron table entries. Say, for example, that you as the root user executed the crontab −e command. To schedule the command /bin/command1 to run at 4:30AM every Friday and /bin/command2 to run at 2:00PM on the first day of every month, you could add the following lines while in the vi editor:

```
30 4 * * 5 /bin/command1
0 14 1 * * /bin/command2
~
~
~
~
~
~
~
```

11

```
~
~
~
~
~
~
~
~
~
"crontab.15233" [Modified] line 1 of 2 --50%-- col 23
```

When a user saves the changes and quits the vi editor, the information is stored in the file /var/spool/cron/username where *username* is the name of the user who executed the crontab —e command. In the example above, the file would be named /var/spool/cron/root.

To list your user cron table, you may use the —l option to the crontab command. The following output lists the cron table created earlier:

```
[root@localhost root]# crontab -l
# DO NOT EDIT THIS FILE - edit the master and reinstall.
# (/tmp/crontab.15233 installed on Fri Jul  5 20:31:56 2003)
# (Cron version -- $Id: crontab.c,v 2.13 1994/01/17 03:20:37 vixie Exp)
30 4 * * 5 /bin/command1
0 14 1 * * /bin/command2
[root@localhost root]# _
```

Furthermore, to remove a cron table and all scheduled jobs, you may use the —r option to the crontab command, as illustrated below:

```
[root@localhost root]# crontab -r
[root@localhost root]# crontab -l
no crontab for root
[root@localhost root]# _
```

The root user may edit, list, or remove any other user's cron table by using the —u option to the crontab command followed by the username. For example, to edit the cron table for the user mary, you could use the command crontab —e —u mary at the command prompt. Similarly, to list and remove mary's cron table, you could execute the commands crontab —l —u mary and crontab —r —u mary, respectively.

The System Cron Table

Linux systems are typically scheduled to run many commands during non-business hours. These commands may perform system maintenance, back up data, or run CPU-intensive programs. Most of these commands are scheduled by the cron daemon from entries in the system cron table /etc/crontab, which can only be edited by the root user. A sample /etc/crontab file is seen in the following output:

```
[root@localhost root]# cat /etc/crontab
SHELL=/bin/bash
PATH=/sbin:/bin:/usr/sbin:/usr/bin
```

```
MAILTO=root
HOME=/

# run-parts
01 * * * * root run-parts /etc/cron.hourly
02 4 * * * root run-parts /etc/cron.daily
22 4 * * 0 root run-parts /etc/cron.weekly
42 4 1 * * root run-parts /etc/cron.monthly

[root@localhost root]# _
```

The initial section of the cron table specifies the environment used while executing commands. The remainder of the file is similar to the format of a user cron table. The first five fields specify the time to run the command, yet the sixth field specifies who to run the command as (the root user in the above output). The remaining fields represent the command to run; the **run-parts** command is used to execute all files in a certain directory listed as an argument.

Thus, the line:

```
01 * * * * root run-parts /etc/cron.hourly
```

in the **/etc/crontab** file listed above executes all files inside the **/etc/cron.hourly** directory as the root user at one minute past the hour, every hour of every day.

Similarly, the line:

```
02 4 * * * root run-parts /etc/cron.daily
```

in the **/etc/crontab** file listed above executes all files inside the **/etc/cron.daily** directory as the root user at 4:02AM, every day.

The remaining lines of the **/etc/crontab** file listed above run any files in the **/etc/cron.weekly** directory at 4:22AM on Sundays and any files in the **/etc/cron.monthly** directory at 4:42AM on the first day of each month.

Since the **/etc/crontab** file organizes tasks hourly, daily, weekly, and monthly, you may simply copy a script file to the appropriate directory to schedule it using the system cron table. To run a script called myscript on a daily basis, you may copy the file to the **/etc/cron.daily** directory. Alternatively, you may simply create a symbolic link in the **/etc/cron.daily** directory that points to the myscript shell script.

You may also place a cron table with the same information in the **/etc/cron.d** directory. Any cron tables found in this directory may have the same format as **/etc/crontab** and will be run by the system. This is useful if the hourly, daily, weekly, and monthly intervals are of no use for a particular task. For example, the **sa1** command is run every 10 minutes as the root user by the cron daemon from the file /etc/cron.d/sysstat, as seen below:

```
[root@localhost root]# cat /etc/cron.d/sysstat
# run system activity accounting tool every 10 minutes
*/10 * * * * root /usr/lib/sa/sa1 1 1

[root@localhost root]# _
```

Notice from the output above that the special notation */10 was used in the first column to indicate all minutes at 10 minute intervals. Instead, you could have used 0–59/10 to specify running the sa1 command from the 0th to 59th minute at 10 minute intervals.

CHAPTER SUMMARY

- Processes are programs that are executing on the system.

- User processes are run in the same terminal as the user who executed them, whereas daemon processes are system processes that do not run on a terminal.

- Every process has a parent process associated with it and, optionally, several child processes.

- Process information is stored in the /proc filesystem; the ps and top commands can be used to view this information.

- Zombie and rogue processes that exist for long periods of time use up system resources and should be killed to improve system performance.

- You may send kill signals to a process using the kill, killall, and top commands.

- The BASH shell forks a subshell to execute most commands.

- Processes may be run in the background by appending an & to the command name; the BASH shell assigns each background process a background job ID so that it may be manipulated afterwards.

- The priority of a process may be affected indirectly by altering its nice value; nice values range from −20 (high priority) to +19 (low priority). Only the root user may increase the priority of a process.

- Commands may be scheduled to run at a later time using the at and cron daemons. The at daemon schedules tasks to occur once at a later time, whereas the cron daemon uses cron tables to schedule tasks to occur repetitively in the future.

KEY TERMS

/etc/at.allow — A file listing all users who can use the at command.

/etc/at.deny — A file listing all users who cannot access the at command.

/etc/cron.allow — A file listing all users who can use the cron command.

/etc/cron.d — A directory that contains additional system cron tables.

/etc/cron.deny — A file listing all users who cannot access the cron command.

/etc/crontab — The default system cron table.

/var/spool/at — A directory that stores the information used to schedule commands using the at daemon.

/var/spool/cron — A directory that stores user cron tables.

at command — The command used to schedule commands and tasks to run at a preset time in the future.

at daemon (atd) — The system daemon that executes tasks at a future time; it is configured with the at command.

background process — A process that does not require the BASH shell to wait for its termination; upon execution, the user receives the BASH shell prompt immediately.

background (bg) command — The command used to run a foreground process in the background.

child process — Refers to a process that was started by another process (parent process).

cron daemon (crond) — The system daemon that executes tasks repetitively in the future—it is configured using cron tables.

cron table — A file specifying tasks to be run by the cron daemon; there are user cron tables and system cron tables.

crontab command — The command used to view and edit user cron tables.

daemon process — A system process that is not associated with a terminal.

foreground (fg) command — The command used to run a background process in the foreground.

foreground process — A process for which the BASH shell that executed it must wait for its termination.

forking — The act of creating a new BASH shell child process from a parent BASH shell process.

jobs command — The command used to see the list of background processes running in the current shell.

kill command — The command used to kill or terminate a process.

kill signal — The type of signal sent to a process by the kill command; different kill signals affect processes in different ways.

killall command — The command that kills all instances of a process by command name.

nice command — The command used to change the priority of a process as it is started.

11

nice value (NI) — The value that indirectly represents the priority of a process; the higher the value, the lower the priority.

parent process — A process that has started other processes (child processes).

parent process ID (PPID) — The PID of the parent process that created the current process.

process — A program currently loaded into physical memory and running on the system.

process ID (PID) — A unique identifier assigned to every process as it begins.

process priority (PRI) — A number assigned to a process, used to determine how many time slices on the processor it will receive; the higher the number, the lower the priority.

process state — The current state of the process on the processor; most processes are in the sleeping or running state.

program — A structured set of commands stored in an executable file on a filesystem; it may be executed to create a process.

ps command — The command used to obtain information about processes currently running on the system.

renice command — The command used to alter the nice value of a process currently running on the system.

rogue process — A process that has become faulty in some way and continues to consume far more system resources than it should.

time slice — The amount of time a process is given on a CPU in a multiprocessing operating system.

top command — The command used to give real-time information about the most active processes on the system; it may also be used to renice or kill processes.

trapping — The process of ignoring a kill signal.

user process — A process begun by a user that runs on a terminal.

zombie process — A process that has finished executing, but whose parent has not yet released its PID; it still retains a spot in the kernel's process table.

REVIEW QUESTIONS

1. A program is an executable or set of executables stored on physical storage media that can be loaded into physical memory and run. True or False?

2. Which command entered without arguments is used to display a list of processes running on the current shell?

   a. `ppid`

   b. `list`

   c. `pid`

   d. `ps`

3. Only system processes or daemons can be run in the background; all user initiated processes must be associated with a terminal and run in the foreground. True or False?

4. What is the only kill signal that cannot be trapped by a process?

   a. SIGKILL

   b. SIGQUIT

   c. SIGINT

   d. SIGTERM

   e. killall

   f. None, as a process will be terminated by the kill command; the signal is just how it exits.

5. If the `nice` command is run and no value is specified, what is the default value that the system will assume?

   a. 0

   b. None; a value must be specified.

   c. 19

   d. −20

   e. 10

6. Only the root user can edit tasks stored in `/etc/crontab`. True or False?

7. Which of the following statements is true? (Choose all that apply.)

   a. If `/etc/at.allow` exists only users listed in it can use the `at` command.

   b. If `/etc/cron.allow` exists only users listed in it can use the `cron` command.

   c. If `/etc/cron.deny` exists and `/etc/cron.allow` does not exist, then any user not listed in `/etc/cron.deny` can use the `cron` command.

   d. If `/etc/cron.allow` and `/etc/cron.deny` exist, only users listed in the former can use the `cron` command and any listed in the latter are denied access to the `cron` command.

   e. If a user is listed in both `/etc/cron.allow` and `/etc/cron.deny` then `/etc/cron.deny` takes precedence and the user cannot access the `crontab` command.

8. Where are individual user tasks scheduled to run with the cron daemon stored?

   a. `/etc/crontab`

   b. `/etc/cron/(the user's login name)`

   c. `/var/spool/cron`

   d. `/var/spool/cron/(the user's login name)`

9. Which process will always have a PID of 1 and a PPID of 0?

    a. the kernel itself

    b. ps

    c. init

    d. top

    e. none, as PIDs are randomly assigned

10. What option do you use with the `kill` command to see the available kill signals that can be sent?

    a. −l

    b. /l

    c. /?

    d. −?

    e. /help

    f. −help

11. The term used to describe a process spawning or initiating another process is referred to as _____.

    a. child process

    b. forking

    c. branching

    d. parenting

12. Only the root user can lower the nice values of processes and hence raise their priority. True or False?

13. A process is a(n) _____.

    a. program loaded into physical memory and running

    b. predefined way of doing something

    c. executable or set of executables stored on a hard disk drive

    d. program that must be initiated by a user logged into a terminal

14. As daemon processes are not associated with a terminal, you have to use the −e switch with **ps** to view them. True or False?

15. Which of the following commands will most increase the chance of a process receiving more time slices?

    a. `renice 0`

    b. `renice 15`

    c. `renice −12`

    d. `renice 19`

16. How do you bypass the wait function and send a process to the background?

    a. This cannot happen once a process is executing; it can only be done when the command is entered by placing an ampersand (&) after it.

    b. Only daemon processes can run in the background.

    c. by using the **ps** command.

    d. by using the **bg** command.

17. The **at** command is used to _____.

    a. schedule processes to run periodically in the background

    b. schedule processes to run periodically on a recurring basis in the future

    c. schedule processes to run at a single instance in the future

    d. schedule processes to run in the foreground

18. Every process on a Linux system including the init daemon has a process ID and a parent process ID. True or False?

19. The higher the priority of a process the more time slices it has on the CPU. True or False?

20. What command is used to view and modify user jobs scheduled to run with cron?

    a. **crontab**

    b. **cron**

    c. **ps**

    d. **sched**

21. When the **at** command is used to schedule a process to run, where is the information on what shell to use when executing the process stored?

    a. All processes scheduled with at are run in the BASH shell.

    b. **/var/spool/at**

    c. **/etc/at**

    d. **/etc/at/shell**

22. Every process has a process ID and a _____.

    a. fork process

    b. daemon

    c. child process

    d. parent process ID

23. The **killall** command will terminate _____.

    a. all instances of a process with the same PPID

    b. all instances of a process with the same PID

    c. all instances of a process with the same priority

    d. all instances of a process with the same name

11

24. What is the preferred way to kill a zombie process?

    a. Kill its parent process.

    b. `Kill -9`

    c. `Kill -15`

    d. It cannot be killed, hence the name zombie.

25. Nice values used to affect process priorities range between _____.

    a. 0 and 20

    b. 0 and −19

    c. −19 and 20

    d. 0 and 127

    e. −20 and 19

26. What is the name given to a process not associated with a terminal?

    a. child process

    b. parent process

    c. user process

    d. daemon process

27. In order to kill a process running in the background you must place a % character before its process ID. True or False?

28. What kill level signal cannot be trapped?

    a. 1

    b. 9

    c. 3

    d. 15

29. A runaway process that is faulty and consuming mass amounts of system resources _____.

    a. is a zombie process

    b. is an orphaned process

    c. has a PID of 1

    d. has a PPID of 0

    e. is a rogue process

30. When you run the `ps` command, how are daemon processes recognized?

    a. The terminal is listed a tty0.

    b. There is a question mark in the TTY column.

    c. There is no way to do this with ps; you must use the `top` command

    d. There is a d for daemon in the terminal identification column.

31. When renice is used to affect a process's priority by lowering the nice value it has _____ than it had before.

    a. more priority

    b. less priority

    c. the same priority

    d. Does not work; it is the `nice` command, not `renice`.

32. Only the root user can run a process in the foreground as they monopolize the terminal and processor until they are completed. True or False?

33. What command is used to gain real-time information about processes running on the system with the most processor intensive processes listed at the beginning of the list?

    a. `ps`

    b. `ps -elf`

    c. `top`

    d. `top -1`

34. What command can be used to see processes running in the background?

    a. `bg`

    b. `jobs`

    c. `ps -%`

    d. They cannot be seen or listed as they are running in the background; only foreground processes can be seen.

35. The `top` command can be used to change a process's priority or to kill a process if need be. True or False?

HANDS-ON PROJECTS

These projects should be completed in the order given. All hands-on projects should take a total of three hours to complete. The requirements for this lab include:

- ❐ A computer with Red Hat 7.2 installed according to Hands-on Project 7-2

Project 11-1

In this hands-on project, you view characteristics of processes using the `ps` command.

1. Turn on your computer. Once your Linux system has been loaded, switch to a command-line terminal (tty2) by pressing **Ctrl-Alt-F2** and log into the terminal using the username of **root** and the password of **secret**.

2. At the command prompt, type **ps -ef | more** and press **Enter** to view the first processes started on the entire Linux system.

3. Fill in the following information from the data displayed on the terminal screen after typing the command:

   a. Which process has a Process ID of 1? (PID = 1) _____

   b. What character do most processes have in the terminal column (tty)?

      _____

   c. What does this character in the terminal column indicate? _____

   d. Which user started most of these processes? _____

4. Most processes that are displayed on the screen are started by a certain parent process indicated in the Parent Process ID column (PPID). Which process is the parent to most processes? _____

   Type **q** at the MORE prompt to quit.

5. At the command prompt, type **ps −el | more** and press **Enter** to view the process states for the first processes started on the entire Linux system.

6. Fill in the following information from the data displayed on the terminal screen after typing the command:

   a. What character exists in the State (S) column for most processes, and what does this character indicate? _____

   b. What range of numbers are possible to have in the nice (NI) column?

      _____

   c. Which process has the number 100 in the Flag (F) column and what does this number indicate? _____

   Type **q** at the MORE prompt to quit.

7. At the command prompt, type **ps −el | grep Z** and press **Enter** to display zombie processes on your Linux system. Are there any zombie processes indicated in the State (S) column?

8. Type **exit** and press **Enter** to log out of your shell.

Project 11-2

In this hands-on project, you use `kill` command signals to terminate processes on your system.

1. Switch to a command-line terminal (tty2) by pressing **Ctrl-Alt-F2** and log into the terminal using the username of **root** and the password of **secret**.

2. At the command prompt, type **ps −ef | grep bash** and press **Enter** to view the bash shells that are running in memory on your computer. Record the PID of the bash shell running in your terminal (tty2): _____

3. At the command prompt, type **kill −l** and press **Enter** to list the available kill signals that you may send to a process.

4. At the command prompt, type **kill −2 PID** (where PID is the PID that you recorded in question 2) and press **Enter**. Did your shell terminate?

5. At the command prompt, type **kill −3 PID** (where PID is the PID that you recorded in question 2) and press **Enter**. Did your shell terminate?

6. At the command prompt, type **kill −15 PID** (where PID is the PID that you recorded in question 2) and press **Enter**. Did your shell terminate?

7. At the command prompt, type **kill −9 PID** (where PID is the PID that you recorded in question 2) and press **Enter**. Did your shell terminate? Why did this command work when the others did not?

8. Type **exit** and press **Enter** to log out of your shell.

Project 11-3

In this hands-on project, you run processes in the background, kill them using the `kill` and `killall` commands, and change their priorities using the `nice` and `renice` commands.

1. Switch to a command-line terminal (tty2) by pressing **Ctrl-Alt-F2** and log into the terminal using the username of **root** and the password of **secret**.

2. At the command prompt, type **sleep 6000** and press **Enter** to start the sleep command, which waits 6000 seconds in the foreground. Do you get your prompt back once you enter this command? Why? Send the process an INT signal by typing the **Ctrl-c** key combination.

3. At the command prompt, type **sleep 6000&** and press **Enter** to start the sleep command, which waits 6000 seconds in the background. Observe the background Job ID and PID that is returned.

4. Bring the background sleep process to the foreground by typing **fg %1** at the command prompt and pressing **Enter**. Send the process an INT signal by typing the **Ctrl-c** key combination.

5. Place another sleep command in memory by typing the **sleep 6000&** command and pressing **Enter**. Repeat this command three more times to place a total of four sleep commands in memory.

6. At the command prompt, type **jobs** and press **Enter** to view the jobs running in the background. What does the + symbol indicate?

7. At the command prompt, type **kill %** and press **Enter** to terminate the most recent process and view the output.

8. At the command prompt, type **killall sleep** and press **Enter** to terminate the remaining sleep processes in memory. Verify that there are no more sleep processes in memory by typing the **jobs** command and pressing **Enter**.

9. Place a sleep command in memory by typing **sleep 6000&** at a command prompt and pressing **Enter**.

10. Place a sleep command in memory with a lower priority by typing **nice −n 19 sleep 6000&** at a command prompt and pressing **Enter**.

11

11. Verify that these 2 processes have different nice values by typing the command **ps –el | grep sleep** at the command prompt and pressing **Enter**. Record the PID of the process with a nice value of 0: _____

12. At the command prompt, type **renice +10 PID** (where PID is the PID you recorded in the previous question) to change the priority of the process. Type the command **ps –el | grep sleep** and press **Enter** to verify the new priority.

13. Type **exit** and press **Enter** to log out of your shell.

Project 11-4

In this hands–on project, you view and manage processes using the top command-line utility.

1. Switch to a command–line terminal (tty2) by pressing **Ctrl–Alt–F2** and log into the terminal using the username of **root** and the password of **secret**.

2. At the command prompt, type **top** and press **Enter**.

3. From the output on the terminal screen, record the following information:

   a. Number of processes: _____

   b. Number of sleeping processes: _____

   c. Amount of memory (K): _____

   d. Amount of swap memory (K): _____

4. While in the top utility, press the **h** key and observe the output. When finished, press any key to return to the previous top output.

5. By observing the output under the COMMAND column on your terminal screen, identify the PID of the top command in the output and record it:
   _____

6. Type **r** in the top utility to change the priority of a running process. When asked which process to change (renice), type in the **PID** from the previous question. When asked which value to use, type **10** to lower the priority of the top process to 10. Does this new priority take effect immediately?

7. Type **k** in the top utility to send a kill signal to a process. When asked which process, type in the **PID** used in Step 5. When asked which signal to send it, type **2** to send it an INT signal. Did the top utility terminate?

8. At the command prompt, type **top** and press **Enter**.

9. By observing the output under the COMMAND column on your terminal screen, identify the PID of the top command in the output and record it:
   _____

10. Type **k** in the top utility to send a kill signal to a process. When asked which process, type in the **PID** from the previous question. When asked which signal to send it, type **15** to send it a TERM signal. Did the TERM signal allow top to exit cleanly?

11. At the command prompt, type **clear** and press **Enter** to clear the screen.

12. Type **exit** and press **Enter** to log out of your shell.

Project 11-5

In this hands-on project, you will schedule processes by using the `at` and `crontab` utilities.

1. Switch to a command-line terminal (tty2) by pressing **Ctrl-Alt-F2** and log into the terminal using the username of **root** and the password of **secret**.

2. Schedule processes to run 1 minute in the future by typing the command **at now + 1 minute** at a command prompt and press **Enter**.

3. When the at> prompt appears, type the word **date** and press **Enter**.

4. When the second at> prompt appears, type the word **who** and press **Enter**.

5. When the third at> prompt appears, press the **Ctrl-d** key combination to finish the scheduling and observe the output. When will your job run? Where will the output of the **date** and **who** commands be sent?

6. In approximately one minute, check your mail by typing **mail** at the command line and pressing **Enter**. Look for the e-mail with the subject "Output from your job" and record the number: _____

7. At the & prompt, type the number that corresponds to the e-mail in the previous question, press **Enter**, and observe the output. When finished, type **q** at the & prompt and press **Enter** to exit the mail program.

8. At the command prompt, type **crontab –l** and press **Enter** to list your cron table. Do you have one?

9. At the command prompt, type **crontab –e** and press **Enter** to edit a new cron table for the root user. When the vi editor appears, add the line:

   30 20 * * 5 /bin/false

10. When finished typing, save and quit the vi editor and observe the output on the terminal screen.

11. At the command prompt, type **crontab –l** and press **Enter** to list your cron table. When will the **/bin/false** command run?

12. At the command prompt, type **cat /var/spool/cron/root** and press **Enter** to list your cron table from the **cron** directory. Is it the same as the output from the previous command?

13. At the command prompt, type **crontab –r** and press **Enter** to remove your cron table.

14. Type **exit** and press **Enter** to log out of your shell.

11

Project 11-6

In this hands-on project, you will view information that is exported by the Linux kernel to the /proc directory.

1. Switch to a command-line terminal (tty2) by pressing **Ctrl–Alt–F2** and log into the terminal using the username of **root** and the password of **secret**.

2. At the command prompt, type **cd /proc** and press **Enter** to change your current directory to **/proc**. Then, type **ls** to list the directory contents and examine the output on the terminal screen. Why are the subdirectories named using numbers?

3. At the command prompt, type **cat meminfo** and press **Enter** to list information about total and available memory. How does the value for total memory (MemTotal) compare to the information from Step 3 in Project 11-4?

4. At the command prompt, type **cat swaps** and press **Enter** to list information about total and available swap memory. How does the value for total swap memory (Size) compare to the information from Step 3 in Project 11-4?

5. At the command prompt, type **cd 1** and press **Enter** to enter the subdirectory that contains information about the **init** daemon (PID = 1).

6. At the command prompt, type **ls** and press **Enter** to list the files in the **/proc/1** directory. Next, type **cat status** and press **Enter**. What is the status of the **init** daemon? Does it list the correct PID and PPID?

7. Type **exit** and press **Enter** to log out of your shell.

DISCOVERY EXERCISES

1. Type the command **sleep 5** at a command prompt and press **Enter**. When did you receive your shell prompt back? Explain the events that occurred by referencing Figure 11-3. Next, type **exec sleep 5** at a command prompt and press **Enter**. What happened? Can you explain the results using Figure 11-3? Redraw Figure 11-3 to indicate what happens when a command is directly executed.

2. Using the man or info pages, research four more options to the **ps** command. What processes does each option display? What information is given about each process?

3. Log into the GNOME desktop and open a command-line terminal. At the shell prompt, type **xcalc** to execute the X Windows calculator. Does the terminal window stay open? Click on the terminal window to bring it to the foreground. Do you see your shell prompt? Why? Close your terminal window by clicking on the X symbol in the upper-right corner. What happened to the X Windows calculator? Why? Next, open another command-line terminal and type **xcalc&** at the command prompt to execute the X Windows calculator in the background. Click on the terminal window to bring it to the foreground. Do you see your shell prompt? Why? Close your terminal window by clicking on the X symbol in the upper-right corner. What happened to the X Windows calculator? Why?

4. There is a graphical version of the **top** utility called **gtop (GNOME top)**. Log into the GNOME desktop environment and open a BASH prompt. Next, type **gtop&** and view the utility. Does it display the same information as **top**? Does it allow you to kill processes and change process priorities?

5. You are the systems administrator for a large trust company. Most of the Linux servers in the company host databases that are accessed frequently by company employees. One particular Linux server has been reported as being very slow today. Upon further investigation using the **top** utility, you have found a rogue process that is wasting a great deal of system resources. Unfortunately, the rogue process is a database maintenance program and should be killed with caution. Which kill signal would you send this process and why? If the rogue process traps this signal, which other kill signals would you try? Which command could you use as a last resort to kill the rogue process?

6. Write the lines that you could use in your user cron table to schedule the **/bin/myscript** command to run:

   a) every Wednesday afternoon at 2:15PM

   b) every hour on the hour every day of the week

   c) every 15 minutes on the first of every month

   d) only on February 25th at 6:00PM

   e) on the first Monday of every month at 12:10PM

11

12

COMMON ADMINISTRATIVE TASKS

After completing this chapter, you will be able to:

♦ Set up, manage, and print to printers on a Linux system

♦ Understand the purpose of log files and how they are administered

♦ Create, modify, manage, and delete user and group accounts using command-line utilities and the Red Hat User Manager

In previous chapters, you learned how to administer filesystems, X Windows, and system startup and processes. In this chapter you examine other essential areas of Linux administration. First, you learn about the print process and how to administer and set up printers, followed by a discussion on managing log files using the system log daemon and the logrotate utility. Next, you examine the system databases that store user and group information, and the command-line utilities that may be used to create, modify, and delete user and group accounts on a Linux system. Finally, you learn about using the Red Hat User Manager to manage user and group accounts.

PRINTER ADMINISTRATION

Printing work files is commonly required by most users on a Linux system, and printing log files and system configuration information is good procedure in case of a system failure. Thus, a firm understanding of how to set up, manage, and print to printers is vital for those who set up and administer Linux servers.

The Print Process

Fundamental to printing on a Linux system is an understanding of the process by which information is sent to a printer. A set of information that is sent to a printer at the same time is called a **print job**. Print jobs may consist of a file, several files, or the output of a command. To send a print job to a printer, you must first use the **lpr command** and specify what to print.

Next, the **line printer daemon (lpd)** assigns the print job a unique **print job ID** and places a copy of the print job into a temporary directory on the filesystem called the **print queue**, provided the printer is **enabled**. If the printer is **disabled**, then the line printer daemon prints an error message stating that the printer is not accepting print jobs.

Accepting print jobs into a print queue is commonly called **spooling**.

The print queue for a printer is typically /var/spool/lpd/printername where *printername* is the name given to the printer. Since you may have several printers on a single Linux system, there is a separate print queue for each printer.

Once a print job is in the print queue, it is ready to be printed. If the printer is **started**, and ready to accept the print job, the line printer daemon then sends the print job from the print queue to the printer and removes the copy of the print job in the print queue. Conversely, if the printer is **stopped**, then the print job remains in the print queue.

Sending print jobs from a print queue to a printer is commonly called **printing**.

An example of this process for a printer called printer1 is illustrated in Figure 12-1.

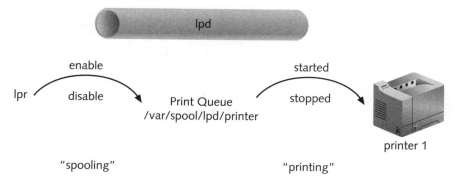

Figure 12-1   The print process

To see a list of all printers on the system and their status, you may use the **-a** (all) option to the **lpc command** followed by the argument **status**, as seen below:

```
[root@localhost root]# lpc -a status
Printer               Printing Spooling Jobs  Server Subserver Redirect Status/(Debug)
printer1@localhost  enabled  enabled    0    none
[root@localhost root]# _
```

The output above indicates that there is only one printer on the system, called *printer1*, and that there are no print jobs in its print queue. In addition, the line printer daemon is accepting jobs into the print queue for this printer since spooling is enabled, and the line printer daemon will send jobs from the print queue to the printer since printing is enabled.

You may manipulate the status of the printer using the **lpc** command by specifying the printer name after the **-P** (printer) option followed by the appropriate keyword listed in Table 12-1.

Table 12-1   Common keywords used in the lpc command

Option	Description
enable	Enables spooling (see Figure 12-1)
disable	Disables spooling (see Figure 12-1)
start	Enables printing (see Figure 12-1)
stop	Disables printing (see Figure 12-1)
up	Enables spooling and printing
down	Disables spooling and printing

Thus, to enable spooling and disable printing for the printer printer1, you could use the following commands:

```
[root@localhost root]# lpc -P printer1 enable
Printer: printer1@localhost
kill server PID 0 with User defined signal 1
printer1@localhost.localdomain: enabled
[root@localhost root]# lpc -P printer1 stop
Printer: printer1@localhost
kill server PID 0 with User defined signal 1
printer1@localhost.localdomain: stopped
[root@localhost root]# _
```

Any print jobs now sent to printer1 will be sent to the print queue, but will remain in the print queue until the printer is started again.

Managing Print Jobs

Recall that you create a print job by using the `lpr` command. To print a copy of the `/etc/inittab` file to the printer *printer1* seen in earlier examples, you may use the following command:

```
[root@localhost root]# lpr -P printer1 /etc/inittab
[root@localhost root]# _
```

As with the `lpc` command, the `lpr` command uses the `-P` option to specify the printer name. If this option is omitted, the `lpr` command will assume the default printer on the system. Since *printer1* is the only printer on the system and hence the default printer, the command `lpr /etc/innitab` is equivalent to the one used in the output above.

Each user on a Linux system may specify their own default printer by using the PRINTER variable. To specify *printer2* as the default printer, you may add the following line to an environment in your home directory such as `.bash_profile`:

```
export PRINTER=printer2
```

Some common options to the `lpr` command are listed in Table 12-2.

Table 12-2 Common options to the lpr command

Option	Description
-r	Removes the file after printing
-h	Prints without a banner page
-#n	Prints n copies of the file
-m user	Mails confirmation of print job completion to the user
-P printer	Prints to the specified printer

You may also specify several files to be printed using a single lpr command by specifying the files as arguments. In this case, only one print job is created to print all of the files. To print the files /etc/hosts and /etc/issue to the printer *printer1*, you could execute the following command:

```
[root@localhost root]# lpr -P printer1 /etc/hosts /etc/issue
[root@localhost root]# _
```

The lpr command accepts information from Standard Input; thus, you may place the lpr command at the end of a pipe to print information. To print a list of logged-in users, you could use the following pipe:

```
[root@localhost root]# who | lpr -P printer1
[root@localhost root]# _
```

Sometimes, you may need to print a file that is of a different format than plain text. The most common of these formats is called **Postscript**. To print a Postscript file, you may specify the file and printer to use with the **enscript command**, as seen below:

```
[root@localhost root]# enscript samplefile.ps -P printer1
[ 1 pages * 1 copy ] sent to p1
[root@localhost root]# _
```

You may also use the **a2ps command** to send Postscript formatted files to a printer; the command a2ps samplefile.ps -P printer1 is equivalent to the one used in the previous output.

To see a list of print jobs in the queue for a printer, you may use the **lpq command** followed by the -P option and printer name, as seen below:

```
[root@localhost root]# lpq -P printer1
Printer: printer1@localhost (printing disabled)
 Queue: 3 printable jobs
 Server: no server active
 Rank    Owner/ID            Class Job Files              Size Time
1        root@localhost+823    A   823 /etc/inittab       1756 23:01:43
2        root@localhost+825    A   825 /etc/hosts,/etc/issue 202 23:01:49
3        root@localhost+832    A   832 (STDIN)              77 23:02:22
[root@localhost root]# _
```

If the -P option is omitted, the lpq command lists the contents of all print queues on the system.

From above, we see that printing is disabled; thus any print jobs in the print queue will not be sent to the printer. The print job ID for the /etc/inittab print job created

12

earlier is 823, whereas the print job ID for the `/etc/hosts,/etc/issue` print job created earlier is 825. The listing of logged-in users is represented by STDIN and has a print job ID of 832.

Other options that may be used with the `lpq` command are listed in Table 12-3.

Table 12-3   Common options to the lpq command

Option	Description
-a	Displays the contents of the print queues for all printers on the system; it is equivalent to the -P all option
-l	Displays a long list of information about each print job in the print queue
-L	Displays a very long list of information about each print job in the print queue
-P *printername*	Displays the contents of the print queue for the printer printername
-s	Displays a summary of all printers configured on the system and the number of jobs waiting in their print queues

To remove a print job that is in the print queue, you may use the **lprm command** and specify the printer and print job ID of the job to remove. To remove the print job IDs 823 and 825 created earlier, you may use the following command:

```
[root@localhost root]# lprm 823 825
Printer printer1@localhost:
  checking perms 'root@localhost+823'
  dequeued 'root@localhost+823'
  checking perms 'root@localhost+825'
  dequeued 'root@localhost+825'
[root@localhost root]# _
```

You may instead remove all jobs started by a certain user; simply specify the username instead of the print job IDs in the `lprm` command.

To remove all jobs in a print queue, you may use keyword `all`, as seen in the following output, when deleting all print jobs in the print queue for *printer1*:

```
[root@localhost root]# lprm -P printer1 all
Printer printer1@localhost:
  checking perms 'root@localhost+832'
  dequeued 'root@localhost+832'
[root@localhost root]# _
```

To remove all print jobs in all print queues, you may use the command `lprm -a all`.

Configuring Printers

Recall that the core component of printing is the line printer daemon (lpd), which accepts print jobs into a queue and sends them to the printer. The configuration file for lpd is **/etc/printcap**; it contains the configuration information for each printer installed on the system. The easiest way to edit the information in /etc/printcap is to use the **Red Hat Printer Configuration Tool** as seen in Figure 12-2.

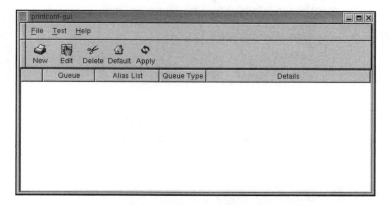

Figure 12-2   The Red Hat Printer Configuration Tool

To start the Red Hat Printer Configuration Tool from within the GNOME desktop environment, simply navigate to the Taskbar, GNOME button, Programs, System, Printer Configuration. To start the Red Hat Printer Configuration Tool from within the KDE desktop environment, simply navigate to the Taskbar, KDE button, System, Printer Configuration.

Alternatively, you may open a command-line terminal from within any graphical environment and type the command **printconf-gui** at the BASH shell prompt.

The Red Hat Printer Configuration Tool depicted in Figure 12-2 indicates that there are no configured printers on the system. To add a printer, you may click the New button and receive the screen shown in Figure 12-3.

Since the print process involves sending jobs to a print queue before sending them to a printer, the Red Hat Printer Configuration Tool is used to configure the queue instead of the printer; the printer name is often referred to as the queue name for the same reason. Once you click the Next button from Figure 12-3, you are prompted for the printer name and type, as seen in Figure 12-4.

12

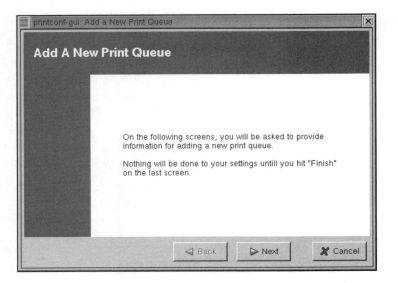

Figure 12-3   Creating a new printer

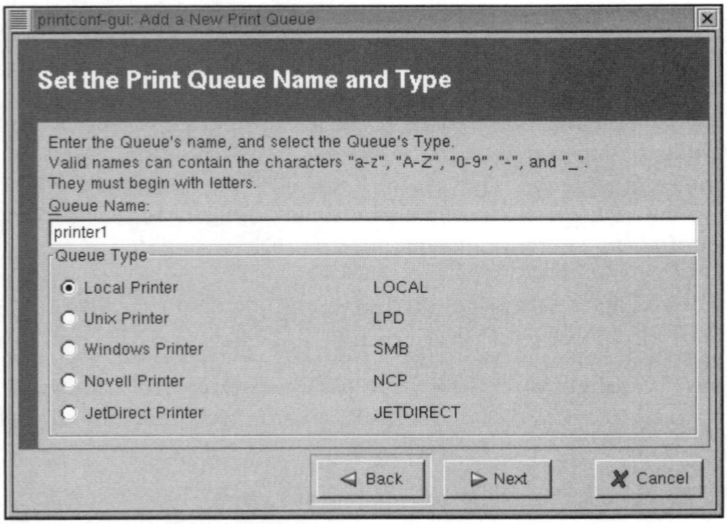

Figure 12-4   Specifying the name and type of a printer

There are several different printer types that may be configured in the screen shown in Figure 12-4. You would choose Local Printer if the printer is attached to the local computer via a serial, parallel, or USB cable. If the printer is attached to a remote UNIX or Linux server across the network running the line printer daemon, then you would select Unix Printer.

Alternatively, you may print to a printer that is connected to a Windows computer and shared to network users via the Server Message Block (SMB) protocol. In this case, you would choose Windows Printer from the list of options. Likewise, you would choose Novell Printer if the printer resides on a Novell Netware server and is made available across the network via Netware Core Protocol (NCP). Many printers used today are attached directly to the network, and do not require a network server to be present. Hewlett Packard JetDirect printers are the most common of these. To configure a JetDirect printer, simply select JetDirect Printer.

Once the type of printer is chosen, you are prompted for specific information about the printer. For a local printer, you are prompted to specify the port that connects to the printer. For a local printer connecting via the first LPT port, you would specify `/dev/lp0` as seen in Figure 12-5.

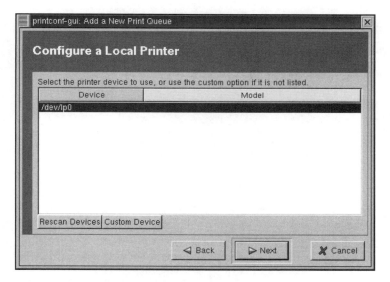

Figure 12-5   Configuring a local printer

However, if the printer is attached to a remote UNIX or Linux computer, then you must specify the remote computer name or IP address, as well as the name of the printer on the remote computer, as seen in Figure 12-6.

Similarly, if the printer is attached to a remote Windows server, then you must supply the IP address of the remote server, the Windows workgroup name, the name of the shared printer, and the **user account** and password to use when printing to it. A sample Windows printer configuration is shown in Figure 12-7.

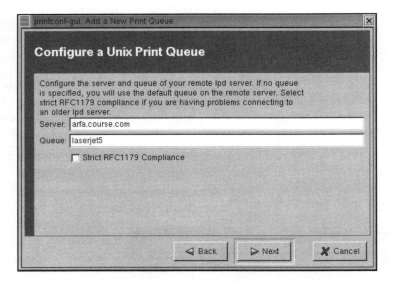

Figure 12-6   Configuring a UNIX printer

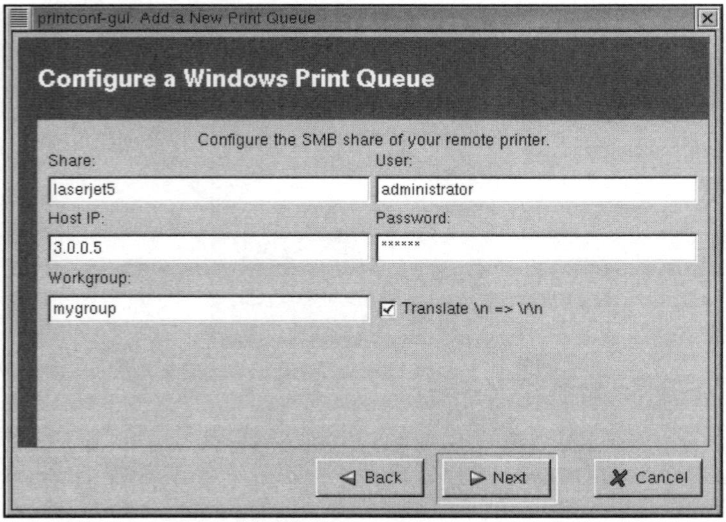

Figure 12-7   Configuring a Windows printer

Like a Windows printer, a Novell printer requires a user account and password to be configured, along with the server name and queue name, as shown in Figure 12-8. A JetDirect printer requires only the IP address and port of the printer, as depicted in Figure 12-9.

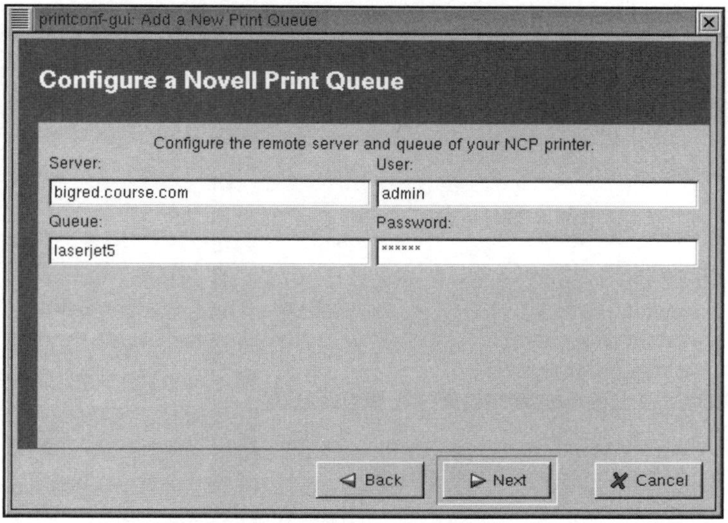

Figure 12-8   Configuring a Novell printer

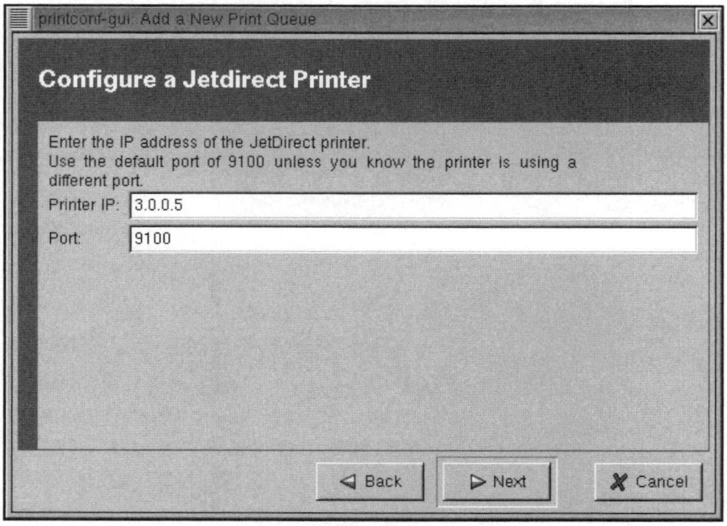

Figure 12-9   Configuring a JetDirect printer

Once the printer type has been configured, the Red Hat Printer Configuration Tool prompts for the printer driver (sometimes referred to as a print filter). Say, for example, that you are configuring a local Canon BJ10e printer that prints to `/dev/lp0`; you would select the appropriate entry from the list shown in Figure 12-10 and confirm the creation of the printer, as seen in Figure 12-11.

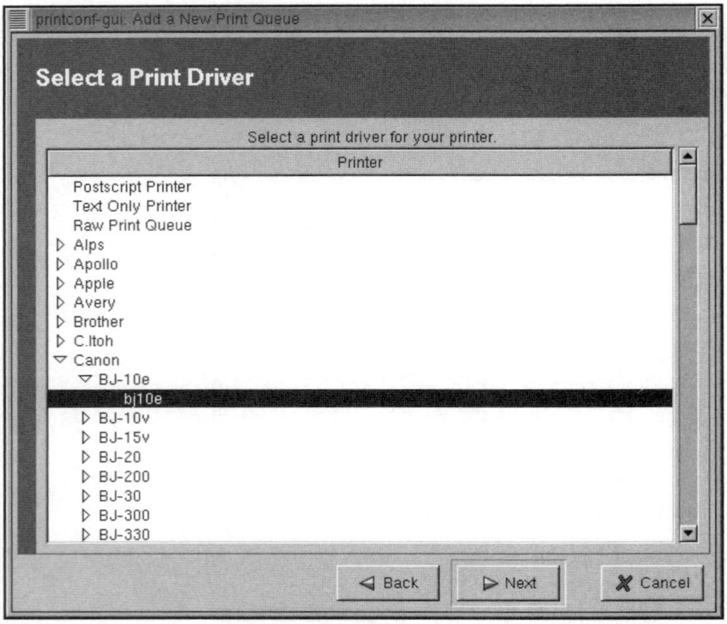

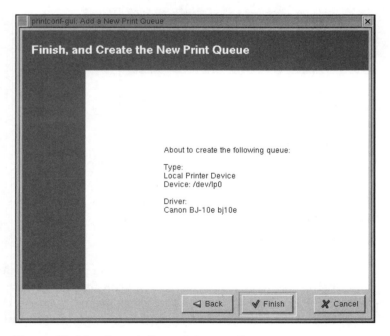

Figure 12-10   Selecting a printer driver

Figure 12-11   Completing printer creation

After a printer has been added, a line for that printer will appear in the Red Hat Printer Configuration Tool, as shown in Figure 12-12.

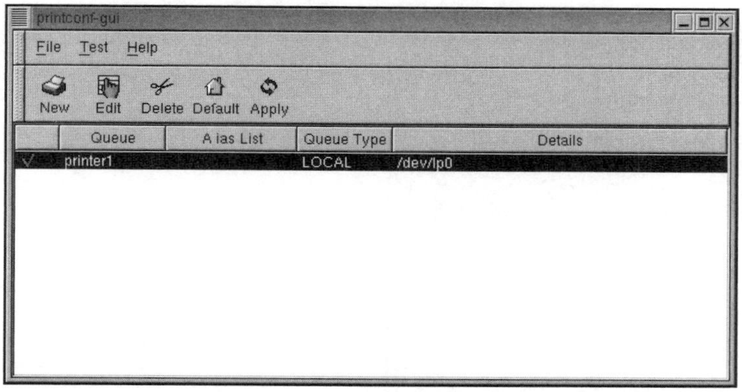

Figure 12-12   Viewing printer in the Red Hat Printer Configuration Tool

The checkmark beside the printer name indicates that it is the default printer. When multiple printers are configured, you may select a printer and click the Default button to make it the default printer for all users.

Additionally, you may choose to edit the properties of a printer after creation by clicking the Edit button, as depicted in Figure 12-13.

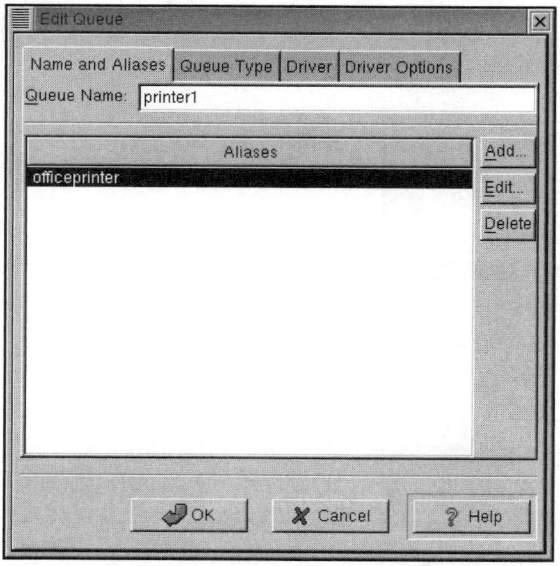

Figure 12-13   Creating a printer alias

12

This allows you to specify alternate names for a printer, known as **printer aliases**. You may also edit the printer details, driver, and additional options, as shown in Figures 12-14, 12-15, and 12-16, respectively.

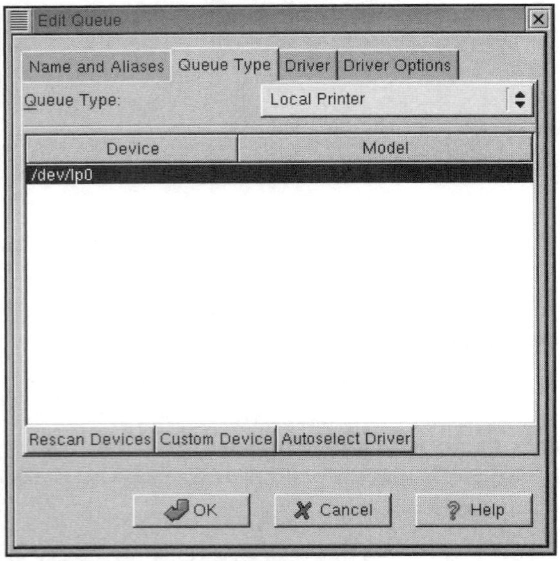

Figure 12-14   Editing the device used for a local printer

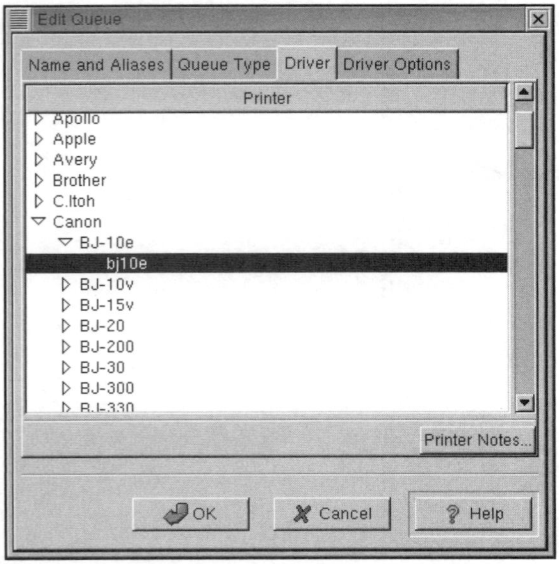

Figure 12-15   Editing the print driver

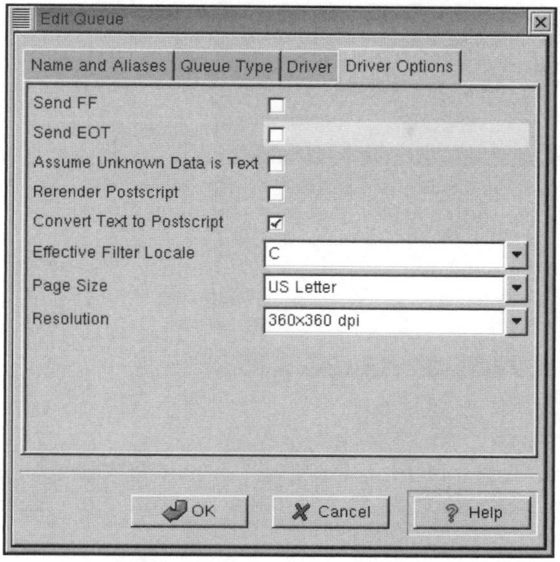

Figure 12-16   Editing printer options

Once a printer has been added or modified, you must save your changes to
`/etc/printcap` and restart the line printer daemon to allow the changes to take effect.
You may do this by using the Apply button shown in Figure 12-12 or by selecting each
action from the File menu, as depicted in Figure 12-17.

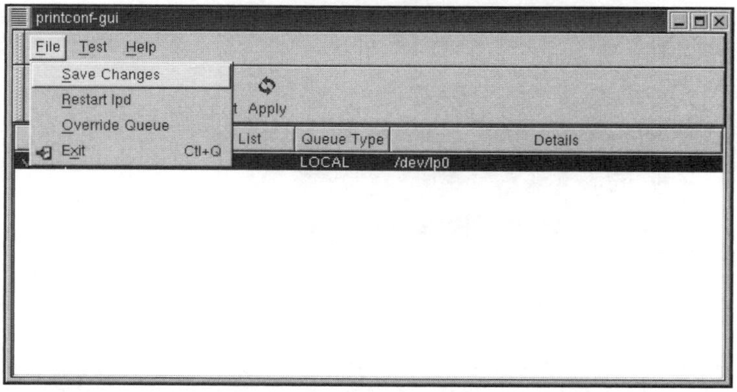

12

Figure 12-17   Saving changes and restarting lpd

To test a newly installed printer, you may simply print a file of your choice or select a
sample file to print from the Test menu, as shown in Figure 12-18.

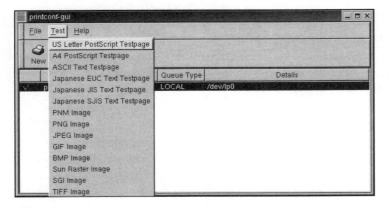

Figure 12-18   Printing a test page

Alternatively, you may run the Red Hat Printer Configuration Tool from a command-line terminal by typing `printconf-tui` at the BASH shell prompt. An example of this interface is shown in Figure 12-19.

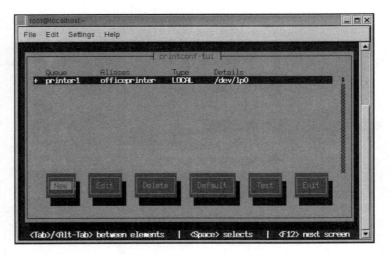

Figure 12-19   The Red Hat Printer Configuration Tool (terminal interface)

Although the Red Hat Printer Configuration Tool is the easiest method for creating printers, you may also add printers by editing the **/etc/printcap.local** file. This file is initially left empty; any entries added to it are incorporated into the `/etc/printcap` file alongside any other printer entries when the line printer daemon is started. The format of the `/etc/printcap` file is rigid; any errors in this file will prevent the line printer daemon from functioning. Thus, when adding entries to the `/etc/printcap.local` file, ensure that there are no typographical errors. An example of the `/etc/printcap` file is seen below:

```
[root@localhost root]# cat /etc/printcap
# /etc/printcap
#
# DO NOT EDIT! MANUAL CHANGES WILL BE LOST!
# This file is autogenerated by printconf-backend during lpd init.
#
# Hand edited changes can be put in /etc/printcap.local, and will be
# included.

printer1|officeprinter:\
        :sh:\
        :mx=0:\
        :sd=/var/spool/lpd/printer1:\
        :af=/var/spool/lpd/printer1/printer1.acct:\
        :lp=/dev/lp0:\
        :if=/usr/share/printconf/util/mf_wrapper:

######################################################################
#Everything below here is included verbatim from /etc/printcap.local#
######################################################################
# printcap.local
#
# This file is included by printconf's generated printcap,
# and can be used to specify custom hand edited printers.

[root@localhost root]# _
```

The output above indicates that there is only one printer on the system, called printer1 and that it has an alias called officeprinter and prints to `/dev/lp0`.

There is a paragraph in the `/etc/printcap` file for each printer installed on the system; each line ends with a \ character except for the last line in each paragraph. Each line in the paragraph contains a tag indicating a certain type of information about the printer itself. There are many different tags that may be used in the `/etc/printcap` file; a description of each of them may be obtained from the man page or info page for the `printcap` file. A list of common tags found in `/etc/printcap` is seen in Table 12-4.

12

Table 12-4   Common keywords used in the /etc/printcap file

Option	Description
af	Specifies the accounting file that contains a history of print jobs
if	Specifies the file used to filter information through before sending it to the printer
lp	Specifies the device file used for a local printer
mx	Maximum allowable size of print jobs in kilobytes; a value of zero indicates unlimited
rm	Specifies the name or IP address of a remote printer
rp	Specifies the name of a remote printer
sd	Specifies the spool directory (print queue)
sh	Prevents a header page from being printed before each print job

Once entries are added to the `/etc/printcap.local` file, the `printconf-backend` command must be run to incorporate the changes into the `/etc/printcap` file and the line printer daemon must be restarted to activate the new configuration. The easiest method to restart the line printer daemon is to send it a SIGHUP signal, as seen in the following example:

```
[root@localhost root]# ps -ef | grep lpd
lp          1626      1   0 10:07 ?        00:00:00 lpd Waiting
root        2415   2189   0 11:47 pts/1    00:00:00 grep lpd
[root@localhost root]# kill -1 1626
[root@localhost root]# _
```

LOG FILE ADMINISTRATION

To identify and troubleshoot problems on a Linux system, you must view the events that occur over time. Since administrators cannot observe all events that take place on a Linux system, most daemons record information and error messages to files stored on the filesystem. These files are referred to as **log files** and are typically stored in the **/var/log** directory or a subdirectory within it. For example, the `/var/log/samba` directory contains the log files created by the samba file sharing daemons. Some common log files found in the `/var/log` directory and their descriptions are found in Table 12-5.

Table 12-5   Common Linux log files found in /var/log

Log File	Description
boot.log	Contains information regarding daemon startup obtained during system initialization
cron	Contains information and error messages generated by the cron and at daemons
dmesg	Contains detected hardware information obtained during system startup

Table 12-5   Common Linux log files found in /var/log (continued)

Log File	Description
maillog	Contains information and error messages generated by the sendmail daemon
secure	Contains information and error messages regarding network access generated by the sshd and xinetd daemons
wtmp	Contains a history of all login sessions
rpmpkgs	Contains a list of packages installed by the Red Hat Package Manager and related error messages
xferlog	Contains information and error messages generated by the FTP daemon
XFree86	Contains information and error messages generated by X Windows
lastlog	Contains a list of users and their last login time; must be viewed using the lastlog command
messages	Contains information regarding daemon startup obtained at system initialization as well as important system messages produced after system initialization
uucp	Contains information and error messages generated by the uucp (UNIX to UNIX copy) daemon; these messages typically involve modem communication

The System Log Daemon

The logging of most events is handled centrally in Linux via the **system log daemon (syslogd)**. When this daemon is loaded upon system startup, it creates a socket (`/dev/log`) for other system processes to write to. It then reads any information written to this socket and saves the information in the appropriate log file according to entries in the `/etc/syslog.conf` file. A sample `/etc/syslog.conf` file is seen in the following output:

```
[root@localhost root]# cat /etc/syslog.conf
# Log all kernel messages to the console.
# Logging much else clutters up the screen.
#kern.*                                      /dev/console

# Log anything (except mail) of level info or higher.
# Don't log private authentication messages!
*.info;mail.none;authpriv.none;cron.none    /var/log/messages

# The authpriv file has restricted access.
authpriv.*                                   /var/log/secure

# Log all the mail messages in one place.
mail.*                                       /var/log/maillog
```

12

```
# Log cron stuff
cron.*                                    /var/log/cron

# Everybody gets emergency messages
*.emerg                                   *

# Save news errors of level crit and higher in a special file.
uucp,news.crit                            /var/log/spooler

# Save boot messages also to boot.log
local7.*                                  /var/log/boot.log

#
# INN
#
news.=crit                                /var/log/news/news.crit
news.=err                                 /var/log/news/news.err
news.notice                               /var/log/news/news.notice
[root@localhost root]# _
```

Any line that starts with a # character is a comment in the /etc/syslog.conf file. All other entries have the following format:

```
facility.priority     /var/log/logfile
```

The **facility** is the area of the system to listen to, whereas the **priority** refers to the importance of the information. For example, a facility of kern and priority of warning indicates that the system log daemon should listen for kernel messages of priority warning and more serious. When found, the system log daemon will place these messages in the /var/log/logfile file. The aforementioned entry would read:

```
kern.warning     /var/log/logfile
```

To log only warning messages from the kernel to /var/log/logfile, you may use the following entry instead:

```
kern.=warning     /var/log/logfile
```

Alternatively, you may log all error messages from the kernel to /var/log/logfile by using the * wildcard, as seen in the following entry:

```
kern.*     /var/log/logfile
```

In addition, you may specify multiple facilities and priorities; to log all error messages except warnings from the kernel to /var/log/logfile you could use the following entry:

```
kern.*;kern.!=warn     /var/log/logfile
```

To log all error messages from the kernel and news daemons, you could use the following entry:

```
kern,news.*        /var/log/logfile
```

To log all warnings from all facilities except for the kernel, you could use the "none" keyword as seen in following entry:

```
*.=warn;kern.none    /var/log/logfile
```

The different facilities available and their descriptions are listed in Table 12-6.

Table 12-6 Facilities used by the system log daemon

Facility	Description
auth or **security**	Specifies messages from the login system such as the login program, the getty program, and the su command
authpriv	Specifies messages from the login system when authenticating users across the network or to system databases
cron	Specifies messages from the cron and at daemons
daemon	Specifies messages from system daemons such as the FTP daemon
kern	Specifies messages from the Linux kernel
lpr	Specifies messages from the printing system (lpd)
mail	Specifies messages from the e-mail system (sendmail)
mark	Used internally only; specifies timestamps used by syslogd
news	Specifies messages from the Inter Network News daemon and other USENET daemons
syslog	Specifies messages from syslogd
user	Specifies messages from user processes
uucp	Specifies messages from the uucp (UNIX to UNIX copy) daemon
local0-7	Specifies local messages; these are not used by default but may be defined for custom use

12

The different priorities available are listed in ascending order in Table 12-7.

Table 12-7   Priorities used by the system log daemon

Priority	Description
debug	Indicates all information from a certain facility
info	Indicates normal information messages as a result of system operations
notice	Indicates information that should be noted for future reference, yet does not indicate a problem
warning or warn	Indicates messages that may be the result of an error but are not critical to system operations
error or err	Indicates all other error messages not described by other priorities
crit	Indicates critical system errors such as hard disk failure
alert	Indicates an error that should be rectified immediately, such as a corrupt system database
emerg or panic	Indicates very serious system conditions that would normally be broadcast to all users

Managing Log Files

Although log files may contain important system information, they may take up unnecessary space on the filesystem over time. Thus, it is important to clear the contents of log files from time to time.

Do not remove log files, as the permissions and ownership will be removed as well.

Before clearing log files, it is good form to print them and store them in a safe place for future reference. To clear a log file, recall that you may use a > redirection symbol. The commands below display the size of the /var/log/messages logfile before and after it has been printed and cleared:

```
[root@localhost root]# ls -l /var/log/messages
-rw--------   1 root     root    21705 Jul 14 10:52 /var/log/messages
[root@localhost root]# lpr -P printer1 /var/log/messages
[root@localhost root]# >/var/log/messages
[root@localhost root]# ls -l /var/log/messages
-rw--------   1 root     root        0 Jul 14 10:52 /var/log/messages
[root@localhost root]# _
```

You may also schedule commands to print and clear log files on a repetitive basis using the cron daemon.

Alternatively, you may schedule the logrotate utility to back up and clear log files from entries stored in the **/etc/logrotate.conf** file and files stored in the /etc/logrotate.d directory. The **logrotate command** typically renames log files on a cyclic basis; a log file called `test.log` will be renamed `test.log.1` on the first cycle and a new `test.log` will be created to accept system information. On the second cycle, `test.log.1` will be renamed `test.log.2`, `test.log` will be renamed `test.log.1`, and a new `test.log` file will be created to accept system information.

You may specify the number of logfiles that logrotate will keep. If logrotate is configured to keep only two copies of old log files, such as the files `test.log.1` and `test.log.2`, then `test.log.2` will be removed on the next cycle.

An example of the /etc/logrotate.conf file is seen in the following output:

```
[root@localhost root]# cat /etc/logrotate.conf
# see "man logrotate" for details
# rotate log files weekly
weekly

# keep 4 weeks worth of backlogs
rotate 4

# create new (empty) log files after rotating old ones
create

# uncomment this if you want your log files compressed
#compress

# RPM packages drop log rotation information into this directory
include /etc/logrotate.d

# no packages own lastlog or wtmp — we'll rotate them here
/var/log/wtmp {
    monthly
    create 0664 root utmp
    rotate 1
}

# system-specific logs may be also be configured here.
[root@localhost root]# _
```

In the output above, any # characters indicate a comment and are ignored. The other lines indicate that log files contained in this file and all other files in the /etc/logrotate.d directory (`include /etc/logrotate.d`) are rotated on a weekly basis unless otherwise specified. In addition, four copies of old log files will be kept (`rotate 4`). For the file /var/log/wtmp, this rotation will occur monthly instead of weekly, only one old log file will be kept, and the new log file created will have the permissions "0664" (rw-rw-r--), the owner "root," and the group "utmp."

The /etc/logrotate.conf file specifies the default parameters used by the **logrotate** command; however, most rotation information regarding log files is stored in the /etc/logrotate.d directory. Take the file /etc/logrotate.d/psacct as an example:

```
[root@localhost root]# cat /etc/logrotate.d/psacct
# Logrotate file for psacct RPM

/var/log/pacct {
prerotate
        /usr/sbin/accton
endscript
        compress
        notifempty
        daily
        rotate 31
postrotate
        /usr/sbin/accton  /var/log/pacct
endscript
}

[root@localhost root]# _
```

The file seen above indicates that the /var/log/pacct file should be rotated daily, and that log files will only be rotated if they are not empty. Log files will be compressed once rotated, and up to 31 copies of old log files may exist. In addition, the /usr/sbin/accton program will be run before each rotation and the /usr/sbin/accton /var/log/pacct programs will be run after each rotation.

On Red Hat Linux systems, the logrotate utility is automatically scheduled to run daily via the file /etc/cron.daily/logrotate; however, you may choose to run it manually by typing the command **logrotate /etc/logrotate.conf** at a command prompt.

Over time, the **logrotate** command will generate several copies of each log file, as seen in the following listing of the /var/log directory:

```
[root@localhost root]# ls /var/log
boot.log        ksyms.4       pacct          pacct.3.gz    spooler.1
boot.log.1      ksyms.5       pacct.10.gz    pacct.4.gz    spooler.2
boot.log.2      ksyms.6       pacct.11.gz    pacct.5.gz    spooler.3
boot.log.3      lastlog       pacct.12.gz    pacct.6.gz    spooler.4
boot.log.4      maillog       pacct.13.gz    pacct.7.gz    squid
cron            maillog.1     pacct.14.gz    pacct.8.gz    usracct
```

```
cron.1          maillog.2       pacct.15.gz     pacct.9.gz      uucp
cron.2          maillog.3       pacct.16.gz     pgsql           vbox
cron.3          maillog.4       pacct.17.gz     rpmpkgs         wtmp
cron.4          messages        pacct.18.gz     rpmpkgs.1       wtmp.1
dmesg           messages.1      pacct.19.gz     rpmpkgs.2       xferlog
fax             messages.2      pacct.1.gz      rpmpkgs.3       xferlog.1
gdm             messages.3      pacct.20.gz     rpmpkgs.4       xferlog.2
htmlaccess.log  messages.4      pacct.21.gz     sa              xferlog.3
httpd           mysqld.log      pacct.22.gz     samba           xferlog.4
iptraf          mysqld.log.1    pacct.23.gz     savacct         XFree86.0.log
iscsi.log       mysqld.log.2    pacct.24.gz     secure          XFree86.9.log
junkbuster      mysqld.log.3    pacct.25.gz     secure.1        zebra
ksyms.0         mysqld.log.4    pacct.26.gz     secure.2
ksyms.1         netconf.log     pacct.27.gz     secure.3
ksyms.2         netconf.log.1   pacct.28.gz     secure.4
ksyms.3         news            pacct.2.gz      spooler
[root@localhost root]# _
```

Given the `boot.log*` files in the above output, the most recent events will be recorded in the `boot.log` file, followed by the `boot.log.1` file, followed by the `boot.log.2` file, and so on.

ADMINISTERING USERS AND GROUPS

You must log in to a Linux system with a valid username and password before a BASH shell is granted. This process is called **authentication**, since the username and password are authenticated against a system database that contains all user account information. Authenticated users are then granted access to files, directories, and other resources on the system based on their user account.

The system database that contains user account information typically consists of two files: **/etc/passwd** and **/etc/shadow**. Every user typically has a line that describes the user account in **/etc/passwd** and a line that contains the encrypted password and expiration information in **/etc/shadow**.

Older Linux systems stored the encrypted password in the **/etc/passwd** file and did not use an **/etc/shadow** file at all. This is considered poor security today since processes often require access to the user information in **/etc/passwd**. Storing the encrypted password in a separate file that cannot be accessed by processes prevents a process from obtaining all user account information. Recall that you are prompted whether to use "Shadow passwords" during installation; if this item is not selected, then only the **/etc/passwd** file will exist after installation. To convert the system so that it will use an **/etc/shadow** file to store the encrypted password after installation, you may run the **pwconv command**. Alternatively, the **pwunconv command** may be used to revert back to using an **/etc/passwd** file only.

12

Each line of the `/etc/passwd` file has the following colon-delimited format:

```
name:password:UID:GID:GECOS:homedirectory:shell
```

The name in the output above refers to the name of the user. If an `/etc/shadow` file is not used, then the password field contains the encrypted password for the user; otherwise, it just contains an x character as a placeholder for the password stored in `/etc/shadow`.

The **User Identifier (UID)** specifies the unique User ID that is assigned to each user. Typically, UIDs from 1 to 100 refer to user accounts that are used by daemons when logging into the system. The root user always has a UID of zero.

The **Group Identifier (GID)** is the primary Group ID for the user. Each user may a member of several groups, but only one of those groups may be the **primary group**. The primary group of a user is the group that is made the group owner of any file or directory that the user creates. Similarly, when a user creates a file or directory, that user becomes the owner of that file or directory.

GECOS represents a text description of the user and is typically left blank; this information was originally used in the **General Electric Comprehensive Operating System (GECOS)**. The last two fields represent the absolute pathname to the user's home directory and the shell, respectively.

An example of an `/etc/passwd` file is seen below:

```
[root@localhost root]# cat /etc/passwd
root:x:0:0:root:/root:/bin/bash
bin:x:1:1:bin:/bin:/sbin/nologin
daemon:x:2:2:daemon:/sbin:/sbin/nologin
adm:x:3:4:adm:/var/adm:/sbin/nologin
lp:x:4:7:lp:/var/spool/lpd:/sbin/nologin
sync:x:5:0:sync:/sbin:/bin/sync
shutdown:x:6:0:shutdown:/sbin:/sbin/shutdown
halt:x:7:0:halt:/sbin:/sbin/halt
mail:x:8:12:mail:/var/spool/mail:/sbin/nologin
news:x:9:13:news:/var/spool/news:
uucp:x:10:14:uucp:/var/spool/uucp:/sbin/nologin
operator:x:11:0:operator:/root:/sbin/nologin
games:x:12:100:games:/usr/games:/sbin/nologin
gopher:x:13:30:gopher:/var/gopher:/sbin/nologin
ftp:x:14:50:FTP User:/var/ftp:/sbin/nologin
nobody:x:99:99:Nobody:/:/sbin/nologin
mailnull:x:47:47::/var/spool/mqueue:/dev/null
rpm:x:37:37::/var/lib/rpm:/bin/bash
xfs:x:43:43:X Font Server:/etc/X11/fs:/bin/false
ntp:x:38:38::/etc/ntp:/sbin/nologin
```

```
rpc:x:32:32:Portmapper RPC user:/:/bin/false
gdm:x:42:42::/var/gdm:/sbin/nologin
rpcuser:x:29:29:RPC Service User:/var/lib/nfs:/sbin/nologin
nfsnobody:x:65534:65534:Anonymous NFS User:/var/lib/nfs:/sbin/nologin
nscd:x:28:28:NSCD Daemon:/:/bin/false
ident:x:98:98:pident user:/:/sbin/nologin
radvd:x:75:75:radvd user:/:/bin/false
postgres:x:26:26:PostgreSQL Server:/var/lib/pgsql:/bin/bash
apache:x:48:48:Apache:/var/www:/bin/false
squid:x:23:23::/var/spool/squid:/dev/null
named:x:25:25:Named:/var/named:/bin/false
pcap:x:77:77::/var/arpwatch:/bin/nologin
amanda:x:33:6:Amanda user:/var/lib/amanda:/bin/bash
junkbust:x:73:73::/etc/junkbuster:/bin/bash
mailman:x:41:41:GNU Mailing List Manager:/var/mailman:/bin/false
mysql:x:27:27:MySQL Server:/var/lib/mysql:/bin/bash
ldap:x:55:55:LDAP User:/var/lib/ldap:/bin/false
pvm:x:24:24::/usr/share/pvm3:/bin/bash
user1:x:500:500:sample user one:/home/user1:/bin/bash
[root@localhost root]# _
```

The root user is usually listed at the top of the `/etc/passwd` file as seen above, followed by user accounts used by daemons when logging into the system, followed by regular user accounts. The last line of the output above indicates that the user "user1" has a UID of 500, a primary GID of 500, a GECOS of "sample user one," and the home directory `/home/user1`, and uses the BASH shell.

Like `/etc/passwd`, the `/etc/shadow` file is colon-delimited, yet has the following format:

> `name:password:lastchange:min:max:warn:disable1:disable2:`

Although the first two fields in the `/etc/shadow` file are the same as those `/etc/passwd`, the contents of the password field will be different; the password field in the `/etc/shadow` file will contain the encrypted password, instead of the x character used in `/etc/passwd`.

The lastchange field represents the date of the most recent password change; it is measured in the number of days since January 1st, 1970. For example, the number 10957 represents January 1st, 2000 since January 1st, 2000 is 10957 days after January 1st, 1970.

 Traditionally, a calendar date was represented by a number indicating the number of days since January 1st, 1970. Today, many calendar dates found in configuration files follow the same convention.

To prevent unauthorized access to a Linux system, it is good form to change passwords for user accounts regularly; thus passwords may be set to expire at certain intervals. The next three fields of the /etc/shadow file indicate information about password expiration; min represents the number of days you must wait before you change your password after receiving a new one, max represents the number of days you may use the same password without changing it, and warn represents the number of days before a password expires that you are warned to change your password.

By default on Red Hat Linux systems, min is equal to zero days, max is equal to 99999 days and warn is equal to seven days. Thus, you may change your password immediately after receiving a new one, your password expires in 99999 days, and you are warned seven days in advance before your password needs to be changed.

When a password has expired, you are still allowed to log into the system for a certain period of time, after which you are disabled from logging in. The number of days after a password expires that a user account is disabled is represented by the disable1 field in /etc/shadow. In addition, you may choose to disable a user from logging in at a certain date, such as the end of an employment contract. The disable2 field in /etc/shadow represents the number of days since January 1st, 1970 that a user account will be disabled.

An example /etc/shadow file is seen below:

```
[root@localhost root]# cat /etc/shadow
root:$1$_r2VJ_UW$Cx.7teI4iU8jZx4JAeMD2.:11884:0:99999:7:::
bin:*:11884:0:99999:7:::
daemon:*:11884:0:99999:7:::
adm:*:11884:0:99999:7:::
lp:*:11884:0:99999:7:::
sync:*:11884:0:99999:7:::
shutdown:*:11884:0:99999:7:::
halt:*:11884:0:99999:7:::
mail:*:11884:0:99999:7:::
news:*:11884:0:99999:7:::
uucp:*:11884:0:99999:7:::
operator:*:11884:0:99999:7:::
games:*:11884:0:99999:7:::
gopher:*:11884:0:99999:7:::
ftp:*:11884:0:99999:7:::
nobody:*:11884:0:99999:7:::
mailnull:!!:11884:0:99999:7:::
rpm:!!:11884:0:99999:7:::
xfs:!!:11884:0:99999:7:::
ntp:!!:11884:0:99999:7:::
rpc:!!:11884:0:99999:7:::
gdm:!!:11884:0:99999:7:::
rpcuser:!!:11884:0:99999:7:::
nfsnobody:!!:11884:0:99999:7:::
```

```
nscd:!!:11884:0:99999:7:::
ident:!!:11884:0:99999:7:::
radvd:!!:11884:0:99999:7:::
postgres:!!:11884:0:99999:7:::
apache:!!:11884:0:99999:7:::
squid:!!:11884:0:99999:7:::
named:!!:11884:0:99999:7:::
pcap:!!:11884:0:99999:7:::
amanda:!!:11884:0:99999:7:::
junkbust:!!:11884:0:99999:7:::
mailman:!!:11884:0:99999:7:::
mysql:!!:11884:0:99999:7:::
ldap:!!:11884:0:99999:7:::
pvm:!!:11884:0:99999:7:::
user1:$1$abHHvXWX$5w0Z75u7CwqvC4u/eVbyW0:11885:0:99999:7:::
[root@localhost root]# _
```

Note from the above output that most user accounts used by daemons do not receive an encrypted password.

Although every user must have a primary group listed in the `/etc/passwd` file, each user may be a member of multiple groups. All groups and their members are listed in the `/etc/group` file. The `/etc/group` file has the following colon-delimited fields:

```
name:password:GID:members
```

The first field is the name of the group, followed by a group password.

The password field usually contains an x, as group passwords are rarely used today. If used, you will need to specify a password to change your primary group membership using the **newgrp command** discussed later in this chapter. These passwords are set using the `gpasswd` command and may be stored in the `/etc/gshadow` file for added security. Refer to the gpasswd manual or info page for more information.

12

GID represents the unique Group ID for the group, and the members field indicates the list of group members. An example `/etc/group` file is seen below:

```
[root@localhost root]# cat /etc/group
root:x:0:root
bin:x:1:root,bin,daemon
daemon:x:2:root,bin,daemon
sys:x:3:root,bin,adm
adm:x:4:root,adm,daemon
tty:x:5:
disk:x:6:root
lp:x:7:daemon,lp
mem:x:8:
kmem:x:9:
```

```
wheel:x:10:root
mail:x:12:mail
news:x:13:news
uucp:x:14:uucp
man:x:15:
games:x:20:
gopher:x:30:
dip:x:40:
ftp:x:50:
lock:x:54:
nobody:x:99:
users:x:100:
slocate:x:21:
floppy:x:19:
utmp:x:22:
mailnull:x:47:
rpm:x:37:
xfs:x:43:
ntp:x:38:
rpc:x:32:
gdm:x:42:
rpcuser:x:29:
nfsnobody:x:65534:
nscd:x:28:
ident:x:98:
radvd:x:75:
postgres:x:26:
apache:x:48:
squid:x:23:
named:x:25:
pcap:x:77:
wine:x:101:
junkbust:x:73:
pppusers:x:44:
popusers:x:45:
slipusers:x:46:
mailman:x:41:
mysql:x:27:
ldap:x:55:
pvm:x:24:
user1:x:500:
[root@localhost root]# _
```

From the above output, the "bin" group has a GID of 1, and three users as members: root, bin, and daemon.

Creating User Accounts

You may create user accounts on the Linux system by using the **useradd command**, specifying the username as an argument, as seen below:

```
[root@localhost root]# useradd bobg
[root@localhost root]# _
```

In this case, all other information such as the UID, shell, and home directory location are taken from two files that contain user account creation default values.

The first file, **/etc/login.defs**, contains parameters that set the default location for e-mail, password expiration information, minimum password length, and range of UIDs and GIDs available for use, as well as specifying whether to create home directories by default.

A sample /etc/login.defs file is depicted below:

```
[root@localhost root]# cat /etc/login.defs
# *REQUIRED*
# Directory where mailboxes reside, _or_ name of file, relative to the
# home directory.  If you _do_ define both, MAIL_DIR takes precedence.
#    QMAIL_DIR is for Qmail
#
#QMAIL_DIR      Maildir
MAIL_DIR        /var/spool/mail
#MAIL_FILE      .mail

# Password aging controls:
#
#     PASS_MAX_DAYS   Maximum number of days a password may be used.
#     PASS_MIN_DAYS   Minimum number of days allowed between password
#                     changes.
#     PASS_MIN_LEN    Minimum acceptable password length.
#     PASS_WARN_AGE   Number of days warning given before a password
#                     expires.
#
PASS_MAX_DAYS   99999
PASS_MIN_DAYS   0
PASS_MIN_LEN    5
PASS_WARN_AGE   7


#
# Min/max values for automatic uid selection in useradd
#
UID_MIN                 500
UID_MAX                 60000

#
# Min/max values for automatic gid selection in groupadd
```

12

```
#
GID_MIN                         500
GID_MAX                         60000


#
# If defined, this command is run when removing a user.
# It should remove any at/cron/print jobs etc. owned by
# the user to be removed (passed as the first argument).
#
#USERDEL_CMD     /usr/sbin/userdel_local


#
# If useradd should create home directories for users by default
# On RH systems, we do. This option is ORed with the -m flag on
# useradd command line.
#
CREATE_HOME      yes

[root@localhost root]# _
```

The second file, **/etc/default/useradd**, contains information regarding the default primary group, location of home directories, default number of days to disable accounts with an expired password, date to disable user accounts, the shell used, and the skeleton directory used. The **skeleton directory** on most Linux systems is /etc/skel and contains files that are copied to all new users' home directories when the home directory is created. Most of these files are environment files such as `.bash_profile` and `.bashrc`.

A sample `/etc/default/useradd` file is seen in the following output:

```
[root@localhost root]# cat /etc/default/useradd
# useradd defaults file
GROUP=
HOME=/home
INACTIVE=
EXPIRE=
SHELL=/bin/bash
SKEL=/etc/skel
[root@localhost root]# _
```

To override any of the default parameters in `/etc/login.defs` and `/etc/default/useradd` for a user, you may specify options to the `useradd` command when creating user accounts. For example, to create a user named maryj with a UID of 762, you may use the `-u` option to the `useradd` command, as seen below:

```
[root@localhost root]# useradd -u 762 maryj
[root@localhost root]# _
```

Some common options available to the useradd command and their descriptions are listed in Table 12-8.

Table 12-8 Common options to the useradd command

Option	Description
-c "description"	Adds a description for the user to the GECOS field of /etc/passwd
-d homedirectory	Specifies the absolute pathname to the user's home directory
-e expirydate	Specifies a date to disable the account from logging in
-f days	Specifies the number of days after a user account with an expired password is disabled
-g group	Specifies the primary group for the user account; by default in Red Hat Linux, a group is created with the same name as the user and made the primary group for that user
-G group1, group2, etc.	Specifies all other group memberships for the user account
-m	Specifies that a home directory should be created for the user account; by default in Red Hat Linux, home directories are created for all users via an entry in the /etc/login.defs file
-k directory	Specifies the skeleton directory used when copying files to a new home directory
-s shell	Specifies the absolute pathname to the shell used for the user account
-u UID	Specifies the UID of the user account

Once a user account has been added, the password field in the /etc/shadow file will contain two ! characters, indicating that no password has been set for the user account. To set the password, type the **passwd command** followed by the name of the new user account at a command prompt, and supply the appropriate password when prompted. An example of setting the password for the user bobg is seen below:

```
[root@localhost root]# passwd bobg
Changing password for user bobg
New password:
Retype new password:
passwd: all authentication tokens updated successfully
[root@localhost root]# _
```

 Without arguments, the passwd command changes the password for the current user.

All user accounts must have a password set before they are used to log into the system.

The root user may set the password on any user account using the `passwd` command; however, regular users may change only their password using this command.

Passwords should be difficult to guess and contain a combination of upper-case, lowercase, and special characters to increase system security. An example of a good password to choose is C2Jr1;Pwr.

Modifying User Accounts

To modify the information regarding a user account after creating it, you may edit the `/etc/passwd` or `/etc/shadow` file; however, this is not recommended practice since typographical errors in these files may prevent the system from functioning. The **usermod command** may be used to modify most information regarding user accounts. For example, to change the login name of the user bobg to barbg, you may use the `-l` option to the `usermod` command:

```
[root@localhost root]# usermod -l barbg bobg
[root@localhost root]# _
```

A complete list of options used with the `usermod` command to modify user accounts can be found in Table 12-9.

Table 12-9 Common options to the usermod command

Option	Description
-c *"description"*	Specifies a new description for the user in the GECOS field of /etc/passwd
-d *homedirectory*	Specifies the absolute pathname to a new home directory
-e *expirydate*	Specifies a date to disable the account from logging in
-f *days*	Specifies the number of days after a user account with an expired password is disabled
-g *group*	Specifies a new primary group for the user account
-G *group1, group2, etc.*	Specifies all other group memberships for the user account
-l *name*	Specifies a new login name
-s *shell*	Specifies the absolute pathname to a new shell used for the user account
-u *UID*	Specifies a new UID for the user account

The only user account information that the `usermod` command cannot modify is the password expiration information stored in `/etc/shadow` (min, max, warn) discussed earlier. To change this information, you may use the **chage command** with the appropriate option. For example, to specify that the user bobg must wait 2 days before changing his password after receiving a new password, as well as specify that his password expires every

50 days with 7 days of warning prior to expiration, you may use the following options to the `chage` command:

```
[root@localhost root]# chage -m 2 -M 50 -W 7 bobg
[root@localhost root]# _
```

It may be necessary in certain situations to prevent a user from logging in temporarily; this is commonly called **locking an account.** To lock an account, you may use the command `usermod -L` *username* at the command prompt. This will place a ! character at the beginning of the encrypted password field in the `/etc/shadow` file. To unlock the account, simply type `usermod -U` *username* at the command prompt, which removes the ! character from the password field in the `/etc/shadow` file.

Alternatively, you may use the `passwd -l` *username* command to lock a user account and the `passwd -u` *username* command to unlock a user account.

Yet another method commonly used to lock a user account is to change the shell specified in `/etc/passwd` for a user account from `/bin/bash` to an invalid shell such as `/bin/false`. Without a valid shell, a user will not be able to use the system. To lock a user account this way, you could edit the `/etc/passwd` file and make the appropriate change, use the `-s` option to the `usermod` command, or use the **chsh** command. The following example uses the `chsh` command to change the shell to `/bin/false` for the user bobg:

```
[root@localhost root]# chsh -s /bin/false bobg
Changing shell for bobg.
Warning: "/bin/false" is not listed in /etc/shells
Shell changed.
[root@localhost root]# _
```

Deleting User Accounts

To delete a user account, you may use the **userdel command** and specify the user name as an argument; this will remove entries from both `/etc/passwd` and `/etc/shadow` corresponding to the user account. Furthermore, you may specify the `-r` option to the `userdel` command to remove the home directory for the user and all of its contents.

When a user account is deleted, any files that were previously owned by the user become owned by a number that represents the UID of the deleted user. Any future user account that is given the same UID then becomes the owner of those files.

Say, for example, that the user bobg leaves the company. To delete bobg's user account and display the ownership of his old files, you may use the following commands:

```
[root@localhost root]# userdel bobg
[root@localhost root]# ls -la /home/bobg
total 40
drwx--    3 502      502         4096 Jul 17 15:37 .
drwxr-xr-x 5 root     root        4096 Jul 17 15:37 ..
-rw-r--r-- 1 502      502           24 Jul 17 15:37 .bash_logout
```

12

```
-rw-r--r--    1 502         502            191 Jul 17 15:37 .bash_profile
-rw-r--r--    1 502         502            124 Jul 17 15:37 .bashrc
-rw-r--r--    1 502         502            820 Jul 17 15:37 .emacs
-rw-r--r--    1 502         502            118 Jul 17 15:37 .gtkrc
-rw-r--r--    1 502         502           1756 Jul 17 15:37 inittab
drwxr-xr-x    3 502         502           4096 Jul 17 15:37 .kde
-rw-r--r--    1 502         502           3511 Jul 17 15:37 .screenrc
[root@localhost root]# _
```

From the above output, we see that the UID of the bobg user was 502. If the user sueb was hired by the company to replace bobg, you may assign the UID of 502 to her user account so that she may own all of bobg's old files and reuse them as needed.

To create the user sueb with a UID of 502 and list the ownership of the files in bobg's home directory, you may use the following commands:

```
[root@localhost root]# useradd -u 502 sueb
[root@localhost root]# ls -la /home/bobg
total 40
drwx------    3 sueb       sueb          4096 Jul 17 15:37 .
drwxr-xr-x    6 root       root          4096 Jul 17 18:56 ..
-rw-r--r--    1 sueb       sueb            24 Jul 17 15:37 .bash_logout
-rw-r--r--    1 sueb       sueb           191 Jul 17 15:37 .bash_profile
-rw-r--r--    1 sueb       sueb           124 Jul 17 15:37 .bashrc
-rw-r--r--    1 sueb       sueb           820 Jul 17 15:37 .emacs
-rw-r--r--    1 sueb       sueb           118 Jul 17 15:37 .gtkrc
-rw-r--r--    1 sueb       sueb          1756 Jul 17 15:37 inittab
drwxr-xr-x    3 sueb       sueb          4096 Jul 17 15:37 .kde
-rw-r--r--    1 sueb       sueb          3511 Jul 17 15:37 .screenrc
[root@localhost root]# _
```

Managing Groups

By far the easiest method to add groups to a system is to edit the /etc/group file using a text editor. However, another method is to use the **groupadd command**. To add a group called group1 to the system and assign it a GID of 492, you may use the following command:

```
[root@localhost root]# groupadd -g 492 group1
[root@localhost root]# _
```

Then, you may use the −G option to the usermod command to add members to the group. To add the user maryj to this group and view the addition, you may use the usermod command seen below:

```
[root@localhost root]# usermod -G group1 maryj
[root@localhost root]# tail -1 /etc/group
group1:x:492:maryj
[root@localhost root]# _
```

There also exists a **groupmod command** that can be used to modify the group name and GID, as well as a **groupdel command**, which can be used to remove groups from the system.

To see a list of groups that you are a member of, simply run the `groups` command; to see the GIDs for each group, simply run the `id` command. The primary group is always listed first by each command. The following output shows the output of these commands when executed by the root user:

```
[root@localhost root]# groups
root bin daemon sys adm disk wheel groupies
[root@localhost root]# id
uid=0(root) gid=0(root)
groups=0(root),1(bin),2(daemon),3(sys),4(adm),6(disk),10(wheel),
1234(groupies)
[root@localhost root]# _
```

You can see from the output above that the primary group for the root user is the root group. This group will be attached as the group owner for all files that are created by the root user, as seen in the following output:

```
[root@localhost root]# touch samplefile1
[root@localhost root]# ls -l samplefile1
-rw-r--r--    1 root       root          0 Jul 17 19:22 samplefile1
[root@localhost root]# _
```

To change the primary group temporarily to another group that is listed in the output of the `groups` and `id` commands, you may use the `newgrp` command. Any new files created afterwards will then have the new group owner. The following output demonstrates how changing the primary group for the root user affects file ownership:

```
[root@localhost root]# newgrp sys
[root@localhost root]# id
uid=0(root) gid=3(sys)
groups=0(root),1(bin),2(daemon),3(sys),4(adm),6(disk),10(wheel),
1234(groupies)
[root@localhost root]# touch samplefile2
[root@localhost root]# ls -l samplefile2
-rw-r--r--    1 root       sys           0 Jul 17 19:28 samplefile2
[root@localhost root]# _
```

12

Note

If you use group passwords as described earlier in this section, you may use the `newgrp` command to change your primary group to a group that you are not a member of, provided you supply the appropriate password when prompted.

Using the Red Hat User Manager

Although command-line utilities are commonly used to administer users and groups, you may instead use a graphical utility to create, modify, and delete user and group accounts on the system. These utilities run the appropriate command-line utility in the background. Although there are several graphical utilities that can manage users and groups, the most common is the **Red Hat User Manager**, shown in Figure 12-20.

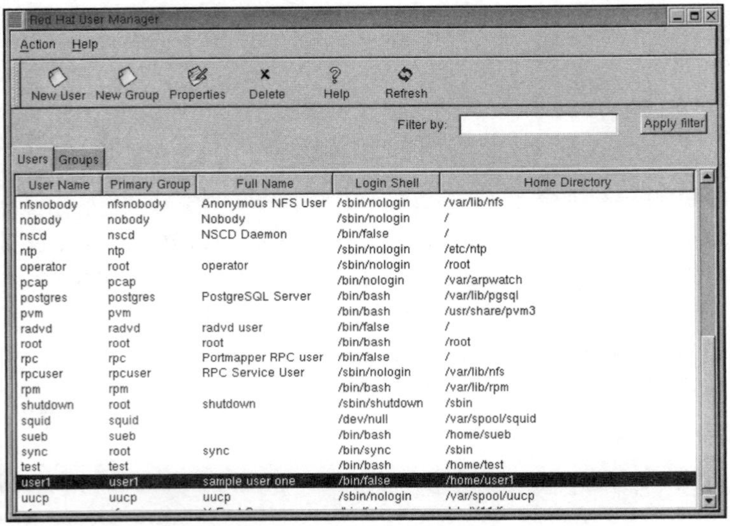

Figure 12-20   The Red Hat User Manager

To start the Red Hat User Manager from the GNOME desktop environment, navigate to the toolbar, GNOME button, Programs, System, User Manager. To start the Red Hat User Manager from the KDE desktop environment, navigate to the toolbar, K button, System, User Manager (with the Red Hat logo).

By default, the Red Hat User Manager displays a list of user accounts on the system; to display a list of groups, you may click the Groups tab, as seen in Figure 12-21.

To create a new user, you may use the New User button and supply the appropriate information. Figure 12-22 illustrates the creation of a user account named bobg that has a GECOS of `Bob G's User Account`, a shell of `/bin/bash`, and a home directory of `/home/bobg`.

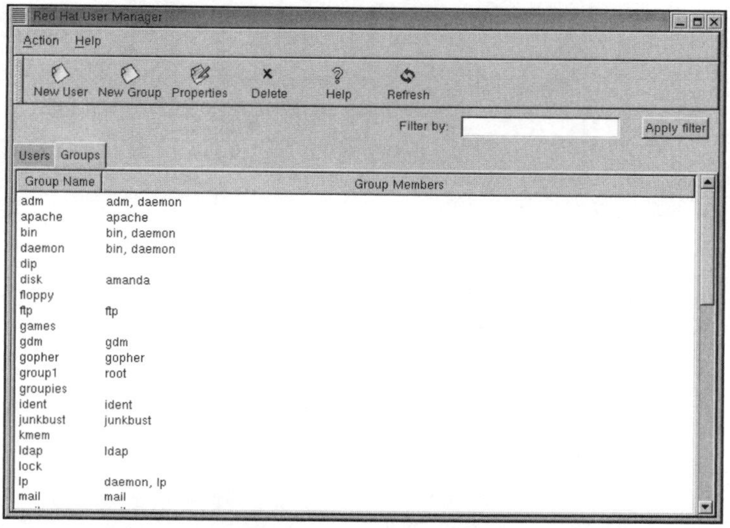

Figure 12-21   Viewing groups in the Red Hat User Manager

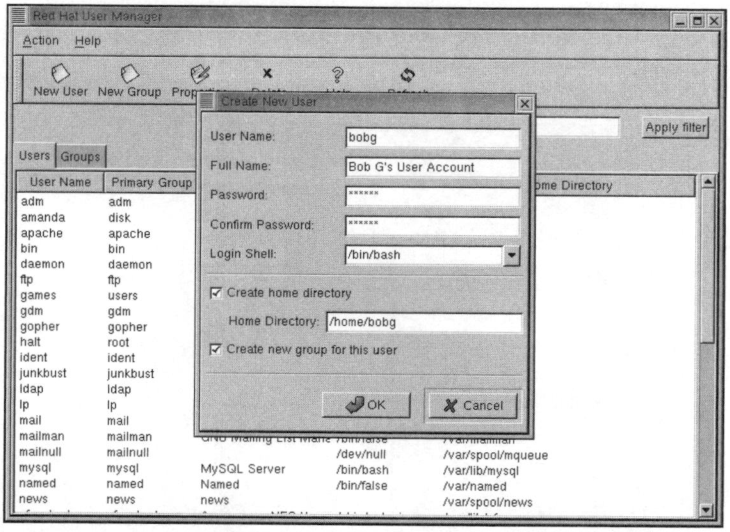

Figure 12-22   Creating a new user account

Similarly, you may use the New Group button to specify a new system group, as depicted in Figure 12-23.

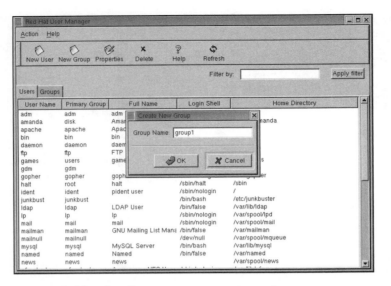

Figure 12-23   Creating a new group account

The Red Hat User Manager also provides an easy way to modify user accounts; you may edit the properties of a user by highlighting the user in the list and clicking on the Properties button, as seen in Figure 12-24.

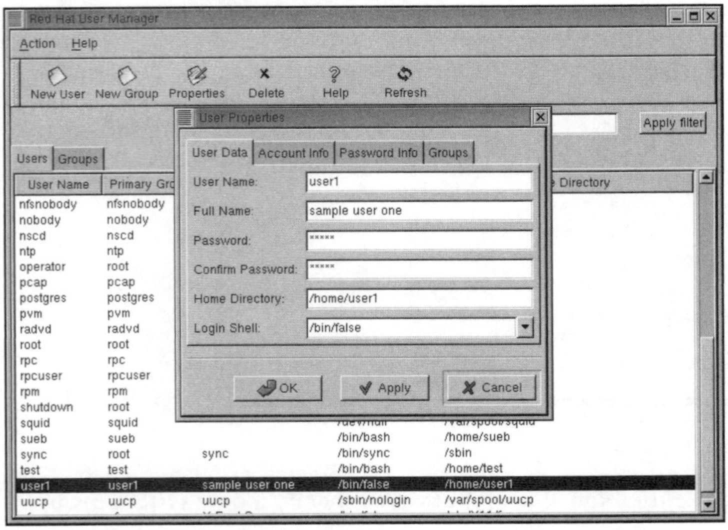

Figure 12-24   Editing the properties of a user account

You may also use the different tabs in the User Properties dialog box seen in Figure 12-24 to modify the date that the account is disabled or lock the user account (Figure 12-25), change the password expiration information for the user account (Figure 12-26), or add the user to various groups on the system (Figure 12-27).

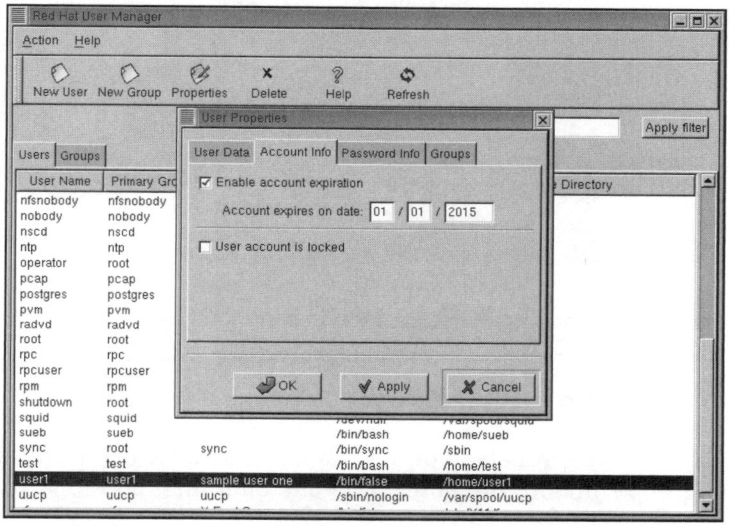

Figure 12-25   Editing the disable date and lockout of a user account

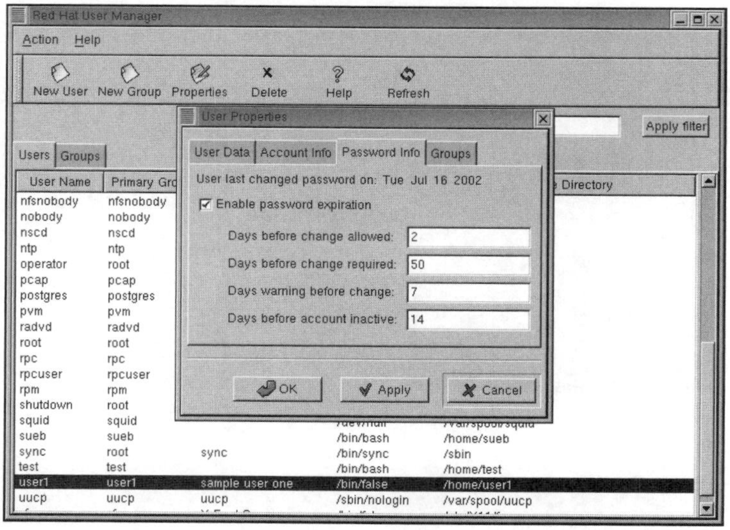

Figure 12-26   Editing the password expiration parameters for a user account

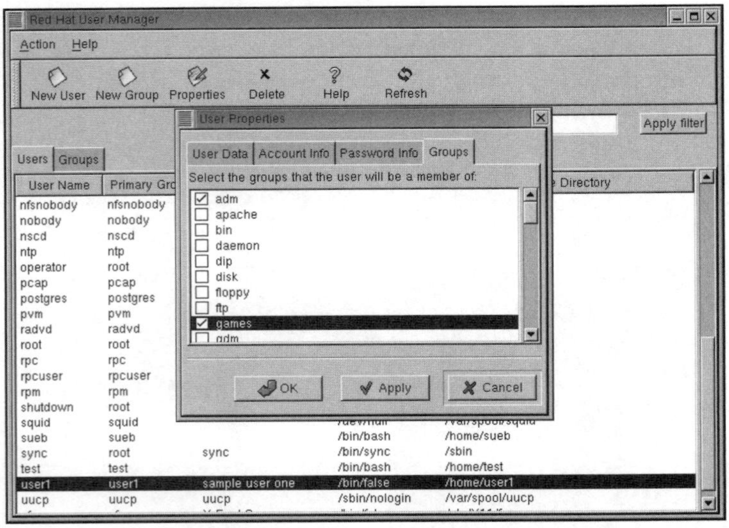

Figure 12-27 Editing the group membership of a user account

In addition, you may edit the properties of a group, including its name and members, by highlighting the group name from Figure 12-21 and choosing the Properties button, as seen in Figures 12-28 and 12-29.

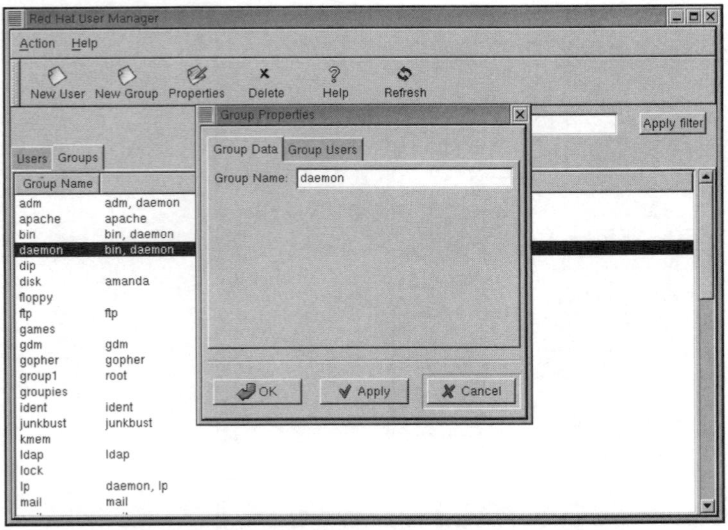

Figure 12-28 Editing a group name

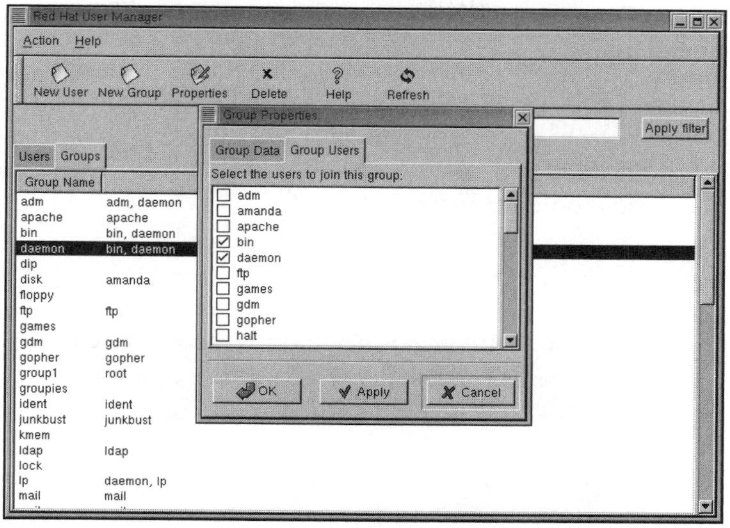

Figure 12-29   Editing the members of a group

CHAPTER SUMMARY

- ❑ Print jobs are spooled to a print queue before being printed to a printer.

- ❑ You may disable spooling or printing for a printer by using the `lpc` command.

- ❑ Print jobs are created using the `lpr` command, may be viewed in the print queue using the `lpq` command, and may be removed from the print queue using the the `lprm` command.

- ❑ You may create local and remote printers using the Red Hat Printer Configuration tool or by modifying the `/etc/printcap.local` file.

- ❑ Most log files on a Linux system are stored in the `/var/log` directory.

- ❑ System events are typically logged to files by the system log daemon.

- ❑ Log files should be cleared or rotated over time to save disk space; the logrotate utility may be used to rotate log files.

- ❑ User and group account information is typically stored in the `/etc/passwd`, `/etc/shadow`, and `/etc/group` files.

- ❑ You may use the **useradd** command to create users and the **groupadd** command to create groups.

- ❑ All users must have a valid password before logging into a Linux system.

12

❑ Users may be modified with the **usermod, chage, chsh,** and **passwd** commands, and groups may be modified using the **groupmod** command.

❑ The **userdel** and **groupdel** commands may be used to remove users and groups from the system, respectively.

❑ The Red Hat User Manager is a graphical utility that can manage users and groups on the system from a desktop environment.

KEY TERMS

/etc/default/useradd — A file that contains default values for user creation.

/etc/login.defs — A file that contains default values for user creation.

/etc/logrotate.conf — The file used by the logrotate utility to specify rotation parameters for logfiles.

/etc/passwd — The file that contains user account information.

/etc/printcap — The file that holds the configuration information for each printer installed on the system.

/etc/printcap.local — A file that holds printer configuration that may be edited by users; it is incorporated into the /etc/printcap file.

/etc/shadow — The file that contains the encrypted password as well as password and account expiry parameters for each user account.

/etc/skel — A directory that contains files that are copied to all new users' home directories upon creation.

/etc/syslog.conf — The file that specifies the events that the system log daemon listens for and the logfiles that it saves the events to.

/var/log — A directory that contains most log files on a Linux system.

authentication — The act of verifying a user's identity by comparing a username and password to a system database (/etc/passwd and /etc/shadow).

a2ps command — The command used to print Postscript formatted files.

chage command — The command used to modify password expiry information for user accounts.

chsh command — The command used to change a valid shell to an invalid shell.

disabled printer — Refers to a printer that will not accept print jobs into the print queue.

enabled printer — Refers to a printer that will accept print jobs into the print queue.

enscript command — The command used to print Postscript formatted files.

facility — When logging system events, refers to the area of the system from which information is gathered.

General Electric Comprehensive Operating System (GECOS) field — The field in the /etc/passwd file that contains a description of the user account.

Group Identifier (GID) — A unique number given to each group.

groupadd command — The command used to add a group to the system.

groupdel command — The command used to delete a group from the system.

groupmod command — The command used to modify the name or GID of a group on the system.

line printer daemon (lpd) — The daemon that accepts print jobs into the print queue and prints them to the printer.

locking an account — Making an account temporarily unusable by altering the password information for it stored on the system.

log file — A file containing information about the Linux system.

logrotate command — The command used to rotate log files; typically uses the configuration information stored in /etc/logrotate.conf.

lpc command — The command used to view the status of and control (start, stop, enable, disable) printers on the system.

lpd command — The command used to start line printer daemon.

lpq command — The command used to view the contents of print queues.

lpr command — The command used to create print jobs in the print queue.

lprm command — The command used to remove print jobs from the print queue.

newgrp command — The command used to change temporarily the primary group of a user.

passwd command — The command used to modify the password associated with a user account.

Postscript — A non-text file format that is commonly used in documents.

primary group — The group that is specified for a user in the /etc/passwd file and that is specified as group owner for all files created by a user.

print job — Information sent to a printer for printing.

print job ID — A unique numeric identifier used to mark and distinguish each print job.

print queue — A directory on the filesystem that holds print jobs that are waiting to be printed.

printer aliases — An alternate name by which a printer can be identified.

printing — The process by which print jobs are sent from a print queue to a printer.

priority — The importance of system information when logging system events.

pwconv command — The command used to enable the use of the /etc/shadow file.

pwunconv command — The command used to disable the use of the /etc/shadow file.

Red Hat Printer Configuration Tool — A graphical utility used to configure printers on the system.

Red Hat User Manager — A graphical utility used to manage users and groups on the system.

skeleton directory — A directory that contains files that are copied to all new users' home directories upon creation; the default skeleton directory on Linux systems is /etc/skel.

12

spooling — The process of accepting a print job into a print queue.

started printer — A printer that will send print jobs from the print queue to a printer.

stopped printer — A printer that will not send print jobs from the print queue to a printer.

system log daemon (syslogd) — The daemon that logs system events to various log files via information stored in /etc/syslog.conf.

user account — Information regarding a user that is stored in a system database (/etc/passwd and /etc/shadow), which may be used to log in to the system and gain access to system resources.

User Identifier (UID) — A unique number assigned to each user account.

useradd command — The command used to add a user account to the system.

userdel command — The command used to remove a user account from the system.

usermod command — The command used to modify the properties of a user account on the system.

REVIEW QUESTIONS

1. If a system has three printers attached to it, only one can be designated as the default printer and this default printer applies to all users on the system. True or False?

2. The process of sending print jobs from the print queue to the printer is called
   _____.
   a. spooling
   b. queuing
   c. sorting
   d. sending
   e. redirecting
   f. printing

3. You may clear a log file simply by redirecting nothing into it. True or False?

4. When a printer is disabled, _____.
   a. the print queue will not accept jobs and will send a message to the user noting that the printer is unavailable
   b. the print queue will accept jobs into the print queue and hold them there until the printer is started again
   c. the printer will appear as off line when an lpc request is sent
   d. the print queue will redirect all print jobs sent to it to `/dev/null`

5. What is the name used to describe a user providing a user name and password to log into a system?

   a. validation

   b. authorization

   c. logon

   d. authentication

   e. certification

   f. substantiation

   g. confirmation

6. Although both users and groups may have passwords attached to them, groups typically do not have passwords assigned to them. True or False?

7. What command may you use to lock a user account?

   a. `lock username`

   b. `close username`

   c. `secure username`

   d. `usermod -L username`

   e. `useradd -L username`

8. What command is used to alter the primary group associated with a given user temporarily?

   a. It cannot be done, as a user's primary group is important and set.

   b. `chggrp`

   c. `gpasswd`

   d. `newgrp`

9. Which command can be used to send a print job to the default printer named Printer1? (Choose all that apply.)

   a. `lpr -P Printer1 file`

   b. `lpr Printer1 file`

   c. `lpr  file`

   d. `lpc -P Printer 1 file`

   e. `lpq Printer1 file`

   f. `lpd Printer1 file`

12

10. You look at the appropriate field in /etc/shadow to see when a password was last changed and observe a value indicating 11000. What does this value indicate?

    a. You are looking at the wrong field.

    b. You are looking in the wrong file; it should be /etc/passwd.

    c. Like the user's password, the date it was last changed is encrypted for security reasons.

    d. It is in a measure of time in hours since January 1, 1980.

    e. It is in a measure of time in days since January 1, 1970.

11. When creating a user from the GUI you cannot specify the UID; this can only be done from the command-line. True or False?

12. What is the name of the file that contains a listing of all users on the system?

    a. /etc/passwd

    b. /etc/passwrd

    c. /etc/users/conf

    d. /etc/shadow

    e. /etc/password

13. UIDs and GIDs are unique to the system and once used can never be reused. True or False?

14. What command is used to view or alter the status of printers on the system ?

    a. lpq

    b. lpr

    c. lpd

    d. lpc

15. What is the name of the utility used to rotate log files?

    a. There is none.

    b. jetpack

    c. logrotate

    d. logbackup

16. You can lock a user account by changing the default login shell to an invalid shell in /etc/passwd. True or False?

17. When a printer is stopped, _____.

    a. the print queue will not accept jobs and will send a message to the user noting that the printer is unavailable

    b. the print queue will accept jobs into the print queue and hold them there until the printer is started again

    c. the printer will appear as off line when an lpc request is sent

    d. the print queue will redirect all print jobs sent to it to /dev/null

18. When referring to the `/etc/syslog.conf` file, _____ specifies information from a certain area of the system whereas _____ is the level of importance of that information.

    a. section, priority

    b. service, precedents

    c. process, degree

    d. facility, priority

19. Most log files on the system will be found in which directory?

    a. `/etc/logfiles`

    b. `/etc/log`

    c. `/etc/var/log`

    d. `/var/log`

    e. `/dev/log`

20. What file contains default information such as UID and GID ranges and minimum password length to be used at user creation?

    a. `/etc/skel`

    b. `/etc/passwd`

    c. `/etc/login.defs`

    d. `/etc/default useradd`

21. What is the background process responsible for printing on Linux?

    a. `lpc`

    b. `lpr`

    c. `lpd`

    d. `lpd.d`

    e. `lpq`

22. What command would you use to unlock a user account?

    a. `unlock username`

    b. `open username`

    c. `free username`

    d. `usermod -U username`

    e. `useradd -U username`

23. If you run `pwconv`, where will passwords be stored on the system?

    a. `/etc/passwrd`

    b. `/etc/passwd`

    c. `/etc/shadow`

    d. `/etc/skel`

12

24. Along with a listing of user accounts, the `/etc/passwd` file also contains information on account expiration. True or False?

25. You use `lpq` and determine that a user named User1 has placed two large print jobs in the queue for Printer1 that have yet to start printing. They have print job ID's of 455 and 457, respectively. What command would you use to remove these two jobs from the print queue?

    a. `lpq -r 455 457 Printer1`

    b. `lprm -P Printer1 User1`

    c. `lprm -P Printer1 455 457`

    d. `lpq -r -P Printer1 455 457`

26. Where are the default home directory path and login shell stored?

    a. `/etc/skel`

    b. `/etc/passwd`

    c. `/etc/login.defs`

    d. `/etc/default useradd`

27. You are aware that `/etc/printcap` has a very particular syntax and structure; you painstakingly modify it and restart the printer daemon and you try, but fail to use your printer. You then view the /etc/printcap file and notice that all your hard work has disappeared. What should you do?

    a. You must use the Red Hat Printer Configuration Tool, as `/etc/printcap` is read-only.

    b. Log on as root and ensure your primary group is root.

    c. Make the very same careful changes you made before, but this time to the `/etc/printcap.local` file. After editing this file, run the command `printconf-backend` to merge the changes into `/etc/printcap`.

    d. Make the very same careful changes you made before, but this time to `/etc/printconf-edit`.

28. What option used with the `lpc` command will both enable and start a printer?

    a. `start`

    b. `enable`

    c. `up`

    d. `launch`

29. What command is used to delete a user account?

    a. `usermod -d username`

    b. `del username`

    c. `userdel username`

    d. `rm username`

30. The system log daemon obtains information on what data to read and where to store the information from _____.

    a. /syslogd.config

    b. /dev/log/conf

    c. /etc/syslog.conf

    d. /var/syslog.conf

31. The process of sending print jobs to the print queue to be held until the printer is ready is called _____.

    a. spinning

    b. queuing

    c. spooling

    d. sorting

32. You can add users to groups on the system by modifying the last field in /etc/group. True or False?

HANDS-ON PROJECTS

These projects should be completed in the order given. All hands-on projects should take a total of three hours to complete. The requirements for this lab include:

> ❐ A computer with Red Hat 7.2 installed according to Hands-on Project 7-2

Project 12-1

In this hands-on project, you will create a local printer using the Red Hat Printer Configuration Tool.

1. Turn on your computer. Once your Linux system has been loaded, log into the graphical terminal (tty7) using the username of **root** and the password of **secret**.

2. Once the GNOME desktop environment has loaded, open a new command-line terminal by clicking the appropriate icon on your toolbar.

3. At the command prompt, type **printconf-gui &** and press **Enter** to start the Red Hat Printer Configuration Tool. Are there any printers configured? List two other methods that may be used to start the Red Hat Printer Configuration Tool.

4. Create a new printer by selecting the **New** button with your mouse. Click the **Next** button.

5. At the "Set the Print Queue Name and Type" screen, type **fakeprinter** in the Queue Name box. Next, select **Local Printer** under Queue Type and click the **Next** button.

6. At the "Configure a Local Printer" screen, observe the entries. Which devices are listed? Why? Select the button entitled **Custom Device**. When prompted, type the filename **/dev/null** into the dialog box and click the **OK** button. Click the **Next** button.

12

The special device /dev/null represents nothing; any print jobs sent to this device will be discarded.

7. At the "Select Print Driver" screen, highlight **Text Only Printer** and click the **Next** button.

8. At the "Finish" screen, observe the information and click the **Finish** button.

9. Observe the line representing the printer you just created in the Red Hat Printer Configuration Tool. Is it the default printer? How do you know?

10. Click the **Edit** button. At the "Name and Aliases" tab of the "Edit Queue" screen, click the **Add** button. When prompted, type in the Alias **printer1** and click the **OK** button. Does the alias appear in the list? Click the **OK** button to close the "Edit Queue" screen. Does the alias appear in the printer description?

11. Click the **Apply** button. At the **Information** screen, click **OK**. What does this button do?

12. Close the Red Hat Printer Configuration Tool by clicking the **X** in the upper-right corner of the window.

13. At the terminal screen prompt, type **cat /etc/printcap** and press **Enter**. Observe the entries in this file. Can you see the name and aliases for your printer in this file? Which line determines the local device to print to? Which line specifies the path to the print queue?

14. Type **exit** and press **Enter** to close the terminal screen.

15. Press the **Ctrl-Alt-Bkspce** key combination to log out of the GNOME desktop environment.

Project 12-2

In this hands-on project, you will create a network printer using the Red Hat Printer Configuration Tool.

1. Log into the graphical terminal (tty7) using the username of **root** and the password of **secret**.

2. Once the GNOME desktop environment has loaded, open a new command-line terminal by pressing the appropriate icon on your toolbar.

3. At the command prompt, type **printconf-gui &** and press **Enter** to start the Red Hat Printer Configuration Tool. What printer is configured?

4. Create a new printer by selecting the **New** button with your mouse. Click the **Next** button.

5. At the "Set the Print Queue Name and Type" screen, type **netprinter** in the Queue Name box. Next, select **Unix Printer** under Queue Type and click the **Next** button.

6. At the "Configure a Unix Print Queue" screen, type **127.0.0.1** in the Server box. Next, type **fakeprinter** in the Queue box. This will print across the network to the printer called `fakeprinter` on the local computer. Click the **Next** button.

 The IP Address of 127.0.0.1 always refers to the local computer.

7. At the "Select a Print Driver" screen, highlight **Text Only Printer** and click the **Next** button.

8. At the "Finish" screen, observe the information and click the **Finish** button.

9. Observe the line representing the printer you just created in the Red Hat Printer Configuration Tool.

10. Click the **Default** button. What happened? Is there another method that you may use to specify **netprinter** as the default printer on the system? Explain.

11. Click the **Apply** button. At the **Information** screen, click **OK**.

12. Close the Red Hat Printer Configuration Tool by clicking the **X** in the upper-right corner of the window.

13. At the terminal screen prompt, type **less /etc/printcap** and press **Enter**. Observe the entries in this file. Does `netprinter` have any aliases? Which lines specify the remote computer and printer names? Which line specifies the path to the print queue?

14. Press **q** to quit the `less` utility.

15. Type **exit** and press **Enter** to close the terminal window.

16. Press the **Ctrl-Alt-Bkspce** key combination to log out of the GNOME desktop environment.

Project 12-3

In this hands-on project, you will control the print process, create print jobs, and manage them in the print queue.

1. Switch to a command-line terminal (tty2) by pressing **Ctrl-Alt-F2** and log into the terminal using the username of **root** and the password of **secret**.

2. At the command prompt, type **lpc status** and press **Enter**. Which printer(s) is/are listed? Why? Next, type **lpc -a status** at the command prompt and press **Enter** to view the status of all printers on the system. Answer the following questions:

Is printing enabled for fakeprinter? _____

Is spooling enabled for fakeprinter? _____

Is printing enabled for netprinter? _____

Is spooling enabled for netprinter? _____

12

3. At the command prompt, type **lpc -P netprinter stop** and press **Enter** to prevent printing for the netprinter printer.

4. At the command prompt, type **lpc -P fakeprinter stop** and press **Enter** to prevent printing for the fakeprinter printer.

5. Next, type **lpc -a status** at the command prompt and press **Enter** to view the status of all printers on the system. Answer the following questions:

   Is printing enabled for fakeprinter? _____

   Is spooling enabled for fakeprinter? _____

   Is printing enabled for netprinter? _____

   Is spooling enabled for netprinter? _____

6. At the command prompt, type **lpr /etc/hosts** and press **Enter** to print the file /etc/hosts to the default printer. Which printer will receive this print job?

7. At the command prompt, type **lpq** and press **Enter** to view the contents of all print queues. Is your print job there? What is its print job ID? _____

8. At the command prompt, type **lpr -P fakeprinter /etc/hosts** and press **Enter** to print the file /etc/hosts to fakeprinter.

9. At the command prompt, type **sort /etc/hosts | lpr -P printer1** and press **Enter** to sort the file /etc/hosts and send the output to printer1. Which printer will receive this print job? Why?

10. At the command prompt, type **lpq** and press **Enter** to view the contents of all print queues. What print jobs do you see? Why? Can you tell which print job came from Standard Input? Record the print job IDs for the two print jobs that were created in Step 8 _____ and Step 9 _____.

11. At the command prompt, type **lprm A B** where **A** is the print job ID for the print job created in Step 8 and **B** is the print job ID for the print job created in Step 9. What was displayed?

12. At the command prompt, type **lpq** and press **Enter** to verify that the print jobs were removed successfully. Are there any print jobs in the print queue for netprinter?

13. At the command prompt, type **lpc -P netprinter start** and press **Enter** to enable printing for netprinter. Where will the print jobs be printed to?

14. At the command prompt, type **lpq** and press **Enter**. Are there any print jobs in the print queue for netprinter? Are there any print jobs in the print queue for fakeprinter? Why? Compare the print job ID for the print job displayed to the print job ID recorded in Step 7.

15. At the command prompt, type **lprm -a all** to remove all print jobs in all print queues on the system. What was displayed?

16. Type **exit** and press **Enter** to log out of your shell.

Project 12-4

In this hands-on project, you will view the configuration of the system log daemon and the `logrotate` utility.

1. Switch to a command-line terminal (tty2) by pressing **Ctrl-Alt-F2** and log into the terminal using the username of **root** and the password of **secret**.

2. At the command prompt, type **ls –l /dev/log** and press **Enter**. What is the file type? Which daemon uses this file and what is its purpose?

3. At the command prompt, type **less /etc/syslog.conf** and press **Enter** to view the configuration file for the system log daemon. Observe the entries. To which file does all information from the `cron` daemon get logged to. Why? Press **q** when finished to quit the `less` utility.

4. At the command prompt, type **tail /var/log/cron** and observe the entries. Write down the last entry that you see in this file: _____

5. At the command prompt, type **killall –9 crond** and press **Enter** to stop the `cron` daemon.

6. At the command prompt, type **crond** and press **Enter** to start the `cron` daemon.

7. At the command prompt, type **tail /var/log/cron** and observe the entries. Compare the output from Step 4 with the output on your terminal screen. What is the last entry? Why?

8. At the command prompt, type **cat /etc/cron.daily/logrotate** and press **Enter** to observe the `logrotate` command that is run each day. Next, type **cat /etc/crontab** at the command prompt and press **Enter**. At what time each day are the contents of the `/etc/cron.daily` directory run?

9. At the command prompt, type **less /etc/logrotate.conf** and press **Enter** to view the configuration file for the `logrotate` command. When are log files rotated by default? _____ How many copies of old log files are kept by default? _____ When finished, press **q** to quit the `less` utility.

10. At the command prompt, type **ls /etc/logrotate.d** and press **Enter**. How many files are in this directory? Will entries in these files override the same entries in `/etc/logrotate.conf`?

11. At the command prompt, type **cat /etc/logrotate.d/psacct** and press **Enter**. How many copies of old log files are kept for this log file? _____

12. At the command prompt, type **ls /var/log** and press **Enter**. How many log files are present? What do the subdirectories represent? Are there any old log files? Observe the number of old log files for **boot.log** and compare this to the number of old log files for **psacct**. Can you explain the difference?

13. Type **exit** and press **Enter** to log out of your shell.

12

Project 12-5

In this hands-on project, you will observe user account databases and create a user account using command-line utilities.

1. Switch to a command-line terminal (tty2) by pressing **Ctrl–Alt–F2** and log into the terminal using the username of **root** and the password of **secret**.

2. At the command prompt, type **less /etc/passwd** and press **Enter**. Where is the line that describes the "root" user located in this file? Where is the line that describes the "user1" user in this file? How many daemon accounts are present? What is in the password field for all accounts? When finished, press the **q** key to quit the less utility.

3. At the command prompt, type **ls –l /etc/passwd** and press **Enter**. Who are the owner and group owner of this file? Who has permission to read this file?

4. At the command prompt, type **less /etc/shadow** and press **Enter**. What is in the password field for the "root" user and "user1" user accounts? What is in the password field for most daemon accounts? Press **q** to quit the less utility.

5. At the command prompt, type **ls –l /etc/shadow** and press **Enter**. Who are the owner and group owner of this file? Who has permission to read this file? Compare the permissions for /etc/shadow to those of /etc/passwd obtained in Step 3 and explain the difference.

6. At the command prompt, type **pwunconv** and press **Enter**. Next, type **less /etc/shadow** at the command prompt and press **Enter**. What error message do you receive? Why?

7. At the command prompt, type **less /etc/passwd** and press **Enter**. What is in the password field for all accounts? Why? When finished, press the **q** key to quit the less utility.

8. At the command prompt, type **pwconv** and press **Enter**. What does this command do?

9. Next, type **less /etc/shadow** at the command prompt and press **Enter**. Verify that the file has contents and press **q** when finished. Next, type **less /etc/passwd** at the command prompt and press **Enter**. Verify that the file has contents and press **q** when finished.

10. At the command prompt, type **cat /etc/default/useradd** and press **Enter**. What is the default shell used when creating users? What is the default location of the skel directory used when creating users? Where are user home directories created by default?

11. At the command prompt, type **ls –a /etc/skel** and press **Enter**. What files are stored in this directory? What is the purpose of this directory when creating users?

12. At the command prompt, type **cp /etc/inittab /etc/skel** and press **Enter** to create a copy of the init table in the /etc/skel directory.

13. At the command prompt, type **useradd –m bozo** and press **Enter**. What does the -m option specify? From where is the default shell, home directory information taken?

14. At the command prompt, type **cat /etc/passwd** and press **Enter**. What shell and home directory does bozo have? What is bozo's UID?

15. At the command prompt, type **cat /etc/shadow** and press **Enter**. Does bozo have a password? Can bozo log into the system?

16. At the command prompt, type **passwd bozo** and press **Enter**. Enter the password of **secret** and press **Enter**. Enter the password of **secret** again to confirm and press **Enter**. (*Note*: You may receive a message that this is a BAD PASSWORD. Don't worry. Your password has been accepted. This message is there to remind you to use complex passwords as a good practice.)

17. At the command prompt, type **ls –a /home/bozo** and press **Enter**. How many files are in this directory? Compare this list to the one obtained in Step 11. Is the inittab file present?

18. Type **exit** and press **Enter** to log out of your shell.

Project 12-6

In this hands-on project, you will modify user accounts using command-line utilities.

1. Switch to a command-line terminal (tty2) by pressing **Ctrl–Alt–F2** and log into the terminal using the username of **root** and the password of **secret**.

2. At the command prompt, type **cat /etc/passwd** and press **Enter**. Record the line used to describe the user bozo:

   _____

3. At the command prompt, type **cat /etc/shadow** and press **Enter**. Record the line used to describe the user bozo:

   _____

4. At the command prompt, type **usermod –l bozo2 bozo** and press **Enter** to change the login name for the user bozo to bozo2. Next, type **cat /etc/passwd** at the command prompt and press **Enter**. Was the login name changed from bozo to bozo2? Was the UID changed? Was the home directory changed?

5. At the command prompt, type **usermod –l bozo bozo2** and press **Enter** to change the login name for the user bozo2 back to bozo.

6. At the command prompt, type **usermod –u 666 bozo** and press **Enter** to change the UID of the user bozo to 666. Next, type **cat /etc/passwd** at the command prompt and press **Enter**. Was the UID changed?

7. At the command prompt, type **usermod –f 14 bozo** and press **Enter** to disable bozo's user account 14 days after the password expires. Next, type **cat /etc/shadow** at the command prompt and press **Enter**. Which field was changed?

12

8. At the command prompt, type **usermod -e "2020/01/01" bozo** and press **Enter** to expire bozo's user account on January 1ˢᵗ, 2020. Next, type **cat /etc/shadow** at the command prompt and press **Enter**. Which field was changed? What does the number represent in this field?

9. At the command prompt, type **chage -m 2 bozo** and press **Enter** to require that the user bozo wait at least 2 days before password changes. Next, type **cat /etc/shadow** at the command prompt and press **Enter**. Which field was changed?

10. At the command prompt, type **chage -M 40 bozo** and press **Enter** to require that the user bozo change passwords every 40 days. Next, type **cat /etc/shadow** at the command prompt and press **Enter**. Which field was changed?

11. At the command prompt, type **chage -W 5 bozo** and press **Enter** to warn the user bozo 5 days in advance before a password change is required. Next, type **cat /etc/shadow** at the command prompt and press **Enter**. Which field was changed?

12. Type **exit** and press **Enter** to log out of your shell.

Project 12-7

In this hands-on project, you lock and unlock user accounts using command-line utilities.

1. Switch to a command-line terminal (tty2) by pressing **Ctrl-Alt-F2** and log into the terminal using the username of **root** and the password of **secret**.

2. At the command prompt, type **cat /etc/shadow** and press **Enter**. Record the encrypted password for bozo's user account: _____

3. At the command prompt, type **passwd -l bozo** and press **Enter** to lock bozo's user account.

4. At the command prompt, type **cat /etc/shadow** and press **Enter**. What has been changed regarding the original encrypted password recorded in Step 2?

5. Switch to a command-line terminal (tty5) by pressing **Ctrl-Alt-F5** and attempt to log into the terminal using the username of **bozo** and the password of **secret**. Were you successful?

6. Switch back to the command-line terminal (tty2) by pressing **Ctrl-Alt-F2**.

7. At the command prompt, type **passwd -u bozo** and press **Enter** to unlock bozo's user account.

8. At the command prompt, type **cat /etc/shadow** and press **Enter**. Compare the encrypted password for bozo's user account to the one recorded in Step 2.

9. Switch to a command-line terminal (tty5) by pressing **Ctrl-Alt-F5** and attempt to log into the terminal using the username of **bozo** and the password of **secret**. Were you successful?

10. Type **exit** and press **Enter** to log out of your shell.

11. Switch back to the command-line terminal (tty2) by pressing **Ctrl-Alt-F2**.

12. At the command prompt, type **chsh –s /bin/false bozo** and press **Enter** to change bozo's shell to **/bin/false**. What message did you receive? Was the shell changed? Type **cat /etc/passwd** at a command prompt to verify that the shell was changed to **/bin/false** for bozo's user account.

13. Switch to a command-line terminal (tty5) by pressing **Ctrl-Alt-F5** and attempt to log into the terminal using the username of **bozo** and the password of **secret**. Were you successful?

14. Switch back to the command-line terminal (tty2) by pressing **Ctrl-Alt-F2**.

15. At the command prompt, type **chsh –s /bin/bash bozo** and press **Enter** to change bozo's shell to **/bin/bash**.

16. Switch to a command-line terminal (tty5) by pressing **Ctrl-Alt-F5** and attempt to log into the terminal using the username of **bozo** and the password of **secret**. Were you successful?

17. Type **exit** and press **Enter** to log out of your shell.

18. Switch back to the command-line terminal (tty2) by pressing **Ctrl-Alt-F2**.

19. Type **exit** and press **Enter** to log out of your shell.

Project 12-8

In this hands-on project, you remove a user account and create a new user account in its place using command-line utilities.

1. Switch to a command-line terminal (tty2) by pressing **Ctrl-Alt-F2** and log into the terminal using the username of **root** and the password of **secret**.

2. At the command prompt, type **ls –la /home/bozo** and press **Enter**. Who owns most files in this directory? Why?

3. At the command prompt, type **userdel bozo** and press **Enter**. Was the home directory for bozo removed as well?

4. At the command prompt, type **ls –la /home/bozo** and press **Enter**. Who owns most files in this directory? Why?

5. At the command prompt, type **useradd –m –u 666 bozoette** and press **Enter**. What do the **–m** and the **–u** options do in this command?

6. At the command prompt, type **passwd bozoette** and press **Enter**. Enter the password of **secret** and press **Enter**. Enter the password of **secret** again to confirm and press **Enter**.

7. At the command prompt, type **cat /etc/passwd** and press **Enter**. What is bozoette's home directory? What is bozoette's UID?

8. At the command prompt, type **ls –la /home/bozo** and press **Enter**. Who owns most files in this directory? Why? Can bozoette manage these files?

9. Type **exit** and press **Enter** to log out of your shell.

12

Project 12-9

In this hands-on project, you create, use, and delete groups using command-line utilities.

1. Switch to a command-line terminal (tty2) by pressing **Ctrl–Alt–F2** and log into the terminal using the username of **root** and the password of **secret**.

2. At the command prompt, type **vi /etc/group** and press **Enter** to open the /etc/group file in the vi editor. Add a line to the bottom of this file, which reads:

   ```
   groupies:x:1234:root,bozoette
   ```

   This will add a group to the system with a GID of 1234 and the members root and bozoette. When finished, save and quit the vi editor.

3. Switch to a command-line terminal (tty5) by pressing **Ctrl–Alt–F5** and log into the terminal using the username of **bozoette** and the password of **secret**.

4. At the command prompt, type **groups** and press **Enter**. What groups is bozoette a member of?

5. At the command prompt, type **id** and press **Enter**. Which group is the primary group for the user bozoette?

6. At the command prompt, type **touch file1** and press **Enter** to create a new file called file1 in the current directory.

7. At the command prompt, type **ls –l** and press **Enter**. Who are the owner and group owner of the file file1? Why?

8. At the command prompt, type **newgrp groupies** and press **Enter** to change temporarily bozoette's primary group to groupies.

9. At the command prompt, type **touch file2** and press **Enter** to create a new file called file2 in the current directory.

10. At the command prompt, type **ls –l** and press **Enter**. Who are the owner and group owner of the file file2? Why?

11. Type **exit** and press **Enter** to log out of your shell.

12. Switch back to the command-line terminal (tty2) by pressing **Ctrl–Alt–F2**.

13. At the command prompt, type **groupdel groupies** and press **Enter** to remove the group groupies from the system. Which file is edited by the groupdel command?

14. Type **exit** and press **Enter** to log out of your shell.

Discovery Exercises

1. Which entry could you add to **/etc/syslog.conf** to:

   a. log all critical messages from the kernel to **/var/log/alert**?

   b. log all messages from the user processes to **/var/log/userlog**?

   c. log all debug messages and more serious from the printing daemon to **/var/log/printer**?

   d. log all messages except notices from the mail daemon to **/var/log/mailman**?

   e. log all alerts and critical error messages to **/var/log/serious**?

   f. log all warnings and errors from the kernel and the printing daemon to **/var/log/shared**?

2. Use the man or info pages to find a description of the **-D** option to the **useradd** command. What does this option do? What file does it edit? Use this option with the **useradd** command to set the date that all new user accounts will be disabled to March 5th, 2015. What command did you use?

3. Configure the system log daemon on your Linux system to log all warnings and more serious messages to the **/var/log/sample.log** file. Next, configure the **logrotate** command to rotate this log file each day, keeping up to 6 old log files, which should be compressed. Which files did you change? What entries did you add?

4. Create a user called **testuser** using the Red Hat User Manager, which has a GECOS of "Test User Account", password of "secret", and home directory of **/home/test**. Passwords for this user should expire every 60 days with 10 days of warning beforehand. After a password has been changed, the user must wait 5 days to change it again. The user account should expire on April 1st, 2018 and should be a member of the sys and adm groups.

5. When adding several user accounts, you may wish to use the **newusers** utility, which can process a text file full of entries to add user accounts. Use the man or info page to find out how to use this utility and use it to add three users. When finished, view the **/etc/passwd**, **/etc/shadow**, and **/etc/group** files to verify that the users were added successfully.

6. Which paragraph could you add to **/etc/printconf.local** that would create a printer called **laserjet6MP** that prints to the first LPT port on your computer? This printer should have an alias called **officeprinter** and should suppress header pages and allow an unlimited print job size. Explain each line.

7. Write commands to accomplish the following: (use the manual or info pages if necessary)

   ❑ Create a user with a login name of bsmith, a UID of 733, a GECOS field entry of "accounting manager," and a password of Gxj234.

   ❑ Delete the user jdoe, but leave the home directory intact.

12

- ❑ Change the properties of the existing user wjones such that the user has a new comment field of "shipping" and an account expiry of March 23, 2011.

- ❑ Lock the account of wjenkins.

- ❑ Change the password of bsmith to We34Rt.

- ❑ Change the properties of the existing user tbanks such that the user is a member of the managers group, and has a login name of artbanks.

- ❑ Create a user with the same UID and primary group as root and a login name of wjones.

- ❑ Create a new user with a login name of jdoe, who has a password of he789R and no home directory.

- ❑ Change the primary group of the user wsmith to root.

- ❑ Add the users tbanks and jdoe to the group acctg.

13

COMPRESSION, SYSTEM BACK-UP, AND SOFTWARE INSTALLATION

After completing this chapter, you will be able to:

♦ Outline the features of common compression utilities

♦ Compress and decompress files using common compression utilities

♦ Perform system back-ups using the `tar`, `cpio`, and `dump` commands

♦ View and extract archives using the `tar`, `cpio`, and `restore` commands

♦ Describe common types of Linux software

♦ Compile and install software packages from source code

♦ Use the Red Hat Package Manager to install, manage, and remove software packages

In the last chapter, you examined common administrative tasks that are performed on a regular basis. In this chapter you also learn about tasks that are performed frequently, but you focus on file- and software-related administration. You begin in this chapter learning about utilities commonly used to compress files on filesystems, followed by a discussion of system back-up and archiving utilities. Finally, you learn about the different forms of software available for Linux systems, how to compile source code into functional programs, and the features and usage of the Red Hat Package Manager.

COMPRESSION

There may be times when you wish to reduce the size of a file or set of files due to limited disk space. You may also wish to compress files that are sent across a computer network such as the Internet to decrease transfer time. In either case, there are several utilities that can perform a standard set of instructions on a file to reduce its size by stripping out characters. This procedure is called **compression**, and the standard set of instructions used to compress a file is known as a **compression algorithm**. To decompress a file, you may simply run the compression algorithm in reverse.

Since compression utilities use different compression algorithms, they achieve different rates of compression for similar types of files. The rate of compression is known as a **compression ratio**; if a compression utility compressed a file to 52% of its original size, we say that it has a compression ratio of 48%.

There are many compression utilities available to Linux users. In the following sections, you learn about the three most common ones, which are:

- compress
- gzip
- bzip2

The compress Utility

The compress utility is one of the oldest compression utilities common to most UNIX and Linux systems. The compression algorithm that it uses is called Adaptive Lempel-Ziv coding (LZW), and it has an average compression ratio of 40–50%.

To compress a file using the compress utility, you may specify the files to compress as arguments to the **compress** command. Each file will be renamed with a **.Z** filename extension to indicate that it is compressed. Additionally, you may use the verbose (**–v**) option to the **compress command** to display the compression ratio during compression. The following output displays the filenames and size of **samplefile** and **samplefile2** before and after compression:

```
[root@localhost root]# ls —l
total 28
drwx------    3 root     root     4096 Jul 21 08:15 Desktop
-rw-r--r--    1 root     root     20239 Jul 21 08:15 samplefile
-rw-rw-r--    1 root     root      574 Jul 21 08:18 samplefile2
[root@localhost root]# compress —v samplefile samplefile2
samplefile:  -- replaced with samplefile.Z Compression: 48.06%
samplefile2: -- replaced with samplefile2.Z Compression: 26.13%
[root@localhost root]# ls —l
total 20
drwx------    3 root     root     4096 Jul 21 08:15 Desktop
-rw-rw-r--    1 root     root      424 Jul 21 08:18 samplefile2.Z
-rw-r--r--    1 root     root     10512 Jul 21 08:15 samplefile.Z
[root@localhost root]# _
```

The compress utility preserves the original ownership, modification, and access time for each file that it compresses.

By default, the compress utility will not compress symbolic links or very small files. To force the compress utility to compress these files, you must use the —f option. You may compress all of the files in a certain directory by using the —r option and specifying the directory name as an argument to the compress command.

Once compressed, the **zcat command** can be used to display the contents of a compressed file, as seen in the following output:

```
[root@localhost root]# zcat samplefile2.Z
Hi there, I hope this day finds you well.

Unfortunately we were not able to make it to your dining
room this year while vacationing in Algonquin Park — I
especially wished to see the model of the Highland Inn
and the train station in the dining room.

I have been reading on the history of Algonquin Park but
no where could I find a description of where the Highland
Inn was originally located on Cache lake.

If it is no trouble, could you kindly let me know such that
I need not wait until next year when I visit your lodge?

Regards,
Mackenzie Elizabeth

[root@localhost root]# _
```

There also exists a **zmore command**, which can be used to view the contents of a compressed file page-by-page.

To decompress files that have been compressed with the compress utility, simply use the **uncompress command** followed by the names of the files to be decompressed. This will restore the original filenames. The following output decompresses and displays the filenames for the samplefile.Z and samplefile2.Z files created earlier:

```
[root@localhost root]# uncompress —v samplefile.Z samplefile2.Z
samplefile.Z:  -- replaced with samplefile
samplefile2.Z:  -- replaced with samplefile2
[root@localhost root]# ls —l
total 28
drwx------    3 root     root          4096 Jul 21 08:15 Desktop
-rw-r--r--    1 root     root         20239 Jul 21 08:15 samplefile
-rw-rw-r--    1 root     root           574 Jul 21 08:18 samplefile2
[root@localhost root]# _
```

You will be prompted for confirmation if any existing files will be overwritten during decompression. To prevent this, you may use the −f option to the uncompress command.

You may omit the `.Z` extension when using the uncompress command. The command `uncompress −v samplefile samplefile2` would achieve the same results as the command seen in the output above.

Furthermore, the compress utility is a filter command that can take information from Standard Input and send to Standard Output. For example, to send the output of the `who` command to the compress utility and save the compressed information to a file called `file.Z`, you may execute the command seen below:

```
[root@localhost root]# who | compress −v >file.Z
Compression: 21.35%
[root@localhost root]# _
```

Following this, you may display the contents of `file.Z` using the `zcat` command or decompress it using the `uncompress` command, as seen in the following output:

```
[root@localhost root]# zcat file.Z
root        pts/1      Jul 20 19:22 (3.0.0.2)
root        tty5       Jul 15 19:03
root        pts/1      Jul 17 19:58
[root@localhost root]# uncompress −v file.Z
file.Z:  -- replaced with file
[root@localhost root]# _
```

A summary of options commonly used with the compress utility is shown in Table 13-1.

Table 13-1   Common options used with the compress utility

Option	Description
−c	When used with the uncompress command, displays the contents of the compress file to Standard Output (same function as the zcat command)
−f	When used with the compress command, can be used to compress symbolic links; when used with the uncompress command, overwrites any existing files without prompting the user
−r	Specifies whether to compress or decompress all files recursively within a specified directory
−v	Displays verbose output (compression ratio and filenames) during compression and decompression

The gzip Utility

The **GNU zip (gzip)** utility uses a Lempel-Ziv compression algorithm (LZ77) that varies slightly from the one used by the compress utility. Typically, this algorithm yields better compression than the one used by compress; the average compression ratio for gzip is 60–70%.

Like the compress utility, symbolic links are not compressed by the gzip utility unless the −f option is given, and the −r option may be used to compress all files in a certain directory. In addition, the ownership, modification, and access times of compressed files are preserved by default, and the −v option to the gzip command can be used to display the compression ratio and filename. However, gzip uses the .gz filename extension by default.

To compress the samplefile and samplefile2 files seen earlier and view the compression ratio, you may use the following command:

```
[root@localhost root]# gzip −v samplefile samplefile2
samplefile:                56.8% -- replaced with samplefile.gz
samplefile2:               40.7% -- replaced with samplefile2.gz
[root@localhost root]# _
```

You may also use the zcat and zmore commands to send the contents of a compressed file to Standard Output. Along the same lines, the gzip command can accept information via Standard Input. Thus, to compress the output of the date command to a file called file.gz and view its contents afterwards, you may use the following commands:

```
[root@localhost root]# date | gzip −v >file.gz
- 6.8%
[root@localhost root]# zcat file.gz
Mon Jul 22 19:24:56 EDT 2003
[root@localhost root]# _
```

To decompress the file.gz file in the above output, you may use the −d option to the gzip command, or the **gunzip command**, as seen below:

```
[root@localhost root]# gunzip −v file.gz
file.gz:                   - 6.8% -- replaced with file
[root@localhost root]# _
```

Like the uncompress command, the gunzip command will prompt you to overwrite existing files unless the −f option is specified. Furthermore, you may omit the .gz extension when decompressing files, as seen in the following example:

```
[root@localhost root]# ls −l
total 20
drwx------      3 root      root           4096 Jul 21 08:15 Desktop
-rw-rw-r--      1 root      root            370 Jul 21 08:18 samplefile2.gz
-rw-r--r--      1 root      root           8763 Jul 21 08:15 samplefile.gz
[root@localhost root]# gunzip −v samplefile samplefile2
samplefile.gz:             56.8% -- replaced with samplefile
samplefile2.gz:            40.7% -- replaced with samplefile2
[root@localhost root]# ls −l
total 28
drwx------      3 root      root           4096 Jul 21 08:15 Desktop
-rw-r--r--      1 root      root          20239 Jul 21 08:15 samplefile
-rw-rw-r--      1 root      root            574 Jul 21 08:18 samplefile2
[root@localhost root]# _
```

13

One of the largest advantages that the gzip utility has over the compress utility is its ability to control the level of compression via a numeric option. The −1 option is also known as fast compression and results in a lower compression ratio. Alternatively, the −9 option is known as best compression and results in the highest compression ratio at the expense of time. If no level of compression is specified, the `gzip` command assumes the number 6.

The following command will compress the `samplefile` file seen earlier using fast compression and display the compression ratio:

```
[root@localhost root]# gzip −v −1 samplefile
samplefile:             51.3% -- replaced with samplefile.gz
[root@localhost root]# _
```

Notice from the above output that `samplefile` was compressed with a compression ratio of 51.3%, which is much lower than the compression ratio of 56.8% obtained earlier when `samplefile` was compressed with the default level of 6.

You need not specify the level of compression when decompressing files, as it is built into the compressed file itself.

There are many more options available to the gzip utility than the compress utility, and many of these options have a POSIX option equivalent. A list of these options is found in Table 13-2.

Table 13-2   Common options used with the gzip utility

Option	Description
-#	Specifies how thorough the compression will be, where # may be the number 1–9 (the option –1 represents fast compression, which takes less time to compress but results in a lower compression ratio; the option –9 represents thorough compression, which takes more time but results in a higher compression ratio)
--best	Same as the –9 option; results in a higher compression ratio
-c --stdout --to-stdout	When used with the gunzip command, displays the contents of the com pressed file to Standard Output (same function as the zcat command)
-d --decompress --uncompress	When used with the gzip command, decompresses the files specified (same as the gunzip command)
-f --force	When used with the gzip command, can be used to compress symbolic links; when used with the gunzip command, overwrites any existing files without prompting the user
--fast	Same as the –1 option; results in a lower compression ratio
-h --help	Displays the syntax and available options for the gzip and gunzip commands

Table 13-2   Common options used with the gzip utility (continued)

Option	Description
-l --list	Lists the compression ratio for files that have been compressed with gzip
-n --no-name	Does not allow gzip and gunzip to preserve the original modification and access time for files
-q --quiet	Suppresses all warning messages
-r --recursive	Specifies to compress or decompress all files recursively within a specified directory
-S .suffix --suffix .suffix	Specifies a file suffix other than .gz when compressing or decompressing files
-t --test	When used with the gunzip command, performs a test decompression such that a user may view any error messages before decompression; does not decompress files
-v --verbose	Displays verbose output (compression ratio and filenames) during compression and decompression

The bzip2 Utility

The **bzip2** utility differs from the compress and gzip utilities previously discussed, in that it uses the Burrows-Wheeler Block Sorting Huffman Coding algorithm when compressing files. In addition, the bzip2 utility cannot be used to compress a directory full of files, the `zcat` and `zmore` commands cannot be used to view files compressed with bzip2, and the compression ratio is 50–75% on average.

Like the compress and gzip utilities, symbolic links are only compressed if the —f option is used, and the —v option can be used to display compression ratios. Also, file ownership, modification, and access time are preserved during compression.

The filename extension given to files compressed with bzip2 is `.bz2`. To compress the `samplefile` and `samplefile2` files and view their compression ratio and filenames, you may use the following commands:

```
[root@localhost root]# bzip2 —v samplefile samplefile2
samplefile:  2.637:1, 3.034 bits/byte, 62.08% saved, 20239 in,7675 out.
samplefile2: 1.483:1, 5.394 bits/byte, 32.58% saved, 574 in,387 out.
[root@localhost root]# ls —l
total 16
drwx------   3 root      root          4096 Jul 21 08:15 Desktop
-rw-rw-r--   1 root      root           387 Jul 21 08:18 samplefile2.bz2
-rw-r--r--   1 root      root          7675 Jul 21 08:15 samplefile.bz2
[root@localhost root]# _
```

13

Since the compression algorithm is different from the one used by the `compress` and `gzip` utilities, you must use the **bzcat command** to display the contents of compressed files to Standard Output, as seen below:

```
[root@localhost root]# bzcat samplefile2.bz2
Hi there, I hope this day finds you well.

Unfortunately we were not able to make it to your dining
room this year while vacationing in Algonquin Park — I
especially wished to see the model of the Highland Inn
and the train station in the dining room.

I have been reading on the history of Algonquin Park but
no where could I find a description of where the Highland
Inn was originally located on Cache lake.

If it is no trouble, could you kindly let me know such that
I need not wait until next year when I visit your lodge?

Regards,
Mackenzie Elizabeth

[root@localhost root]# _
```

To decompress files, you may use the **bunzip2 command** followed by the filename(s) to decompress; unlike `compress` and `gzip`, you must include the filename extension when decompressing files. To decompress the `samplefile` and `samplefile2` files created earlier and view the results, you may use the following command:

```
[root@localhost root]# bunzip2 —v samplefile.bz2 samplefile2.bz2
  samplefile.bz2:  done
  samplefile2.bz2: done
[root@localhost root]# _
```

The `bunzip2` command will prompt you for confirmation if any files are to be over-written, unless the —f option is specified. Other common options used with the bzip2 utility are listed in Table 13-3.

Table 13-3   Common options used with the bzip2 utility

Option	Description
-#	Specifies the block size used during compression; –1 indicates a block size of 100KB whereas –9 indicates a block size of 900KB
-c --stdout	When used with the bunzip2 command, displays the contents of the compressed file to Standard Output
-d --decompress	When used with the bzip2 command, decompresses the files specified (same as the bunzip2 command)

Table 13-3   Common options used with the bzip2 utility (continued)

Option	Description
-f --force	When used with the bzip2 command, can be used to compress symbolic links; when used with the bunzip2 command, overwrites any existing files without prompting the user
-k --keep	Keeps the original file during compression; a new file will be created with the extension .bz2
-q --quiet	Suppresses all warning messages
-s --small	Minimizes memory usage during compression
-t --test	When used with the bunzip2 command, performs a test decompression such that a user may view any error messages before decompression; does not decompress files
-v --verbose	Displays verbose output (compression ratio) during compression and decompression

SYSTEM BACK-UP

Files and directories may be copied to an alternate location at regular intervals. These back-up copies may then be distributed to other computers or used to restore files if a system failure occurs that results in a loss of information. This entire process is known as **system back-up**, and the back-up copies of files and directories are called **archives**.

Archives may be created on many different types of media such as tapes, zip disks, floppy disks, CD-RW discs, or hard disks. The most common medium used to back up data on Linux systems, however, is tape. A list of some common device files for use with different tape devices is shown in Table 13-4.

Table 13-4   Common tape device files

Device File	Description
/dev/st0	First SCSI tape device (rewinding)
/dev/st1	Second SCSI tape device (rewinding)
/dev/st2	Third SCSI tape device (rewinding)
/dev/nst0	First SCSI tape device (non-rewinding)
/dev/ht0	First ATAPI IDE tape device (rewinding)
/dev/nht0	First ATAPI IDE tape device (non-rewinding)
/dev/ft0	First floppy tape device (rewinding)
/dev/nft0	First floppy tape device (non-rewinding)

The **magnetic tape (mt) command** can be used to manipulate tape devices or prepare a tape for system back-up. For example, to rewind the first SCSI tape device on a system, you could use the command mt –f /dev/st0 rewind.

A typical Linux system may have hundreds of thousands of files on it, but not all of these files need be included in an archive. Temporary files in the /tmp and /var/tmp directories need not be included, nor do any cached Internet content found in the .netscape (for the Netscape Navigator Web browser) or .mozilla (for the Mozilla Web browser) directories under each user's home directory.

As a general rule of thumb, you should back up user files from home directories and any important system configuration files such as /etc/passwd. In addition to this, you may wish to back up files used by system services. For example, you would back up Web site files if the Linux computer was used as a Web server. Programs such as grep and vi need not be backed up since they may be restored from the original installation media in the event of a system failure.

Once files have been selected for system back-up, you may use a back-up utility to copy the files to the appropriate media. There are several back-up utilities available to Linux administrators; the most common are:

- tar
- cpio
- dump/restore

The tar Utility

The **tape archive (tar)** utility is one of the oldest and most common back-up utilities; it can create an archive in a file on a filesystem or directly on a device.

Like the compression utilities discussed earlier, the tar utility accepts options to determine the location of the archive and the action to perform on the archive; any arguments specified to the **tar** command list the file(s) to place in the archive. A list of common options used with the **tar** command is depicted in Table 13-5.

Table 13-5 Common options used with the tar utility

Option	Description
-A --catenate --concatenate	Appends whole archives to another archive
-c --create	Creates a new archive
--exclude *FILENAME*	Excludes *FILENAME* when creating an archive
-f *FILENAME* --file *FILENAME*	Specifies the location of the archive (*FILENAME*); may be a file on a filesystem or a device file

Table 13-5   Common options used with the tar utility (continued)

Option	Description
-h --dereference	Will prevent tar from backing up symbolic links; instead, tar will back up the target files of symbolic links
-j --bzip	Compresses/decompresses the archive using the bzip2 utility
-P --absolute-paths	Stores filenames in an archive using absolute pathnames
-r --append	Appends files to an existing archive
--remove-files	Removes files after adding them to an archive
-t --list	Lists the filename contents (table of contents) of an existing archive
-u --update	Appends files to an existing archive only if they are newer than the same filename inside the archive.
-v --verbose	Displays verbose output (file & directory information) when manipulating archives
-w --interactive --confirmation	Prompts the user for confirmation of each action
-W --verify	Verifies the contents of each archive after creation
-x --extract --get	Extracts the contents of an archive
-z --gzip --ungzip	Compresses/decompresses the archive using the gzip utility
-Z --compress --uncompress	Compresses/decompresses the archive using the compress utility

13

To create an archive called /backup.tar that contains the contents of the current directory and view the results, you may use the following commands:

```
[root@localhost root]# tar —cvf /backup.tar  *
Desktop/
Desktop/Home
Desktop/Trash/
Desktop/Trash/.directory
Desktop/www.redhat.com
Desktop/cdrom
Desktop/.directory
Desktop/floppy
Desktop/KDE Control Panel
```

```
Desktop/Linux Documentation
samplefile
samplefile2
[root@localhost root]# ls -l /backup.tar
-rw-r--r--    1 root      root              40960 Jul 27 10:49 /backup.tar
[root@localhost root]# _
```

Note from the command above that the −f option is followed by the pathname of the archive and that the * metacharacter indicates that all files in the current directory will be added to this archive. Also note that files are backed up recursively by default and stored using relative pathnames; to force the use of absolute pathnames when creating archives, simply use the −P option to the tar command.

The filename used for an archive need not have an extension; however, it is good practice to name archive files with an extension to identify their contents as with /backup.tar in the example above.

The tar utility cannot back up device files or files with filenames longer than 255 characters.

You may view the detailed contents of an archive after creation by specifying the −t (table of contents) option to the tar command and the archive to view. For example, to view the detailed contents of the /backup.tar archive created earlier, you may issue the following command:

```
[root@localhost root]# tar -tvf /backup.tar
drwx------ root/root         0 2002-07-21 08:15:09 Desktop/
-rw-r--r-- root/root      2588 2002-06-21 20:32:48 Desktop/Home
drwx------ root/root         0 2002-07-21 08:15:09 Desktop/Trash/
-rw-r--r-- root/root       757 2002-06-21 20:32:48 Desktop/Trash/.directory
-rw-r--r-- root/root       107 2002-06-21 20:32:48 Desktop/www.redhat.com
-rw------- root/root      1117 2002-06-21 20:32:48 Desktop/cdrom
-rw------- root/root       321 2002-07-18 06:08:35 Desktop/.directory
-rw------- root/root       151 2002-06-21 20:32:48 Desktop/floppy
-rw-r--r-- root/root       149 2002-06-21 20:32:48 Desktop/KDE Control Panel
-rw-r--r-- root/root        80 2002-06-21 20:32:48 Desktop/Linux Documentation
-rw-r--r-- root/root     20239 2002-07-21 08:15:35 samplefile
-rw-rw-r-- root/root       574 2002-07-21 08:18:08 samplefile2
[root@localhost root]# _
```

The −x option may be used with the tar command to extract a specified archive. To extract the contents of the /backup.tar file to a new directory called /tartest and view the results, you may issue the following commands:

```
[root@localhost root]# mkdir /tartest
[root@localhost root]# cd /tartest
[root@localhost tartest]# tar -xvf /backup.tar
Desktop/
Desktop/Home
Desktop/Trash/
```

```
Desktop/Trash/.directory
Desktop/www.redhat.com
Desktop/cdrom
Desktop/.directory
Desktop/floppy
Desktop/KDE Control Panel
Desktop/Linux Documentation
samplefile
samplefile2
[root@localhost tartest]# ls -F
Desktop/   samplefile   samplefile2
[root@localhost tartest]# _
```

Once an archive has been created in a file on a filesystem, that file may be sent to other computers across a network such as the Internet. Unfortunately, the tar utility does not compress files inside the archive; thus the time needed to transfer the archive across a network would be high. To reduce transfer times, you may compress the archive using a compression utility before transmission. Since this is a common task, the `tar` command accepts options that allow you to compress an archive immediately after creation using the `compress`, `gzip`, or `bzip2` utilities.

To create a gzip-compressed archive called `/backup.tar.gz` that contains the contents of the current directory and view the results, you may use the following commands:

```
[root@localhost root]# tar -zcvf /backup.tar.gz  *
Desktop/
Desktop/Home
Desktop/Trash/
Desktop/Trash/.directory
Desktop/www.redhat.com
Desktop/cdrom
Desktop/.directory
Desktop/floppy
Desktop/KDE Control Panel
Desktop/Linux Documentation
samplefile
samplefile2
[root@localhost root]# ls -l /backup.tar*
-rw-r--r--    1 root      root           40960 Jul 27 10:49 /backup.tar
-rw-r--r--    1 root      root           12207 Jul 27 11:18 /backup.tar.gz
[root@localhost root]# _
```

Note from above that the -z option indicated compression using the `gzip` utility, and that we chose to end the filename with the `.tar.gz` extension. In addition, the size of the `/backup.tar.gz` file is much less than the `/backup.tar` file created earlier.

Filenames that end with the .tar.gz or .tgz extensions are commonly called **tarballs** and represent gzip-compressed tar archives.

To view the contents of a gzip-compressed archive, you must use the −z option in addition to the −t option followed by the archive to view. The detailed contents of the /backup.tar.gz file may be viewed using the following command:

```
[root@localhost root]# tar −ztvf /backup.tar.gz
drwx------ root/root          0 2002-07-21 08:15:09 Desktop/
-rw-r--r-- root/root       2588 2002-06-21 20:32:48 Desktop/Home
drwx------ root/root          0 2002-07-21 08:15:09 Desktop/Trash/
-rw-r--r-- root/root        757 2002-06-21 20:32:48 Desktop/Trash/.directory
-rw-r--r-- root/root        107 2002-06-21 20:32:48 Desktop/www.redhat.com
-rw------- root/root       1117 2002-06-21 20:32:48 Desktop/cdrom
-rw------- root/root        321 2002-07-18 06:08:35 Desktop/.directory
-rw------- root/root        151 2002-06-21 20:32:48 Desktop/floppy
-rw-r--r-- root/root        149 2002-06-21 20:32:48 Desktop/KDE Control Panel
-rw-r--r-- root/root         80 2002-06-21 20:32:48 Desktop/Linux Documentation
-rw-r--r-- root/root      20239 2002-07-21 08:15:35 samplefile
-rw-rw-r-- root/root        574 2002-07-21 08:18:08 samplefile2
[root@localhost root]# _
```

Similarly, when extracting a gzip-compressed archive, you must supply the −z option to the tar command. To extract the contents of the /backup.tar.gz file to a new directory called /tartest2 and view the results, you may issue the following commands:

```
[root@localhost root]# mkdir /tartest2
[root@localhost root]# cd /tartest2
[root@localhost tartest2]# tar −zxvf /backup.tar.gz
Desktop/
Desktop/Home
Desktop/Trash/
Desktop/Trash/.directory
Desktop/www.redhat.com
Desktop/cdrom
Desktop/.directory
Desktop/floppy
Desktop/KDE Control Panel
Desktop/Linux Documentation
samplefile
samplefile2
[root@localhost tartest2]# ls −F
Desktop/   samplefile   samplefile2
[root@localhost tartest2]# _
```

Backing up files to a compressed archive on a filesystem is useful when transferring data across a network, but is ill-suited to backing up large amounts of data for system recovery. Devices such as tapes are better suited for this task. To back up files to a device, you may use the −f option to the tar command to specify the pathname to the appropriate device file. Files will then be transferred directly to the device, overwriting any other data or filesystems that may be present.

For example, to create an archive on the first rewinding SCSI tape device containing the contents of the current directory, you may use the following command:

```
[root@localhost root]# tar -cvf /dev/st0  *
Desktop/
Desktop/Home
Desktop/Trash/
Desktop/Trash/.directory
Desktop/www.redhat.com
Desktop/cdrom
Desktop/.directory
Desktop/floppy
Desktop/KDE Control Panel
Desktop/Linux Documentation
samplefile
samplefile2
[root@localhost root]#
```

You may then view the contents of the archive on the tape device used in the above example using the command tar -tvf /dev/st0 or extract the contents of the archive on the tape device using the command tar -xvf /dev/st0 in a similar fashion to the examples seen earlier.

Since tape devices may hold large amounts of information, you may wish to add to a tar archive that already exists on the tape device. To do this, simply replace the -c option with the -r option when using the tar utility. For example, to append a file called samplefile3 to the archive created in the previous output and view the results, you may use the following commands:

```
[root@localhost root]# tar -rvf /dev/st0 samplefile3
samplefile3
[root@localhost root]# tar -tvf /dev/st0
drwx------ root/root        0 2002-07-21 08:15:09 Desktop/
-rw-r--r-- root/root     2588 2002-06-21 20:32:48 Desktop/Home
drwx------ root/root        0 2002-07-21 08:15:09 Desktop/Trash/
-rw-r--r-- root/root      757 2002-06-21 20:32:48 Desktop/Trash/.directory
-rw-r--r-- root/root      107 2002-06-21 20:32:48 Desktop/www.redhat.com
-rw------- root/root     1117 2002-06-21 20:32:48 Desktop/cdrom
-rw------- root/root      321 2002-07-18 06:08:35 Desktop/.directory
-rw------- root/root      151 2002-06-21 20:32:48 Desktop/floppy
-rw-r--r-- root/root      149 2002-06-21 20:32:48 Desktop/KDE Control Panel
-rw-r--r-- root/root       80 2002-06-21 20:32:48 Desktop/Linux Documentation
-rw-r--r-- root/root    20239 2002-07-21 08:15:35 samplefile
-rw-rw-r-- root/root      574 2002-07-21 08:18:08 samplefile2
-rw-r--r-- root/root      147 2002-07-27 16:15:18 samplefile3
[root@localhost root]# _
```

13

The cpio Utility

Another common back-up utility is **copy in/out (cpio)**. Although this utility uses options similar to the tar utility, cpio has some added features including the ability to back up device files and long filenames.

Since its primary use is to back up files in case of system failure, cpio uses absolute path-names by default when archiving. In addition, cpio normally takes a list of files to archive from Standard Input and sends the files "out" to an archive specified by the −O option. Conversely, when extracting an archive, the −I option must be specified to indicate the archive from which to read "in" files.

A list of commonly used options to the cpio command and their descriptions is seen in Table 13-6.

Table 13-6   Common options used with the cpio utility

Option	Description
-A --append	Appends files to an existing archive
-B	Changes the default block size from 512 bytes to 5 kilo bytes, thus speeding up the transfer of information
-c	Uses a storage format (SVR4) that is widely recognized by different versions of cpio for UNIX and Linux
-d --make-directories	Creates directories as needed during extraction
-i --extract	Reads files from an archive
-I FILENAME	Represents the input archive; Filename is the file or device file of the archive used when viewing or extracting files
-L --dereference	Will prevent cpio from backing up symbolic links; instead, cpio will back up the target files of symbolic links
--no-absolute-filenames	Stores filenames in an archive using relative pathnames
-o --create	Creates a new archive
-O FILENAME	Represents the output archive; Filename is the file or device of the target archive when backing up files
-t --list	Lists the filename contents (table of contents) of an existing archive
-u --unconditional	Overwrites existing files during extraction without prompting for user confirmation
-v --verbose	Displays verbose output (file & directory information) when manipulating archives

To create an archive using cpio, a list of filenames must first be generated; this may be accomplished using the find command. To list all filenames underneath the /root/sample directory, you may use the following command:

```
[root@localhost root]# find /root/sample
/root/sample
```

```
/root/sample/samplefile
/root/sample/samplefile2
[root@localhost root]# _
```

Now, you may send this list via Standard Input to the cpio command. For example, to back up all files in /root/sample verbosely to the first rewinding SCSI tape device using a block size of 5 kilobytes and a common format, you may use the following command:

```
[root@localhost root]# find /root/sample | cpio —vocB —O @Code 2nd:/dev/st0
/root/sample
/root/sample/samplefile
/root/sample/samplefile2
5 blocks
[root@localhost root]# _
```

To view the verbose table of contents of this archive, you may use the command shown below:

```
[root@localhost root]# cpio —vitB —I /dev/st0
drwxr-xr-x   2 root      root          0 Jul 27 13:40 /root/sample
-rw-r--r--   1 root      root      20239 Jul 21 08:15 /root/sample/samplefile
-rw-rw-r--   1 root      root        574 Jul 21 08:18 /root/sample/samplefile2
5 blocks
[root@localhost root]# _
```

Following this, you may extract the archive on /dev/st0, creating directories and over-writing files as needed, by using the following command:

```
[root@localhost root]# cpio —vicduB —I /dev/st0
/root/sample
/root/sample/samplefile
/root/sample/samplefile2
5 blocks
[root@localhost root]# _
```

Like tar, the cpio command can be used to create an archive on a file on the current filesystem; to do this, simply specify the filename after the —O option. To create an archive called /root/sample.cpio that contains the files from the directory /root/sample, using a block size of 5 kilobytes as well as a common format, and view the results, you may issue the following commands:

```
[root@localhost root]# find /root/sample | cpio —vocB —O /root/sample.cpio
/root/sample
/root/sample/samplefile
/root/sample/samplefile2
5 blocks
[root@localhost root]# ls —l sample.cpio
-rw-rw-rw-   1 root      root      25600 Jul 27 13:45 sample.cpio
[root@localhost root]# _
```

As with the tar utility, cpio archive filenames need not have an extension to identify their contents. However, it is good practice to use extensions, as seen with /root/sample.cpio in the example above.

The dump/restore Utility

Like the tar and gzip utilities, the **dump/restore** utility can be used to back up files and directories to a device or to a file on the filesystem. However, the dump/restore utility can only work with files on ext2 and ext3 filesystems.

Although the dump/restore utility can be used to back up only certain files and directories, it was designed to back up entire filesystems to an archive and keep track of these filesystems in a file called **/etc/dumpdates**. Since archiving all data on a filesystem (known as a **full back-up**) may take a long time, you may choose to perform a full back-up only on weekends and incremental back-ups each evening during the week. An **incremental back-up** only backs up the data that has been changed since the last back-up. In the case of a system failure, you may restore the information from the full back-up and then restore the information from all subsequent incremental back-ups in sequential order. You may perform up to nine different incremental back-ups using the dump/restore utility; number 0 represents a full back-up, whereas numbers 1 through 9 represent incremental back-ups.

Say, for example, that you perform a full back-up of the /dev/hda3 filesystem on Sunday, perform incremental back-ups from Monday to Wednesday, and on Thursday the /dev/hda3 filesystem becomes corrupted, as depicted in Figure 13-1.

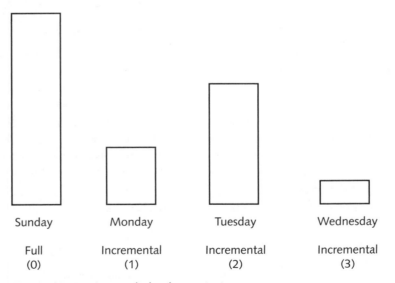

Figure 13-1 A sample back-up strategy

Once the filesystem has been recreated, you should restore the full back-up (0) followed by the first incremental back-up (1), the second incremental back-up (2), and the third incremental back-up (3), to ensure that data has been properly recovered.

The dump/restore utility has many options available to it, as do the tar and cpio utilities. A list of these is shown in Table 13-7.

Table 13-7   Common options used with the dump/restore utility

Option	Description
-#	Specifies the type of back-up when used with the dump command (if # is 0, a full back-up is performed; if # is 1 through 9, then the appropriate incremental back-up is performed)
-b NUM	Specifies a certain block size to use in kilobytes; the default block size is 10 kilobytes
-f FILENAME	Specifies the pathname to the archive; FILENAME may be a file on a filesystem or a device file
-u	Specifies to update the /etc/dumpdates file after a successful back-up
-n	Notifies the user if any errors occur and when the back-up has completed
-r	When used with the restore command, extracts an entire archive
-x FILENAME	When used with the restore command, extracts a certain file or files represented by FILENAME
-i	When used with the restore command, restores files interactively, prompting the user for confirmation for all actions
-t	When used with the restore command, lists the filename contents (table of contents) of an existing archive
-v	Displays verbose output (file & directory information) when manipulating archives

13

Take, for example, the output from the df command shown below:

```
[root@localhost root]# df
Filesystem           1k-blocks     Used Available Use% Mounted on
/dev/hda3             4032124   2840560    986736  75% /
/dev/hda2              101107     10550     85336  12% /boot
none                  192232         0    192232   0% /dev/shm
[root@localhost root]# _
```

To perform a full back-up of the /boot partition (/dev/hda2) to the first rewinding SCSI tape device and update the /etc/dumpdates file when completed, you could issue the following command:

```
[root@localhost root]# dump -0uf /dev/st0 /dev/hda2
  DUMP: Date of this level 0 dump: Sat Jul 27 16:43:09 2003
  DUMP: Dumping /dev/hda2 (/boot) to /dev/st0
  DUMP: Exclude ext3 journal inode 8
  DUMP: Label: /boot
  DUMP: mapping (Pass I) [regular files]
  DUMP: mapping (Pass II) [directories]
```

```
    DUMP: estimated 6485 tape blocks.
    DUMP: Volume 1 started with block 1 at: Sat Jul 27 16:43:10 2003
    DUMP: dumping (Pass III) [directories]
    DUMP: dumping (Pass IV) [regular files]
    DUMP: Closing /dev/st0
    DUMP: Volume 1 completed at: Sat Jul 27 16:43:11 2003
    DUMP: Volume 1 6470 tape blocks (6.32MB)
    DUMP: Volume 1 took 0:00:01
    DUMP: Volume 1 transfer rate: 6470 kB/s
    DUMP: 6470 tape blocks (6.32MB) on 1 volume(s)
    DUMP: finished in 1 seconds, throughput 6470 kBytes/sec
    DUMP: Date of this level 0 dump: Sat Jul 27 16:43:09 2003
    DUMP: Date this dump completed:  Sat Jul 27 16:43:11 2003
    DUMP: Average transfer rate: 6470 kB/s
    DUMP: DUMP IS DONE
[root@localhost root]# _
```

Alternatively, you may specify the filesystem mount point when using the dump command; the command dump −0uf /dev/st0 /boot is equivalent to the one used in the above example.

The contents of the /etc/dumpdates file will now indicate that a full back-up has taken place:

```
[root@localhost root]# cat /etc/dumpdates
/dev/hda2 0 Sat Jul 27 16:43:09 2003
[root@localhost root]# _
```

To perform the first incremental back-up and view the contents of the /etc/dumpdates file, you could place a new tape into the SCSI tape drive and issue the following commands:

```
[root@localhost root]# dump −1uf /dev/st0 /dev/hda2
   DUMP: Date of this level 1 dump: Sat Jul 27 16:50:57 2003
   DUMP: Date of last level 0 dump: Sat Jul 27 16:43:09 2003
   DUMP: Dumping /dev/hda2 (/boot) to /dev/st0
   DUMP: Exclude ext3 journal inode 8
   DUMP: Label: /boot
   DUMP: mapping (Pass I) [regular files]
   DUMP: mapping (Pass II) [directories]
   DUMP: estimated 21 tape blocks.
   DUMP: Volume 1 started with block 1 at: Sat Jul 27 16:50:58 2003
   DUMP: dumping (Pass III) [directories]
   DUMP: dumping (Pass IV) [regular files]
   DUMP: Closing /dev/st0
   DUMP: Volume 1 completed at: Sat Jul 27 16:50:58 2003
   DUMP: Volume 1 20 tape blocks (0.02MB)
   DUMP: 20 tape blocks (0.02MB) on 1 volume(s)
   DUMP: finished in less than a second
   DUMP: Date of this level 1 dump: Sat Jul 27 16:50:57 2003
   DUMP: Date this dump completed:  Sat Jul 27 16:50:58 2003
   DUMP: Average transfer rate: 0 kB/s
   DUMP: DUMP IS DONE
```

```
[root@localhost root]# cat /etc/dumpdates
/dev/hda2 0 Sat Jul 27 16:43:09 2003
/dev/hda2 1 Sat Jul 27 16:50:57 2003
[root@localhost root]# _
```

To view the contents of an archive, you may specify the −t option to the **restore command** followed by the archive information. To view the contents of the full back-up performed earlier, you could place the appropriate tape into the tape drive and execute the following command:

```
[root@localhost root]# restore −tf /dev/st0
Dump    date: Sat Jul 27 16:43:09 2003
Dumped from: the epoch
Level 0 dump of /boot on localhost.localdomain:/dev/hda2
Label: /boot
            2        .
           11        ./lost+found
         4033        ./grub
         4035        ./grub/grub.conf
         4034        ./grub/splash.xpm.gz
         4036        ./grub/menu.lst
         4037        ./grub/device.map
         4038        ./grub/stage1
         4039        ./grub/stage2
         4040        ./grub/e2fs_stage1_5
         4041        ./grub/fat_stage1_5
         4042        ./grub/ffs_stage1_5
         4043        ./grub/minix_stage1_5
         4044        ./grub/reiserfs_stage1_5
         4045        ./grub/vstafs_stage1_5
           16        ./kernel.h-2.4.7
           12        ./boot.b
           13        ./chain.b
           14        ./message
           15        ./os2_d.b
           17        ./kernel.h
           19        ./module-info-2.4.7-10
           18        ./System.map-2.4.7-10
           21        ./vmlinuz
           22        ./System.map
           20        ./vmlinuz-2.4.7-10
           23        ./module-info
           24        ./initrd-2.4.7-10.img
           29        ./initrd-2.4.7-10debug.img
           25        ./System.map-2.4.7-10debug
           26        ./module-info-2.4.7-10debug
           27        ./vmlinux-2.4.7-10debug
           28        ./vmlinuz-2.4.7-10debug
           31        ./boot.0300
           32        ./map
[root@localhost root]# _
```

13

To extract the full back-up seen in the output above, you may specify the —r option to the `restore` command followed by the archive information. Additionally, you may specify the —v option to list the filenames restored as seen below:

```
[root@localhost root]# restore —vrf /dev/st0
Verify tape and initialize maps
Input is from file/pipe
Input block size is 32
Dump   date: Sat Jul 27 16:43:09 2003
Dumped from: the epoch
Level 0 dump of /boot on localhost.localdomain:/dev/hda2
Label: /boot
Begin level 0 restore
Initialize symbol table.
Extract directories from tape
Calculate extraction list.
restore: ./lost+found: File exists
restore: ./grub: File exists
Extract new leaves.
Check pointing the restore
extract file ./boot.b
extract file ./chain.b
extract file ./message
extract file ./os2_d.b
extract file ./kernel.h-2.4.7
extract file ./System.map-2.4.7-10
extract file ./module-info-2.4.7-10
extract file ./vmlinuz-2.4.7-10
extract file ./initrd-2.4.7-10.img
extract file ./System.map-2.4.7-10debug
extract file ./module-info-2.4.7-10debug
extract file ./vmlinux-2.4.7-10debug
extract file ./vmlinuz-2.4.7-10debug
extract file ./initrd-2.4.7-10debug.img
extract file ./boot.0300
extract file ./map
extract file ./grub/splash.xpm.gz
extract file ./grub/grub.conf
extract file ./grub/device.map
extract file ./grub/stage1
extract file ./grub/stage2
extract file ./grub/e2fs_stage1_5
extract file ./grub/fat_stage1_5
extract file ./grub/ffs_stage1_5
extract file ./grub/minix_stage1_5
extract file ./grub/reiserfs_stage1_5
extract file ./grub/vstafs_stage1_5
```

```
Add links
Set directory mode, owner, and times.
Check the symbol table.
Check pointing the restore
[root@localhost root]# _
```

SOFTWARE INSTALLATION

Primary responsibilities of most Linux administrators typically include the installation and maintenance of software packages. Software for Linux may consist of binary program files that have been pre-compiled to run on certain hardware architectures such as Intel, or as source code, which must be compiled on the local architecture before use. The largest advantage to obtaining and compiling source code is that the source code is not created for particular hardware architecture. Once compiled, the program will execute on the architecture from which it was compiled.

 The most common method for obtaining software for Linux is via the Internet; Appendix C lists some common Web sites that host Linux Open Source Software for download.

Program source code is typically distributed in tarball format; the tarball can then be uncompressed and the source code extracted so that it may be compiled. Pre-compiled binary programs may also be distributed in tarball format, but are typically distributed in a format for use with a package manager.

Recall from Chapter 1 that a **package manager** provides a standard format for distributing programs as well as a central database to store information about software packages installed on the system; this allows software packages to be queried and uninstalled easily. The most common package manager used by Linux systems today is the **Red Hat Package Manager (RPM)**.

Compiling Source Code into Programs

The procedure for compiling source code into binary programs is standardized today among most Open Source Software developers. Since most source code comes in tarball format, you must first uncompress and extract the files. This will create a subdirectory under the current directory containing the source code. In addition, this directory typically contains a README file with information about the program and an INSTALL file with instructions for installation.

While inside the source code directory, the first step to installation is to run the `configure` program. This performs a preliminary check for system requirements and creates a list of what to compile inside a file called `Makefile` in the current directory.

13

Next, you may type the **make** command, which looks for **Makefile** and uses the information within to compile the source code into binary programs using the **GNU C Compiler (gcc)** for the local hardware architecture. After this has completed, the binary files that comprise the program are still stored in the source code directory. To copy the files to the appropriate location on the filesystem, such as a directory listed in the PATH variable, you must type **make install**.

 Most Linux programs are installed to a subdirectory of the /usr/local directory.

Once the program has been compiled and copied to the correct location on the filesystem, the source code directory and its contents may be removed from the system.

Say, for example, that you download the source code for LTRIS (Linux Tetris) version 1.0.3 from the Internet at *http://www.sourceforge.net*:

```
[root@localhost root]# ls —F
Desktop/      ltris-1.0.3.tar.gz
[root@localhost root]# _
```

The first step to installing this program is to uncompress and extract the tarball. This will create a directory called **ltris-1.0.3** containing the source code and supporting files, as seen in the output below:

```
[root@localhost root]# tar —zxvf ltris—1.0.3.tar.gz
ltris-1.0.3/
ltris-1.0.3/src/
ltris-1.0.3/src/gfx/
ltris-1.0.3/src/gfx/f_white.bmp
ltris-1.0.3/src/gfx/menuback.bmp
ltris-1.0.3/src/gfx/f_small_white.bmp
ltris-1.0.3/src/gfx/f_small_yellow.bmp
ltris-1.0.3/src/gfx/Makefile.am
ltris-1.0.3/src/gfx/Makefile.in
ltris-1.0.3/src/gfx/blocks.bmp
ltris-1.0.3/src/gfx/f_yellow.bmp
ltris-1.0.3/src/gfx/back0.bmp
ltris-1.0.3/src/gfx/back1.bmp
ltris-1.0.3/src/gfx/back2.bmp
ltris-1.0.3/src/gfx/f_tiny_black.bmp
ltris-1.0.3/src/gfx/back3.bmp
ltris-1.0.3/src/gfx/back4.bmp
ltris-1.0.3/src/gfx/back5.bmp
ltris-1.0.3/src/gfx/balloon_peek.bmp
ltris-1.0.3/src/gfx/logo.bmp
ltris-1.0.3/src/gfx/quest.bmp
ltris-1.0.3/src/gfx/balloon.bmp
```

```
ltris-1.0.3/src/cpu.c
ltris-1.0.3/src/cpu.h
ltris-1.0.3/src/gfx.S
ltris-1.0.3/src/gfx.h
ltris-1.0.3/src/sdl.c
ltris-1.0.3/src/sdl.h
ltris-1.0.3/src/empty.hscr
ltris-1.0.3/src/tetris.c
ltris-1.0.3/src/tetris.h
ltris-1.0.3/src/parser.c
ltris-1.0.3/src/parser.h
ltris-1.0.3/src/figures
ltris-1.0.3/src/event.c
ltris-1.0.3/src/event.h
ltris-1.0.3/src/ltris.h
ltris-1.0.3/src/bowl.c
ltris-1.0.3/src/bowl.h
ltris-1.0.3/src/manager.c
ltris-1.0.3/src/manager.h
ltris-1.0.3/src/config.c
ltris-1.0.3/src/config.h
ltris-1.0.3/src/Makefile.am
ltris-1.0.3/src/Makefile.in
ltris-1.0.3/src/hint.c
ltris-1.0.3/src/hint.h
ltris-1.0.3/src/tools.c
ltris-1.0.3/src/tools.h
ltris-1.0.3/src/item.c
ltris-1.0.3/src/item.h
ltris-1.0.3/src/list.c
ltris-1.0.3/src/list.h
ltris-1.0.3/src/main.c
ltris-1.0.3/src/menu.c
ltris-1.0.3/src/menu.h
ltris-1.0.3/src/value.c
ltris-1.0.3/src/value.h
ltris-1.0.3/src/sounds/
ltris-1.0.3/src/sounds/motion.wav
ltris-1.0.3/src/sounds/explosion.wav
ltris-1.0.3/src/sounds/nextlevel.wav
ltris-1.0.3/src/sounds/excellent.wav
ltris-1.0.3/src/sounds/leftright.wav
ltris-1.0.3/src/sounds/Makefile.am
ltris-1.0.3/src/sounds/Makefile.in
ltris-1.0.3/src/sounds/click.wav
ltris-1.0.3/src/sounds/stop.wav
ltris-1.0.3/src/shrapnells.c
ltris-1.0.3/src/shrapnells.h
ltris-1.0.3/src/audio.c
```

13

```
ltris-1.0.3/src/audio.h
ltris-1.0.3/src/chart.c
ltris-1.0.3/src/chart.h
ltris-1.0.3/NEWS
ltris-1.0.3/TODO
ltris-1.0.3/aclocal.m4
ltris-1.0.3/icons/
ltris-1.0.3/icons/ltris16.xpm
ltris-1.0.3/icons/ltris32.xpm
ltris-1.0.3/icons/ltris48.xpm
ltris-1.0.3/icons/Makefile.am
ltris-1.0.3/icons/Makefile.in
ltris-1.0.3/README
ltris-1.0.3/configure
ltris-1.0.3/configure.in
ltris-1.0.3/install-sh
ltris-1.0.3/missing
ltris-1.0.3/mkinstalldirs
ltris-1.0.3/Makefile.am
ltris-1.0.3/Makefile.in
ltris-1.0.3/config.h.in
ltris-1.0.3/acinclude.m4
ltris-1.0.3/stamp-h.in
ltris-1.0.3/AUTHORS
ltris-1.0.3/INSTALL
ltris-1.0.3/touchall
ltris-1.0.3/ChangeLog
ltris-1.0.3/acconfig.h
ltris-1.0.3/COPYING
[root@localhost root]# _
```

Next, you may move to this directory and view the file contents, as seen below:

```
[root@localhost root]# cd ltris-1.0.3
[root@localhost ltris-1.0.3]# ls -F
acconfig.h     ChangeLog     COPYING     Makefile.am     NEWS      TODO
acinclude.m4   config.h.in   icons/      Makefile.in     README    touchall*
aclocal.m4     configure*    INSTALL     missing*        src/
AUTHORS        configure.in  install-sh* mkinstalldirs*  stamp-h.in
[root@localhost ltris-1.0.3]# _
```

Notice from the above output that a README, INSTALL, and `configure` file exist and that the `configure` file is executable. To execute this file without using the PATH variable, you may enter the following command:

```
[root@localhost ltris-1.0.3]# ./configure
creating cache ./config.cache
checking for a BSD compatible install... /usr/bin/install -c
checking whether build environment is sane... yes
checking whether make sets ${MAKE}... yes
checking for working aclocal... found
checking for working autoconf... found
```

```
checking for working automake... found
checking for working autoheader... found
checking for working makeinfo... found
checking for gcc... gcc
checking whether the C compiler (gcc  ) works... yes
checking whether the C compiler (gcc  ) is a cross-compiler... no
checking whether we are using GNU C... yes
checking whether gcc accepts —g... yes
checking for ranlib... ranlib
checking for main in —lm... yes
checking for sdl-config... /usr/bin/sdl-config
checking for SDL - version >= 1.0.0... yes
checking for sdl-config... (cached) /usr/bin/sdl-config
checking for SDL - version >= 1.1.5... yes
checking for main in -lSDL_mixer... yes
SDL_Mixer found
updating cache ./config.cache
creating ./config.status
creating Makefile
creating src/Makefile
creating icons/Makefile
creating src/sounds/Makefile
creating src/gfx/Makefile
creating config.h
[root@localhost ltris—1.0.3]# _
```

Notice that the `Makefile` file was created near the end of the output above, and that other `Makefile` files may exist in subdirectories of the source code directory. These other files will be referenced by the `Makefile` file in the source code directory.

Next, you must compile the program according to the settings stored in `Makefile` by typing the `make` command while in the source code directory. This will use the gcc program to compile the source code files, as seen in the following output:

```
[root@localhost ltris—1.0.3]# make
make  all-recursive
make[1]: Entering directory '/root/ltris-1.0.3'
Making all in src
make[2]: Entering directory '/root/ltris-1.0.3/src'
Making all in gfx
make[3]: Entering directory '/root/ltris-1.0.3/src/gfx'
make[3]: Nothing to be done for 'all'.
make[3]: Leaving directory '/root/ltris-1.0.3/src/gfx'
Making all in sounds
make[3]: Entering directory '/root/ltris-1.0.3/src/sounds'
make[3]: Nothing to be done for 'all'.
make[3]: Leaving directory '/root/ltris-1.0.3/src/sounds'
make[3]: Entering directory '/root/ltris-1.0.3/src'
gcc -DHAVE_CONFIG_H -DSOUND -DAUDIO_BUFFER_SIZE=256 -
DSRC_DIR=\"/usr/local/share
/games/ltris\" -DHI_DIR=\"/var/lib/games\"     -g -O2 -Wall -I/usr/include/SDL
-D_REENTRANT -DSDL_1_1_5 -c sdl.c
gcc -DHAVE_CONFIG_H -DSOUND -DAUDIO_BUFFER_SIZE=256 -
DSRC_DIR=\"/usr/local/share
```

13

```
/games/ltris\" -DHI_DIR=\"/var/lib/games\"      -g -O2 -Wall -I/usr/include/SDL
-D_REENTRANT -DSDL_1_1_5 -c menu.c
gcc -DHAVE_CONFIG_H -DSOUND -DAUDIO_BUFFER_SIZE=256 -
DSRC_DIR=\"/usr/local/share
/games/ltris\" -DHI_DIR=\"/var/lib/games\"      -g -O2 -Wall -I/usr/include/SDL
-D_REENTRANT -DSDL_1_1_5 -c item.c
gcc -DHAVE_CONFIG_H -DSOUND -DAUDIO_BUFFER_SIZE=256 -
DSRC_DIR=\"/usr/local/share
/games/ltris\" -DHI_DIR=\"/var/lib/games\"      -g -O2 -Wall -I/usr/include/SDL
-D_REENTRANT -DSDL_1_1_5 -c manager.c
gcc -DHAVE_CONFIG_H -DSOUND -DAUDIO_BUFFER_SIZE=256 -
DSRC_DIR=\"/usr/local/share
/games/ltris\" -DHI_DIR=\"/var/lib/games\"      -g -O2 -Wall -I/usr/include/SDL
-D_REENTRANT -DSDL_1_1_5 -c value.c
gcc -DHAVE_CONFIG_H -DSOUND -DAUDIO_BUFFER_SIZE=256 -
DSRC_DIR=\"/usr/local/share
/games/ltris\" -DHI_DIR=\"/var/lib/games\"      -g -O2 -Wall -I/usr/include/SDL
-D_REENTRANT -DSDL_1_1_5 -c main.c
gcc -DHAVE_CONFIG_H -DSOUND -DAUDIO_BUFFER_SIZE=256 -
DSRC_DIR=\"/usr/local/share
/games/ltris\" -DHI_DIR=\"/var/lib/games\"      -g -O2 -Wall -I/usr/include/SDL
-D_REENTRANT -DSDL_1_1_5 -c audio.c
gcc -DHAVE_CONFIG_H -DSOUND -DAUDIO_BUFFER_SIZE=256 -
DSRC_DIR=\"/usr/local/share
/games/ltris\" -DHI_DIR=\"/var/lib/games\"      -g -O2 -Wall -I/usr/include/SDL
-D_REENTRANT -DSDL_1_1_5 -c event.c
gcc -DHAVE_CONFIG_H -DSOUND -DAUDIO_BUFFER_SIZE=256 -
DSRC_DIR=\"/usr/local/share
/games/ltris\" -DHI_DIR=\"/var/lib/games\"      -g -O2 -Wall -I/usr/include/SDL
-D_REENTRANT -DSDL_1_1_5 -c list.c
gcc -DHAVE_CONFIG_H -DSOUND -DAUDIO_BUFFER_SIZE=256 -
DSRC_DIR=\"/usr/local/share
/games/ltris\" -DHI_DIR=\"/var/lib/games\"      -g -O2 -Wall -I/usr/include/SDL
-D_REENTRANT -DSDL_1_1_5 -c tools.c
gcc -DHAVE_CONFIG_H -DSOUND -DAUDIO_BUFFER_SIZE=256 -
DSRC_DIR=\"/usr/local/share
/games/ltris\" -DHI_DIR=\"/var/lib/games\"      -g -O2 -Wall -I/usr/include/SDL
-D_REENTRANT -DSDL_1_1_5 -c config.c
gcc -DHAVE_CONFIG_H -DSOUND -DAUDIO_BUFFER_SIZE=256 -
DSRC_DIR=\"/usr/local/share
/games/ltris\" -DHI_DIR=\"/var/lib/games\"      -g -O2 -Wall -I/usr/include/SDL
-D_REENTRANT -DSDL_1_1_5 -c chart.c
gcc -DHAVE_CONFIG_H -DSOUND -DAUDIO_BUFFER_SIZE=256 -
DSRC_DIR=\"/usr/local/share
/games/ltris\" -DHI_DIR=\"/var/lib/games\"      -g -O2 -Wall -I/usr/include/SDL
-D_REENTRANT -DSDL_1_1_5 -c tetris.c
gcc -DHAVE_CONFIG_H -DSOUND -DAUDIO_BUFFER_SIZE=256 -
DSRC_DIR=\"/usr/local/share
/games/ltris\" -DHI_DIR=\"/var/lib/games\"      -g -O2 -Wall -I/usr/include/SDL
-D_REENTRANT -DSDL_1_1_5 -c bowl.c
gcc -DHAVE_CONFIG_H -DSOUND -DAUDIO_BUFFER_SIZE=256 -
DSRC_DIR=\"/usr/local/share
/games/ltris\" -DHI_DIR=\"/var/lib/games\"      -g -O2 -Wall -I/usr/include/SDL
-D_REENTRANT -DSDL_1_1_5 -c shrapnells.c
gcc -DHAVE_CONFIG_H -DSOUND -DAUDIO_BUFFER_SIZE=256 -
DSRC_DIR=\"/usr/local/share
/games/ltris\" -DHI_DIR=\"/var/lib/games\"      -g -O2 -Wall -I/usr/include/SDL
-D_REENTRANT -DSDL_1_1_5 -c cpu.c
gcc -DHAVE_CONFIG_H -DSOUND -DAUDIO_BUFFER_SIZE=256 -
DSRC_DIR=\"/usr/local/share
/games/ltris\" -DHI_DIR=\"/var/lib/games\"      -g -O2 -Wall -I/usr/include/SDL
```

```
-D_REENTRANT -DSDL_1_1_5 -c hint.c
gcc -DHAVE_CONFIG_H -DSOUND -DAUDIO_BUFFER_SIZE=256 -
DSRC_DIR=\"/usr/local/share
/games/ltris\" -DHI_DIR=\"/var/lib/games\"      -g -O2 -Wall -I/usr/include/SDL
-D_REENTRANT -DSDL_1_1_5 -c parser.c
gcc  -g -O2 -Wall -I/usr/include/SDL -D_REENTRANT -DSDL_1_1_5  -o ltris  sdl.o
m
enu.o item.o manager.o value.o main.o audio.o event.o list.o tools.o config.o
ch
art.o tetris.o bowl.o shrapnells.o cpu.o hint.o parser.o -lSDL_mixer -lm  -
L/usr
/lib -Wl,-rpath,/usr/lib -lSDL -lpthread -lm -L/usr/lib -ldl -lartsc -DPIC -
fPIC
 -lpthread -L/usr/lib -lesd -laudiofile -lm -L/usr/X11R6/lib -lX11 -lXext -
lXxf8
6vm -lXxf86dga -lXv -ldl
make[3]: Leaving directory '/root/ltris-1.0.3/src'
make[2]: Leaving directory '/root/ltris-1.0.3/src'
Making all in icons
make[2]: Entering directory '/root/ltris-1.0.3/icons'
make[2]: Nothing to be done for 'all'.
make[2]: Leaving directory '/root/ltris-1.0.3/icons'
make[2]: Entering directory '/root/ltris-1.0.3'
make[2]: Leaving directory '/root/ltris-1.0.3'
make[1]: Leaving directory '/root/ltris-1.0.3'
[root@localhost ltris—1.0.3]# _
```

Once compiled, these binary programs may then be copied to the correct location on the filesystem by typing the following command:

```
[root@localhost ltris—1.0.3]# make install
Making install in src
make[1]: Entering directory '/root/ltris-1.0.3/src'
Making install in gfx
make[2]: Entering directory '/root/ltris-1.0.3/src/gfx'
make[3]: Entering directory '/root/ltris-1.0.3/src/gfx'
make[3]: Nothing to be done for 'install-exec-am'.
/bin/sh ../../mkinstalldirs /usr/local/share/games/ltris/gfx
mkdir /usr/local/share/games
mkdir /usr/local/share/games/ltris
mkdir /usr/local/share/games/ltris/gfx
make[3]: Leaving directory '/root/ltris-1.0.3/src/gfx'
make[2]: Leaving directory '/root/ltris-1.0.3/src/gfx'
Making install in sounds
make[2]: Entering directory '/root/ltris-1.0.3/src/sounds'
make[3]: Entering directory '/root/ltris-1.0.3/src/sounds'
make[3]: Nothing to be done for 'install-exec-am'.
/bin/sh ../../mkinstalldirs /usr/local/share/games/ltris/sounds
mkdir /usr/local/share/games/ltris/sounds
make[3]: Leaving directory '/root/ltris-1.0.3/src/sounds'
make[2]: Leaving directory '/root/ltris-1.0.3/src/sounds'
make[2]: Entering directory '/root/ltris-1.0.3/src'
make[3]: Entering directory '/root/ltris-1.0.3/src'
/bin/sh ../mkinstalldirs /usr/local/bin
  /usr/bin/install -c  ltris /usr/local/bin/ltris
/bin/sh ../mkinstalldirs /usr/local/share/games/ltris
/usr/bin/install -c -m 644 figures /usr/local/share/games/ltris/figures
/bin/sh ../mkinstalldirs /var/lib/games
if ! test -f /var/lib/games/ltris.hscr; then \
  /usr/bin/install -c -m 644 —mode=666 empty.hscr /var/lib/games/ltris.hscr; \
fi;
```

13

```
make[3]: Leaving directory '/root/ltris-1.0.3/src'
make[2]: Leaving directory '/root/ltris-1.0.3/src'
make[1]: Leaving directory '/root/ltris-1.0.3/src'
Making install in icons
make[1]: Entering directory '/root/ltris-1.0.3/icons'
make[2]: Entering directory '/root/ltris-1.0.3/icons'
make[2]: Nothing to be done for 'install-exec-am'.
make[2]: Nothing to be done for 'install-data-am'.
make[2]: Leaving directory '/root/ltris-1.0.3/icons'
make[1]: Leaving directory '/root/ltris-1.0.3/icons'
make[1]: Entering directory '/root/ltris-1.0.3'
make[2]: Entering directory '/root/ltris-1.0.3'
make[2]: Nothing to be done for 'install-exec-am'.
make[2]: Nothing to be done for 'install-data-am'.
make[2]: Leaving directory '/root/ltris-1.0.3'
make[1]: Leaving directory '/root/ltris-1.0.3'
[root@localhost ltris-1.0.3]# _
```

The README file typically contains the location of the program; for LTRIS, the ltris binary program is located in /usr/local/bin, a directory in the PATH variable. Thus, to execute the LTRIS program, you simply log into a desktop environment, open a terminal window and type the command ltris, which results in the program seen in Figure 13-2.

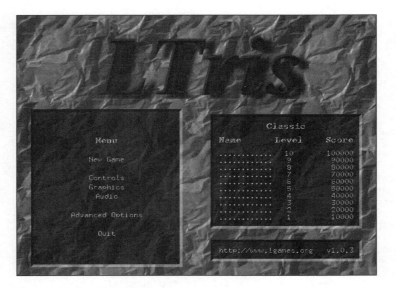

Figure 13-2   The LTRIS program

Installing Programs using RPM

The Red Hat Package Manager format is the most widely used format for pre-compiled Linux software distributed via the Internet. Packages in this format have filenames that indicate the hardware architecture the software was compiled for, and end with the

.rpm extension. The following output indicates that the bluefish RPM package (a Web page editor) version 0.7-fr1 was compiled for the Intel i386 platform:

```
[root@localhost root]# ls —F
Desktop/     bluefish-0.7-fr1.i386.rpm
[root@localhost root]# _
```

To install an RPM package, you may use the —i option to the **rpm command**. Additionally, you may use the —v and —h options to print the verbose information and hash marks respectively during installation. The following command installs the bluefish RPM package using these options:

```
[root@localhost root]# rpm —ivh bluefish-0.7-fr1.i386.rpm
Preparing...          ######################################### [100%]
   1:bluefish          ######################################### [100%]
 [root@localhost root]# _
```

Once installed, the RPM database (stored in subdirectories of /var/lib/rpm) contains information about the package and the files contained within. To query the full package name after installation you may use the —q option to the rpm command followed by the common name of the package:

```
[root@localhost root]# rpm —q bluefish
bluefish-0.7-fr1
[root@localhost root]# _
```

In addition, you may add the info (—i) option to the above command to display the detailed package information for the bluefish package:

```
[root@localhost root]# rpm —qi bluefish
Name        : bluefish              Relocations: (not relocateable)
Version     : 0.7                        Vendor: Freshrpms.net
Release     : fr1                    Build Date: Mon 19 Nov 2001 05:43:36
 AM EST
Install date: Sat 27 Jul 2003 09:39:05 PM EDT    Build Host: devel.freshrpms.n
et
Group       : Development/Tools       Source RPM: bluefish-0.7-fr1.src.rpm
Size        : 3510172                    License: GPL
Packager    : Matthias Saou <matthias.saou@est.une.marmotte.net>
URL         : http://bluefish.openoffice.nl/
Summary     : A GTK+ HTML editor for the experienced web designer or
programmer.
Description :
Bluefish is a GTK+ HTML editor for the experienced web designer or
programmer. It is not finished yet, but already a very powerful site
creating environment. Bluefish has extended support for programming
dynamic and interactive websites, there is for example a lot of PHP
support.
[root@localhost root]# _
```

Since the Red Hat Package Manager keeps track of all installed files, you may find the executable file for the bluefish program by using the —q and list (—l) options followed by the package name to list all files contained within the package:

```
[root@localhost root]# rpm —ql bluefish
/usr/bin/bluefish
```

13

```
/usr/lib/bluefish
/usr/lib/bluefish/frameset.dtd
/usr/lib/bluefish/gen_php3_functions
/usr/lib/bluefish/gen_php4_functions
/usr/lib/bluefish/gen_rxml_functions
/usr/lib/bluefish/html-0.dtd
/usr/lib/bluefish/html-0s.dtd
/usr/lib/bluefish/html-1.dtd
/usr/lib/bluefish/html-1s.dtd
/usr/lib/bluefish/html-2.1e.dtd
/usr/lib/bluefish/html-3.2.dtd
/usr/lib/bluefish/html-3.dtd
/usr/lib/bluefish/html-3s.dtd
/usr/lib/bluefish/html-4-frameset.dtd
/usr/lib/bluefish/html-4-strict.dtd
/usr/lib/bluefish/html-4.dtd
/usr/lib/bluefish/html-s.dtd
/usr/lib/bluefish/html.dtd
/usr/lib/bluefish/loose.dtd
/usr/lib/bluefish/man1
/usr/lib/bluefish/php3_functions
/usr/lib/bluefish/php4_functions
/usr/lib/bluefish/rxml_functions
/usr/lib/bluefish/ssi_functions
/usr/lib/bluefish/strict.dtd
/usr/lib/bluefish/xhtml1-frameset.dtd
/usr/lib/bluefish/xhtml1-strict.dtd
/usr/lib/bluefish/xhtml1-transitional.dtd
/usr/share/doc/bluefish-0.7
/usr/share/doc/bluefish-0.7/AUTHORS
/usr/share/doc/bluefish-0.7/BUGS
/usr/share/doc/bluefish-0.7/ChangeLog
/usr/share/doc/bluefish-0.7/NEWS
/usr/share/doc/bluefish-0.7/README
/usr/share/doc/bluefish-0.7/TODO
/usr/share/doc/bluefish-0.7/manual
/usr/share/doc/bluefish-0.7/manual/en
/usr/share/doc/bluefish-0.7/manual/en/chapter1.html
/usr/share/doc/bluefish-0.7/manual/en/chapter2.html
/usr/share/doc/bluefish-0.7/manual/en/chapter3.html
/usr/share/doc/bluefish-0.7/manual/en/chapter4.html
/usr/share/doc/bluefish-0.7/manual/en/index.html
/usr/share/doc/bluefish-0.7/manual/en/manual.book
/usr/share/doc/bluefish-0.7/manual/en/preface.html
/usr/share/doc/bluefish-0.7/manual/index.html
/usr/share/doc/bluefish-0.7/manual/it
/usr/share/doc/bluefish-0.7/manual/it/chapter1.html
/usr/share/doc/bluefish-0.7/manual/it/chapter2.html
/usr/share/doc/bluefish-0.7/manual/it/chapter3.html
```

```
/usr/share/doc/bluefish-0.7/manual/manual.css
/usr/share/gnome/apps/Development/bluefish.desktop
/usr/share/man/man1/bluefish.1.gz
/usr/share/pixmaps/bluefish_icon.xpm
[root@localhost root]# _
```

From the output above, you can see that the pathname to the executable file is /usr/bin/bluefish. Upon execution in a desktop environment, you will see the screen depicted in Figure 13-3.

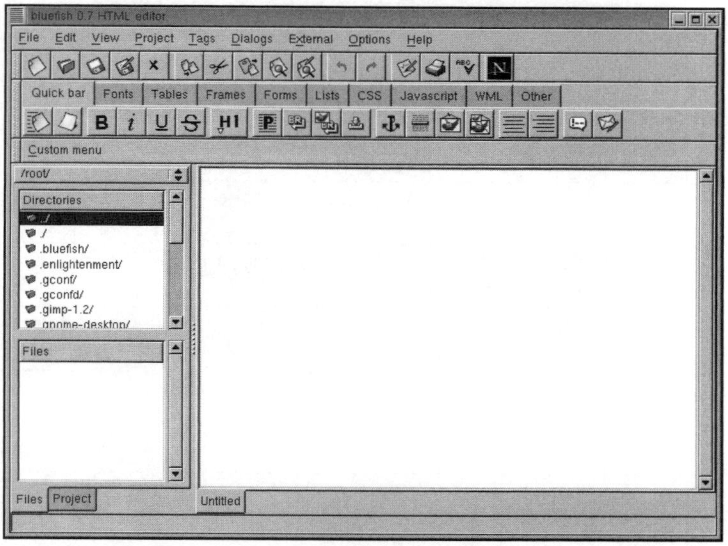

Figure 13-3   The bluefish program

Conversely, you may find out which package a certain file belongs to by using the –q and file (–f) options with the **rpm** command, followed by the filename:

```
[root@localhost root]# rpm –qf /usr/bin/bluefish
bluefish-0.7-fr1
[root@localhost root]# _
```

To remove a package from the system, you may use the –e option to the **rpm** command; all files that belong to the package will be removed as well. To remove the bluefish package and verify its deletion, you may use the following commands:

```
[root@localhost root]# rpm –e bluefish
[root@localhost root]# rpm –q bluefish
package bluefish is not installed
[root@localhost root]# _
```

A list of common options used with the rpm utility is displayed in Table 13-8.

Table 13-8 Common options used with the rpm utility

Option	Description
-a --all	When used with the -q option, displays all package names installed on the system
-e --erase	Removes a specified package from the system
-F --freshen	Upgrades a specified package only if an older version exists on the system
-f --file	When used with the -q option, displays the package that the specified file belongs to
-h --hash	When used with the -i option, prints hash marks on the screen to indicate installation progress
-i --install	Installs a specified package (provided the -q option is not used)
-i --info	When used with the -q option, displays full information about the specified package
-l --list	When used with the -q option, lists the filenames that comprise the specified package
-q --query	Queries information about packages on the system
--test	When used with the -i option, performs a test installation only
-U --upgrade	Upgrades a specified package; the package is installed even if no older version exists on the system
-V --verify	Verifies the location of all files that belong to the specified package
-v	Prints verbose information when installing or manipulating packages

The KDE and GNOME desktop environments contain a graphical interface to the Red Hat Package Manager. For the GNOME desktop environment, you may type `gnorpm` at a terminal prompt or navigate to the toolbar, GNOME Button, Programs, System, GnoRPM to start the **GNOME RPM Manager** depicted in Figure 13-4.

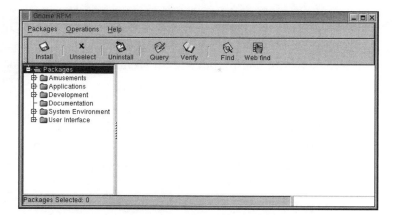

Figure 13-4   The GNOME RPM Manager

Conversely, you may start the **KDE Package Manager** seen in Figure 13-5 from the KDE desktop environment by typing **kpackage** at a terminal prompt or by navigating to the toolbar, K Button, System, Package Manager.

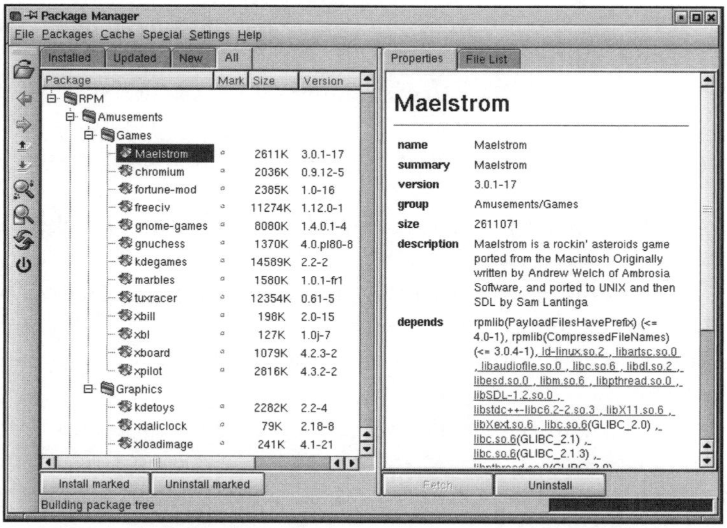

Figure 13-5   The KDE Package Manager

Both the GNOME RPM Manager and KDE Package Manager allow you to query and erase installed software, as well as install new RPM packages.

CHAPTER SUMMARY

❏ There are many compression utilities available for Linux systems; each of them uses a different compression algorithm and produces a different compression ratio.

❏ Files may be backed up to an archive using a back-up utility. Tape devices are the most common medium used for archives.

❏ The tar utility is the most common back-up utility used today; it is typically used to create compressed archives called tarballs.

❏ The source code for Linux software may be obtained and compiled afterwards using the GNU C Compiler; most source code is available in tarball format via the Internet.

❏ Package managers install and manage compiled software of the same format.

❏ The Red Hat Package Manager can be used to install software in Red Hat Package Manager format; these packages may be queried and removed afterwards.

KEY TERMS

/etc/dumpdates — The file used to store information about incremental and full back-ups for use by the dump/restore utility.

archive — The location (file or device) that contains a copy of files; it is typically created by a back-up utility.

bunzip2 command — The command used to decompress files compressed by the bzip2 command.

bzcat command — The command used to view the contents of an archive created with bzip2 to Standard Output.

bzip2 command — The command used to compress files using a Burrows-Wheeler Block Sorting Huffman Coding compression algorithm.

compress command — The command used to compress files using a Lempel-Ziv compression algorithm.

compression — The process in which files are reduced in size by a compression algorithm.

compression algorithm — The set of instructions used to reduce the contents of a file systematically.

compression ratio — The amount of compression that occurred during compression.

copy in/out (cpio) command — A common back-up utility.

dump command — The common utility used to create full and incremental back-ups.

full back-up — An archive of an entire filesystem.

GNOME RPM Manager — A graphical tool that may be used to install RPM packages available with the GNOME desktop environment.

GNU C Compiler (gcc) command — The command used to compile source code into binary programs.

GNU zip (gzip) command — The command used to compress files using a Lempel-Ziv compression algorithm.

gunzip command — The command used to decompress files compressed by the gzip command.

incremental back-up — An archive of a filesystem that contains only files that were modified since the last archive was created.

KDE Package Manager — A graphical tool that may be used to install RPM packages available with the KDE desktop environment.

magnetic tape (mt) command — The command used to control tape devices.

package manager — A system that defines a standard package format and can be used to install, query, and remove packages.

Red Hat Package Manager (RPM) — The most commonly used package manager for Linux.

restore command — The command used to extract archives created with the dump command.

rpm command —The command used to install, query, and remove RPM packages.

system back-up — The process whereby files are copied to an archive.

tape archive (tar) command — The most common utility used to create archives.

tarball — A gzip-compressed tar archive.

uncompress command — The command used to decompress files compressed by the compress command.

zcat command — The command used to view the contents of an archive created with compress or gzip to Standard Output.

zmore command — The command used to view the contents of an archive created with compress or gzip to Standard Output in a page-by-page fashion.

13

REVIEW QUESTIONS

1. Most source code is available on the Internet in tarball format. True or False?

2. Which dump level indicates a full back-up?
    a. 0
    b. 9
    c. 1
    d. f

3. What filename extension indicates a tarball?
    a. `.tar.gz`
    b. `.cpio`
    c. `.dump`
    d. `.tar`

4. Files that have been compressed using the compress utility typically have the
   _____ extension.

   a. `.tar.gz`

   b. `.gz`

   c. `.Z`

   d. `.bz2`

5. Files that have been compressed using the bzip2 utility typically have the
   _____ extension.

   a. `.tar.gz`

   b. `.gz`

   c. `.Z`

   d. `.bz2`

6. The bzip2 and gzip utilities use similar compression algorithms. True or False?

7. When compiling source code into a binary program, which command does the
   compiling using the GNU C Compiler?

   a. `tar`

   b. `./configure`

   c. `make`

   d. `make install`

8. The −9 option to the `gzip` command will result in a higher compression ratio.
   True or False?

9. Which of the following is a graphical interface to the Red Hat Package Manager?
   (Choose all that apply).

   a. GNOME Package Installer

   b. KDE Package Manager

   c. GNOME RPM Manager

   d. KDE RPM Installer

10. You have created a full back-up and 4 incremental backups. In which order must
    you restore these backups?

    a. 0,1,2,3,4

    b. 0,4,3,2,1

    c. 4,3,2,1,0

    d. 1,2,3,4,0

11. Which of the following commands will extract an archive?

    a. `cpio -vocBL /dev/fd0`

    b. `cpio -vicdu —I /dev/fd0`

    c. `cpio -vicdu —O /dev/fd0`

12. Source code is commonly obtained in Red Hat Package Manager format. True or False?

13. Which of the following commands can be used to list the files contained within an installed RPM package?

    a. `rpm -qa packagename`

    b. `rpm -qi packagename`

    c. `rpm -ql packagename`

    d. `rpm -q packagename`

14. How many dump levels are there for use with the dump command?

    a. 1

    b. 5

    c. 9

    d. 10

15. When compiling source code into a binary program, which command copies compiled binary files to the correct location on the filesystem?

    a. `tar`

    b. `./configure`

    c. `make`

    d. `make install`

16. Compiling and installing software from source code updates a central database that can then be used to query and remove the software at a later time. True or False?

17. Which file contains full and incremental backup information for use with the dump/restore utility?

    a. `/etc/dumps`

    b. `/etc/dumpdates`

    c. `/etc/dumpfile`

    d. `/etc/dump.conf`

13

18. Which of the following represents the first non–rewinding SCSI tape device on a system?

    a. /dev/st0

    b. /dev/ht0

    c. /dev/nht0

    d. /dev/nst0

19. What is the most common method for obtaining Linux software?

    a. CD-ROM

    b. floppy

    c. Internet download

    d. e-mail

20. Which option to the rpm command can be used to remove a package from the system?

    a. —r

    b. —e

    c. —u

    d. —U

21. Which of the following commands will create an archive?

    a. tar -cvf /dev/fd0

    b. tar -xvf /dev/fd0

    c. tar -tvf /dev/fd0

    d. tar -zcvf /dev/fd0 *

22. When compiling source code into a binary program, which command performs a system check and creates Makefile?

    a. tar

    b. ./configure

    c. make

    d. make install

23. When decompressing files, you need not specify the extension when using the compress and bzip2 utilities. True or False?

24. Which of the following commands can be used to list detailed information about a package such as its installation date and license?

    a. rpm -qa packagename

    b. rpm -qi packagename

    c. rpm -ql packagename

    d. rpm -q packagename

25. The tar utility can compress symbolically linked files and device files. True or False?

HANDS-ON PROJECTS

These projects should be completed in the order given. All hands-on projects should take a total of three hours to complete. The requirements for this lab include:

❏ A computer with Red Hat 7.2 installed according to Hands-on Project 7-2

❏ A tarball copy of the source code for the ethereal program version 0.8.19 available from the Internet at *http://www.ethereal.com*

❏ A copy of the nmap program version 2.99RC2-1 RPM for the Intel platform available from the Internet at *http://www.nmap.org*

❏ A blank floppy diskette

Project 13-1

In this hands-on project, you will use common compression utilities to compress and uncompress information.

1. Turn on your computer. Once your Linux system has been loaded, switch to a command-line terminal (tty2) by pressing **Ctrl–Alt–F2** and log into the terminal using the username of **root** and the password of **secret**.

2. At the command prompt, type **cp /etc/termcap ~** and press **Enter** to make a copy of the /etc/termcap file in your current directory. Next, type **ls –l** at the command prompt and press **Enter**. How large is the termcap file?

3. At the command prompt, type **compress –v termcap** and press **Enter** to compress the termcap file. What was the compression ratio? Next, type **ls –l** at the command prompt and press **Enter**. What extension does the termcap file have and how large is it?

4. At the command prompt, type **uncompress –v termcap.Z** and press **Enter** to decompress the termcap file.

5. At the command prompt, type **compress –vr Desktop** and press **Enter** to compress the contents of the Desktop subdirectory. Next, type **ls –lR Desktop** at the command prompt and press **Enter** to view the contents of the Desktop directory. Which files were compressed? Which files were left uncompressed? Why? How could you force the compress utility to compress these files as well?

6. At the command prompt, type **uncompress –vr Desktop** and press **Enter** to decompress the contents of the Desktop subdirectory. Next, type **ls –lR Desktop** at the command prompt and press **Enter** to verify that these files were uncompressed.

7. At the command prompt, type **ps –ef | compress –v >psfile.Z** and press **Enter** to compress the output of the ps –ef command to a file called psfile.Z. What was the compression ratio?

8. At the command prompt, type **zmore psfile.Z** and press **Enter** to view the compressed contents of the psfile.Z file. When finished, press **q** to quit the more utility.

13

9. At the command prompt, type **gzip –v termcap** and press **Enter** to compress the `termcap` file. What was the compression ratio? How does this ratio compare to the one obtained in Step 3? Why? Next, type **ls –l** at the command prompt and press **Enter**. What extension does the `termcap` file have and how large is it?

10. At the command prompt, type **gunzip –v termcap.gz** and press **Enter** to decompress the `termcap` file.

11. At the command prompt, type **gzip –v –9 termcap** and press **Enter** to compress the `termcap` file. What was the compression ratio? Why?

12. At the command prompt, type **gunzip –v termcap.gz** and press **Enter** to decompress the `termcap` file.

13. At the command prompt, type **gzip –v –1 termcap** and press **Enter** to compress the `termcap` file. What was the compression ratio? Why?

14. At the command prompt, type **gunzip –v termcap.gz** and press **Enter** to decompress the `termcap` file.

15. At the command prompt, type **bzip2 –v termcap** and press **Enter** to compress the `termcap` file. What was the compression ratio? How does this compare to the ratios from Step 3 and Step 9? Why? Next, type **ls –l** at the command prompt and press **Enter**. What extension does the `termcap` file have and how large is it?

16. At the command prompt, type **bunzip2 –v termcap.bz2** and press **Enter** to decompress the `termcap` file.

17. Type **exit** and press **Enter** to log out of your shell.

Project 13-2

In this hands-on project, you will create, view, and extract archives using the `tar` utility.

1. Switch to a command-line terminal (tty2) by pressing **Ctrl-Alt-F2** and log into the terminal using the username of **root** and the password of **secret**.

2. At the command prompt, type **tar –cvf test1.tar Desktop** and press **Enter** to create an archive called `test1.tar` in the current directory that contains the `Desktop` directory and its contents. Next, type **ls –l** at the command prompt and press **Enter**. How large is the `test1.tar` file?

3. At the command prompt, type **tar –tvf test1.tar** and press **Enter**. What is displayed?

4. At the command prompt, type **mkdir /new1** and press **Enter**. Next, type **cd /new1** at the command prompt and press **Enter** to change the current directory to the `/new1` directory.

5. At the command prompt, type **tar –xvf /root/test1.tar** and press **Enter** to extract the contents of the `test1.tar` archive. Next, type **ls –F** at the command prompt and press **Enter** to view the contents of the `/new1` directory. Was the extraction successful?

6. At the command prompt, type **cd** and press **Enter** to return to your home directory.

7. At the command prompt, type **tar −zcvf test2.tar.gz Desktop** and press **Enter** to create a gzip-compressed archive called test2.tar.gz in the current directory that contains the Desktop subdirectory and its contents. Next, type **ls −l** at the command prompt and press **Enter**. How large is the test2.tar.gz file? How does this compare to the size obtained for test1.tar in Step 2? Why?

8. At the command prompt, type **tar −ztvf test2.tar.gz** and press **Enter**. What is displayed?

9. At the command prompt, type **mkdir /new2** and press **Enter**. Next, type **cd /new2** at the command prompt and press **Enter** to change the current directory to the /new2 directory.

10. At the command prompt, type **tar −zxvf /root/test2.tar.gz** and press **Enter** to uncompress and extract the contents of the test2.tar.gz archive. Next, type **ls −F** at the command prompt and press **Enter** to view the contents of the /new2 directory. Was the extraction successful?

11. At the command prompt, type **cd** and press **Enter** to return to your home directory.

12. Insert a floppy diskette into the floppy disk drive of your computer.

13. At the command prompt, type **tar −cvf /dev/fd0 Desktop** and press **Enter** to create an archive on the device /dev/fd0 that contains the Desktop subdirectory and its contents.

14. At the command prompt, type **tar −tvf /dev/fd0** and press **Enter**. What is displayed?

15. At the command prompt, type **mkdir /new3** and press **Enter**. Next, type **cd /new3** at the command prompt and press **Enter** to change the current directory to the /new3 directory.

16. At the command prompt, type **tar −xvf /dev/fd0** and press **Enter** to extract the contents of the archive stored on the first floppy disk. Next, type **ls −F** at the command prompt and press **Enter** to view the contents of the /new3 directory. Was the extraction successful?

17. At the command prompt, type **mount /dev/fd0** and press **Enter** to mount the floppy from the appropriate entry in /etc/fstab. What error message do you receive and why? Why was the filesystem type not automatically detected? Can this floppy be mounted?

18. At the command prompt, type **rm −rf /new[123]** and press **Enter** to remove the directories created in this hands-on project.

19. At the command prompt, type **rm −f /root/test*** and press **Enter** to remove the tar archives created in this hands-on project.

20. Remove the floppy diskette from your floppy disk drive, type **exit**, and press **Enter** to log out of your shell.

13

Project 13-3

In this hands-on project, you will create, view, and extract archives using the cpio and dump utilities.

1. Switch to a command-line terminal (tty2) by pressing **Ctrl-Alt-F2** and log into the terminal using the username of **root** and the password of **secret**.

2. Insert a floppy diskette into the floppy disk drive of your computer.

3. At the command prompt, type **find /root/Desktop | cpio −ovcBL −O /dev/fd0** and press **Enter** to create an archive on /dev/fd0 that contains the Desktop subdirectory and its contents. What does each option indicate in the aforementioned command?

4. At the command prompt, type **cpio −ivtB −I /dev/fd0** and press **Enter**. What is displayed? What does each option indicate in the aforementioned command?

5. At the command prompt, type **cpio −ivcdumB −I /dev/fd0** and press **Enter** to extract the contents of the archive on the first floppy device. Where were the files extracted to? Were any files overwritten? What does each option indicate in the aforementioned command?

6. At the command prompt, type **dump −0f /dev/fd0 /root/Desktop** and press **Enter** to create an archive of the /root/Desktop directory on the device /dev/fd0. What type of back-up was performed? Will the /etc/dumpdates file be updated?

7. At the command prompt, type **restore −tf /dev/fd0** and press **Enter**. What was displayed? Are the pathnames used absolute or relative pathnames?

8. At the command prompt, type **mkdir /new** and press **Enter**. Next, type **cd /new** at the command prompt and press **Enter** to change the current directory to the /new directory.

9. At the command prompt, type **restore −rf /dev/fd0** and press **Enter** to uncompress and extract the contents of the archive on the first floppy device. Next, type **ls −F** at the command prompt and press **Enter** to view the contents of the /new directory. What is displayed? Next, type **ls −RF** at the command prompt and press **Enter** to view the contents of the /new directory recursively. What is displayed?

10. At the command prompt, type **df** and press **Enter**. Is the /home directory mounted to its own filesystem?

11. At the command prompt, type **dump −0uf /home.0.dump /home** and press **Enter** to create an archive of the /home filesystem in the file /home.0.dump. What type of back-up was performed? Will the /etc/dumpdates file be updated?

12. At the command prompt, type **cat /etc/dumpdates** and press **Enter**. What is displayed?

13. At the command prompt, type **touch /home/newfile** and press **Enter**.

14. At the command prompt, type **dump −1uf /home.1.dump /home** and press **Enter** to create an archive of the /home filesystem in the file /home.1.dump. What type of back-up was performed? Which file(s) will be backed up? Will the /etc/dumpdates file be updated?

15. At the command prompt, type **cat /etc/dumpdates** and press **Enter**. What is displayed?

16. At the command prompt, type **restore −tf /home.0.dump** and press **Enter**. What was displayed? Why?

17. At the command prompt, type **restore −tf /home.1.dump** and press **Enter**. What was displayed? Why? Which commands would you use to restore the /home filesystem from these files? Which order must they be executed in?

18. At the command prompt, type **rm −f /home.*** and press **Enter** to remove the archives created in this hands-on project.

19. Remove the floppy diskette from your floppy disk drive, type **exit,** and press **Enter** to log out of your shell.

Project 13-4

In this hands-on project, you will compile and install a program from source code. Ensure that you have a copy of the Ethereal source code version 0.8.19 in your home directory (ethereal-0.8.19.tar.gz).

1. Switch to a command-line terminal (tty2) by pressing **Ctrl-Alt-F2** and log into the terminal using the username of **root** and the password of **secret**.

2. At the command prompt, type **ls −F** and press **Enter** to view the ethereal source code tarball. Does the filename indicate the architecture that the source code was designed for? Explain.

3. At the command prompt, type **tar −zxvf ethereal-0.8.19.tar.gz** and press **Enter** to uncompress and extract the contents of the tarball. Next, type **ls −F** at the command prompt and press **Enter**. What directory was created?

4. At the command prompt, type **cd ethereal-0.8.19** and press **Enter**. Next, type **ls −F | less** at the command prompt and press **Enter**. Use the cursor keys to scroll through the output on the terminal screen. Is there an executable configure program? Are there README and INSTALL files present? What is the extension of most other files? What do you think this extension represents? When finished, press **q** to quit the less utility.

5. At the command prompt, type **less README** and press **Enter**. Scroll through the output on the terminal screen. What does the ethereal program do? What operating systems are supported? Where could you get more information specific about ethereal for their operating system? When finished, press **q** to quit the less utility.

6. At the command prompt, type **less INSTALL** and press **Enter**. Scroll through the output on the terminal screen. What does this file contain? When finished, press **q** to quit the less utility.

13

7. At the command prompt, type **./configure** and press **Enter**. What does this program do? Near the bottom of the output, can you see whether `Makefile` was created successfully?

8. At the command prompt, type **make** and press **Enter**. This step should take about five minutes depending on the speed of your computer. What does the `make` program do? Which program compiles the different parts of the program?

9. At the command prompt, type **make install** and press **Enter**. What does the `make install` command do?

10. At the command prompt, type **cd** and press **Enter** to return to your home directory. Next type **rm −rf ethereal-0.8.19** to remove the source code directory for `ethereal`.

11. At the command prompt, type **which ethereal** and press **Enter**. Which directory contains the `ethereal` executable program? Is this listed in the PATH variable?

12. Type **exit** and press **Enter** to log out of your shell.

13. Switch to the graphical login screen by pressing **Ctrl-Alt-F7**, and log into the GNOME desktop environment using the username of **root** and the password of **secret**.

14. Once logged in, open a command-line terminal, type **ethereal &** at the command prompt, and press **Enter**. Why is it good form to run **ethereal** in the background? Observe the **ethereal** interface. When finished, close the **ethereal** program, close the terminal shell and log out of the GNOME desktop environment.

Project 13-5

In this hands-on project, you will use the Red Hat Package Manager to install, view, and remove software on your system via a command-line interface. Ensure that you have a copy of the Nmap RPM version 2.99RC2-1 for the Intel architecture in your home directory (nmap-2.99RC2-1.i386.rpm).

1. Switch to a command-line terminal (tty2) by pressing **Ctrl-Alt-F2** and log into the terminal using the username of **root** and the password of **secret**.

2. At the command prompt, type **rpm −qa | less** and press **Enter** to view the RPM packages installed on your computer. Are there many of them? Briefly scroll through the list and press **q** when finished to exit the `less` utility.

3. At the command prompt, type **rpm −qa | grep nmap** and press **Enter** to see whether the `nmap` RPM has been installed on your computer. What files do you see? What version of `nmap` has been installed?

4. At the command prompt, type **rpm −e nmap** and press **Enter**. What error message do you receive?

5. At the command prompt, type **rpm −e nmap-frontend** and press **Enter**. Next, type **rpm −e nmap** at the command prompt and press **Enter**. Did you receive any error messages? Why?

6. At the command prompt, type **rpm −qa | grep nmap** and press **Enter**. Have the nmap packages been removed successfully?

7. At the command prompt, type **rpm −ivh nmap-2.99RC2-1.i386.rpm** and press **Enter**. What architecture is indicated in the filename for this RPM?

8. At the command prompt, type **rpm −qa | grep nmap** and press **Enter**. Have the nmap packages been installed successfully?

9. At the command prompt, type **rpm −qi nmap** and press **Enter** to view the information about the nmap package. What does the nmap program do? What license does this package use?

10. At the command prompt, type **rpm −ql nmap** and press **Enter** to view the locations of all files that belong to the nmap package. Which file is the executable program itself? How do you know?

11. At the command prompt, type **nmap −O localhost** and press **Enter** to view any open network ports on your system as well as the operating system type. What was displayed? Did the nmap program guess the operating system type correctly?

12. At the command prompt, type **rpm −V nmap** and press **Enter**. What does this option to the rpm command do? Did you see any error messages?

13. Type **exit** and press **Enter** to log out of your shell.

DISCOVERY EXERCISES

1. Provided you have Internet access and a functional Web browser, visit *http://www.sourceforge.net* and *http://www.freshmeat.net* and obtain software of your choice to install. Are most packages available as source code in tarball format and as compiled binaries in RPM format? Download two RPM files for your architecture. Use the GNOME RPM Manager to install the first RPM file. Next, use the GNOME RPM Manager to query the detailed information about the package including file locations. Install the second RPM file using the KDE Package Manager. When finished, use the KDE Package Manager to query the detailed package information and file locations. Execute both programs.

2. Write the command that can be used to perform the following:

   a. compress the symbolic link **/root/sfile** using the **compress** utility and display the compression ratio

   b. compress the contents of the directory **/root/dir1** using the **gzip** utility and display the compression ratio

   c. decompress the file **/root/letter.bz2**

   d. compress the file **/root/letter** using **gzip** fast compression

   e. find the compression ratio of the file **/root/letter.gz**

   f. perform a test compression of the file **/root/sample** using the **bzip2** utility

   g. compress the file **/root/sample** using the **bzip2** utility while minimizing memory usage during the compression

3. Write the command that can be used to perform the following:

    a. back up the contents of the **/var** directory (which contains symbolically linked files) to the second non-rewinding SCSI tape device on the system using the **tar** utility

    b. append the file **/etc/inittab** to the archive created in a)

    c. create a tarball called **/stuff.tar.gz** that contains all files in the **/root/stuff** directory

    d. use the **cpio** utility to back up all files in the **/var** directory (which contains symbolically linked files) to the first rewinding IDE tape device with a block size of 5KB

    e. perform a full filesystem back-up of the **/var** filesystem using the **dump** utility and record the event in the **/etc/dumpdates** file

    f. view the contents of the archives created in b) c) d) and e)

    g. extract the contents of the archives created in a) and c) to the **/root** directory

    h. extract the contents of the archives created in d) and e) to their original locations

4. Use the Internet, library, or other sources of information to research two other package managers available for Linux systems. For each package manager, list the command and options required to install, query, and remove packages. Also list the benefits that the package manager offers to Linux users and where it may be downloaded from on the Internet.

CHAPTER

14

TROUBLESHOOTING AND PERFORMANCE

After completing this chapter, you will be able to:

◆ Describe and outline common troubleshooting procedures

◆ Identify good troubleshooting practices

◆ Effectively troubleshoot common hardware-related problems

◆ Effectively troubleshoot common software-related problems

◆ Monitor system performance using command-line and graphical utilities

◆ Understand the purpose and usage of kernel modules

Throughout this textbook, you have examined various areas of a Linux system. In this chapter you focus on fixing common problems that affect these areas. First, you explore system maintenance and troubleshooting procedures. Next, you learn about common hardware-related and software-related problems and their solutions, followed by a discussion of performance-related problems and utilities that can be used to monitor performance. Finally, you learn how to provide support for hardware and kernel features using modules, as well as how to compile this support directly into a new kernel.

TROUBLESHOOTING METHODOLOGY

Once you have successfully installed Linux, configured services on the system, and documented settings, you must maintain the system's integrity over time. This includes monitoring, proactive maintenance, and reactive maintenance, as illustrated in Figure 14-1.

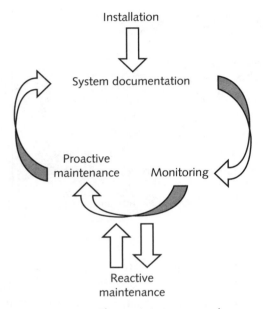

Figure 14-1   The maintenance cycle

Monitoring is the largest activity that Linux administrators do; it involves examining log files and running performance utilities periodically to identify problems and their causes. **Proactive maintenance** involves taking the necessary steps required to minimize the chance of future problems as well as their impact. Performing regular system back-ups and identifying potential problem areas are examples of proactive maintenance. All proactive maintenance tasks should be documented for future reference; this information, along with any data back-ups, is vital to the reconstruction of your system, should it suffer catastrophic failure.

Reactive maintenance is used to correct problems when they arise during monitoring. When a problem is solved, it should be documented and the system adjusted proactively to reduce the likelihood that the same problem will occur in the future. Furthermore, documenting the solution to problems will create a template for action, allowing subsequent or similar problems to be remedied faster.

Any system **documentation** should be printed and kept in a logbook, as this information may be lost during a system failure if kept on the Linux system itself.

Reactive maintenance is further composed of many components known as **troubleshooting procedures**, which can be used to solve a problem efficiently in a systematic manner.

When a problem occurs, you should gather as much information about the problem as possible; this may include examining system log files, viewing the contents of the `/proc` filesystem, as well as running information utilities such as ps or mount. In addition to this, you may research the symptoms of the problem on the Internet; Web sites and newsgroups often list log files and commands that can be used to check for certain problems.

The `tail –f <logfile>` command opens a log file for continuous viewing; this allows you to see entries as they are added, which is useful when gathering information about system problems.

Following this, you should try to isolate the problem by examining the information gathered. Determine whether the problem is persistent or intermittent, and whether it affects all users or just one.

Given this information, you may then generate a list of possible causes and solutions, organized by placing the most probable solution at the top of the list and the least probable solution at the bottom of the list. Using the Internet at this stage is beneficial since solutions for many Linux problems are posted on Web sites or newsgroups. In addition, posing the problem at a local Linux Users Group will likely generate many possible solutions.

Next, you should implement and test each possible solution for results until the problem is resolved. When implementing possible solutions, it is very important that you only apply one change at a time. If you make multiple modifications, it will be unclear as to what worked and why.

Once the problem has been solved, document the solution for future reference and proceed to take proactive maintenance measures to reduce the chance of the same problem reoccurring in the future.

These troubleshooting procedures are outlined in Figure 14-2.

14

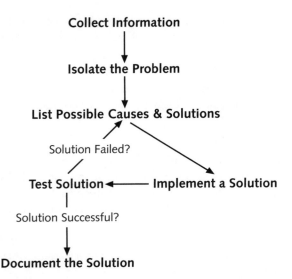

Figure 14-2   Common troubleshooting procedures

Keep in mind that the procedures listed in Figure 14-2 serve as a guideline only; they may need to be adjusted for certain problems, since troubleshooting is an art that you will improve on over time. There are, however, two golden rules that should guide you during any troubleshooting process:

- *Prioritize problems*—If there are multiple problems to be solved, prioritize the problems according to severity and spend a reasonable amount of time on each problem given its priority. Becoming fixated on a small problem and ignoring larger issues results in much lower productivity. If a problem is too difficult to solve in a given period of time, it is good practice to ask for help.

- *Try to solve the root of the problem*—Some solutions may appear successful in the short term, yet the problems reoccur due to an underlying cause that was not discovered. Effective troubleshooting relies a great deal on instinct, which comes from a solid knowledge of the system hardware and configuration. To avoid missing the underlying cause of any problem, try to justify why a certain solution was successful. If it is unclear why a certain solution worked, then there is likely an underlying cause to the problem that may need to be remedied in the future to prevent the same problem from reoccurring.

Resolving Common System Problems

There are many possible problems that can occur on different types of Linux systems. These problems are too numerous to mention here; however, there are some problems common to many Linux systems that will be examined throughout this section. All Linux problems can be divided into two categories: hardware-related and software-related.

Hardware-Related Problems

Although hardware problems may be the result of damaged hardware, many hardware-related problems involve improper hardware or software configuration. This is most likely the case if the hardware problem presents itself immediately after Linux installation.

As discussed in earlier chapters, ensuring that all SCSI drives are properly terminated, that the video card and monitor settings have been configured properly, and that all hardware is on the Hardware Compatibility List will minimize problems later. In addition, if the POST does not complete or alerts you with two or more beeps at system startup, then there is likely a peripheral card, cable, or memory stick that is loose or connected improperly inside the computer.

Some hardware-related problems prevent the use of hardware with the Linux operating system. This may be caused if an IRQ or I/O address is used by two different devices; in this case, neither device will work properly. Error messages indicating these IRQ and I/O address conflicts are typically written to log files during boot time and when applications try to access the device afterwards. Viewing the output of the **dmesg** command or the contents of the **/var/log/boot.log** and **/var/log/messages** log files may isolate the devices with conflicting parameters. Alternatively, you may view device parameters using the KDE Control Center, as depicted in Figure 14-3, by navigating to the K button, Control Center while logged into the KDE desktop environment or by navigating to the GNOME button, KDE menus, Control Center while logged into the GNOME desktop environment.

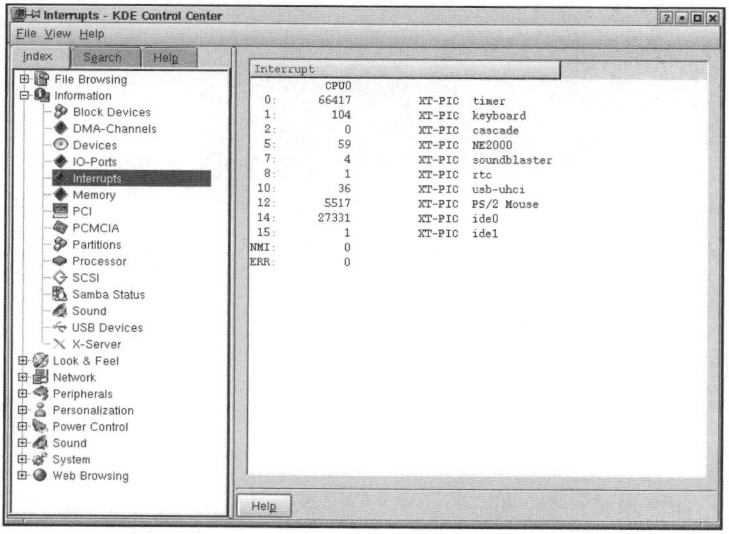

Figure 14-3   The KDE Control Center

Once an IRQ or I/O address conflict has been identified, you may take the necessary steps to resolve it. Many conflicts are the result of PnP selecting parameters for a device when another non-PnP device has already configured itself with the same parameters; to prevent this, reserve all parameters that are used by non-PnP devices in the computer BIOS. Alternatively, you may change the parameters on the non-PnP device manually, since many devices come with a configuration program that allows you to change their IRQ and I/O address parameters on a CMOS chip stored on the peripheral card itself.

The absence of a device driver will also prevent the operating system from using the associated hardware device. Normally, the **kudzu program** runs at each boot time, detects new hardware devices, and configures the device driver for them automatically. For example, if you add a sound card to the system, simply boot the computer and the screen depicted in Figure 14-4 will be displayed. Pressing Enter at this screen will allow you to configure the new hardware, as shown in Figure 14-5.

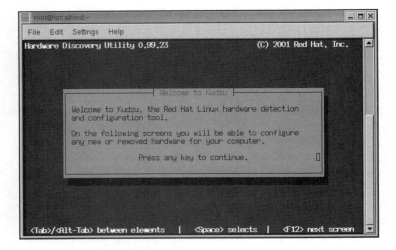

Figure 14-4   The kudzu welcome screen

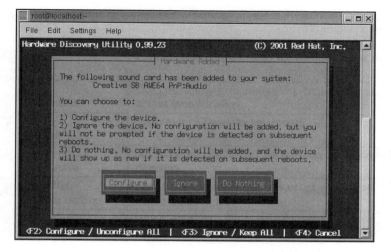

Figure 14-5 Configuring new hardware using kudzu

If a hardware device is not detected by kudzu, then the device driver for it must be configured manually. Device drivers may be inserted into the kernel as modules or may be compiled directly into the kernel. These topics are discussed later in this chapter.

Although less common than other hardware problems, hardware failure may also render a device unusable. In this case, you must replace the hardware and allow kudzu to detect it, or configure the device driver for it manually. Since hard disks are used frequently and consist of moving parts, they are the most common hardware component to fail on Linux systems. If the Linux system uses hardware RAID level 1 or 5, then the data on the hard disk may be regenerated using the configuration utility for the RAID controller. Most SCSI RAID controllers allow you to enter this utility by pressing a key combination such as Ctrl-a when prompted during system startup.

If, however, the Linux system does not use hardware RAID and the hard disk that failed contained partitions that were mounted on non-critical directories such as **/home** or **/var**, then you may perform the following steps:

1. Power down the computer and replace the failed hard disk.

2. Boot the Linux system.

3. Use fdisk to create partitions on the replaced hard disk.

4. Use mkfs to create filesystems on those partitions.

5. Restore the original data using a back-up utility.

6. Ensure that **/etc/fstab** has the appropriate entries to mount the filesystems at system startup.

14

Alternatively, if the hard disk that contains the / filesystem fails, then you should perform the following steps:

1. Power down the computer and replace the failed hard disk.

2. Reinstall Linux on the new hard disk (you may choose to leave partitions on other hard disks intact and mount them to the appropriate directory).

3. Restore the original configuration and data files using a back-up utility.

Software-Related Problems

Software-related problems are typically more difficult to identify and resolve than hardware-related problems. To narrow down the possibilities, you should begin by identifying whether the software-related problem is related to the application software or operating system software.

Application-Related Problems

Applications may fail during execution for a number of reasons, including missing program libraries and files, process restrictions, or conflicting applications.

When software is installed using the Red Hat Package Manager, it does a preliminary check to ensure that all shared program libraries and prerequisite packages (also known as **dependencies**) have been installed; if there are any dependencies missing, the Red Hat Package Manager will print an error message to the screen and quit the installation. Similarly, uninstalling software using the Red Hat Package Manager will fail if the software being uninstalled is a dependency for another package. Also, when compiling source code, the configure script checks for the presence of any dependencies and fails to create `Makefile` if they are absent. Thus you must download and install the necessary shared libraries and/or packages before installing most software packages.

Some programs, however, may fail to check for dependencies during installation, or program dependencies may be accidentally removed from the system over time. If this is the case, certain programs will fail to execute properly.

To identify any missing files in a package or package dependency, recall that you may use the –V option to the `rpm` command followed by the name of the package. The following output indicates that there are two missing files in the `bash` package:

```
[root@localhost root]# rpm -V bash
missing     /usr/share/doc/bash-2.05/NEWS
missing     /usr/share/doc/bash-2.05/NOTES
[root@localhost root]# _
```

To identify which shared libraries are required by a certain program, you may use the **ldd command**. For example, the following output displays the shared libraries required by the /bin/bash program:

```
[root@localhost root]# ldd /bin/bash
```

```
                       libtermcap.so.2 => /lib/libtermcap.so.2 (0x40033000)
                       libdl.so.2 => /lib/libdl.so.2 (0x40037000)
                       libc.so.6 => /lib/i686/libc.so.6 (0x4003b000)
                       /lib/ld-linux.so.2 => /lib/ld-
                       linux.so.2 (0x40000000)
        [root@localhost root]# _
```

If any shared libraries listed by the `ldd` command are missing, you may download the appropriate library from the Internet and install it to the correct location, which is typically underneath the `/lib` or `/usr/lib` directories. After downloading and installing any shared libraries, it is good practice to run the **ldconfig command** to ensure that the list of shared library directories (**/etc/ld.so.conf**) and the list of shared libraries (**/etc/ld.so.cache**) are updated.

Processes are restricted by a number of constraints that may also prevent them from executing properly. Recall that all processes require a PID from the system process table. Too many processes running on the system may use all available PIDs in the process table; this is typically the result of a large number of zombie processes. Killing the parent process of the zombie processes will then free up several entries in the process table.

In addition, processes may initiate numerous connections to files on the filesystem in addition to Standard Input, Standard Output, and Standard Error. These connections are called **filehandles**. The shell restricts the number of filehandles that programs may open to 1024 by default; to increase the maximum number of filehandles to 5000, you may run the command `ulimit -n 5000`. The **ulimit command** can also be used to increase the number of processes that users may start in a shell; this may be required for programs that start a great deal of child processes. For example, to increase the maximum number of user processes to 8000, you may use the command `ulimit -u 8000`.

To isolate application problems that are not related to missing dependencies or restrictions, you should first check the log file produced by the application. Most application log files are stored in the **/var/log directory** or a subdirectory of the `/var/log` directory named for the application. For example, to view the errors for the Apache Web server daemon, you may view the file `/var/log/httpd/error_log`.

Applications may run into difficulties gaining resources during execution and stop functioning. Often, restarting the process solves this problem. This condition may also be caused by another process on the system that attempts to use the same resources. To determine this, you should attempt to start the application when fewer processes are loaded, such as in single user mode. If resource conflict seems to be the cause of the problem, check the Internet for a newer version of the application or an application fix.

Operating System-Related Problems

Most software-related problems are related to the operating system itself. These typically include problems with boot loaders, filesystems, and serial devices.

As discussed in Chapter 9, boot loaders may encounter problems while attempting to load the operating system kernel. For the LILO boot loader, replacing the word compact with the word linear in the /etc/lilo.conf file usually remedies the problem; for the GRUB boot loader, errors are typically the result of a missing file in the /boot directory. Also, ensuring that the Linux kernel resides before the 1024th cylinder of the hard disk and that 32-bit Large Block Addressing (lba32) is specified in the boot loader configuration file eliminates BIOS problems with large hard disks. Recall from Chapter 3 that it is safe practice to create a boot disk during installation; if the boot loader fails to load the kernel after installation, you may then use the boot loader and kernel on the boot disk to mount the root filesystem and continue the boot process.

The **mkbootdisk command** can be used to create a boot disk after installation. To create a boot disk with the 2.4.7-10 kernel on it, you may use the command `mkbootdisk 2.4.7-10` at the command prompt and insert a blank floppy diskette when prompted. This boot disk may then be used to boot into a system so that the boot loader may be repaired.

Since the operating system transfers data to and from the hard disk frequently, the filesystem may become corrupted over time; a corrupted filesystem can be identified by very slow write requests, errors printed to the console, or failure to mount. If the filesystem on a partition mounted to a non-critical directory such as /home or /var becomes corrupted, you should perform the following steps:

1. Unmount the filesystem if mounted.

2. Run the `fsck` command with the —f (full) option on the filesystem device.

3. If the `fsck` command cannot repair the filesystem, use the `mkfs` command to recreate the filesystem.

4. Restore the original data for the filesystem using a back-up utility.

 Do not restore data onto a damaged filesystem; ensure that the filesystem has been recreated first.

If the / filesystem becomes corrupted, the system is unstable and must be turned off. Following this, you may use a copy of Linux on the installation media to remedy the problem using the following troubleshooting steps:

1. Place the first Red Hat installation CD-ROM in the CD-ROM drive and turn on the computer.

2. At the welcome screen shown in Figure 14-6, type linux rescue and press Enter. When prompted for language and keyboard layout, choose English and U.S., respectively.

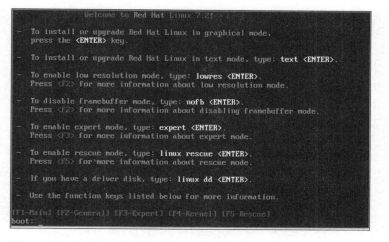

Figure 14-6   The Red Hat Linux installation welcome screen

3. At the screen depicted in Figure 14-7, choose Skip to enter a shell for the Linux system on the CD-ROM. This system contains utilities in the /usr/bin and /usr/sbin directories required to restore the filesystem on the hard disk as shown in Figure 14-8.

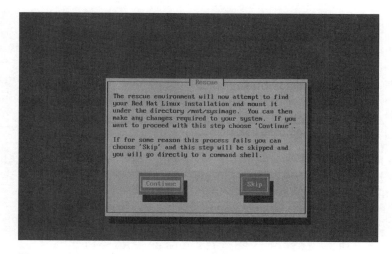

Figure 14-7   Obtaining a shell in rescue mode

14

Figure 14-8 The command-line shell used in rescue mode

4. Use the `mkfs` command on the CD-ROM Linux system to create a new `/` filesystem on the appropriate partition on the hard disk.

5. Use a back-up utility on the CD-ROM Linux system (`tar` or `cpio`) to restore the original data to the recreated `/`filesystem.

6. Type exit at the shell prompt and reboot the system.

Another common problem encountered on Linux systems is improper serial port configuration. Modem devices are identified as serial devices to the system; however, many modems use the same IRQ and I/O address settings as a serial port that is connected to the mainboard of the computer, which will result in parameter conflicts. In addition to this, some serial devices such as serial printers and terminal stations require communication at a set speed, rather than the default speed of 115KB/s for most serial ports. To remedy these problems, you may use keyword arguments to the setserial program to set the IRQ, I/O address, and speed of a specified serial device. For example, to set the IRQ of the first serial port (`/dev/ttyS0`) to 11 and the I/O address to 0x03f8, and view the results, you may use the following commands:

```
[root@localhost root]# setserial /dev/ttyS0 irq 11 port 0x03f8
[root@localhost root]# setserial /dev/ttyS0
/dev/ttyS0, UART: 16550A, Port: 0x03f8, IRQ: 11
[root@localhost root]# _
```

Other keywords that may be used with the **setserial command** are listed in Table 14-1.

Table 14-1   Common keywords used with the setserial utility

Option	Description
port n	Sets the I/O address to n for a serial device
irq n	Sets the IRQ to n for a serial device
auto_irq	Attempts automatically to detect the IRQ setting for a serial device
spd_hi	Sets the speed of a serial port to 56KB/s
spd_vhi	Sets the speed of a serial port to 115KB/s
spd_normal	Sets the speed of a serial port to 38.4KB/s

PERFORMANCE MONITORING

Some problems that you will encounter on a Linux system are not as noticeable as those discussed in the previous section; such problems may affect the overall performance of the Linux system. Like the problems discussed earlier, performance problems may be caused by software or hardware or a combination of the two.

Hardware that is improperly configured may still work, but at a slower speed. In addition, when hardware ages, it may start to malfunction and send large amounts of information to the CPU when not in use; this process is known as **jabbering** and can slow down a CPU and hence the rest of the Linux system. To avoid this hardware malfunction, most companies retire computer equipment after 2–3 years of use.

Software may also affect the overall performance of a system; software that requires too many system resources will monopolize the CPU, memory, and peripheral devices. Poor performance may also be the result of too many processes running on a computer, processes that make a great deal of read/write requests to the hard disk (such as databases), or rogue processes. To remedy most software performance issues, you may remove software from the system to free up system resources; if this software is needed for business activity, you may instead choose to move the software to another Linux system that has more free system resources.

Software performance problems may also sometimes be remedied by altering the hardware. Upgrading or adding another CPU will allow the Linux system to execute processes faster and reduce the number of processes running concurrently on the CPU. Alternatively, some peripheral devices can perform a great deal of processing that is normally performed by the CPU; this is known as **bus mastering**. Using bus mastering peripheral components will reduce the amount of processing the CPU must perform and hence increase system speed.

Adding RAM to the computer will also increase system speed, as processes will have more working space in memory and the system will swap much less information to and from the hard disk. Since the operating system, peripheral components, and all processes

14

use RAM constantly, adding RAM to any system often has a profound impact on system performance.

In addition to this, replacing slower hard disk drives with faster ones or using Disk Striping RAID will improve the performance of programs that require frequent access to filesystems. Recall from earlier that SCSI hard disks typically have faster access speeds than their IDE counterparts; many Linux servers use SCSI hard disks for this reason. In addition, CD-ROMs have a slower access speed than hard disks; thus, keeping CD-ROM drives and hard disk drives on separate controllers will also improve hard disk performance.

The size of the Linux kernel itself has an impact on system performance; a smaller kernel can execute faster on the CPU than a larger one. Thus, recompiling the kernel (discussed later in this chapter) to remove unnecessary components and reduce its size will improve overall system performance.

To ease the identification of performance problems, you should run performance utilities on a healthy Linux system on a regular basis during normal business hours and record the results in a system log book. The average results of these performance utilities are known as **baseline** values since they represent normal system activity. When performance issues arise, you may compare the output of performance utilities to the baseline values found in the system log book; values that have changed dramatically from the baseline may indicate the source of the performance problem.

Although there are many performance utilities available to Linux administrators, the most common of these belong to the sysstat package.

Monitoring Performance with sysstat Utilities

The **System Statistics (sysstat) package** contains a wide range of utilities that monitor the system using information from the /proc directory and system devices.

To monitor CPU performance, you may use the **Multiple Processor Statistics (mpstat) utility**. Without arguments, the mpstat utility gives average CPU statistics for all processors on the system since the most previous system boot, as seen in the output below:

```
[root@localhost cron.d]# mpstat
Linux 2.4.7-10 (localhost.localdomain)  07/14/2003
02:35:10 PM  CPU   %user   %nice %system   %idle    intr/s
02:35:10 PM  all   66.64    0.00    2.60   30.77    107.92
[root@localhost root]# _
```

If your system has multiple CPUs, you may measure the performance of a single CPU by specifying the −P # option to the mpstat command where # represents the number of the processor, starting from zero. Thus, the command mpstat −P 0 would display statistics for the first processor on the system.

The %user value seen in the output above indicates the amount of time the processor spent executing user programs and daemons, whereas the %nice value indicates the amount of time the processor spent executing user programs and daemons that had non-default nice values. These numbers combined should be greater than the value of %system, which indicates the amount of time the system spent maintaining itself in order to execute user programs and daemons.

A system that has a high %system compared to %user and %nice is likely executing too many resource-intensive programs.

The %idle value indicates the percentage of time the CPU did not spend executing tasks. Although it may be zero for short periods of time, %idle should be greater than 25% over a long period of time.

A system that has a %idle less than 25% over a long period of time may require a faster or additional CPU.

The intr/s value is the number of interrupts or requests that a CPU receives from peripheral devices on average per second; a very high value compared to the average baseline value may be the result of a jabbering peripheral device.

Although the average values given by the mpstat command are very useful in determining the CPU health of a Linux system, you may also choose to take current measurements using mpstat. To do this, simply specify the interval in seconds and number of measurements as arguments to the mpstat command; for example, the following command takes five current measurements, one per second:

```
[root@localhost root]# mpstat 1 5
Linux 2.4.7-10 (localhost.localdomain)   07/14/2003

03:16:39 AM  CPU   %user   %nice %system   %idle    intr/s
03:16:40 AM  all   39.00    0.00    6.00   55.00    257.00
03:16:41 AM  all   93.00    0.00    6.00    1.00    123.00
03:16:42 AM  all   73.00    0.00   21.00    6.00    114.00
03:16:43 AM  all   79.00    0.00   19.00    2.00    109.00
03:16:44 AM  all   57.00    0.00   33.00   10.00    128.00
Average:     all   68.20    0.00   17.00   14.80    146.20
[root@localhost root]# _
```

The output above must be used with caution since it was taken over a short period of time; although the %idle values are under 25% on average, they are not necessarily abnormal.

Another utility in the sysstat package is **Input/Output Statistics (iostat)**; this utility measures the flow of information to and from disk devices. Without any arguments, the iostat command displays CPU statistics similar to mpstat, followed by statistics for

14

each disk device on the system. Disk devices are named by their major number and given a sequence number. If the Linux system has one IDE hard disk drive (/dev/hda) and one IDE CD-ROM drive (/dev/hdc), then the iostat command will produce output similar to the following:

```
[root@localhost cron.d]# iostat
Linux 2.4.7-10 (localhost.localdomain)  07/14/2003

avg-cpu:  %user    %nice    %sys    %idle
          78.61     0.00    2.68    18.71

Device:   tps   Blk_read/s   Blk_wrtn/s   Blk_read   Blk_wrtn
dev3-0   6.22    122.47        57.45       204832     96094
dev22-1  0.00      0.00         0.00            4         0
[root@localhost root]# _
```

The device dev3-0 represents the hard disk drive since /dev/hda has a major number of 3. The device dev22-1 represents the CD-ROM drive since /dev/hdc has a major number of 22. The -0 and -1 extensions label each device in sequence.

The output from iostat displays the number of transfers per second (tps) as well as the number of blocks read per second (Blk_read/s) and written per second (Blk_wrtn/s), followed by the total number of blocks read (Blk_read) and written (Blk_wrtn) for the device since the last boot. An increase over time in these values indicates an increase in disk usage by processes. If this increase results in slow performance, the hard disks should be replaced with faster ones or a RAID Disk Stripe. Like mpstat, the iostat command can take current measurements of the system. Simply specify the interval in seconds followed by the number of measurements as arguments to the iostat command.

Although iostat and mpstat can be used to get quick information about system status, they are limited in their abilities. The **System Activity Reporter (sar) command** that is contained in the sysstat package can be used to display far more information than iostat and mpstat; as such, it is the most widely used performance monitoring tool on UNIX and Linux systems.

By default, sar commands are scheduled using the cron daemon to run every 10 minutes in Red Hat Linux. All performance information obtained is logged to a file in the /var/log/sa directory called sa#, where # represents the day of the month. If today were the 14th day of the month, then the output from the sar command that is run every 10 minutes would be logged to the file /var/log/sa/sa14. Next month, this file will be overwritten on the 14th day; thus only one month of records is kept at any one time in the /var/log/sa directory.

You may change the sar logging interval by editing the cron table /etc/cron.d/sysstat.

Without arguments, the sar command displays the CPU statistics taken every 10 minutes for the current day as seen below:

```
[root@localhost root]# sar
Linux 2.4.7-10 (localhost.localdomain)   07/14/2003

12:00:00 PM        CPU      %user      %nice     %system       %idle
12:10:01 PM        all       1.14       0.00        0.14       98.72
12:20:01 PM        all       1.10       0.00        0.17       98.73
12:30:01 PM        all       0.98       0.00        0.15       98.87
12:40:01 PM        all       1.01       0.00        0.13       98.86
12:50:01 PM        all       1.02       0.00        0.12       98.86
01:00:00 PM        all       1.08       0.00        0.16       98.76

01:00:00 PM        CPU      %user      %nice     %system       %idle
01:10:01 PM        all       1.05       0.00        0.14       98.81
01:20:00 PM        all       1.00       0.00        0.12       98.88
01:30:00 PM        all       1.02       0.00        0.12       98.86
01:40:00 PM        all       1.04       0.00        0.12       98.84
01:50:00 PM        all       1.04       0.00        0.13       98.82
02:00:00 PM        all       1.00       0.00        0.12       98.88
02:10:00 PM        all       1.04       0.00        0.15       98.81
02:20:00 PM        all       1.02       0.00        0.13       98.85
02:30:01 PM        all       1.01       0.00        0.12       98.87
02:40:01 PM        all       0.98       0.00        0.15       98.87
02:50:01 PM        all       0.98       0.00        0.15       98.87

02:50:01 PM        CPU      %user      %nice     %system       %idle
03:00:01 PM        all       1.02       0.00        0.13       98.86
03:10:01 PM        all       1.03       0.00        0.13       98.83
03:20:01 PM        all       1.01       0.00        0.13       98.86
03:30:01 PM        all       1.00       0.00        0.13       98.87
03:40:01 PM        all       1.01       0.00        0.12       98.87
03:50:00 PM        all       0.99       0.00        0.14       98.87
04:00:00 PM        all       1.11       0.00        0.15       98.74
04:10:00 PM        all       1.19       0.00        0.18       98.63
04:20:00 PM        all       1.02       0.00        0.13       98.85
04:30:00 PM        all       1.02       0.00        0.12       98.86
04:40:00 PM        all       1.03       0.00        0.11       98.86
04:50:01 PM        all       1.01       0.00        0.23       98.76
Average:           all       1.03       0.00        0.14       98.82
[root@localhost root]# _
```

14

Note from the output above that a new set of column headers is printed each time the computer is rebooted.

To view the CPU statistics for the 10th of the month, you may specify the pathname to the file using the —f option to the sar command:

```
[root@localhost root]# sar -f /var/log/sa/sa10
Linux 2.4.7-10 (localhost.localdomain)   07/10/2003

09:50:01 PM       CPU      %user      %nice     %system      %idle
10:00:01 PM       all       0.97       0.00        0.14      98.89
10:10:01 PM       all       1.04       0.00        0.11      98.84
10:20:00 PM       all       0.98       0.00        0.14      98.88
10:30:00 PM       all       1.01       0.00        0.11      98.89
10:40:00 PM       all       1.01       0.00        0.11      98.88
10:50:01 PM       all       1.00       0.00        0.13      98.87
11:00:01 PM       all       1.01       0.00        0.11      98.88

11:00:01 PM       CPU      %user      %nice     %system      %idle
11:10:01 PM       all       1.04       0.00        0.11      98.84
11:20:01 PM       all       1.01       0.00        0.11      98.89
11:30:00 PM       all       1.02       0.00        0.11      98.88
11:40:00 PM       all       1.01       0.00        0.12      98.88
11:50:01 PM       all       0.99       0.00        0.12      98.88
Average:          all     100.00     100.01      100.00       0.00

[root@localhost root]# _
```

You must use the —f option to the sar command to view files in the /var/log/sa directory with the aforementioned filenames since they contain binary information. However, a text version of each file is automatically created on the next day and stored as sar# in the /var/log/sa directory where # is the day of the month. These files may then be viewed with text utilities such as less and grep, or printed for use in a system log book.

As with the iostat and mpstat commands, the sar command can be used to take current system measurements. To take four CPU statistics every two seconds, you could use the following command:

```
[root@localhost root]# sar 2 4
Linux 2.4.7-10 (localhost.localdomain)   07/14/2003

05:13:44 AM       CPU      %user      %nice     %system      %idle
05:13:46 AM       all       0.00       0.00        0.50      99.50
05:13:48 AM       all       0.50       0.00        0.00      99.50
05:13:50 AM       all       0.50       0.00        0.00      99.50
05:13:52 AM       all       0.50       0.00        0.00      99.50
Average:          all       0.38       0.00        0.12      99.50
[root@localhost root]# _
```

Although the `sar` command displays CPU statistics by default, you may display different statistics by specifying options to the `sar` command. Table 14-2 lists common options used with the `sar` command.

Table 14-2   Common options to the sar command

Option	Description
-A	Equivalent to all options; displays the most information
-b	Displays I/O statistics
-B	Displays swap statistics
-c	Displays the number of processes created per second
-d	Displays Input/Output statistics for each block device on the system
-f *FILENAME*	Displays information from the specified file; these files typically reside in the /var/log/sa directory
-n FULL	Reports full network statistics; network monitoring will be discussed in the next chapter
-o *FILENAME*	Saves the output to a file in binary format
-q	Displays statistics for the processor queue
-r	Displays memory and swap statistics
-R	Displays memory statistics
-u	Displays CPU statistics; this is the default action when no options are specified
-U #	Displays CPU statistics for a given CPU, where # is the number of the CPU starting from zero
-v	Displays kernel-related filesystem statistics
-W	Displays swapping statistics

14

From Table 14-2, you can see that the −b and −d options to the `sar` command display information similar to the output of the `iostat` command. In addition, the −u and −U options display CPU statistics equivalent to the output of the `mpstat` command.

Another important option to the `sar` command is −q, which shows processor queue statistics. Recall that a queue, also known as a cache, is used to store information temporarily for a certain device. The queues that surround the CPU are known as L1 and L2 cache. To view processor queue statistics every second five times, you may execute the following command:

```
[root@localhost root]# sar -q 1 5
Linux 2.4.7-10 (localhost.localdomain)   07/14/2003

09:23:04 AM   runq-sz   plist-sz   ldavg-1   ldavg-5
09:23:05 AM         1         57      0.01      0.02
```

```
09:23:06 AM          1          55       0.01       0.02
09:23:07 AM          1          57       0.09       0.04
09:23:08 AM          1          55       0.09       0.04
09:23:09 AM          1          57       0.09       0.04
Average:             1          56       0.06       0.03
[root@localhost root]# _
```

The `runq-sz` (run queue size) value indicates the number of processes that are waiting for execution on the processor run queue. For most Intel architectures, this number is typically two or less on average.

 A `runq-sz` much greater than two for long periods of time indicates that the CPU is too slow to respond to system requests.

The `plist-sz` (process list size) value indicates the number of processes currently running in memory, and the `ldavg-1` (load average — 1 minute) and `ldavg-5` (load average — 5 minutes) values represent an average CPU load for the last 1 minute and 5 minutes respectively. These three statistics display an overall picture of processor activity. A rapid increase in these values is typically caused by software that is running on the system.

Recall that all Linux systems use a swap partition to store information that cannot fit into physical memory; this information is sent to and from the swap partition in units called pages. The number of pages that are sent to the swap partition (`pswpin/s`) and the pages that are taken from the swap partition (`pswpout/s`) can be viewed using the —W option to the `sar` command as seen below:

```
[root@localhost root]# sar -W 1 5
Linux 2.4.7-10 (localhost.localdomain)   07/14/2003

09:39:24 AM   pswpin/s pswpout/s
09:39:25 AM      0.00      0.54
09:39:26 AM      1.32      1.93
09:39:27 AM      0.38      0.00
09:39:28 AM      0.00      0.00
09:39:29 AM      0.00      0.00
Average:         0.00      0.00
[root@localhost root]# _
```

If there are a large number of pages being sent to and taken from the swap partition, then the system will suffer from slower performance. To remedy this, you could add more physical memory (RAM) to the system.

The sysstat package also contains a program that can create graphs using the information stored in the /var/log/sa directory. This program is called the Interactive System Activity Grapher and may be started by typing `isag` at a command prompt while in a desktop environment. The **Interactive System Activity Grapher (isag) command** allows you to choose the file to view (see Figure 14-9) as well as the information in that file that corresponds to various `sar` command options (see Figure 14-10).

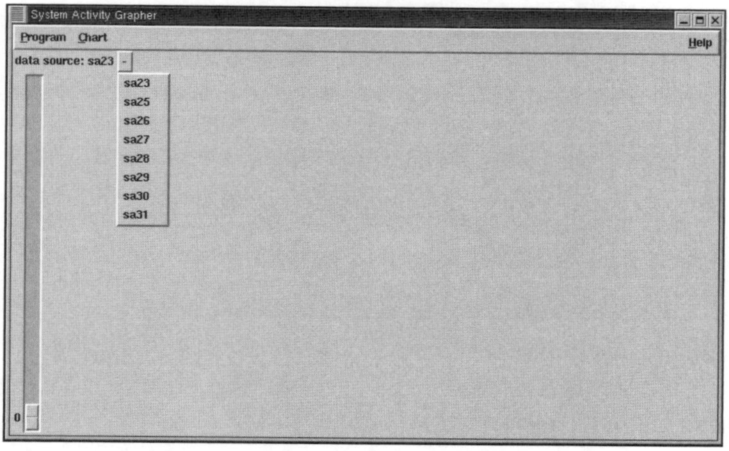

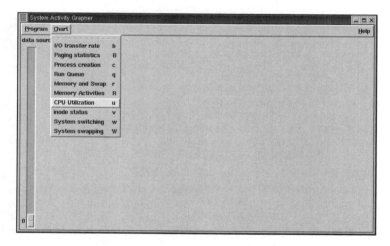

Figure 14-9   Choosing a file to view using the System Activity Grapher

Figure 14-10   Choosing statistics using the System Activity Grapher

Once chosen, the Interactive System Activity Grapher displays the information in a line graph; a sample graph showing CPU statistics from the 28th day of the month (`/var/log/sa/sa28`) is depicted in Figure 14-11.

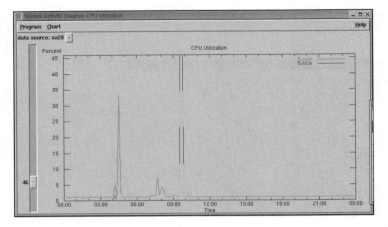

Figure 14-11   Viewing user statistics using the System Activity Grapher

Other Performance Monitoring Utilities

The sysstat package utilities are not the only performance monitoring utilities available on Red Hat Linux. The top utility discussed in Chapter 11 also displays CPU statistics, including memory usage, swap usage, and average CPU load, at the top of the screen as seen below:

```
10:23am  up  7:18,  1 user,  load average: 0.00, 0.01, 0.09
58 processes: 57 sleeping, 1 running, 0 zombie, 0 stopped
CPU states:  0.0% user,  1.1% system,  0.0% nice, 98.8% idle
Mem:   384468K av, 332616K used, 51852K free, 900K shrd, 32492K buff
Swap:  514040K av,      0K used,514040K free              150512K cached

  PID USER      PRI  NI  SIZE  RSS SHARE STAT %CPU %MEM   TIME COMMAND
12570 root       17   0  1044 1044   836 R    0.7  0.2  0:00 top
 9346 root       14   0  3164 3164  2600 S    0.5  0.8  0:13 magicdev
    1 root        8   0   520  520   452 S    0.0  0.1  0:04 init
    2 root        8   0     0    0     0 SW   0.0  0.0  0:00 keventd
    5 root        9   0     0    0     0 SW   0.0  0.0  0:00 kswapd
    6 root        9   0     0    0     0 SW   0.0  0.0  0:00 kreclaimd
    7 root        9   0     0    0     0 SW   0.0  0.0  0:00 bdflush
    8 root        9   0     0    0     0 SW   0.0  0.0  0:00 kupdated
   13 root        9   0     0    0     0 SW   0.0  0.0  0:00 kjournald
   88 root        9   0     0    0     0 SW   0.0  0.0  0:00 khubd
  202 root        9   0     0    0     0 SW   0.0  0.0  0:00 kjournald
  661 root        9   0   592  592   496 S    0.0  0.1  0:00 syslogd
  666 root        9   0  1100 1100   448 S    0.0  0.2  0:00 klogd
  686 rpc         9   0   592  592   504 S    0.0  0.1  0:00 portmap
  714 rpcuser     9   0   764  764   664 S    0.0  0.1  0:00 rpc.statd
```

Furthermore, the **free command** can be used to display the total amounts of physical and swap memory in kilobytes and their utilizations as seen in the following output:

```
[root@localhost root]# free
              total       used        free     shared    buffers     cached
Mem:         384468     333348       51120        900      32736     150520
-/+ buffers/cache:      150092      234376
Swap:        514040          0      514040
[root@localhost root]# _
```

The Linux kernel reserves some memory for its own use (cached) to hold requests from hardware devices (buffers); the total memory in the above output is calculated with and without these values to indicate how much memory the system has reserved. The output from the **free** command above indicates that there is sufficient memory in the system since no swap is used and there is a great deal of free physical memory.

Like the free utility, the vmstat utility can be used to indicate whether more physical memory is required by measuring swap performance:

```
[root@localhost root]# vmstat
   procs                      memory      swap          io     system          cpu
 r  b  w   swpd   free   buff  cache   si   so    bi    bo   in    cs  us  sy  id
 0  0  0      0  51120  32740 150532    0    0     8    17  105    27   4   1  95
[root@localhost root]# _
```

The **vmstat command** shown above indicates more information than the **free** command used earlier, including:

- the number of processes waiting to be run (**r**)
- the number of sleeping processes (**b**)
- the number of processes in swap memory (**w**)
- the amount of swap memory used in kilobytes (**swpd**)
- the amount of free physical memory (**free**)
- the amount of memory used by buffers in kilobytes (**buff**)
- the amount of physical memory used by caches (**cache**)
- the amount of memory in kilobytes per second swapped in from the disk (**si**)
- the amount of memory in kilobytes per second swapped out to the disk (**so**)
- the number of blocks per second sent to block devices (**bi**)
- the number of blocks per second received from block devices (**bo**)
- the number of interrupts sent to the CPU per second (**in**)
- the number of context changes sent to the CPU per second (**cs**)

14

- the CPU user time (`us`)
- the CPU system time (`sy`)
- the CPU idle time (`id`)

Thus, the output from **vmstat** seen above indicates that there is no swap memory being used since **w**, **swpd**, **si**, and **so** are all zero; however, it also indicates that the reason for this is that the system is not running many processes at the current time (`r=0, id=95`).

CUSTOMIZING THE KERNEL

Since the Linux kernel interfaces with the computer hardware, you may provide additional hardware support or change existing hardware support by altering the way in which the kernel works. This may be done by inserting a module into the kernel or recompiling the kernel to incorporate different features. Alternatively, it may be necessary to download and compile a new kernel to obtain certain hardware support that is not available in the current version. In addition, the Linux kernel also affects performance; recompiling the kernel to remove unnecessary features will reduce its size and increase its speed.

Kernel Modules

Many device drivers and kernel features are compiled into the kernel. However, these may also be inserted into the kernel as modules to reduce the size of the kernel. It is good form to compile standard device support into the kernel and leave support for other devices and features as modules. Since there is a wide variety of sound card and NIC card manufacturers, drivers for these components are typically represented by modules that can be inserted into the kernel, as compared to IDE hard disk support, which is typically compiled directly into the kernel since it is so often needed.

Some kernel features are available as modules; these modules must be manually inserted into the kernel. In addition, if kudzu does not detect new hardware properly, then you will need to load the appropriate module into the kernel to provide the necessary hardware support.

Modules are typically stored in subdirectories of the `/lib/modules/<kernel-version>` directory. For example, to see a partial list of NIC driver modules for the 2.4.7-10 kernel, you could list the contents of the `/lib/modules/2.4.7-10/kernel/drivers/net` directory:

```
[root@localhost root]# ls -F /lib/modules/2.4.7-10/kernel/drivers/net/
3c501.o          bcm/          epic100.o    ni52.o        starfire.o
3c503.o          bonding.o     eql.o        ni65.o        strip.o
3c505.o          bsd_comp.o    es3210.o     ns83820.o     sundance.o
3c507.o          cipe/         eth16i.o     pcmcia/       sungem.o
3c509.o          cs89x0.o      ethertap.o   pcnet32.o     sunhme.o
3c515.o          de4x5.o       ewrk3.o      plip.o        tlan.o
```

```
3c59x.o              de600.o        fc/          ppp_async.o     tokenring/
8139too.o            de620.o        hamachi.o    ppp_deflate.o   tulip/
82596.o              defxx.o        hp100.o      ppp_generic.o   tulip_old/
8390.o               depca.o        hp.o         ppp_synctty.o   tun.o
ac3200.o             dgrs.o         hp-plus.o    rcpci.o         via-rhine.o
acenic.o             dl2k.o         irda/        sb1000.o        wan/
aironet4500_card.o   dmfe.o         lance.o      shaper.o        wavelan.o
aironet4500_core.o   dummy.o        lne390.o     sis900.o        wd.o
aironet4500_proc.o   e1000.o        lp486e.o     sk98lin/        winbond-
840.o
appletalk/           e100.o         natsemi.o    skfp/           wireless/
arlan.o              e2100.o        ne2k-pci.o   slhc.o          yellowfin.o
arlan-proc.o         eepro100.o     ne3210.o     slip.o
at1700.o             eepro.o        ne.o         smc-ultra32.o
atp.o                eexpress.o     ni5010.o     smc-ultra.o
[root@localhost root]# _
```

Most files seen in the above output have the .o extension that indicates that they are compiled and ready to be inserted into the kernel. If there exists a PnP NE2000 NIC in the Linux computer, you could use the insmod ne command to insert the module into the kernel. The **insmod command** does not require the full path to the module underneath the /lib/modules/<kernel-version> directory as it searches there by default and will locate the ne.o file seen in the above output.

Alternatively, you may use the modprobe ne command to insert the module into the kernel. The **modprobe command** checks to make sure that any prerequisite modules have been loaded first and loads them if needed before loading the specified module.

Some modules may require extra parameters when inserted into the kernel. For example, a non-PnP NE2000 NIC will require the IRQ and I/O address to be specified alongside its module name; to insert this module into the kernel for a NIC that uses IRQ 10 and an I/O address range of 0x300-31F, you could use the command insmod ne irq=10 io=0x300.

Both the insmod and modprobe commands will fail to insert a driver module if the associated device is not present.

To see a list of modules that have been inserted into the Linux kernel, you may use the **lsmod command**:

```
[root@localhost root]# lsmod
Module             Size   Used by
iptable_mangle     2256   0   (autoclean) (unused)
iptable_nat        18224  0   (autoclean) (unused)
ip_conntrack       16944  1   (autoclean) [iptable_nat]
iptable_filter     2256   0   (autoclean) (unused)
ip_tables          11392  5   [iptable_mangle iptable_nat iptable_filter]
binfmt_misc        6416   1
iscsi              1984   0   (unused)
scsi_mod           5696   1   [iscsi]
autofs             11520  0   (autoclean) (unused)
```

```
ne                    7456   1
8390                  6752   0   [ne]
appletalk            20912   0   (autoclean)
ipx                  16448   0   (autoclean)
usb-uhci             21536   0   (unused)
usbcore              51712   1   [usb-uhci]
ext3                 64624   2
jbd                  40992   2   [ext3]
[root@localhost root]# _
```

The lsmod command can also be used to show module dependencies. From the above output, the ne module requires the 8390 module since the 8390 module is used by ne.

To remove a module from the kernel, you may use the **rmmod command**. To remove the ne module seen in the previous output, you could type the command rmmod ne at the command prompt.

Normally, modules are inserted into the kernel automatically at boot time from entries in the **/etc/modules.conf file**. An example of this file is seen below:

```
[root@localhost root]# cat /etc/modules.conf
alias parport_lowlevel parport_pc
alias usb-controller usb-uhci
alias eth0 ne
alias sound-slot-0 sb
alias synth0 awe_wave
[root@localhost root]# _
```

The above output loads the ne module at boot time for a PnP NE2000 NIC and gives it an alias name of eth0; if the NIC is not PnP, you would also need to specify the IRQ and I/O address options, as seen in the following /etc/modules.conf file:

```
[root@localhost root]# cat /etc/modules.conf
alias parport_lowlevel parport_pc
alias usb-controller usb-uhci
alias eth0 ne
options ne irq=10 io=0x300
alias sound-slot-0 sb
alias synth0 awe_wave
[root@localhost root]# _
```

You may edit the /etc/modules.conf file and add a line to load a particular module on system startup if hardware is not detected properly or certain kernel features are required. Alternatively, you may place the appropriate insmod or modprobe command in the **/etc/rc.d/rc.local file**, which is executed at the end of system startup.

Compiling a New Linux Kernel

To gain certain hardware or kernel support, it may be necessary to recompile the current kernel with different features or download the source code for a newer kernel and compile it.

Kernel source code is stored under the **/usr/src/<kernel-version>** directory. The source code for the current kernel version is present underneath this directory. You may instead choose to download source code in tarball format for a newer kernel and place the tarball in the **/usr/src** directory. Upon extraction, the appropriate **<kernel-version>** directory will be created underneath **/usr/src**.

Regardless of whether you are recompiling the current kernel version or a new one, the remaining steps are identical. The next step is to create a symbolic link called **/usr/src/linux** to the correct kernel version directory **/usr/src/<kernel-version>**. Next, change to this directory and execute one of many **make** commands.

If the source code has been compiled previously, you may optionally use the **make mrproper** command to remove any files created by previous kernel compilations; this will speed up compiling the new kernel. In addition, if you are compiling the same kernel version that is currently being used, you may use the **make oldconfig** command to record the current kernel features and settings that can then be used as a starting point for further configuration.

Next, you must choose the certain features required for the kernel; this can be done using one of three commands:

- **make config**, which provides a text-based interface that prompts you for information regarding kernel configuration in a question-by-question format as seen below:

```
[root@localhost linux]# make config
rm -f include/asm
( cd include ; ln -sf asm-i386 asm)
/bin/sh scripts/Configure arch/i386/config.in
#
# Using defaults found in configs/kernel-2.4.7-i686.config
#
*
* Code maturity level options
*
Prompt for development and/or incomplete code/drivers
(CONFIG_EXPERIMENTAL) [Y/n/?]
```

- **make menuconfig**, which provides a text-based menu that allows easy navigation of kernel features for configuration as seen in Figure 14-12

14

Figure 14-12 The make menuconfig interface

- `make xconfig`, which must be run in a GUI environment and allows the easiest navigation of kernel features via a graphical interface as depicted in Figure 14–13

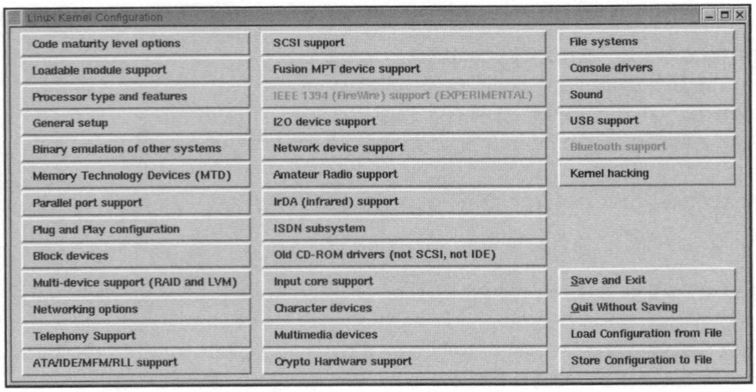

Figure 14-13 The make xconfig interface

The easiest method for choosing kernel features and support is by using `make xconfig`; hence we will discuss this method further.

From Figure 14–13, the first configuration button is "Code maturity level options"; clicking on this button will result in the screen seen in Figure 14–14.

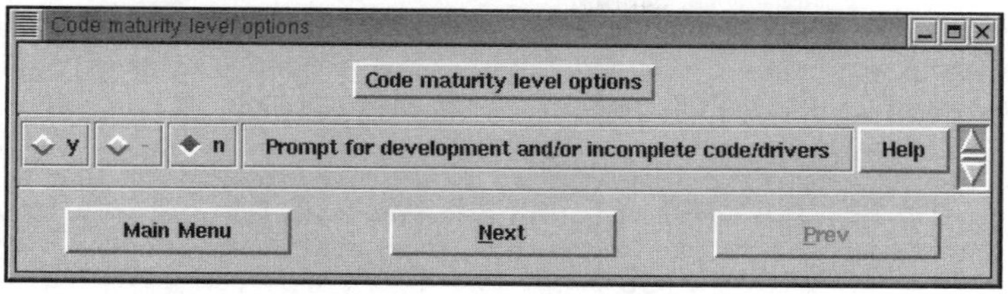

Figure 14-14   Configuring code maturity level options

Selecting y from Figure 14-14 will display any experimental features or drivers that may be configured into the Linux kernel throughout the other menus listed in Figure 14-13. If you are building a production server, it is good practice to avoid viewing these experimental options; this will prevent them from being accidentally chosen during kernel configuration.

Most other buttons displayed in Figure 14-13 are used to configure different aspects of the Linux kernel; clicking on "USB support" will display the screen seen in Figure 14-15.

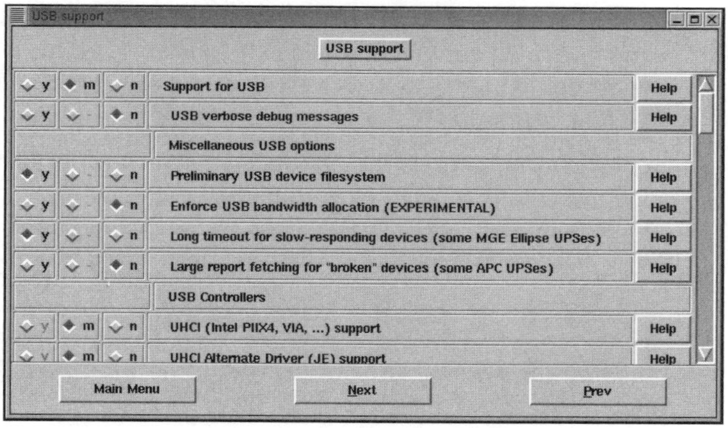

Figure 14-15   Configuring USB support

From Figure 14-15, notice that there are three options for specifying kernel support:

- *y* indicates that the support will be compiled into the kernel
- *m* indicates that the support will be compiled into a module that may be inserted into the Linux kernel
- *n* disables support for a certain kernel feature

All three choices may not be available for some features.

You should disable support for unused kernel features to reduce the size of the Linux kernel and increase its speed. For the same reason, you should compile rarely used features as modules.

According to Figure 14-15, USB support is compiled as a module whereas support for a preliminary USB filesystem is compiled directly into the kernel. Since many features may be misunderstood, you may press the "Help" button beside each option in Figure 14-15 to receive a description of each feature and recommended settings.

When configuring a new kernel, it is good form to click on each button in Figure 14-13 to ensure that all required support is chosen. When finished, you may select the "Save and Exit" button from Figure 14-13 and return to the command prompt.

Once the kernel features have been selected, you must run the command `make dep` to ensure that any features compiled as modules will have the necessary prerequisite modules created as well. Next, you should run the `make clean` command to remove any files that will not be required for compiling the kernel; this will speed up the time it takes to compile the kernel.

Next, you may compile the kernel by typing `make bzImage`; for the Intel x86 architecture, this will create a bzip2 compressed kernel called `/usr/src/linux/ arch/i386/boot/bzImage`, which can be copied to the `/boot` directory and renamed `vmlinuz-<kernel version>`.

Following this, you may then compile the kernel modules by typing `make modules` at a command prompt. These modules then need to be copied to the correct location under the `/lib/modules` directory by using the command `make modules_install`.

Next, you may configure the boot loader to boot the new kernel. It is good form to dual boot the new kernel with the old one; if the new kernel does not work, you may boot into the old kernel and fix the problem. To dual boot a kernel called `/boot/vmlinuz-2.4.7-10-new` with a previous kernel using LILO, simply add the following entries to `/etc/lilo.conf`:

```
prompt
timeout=50
default=RedHatLinux
boot=/dev/hda
map=/boot/map
install=/boot/boot.b
message=/boot/message
lba32

image=/boot/vmlinuz-2.4.7-10
        label=RedHatLinux
        read-only
        root=/dev/hda1
```

```
image=/boot/vmlinuz-2.4.7-10-new
        label=RedHatLinuxNew
        read-only
        root=/dev/hda1
```

Next, you must run the lilo command to reinstall LILO. To use GRUB to dual boot the /boot/vmlinuz-2.4.7-10-new kernel with the previous one, you may alternatively add the following entries to /boot/grub/grub.conf:

```
default=1
timeout=10
splashimage=(hd0,1)/grub/splash.xpm.gz
title Red Hat Linux (2.4.7-10)
        root (hd0,1)
        kernel /vmlinuz-2.4.7-10 ro root=/dev/hda1
title Red Hat Linux New (2.4.7-10)
        root (hd0,1)
        kernel /vmlinuz-2.4.7-10-new ro root=/dev/hda1
```

If the system requires kernel features or device support while the kernel is being loaded at boot time, you should create a kernel ramdisk image and reference it appropriately with LILO or GRUB; this is common if the /boot directory lies on a SCSI hard disk. To create a kernel ramdisk image, you may use the command mkinitrd -v /boot/ initrd-<kernel version>.img <kernel version>. To configure LILO to use the kernel ramdisk image, simply add the line initrd = /boot/initrd-<kernel version>.img to the correct image= paragraph in /etc/lilo.conf and run the lilo command afterwards. To configure GRUB to use the kernel ramdisk image, simply add the line initrd /initrd-<kernel version>.img to the correct title paragraph in the /boot/grub/grub.conf file.

Patching the Linux Kernel

14

To install a more current Linux kernel version, you normally download the source code for that kernel and place it in a directory that will be referenced by /usr/src/linux. If the /usr/src/linux directory already contains the source code for the current kernel, you may instead choose to download and apply patch files to this source code to change it into the desired version. Patches are not cumulative; to patch the Linux kernel version 2.4.7 to 2.4.9, you must apply the Linux kernel patches 2.4.8 and 2.4.9.

Patches are typically distributed in compressed form; to apply a patch, simply download and uncompress the patch file into the /usr/src/linux directory and execute the **patch command**. To execute a kernel patch, you could type patch < patchfile. When all patches have been applied, you may compile the kernel as described in the previous section.

CHAPTER SUMMARY

- After installation, Linux administrators monitor the system, perform proactive and reactive maintenance, and document important system information.

- Common troubleshooting procedures involve collecting data to isolate and determine the cause of system problems, as well as implementing and testing solutions that can be documented for future use.

- System problems may be categorized as hardware- or software-related.

- IRQ conflicts, invalid hardware settings, absense of kernel support, and hard disk failure are common hardware-related problems on Linux systems.

- Software-related problems may be further categorized as application-related or operating system-related.

- Absence of program dependencies, program limits, and resource conflicts are common application-related problems, whereas boot failure, filesystem corruption, and the misconfiguration of serial devices are common operating system-related problems.

- System performance is affected by a variety of hardware and software factors including the amount of RAM, CPU speed, kernel size, and process load.

- Using performance monitoring utilities to create a baseline is helpful when diagnosing performance problems in the future. The sysstat package contains many useful performance monitoring commands.

- System features and hardware support may be compiled into the Linux kernel or provided by a kernel module.

- You may compile a Linux kernel with only the necessary features and support in order to increase system performance.

KEY TERMS

/etc/ld.so.cache file — The file that contains the location of shared library files.

/etc/ld.so.conf file — The file that contains a list of directories that contain shared libraries.

/etc/modules.conf file — The file used to load and alias modules at system initialization.

/etc/rc.d/rc.local file — The file that can be used to load modules at system initialization.

/usr/src/linux directory — The directory that contains source code for the Linux kernel during compilation.

/var/log directory — The directory that contains most system log files.

baseline — A measure of normal system activity.

bus mastering — The process by which peripheral components perform tasks normally executed by the CPU.

dependencies — The prerequisites required for program execution such as shared libraries or other packages.

documentation — System information that is stored in a log book for future reference.

filehandles — The connections that a program makes to files on a filesystem.

free command — The command used to display memory and swap statistics.

Input/Output Statistics (iostat) command — The command that displays Input/Output statistics for block devices.

insmod command — The command used to insert a module into the Linux kernel.

Interactive System Activity Grapher (isag) command — The command used to graph system performance information stored in the /var/log/sa directory.

jabbering — The process by which failing hardware components send large amounts of information to the CPU.

kudzu program — The program used to detect and install support for new hardware.

ldconfig command — The command that updates the /etc/ld.so.conf and /etc/ld.so.cache files.

ldd command — The command used to display the shared libraries used by a certain program.

lsmod command — The command that lists modules currently used by the Linux kernel.

mkbootdisk command — The command used to create a boot floppy diskette.

modprobe command — The command used to insert a module and all necessary prerequisite modules into the Linux kernel.

monitoring — The process by which system areas are observed for problems or irregularities.

Multiple Processor Statistics (mpstat) command — The command that displays CPU statistics.

patch command — The command used to apply a patch to the Linux kernel source code.

proactive maintenance — The measures taken to reduce future system problems.

reactive maintenance — The measures taken when system problems arise.

rmmod command — The command that removes a module from the Linux kernel.

setserial command — The command used to set the parameters of serial device.

System Activity Reporter (sar) command — The command that displays various system statistics.

System Statistics (sysstat) package — A software package that contains common performance monitoring utilities such as mpstat, iostat, sar, and isag.

troubleshooting procedures — The tasks performed when solving system problems.

ulimit command — The command used to modify process limit parameters in the current shell.

vmstat command — The command used to display memory, CPU, and swap statistics.

14

REVIEW QUESTIONS

1. On which part of the Maintenance Cycle do Linux administrators spend the most time?

   a. monitoring

   b. proactive maintenance

   c. reactive maintenance

   d. documentation

2. Backing up system data on a regular basis is a type of reactive maintenance. True or False?

3. Linux administrators should always keep a copy of all documentation in a reserved directory on the filesystem. True or False?

4. Which of the following files is likely to be found in the `/var/log/sa` directory over time? (Choose all that apply).

   a. `sar15`

   b. `sa39`

   c. `sa19`

   d. `sar00`

5. Which of the following commands can be used to display memory statistics? (Choose all that apply.)

   a. `free`

   b. `sar`

   c. `vmstat`

   d. `iostat`

6. Which command will indicate the shared libraries required by a certain executable program?

   a. `ldconfig`

   b. `ldd`

   c. `rpm -V`

   d. `slconfig`

7. Which directory must you be in to compile the Linux kernel?

   a. `/lib/modules`

   b. `/usr/src/linux`

   c. `/lib/modules/<kernel-version>`

   d. `/usr/src/linux/<kernel-version>`

8. Which command can be used to create a ramdisk that will be used at boot time to load SCSI support?

a. `mkramdisk`

b. `load ramdisk`

c. `image=ramdisk`

d. `mkinitrd`

9. Which key combination will enter the configuration utility for many SCSI RAID controllers at boot time?

a. `Ctrl-x`

b. `Delete`

c. `Ctrl-a`

d. `Shift-Delete`

10. Which command can be used to apply a patch to kernel source code?

a. `patch`

b. `P0patch`

c. `make patch`

d. `make patch_install`

11. When an application stops functioning, what should you try first?

a. Restart the application.

b. Research the solution using the Internet.

c. Switch to single user mode.

d. Kill all other applications running in memory.

12. Which of the following steps is not a common troubleshooting procedure?

a. test solution

b. isolate the problem

c. delegate responsibility

d. collect information

13. You may recompile the kernel to _____. (Choose all that apply.)

a. add support for a certain hardware device

b. remove support for a certain hardware device

c. change kernel features

d. improve system performance

14

14. Which command can be used to insert a module into the Linux kernel? (Choose all that apply.)

    a. `insmod`

    b. `rmmod`

    c. `lsmod`

    d. `modprobe`

15. Applications that fail to execute properly may be missing key files or shared libraries known as dependencies. True or False?

16. The cron daemon takes system statistics every _____ by default on Red Hat Linux systems.

    a. 10 seconds

    b. 10 minutes

    c. 1 hour

    d. 10 hours

17. Which files may be used to load modules upon system startup? (Choose all that apply.)

    a. `/etc/modules.conf`

    b. `/etc/fstab`

    c. `/etc/modtab`

    d. `/etc/rc.d/rc.local`

18. Which of the following programs detects and installs new hardware detected at boot time?

    a. insmod

    b. kudzu

    c. lba32

    d. LILO

19. Which command can increase the number of filehandles that programs may open in a certain shell?

    a. `ldd`

    b. `ulimit`

    c. `lba32`

    d. `top`

20. The smaller the Linux kernel, the better it will perform on the system hardware. True or False?

21. Which command can be used to configure options for the kernel using a graphical interface only available in a desktop environment?

    a. `make config`

    b. `make xconfig`

    c. `make menuconfig`

    d. `make gnomeconfig`

22. Which of the following common troubleshooting steps should be performed first?

    a. test solution

    b. isolate the problem

    c. delegate responsibility

    d. collect information

23. When compiling a new Linux kernel, which command compiles the actual kernel itself?

    a. `make clean`

    b. `make bzImage`

    c. `make dep`

    d. `make oldconfig`

24. Which command can be used to create a system boot disk?

    a. `makeboot`

    b. `bootdisk`

    c. `mkboot`

    d. `mkbootdisk`

25. What will the command `sar -W 3 50` do?

    a. take 3 swap statistics, once every 50 seconds

    b. take 50 swap statistics, once every 3 seconds

    c. take 3 CPU statistics, once every 50 seconds

    d. take 50 CPU statistics, once every 3 seconds

26. Which option to the `rpm` command can be used to verify the existence of required files within an RPM package?

    a. `-q`

    b. `-V`

    c. `-f`

    d. `-i`

27. Documentation is only required if all proposed solutions to a certain problem fail when tested. True or False?

14

28. Which directory stores most modules on a Linux system?

    a. `/lib/modules/<kernel-version>`

    b. `/usr/src/linux-<kernel-version>`

    c. `/usr/lib/modules/<kernel-version>`

    d. `/usr/src/linux`

29. When the `fsck` command cannot repair a non-root filesystem, you should immediately restore all data from tape back-up. True or False?

30. When performing a `sar -u` command, you notice that `%idle` is consistently 10%; is this good or bad?

    a. good, since the processor should be idle more than 5% of the time

    b. good, since the processor is idle 90% of the time

    c. bad, since the processor is idle 10% of the time and perhaps a faster CPU is required

    d. bad, since the processor is idle 10% of the time and perhaps a new hard disk is required

31. The contents of the `/var/log/sa` directory are never more than one month old. True or False?

32. Which of the following commands can be used to view processor statistics? (Choose all that apply.)

    a. `iostat`

    b. `mpstat`

    c. `sar`

    d. `top`

33. Which of the following are good practices when troubleshooting? (Choose all that apply.)

    a. Try to find the quickest solution to the problem.

    b. Try to remedy the root of the problem.

    c. Prioritize problems according to their severity.

    d. Spend the same amount time documenting solutions as it took to fix them.

34. Which keyword can you place in `/etc/lilo.conf` or `/boot/grub/grub.conf` to fix problems with large hard disk support?

    a. `large-disk`

    b. `image`

    c. `lba32`

    d. `LIL?`

35. Which option to the `tail` command can be used to view the end of a log file continuously?

   a. `-c`

   b. `-f`

   c. `-l`

   d. `-a`

36. Which command can be used to modify the IRQ and I/O address settings of a serial device?

   a. `setserial`

   b. `modserial`

   c. `serial2K`

   d. `lsmod`

37. Given Figure 14-16 below, which of the following statements is true?

   a. SCSI support will be compiled into the kernel.

   b. SCSI support will be available as a module.

   c. SCSI support will not be available.

   d. SCSI support will be available as a module or compiled into the kernel at the discretion of the user upon system startup.

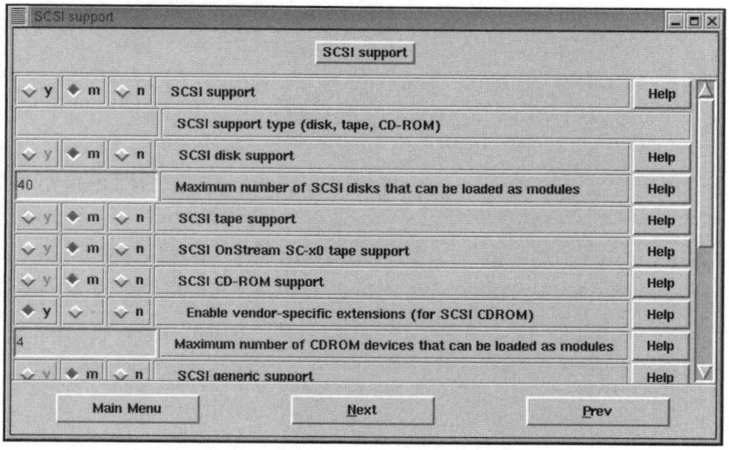

Figure 14-16   Configuring SCSI support

38. When performing a `sar -q` command, you notice that the `runq-sz` value is consistently 2; is this good or bad?

   a. good, since that is the average value

       b. good, since the `runq-sz` should be greater than 0

       c. bad, since the `runq-sz` should be less than 2

       d. bad, since the `runq-sz` should be greater than 2

HANDS-ON PROJECTS

These projects should be completed in the order given. All hands-on projects should take a total of three hours to complete. The requirements for this lab include:

❑ A computer with Red Hat Linux 7.2 installed according to Hands-on Project 7-2

Project 14-1

In this hands-on project, you will view and modify package dependencies.

1. Turn on your computer. Once your Linux system has been loaded, switch to a command-line terminal (tty2) by pressing **Ctrl-Alt-F2** and log into the terminal using the username of **root** and the password of **secret**.

2. At the command prompt, type **rpm –ql grep | less** and press **Enter** to view the file contents of the `grep` package on the system. When finished, press **q** to quit the `less` utility. Next, type **rpm –V grep** at the command prompt and press **Enter** to verify the existence of these files on the filesystem. Were any errors reported? Why?

3. At the command prompt, type **rm –f /usr/share/doc/grep-2.4.2/AUTHORS** and press **Enter** to remove a file that belongs to the `grep` package. Next, type **rpm –V grep** at the command prompt and press **Enter** to verify the existence of all files in the `grep` package. Were any errors reported? Why? If critical files were missing from this package, how could they be recovered?

4. Next, type **ldd /bin/grep** at the command prompt and press **Enter** to determine which shared libraries are used by the `grep` command.

5. At the command prompt, type **ls –l /lib/i686/libc.so.6 /lib/ld-linux.so.2** and press **Enter** to verify that these shared library files are available. If these libraries were missing, what should you do to regain them?

6. Type **exit** and press **Enter** to log out of your shell.

Project 14-2

In this hands-on project, you will monitor system performance using command-line utilities included in the sysstat package.

1. Switch to a command-line terminal (tty2) by pressing **Ctrl–Alt–F2** and log into the terminal using the username of **root** and the password of **secret**.

2. At the command prompt, type **mpstat** and press **Enter** to view average CPU statistics for your system since the last boot time. What is the value for %user? Is this higher or lower or the same as %system? Why? What is the value for %idle? What should this value be over?

3. At the command prompt, type **mpstat 1 5** and press **Enter** to view 5 CPU statistic measurements, one per second. How do these values compare to the ones seen in Step 2? Why?

4. Switch to a graphical terminal (tty7) by pressing **Ctrl-Alt-F7** and log into the GNOME desktop using the username of **root** and the password of **secret**.

5. Navigate to GNOME button, Programs, Games, Tux Racer. Observe the Tux Racer program menu.

6. Switch back to your command-line terminal (tty2) by pressing **Ctrl-Alt-F2**, type **mpstat 1 5** at the command prompt, and press **Enter** to view 5 CPU statistic measurements, one per second. How do these values compare to the ones seen in Step 3? Why?

7. Switch back to the graphical terminal (tty7) by pressing **Ctrl-Alt-F7** and quit out of the Tux Racer game.

8. Switch back to your command-line terminal (tty2) by pressing **Ctrl-Alt-F2**, type **iostat** at the command prompt, and press **Enter** to view average device I/O statistics since the last boot time. What devices are displayed? Which one is your hard disk? (Hint: look at device files in the /dev directory. How many blocks were read from and written to your hard disk since the last boot time on average?

9. At the command prompt, type **iostat 1 5** and press **Enter** to view 5 I/O statistic measurements, one per second. How do these values compare to the ones seen in Step 8? Why?

10. Switch to a graphical terminal (tty7) by pressing **Ctrl-Alt-F7** and navigate to GNOME button, Programs, Games, Tux Racer.

11. Switch back to your command-line terminal (tty2) by pressing **Ctrl-Alt-F2**, type **iostat 1 5** at the command prompt, and press **Enter** to view 5 I/O statistic measurements, one per second. How do these values compare to the ones seen in Step 9? Were there any significant changes? Why?

12. Switch back to the graphical terminal (tty7) by pressing **Ctrl-Alt-F7** and quit out of the Tux Racer game.

13. Switch back to your command-line terminal (tty2) by pressing **Ctrl-Alt-F2**, type **sar** at the command prompt, and press **Enter**. What statistics are displayed by default? What times were the statistics taken?

14. At the command prompt, type **sar -q** and press **Enter** to view queue statistics. What times were the statistics taken? How does this compare to Step 13? What is the queue size? What is the average load for the last minute? What is the average load for the last 5 minutes?

14

15. At the command prompt, type **sar -q 1 5** and press **Enter** to view 5 queue statistics, one per second. How do these values compare to those taken in Step 14? Why?

16. Switch to a graphical terminal (tty7) by pressing **Ctrl-Alt-F7** and navigate to GNOME button, Programs, Games, Tux Racer.

17. Switch back to your command-line terminal (tty2) by pressing **Ctrl-Alt-F2**, type **sar -q 1 5** at the command prompt, and press **Enter** to view 5 queue statistic measurements, one per second. How do these values compare to the ones seen in Step 15? Why?

18. Switch back to the graphical terminal (tty7) by pressing **Ctrl-Alt-F7** and quit out of the Tux Racer game.

19. Switch back to your command-line terminal (tty2) by pressing **Ctrl-Alt-F2**, type **sar -W** at the command prompt, and press **Enter**. How many pages were swapped to and from the swap partition today on average?

20. At the command prompt, type **sar -W 1 5** and press **Enter** to view 5 swap statistics, one per second. How do these values compare to those taken in Step 19? Why?

21. Switch to a graphical terminal (tty7) by pressing **Ctrl-Alt-F7** and navigate to GNOME button, Programs, Games, Tux Racer.

22. Switch back to your command-line terminal (tty2) by pressing **Ctrl-Alt-F2**, type **sar -W 1 5** at the command prompt, and press **Enter** to view 5 swap statistic measurements, one per second. How do these values compare to the ones seen in Step 20? Why?

23. Switch back to the graphical terminal (tty7) by pressing **Ctrl-Alt-F7** and quit out of the Tux Racer game. Next, log out of the GNOME desktop environment.

24. Switch back to your command-line terminal (tty2) by pressing **Ctrl-Alt-F2**.

25. Type **exit** and press **Enter** to log out of your shell.

Project 14-3

In this hands-on project, you will monitor system performance statistics taken from previous days using command-line and graphical utilities included in the sysstat package.

1. Switch to a command-line terminal (tty2) by pressing **Ctrl-Alt-F2** and log into the terminal using the username of **root** and the password of **secret**.

2. At the command prompt, type **cd /var/log/sa** and press **Enter** to change to the directory that contains recorded performance statistics.

3. Next, type **ls** at the command prompt and press **Enter**. What files are available? What are their filenames? Which files in this directory are safe to view using a text utility? Which file contains binary system statistics for the current day? Is there a text file in this directory that contains readable statistics for the current day? Why? Record the name of a file that contains binary system statistics for a previous day: _____. Record the name of a file that contains system statistics in text format for a previous day: _____.

4. At the command prompt, type **sar -q -f FILE1 | less** and press **Enter** where **FILE1** is the first filename recorded in Step 3. Scroll through the output. How many measurements were taken and when? Was your computer rebooted during that day? How can you tell? When finished, press **q** to quit the **less** utility.

5. At the command prompt, type **less FILE2** and press **Enter** where **FILE2** is the second filename recorded in Step 3. Scroll through the output. How many measurements were taken and when? When finished, press **q** to quit the **less** utility.

6. Switch to a graphical terminal (tty7) by pressing **Ctrl-Alt-F7** and log into the GNOME desktop using the username of **root** and the password of **secret**.

7. Open a terminal in the GNOME desktop, type **isag&** at the command prompt, and press **Enter**.

8. Click on the button to the right of **(no file)** and choose the first filename recorded in Step 3. What is the data source?

9. Click on the **Chart** menu and choose **Run Queue** to view queue statistics from this file. What is displayed on the screen? What times are listed? How does this compare to the figures observed in Step 4?

10. Close the Interactive System Activity Grapher and log out of the GNOME desktop environment.

11. Switch back to your command-line terminal (tty 2) by pressing **Ctrl-Alt-F2**.

12. Type **exit** and press **Enter** to log out of your shell.

Project 14-4

In this hands-on project, you will monitor memory and swap performance using the **top**, **free**, and **vmstat** commands.

1. Switch to a command-line terminal (tty2) by pressing **Ctrl-Alt-F2** and log into the terminal using the username of **root** and the password of **secret**.

2. At the command prompt, type **top** and press **Enter**. From the information displayed, answer the following questions:

   How many processes are currently running? _____

   How much memory does your system have in total? _____

   How much memory is being used? _____

   How much memory is used by buffers? _____

   How much swap memory does your system have in total? _____

   How much swap memory is being used? _____

3. Type **q** to quit the **top** utility.

4. At the command prompt, type **free** and press **Enter**. Does this utility give more or less information regarding memory and swap memory than the **top** utility? How do the values shown by the **free** command compare to those from Step 2?

14

5. At the command prompt, type **vmstat** and press **Enter**. Does this utility give more or less information regarding memory and swap memory than the top and free utilities? How do the values shown by the **vmstat** command compare to those from Step 2? What other information is provided by the **vmstat** command?

6. Type **exit** and press **Enter** to log out of your shell.

Project 14-5

In this hands-on project, you manage kernel modules on the system.

1. Switch to a command-line terminal (tty2) by pressing **Ctrl–Alt–F2** and log into the terminal using the username of **root** and the password of **secret**.

2. At the command prompt, type **lsmod** and press **Enter**. What modules are listed? Why? Do you see any modules that provide USB support? If so, write down their names here as they will be used in a later exercise: _____ .

3. At the command prompt, type **insmod dummy** and press **Enter**. What module was loaded from which directory? What do you think this module does? Type **lsmod** at the command prompt and press **Enter** to verify that it was inserted into the kernel. What could you do to load this module automatically at boot time?

4. At the command prompt, type **rmmod dummy** and press **Enter**. Next, type **lsmod** at the command prompt and press **Enter** to verify that the module was removed from the kernel properly.

5. At the command prompt, type **less /etc/modules.conf** and press **Enter**. What entries are listed? How do they compare to the output of the **lsmod** command from Step 2? What is another method for loading modules at boot time? Type **q** to quit the less command.

6. Use a text editor such as vito insert a line at the bottom of the /etc/rc.d/rc.local file that reads:

   ```
   insmod dummy
   ```

   When finished, save your changes.

7. At the command prompt, type **reboot** and press **Enter** to reboot the system.

8. Once your Linux system has been loaded, switch to a command-line terminal (tty2) by pressing **Ctrl–Alt–F2** and log into the terminal using the username of **root** and the password of **secret**.

9. At the command prompt, type **lsmod** and press **Enter**. Is the dummy module listed? Why?

10. Type **exit** and press **Enter** to log out of your shell.

Project 14-6

In this hands-on project, you will compile and use a new Linux kernel.

1. Switch to a graphical terminal (tty7) by pressing **Ctrl–Alt–F7** and log into the GNOME desktop using the username of **root** and the password of **secret**. Once loaded, open a command-line terminal.

2. At the command prompt, type **cd /usr/src** and press **Enter**. Type the **ls** command. What directories are shown? Next, type **ln –s linux-2.4.7-10 linux** to create a symbolic link called `/usr/src/linux` to the `/usr/src/linux-2.4.7-10` directory.

3. At the command prompt, type **cd linux** and press **Enter**. Next, type **ls –F** at the command prompt and press **Enter**. What files do you see? Is there a `Makefile`?

4. At the command prompt, type **make oldconfig** and press **Enter**. What does this command do?

5. At the command prompt, type **make xconfig** and press **Enter** to configure the settings that will be used when compiling the new kernel.

6. At the Linux Kernel Configuration screen, select **Code Maturity Level Options**.

7. At the Code maturity level options screen, ensure that **y** is selected. What does this option do?

8. Click the **Main Menu** button to return to the Linux Kernel Configuration screen.

9. At the Linux Kernel Configuration screen, select **Processor type and features**.

10. At the Processor type and features screen, ensure that **y** is selected beside `Symmetric multi-processing support`. What does the **y** indicate?

11. Next, click the **Help** button beside `Symmetric multi-processing support`. What does it say about using this support with ACPI? Click **OK**.

12. Click the **Main Menu** button to return to the Linux Kernel Configuration screen.

13. At the Linux Kernel Configuration screen, select **SCSI support**.

14. At the SCSI support screen, ensure that **m** is selected next to `SCSI support`, `SCSI disk support`, `SCSI tape support`, and `SCSI CD-ROM support`. What does the m indicate for these features?

15. Click the **Main Menu** button to return to the Linux Kernel Configuration screen.

16. At the Linux Kernel Configuration screen, select **USB support**.

17. At the USB support screen, ensure that **y** is selected beside `Support for USB`.

18. Click the **Main Menu** button to return to the Linux Kernel Configuration screen.

19. At the Linux Kernel Configuration screen, select **Save and Exit**. At the Kernel build instructions screen, click **OK**.

20. At the command prompt, type **make dep** and press **Enter**. What does this command do?

21. At the command prompt, type **make clean** and press **Enter**. What does this command do?

22. At the command prompt, type **make bzImage** and press **Enter**. What does this command do? Where will the results be placed? This step should take 15–30 minutes on most Linux systems.

23. At the command prompt, type **make modules** and press **Enter**. What does this command do? This step should take 30–45 minutes on most Linux systems.

14

24. At the command prompt, type **make modules_install** and press **Enter**. What does this command do?

25. At the command prompt, type **cp /usr/src/linux/arch/i386/boot/bzImage /boot/vmlinuz-2.4.7-10new** and press **Enter**. What does this command do?

26. Edit the **/etc/lilo.conf** file using a text editor such as **vi**. At the bottom of this file, add the following entries:

    ```
    image=/boot/vmlinuz-2.4.7-10new
            label=RedHatLinuxNew
            read-only
            root=/dev/hda1
    ```

    Note: If your **/boot** partition is not **/dev/hda1**, use the appropriate device file instead.

    When finished, save your changes and quit the editor.

27. At the command prompt, type **lilo** and press **Enter** to activate the changes made to the LILO boot loader.

28. At the command prompt, type **reboot** and press **Enter**. When the LILO `boot:` prompt appears, press the **Tab** key. What entries are listed and why? Type **RedHatLinuxNew** at the LILO `boot:` prompt and press **Enter**.

29. Once your Linux system has been loaded, switch to a command-line terminal (tty2) by pressing **Ctrl-Alt-F2**. What version of the kernel is displayed on the login banner? Why? Log into the terminal using the username of **root** and the password of **secret**.

30. At the command prompt, type **lsmod** and press **Enter**. Do you see any SCSI modules? Do you see any USB modules? Compare this to the results of Project 14-5 Step 2. Explain your findings.

31. Type **exit** and press **Enter** to log out of your shell.

DISCOVERY EXERCISES

1. Given the following situations, list any log files or commands that you would use when collecting information during the troubleshooting process:

    a. A CD-ROM device that worked previously with Linux does not respond to the **mount** command.

    b. The system was unable to mount the **/home** filesystem (**/dev/hda6**).

    c. A new database application fails to start successfully.

    d. The modem configuration utility that you have installed cannot recognize any modems on the system.

    e. You have installed a new sound card in the Linux system, but it is not detected by kudzu during system startup.

2. For each problem in Question 1, list as many possible causes and solutions that you can think of given the material presented throughout this textbook. Next, research other possible causes using resources such as the Internet, books, local HOWTOs, magazines, or LUGs.

3. You are the administrator of a Linux system that provides file and print services to over 100 clients in your company. The system uses several IDE hard disks and has a Pentium II processor with 128 MB of RAM. Since its installation, you have installed database software that is used by a few users only. Unfortunately, you have rarely monitored and documented performance information of this system in the past. Recently, users have begun to complain that the performance of the server is very poor. What commands could you use to narrow down the problem? Are there any other troubleshooting methods that may be useful when solving this problem?

4. Briefly describe the purpose of a baseline. What areas of the system would you include in a baseline for your Linux system? Which commands would you use to obtain the information about these areas? Use these commands to generate baseline information for your system (for the current day only) and place this information in a system log book (small binder) for later use. Next, monitor the normal activity of your system for 3 consecutive days and compare the results to the baseline that you have printed out. Are there any differences? Incorporate this new information into your baseline by averaging the results. Are these new values a more accurate indication of normal activity? Why or why not?

5. When new hardware devices are released by manufacturers, it takes some time for Linux drivers to be made and included in most Linux distributions. Often, you may download the source code for a module, which acts as the driver for a new hardware device. Pretend that you have just downloaded the source code for a new module and wish to compile it and insert it into the kernel so that the new hardware may be used with the Linux operating system. This new source code looks like the following:

```
#define MODULE
#include <linux/module.h>
int init_module(void)
{
     return 0;
}
```

Enter the code above into a file called **sample.c** using a text editor such as **vi**. Next, compile the **sample.c** file by executing the command **gcc -O -c sample.c**; this will create a compiled module file called **sample.o** in your current directory. Insert this module into the Linux kernel and verify that it was inserted successfully. Next, remove the module and configure it to be loaded upon boot time. (*Hint*: The module is not in the **/lib/modules/<kernel-version>** directory.)

14

CHAPTER

15

LINUX NETWORKING

After completing this chapter, you will be able to:

♦ Describe the purpose and types of networks, protocols, and media access methods

♦ Understand the basic configuration of the TCP/IP protocol

♦ Configure a NIC interface to use the TCP/IP protocol

♦ Configure a modem, ISDN, and DSL interface to use the PPP and TCP/IP protocols

♦ Understand the purpose of hostnames and how they are resolved to IP addresses

♦ Use common network utilities to interact with network services

♦ Identify and configure common network services

Throughout this textbook, you have examined the installation and administration of local Linux services. In this chapter you focus on configuring Linux to participate on a network. First, you become acquainted with some common network terminology, and then learn about the TCP/IP protocol and the procedure for configuring a network interface. Next, you learn about the Domain Name Space and the processes by which hostnames are resolved to IP addresses. Finally, you learn about the various network utilities and services that may be used on a Linux system.

NETWORKS AND TCP/IP

Most functions that computers perform today involve the sharing of information between computers. Information is usually transmitted from computer to computer via media such as fiber optic, telephone, coaxial, or UTP (Unshielded Twisted Pair) cable, but may also be transmitted via wireless media such as radio, micro-, or infrared waves. This media typically attaches to a peripheral card on the computer such as a Network Interface Card (NIC) or modem device.

Two or more computers that are connected with media that can exchange information are called a **network**. Networks that connect computers within close proximity are called **Local Area Networks (LANs)** whereas networks that connect computers separated by large distances are called **Wide Area Networks (WANs)**.

Many companies use LANs to allow employees to connect to databases and other shared resources such as printers. Home users may also use a LAN to connect several home computers together. Alternatively, home users may use a WAN to connect home computers to an Internet Service Provider to gain access to resources such as Web sites on the world-wide public network called the Internet.

 The Internet (Internetwork) is merely several public networks that are interconnected; both home and company networks may be part of the Internet. Special computers called **routers** transfer information from one network to another.

Computers that are connected via network media still require a method for sending and receiving information to and from other computers on the network. This is achieved by using a network **protocol** that formats information into packages of information called **packets**, as well as a **media access method** that can send these packets onto the media itself.

There are many different LAN protocols that you may configure in Linux, including but not limited to:

- TCP/IP (Transfer Control Protocol/Internet Protocol)
- UDP/IP (User Datagram Protocol/Internet Protocol)
- IPX/SPX (Internetwork Packet Exchange/Sequenced Packet Exchange)
- Appletalk
- DLC (Data Link Control)
- DECnet (Digital Equipment Corporation network)

 The most common LAN protocol used today is TCP/IP; it is the standard protocol used to transmit information across the Internet and the one discussed in this chapter.

When transmitting information across a WAN, you may also use a WAN protocol in addition to a specific LAN protocol to format packets for safer transmission. The two most common WAN protocols are SLIP (Serial Line Internet Protocol) and PPP (Point-to-Point Protocol).

Although there are many media access methods available, the most common one used to send TCP/IP packets onto network media is called **Ethernet**; it ensures that any TCP/IP packets are retransmitted onto the network if network error occurs. Another popular media access method is called **Token Ring**, which gives the computer that has a special token the ability to transmit information on a network; the token is passed from computer to computer to allow multiple computers to communicate. The media access method is usually contained within the hardware on the NIC or modem.

The TCP/IP Protocol

Each computer that participates on a TCP/IP network must have an **Internet Protocol (IP) address** and **subnet mask** to identify itself to other computers. IP addresses are normally comprised of four numbers (0–255) separated by periods; each number represents an 8-bit binary number. Thus, the IP address 192.168.0.1 can be represented as the number 11000000.10101000.00000000.00000001 in binary format.

Like IP addresses, subnet masks are also comprised of four 8-bit binary numbers, but are used to divide the IP address into two parts; one part identifies the network that the computer is on, and the other part represents the host computer itself. A subnet mask of 255.255.0.0 can be represented as 11111111.11111111.00000000.00000000 in binary format; the binary 1's in the subnet mask determine the network portion of the IP address, whereas the binary 0's in the subnet mask determine the host portion of the IP address as seen in Figure 15-1.

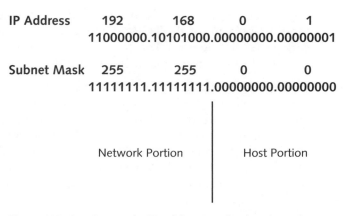

IP Address	192	168	0	1

11000000.10101000.00000000.00000001

Subnet Mask	255	255	0	0

11111111.11111111.00000000.00000000

Network Portion   Host Portion

15

Figure 15-1   A sample IP address and subnet mask

Thus, the IP address shown in Figure 15-1 identifies the first computer (host portion 0.1) on the 192.168 network (network portion 192.168).

The IP addresses 0.0.0.0 and 255.255.255.255 are not allowed to be assigned to a host computer since they refer to all computers on all networks. Similarly, using the number 255 (all 1's in binary format) in an IP address specifies many hosts. For example, the IP address 192.168.255.255 refers to all hosts on the 192.168 network; this IP address is also called the broadcast address for the 192.168 network.

Typically, all computers on a LAN are configured with the same network portion and different host portions. A LAN may connect to another LAN by means of a router, which has IP addresses for both LANs and can forward packets to and from each network. Each computer on a LAN may specify the IP address of a router in its TCP/IP configuration; any packets that are not destined for the local LAN will then be sent to the router, which can then forward the packet to the appropriate network or to another router. This router IP address is called the **default gateway**.

 The IP address 127.0.0.1 is called the loopback IP address; it always refers to the local computer.

CONFIGURING A NIC INTERFACE

Linux computers in a business environment typically connect to the company network via a Network Interface Card (NIC). At home, more and more people are connecting to the Internet by means of a NIC using technologies such as Digital Subscriber Line and (DSL) and Broadband Cable Networks (BCN).

If the NIC was detected during installation, Red Hat Linux automatically configures the appropriate driver module and prompts you for the TCP/IP configuration required for the business or home network (refer to Figure 3-13); however, some NICs are not detected upon installation and must be configured manually afterwards.

NIC drivers are usually contained within modules that may be inserted into the Linux kernel; you may use your computer manual, the Internet, or other sources of information to find which Linux module underneath the `/lib/modules` directory to use for a particular NIC. If there is no module for that NIC underneath `/lib/modules`, you may need to download a module from Internet. Once the module has been identified or downloaded, this module may be inserted into the kernel using the insmod or modprobe commands discussed in the previous chapter. To load this module at boot time, you should edit the `/etc/modules.conf` file.

The `/etc/modules.conf` file also assigns an alias to the module that may be used when referencing the module in a configuration command since modules do not have a corresponding file in the /dev directory. The first Ethernet NIC is given the alias eth0, the second Ethernet NIC is given the alias eth1, and so on. Thus, to load the driver module for the first NIC of type NE2000, you would place the following line in /etc/modules.conf:

```
alias eth0 ne
```

Along the same line, to load the driver module for the second NIC of type DEC Tulip, you would place the following line in /etc/modules.conf:

```
alias eth1 tulip
```

Once the driver module for the NIC has been loaded into the Linux kernel, you may configure it to use the TCP/IP protocol. The **ifconfig command** can be used to assign a TCP/IP configuration to a NIC as well as view the configuration of all network interfaces in the computer. To assign eth0 the IP address of 3.4.5.6 with a subnet mask of 255.0.0.0 and broadcast address of 3.255.255.255, you could use the following command at a command prompt:

```
ifconfig eth0 3.4.5.6 netmask 255.0.0.0 broadcast 3.255.255.255
```

Alternatively, you may receive TCP/IP configuration from a DHCP (Dynamic Host Configuration Protocol) or BOOTP (Boot Protocol) server on the network. To obtain and configure TCP/IP information from a server on the network for the first Ethernet adapter, you may use the command **pump —i eth0** or the command **dhcpcd eth0** at the command prompt.

To view the configuration of all interfaces, you may use the **ifconfig** command without any arguments as seen in the following output:

```
[root@localhost root]# ifconfig
eth0      Link encap:Ethernet  HWaddr 00:80:C8:D6:74:43
          inet addr:3.4.5.6  Bcast:3.255.255.255  Mask:255.0.0.0
          UP BROADCAST RUNNING MULTICAST  MTU:1500  Metric:1
          RX packets:975 errors:0 dropped:0 overruns:0 frame:0
          TX packets:806 errors:0 dropped:0 overruns:0 carrier:0
          collisions:0
          RX bytes:61250 (59.8 Kb)  TX bytes:110294 (107.7 Kb)

lo        Link encap:Local Loopback
          inet addr:127.0.0.1  Mask:255.0.0.0
          UP LOOPBACK RUNNING  MTU:16436  Metric:1
          RX packets:10 errors:0 dropped:0 overruns:0 frame:0
          TX packets:10 errors:0 dropped:0 overruns:0 carrier:0
          collisions:0
          RX bytes:750 (750.0 b)  TX bytes:750 (750.0 b)

[root@localhost root]# _
```

The output of the **ifconfig** command will also show interface statistics and the special loopback adapter (lo) with the IP address 127.0.0.1; this IP address represents the local computer and is required on all computers that use TCP/IP.

15

The `netstat -i` command may also be used to show interface statistics.

If you restart the computer, the TCP/IP information configured for eth0 above will be lost. To allow the system to activate and configure the TCP/IP information for an interface at each boot time, you should place entries in the `/etc/sysconfig/network-scripts/ifcfg-interface` file. An example of the configuration file for the first Ethernet interface (eth0) is seen in the following output:

```
[root@localhost root]# cat /etc/sysconfig/network-scripts/ifcfg-eth0
DEVICE=eth0
ONBOOT=yes
BOOTPROTO=static
IPADDR=3.4.5.6
NETMASK=255.0.0.0
GATEWAY=3.0.0.1
[root@localhost root]# _
```

The entries in the output above indicate that the TCP/IP configuration for the first Ethernet adapter (eth0) will be activated at boot time (ONBOOT=yes). In addition, the NIC is statically configured using the IP address 3.4.5.6, subnet mask of 255.0.0.0, and default gateway of 3.0.0.1. The broadcast need not be included in this file since it can easily be calculated by the system given the subnet mask. Also, you may change **BOOT-PROTO=static** to **BOOTPROTO=dhcp** or **BOOTPROTO=bootp** to gain all TCP/IP configuration information from a DHCP or BOOTP server on the network, respectively.

The `/etc/sysconfig/network-scripts/ifcfg-eth0` file may also contain information regarding the configuration of other network protocols such as IPX/SPX.

After editing the `/etc/sysconfig/network-scripts/ifcfg-eth0` file, you need not reboot the system to have the new TCP/IP configuration take effect; simply run the command `ifdown eth0` to un-configure the eth0 interface, followed by `ifup eth0` to configure the eth0 interface using the new settings in the /etc/sysconfig/network-scripts/ifcfg-eth0 file.

Once a NIC has been configured to use the TCP/IP protocol, you should test the configuration by using the **packet internet groper (ping) command**. The `ping` command sends a small TCP/IP packet to another IP address and awaits a response. By default, the `ping` command sends packets continuously every second until the `Ctrl-c` key combination is pressed; to send only five ping requests to the loopback adapter, you may use the `-c` option to the `ping` command, as seen below:

```
[root@localhost root]# ping -c 5 127.0.0.1
PING 127.0.0.1 (127.0.0.1) from 127.0.0.1 : 56(84) bytes of data.
64 bytes from 127.0.0.1: icmp_seq=0 ttl=255 time=246 usec
```

```
64 bytes from 127.0.0.1: icmp_seq=1 ttl=255 time=84 usec
64 bytes from 127.0.0.1: icmp_seq=2 ttl=255 time=110 usec
64 bytes from 127.0.0.1: icmp_seq=3 ttl=255 time=76 usec
64 bytes from 127.0.0.1: icmp_seq=4 ttl=255 time=87 usec

--- 127.0.0.1 ping statistics ---
5 packets transmitted, 5 packets received, 0% packet loss
round-trip min/avg/max/mdev = 0.076/0.120/0.246/0.064 ms

[root@localhost root]# _
```

If the ping command fails to receive any responses from the loopback adapter, then there is a problem with the TCP/IP protocol itself.

In addition, to send five ping requests to the IP address configured earlier, you may use the following command:

```
[root@localhost root]# ping -c 5 3.4.5.6
PING 3.4.5.6 (3.4.5.6) from 3.4.5.6 : 56(84) bytes of data.
64 bytes from 3.4.5.6: icmp_seq=0 ttl=255 time=1.693 msec
64 bytes from 3.4.5.6: icmp_seq=1 ttl=255 time=104 usec
64 bytes from 3.4.5.6: icmp_seq=2 ttl=255 time=62 usec
64 bytes from 3.4.5.6: icmp_seq=3 ttl=255 time=148 usec
64 bytes from 3.4.5.6: icmp_seq=4 ttl=255 time=133 usec

--- 3.4.5.6 ping statistics ---
5 packets transmitted, 5 packets received, 0% packet loss
round-trip min/avg/max/mdev = 0.062/0.428/1.693/0.633 ms

[root@localhost root]# _
```

If the ping command fails to receive any responses from the newly configured IP address, then there is a problem with the TCP/IP configuration for the NIC.

15

Next, you should test to see whether the Linux computer can ping other computers on the same network; the following command can be used to send five ping requests to the computer that has the IP address 3.0.0.2 configured:

```
[root@localhost root]# ping -c 5 3.0.0.2
PING 3.0.0.2 (3.0.0.2) from 3.0.0.88 : 56(84) bytes of data.
64 bytes from 3.0.0.2: icmp_seq=0 ttl=128 time=353 usec
64 bytes from 3.0.0.2: icmp_seq=1 ttl=128 time=981 usec
64 bytes from 3.0.0.2: icmp_seq=2 ttl=128 time=629 usec
64 bytes from 3.0.0.2: icmp_seq=3 ttl=128 time=690 usec
64 bytes from 3.0.0.2: icmp_seq=4 ttl=128 time=626 usec
```

```
--- 3.0.0.2 ping statistics ---
5 packets transmitted, 5 packets received, 0% packet loss
round-trip min/avg/max/mdev = 0.353/0.655/0.981/0.202 ms

[root@localhost root]# _
```

 If the `ping` command fails to receive any responses from other computers on the network, there is a problem with the network media.

Configuring a NIC interface can also be done from a GUI environment as seen in Figure 15-2; if you are using the GNOME desktop environment, navigate to GNOME button, Programs, System, Network Configuration; or navigate to OK button, System, Network Configuration if you are using the KDE desktop environment.

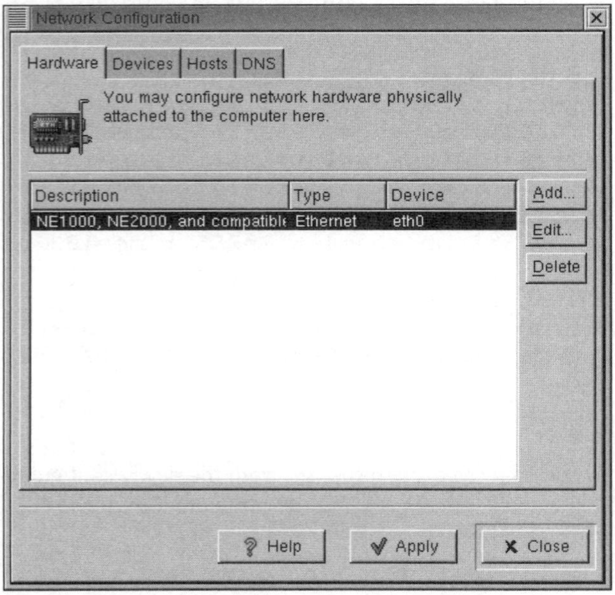

Figure 15-2   Configuring network hardware

The Hardware tab seen Figure 15-2 can be used to add or modify NIC driver modules, whereas the Devices tab shown in Figure 15-3 allows you to modify the interface information.

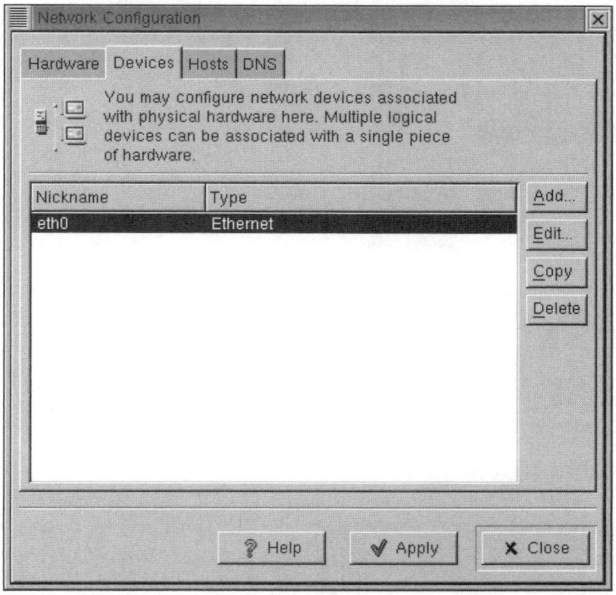

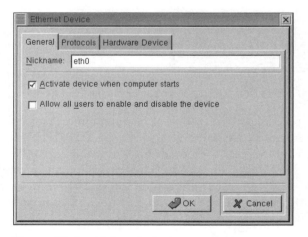

Figure 15-3   Configuring a network device

Editing the eth0 interface shown in Figure 15-3 will bring up the screen seen in Figure 15-4 that allows you to change the alias of the interface and whether it will be configured at boot time. The Protocols tab from Figure 15-4 is shown in Figure 15-5; editing the TCP/IP protocol will allow you to set the TCP/IP configuration as shown in Figure 15-6.

Figure 15-4   Network device properties

15

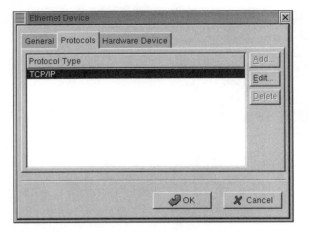

Figure 15-5   Configuring a network protocol

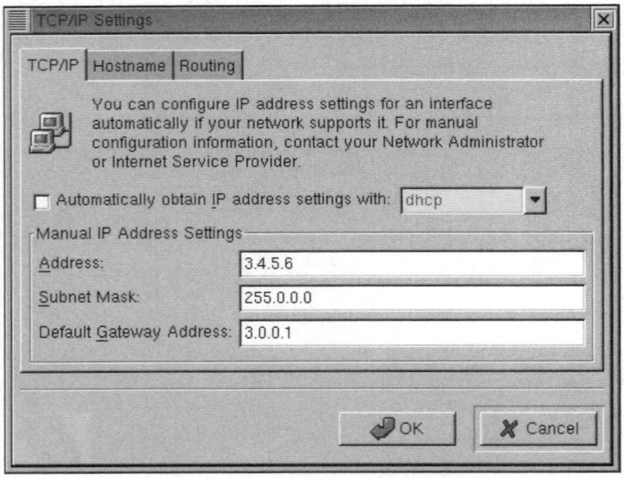

Figure 15-6   Network protocol properties

The Network Configuration tool used above is one of many graphical network config-uration tools; all of these tools modify the same files to set the TCP/IP configuration, yet have different features and appearances. Two other tools available in Red Hat Linux for configuring the network are **Linuxconf** and **netconfig**. Linuxconf is depicted in Figure 15-7 and may be started by typing `linuxconf` at a terminal prompt while in a desktop environment. Similarly, typing `netconfig` at a command prompt will allow you to configure TCP/IP as depicted in Figure 15-8.

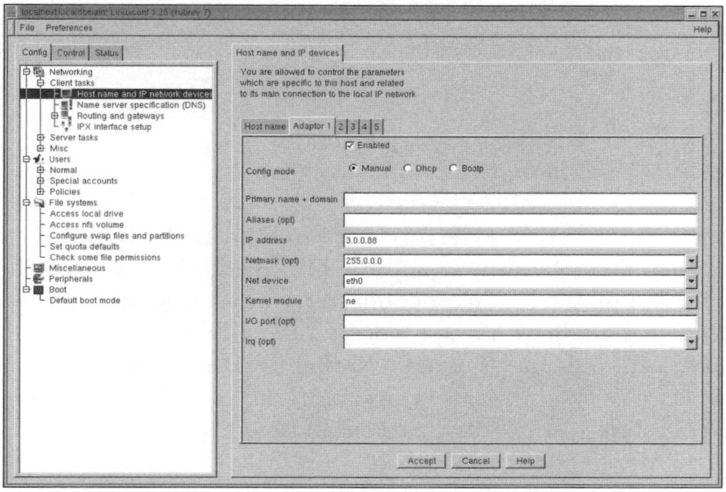

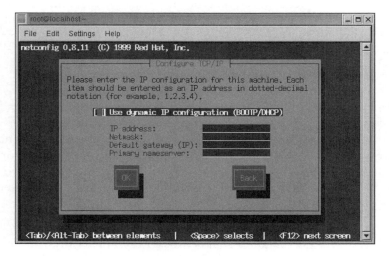

Figure 15-7   The linuxconf utility

Figure 15-8   The netconfig utility

CONFIGURING A PPP INTERFACE

Instead of configuring TCP/IP to run on a NIC to gain network access, you may instead run TCP/IP over serial lines using a WAN protocol, such as SLIP (Serial Line Interface Protocol) or PPP (Point-to-Point Protocol). PPP is a newer technology than SLIP and incorporates all of SLIP's features; thus PPP is the standard protocol used today to connect to remote networks over serial lines.

There are three common technologies that use PPP today to connect computers to a network such as the Internet:

- modems
- ISDN
- DSL

Modem (modulator-demodulator) devices use PPP to send TCP/IP information across normal telephone lines; they were the most common method for home users to gain Internet access in the last decade. Modem connections are considered slow today compared to most other technologies; most modems can only transmit data at 56KB/s. Modems are typically detected and configured during installation or by the `kudzu` program afterwards. Since modems transmit information on a serial port, the system typically makes a symbolic link called **/dev/modem** that points to the correct serial port device, such as **/dev/ttyS0** for COM1.

ISDN (Integrated Services Digital Network) was originally intended to replace normal telephone lines and allows data to be transferred at 128KB/s. ISDN uses an ISDN modem device to connect to a different type of media than regular phone lines. Although ISDN is popular in Europe, it does not have a large presence in North America. Like modems, ISDN modems are typically detected and configured by `kudzu` or during installation.

One of the most popular connection technologies in North America is DSL (Digital Subscriber Line). DSL has many variants such as ADSL (Asynchronous DSL), which is the most common DSL used in homes across North America, and HDSL (High bit-rate DSL), which is common in business environments; for simplification all variants of DSL are referred to as xDSL. You use an Ethernet NIC on your computer to connect to a DSL modem using TCP/IP over PPP; the DSL modem then transmits information across normal telephone lines at speeds that can exceed 8Mb/s. Since DSL modems are connected to a NIC via some type of media, they are not normally configured automatically during installation or by the `kudzu` program; instead they must be configured manually.

Configuring a PPP connection requires support for PPP compiled into the kernel or available as a module, the pppd (PPP daemon), and a series of supporting utilities such as the chat program that is used to communicate with a modem. PPP configuration in the past was tedious at best; you needed to create a chat script that contained the necessary information to establish a PPP connection (username, password, etc.) and a connection script that contained device parameters used by the PPP daemon, and then use a program such as `minicom` to initiate network communication. Today, because the TCP/IP configuration is typically assigned by the Internet Service Provider that you connect to, it rarely needs to be configured during the process.

Today, there are a wide variety of graphical programs that can configure the necessary files and start the necessary utilities to allow PPP network communication. The most common utility used to configure a PPP device in Red Hat Linux is the Internet Configuration Wizard shown in Figure 15-9. To start the Internet Configuration Wizard from within the GNOME desktop environment, simply navigate to GNOME button, Programs, System, Internet Configuration Wizard. To start the Internet Configuration Wizard while in the KDE desktop environment, navigate to K button, System, Internet Configuration Wizard.

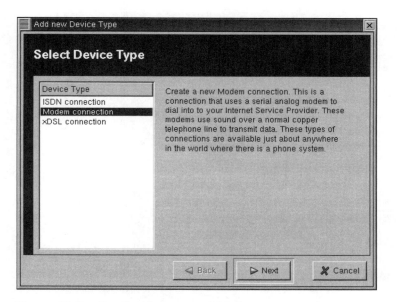

Figure 15-9   Configuring a new PPP device

If you choose to configure a modem device from Figure 15-9, then you will be prompted for the device information seen in Figure 15-10 and the Internet Service Provider information seen in Figure 15-11.

15

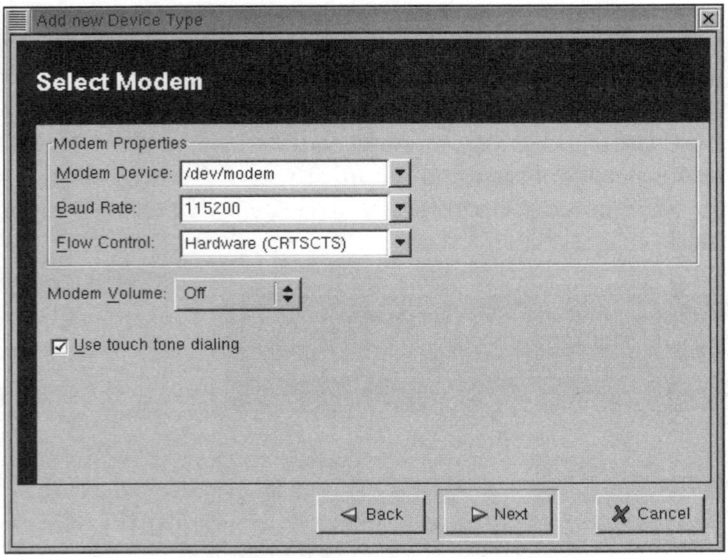

Figure 15-10   Configuring a modem device

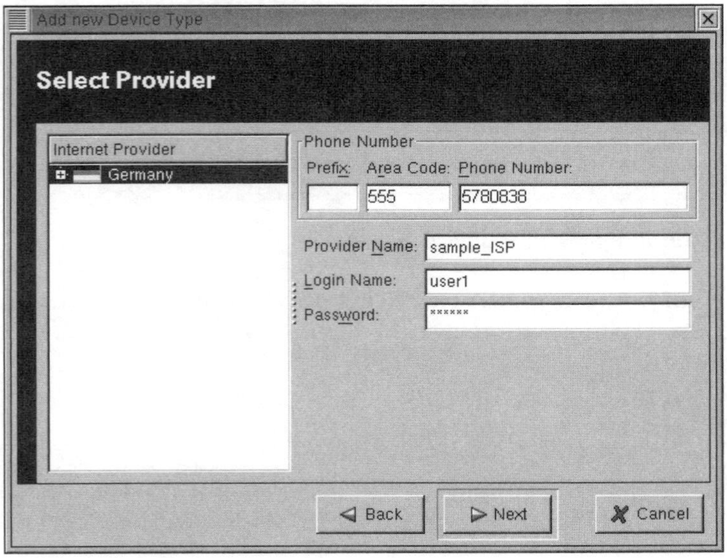

Figure 15-11   Configuring user account information

Alternatively, if you choose to configure an ISDN modem, then you will be required to choose the model of the ISDN modem as seen in Figure 15-12 as well as the Internet Service Provider information shown in Figure 15-13.

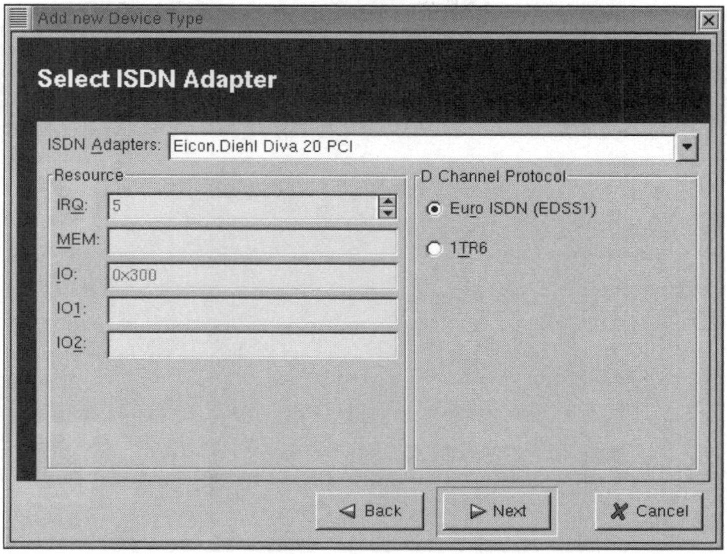

Figure 15-12   Configuring ISDN hardware

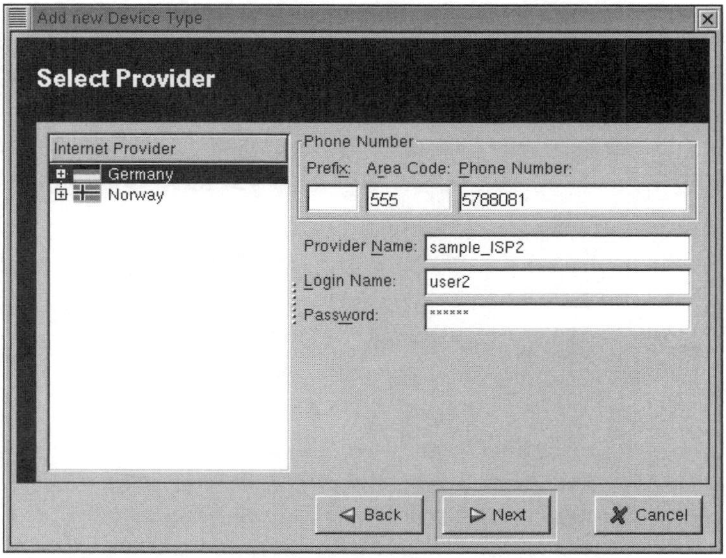

Figure 15-13   Configuring user account information

If you chose to set up a DSL connection from Figure 15-9, then you will be prompted to choose the Ethernet interface that is connected to the DSL modem as well as the Internet Service Provider information as depicted in Figure 15-14.

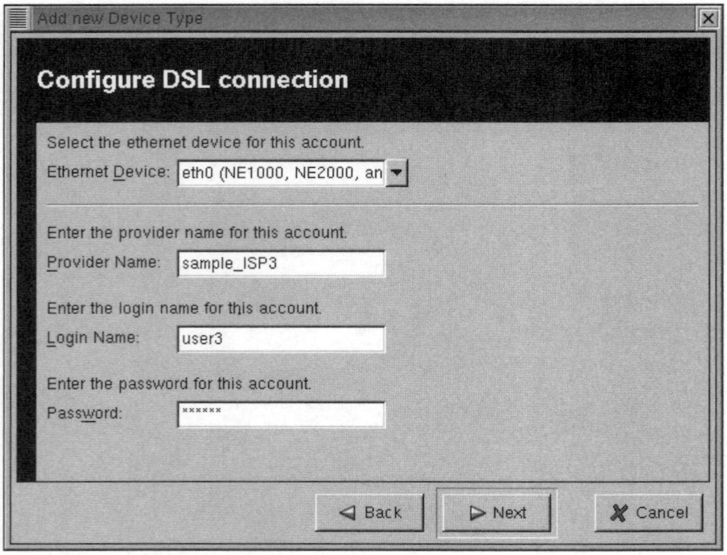

Figure 15-14   Configuring a DSL connection

Like configuring a NIC, the Internet Configuration Wizard stores information about each device in files underneath the /etc/sysconfig/network-scripts directory. The modem information configured earlier is stored in the /etc/sysconfig/network-scripts/ifcfg-ppp0 file, whereas the ISDN information is stored in /etc/sysconfig/network-scripts/ifcfg-isdn0 and the DSL information is stored in /etc/sysconfig/network-scripts/ifcfg-ppp1. These files are shown in the following output:

```
[root@localhost root]# cat /etc/sysconfig/network-scripts/ifcfg-ppp0
USERCTL=yes
BOOTPROTO=dialup
NAME=sample_ISP
DEVICE=ppp0
TYPE=Modem
ONBOOT=no
BSDCOMP=off
CCP=off
VJCCOMP=off
AC=off
VJ=off
PC=off
LINESPEED=115200
MODEMPORT=/dev/modem
DEMAND=no
PROVIDER=sample_ISP
DEFROUTE=no
PERSIST=no
PAPNAME=user1
WVDIALSECT=sample_ISP
```

```
MODEMNAME=Modem0
PEERDNS=yes
[root@localhost root]# cat /etc/sysconfig/network-scripts/ifcfg-isdn0
USERCTL=yes
BOOTPROTO=dialup
DEVICE=isdn0
TYPE=ISDN
ONBOOT=no
BUNDLING=off
DEFROUTE=yes
SECURE=off
PERSIST=off
PROVIDER=sample_ISP2
AREACODE=578
PREFIX=519
PHONE_OUT=8081
USER=user2
PASSWORD=secret
PEERDNS=yes
BSDCOMP=off
CCP=off
VJCCOMP=off
AC=off
VJ=off
PC=off
[root@localhost root]# cat /etc/sysconfig/network-scripts/ifcfg-ppp1
USERCTL=yes
BOOTPROTO=dialup
DEVICE=ppp1
TYPE=xDSL
ONBOOT=no
PIDFILE=/var/run/pppoe-adsl.pid
FIREWALL=NONE
PING=.
PPPOE_TIMEOUT=20
LCP_FAILURE=3
LCP_INTERVAL=20
CLAMPMSS=1412
CONNECT_POLL=6
CONNECT_TIMEOUT=60
DEFROUTE=yes
SYNCHRONOUS=no
PERSIST=no
ETH=eth0
PROVIDER=sample_ISP3
USER=user3
PASS=secret
PEERDNS=yes
[root@localhost root]# _
```

15

Other configurations used by the PPP daemon are stored in the /etc/ppp and
/etc/isdn directories. It is good form to double check the passwords used to connect
to the Internet Service Provider, as incorrect passwords represent the most common

problem with PPP connections. These passwords are stored in two files: /etc/ppp/pap-secrets (Password Authentication Protocol secrets) and /etc/ppp/chap-secrets (Challenge Handshake Authentication Protocol secrets). If the Internet Service Provider accepts passwords sent across the network in text form, then the /etc/ppp/pap-secrets file will be consulted for the correct password; however, if the Internet Service Provider requires a more secure method for validating the identity of a user, the passwords in the /etc/ppp/chap-secrets file will be used. The Internet Configuration Wizard used earlier adds the passwords specified to both files as seen in the following output:

```
[root@localhost root]# cat /etc/ppp/pap-secrets
# Secrets for authentication using PAP
# client          server  secret                IP addresses
####### redhat-config-network will overwrite this part!!! (begin) ####
"user3"          *        "secret"
"user2"          *        "secret"
"user1"          *        "secret"
####### redhat-config-network will overwrite this part!!! (end) ######
[root@localhost root]# cat /etc/ppp/chap-secrets
# Secrets for authentication using CHAP
# client          server  secret                IP addresses
####### redhat-config-network will overwrite this part!!! (begin) ####
"user3"          *        "secret"
"user2"          *        "secret"
"user1"          *        "secret"
####### redhat-config-network will overwrite this part!!! (end) ######
[root@localhost root]# _
```

After a PPP device has been configured, that device must be activated by connecting to (or dialing) the Internet Service Provider; this may be done using the Red Hat PPP Dialer as shown in Figure 15-15. To start the Red Hat PPP Dialer, you may navigate to GNOME button, Programs, Internet, RH PPP Dialer while in the GNOME desktop environment or by navigating to K button, Internet, RH PPP Dialer while in the KDE desktop environment.

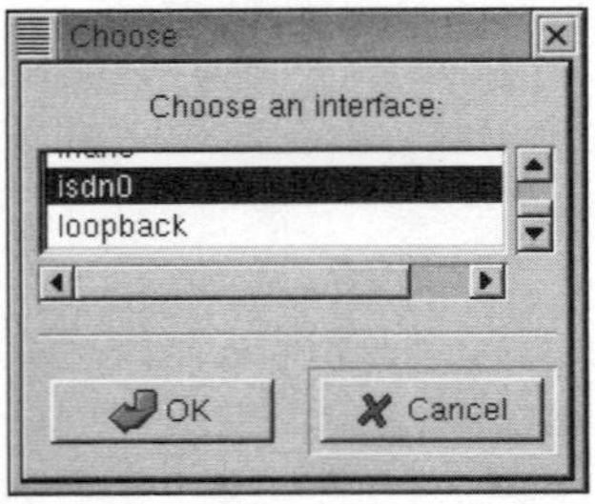

Figure 15-15   Activating a PPP connection

Once activated, the `ifconfig` command will indicate the interface using the appropriate names such as ppp0, isdn0, and ppp1 used in the examples above, as well as the IP address obtained from the Internet Service Provider. The following output depicts the output of the `ifconfig` command when the ppp0 interface is activated:

```
[root@localhost root]# ifconfig
eth0      Link encap:Ethernet  HWaddr 00:80:C8:D6:74:43
          inet addr:3.0.0.88  Bcast:3.255.255.255  Mask:255.0.0.0
          UP BROADCAST RUNNING  MTU:1500  Metric:1
          RX packets:23068 errors:0 dropped:0 overruns:0 frame:9
          TX packets:29730 errors:0 dropped:0 overruns:0 carrier:0
          collisions:0
          RX bytes:1908993 (1.8 Mb)  TX bytes:32792075 (31.2 Mb)

lo        Link encap:Local Loopback
          inet addr:127.0.0.1  Mask:255.0.0.0
          UP LOOPBACK RUNNING  MTU:16436  Metric:1
          RX packets:508 errors:0 dropped:0 overruns:0 frame:0
          TX packets:508 errors:0 dropped:0 overruns:0 carrier:0
          collisions:0
          RX bytes:34319 (33.5 Kb)  TX bytes:34319 (33.5 Kb)

ppp0      Link encap:Point-to-Point Protocol
          inet addr:65.95.13.63  P-t-P:65.95.13.1  Mask:255.255.255.255
          UP POINTOPOINT RUNNING NOARP MULTICAST  MTU:1492  Metric:1
          RX packets:5 errors:0 dropped:0 overruns:0 frame:0
          TX packets:3 errors:0 dropped:0 overruns:0 carrier:0
          collisions:0
          RX bytes:110 (110.0 b)  TX bytes:54 (54.0 b)

[root@localhost root]# _
```

There are many other utilities that you may use to configure and activate a PPP interface, such as Linuxconf described in the previous section. Most of these utilities perform the same tasks but in a different fashion. One of the most common utilities for configuring and dialing modem connections is KDE PPP Manager seen in Figure 15-16, which can be started by typing `kppp` at a terminal prompt while logged into a desktop environment.

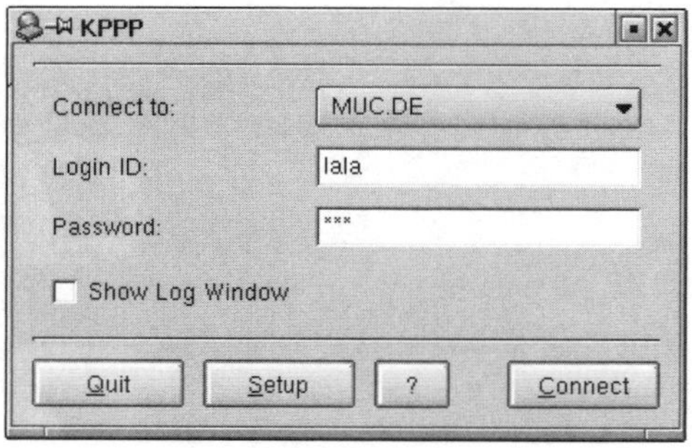

15

Figure 15-16   The kppp utility

NAME RESOLUTION

Computers that communicate on a TCP/IP network identify themselves using unique IP addresses; however, this identification scheme is impractical for human use since it is difficult to remember IP addresses. As a result, we identify a computer by a name; since each computer on a network is commonly called a host, computer names are called **hostnames**.

For computers that participate on the Internet, simple hostnames are rarely used; instead, you may give a computer a hostname called a **Fully Qualified Domain Name (FQDN)** according to a hierarchical naming scheme called the **Domain Name Space (DNS)**. The Domain Name Space consists of an imaginary root with several top-level domain names that identify the type of organization that runs the network that your computer is on. Several second-level domains exist underneath each top-level domain name to identify the name of the organization, and simple hostnames are listed underneath the second-level domains as depicted in Figure 15-17.

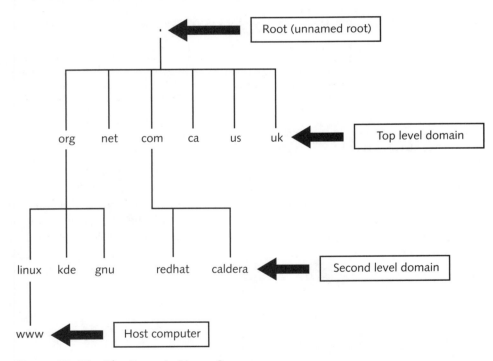

Figure 15-17   The Domain Name Space

Thus, the host computer shown in Figure 15-17 has an FQDN of www.linux.org.

You may view or set the hostname for a Linux computer using the **hostname command** as seen in the following output:

```
[root@localhost root]# hostname
ocalhost.localdomain
[root@localhost root]# hostname computer1.sampledomain.com
[root@localhost root]# hostname
computer1.sampledomain.com
[root@localhost root]# _
```

To configure the hostname seen in the above output at every boot time, simply modify the HOSTNAME line in the /etc/sysconfig/network file as seen below:

```
[root@localhost root]# cat /etc/sysconfig/network
NETWORKING=yes
HOSTNAME=localhost.localdomain
[root@localhost root]# _
```

 Planning an appropriate hostname prior to installation is good practice since many applications record this hostname in their configuration files during installation; you may need to change these files if you change the hostname after installation.

Although hostnames are easier to use when specifying computers on the network, the TCP/IP protocol cannot use them to identify computers. Thus, you must map hostnames to their associated IP addresses such that applications that contact other computers across the network can find the appropriate IP address for a hostname.

The simplest method for mapping hostnames to IP addresses is by placing entries into the /etc/hosts file as seen below:

```
[root@localhost root]# cat /etc/hosts
# Do not remove the following line, or various programs
# that require network functionality will fail.
127.0.0.1    localhost.localdomain   localhost
3.0.0.2      ftp.sampledomain.com    fileserver
192.168.0.1  alpha
[root@localhost root]# _
```

The entries in the above output identify the local computer, 127.0.0.1, by the hostnames localhost.localdomain and localhost. Similarly, you may use the hostname ftp.sampledomain.com or the hostname fileserver to refer to the computer with the IP address of 3.0.0.2. Also, the computer with the IP address of 192.168.0.1 is mapped to the hostname alpha.

 You may use the Network Information Service (NIS) to share the /etc/hosts configuration file amongst several Linux computers on the network; NIS will be discussed later in this chapter.

15

Since it would be cumbersome to list names for all hosts on the Internet in the /etc/hosts file, Internet Service Providers can list FQDNs in DNS servers on the Internet. An application may then ask DNS servers for the IP address associated with a certain FQDN. To configure your system to resolve names to IP addresses by contacting a DNS server, simply specify the IP address of the DNS server in the /etc/resolv.conf file. This file may contain up to three DNS servers; if the first DNS server is unavailable, the system will attempt to contact the second DNS server followed by the third DNS server listed in the file. An example /etc/resolv.conf file is seen in the following output:

```
[root@localhost root]# cat /etc/resolv.conf
nameserver 209.121.197.2
nameserver 192.139.188.144
nameserver 6.0.4.211
[root@localhost root]# _
```

 To test the DNS configuration by resolving a name to an IP address, you may use the command nslookup hostname, dig hostname, or host hostname.

When you specify a hostname while using a certain application, that application must then resolve that hostname to the appropriate IP address by searching either the local /etc/hosts file, a DNS server, or an NIS server. The order that applications use to resolve hostnames is determined by the hosts line in the /etc/nsswitch.conf file as seen below:

```
[root@localhost root]# grep hosts /etc/nsswitch.conf
hosts:          files dns nis
[root@localhost root]# _
```

The output above indicates that applications will first try to resolve hostnames using the /etc/hosts file (files). If unsuccessful, applications will contact the DNS servers listed in /etc/resolv.conf (dns) followed by an NIS server (nis) if one is configured.

On older Linux computers, the /etc/host.conf file was used instead of /etc/nsswitch.conf; the /etc/host.conf file still exists today to support older application programs and should contain the same name resolution order as /etc/nsswitch.conf. An example /etc/host.conf file that tells applications to search the /etc/hosts file followed by DNS servers (bind) and NIS servers is seen in the following output:

```
[root@localhost root]# cat /etc/host.conf
order hosts,bind,nis
[root@localhost root]# _
```

CONNECTING TO NETWORK RESOURCES

Once an interface to a network has been configured, a Linux computer may use resources on the network such as shared printers, applications, and files. To use a network resource, you must first have the appropriate network utility that can connect to that resource. Some network utilities are easy to use, such as a Web browser to access Web pages from a Web server on the network, whereas other network utilities such as FTP require that you learn specific commands before use.

In this section, we shall examine the most common network utilities used to perform various network tasks on the system.

Downloading Files using FTP

The most common method for transferring files across the Internet is by using the File Transfer Protocol as discussed in Chapter 1. Most Web browsers have a built-in FTP utility that allows you to enter an FQDN in the form of *ftp://ftp.sampledomain.com* and view publicly available files and directories on a remote computer using the Web browser screen as depicted in Figure 15-18.

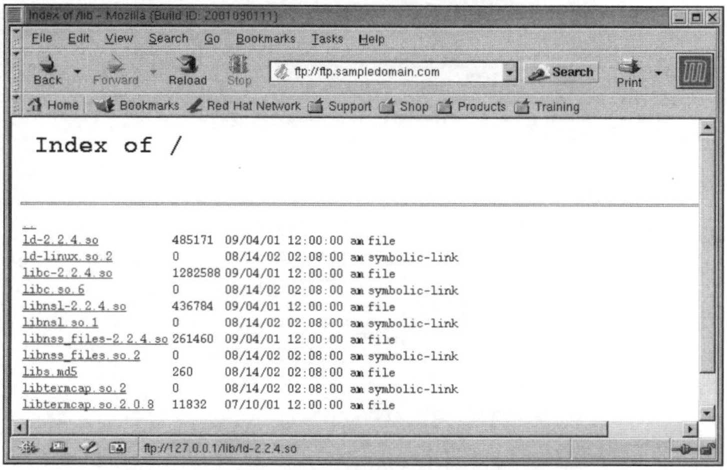

Figure 15-18   Using a Web browser FTP client

You may also use *ftp://IP_address* to connect to a public FTP server.

Using the mouse to click on a file displayed in Figure 15-18 will result in a dialog box that allows you to save the file to the appropriate location on a local filesystem.

Alternatively, you may specify the hostname or IP address of a computer running the FTP service as an argument to the FTP command-line utility to open a connection that will allow the transfer of files to and from that computer. Following this, you may then log in as a valid user on that computer and be placed in your home directory, or log in as the user anonymous and be placed in a publicly available FTP directory (`/var/ftp`). Once logged in, you receive an `ftp>` prompt that will accept FTP commands; a list of common FTP commands is depicted in Table 15-1.

 Most FTP servers require that you enter a password when logging in as the anonymous user; this password is typically your e-mail address.

Table 15-1   Common FTP commands

Command	Description
help	Displays a list of commands
pwd	Displays the current directory on the remote computer
dir ls	Displays a directory listing from the remote computer
cd *directory*	Changes the current directory to *directory* on the remote computer
lcd *directory*	Changes the current directory to *directory* on the local computer
get *filename*	Downloads *filename* to the current directory on the local computer
ascii	Used to specify text file downloads (default)
binary	Used to specify binary file downloads
mget *filename*	Downloads *filename* to the current directory on the local computer; also allows the use of wildcard metacharacters to specify *filename*
put *filename*	Uploads *filename* from the current directory on the local computer to the current directory on the remote computer
mput *filename*	Uploads *filename* from the current directory on the local computer to the current directory on the remote computer; also allows the use of wildcard metacharacters to specify *filename*
!	Runs a shell on the local computer
close	Closes the FTP connection to the remote computer
open *hostname* or *IP*	Opens an FTP connection to the *hostname* or *IP* address specified
bye quit	Quits the **FTP** utility

Connecting to the FTP server named www.sampledomain.com as the root user is depicted below:

```
[root@localhost root]# ftp www.sampledomain.com
Connected to www.sampledomain.com.
220 www.sampledomain.com FTP server (Version wu-2.6.1-18) ready.
```

```
530 Please login with USER and PASS.
530 Please login with USER and PASS.
KERBEROS_V4 rejected as an authentication type
Name (localhost:root): root
331 Password required for root.
Password:
230 User root logged in.
Remote system type is UNIX.
Using binary mode to transfer files.
ftp>
```

Passwords are not displayed when typed into the FTP utility.

The current directory on the remote computer is the home directory for the root user in the above output. To verify this and see a list of files to download, you may use the following commands at the ftp> prompt:

```
ftp> pwd
257 "/root" is current directory.
ftp> ls
227 Entering Passive Mode (192,168,0,1,56,88)
150 Opening ASCII mode data connection for directory listing.
total 2064
-rw-r--r--    1 root     root          1756 Aug 14 08:48 file1
-rw-r--r--    1 root     root           160 Aug 14 08:48 file2
-rw-r--r--    1 root     root       1039996 Aug 14 08:39 file3
drwxr-xr-x    2 root     root          4096 Aug 14 08:50 stuff
226 Transfer complete.
ftp>
```

The output above shows three files and one subdirectory. To download `file3` to the current directory on the local computer, you may use the following command:

```
ftp> get file3
local: file3 remote: file3
227 Entering Passive Mode (192,168,0,1,137,37)
150 Opening BINARY mode data connection for file3 (1039996 bytes).
226 Transfer complete.
ftp>
```

If your Internet connection is slow, you may instead use the get file3.gz command; the FTP service will automatically compress file3 with the gzip utility before transmission.

Similarly, to change the current directory on the remote computer to /root/stuff and upload a copy of file4 from the current directory on the local computer to it, as well as view the results and then exit the FTP utility, you may use the following commands at the ftp> prompt:

```
ftp> cd stuff
250 CWD command successful.
ftp> pwd
257 "/root/stuff" is current directory.
ftp> mput file4
mput file4? y
227 Entering Passive Mode (192,168,0,1,70,109)
150 Opening BINARY mode data connection for file4.
226 Transfer complete.
929 bytes sent in 0.00019 seconds (4.8e+03 Kbytes/s)
ftp> ls
227 Entering Passive Mode (192,168,0,1,235,35)
150 Opening ASCII mode data connection for directory listing.
total 8
-rw-r--r--   1 root      root          929 Aug 14 09:26 file4
226 Transfer complete.
ftp> bye
[root@localhost root]# _
```

Accessing Files with NFS

Although not as common as FTP, the Network File System (NFS) is another common method for transferring files amongst UNIX and Linux computers. To access files using NFS, you simply mount a directory from a remote computer on the network that has the NFS daemons started to a local directory. Simply specify the nfs filesystem type, servername or IP address, remote directory, and local directory as arguments to the mount command. For example, to mount the /var directory on the remote computer named www.sampledomain.com (IP address 192.168.0.1) to the /mnt directory on the local computer using NFS and view the results, you could use the following commands:

```
[root@localhost root]# mount -t nfs www.sampledomain.com:/var /mnt
[root@localhost root]# mount
/dev/hda3 on / type ext3 (rw)
none on /proc type proc (rw)
usbdevfs on /proc/bus/usb type usbdevfs (rw)
/dev/hda2 on /boot type ext3 (rw)
none on /dev/pts type devpts (rw,gid=5,mode=620)
none on /dev/shm type tmpfs (rw)
none on /proc/sys/fs/binfmt_misc type binfmt_misc (rw)
192.168.0.1:/var on /mnt type nfs (rw,addr=192.168.0.1)
[root@localhost root]# ls /mnt
arpwatch   ftp       kerberos   lock   mailman    nis        run      tux
cache      gdm       lib        log    mars_nwe   opt        spool    www
db         iptraf    local      mail   named      preserve   tmp      yp
[root@localhost root]# _
```

Now, you may use the /mnt directory as any other local directory; all file operations will be performed in the /var directory on the remote computer. The NFS filesystem can then be dismounted normally using the umount command.

Accessing Windows Files

NFS is a common method for transferring information to and from Linux and UNIX computers; however, it is difficult to find NFS software for the Microsoft Windows operating system. To transfer information to and from a shared Windows directory, you may mount that directory to a local Linux directory much like NFS; however, the filesystem type must be smbfs.

SMB stands for Server Message Blocks; it defines the format that Microsoft computers use for information transfer across networks.

For example, to mount the shared directory called accounting on the Windows computer named windowsxp to the /mnt directory and view the results, you could use the following commands:

```
[root@localhost root]# mount -t smbfs //windowsxp/accounting /mnt
[root@localhost root]# mount
/dev/hda3 on / type ext3 (rw)
none on /proc type proc (rw)
usbdevfs on /proc/bus/usb type usbdevfs (rw)
/dev/hda2 on /boot type ext3 (rw)
none on /dev/pts type devpts (rw,gid=5,mode=620)
none on /dev/shm type tmpfs (rw)
none on /proc/sys/fs/binfmt_misc type binfmt_misc (rw)
//windowsxp/accounting on /mnt type smbfs (0)
[root@localhost root]# ls /mnt
Final Exam.doc          Part 0.DOC   Part 2.doc   Part 4.doc   Part 6.doc
homework questions.doc  Part 1.DOC   Part 3.DOC   Part 5.DOC   TOC.doc
[root@localhost root]# _
```

The **smbmount command** can also be used to mount a Windows shared directory; the command smbmount //windowsxp/accounting /mnt is equivalent to the command used to mount the accounting directory in the above output.

Like NFS, the umount command can be used to unmount the Windows shared directory from the local /mnt directory.

15

Another useful utility when sharing files between Linux and Windows computers is the
smbclient utility. To see information about the windowsxp computer used earlier, you
may use the following command:

```
[root@localhost root]# smbclient -L windowsxp
added interface ip=192.168.0.1 bcast=192.168.255.255 nmask=255.255.0.0
Got a positive name query response from 192.168.0.1 ( 192.168.0.1
65.95.13.77 )
Password:
Domain=[HOME] OS=[Windows 5.1] Server=[Windows 2000 LAN Manager]

        Sharename       Type        Comment
        ---------       ----        -------
        IPC$            IPC         Remote IPC
        print$          Disk        Printer Drivers
        movies          Disk
        My Jams         Disk
        HPLaserJ        Printer     HP LaserJet 6P/6MP PostScript
        accounting      Disk
        ADMIN$          Disk        Remote Admin
        C$              Disk        Default share

        Server                  Comment
        ---------               -------
        WINDOWSXP

        Workgroup               Master
        ---------               -------
        HOME                    WINDOWSXP
[root@localhost root]# _
```

The smbclient utility also offers an FTP-like interface for transferring files to and from
shared directories on Windows computers, as seen in the following output when connecting to the **accounting** shared directory seen earlier:

```
[root@localhost root]# smbclient //windowsxp/accounting
added interface ip=192.168.0.1 bcast=192.168.255.255 nmask=255.255.0.0
Got a positive name query response from 192.168.0.1 ( 192.168.0.1
65.95.13.77 )
Password:
Domain=[HOME] OS=[Windows 5.1] Server=[Windows 2000 LAN Manager]
smb: \> dir
  .                         D        0   Wed Aug 14 22:28:12 2002
  ..                        D        0   Wed Aug 14 22:28:12 2002
  Final Exam.doc            A    26624   Tue Aug  6 23:17:30 2002
  homework questions.doc    A    46080   Tue Aug  6 23:33:03 2002
  Part 0.DOC                A    13312   Tue Aug  6 23:27:51 2002
  Part 1.DOC                A    35328   Tue Aug  6 23:24:44 2002
  Part 2.doc                A    70656   Tue Aug  6 23:25:28 2002
  Part 3.DOC                A    38912   Tue Aug  6 23:26:07 2002
```

```
Part 4.doc                      A     75776   Tue Aug  6 23:26:57 2002
Part 5.DOC                      A     26624   Tue Aug  6 23:27:23 2002
Part 6.doc                      A     59904   Tue Aug  6 23:05:32 2002
TOC.doc                         A     58880   Tue Aug  6 23:09:16 2002
                39032 blocks of size 262144. 14180 blocks available

smb: \> help
ls              dir             du              lcd             cd
pwd             get             mget            put             mput
rename          more            mask            del             open
rm              mkdir           md              rmdir           rd
prompt          recurse         translate       lowercase       print
printmode       queue           cancel          quit            q
exit            newer           archive         tar             blocksize
tarmode         setmode         help            ?               history
!
smb: \> get TOC.doc
Get file TOC.doc? y
getting file TOC.doc of size 58880 as TOC.doc (3.9 kb/s) (average 3.9 kb/s)
smb: \> exit
[root@localhost root]# _
```

Running Remote Applications

On large Linux systems, users typically gain access to a BASH shell by using a utility that connects to the server across the network. The most common utility used to obtain a BASH shell from a remote Linux computer on the network is telnet; most operating systems today such as Windows, Macintosh, and UNIX come with a telnet utility. Simply specify the hostname or IP address of the target computer to the telnet command and log in as the appropriate user and password. A shell obtained during a telnet session runs on a pseudo terminal rather than a local terminal and works in much the same way as a normal shell does; you may execute commands and use the **exit** command to kill the BASH shell and end the session. A sample telnet session is seen in the following output using a computer with an IP address of 3.0.0.88:

15

```
[root@localhost root]# telnet 3.0.0.88
Trying 3.0.0.88...
Connected to localhost.localdomain (3.0.0.88).
Escape character is '^]'.
Red Hat Linux release 7.2 (Enigma)
Kernel 2.4.7-10 on an i686
login: root
Password:
Last login: Wed Aug 14 10:41:41 from localhost
You have new mail.
[root@localhost root]# who
root      pts/0    Aug 14 10:42 (localhost)
root      tty2     Aug 14 10:14
[root@localhost root]# exit
```

```
Connection closed by foreign host.
[root@localhost root]# _
```

Another utility that can be used to obtain a shell from a remote computer on the network is rlogin. This utility is one of several "r" utilities that can allow you access to remote systems on the network without specifying a password; the rcp utility can be used to copy files between computers and the rsh utility can be used to execute a command on a remote computer.

The "r" utilities allow access to remote computers without a password, provided the remote computer has **trusted access** set up. One method of setting up trusted access is to add the hostnames of computers to the /etc/hosts.equiv file on the remote computer; the following /etc/hosts.equiv file allows users who have logged into the computers www.sampledomain.com and www.sampledomain2.com to use the rlogin, rcp, and rsh utilities to connect to the computer as the same user without specifying a password:

```
[root@localhost root]# cat /etc/hosts.equiv
www.sampledomain.com
www.sampledomain2.com
[root@localhost root]# _
```

Thus, if the user mary logs into the remote computer www.sampledomain.com and uses an "r" utility to connect to the local computer, she will automatically be logged into the system using the local mary account without having to specify a password. The only user that cannot be trusted using the /etc/hosts.equiv file is the root user. Trusted access is common in companies that have several Linux servers that have the same user accounts; setting up trusted access allows users that log into one Linux computer to access other computers without having to re-enter their password.

Another method for setting trusted access is to create a .rhosts file in the home directory on the local computer of each user who wishes to connect using trusted access. Consider the following /home/mary/.rhosts file:

```
[root@localhost root]# cat /home/mary/.rhosts
www.sampledomain.com
www.sampledomain2.com
[root@localhost root]# _
```

This will allow the user mary on the computers www.sampledomain.com and www.sampledomain2.com to use the "r" utilities to connect to the local Linux computer as the user mary without specifying a password. In addition to this, the /root/.rhosts file can be used to allow the root user on other trusted computers to use "r" utilities to connect to the local computer without specifying a password.

Say that a remote computer called remoteserver has trusted access set up; you may use the following command to obtain a shell:

```
[root@localhost root]# rlogin remoteserver
Last login: Thu Aug 15 13:16:51 from 100.6.6.0
You have new mail.
[root@localhost root]# _
```

Similarly, you may copy the /etc/hosts file from the computer remoteserver to the /root directory of the local computer by using the following command:

```
[root@localhost root]# rcp remoteserver:/etc/hosts localhost:/root
[root@localhost root]# ls —F /root
Desktop/  hosts
[root@localhost root]# _
```

In addition, to run the who command on the computer remoteserver and display the results to the local terminal, you may use the following command:

```
[root@localhost root]# rsh remoteserver who
root      tty2      Aug 15 12:26
root      pts/0     Aug 15 13:16 (100.6.6.0)
[root@localhost root]# _
```

Today, the rsh and rlogin commands may be replaced by the ssh (secure shell) command; this command enhances security by encrypting communication between computers on the network.

Accessing E-mail

Recall from Chapter 1 that network users may use a variety of mail user agent (MUA) programs to obtain e-mail from an e-mail server. E-mail is typically downloaded from an e-mail server via a protocol called POP (Post Office Protocol) or IMAP (Interactive Mail Access Protocol). POP usually downloads e-mail messages from the e-mail server to the client computer, whereas IMAP typically stores e-mail messages on the e-mail server and views them across the network. Regardless of the method used to send e-mail from the e-mail server to the mail user agent, mail is sent from the mail user agent to the e-mail server via SMTP (Simple Mail Transfer Protocol). The address of the necessary POP, IMAP, and SMTP servers should be configured to the appropriate values in the mail user agent program.

The most common mail user agent used in Red Hat Linux is Mozilla, which can also function as a Web browser, FTP client, and newsgroup reader. To open Mozilla, simply use the mouse to click on the Mozilla icon on the toolbar of the KDE or GNOME desktops. Once open, navigate to the Tasks menu and choose Mail; if no mail accounts have been configured, the Account Wizard will appear as shown in Figure 15-19.

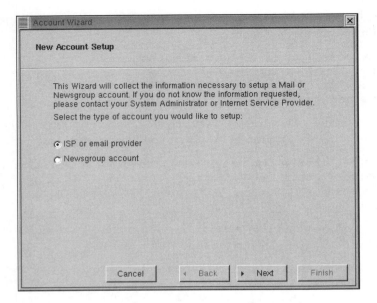

Figure 15-19 Configuring a new e-mail account

Choosing "ISP or email provider" from Figure 15-19 and clicking on the Next button will prompt you for the username, POP/IMAP, SMTP, and account information as seen in Figures 15–20, 15–21, 15–22, and 15–23.

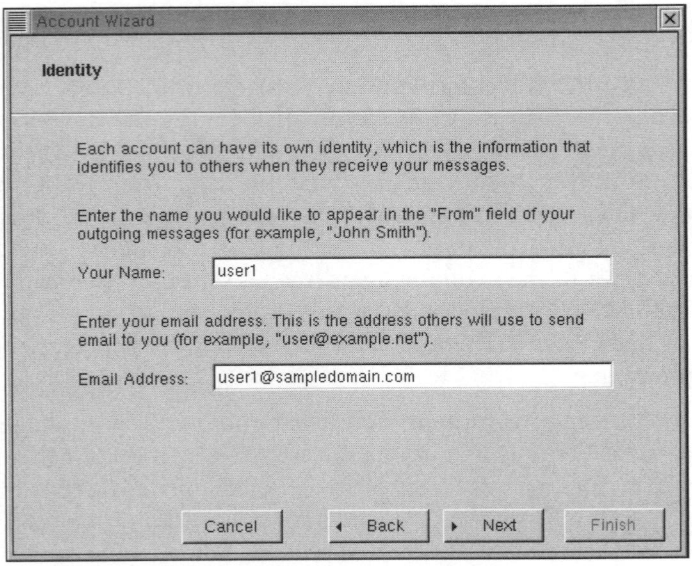

Figure 15-20 Specifying user information

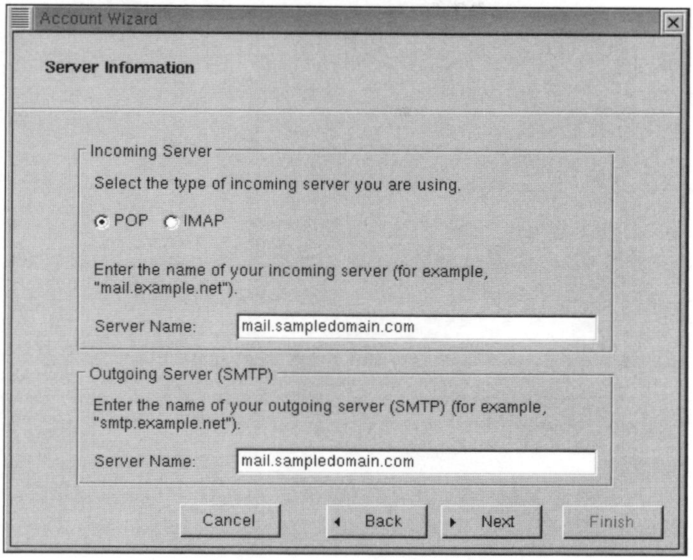

Figure 15-21   Configuring a POP, IMAP, and SMTP server

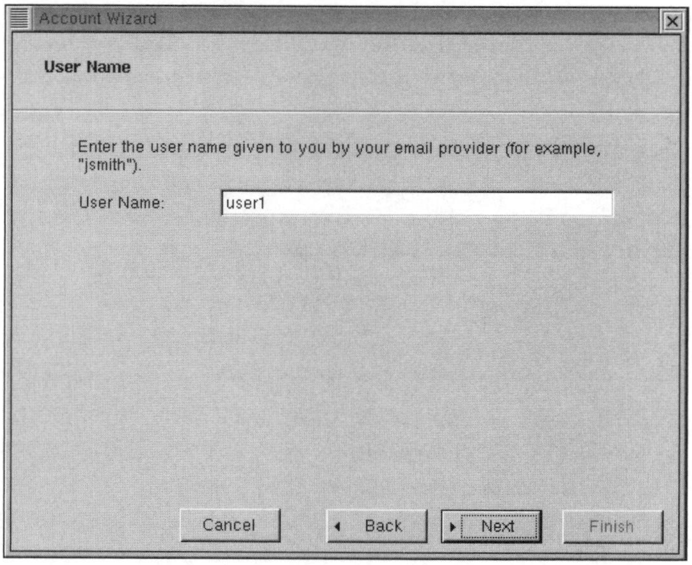

Figure 15-22   Specifying a user name

15

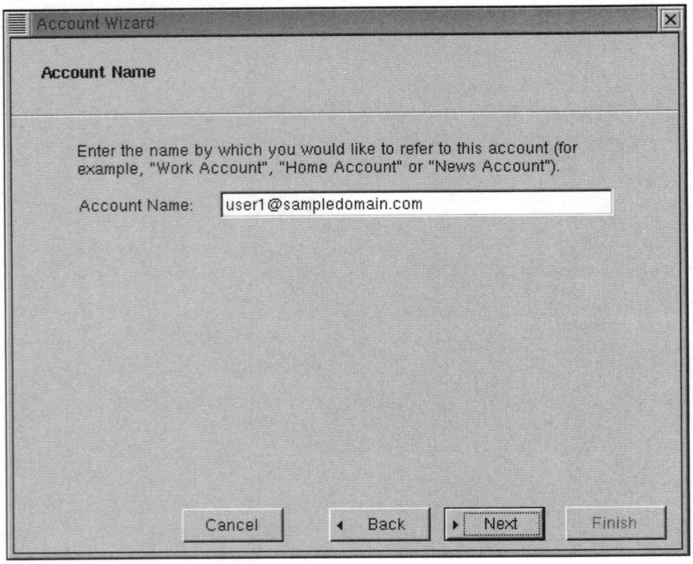

Figure 15-23   Specifying an account name

Once the server and account information has been configured, navigating to the Tasks menu and choosing Mail will bring up the Mozilla mail user agent depicted in Figure 15-24, which can be used to send and receive e-mail messages.

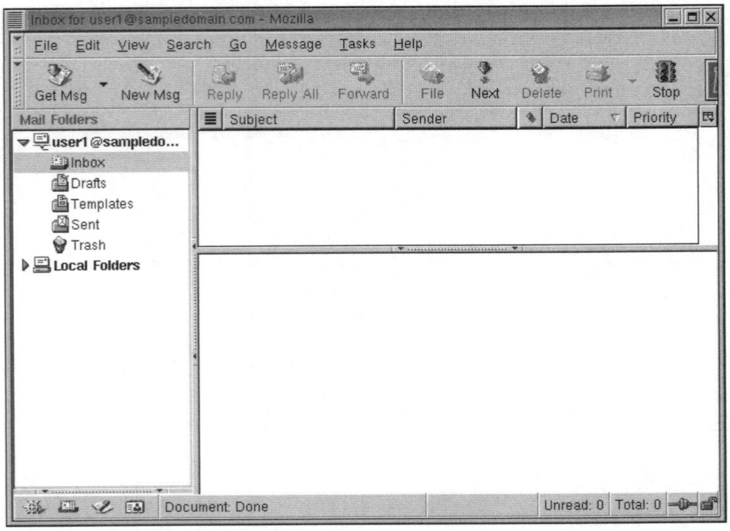

Figure 15-24   The Mozilla e-mail client

COMMON NETWORK SERVICES

Recall from Chapter 1 that Linux provides a wide variety of services that are available to users across a network. These services are often represented by a series of daemon processes that listen for certain requests on the network. Daemons identify which packets they should respond to by listening only for packets that have a certain number; this number is called a **port** and uniquely identifies a particular service. Ports and their associated protocol are defined in the `/etc/services` file; to see which port the telnet daemon listens to, you may use the following command:

```
[root@localhost root]# grep telnet /etc/services
telnet          23/tcp
telnet          23/udp
rtelnet         107/tcp                              # Remote Telnet
rtelnet         107/udp
telnets         992/tcp
telnets         992/udp
[root@localhost root]# _
```

The output above indicates that the telnet daemon listens on port 23 using both the TCP/IP and UDP/IP protocols.

Ports range from 0 to 65534. The ports 0–1023 are called **well-known ports** since they represent commonly used services.

In addition, network utilities may connect to daemons that provide network services directly, or they may connect to network daemons via the **Internet Super Daemon (xinetd)** as seen in Figure 15-25.

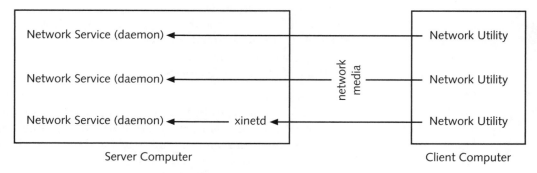

15

Figure 15-25 Interacting with network services

The Internet Super Daemon is typically used to start and manage connections for smaller network daemons such as the telnet and FTP daemons. It is started automatically at boot time and uses the configuration file `/etc/xinetd.conf`; normally, this file incorporates all of the files in the `/etc/xinetd.d` directory as well. Most daemons that are managed by the Internet Super Daemon are configured by files in the `/etc/xinetd.d` directory named after the daemons; for example, the telnet daemon is configured by the Internet Super Daemon via the `/etc/xinetd.d/telnet` file as seen in the following output:

```
[root@localhost root]# cat /etc/xinetd.d/telnet
# description: The telnet server serves telnet sessions; it uses \
#        unencrypted username/password pairs for authentication.
service telnet
{
        flags           = REUSE
        socket_type     = stream
        wait            = no
        user            = root
        server          = /usr/sbin/in.telnetd
        log_on_failure  += USERID
        disable         = yes
}
[root@localhost root]# _
```

The above output displays the full path to the telnet daemon (`/usr/sbin/in.telnetd`). In addition to this, the `disable = yes` line in the `/etc/xinetd.d/telnet` file indicates that the telnet daemon is currently disabled on this computer.

 After a Red Hat Linux installation, most files in the `/etc/xinetd.d` directory have the line `disable = yes` in them to prevent them from being used. Ensure that any unused xinetd-managed daemons are disabled in the same manner for both security and performance reasons.

Large network daemons are rarely started by the Internet Super Daemon and are hence called **standalone daemons**. Standalone daemons are typically started at boot time from files in the `/etc/rc.d/rc*.d` directories; the `ntsysv` utility discussed in Chapter 9 can be used to configure most standalone daemons to start in various runlevels. In addition, most standalone daemons may be started manually from files in the `/etc/init.d` or `/etc/rc.d/init.d` directories.

Many standalone and xinetd-managed daemons also have configuration files that control how they operate and indicate the pathname to other important files used by the daemon. For simplicity, many of these daemons store all information in only one configuration file that contains comments that indicate the syntax and purpose of each line. As a result, these configuration files may be very large; the configuration file used by the Apache Web server is almost 1500 lines long. In addition to this, most standalone network daemons do not use the syslog daemon to log information related to their operation; instead, they log this information themselves to subdirectories of the same name underneath the `/var/log` directory. For example, log files for the Samba daemon are located in the `/var/log/samba` directory.

The location of configuration and log files for network daemons may vary between different Linux distributions; the locations discussed in this chapter are for Red Hat Linux only.

Table 15–2 lists common network services and their features.

Table 15-2 Common network services

Network Service	Type	Port	Description
Apache Web server (httpd)	standalone	80	Used to serve Web pages to other computers on the network that have a Web browser; configuration file: `/etc/httpd/conf/httpd.conf`
BIND / DNS (named)	standalone	53	Resolves Fully Qualified Domain Names to IP addresses for a certain namespace on the Internet; configuration file: `/etc/named.conf`
FTP Server (in.ftpd)	xinetd	20 21	Used to transfer files to and accept files from other computers on the network with an FTP utility. configuration file: `/etc/ftpaccess` hosts denied FTP access: `/etc/ftphosts` users denied FTP access: `/etc/ftpusers` FTP data compression: `/etc/ftpconversions`
IMAP Server (imapd)	xinetd	143	Allows users with an e-mail reader (Mail User Agent) to obtain e-mail from the server using the Interactive Mail Access Protocol
Internetwork News Server (innd)	standalone	119	Used to accept and manage newsgroup postings and transfer them to other news servers; configuration file: `/etc/news/inn.conf`
NFS Server (rpc.nfsd)	standalone	2049	Shares files to other computers on the network that have an NFS client utility; configuration file: `/etc/exports`
POP3 Server (ipop3d)	xinetd	110	Allows users with an e-mail reader (Mail User Agent) to obtain e-mail from the server using the Post Office Protocol version 3
rlogin Daemon (in.rlogind)	xinetd	513	Allows users that use the rlogin and rcp utilities to copy files and obtain shells on other computers on the network using trusted access
rsh Daemon (in.rshd)	xinetd	514	Allows users that use the rsh utility to run commands on other computers on the network using trusted access
Samba Server (smbd & nmbd)	standalone	137 138 139	Allows Windows users to view shared files and printers on a Linux server; configuration file: `/etc/samba/smb.conf`
Secure Shell Daemon (sshd)	standalone	22	Provides a secure alternative to the rlogin and rsh utilities by using encrypted communication

15

Table 15-2   Common network services (continued)

Network Service	Type	Port	Description
Sendmail Email Server (sendmail)	standalone	25	Used to send e-mail to and accept e-mail from users or other e-mail servers on the Internet using the Simple Mail Transfer Protocol (SMTP); configuration file: `/etc/sendmail.cf`
Squid Proxy Server (squid)	standalone	3128	Also known as a Proxy Server, allows computers on a network to share one connection to the Internet; configuration file: `/etc/squid/squid.conf`
telnet Daemon (in.telnetd)	xinetd	23	Allows users that have a telnet utility to log into the system from across the network and obtain a shell
X Server	standalone	0	Can be used to generate graphics that will be displayed on a computer on the network that has an X-Client using the DISPLAY variable on the X Server

By default, you are prevented from logging in and obtaining a shell as the root user to network services such as telnet due to entries in the `/etc/securetty` file. This file lists terminals that the root user is allowed to access; removing or renaming this file will allow the root user to log in and receive a shell across the network.

Some network services are not provided by network daemons; instead these services are provided by the Linux kernel and do not listen to a particular port. One example of this type of network service is `netfilter/iptables`, which ignores certain network packets according to various criteria, hence creating a security firewall as discussed in Chapter 1. The rules that determine what packets to allow and reject are stored in memory and used directly by the Linux kernel. You may use the `iptables` command to specify these rules or place these rules in the `/etc/sysconfig/iptables` file to have them execute at every boot time.

For more information on how to configure firewall rules using `netfilter/iptables`, consult the man or info page for the `iptables` command.

Older Linux kernels used the ipchains utility to provide firewall services; this utility is not supported by the Linux kernel in Red Hat 7.2 by default.

Another example of a network service that is provided directly by the Linux kernel is routing. Every computer on a network maintains a list of TCP/IP networks so that packets are sent to the appropriate location; this list is called a **route table** and is stored in system memory. To see the route table, you may simply use the **route** command as seen in the following output:

```
[root@localhost root]# route
Kernel IP routing table
Destination    Gateway         Genmask         Flags Metric Ref   Use Iface
192.168.0.0    *               255.255.0.0     U     0      0       0 eth0
127.0.0.0      *               255.0.0.0       U     0      0       0 lo
default        192.168.0.1     0.0.0.0         UG    0      0       0 eth0
[root@localhost root]# _
```

 The netstat —r command is equivalent to the route command.

The route table shown in the above output indicates that all packets destined for the 192.168.0.0 network will be sent to the device eth0. Similarly, all packets destined for the 127.0.0.0 network will be sent to the loopback adapter (lo). Packets that must be sent to any other network will be sent to the default gateway; the last line in the output above indicates that the default gateway is a computer with the IP address 192.168.0.1, which is on the same network as the eth0 device.

You may add more information to the route table using the appropriate arguments to the **route** command; to load this information to the route table at every boot time, simply place the appropriate information in the **/etc/sysconfig/static-routes** file.

If the computer has more than one network interface configured, then the route table will have more entries that define the available TCP/IP networks; computers that have more than one network interface are called **multihomed hosts**. Multihomed hosts can be configured to forward packets from one interface to another to aid a packet in reaching its destination; this process is commonly called **routing** or **IP forwarding**. To enable routing on your Linux computer, simply place the number 1 in the file **/proc/sys/net/ipv4/ip_forward** as seen in the following output:

```
[root@localhost root]# cat /proc/sys/net/ipv4/ip_forward
0
[root@localhost root]# echo 1 > /proc/sys/net/ipv4/ip_forward
[root@localhost root]# cat /proc/sys/net/ipv4/ip_forward
1
[root@localhost root]# _
To enable routing at every boot, ensure that the line
net.ipv4.ip_forward = 1 exists in the /etc/sysctl.conf
file.
```

15

To enable routing at every boot, ensure that the line `net.ipv4.ip_forward = 1` exists in the `/etc/sysctl.conf` file.

A common utility used to troubleshoot routing is the **traceroute command**; it displays all routers between the current computer and a remote computer. To trace the path from the local computer to the computer with the IP address 3.4.5.6, you may use the following command:

```
[root@localhost root]# traceroute 3.4.5.6
traceroute to 3.4.5.6 (3.4.5.6), 30 hops max, 38 byte packets
 1   router1 (192.168.0.1)  2.048 ms   0.560 ms   0.489 ms
 2   apban.pso.com (7.43.111.2)  2.560 ms   0.660 ms   0.429 ms
 3   tfs.ihtfcid.net (3.0.0.1)  3.521 ms   0.513 ms   0.499 ms
 4   sr1.lala.com (3.4.5.6)  5.028 ms   0.710 ms   0.554 ms
[root@localhost root]# _
```

In addition to the network services discussed in this section, some network services involve a large number of daemons and require a great deal of configuration. A good example of this type of network service is Network Information Services (NIS). NIS can be used to coordinate the common configuration files such as /etc/passwd and /etc/hosts across several Linux computers. Each computer that participates in NIS belongs to an NIS domain and uses an NIS map for accessing certain information rather than the local configuration file. Furthermore, you may configure a master NIS server to send all NIS map configurations to NIS slave servers that then hand out these NIS maps to all other Linux computers, known as NIS clients.

The most common configuration file that companies use NIS to coordinate are password databases (/etc/passwd and /etc/shadow); the steps required to set up an NIS server and NIS client for this purpose are listed below:

Setting up the NIS Server:

1. Define the NIS domain by typing the command domainname *NIS_domain* at a command prompt.

2. Add the following line to /etc/sysconfig/network to configure the NIS domain from Step 1 at every boot time:

NISDOMAIN="*NIS_domain*"

3. Edit the file /var/yp/Makefile, navigate to the line that starts with all:, and edit the list of files to be made into maps. If you have no slave servers, also ensure that NOPUSH=true in this file. If you have slave servers, they must be listed in the

/var/yp/ypservers file.

4. Add the names or IP addresses of allowed clients to the /var/yp/securenets file.

5. Allow the clients from Step 4 access to the appropriate maps in the

/etc/ypserv.conf file.

6. Start the NIS server daemon by typing /etc/init.d/ypserv at the command prompt.

7. Start the NIS password server daemon by typing /etc/init.d/yppasswdd at the command prompt.

8. Generate the configuration file maps by typing /usr/lib/yp/ypinit —m at a command prompt.

9. Allow clients to connect by typing **ypbind** at a command prompt.

Setting up the NIS Client:

1. Define the NIS domain by typing the command domainname *NIS_domain* at a command prompt.

2. Add the following line to /etc/sysconfig/network to configure the NIS domain from Step 1 at every boot time:

   NISDOMAIN="*NIS_domain*"

3. Edit the /etc/yp.conf file and add the following line to query a specific NIS server:

   domain *NIS_domain* server *NIS_server*

   Alternatively, you may add the following line to listen for NIS broadcasts on the network:

   domain *NIS_domain* broadcast

4. Start the NIS client program by typing **ypbind** at a command prompt.

5. Locate the NIS server by typing the command **ypwhich** at a command prompt.

6. Add the following line to /etc/passwd to redirect all requests to the NIS server:

   +:*:0:0:::

Once the NIS server and client have been set up, ensure that all users on NIS clients use the **yppasswd** command to change their NIS password; using the **passwd** command will only modify the local password database.

 NIS was originally called Yellow Pages; as a result, many configuration commands and files are prefixed with the letters yp.

CHAPTER SUMMARY

❑ A network is a collection of computers that are connected together and share information.

15

❏ Protocols define the format of information that is transmitted across a network; the protocol used by the Internet and most networks is TCP/IP.

❏ Each computer on a TCP/IP network must have a valid IP address and subnet mask.

❏ The **/etc/sysconfig/network-scripts** directory contains the configuration for NIC and PPP interfaces.

❏ The TCP/IP configuration of a network interface may be specified manually, or obtained automatically from a DHCP or BOOTP server

❏ Hostnames are used to identify computers on a network easily; hostnames that follow the Domain Name Space are called Fully Qualified Domain Names.

❏ Hostnames must be resolved to an IP address before network communication can take place.

❏ Files, applications, and e-mail may be accessed across the network with the appropriate network utility.

❏ Network services are typically provided by daemons that listen to network ports; these daemons may be standalone or managed by the Internet Super Daemon.

❏ Some network services, such as firewall and routing services, are provided by the Linux kernel.

❏ NIS can be used to share key configuration files across Linux computers that participate in an NIS domain.

KEY TERMS

default gateway — The IP address of the router on the network used to send packets to remote networks.

Domain Name Space (DNS) — A network service used to resolve FQDNs to the appropriate IP address.

Ethernet — The most common media access method used in networks today.

Fully Qualified Domain Name (FQDN) — A hostname that follows DNS convention.

hostname — A user-friendly name assigned to a computer.

hostname command — A command used to display and change the hostname of a computer.

ifconfig command — A command used to display and modify the TCP/IP configuration information of a network interface.

Internet Protocol (IP) address — A series of four 8-bit numbers that represent a computer on a network.

Internet Super Daemon (xinetd) — The daemon responsible for initializing and configuring many networking services on a Linux computer.

IP forwarding — The act of forwarding TCP/IP packets from one network to another.

linuxconf — A common graphical configuration program that can configure network interfaces.

Local Area Network (LAN) — A network in which the computers are all in close physical proximity.

media access method — A system that defines how computers on a network share access to the physical medium.

multihomed hosts — A computer that has more than one network interface.

netconfig — A graphical utility used to configure the network card settings of a computer.

network — Two or more computers joined together via network media and able to exchange information.

packet internet groper (ping) command — The command used to check TCP/IP connectivity on a network.

packets — Packages of data formatted by a network protocol.

port — A number that uniquely identifies a network service.

protocol — A set of rules of communication used between computers on a network.

route table — A table of information used to indicate which networks are connected to network interfaces.

routers — Devices capable of transferring packets from one network to another.

routing — The act of forwarding data packets from one network to another.

smbclient utility — The utility used to connect to shared resources on a Windows system.

smbmount command — A command used to mount directories from Windows computers to mount points on Linux computers.

standalone daemons — Daemons normally started at boot-up that configure themselves without assistance from the Internet Super Daemon.

subnet mask — A series of four 8-bit numbers that determine the network and host portions of an IP address.

Token Ring — A popular media access method.

traceroute command — A command used to trace the path a packet takes through routers to a destination host.

trusted access — A configuration where computers are allowed to access a given computer without having to provide a password first.

well-known ports — Of the 65535 possible ports, the ones from 0 to 1024 used by common networking services.

Wide Area Networks (WAN) — A network of computers separated geographically by large distances.

15

REVIEW QUESTIONS

1. A subnet mask is used to differentiate the host portion from the network portion in a TCP/IP address. True or False?

2. When logging in to an FTP server as the anonymous user, what password is usually used?

    a. the user's normal network password

    b. the password stored in `/etc/ftp/pap-secrets`

    c. the password for the user account on the FTP server

    d. the user's e-mail address

3. Like modems and ISDN devices, xDSL devices can be configured using the kudzu utility. True or False?

4. What does the acronym NIC stand for?

    a. Network Installation and Configuration

    b. Network IP Configuration

    c. Network Interface Card

    d. nothing; a NIC is what connects a computer to a network

5. Which networking service lets you mount directories from another Linux computer on the network to a mount point on your computer?

    a. NIS

    b. NFS

    c. SMB

    d. FTP

6. The `/etc/sysconfig/network-scripts` directory holds files that contain configuration information about NICs, ISDN, and PPP connections. True or False?

7. What file stores the TCP/IP addresses of the DNS servers used to resolve hostnames?

    a. `/etc/hosts`

    b. `/etc/host.conf`

    c. `/etc/resolve`

    d. `/etc/resolv.conf`

8. What command would you type to exit the FTP utility?

    a. `close`

    b. `exit`

    c. `bye`

    d. `done`

9. If your NIC is not automatically detected and you have to download a module for it, what file must you edit to have the module load at system boot?

a. `/etc/modules.conf`

b. `/kernel/modules.conf`

c. `/etc/modules/conf`

d. `/modules/conf`

e. none as it can only be added to the kernel via the `insmod` command

10. To allow a user to use a networking service such as telnet to access a computer remotely as the root user, what file would you need to remove?

a. `/etc/secure`

b. `/etc/security`

c. `/etc/securetty`

d. `/etc/passwd`

e. `/etc/shadow`

11. What command would you use to create rules about what packets are allowed to enter the computer from the network, thus creating a firewall, on a Red Hat 7.2 system?

a. `ipchains`

b. `iptables`

c. `ipfirewall`

d. `ipsecurity`

12. Linuxconf and netconfig can be used in addition to ifconfig to view and modify TCP/IP configuration information. True or False?

13. A computer with more than one NIC is referred to as a _____.

a. router

b. multihomed device

c. double suited device

d. none of the above; computers can only have one NIC

14. A hostname should be unique on the network on which it is used. True or False?

15. To test DNS configuration by resolving a hostname to IP address, what command or commands can you use? (Choose all that apply.)

a. `nslookup` *hostname*

b. `dig` *hostname*

c. `host` *hostname*

d. `resolve` *hostname*

15

16. What file holds the methods to be used and the order in which they will be applied for hostname resolution?

    a. `/etc/nsswitch.conf`

    b. `/etc/resolve.conf`

    c. `/etc/hosts`

    d. `/etc/dns.conf`

17. What are two means available to resolve a host name to the appropriate TCP/IP address?

    a. DHCP

    b. DNS

    c. `/etc/hosts`

    d. `/etc/resolve.conf`

18. NIC modules, like all other devices, have a file in the /dev directory. True or False?

19. A WAN covers a greater geographic area than a LAN. True or False?

20. What devices are used to transfer information from one network to another?

    a. routers

    b. LANs

    c. SLIPs

    d. DNS servers

    e. DHCP servers

21. Network services are associated with a particular _____ on which the daemons running the service listen for incoming packets?

    a. station

    b. port

    c. TCP/IP address

    d. allocation number

22. What command can you use to view the TCP/IP configuration on your computer?

    a. `ipconfig`

    b. `insmod`

    c. `showip`

    d. `ifconfig`

23. What is the standard protocol used for communication on the Internet?

    a. TCP/IP

    b. IPX

    c. DLC

    d. AppleTalk

24. What utility allows a Linux-based computer to access shares on a Windows-based computer?

    a. NIS

    b. NFS

    c. SMB

    d. smbclient

25. The TCP/IP address of 127.0.0.1 is also referred to as the _____.

    a. local address

    b. lookup address

    c. local host

    d. loopback address

26. The line that configures the hostname for the computer at boot time can be found in **/etc/sysconfig/network**. True or False?

27. For the FQDN *jim.slim.net*, what is the host name?

    a. jim

    b. slim

    c. net

    d. .

28. What command would be used to activate the NIC aliased as eth0?

    a. `ifup`

    b. `ifup eth0`

    c. `ipup`

    d. `ipup eth0`

    e. `ipdown`

    f. `ifdown eth0`

15

29. What file would you modify to change the TCP/IP address of the first aliased NIC on the system the next time the system is booted or the card is brought up?

    a. `/etc/sysconfig/network-scripts/ifcfg-eth1`

    b. `/etc/sysconfig/network-scripts/ifcfg-eth0`

    c. `/etc/sysconfig/network-scripts/ipcfg-eth0`

    d. `/etc/sysconfig/network-scripts/ipcfg-eth1`

30. Before a computer can use a router it must be provided what configuration information?

    a. routing table

    b. subnet mask

    c. default gateway

    d. default router

31. A TCP/IP address has two portions: a network portion and a host portion. True or False?

32. What commands below can be used to check TCP/IP configuration and test network connectivity? (Choose all that apply.)

    a. `ifconfig`

    b. `ipconfig`

    c. `traceroute`

    d. `ping`

    e. `netstat -i`

    f. `pong`

33. When information is sent between computers over a network it is formatted by the protocol used and sent in the form of _____.

    a. modules

    b. pockets

    c. packets

    d. pings

    e. entities

34. What command is used to mount a directory from a Windows computer to a mount point on Linux computer?

    a. It cannot be done as the filesystems are not compatible.

    b. `NFS`

    c. `smbmount`

    d. `smbclient`

35. A router must have a NIC card or interface on more than one network in order to transfer information between networks. True or False?

HANDS-ON PROJECTS

These projects should be completed in the order given. All Hands-on Projects should take a total of three hours to complete. The requirements for this lab include:

❑ A computer with Red Hat 7.2 installed according to Hands-on Project 7-2

Project 15-1

In this hands-on project, you will modify the TCP/IP configuration of your NIC interface and test the results.

1. Turn on your computer. Once your Linux system has been loaded, log into the GNOME desktop environment using the username of **root** and the password of **secret**.

2. Navigate to GNOME button, Programs, System, Network Configuration.

3. Observe the Hardware tab of the "Network Configuration" screen. Is your NIC hardware listed?

If your NIC was not detected during installation, it may not appear in this list. In this case, add the appropriate NIC at this screen.

4. Use your mouse to highlight the **Devices** tab. What is the name given to your network interface? What media access method does it use?

5. Click the **Edit** button. When the "Ethernet Device" screen appears, use your mouse to highlight the **Protocols** tab. Which protocols are listed?

6. At the "Ethernet Device" screen, click the **Edit** button and observe the current TCP/IP settings. When were these configured?

   NOTE: If the information displayed is not correct, supply the correct values.

7. Click the **OK** button to close the "TCP/IP Settings" screen.

8. Click the **OK** button to close the "Ethernet Device" screen.

9. Click the **Close** button to close the "Network Configuration" screen. When prompted to save your changes, choose **Yes**.

10. Log out of the GNOME desktop environment.

11. Switch to a command-line terminal (tty2) by pressing **Ctrl-Alt-F2** and log into the terminal using the username of **root** and the password of **secret**.

15

12. Using an editor such as vi, edit the **/etc/sysconfig/network-scripts/ ifcfg-eth0** file. Do the entries contain the correct information? Change the fourth number in your IP address such that it is incremented by 1. Save your changes and quit from the editor to return to the command prompt.

13. At the command prompt, type **ifconfig eth0** and press **Enter**. What configuration do you see? Why?

14. At the command prompt, type **reboot** and press **Enter**. When your system has booted, switch to a command-line terminal (tty2) by pressing **Ctrl-Alt-F2** and log into the terminal using the username of **root** and the password of **secret**.

15. At the command prompt, type **ifconfig eth0** and press **Enter**. What configuration do you see? Why?

16. Using an editor such as vi, edit the **/etc/sysconfig/network-scripts/ifcfg-eth0** file and change your IP address back to its original value. Save your changes and quit from the editor to return to the command prompt.

17. Type **exit** and press **Enter** to log out of your shell.

Project 15-2

In this hands-on project, you will view your hostname as well as resolve hostnames using the /etc/hosts file.

1. Switch to a command-line terminal (tty2) by pressing **Ctrl-Alt-F2** and log into the terminal using the username of **root** and the password of **secret**.

2. At the command prompt, type **hostname** and press **Enter**. What is your hostname? Next, type **cat /etc/sysconfig/network** at the command prompt and press **Enter**. What hostname is listed here? Why?

3. At the command prompt, type **cat /etc/resolv.conf** and press **Enter**. Do you have a DNS server configured?

4. At the command prompt, type **cat /etc/nsswitch.conf** and press **Enter**. What method will applications use to resolve hostnames first? Second?

5. Edit the **/etc/hosts** file with a text editor such as vi. What entries are in this file? Add a line to the bottom of the file that reads:

       1.2.3.4   fakehost.fakedomain.com sample

   When finished, save your changes and quit the editor.

6. At the command prompt, type **ping -c 5 localhost.localdomain** and press **Enter**. Was the name resolved correctly?

7. At the command prompt, type **ping -c 5 localhost** and press **Enter**. Was the name resolved correctly?

8. At the command prompt, type **ping -c 5 fakehost.fakedomain.com** and press **Enter**. Was the name resolved correctly? Was the ping command able to contact the host?

9. At the command prompt, type **ping –c 5 sample** and press **Enter**. Was the name resolved correctly? Was the `ping` command able to contact the host?

10. Type **exit** and press **Enter** to log out of your shell.

Project 15-3

In this hands–on project, you will enable the telnet daemon and use the telnet utility to connect to it.

1. Switch to a command-line terminal (tty2) by pressing **Ctrl–Alt–F2** and log into the terminal using the username of **root** and the password of **secret**.

2. At the command prompt, type **telnet localhost** and press **Enter**. What error did you receive? Why?

3. Edit the **/etc/xinetd.d/telnet** file with a text editor such as vi and remove the line that reads:

   ```
   disable = yes
   ```

   When finished, save your changes and quit the editor.

4. At the command prompt, type **telnet localhost** and press **Enter**. Were you able to use the `telnet` utility? Why or why not?

5. At the command prompt, type **/etc/init.d/xinetd restart** and press **Enter** to restart the Internet Super Daemon.

6. At the command prompt, type **telnet localhost** and press **Enter**. Why were you successful? Next, log into the system using the username of **root** and the password of **secret** when prompted. Were you successful? What error message did you receive? Wait 1 minute for the `telnet` utility to close.

7. At the command prompt, type **cat /etc/securetty** and press **Enter**. What does each entry in this file represent? Next, type **rm –f /etc/securetty** at the command prompt and press **Enter**.

8. At the command prompt, type **telnet localhost** and press **Enter**. Next, log into the system using the username of **root** and the password of **secret** when prompted. Were you successful? Why?

9. At the command prompt, type **date** and press **Enter**. Next, type **who** at the command prompt and press **Enter**. Given the output of these commands, can you tell which terminal you are using?

10. Type **exit** and press **Enter** to log out of your shell. Which shell were you logged out of? Next, type **who** at the command prompt and press **Enter**. How can you tell that the `telnet` session has been closed?

11. Type **exit** and press **Enter** to log out of your shell.

15

Project 15-4

In this hands-on project, you will enable the FTP daemon and use the FTP utility to connect to it as the root user as well as anonymously.

1. Switch to a command-line terminal (tty2) by pressing **Ctrl–Alt–F2** and log into the terminal using the username of **root** and the password of **secret**.

2. At the command prompt, type **ftp localhost** and press **Enter**. What error did you receive? Type **bye** at the ftp> prompt and press **Enter** to quit the FTP utility.

3. Edit the **/etc/xinetd.d/wu-ftpd** file with a text editor such as vi and remove the line that reads:

   ```
   disable = yes
   ```

   When finished, save your changes and quit the editor.

4. At the command prompt, type **/etc/init.d/xinetd restart** and press **Enter** to restart the Internet Super Daemon.

5. At the command prompt, type **ftp localhost** and press **Enter**. Why were you successful? Log in using the username of **root** and the password of **secret** when prompted. Were you successful? Next, type **bye** at the ftp> prompt and press **Enter** to quit the FTP utility.

6. Edit the **/etc/ftpusers** file with a text editor such as vi and read the lines. What is the purpose of this file? Remove the line that reads:

   ```
   root
   ```

   When finished, save your changes and quit the editor.

7. At the command prompt, type **ftp localhost** and press **Enter**. Log in using the username of **root** and the password of **secret** when prompted. Were you successful? Next, type **bye** at the ftp> prompt and press **Enter** to quit the FTP utility.

8. Edit the **/etc/ftpaccess** file with a text editor such as vi and remove the lines that read:

   ```
   deny-uid %-99 %65534-
   deny-gid %-99 %65534-
   ```

   What do you suppose those lines do? When finished, save your changes and quit the editor.

9. At the command prompt, type **ftp localhost** and press **Enter**. Log in using the username of **root** and the password of **secret** when prompted. Were you successful?

10. At the ftp> prompt, type the command **dir** and press **Enter**. What is listed? What directory are you in? Type **pwd** and press **Enter**.

11. Next, type **lcd /etc** at the ftp> prompt and press **Enter** to change the local directory on the client to /etc. Now, type **mput initt*** to transfer the inittab file to the **/root** directory on the remote server (localhost). Press **y** and then **Enter** when prompted to "mput inittab?". How long did it take? What is the difference between the mput and put commands?

12. At the ftp> prompt, type **dir** and press **Enter**. Is the `inittab` file there? Next, type **bye** at the ftp> prompt and press **Enter** to quit the FTP utility.

13. At the command prompt, type **ls –F** and press **Enter**. What are the contents of your home directory? Was the `inittab` file transferred successfully?

14. At the command prompt, type **cp inittab /var/ftp** and press **Enter** to copy the **inittab** file to the anonymous FTP directory. Next, type **ls –F /var/ftp** at the command prompt and press **Enter**. Which files and subdirectories are present? Was the `inittab` file copied successfully?

15. At the command prompt, type **ftp localhost** and press **Enter**. Log in using the username of **anonymous** and the password of **user@sample.com** when prompted. Were you successful?

16. At the ftp> prompt, type **dir** and press **Enter**. What do you see? Is the `inittab` file there?

17. Next, type **lcd /** at the ftp> prompt and press **Enter** to change the local directory to the / directory. Now, type **mget in*** at the ftp> prompt and press **Enter**. When prompted to "mget inittab?", press **y** and then **Enter**.

18. At the ftp> prompt, type **cd lib** and press **Enter**. Next, type **pwd** at the ftp> prompt and press **Enter**. What directory are you in?

19. Next, type **mget libs*** at the ftp> prompt and press **Enter**. When prompted to "mget libs.md5?", press **y** and then **Enter**. What error message do you receive? Why? (*Hint*: look at the permissions of the file on the screen output.)

20. Next, type **mget ld-2*** at the ftp> prompt and press **Enter**. When prompted to "mget ld-2.2.4.so?", press **y** and then **Enter**. Did it transfer? Why?

21. Type **bye** at the ftp> prompt and press **Enter** to quit the FTP utility.

22. At the command prompt, type **ls –F /** and press **Enter** to view the contents of the / directory. Are the `inittab` and `ld–2.2.4.so` files there?

23. Type **exit** and press **Enter** to log out of your shell.

15

Project 15-5

In this hands-on project, you will the rcp, rsh, rlogin and ssh utilities to access your computer with trusted access.

1. Switch to a command-line terminal (tty2) by pressing **Ctrl-Alt-F2** and log into the terminal using the username of **root** and the password of **secret**.

2. At the command prompt, type **rlogin localhost** and press **Enter**. What happened? Press the **Ctrl-c** key combination to return to the command prompt.

3. Edit the **/etc/xinetd.d/rlogin** file with a text editor such as vi and remove the line that reads:

```
disable = yes
```

When finished, save your changes and quit the editor.

4. At the command prompt, type **/etc/init.d/xinetd restart** and press **Enter** to restart the Internet Super Daemon.

5. At the command prompt, type **rlogin localhost** and press **Enter**. Were you prompted to enter a password? Why? Enter the password of **secret** and press **Enter**.

6. At the command prompt, type **who** and press **Enter**. What user are you logged in as? What terminal are you using? How can you tell?

7. At the command prompt, type **exit** and press **Enter**. What message did you receive?

8. Edit the **/etc/hosts.equiv** file with a text editor such as vi. Are there any entries? Add a line that reads:

   ```
   localhost
   ```

   When finished, save your changes and quit the editor.

9. At the command prompt, type **rlogin localhost** and press **Enter**. Were you prompted to enter a password? Why? Enter the password of **secret** and press **Enter**.

10. At the command prompt, type **exit** and press **Enter**.

11. Edit the **/root/.rhosts** file with a text editor such as vi. Are there any entries? Add a line that reads:

    ```
    localhost
    ```

    When finished, save your changes and quit the editor.

12. At the command prompt, type **rlogin localhost** and press **Enter**. Were you prompted to enter a password? Why not?

13. At the command prompt, type **exit** and press **Enter**.

14. At the command prompt, type **rcp localhost:/etc/hosts localhost:/root/rcptest** and press **Enter**. Were you required to specify a password? Why? Next, type **ls -F /root** and press **Enter**. Was the /etc/hosts file copied successfully to the /root/rcptest file?

15. At the command prompt, type **rsh localhost date** and press **Enter** to execute the command **date** on the computer localhost. What happened? Press the **Ctrl-c** key combination to return to your shell prompt.

16. Edit the **/etc/xinetd.d/rsh** file with a text editor such as vi and remove the line that reads:

    ```
    disable = yes
    ```

    When finished, save your changes and quit the editor.

17. At the command prompt, type **/etc/init.d/xinetd restart** and press **Enter** to restart the Internet Super Daemon.

18. At the command prompt, type **rsh localhost date** and press **Enter** to execute the command **date** on the computer localhost. Did it work? Why?

19. At the command prompt, type **ssh localhost** and press **Enter** to obtain a shell. Enter the password of **secret** when prompted and press **Enter**. Why did you not need to modify the configuration of the Internet Super Daemon to start the ssh daemon?

20. Type **exit** and press **Enter** to log out of your shell.

Project 15-6

In this hands-on project, you will export the /etc directory using NFS and access it across the network using the `mount` command.

1. Switch to a command-line terminal (tty2) by pressing **Ctrl-Alt-F2** and log into the terminal using the username of **root** and the password of **secret**.

2. Edit the **/etc/exports** file with a text editor such as vi. Are there any entries? Add a line that reads:

    /etc

   When finished, save your changes and quit the editor.

3. At the command prompt, type **/etc/init.d/nfs start** and press **Enter**. What happened?

4. At the command prompt, type **mount –t nfs localhost:/etc /mnt** and press **Enter**.

5. At the command prompt, type **mount** and press **Enter**. What is mounted to the /mnt directory?

6. At the command prompt, type **cd /mnt** and press **Enter**. Next, type **ls –F** at the command prompt and press **Enter**. What directory are you observing? Type **ls –F /etc** at the command prompt and press **Enter**. Is the output on the terminal screen identical?

7. At the command prompt, type **cd** and press **Enter** to return to your home directory. Next, type **umount /mnt** at the command prompt and press **Enter** to unmount the NFS filesystem.

8. Type **exit** and press **Enter** to log out of your shell.

15

DISCOVERY EXERCISES

1. An easy way to use the rsh utility to transfer a text file is to use the syntax

    ```
    rsh remotehostname cat remotefile > localfile
    ```

   Briefly describe how this command achieves this using your knowledge of redirection. Can this be used to transfer a binary file? Explain.

2. Use the Internet, books, or other resources to find out how to register a FQDN on a DNS server for use on the Internet. Describe the procedure and cost involved. Also, find three domain names that would be available for you to register if you wanted to.

3. Use the Internet, books, or other resources to research the history of DNS. How and where did it start? Are there different versions of DNS? If so, what are their differences?

4. Research and configure one of the network services listed in Table 15-2. What sources of information did you use? Was there a configuration file? If so, what was its format?

5. Use the Internet, books, or other resources to research PPP and SLIP. What are the differences between the two? Briefly list the benefits and disadvantages of each.

APPENDIX

A

CERTIFICATION

WHY GET CERTIFIED?

As technology advances, so does the need for educated people to manage technology. One of the principal risks that companies take is the hiring of qualified people to administer, use, or develop programs for Linux. To lower this risk, companies seek people who have demonstrated proficiency in certain technical areas. Although this proficiency may be demonstrated in the form of practical experience, practical experience alone is often not enough for companies when hiring for certain technical positions. Certification tests have become a standard benchmark of technical ability, and those who have passed these tests are sought after by many companies. Certification tests can vary based on the technical certification, but usually involve a multiple-choice computer test administered by an approved testing center. They may also include a "hands-on" portion, in which you will be expected actually to perform the functions on which you are being tested. Hundreds of thousands of computer-related certification tests are written world-wide each year, and the certification process is likely to increase in importance in the future as technology advances.

 It is important to recognize that certification does not replace ability, but demonstrates it. An employer may get 30 qualified applicants for a position, and part of the hiring process will likely be a demonstration of ability. It is unlikely the employer will incur the cost and time it takes to test all 30. It is more likely that the employer will look for benchmark certifications that indicate a base ability, and then test this smaller subgroup.

Furthermore, certifications are an internationally administered and recognized standard. While an employer may not be familiar with the criteria involved in achieving a computer science degree from a particular university in Canada or a certain college in Texas, certification exam criteria is well published on Web sites and hence, well known. In addition, it does not matter in which country the certification exam was taken, as the tests are standardized and administered by the same authenticating authority using common rules.

Certifications come in two broad categories, vendor-specific and vendor-neutral. Vendor-specific certifications are ones where the vendor of a particular operating system or program sets the standards to be met and creates the exams. Obtaining one of these certifications demonstrates knowledge of, or on, a particular product or operating system. Microsoft, Novell, and Oracle, for example, all provide vendor-specific certifications for their products. Vendor-neutral exams, such as those offered by the Computing Technology Industry Association (CompTIA), demonstrate knowledge in a particular

745

area, but not on any specific product or brand of product. In either case, the organizations that create the certification exams and set the standards strive to ensure that they are of the highest quality and integrity to be used as a true benchmark worldwide. One globally recognized and vendor-neutral Linux certification used by industry is CompTIA's Linux+ certification.

Linux is a general category of operating system software that shares a common operating system kernel and utilities. What differentiates one Linux distribution from another are the various accompanying software applications, which modify the look and feel of the operating system. Vendor-neutral certification suits Linux particularly well, as there is no one specific vendor. Linux distributions may have different brands attached to them, but all essentially work in the same fashion. To certify on one particular distribution may well indicate the ability to port to and work well on another distribution, but with the varied number of distributions it is probably best to show proficiency on the most common features of Linux that the majority of distributions share. The CompTIA Linux+ certification exam achieves this well and tests a wide body of knowledge on the various ways Linux is distributed and installed, as well as common commands, procedures, and user interfaces. The exam may be taken at any participating VUE or Sylvan Prometric testing center world-wide and involves 95 questions to be answered within a two hour timeframe.

 To find out more about the Linux+ certification exam, visit the CompTIA Web site on the Internet at *http://www.comptia.org/certification/linuxplus/*.

LINUX+ CERTIFICATION OBJECTIVES

The following tables identify where certification topics are covered in this book. Each table represents a separate domain measured by the exam.

Table A-1   Domain 1.0 Planning the implementation

Objective	Chapter
1.1 Identify purpose of Linux machine based on predetermined customer requirements	7
1.2 Identify all system hardware required and validate that it is supported by Linux	7
1.3 Determine what software and services should be installed, check requirements, and validate that it is supported by Linux	7
1.4 Determine how storage space will be allocated to file systems	7
1.5 Compare and contrast how major Linux licensing schemes work	1

Table A-1   Domain 1.0 Planning the implementation (continued)

Objective	Chapter
1.6 Identify the function of different Linux services	1, 15
1.7 Identify strengths and weaknesses of different distributions and their packaging solutions	1
1.8 Describe the functions, features, and benefits of a Linux solution, as compared with other operating systems	1
1.9 Identify how the Linux kernel version numbering works	1
1.10 Identify where to obtain software and resources	1
1.11 Determine customer resources for a solution	1

Table A-2   Domain 2.0 Installation

Objective	Chapter
2.1 Determine the appropriate method of installation based on the environment	2, 3, 6
2.2 Describe the different types of Linux installation interactions and determine which to use in a given situation	2, 3, 6
2.3 Select appropriate parameters for Linux installation	2, 3, 6
2.4 Select packages based on the machine's "role"	2, 3, 6
2.5 Select appropriate options for partitions based on pre-installation choices	2, 3, 6
2.6 Partition according to your pre-installation plan using FDISK	2, 3, 6
2.7 Configure filesystems	2, 3, 6
2.8 Select appropriate networking configuration and protocols	2, 3, 6
2.9 Select appropriate security settings	2, 3, 6
2.10 Create users and passwords during installation	2, 3, 6
2.11 Install and configure Xfree86 server	2, 3, 6
2.12 Select video card support	2, 3, 6
2.13 Select appropriate monitor manufacturer and settings	2, 3, 6
2.14 Select the appropriate window managers or desktop environment	2, 3, 6
2.15 Explain when and why the kernel will need to be recompiled	14
2.16 Install boot loader	9
2.17 Install and uninstall applications after installing the operating system	13
2.18 Read the logfiles created during installation to verify the success of the installation	7
2.19 Validate that an installed application is performing correctly in both a test and a production environment	11

Table A-3 Domain 3.0 Configuration

Objective	Chapter
3.1 Reconfigure the X Windows system with automated utilities	9
3.2 Configure the client's workstation for remote access	15
3.3 Set environment variables	8
3.4 Configure basic network services and settings	15
3.5 Configure basic server services	15
3.6 Configure basic Internet services	15
3.7 Identify when swap space needs to be increased	14
3.8 Add and configure printers	12
3.9 Install and configure add-in hardware	14
3.10 Reconfigure boot loader	9
3.11 Identify the purpose and characteristics of configuration files	5, 6, 9
3.12 Edit basic configuration files	8
3.13 Load, remove, and edit list modules	14
3.14 Document the installation of the operating system, including configuration	7
3.15 Configure access rights	15

Table A-4 Domain 4.0 Administration

Objective	Chapter
4.1 Create and delete users	12
4.2 Modify existing users	12
4.3 Create, modify, and delete groups	12
4.4 Identify and change file permissions, modes, and types by using chmod, chown, and chgrp	5
4.5 Manage and navigate the Linux hierarchy	5
4.6 Manage and navigate the standard Linux file system	5
4.7 Perform administrative tasks while logged in as root, or by using the su command	12
4.8 Mount and image filesystems and devices	6
4.9 Describe and use the features of the multiuser environment	3
4.10 Use common shell commands and expressions	3
4.11 Use network commands to connect to and manage remote systems	15
4.12 Create, extract, and edit file and tape archives using tar	13
4.13 Manage runlevels using init and shutdown	9
4.14 Stop, start, and restart services (daemons) as needed	9

A

Table A-4   Domain 4.0 Administration (continued)

Objective	Chapter
4.15 Manage print spools and queues	12
4.16 Create, edit, and save files using vi	4
4.17 Manage and navigate the graphical user interface	10
4.18 Program basic shell scripts using common shell commands	8

Table A-5   Domain 5.0 System maintenance

Objective	Chapter
5.1 Create and manage local storage devices and filesystems	6
5.2 Verify user and root cron jobs and understand the function of cron	11
5.3 Identify core dumps and remove or forward as appropriate	11
5.4 Run and interpret `ifconfig`	15
5.5 Download and install patches and updates	14
5.6 Differentiate core services from non-critical services	11
5.7 Identify, execute, and kill processes	11
5.8 Monitor system log files regularly for errors, logins, and unusual activity	12
5.9 Document work performed on a system	14
5.10 Perform and verify back-ups and restores	13
5.11 Perform and verify security best practices	12
5.12 Assess security risks	5, 12
5.13 Set daemon and process permissions	5

Table A-6   Domain 6.0 Troubleshooting

Objective	Chapter
6.1 Identify and locate a problem by determining whether the problem is due to hardware, operating system, application software, configuration, or the user	14
6.2 Describe troubleshooting best practices	14
6.3 Examine and edit configuration files based on symptoms of a problem using system utilities	14
6.4 Examine, start, and stop processes based on the signs and symptoms of a problem	14
6.5 Use system status tools to examine system resources and statuses	14
6.6 Use the system boot disk and root disk on a workstation and server to diagnose and rescue a filesystem	14
6.7 Inspect and determine the cause of errors from system log files	14

Table A-6   Domain 6.0 Troubleshooting (continued)

Objective	Chapter
6.8 Use disk utilities to solve filesystem problems	14
6.9 Resolve problems based on user feedback	14
6.10 Recognize common errors	14
6.11 Take appropriate action on boot errors	14
6.12 Identify back-up and restore errors	14
6.13 Identify application failure on a server	14
6.14 Identify and use troubleshooting commands	14
6.15 Locate troubleshooting resources and update as allowable	12
6.16 Use network utilities to identify network and connectivity problems	15

Table A-7   Domain 7.0 Identify, install, and maintain system hardware

Objective	Chapter
7.1 Identify basic terms, concepts, and functions of system components, including how each component should work during normal operation and during the boot process	7, 14
7.2 Assure that system hardware is configured correctly prior to installation by identifying proper procedures for installing and configuring ATA devices	7, 14
7.3 Assure that system hardware is configured correctly prior to installation by identifying proper procedures for installing and configuring SCSI and IEEE 1394 devices	7, 14
7.4 Assure that system hardware is configured correctly prior to installation by identifying proper procedures for installing and configuring peripheral devices	7, 14
7.5 Assure that system hardware is configured correctly prior to installation by identifying available IRQs, DMAs, and I/O addresses and procedures for device installation and configuration	7, 14
7.6 Remove and replace hardware and accessories based on symptoms of a problem by identifying basic procedures for adding and removing field replaceable components	7, 14
7.7 Remove and replace hardware and accessories based on symptoms of a problem by identifying common symptoms and problems associated with each component and how to troubleshoot and isolate the problems	7, 14
7.8 Identify basic networking concepts, including how a network works	7, 14

Table A-7   Domain 7.0 Identify, install, and maintain system hardware (continued)

Objective	Chapter
7.9 Identify proper procedures for diagnosing and troubleshooting ATA devices	7, 14
7.10 Identify proper procedures for diagnosing and troubleshooting SCSI devices	7, 14
7.11 Identify proper procedures for diagnosing and troubleshooting peripheral devices	7, 14
7.12 Identify proper procedures for diagnosing and troubleshooting core system hardware	7, 14
7.13 Identify and maintain mobile system hardware	7, 14

GNU PUBLIC LICENSE

A copy of the GNU public license referred to in Chapter 1 is shown here
in Figure B-1. It may also be found on the Internet at *http://www.gnu.org/
copyleft/gpl.*

```
GNU GENERAL PUBLIC LICENSE
               Version 2, June 1991

 Copyright (C) 1989, 1991 Free Software Foundation, Inc.
 59 Temple Place, Suite 330, Boston, MA  02111-1307  USA
 Everyone is permitted to copy and distribute verbatim copies
 of this license document, but changing it is not allowed.

                       Preamble

   The licenses for most software are designed to take away your
 freedom to share and change it.  By contrast, the GNU General Public
 License is intended to guarantee your freedom to share and change free
 software--to make sure the software is free for all its users.  This
 General Public License applies to most of the Free Software
 Foundation's software and to any other program whose authors commit to
 using it.  (Some other Free Software Foundation software is covered by
 the GNU Library General Public License instead.)  You can apply it to
 your programs, too.

   When we speak of free software, we are referring to freedom, not
 price.  Our General Public Licenses are designed to make sure that you
 have the freedom to distribute copies of free software (and charge for
 this service if you wish), that you receive source code or can get it
 if you want it, that you can change the software or use pieces of it
 in new free programs; and that you know you can do these things.

   To protect your rights, we need to make restrictions that forbid
 anyone to deny you these rights or to ask you to surrender the rights.
 These restrictions translate to certain responsibilities for you if you
 distribute copies of the software, or if you modify it.

   For example, if you distribute copies of such a program, whether
 gratis or for a fee, you must give the recipients all the rights that
 you have.  You must make sure that they, too, receive or can get the
 source code.  And you must show them these terms so they know their
 rights.

   We protect your rights with two steps: (1) copyright the software, and
 (2) offer you this license which gives you legal permission to copy,
 distribute and/or modify the software.

   Also, for each author's protection and ours, we want to make certain
 that everyone understands that there is no warranty for this free
 software.  If the software is modified by someone else and passed on, we
 want its recipients to know that what they have is not the original, so
 that any problems introduced by others will not reflect on the original
 authors' reputations.

   Finally, any free program is threatened constantly by software
 patents.  We wish to avoid the danger that redistributors of a free
 program will individually obtain patent licenses, in effect making the
 program proprietary.  To prevent this, we have made it clear that any
 patent must be licensed for everyone's free use or not licensed at all.

   The precise terms and conditions for copying, distribution and
 modification follow.

                 GNU GENERAL PUBLIC LICENSE
  TERMS AND CONDITIONS FOR COPYING, DISTRIBUTION AND MODIFICATION

   0. This License applies to any program or other work which contains
 a notice placed by the copyright holder saying it may be distributed
 under the terms of this General Public License.  The "Program", below,
 refers to any such program or work, and a "work based on the Program"
 means either the Program or any derivative work under copyright law:
 that is to say, a work containing the Program or a portion of it,
 either verbatim or with modifications and/or translated into another
 language.  (Hereinafter, translation is included without limitation in
 the term "modification".)  Each licensee is addressed as "you".
```

Activities other than copying, distribution and modification are not covered by this License; they are outside its scope. The act of running the Program is not restricted, and the output from the Program is covered only if its contents constitute a work based on the Program (independent of having been made by running the Program). Whether that is true depends on what the Program does.

   1. You may copy and distribute verbatim copies of the Program's source code as you receive it, in any medium, provided that you conspicuously and appropriately publish on each copy an appropriate copyright notice and disclaimer of warranty; keep intact all the notices that refer to this License and to the absence of any warranty; and give any other recipients of the Program a copy of this License along with the Program.

You may charge a fee for the physical act of transferring a copy, and you may at your option offer warranty protection in exchange for a fee.

   2. You may modify your copy or copies of the Program or any portion of it, thus forming a work based on the Program, and copy and distribute such modifications or work under the terms of Section 1 above, provided that you also meet all of these conditions:

   a) You must cause the modified files to carry prominent notices
   stating that you changed the files and the date of any change.

   b) You must cause any work that you distribute or publish, that in
   whole or in part contains or is derived from the Program or any
   part thereof, to be licensed as a whole at no charge to all third
   parties under the terms of this License.

   c) If the modified program normally reads commands interactively
   when run, you must cause it, when started running for such
   interactive use in the most ordinary way, to print or display an
   announcement including an appropriate copyright notice and a
   notice that there is no warranty (or else, saying that you provide
   a warranty) and that users may redistribute the program under
   these conditions, and telling the user how to view a copy of this
   License. (Exception: if the Program itself is interactive but
   does not normally print such an announcement, your work based on
   the Program is not required to print an announcement.)

These requirements apply to the modified work as a whole. If identifiable sections of that work are not derived from the Program, and can be reasonably considered independent and separate works in themselves, then this License, and its terms, do not apply to those sections when you distribute them as separate works. But when you distribute the same sections as part of a whole which is a work based on the Program, the distribution of the whole must be on the terms of this License, whose permissions for other licensees extend to the entire whole, and thus to each and every part regardless of who wrote it.

Thus, it is not the intent of this section to claim rights or contest your rights to work written entirely by you; rather, the intent is to exercise the right to control the distribution of derivative or collective works based on the Program.

In addition, mere aggregation of another work not based on the Program with the Program (or with a work based on the Program) on a volume of a storage or distribution medium does not bring the other work under the scope of this License.

   3. You may copy and distribute the Program (or a work based on it, under Section 2) in object code or executable form under the terms of Sections 1 and 2 above provided that you also do one of the following:

   a) Accompany it with the complete corresponding machine-readable
   source code, which must be distributed under the terms of Sections
   1 and 2 above on a medium customarily used for software interchange; or,

   b) Accompany it with a written offer, valid for at least three

years, to give any third party, for a charge no more than your
cost of physically performing source distribution, a complete
machine-readable copy of the corresponding source code, to be
distributed under the terms of Sections 1 and 2 above on a medium
customarily used for software interchange; or,

c) Accompany it with the information you received as to the offer
to distribute corresponding source code. (This alternative is
allowed only for noncommercial distribution and only if you
received the program in object code or executable form with such
an offer, in accord with Subsection b above.)

The source code for a work means the preferred form of the work for
making modifications to it. For an executable work, complete source
code means all the source code for all modules it contains, plus any
associated interface definition files, plus the scripts used to
control compilation and installation of the executable. However, as a
special exception, the source code distributed need not include
anything that is normally distributed (in either source or binary
form) with the major components (compiler, kernel, and so on) of the
operating system on which the executable runs, unless that component
itself accompanies the executable.

If distribution of executable or object code is made by offering
access to copy from a designated place, then offering equivalent
access to copy the source code from the same place counts as
distribution of the source code, even though third parties are not
compelled to copy the source along with the object code.

4. You may not copy, modify, sublicense, or distribute the Program
except as expressly provided under this License. Any attempt
otherwise to copy, modify, sublicense or distribute the Program is
void, and will automatically terminate your rights under this License.
However, parties who have received copies, or rights, from you under
this License will not have their licenses terminated so long as such
parties remain in full compliance.

5. You are not required to accept this License, since you have not
signed it. However, nothing else grants you permission to modify or
distribute the Program or its derivative works. These actions are
prohibited by law if you do not accept this License. Therefore, by
modifying or distributing the Program (or any work based on the
Program), you indicate your acceptance of this License to do so, and
all its terms and conditions for copying, distributing or modifying
the Program or works based on it.

6. Each time you redistribute the Program (or any work based on the
Program), the recipient automatically receives a license from the
original licensor to copy, distribute or modify the Program subject to
these terms and conditions. You may not impose any further
restrictions on the recipients' exercise of the rights granted herein.
You are not responsible for enforcing compliance by third parties to
this License.

7. If, as a consequence of a court judgment or allegation of patent
infringement or for any other reason (not limited to patent issues),
conditions are imposed on you (whether by court order, agreement or
otherwise) that contradict the conditions of this License, they do not
excuse you from the conditions of this License. If you cannot
distribute so as to satisfy simultaneously your obligations under this
License and any other pertinent obligations, then as a consequence you
may not distribute the Program at all. For example, if a patent
license would not permit royalty-free redistribution of the Program by
all those who receive copies directly or indirectly through you, then
the only way you could satisfy both it and this License would be to
refrain entirely from distribution of the Program.

If any portion of this section is held invalid or unenforceable under
any particular circumstance, the balance of the section is intended to
apply and the section as a whole is intended to apply in other
circumstances.

It is not the purpose of this section to induce you to infringe any
patents or other property right claims or to contest validity of any
such claims; this section has the sole purpose of protecting the
integrity of the free software distribution system, which is
implemented by public license practices. Many people have made
generous contributions to the wide range of software distributed
through that system in reliance on consistent application of that
system; it is up to the author/donor to decide if he or she is willing
to distribute software through any other system and a licensee cannot
impose that choice.

This section is intended to make thoroughly clear what is believed to
be a consequence of the rest of this License.

  8. If the distribution and/or use of the Program is restricted in
certain countries either by patents or by copyrighted interfaces, the
original copyright holder who places the Program under this License
may add an explicit geographical distribution limitation excluding
those countries, so that distribution is permitted only in or among
countries not thus excluded. In such case, this License incorporates
the limitation as if written in the body of this License.

  9. The Free Software Foundation may publish revised and/or new versions
of the General Public License from time to time. Such new versions will
be similar in spirit to the present version, but may differ in detail to
address new problems or concerns.

Each version is given a distinguishing version number. If the Program
specifies a version number of this License which applies to it and "any
later version", you have the option of following the terms and conditions
either of that version or of any later version published by the Free
Software Foundation. If the Program does not specify a version number of
this License, you may choose any version ever published by the Free Software
Foundation.

  10. If you wish to incorporate parts of the Program into other free
programs whose distribution conditions are different, write to the author
to ask for permission. For software which is copyrighted by the Free
Software Foundation, write to the Free Software Foundation; we sometimes
make exceptions for this. Our decision will be guided by the two goals
of preserving the free status of all derivatives of our free software and
of promoting the sharing and reuse of software generally.

                               NO WARRANTY

  11. BECAUSE THE PROGRAM IS LICENSED FREE OF CHARGE, THERE IS NO WARRANTY
FOR THE PROGRAM, TO THE EXTENT PERMITTED BY APPLICABLE LAW. EXCEPT WHEN
OTHERWISE STATED IN WRITING THE COPYRIGHT HOLDERS AND/OR OTHER PARTIES
PROVIDE THE PROGRAM "AS IS" WITHOUT WARRANTY OF ANY KIND, EITHER EXPRESSED
OR IMPLIED, INCLUDING, BUT NOT LIMITED TO, THE IMPLIED WARRANTIES OF
MERCHANTABILITY AND FITNESS FOR A PARTICULAR PURPOSE. THE ENTIRE RISK AS
TO THE QUALITY AND PERFORMANCE OF THE PROGRAM IS WITH YOU. SHOULD THE
PROGRAM PROVE DEFECTIVE, YOU ASSUME THE COST OF ALL NECESSARY SERVICING,
REPAIR OR CORRECTION.

  12. IN NO EVENT UNLESS REQUIRED BY APPLICABLE LAW OR AGREED TO IN WRITING
WILL ANY COPYRIGHT HOLDER, OR ANY OTHER PARTY WHO MAY MODIFY AND/OR
REDISTRIBUTE THE PROGRAM AS PERMITTED ABOVE, BE LIABLE TO YOU FOR DAMAGES,
INCLUDING ANY GENERAL, SPECIAL, INCIDENTAL OR CONSEQUENTIAL DAMAGES ARISING
OUT OF THE USE OR INABILITY TO USE THE PROGRAM (INCLUDING BUT NOT LIMITED
TO LOSS OF DATA OR DATA BEING RENDERED INACCURATE OR LOSSES SUSTAINED BY
YOU OR THIRD PARTIES OR A FAILURE OF THE PROGRAM TO OPERATE WITH ANY OTHER
PROGRAMS), EVEN IF SUCH HOLDER OR OTHER PARTY HAS BEEN ADVISED OF THE
POSSIBILITY OF SUCH DAMAGES.

                    END OF TERMS AND CONDITIONS

               How to Apply These Terms to Your New Programs

  If you develop a new program, and you want it to be of the greatest

B

possible use to the public, the best way to achieve this is to make it
free software which everyone can redistribute and change under these terms.

    To do so, attach the following notices to the program. It is safest
to attach them to the start of each source file to most effectively
convey the exclusion of warranty; and each file should have at least
the "copyright" line and a pointer to where the full notice is found.

    , 1 April 1989
    Ty Coon, President of Vice

This General Public License does not permit incorporating your program into
proprietary programs. If your program is a subroutine library, you may
consider it more useful to permit linking proprietary applications with the
library. If this is what you want to do, use the GNU Library General
Public License instead of this License.

APPENDIX
C

FINDING LINUX RESOURCES ON THE INTERNET

Open Source development has made Linux a powerful and versatile operating system. However, this development has also increased the complexity of Linux and Linux resources available on the Internet. Newcomers to Linux may find this bounty of resources intimidating, but there are some simple rules that make finding particular types of Linux resources easier. Understanding how to navigate the Internet to find these resources is a valuable skill to develop.

By far the easiest way to locate resources on any topic is by using a search engine such as *http://www.google.com*, where you can simply type in a phrase representing what you are searching for and receive a list of Web sites that contain relevant material. However, since there is a plethora of Linux-related Web sites on the Internet, a search of the word Linux will yield thousands of results. You may need to narrow down and be more specific in your request to a search engine in order to obtain a list of Web sites that likely contain the information you desire. Thus, it is very important to approach Linux documentation by topic; otherwise, you may be searching for hours through numerous Web sites to find the resources you need.

There are many Web sites that describe the features of Linux and Open Source Software. Many of these Web sites contain links to other Linux resources organized by topic, and hence are a good place for people to start if they are new to Linux and desire some background or terminology. Unfortunately, many of the sites do not follow a common naming scheme. Table C-1 is a partial list of some valuable Web sites offering general Linux information.

Table C-1   General Linux & Open Source Web sites

Description	Web site
Linux Online	http://www.linux.org
Linux International	http://www.li.org
Linux Jargon File (Terminology)	http://www.tuxedo.org/~esr/jargon/
The Cathedral & the Bazaar (History of Open Source)	http://www.tuxedo.org/~esr/writings/cathedral-bazaar/
The Free Software Foundation	http://www.gnu.org

Other important sources of information for inexperienced and expert Linux users alike are Linux news sites. Some of these Web sites are hosted by organizations that publish trade magazines, and as a result share the same name as the magazine with a *.com* suffix making the Web site easier to find. An example is the Linux Journal, which can be found at *http://www.linuxjournal.com*. Often, these sites contain more than just Linux news. They also contain tutorials, Frequently Asked Questions (FAQs), and links to other Linux resources. Table C-2 lists some common Linux news Web sites.

Table C-2   Common Linux news Web sites

Description	Web site
Linux Journal (magazine)	http://www.linuxjournal.com
Linux Today (magazine)	http://www.linuxtoday.com
Slashdot	http://www.slahdot.org
Linux Weekly News	http://www.lwn.net
Linux News	http://www.linuxnews.com
Linux Gazette (magazine)	http://www.linuxgazette.com
Linux Focus	http://www.linuxfocus.org
Linux Magazine (magazine)	http://www.linux-mag.com
SysAdmin Magazine (magazine)	http://www.samag.com
Open Magazine (magazine)	http://www.open-magazine.com

Although there are many Web sites offering general information and news regarding Linux and Open Source Software, the most important resources the Internet offers are help files and product documentation. These resources take many forms, including instructions for completing tasks (HOWTO documents), FAQs, supporting documentation (text files & HTML files), and newsgroup postings (Usenet). Almost every Web site containing Linux information of some type provides at least one of these resources; however, there are many centralized Web sites that make finding this information easier. Table C-3 lists some common Web sites that make locating documentation and help files easier.

Table C-3   Common Linux documentation & help resources

Description	Web site
Linux Documentation Project (HOWTOs)	*http://www.linuxdoc.org*
Linux Online	*http://www.linux.org/docs/*
Linux Help Network	*http://www.linuxhelp.net*
Google Newsgroups (formerly Deja News)	*http://groups.google.com*
Usenet (newsgroups)	*http://www.usenet.org*

In many cases, you can find help on a particular Open Source Software component for Linux by visiting its development Web site. Most large Open Source Software projects, such as the KDE project, have their own Web site where information and news regarding the software is available and the latest release can be downloaded. These Web sites usually follow the naming convention *http://www.projectname.org*, where "*projectname*" is the name of the project, and thus they are easy to locate without the use of a search engine. Table C-4 is a partial list of common Open Source Software project Web sites available on the Internet.

Table C-4   Open Source Software project Web sites

Description	Web site
The Apache Web server	*http://www.apache.org*
The KDE Desktop	*http://www.kde.org*
The GNOME Desktop	*http://www.gnome.org*
The Xfree86 Project (X Windows)	*http://www.xfree86.org*
The Linux Kernel	*http://www.kernel.org*

Smaller Open Source Software packages and projects rarely have Web sites hosting the development. Instead, they are listed on Open Source Software repository Web sites, also known as Open Source Software archives, which contain thousands of software packages available for download. Often these Web sites offer several different distributions of Linux as well, conveniently saving a visit to a distribution Web site in order to obtain one. There are many repository Web sites, a sampling of which is listed in Table C-5.

Table C-5   Common Open Source Software archives

Description	Web site
Freshmeat	*http://www.freshmeat.net*
SourceForge	*http://www.sourceforge.net*
Linux Applications	*http://www.linuxapps.com*

Table C-5   Common Open Source Software archives (continued)

Description	Web site
Tucows	*http://linux.tucows.com*
CERN	*http://linux.web.cern.ch/linux/lsr/*
Linux Online	*http://www.linux.org/apps/*
Ibiblio	*http://www.ibiblio.org/pub/Linux/*

Glossary

| — A shell metacharacter used to pipe Standard Output from one command to the Standard Input of another command.

. **(metacharacter)** — A special metacharacter used to indicate the user's current directory in the directory tree.

.. **(metacharacter)** — A special metacharacter used to represent the user's parent directory in the directory tree.

~ **(metacharacter)** — A metacharacter used to represent a user's home directory.

/bin directory — Contains binary commands for use by all users.

/boot directory — Contains the Linux kernel and files used by the boot loader data block.

/boot/grub/grub.conf — The GRUB configuration file.

/dev directory — The directory off the root where device files are typically stored.

/dev/MAKEDEV — The command used to recreate a device file if one or more of the following pieces of device information is unknown: major number, minor number, or type (character or block).

/dev/mouse — A symbolic link to the device file used for the mouse configured at installation.

/etc directory — Contains system-specific configuration files.

/etc/at.allow — A file listing all users who can use the at command.

/etc/at.deny — A file listing all users who cannot access the at command.

/etc/cron.allow — A file listing all users who can use the cron command.

/etc/cron.d — A directory that contains additional system cron tables.

/etc/cron.deny — A file listing all users who cannot access the cron command.

/etc/crontab — The default system cron table.

/etc/default/useradd — A file that contains default values for user creation.

/etc/dumpdates — The file used to store information about incremental and full back-ups for use by the dump/restore utility.

/etc/fstab — A file used to specify which filesystems to mount automatically at boot time and queried by the mount command if an insufficient number of arguments are specified.

/etc/inittab — The configuration file for the init daemon.

/etc/ld.so.cache file — The file that contains the location of shared library files.

/etc/ld.so.conf file — The file that contains a list of directories that contain shared libraries.

/etc/lilo.conf — The LILO configuration file.

/etc/login.defs — A file that contains default values for user creation.

/etc/logrotate.conf — The file used by the logrotate utility to specify rotation parameters for logfiles.

/etc/modules.conf file — The file used to load and alias modules at system initialization.

/etc/mtab — A file that stores a list of currently mounted filesystems.

/etc/passwd — The file that contains user account information.

/etc/printcap — The file that holds the configuration information for each printer installed on the system.

/etc/printcap.local — A file that holds printer configuration that may be edited by users; it is incorporated into the /etc/printcap file.

/etc/rc.d/init.d — The directory in which most daemons are located.

/etc/rc.d/rc — The script that executes files in the /etc/rc.d/rc*.d directories.

/etc/rc.d/rc*.d — The directories used to start and kill daemons in each runlevel.

/etc/rc.d/rc.local — The final script executed during system startup.

/etc/rc.d/rc.sysinit — The first script executed during system startup.

/etc/shadow — The file that contains the encrypted password as well as password and account expiry parameters for each user account.

/etc/skel — A directory that contains files that are copied to all new users' home directories upon creation.

/etc/syslog.conf — The file that specifies the events that the system log daemon listens for and the logfiles that it saves the events to.

/etc/X11/gdm/gdm.conf — The file that contains the configuration of the GNOME Desktop Manager.

/etc/X11/XF86Config — The configuration file used by X Windows.

/home directory — Default location for user home directories.

/lib directory — Contains shared program libraries (used by the commands in /bin and /sbin) as well as kernel modules.

/mnt directory — Empty directory used for accessing (mounting) disks such as floppy disks and CD-ROMs.

/opt directory — Stores additional software programs.

/proc directory — Contains process and kernel information.

/proc/cpuinfo — The directory that contains information on current CPU setup on the system.

/proc/devices — A file that contains currently used device information.

/proc/dma — The directory that contains information on current Direct Memory Access assignments on the system.

/proc/interrupts — The directory that contains information on current Interrupt Request assignments on the system.

/proc/ioports — The directory that contains information on current Input/Output address assignments on the system.

/proc/meminfo — The directory that contains information on the current memory usage situation, both physical and virtual, on the system.

/proc/modules — The directory that contains information on what modules are current incorporated into the kernel.

/root directory — The root user's home directory.

/sbin directory — Contains system binary commands (used for administration).

/tmp directory — Holds temporary files created by programs.

/usr directory — Contains most system commands and utilities.

/usr/local directory — Location for most additional programs.

/usr/src/linux directory — The directory that contains source code for the Linux kernel during compilation.

/var directory — Contains log files and spools.

/var/log directory — The directory that contains most system log files.

/var/spool/at — A directory that stores the information used to schedule commands using the at daemon.

/var/spool/cron — A directory that stores user cron tables.

< — A shell metacharacter used to obtain Standard Input from a file.

> — A shell metacharacter used to redirect Standard Output and Standard Error to a file.

a2ps command — The command used to print Postscript formatted files.

ABOOT — The boot loader for Alpha architecture platforms.

absolute pathname — The full pathname to a certain file or directory starting from the root directory.

Accelerated Graphics Port (AGP) — A motherboard connection slot designed for video card peripherals allowing data transfer speeds of over 66MHz.

active partition — The partition searched for an operating system after the MBR.

Advanced Power Management (APM) — A BIOS feature that shuts off power to peripheral devices not in use to save electricity; this feature is commonly used on laptop computers.

Advanced Technology Attachment (ATA) — *See* Integrated Device Electronics.

AIX — A version of UNIX developed by IBM.

alias command — A command used to create special variables that are shortcuts to longer command strings.

Alpha — A 64-bit processor platform from Compaq.

application — Software that runs on an operating system and provides the user with specific functionality (e.g., word processing or financial calculation).

architecture — The method employed of arranging a computer's integral electronics.

archive — The location (file or device) that contains a copy of files; it is typically created by a back-up utility.

arguments — Text that appears after a command name, does not start with a dash "-" character, and specifies information the command requires to work properly.

arithmetic logic unit — The section of the CPU where all the mathematical calculations and logic-based operations are executed.

artistic license — An Open Source license that allows source code to be distributed freely, but changed only at the discretion of the original author.

ASymmetric Multi-Processing (ASMP) — A system containing more than one processor where each processor is given a certain role or set of tasks to complete independent of the other processors.

at command — The command used to schedule commands and tasks to run at a preset time in the future.

at daemon (atd) — The system daemon that executes tasks at a future time; it is configured with the at command.

authentication — The process whereby each user must log in with a valid username and password before gaining access to the user interface of a system.

background (bg) command — The command used to run a foreground process in the background.

background process — A process that does not require the BASH shell to wait for its termination; upon execution, the user receives the BASH shell prompt immediately.

bad blocks — Those areas of a storage medium unable to store data properly.

baseline — A measure of normal system activity.

BASH Shell — The Bourne Again Shell; it is the default command line interface in Linux.

Basic Input/Output System (BIOS) ROM — The computer chips on a computer mainboard that contain the programs used to initialize hardware components at boot time.

Beowulf cluster — A popular and widespread method of clustering computers together to perform useful tasks using Linux.

binary data file — A file that contains machine language (binary 1s and 0s) and stores information (such as common functions and graphics) used by binary compiled programs.

bit — The smallest unit of information that a computer can compute.

block — The unit of data commonly used by filesystem commands; a block may contain several sectors.

block devices — Storage devices that transfer data to and from the system in chunks of many data bits by caching the information in RAM; they are represented by block device files.

boot disk — A bootable floppy disk that can be used to start a Linux system or initiate a Linux installation.

boot loader — A program used to load an operating system.

boot.ini — The file used to configure NTLOADER.

BSD (Berkeley Software Distribution) — A version of UNIX, developed out of the original UNIX source code, and given away free by AT&T to the University of California at Berkeley.

bunzip2 command — The command used to decompress files compressed by the bzip2 command.

bus — A term that represents the pathway information takes from one hardware device to another via a mainboard.

bus mastering — The process by which peripheral components perform tasks normally executed by the CPU.

bzcat command — The command used to view the contents of an archive created with bzip2 to Standard Output.

bzip2 command — The command used to compress files using a Burrows–Wheeler Block Sorting Huffman Coding compression algorithm.

cache — A temporary store of information used by the processor.

Caldera — A version of Linux supported and distributed by Caldera Systems Inc.

cat command — A Linux command used to display (or concatenate) the entire contents of a text file to the screen.

cd command — A Linux command used to change the current directory in the directory tree.

central processing unit (CPU) — Integrated circuit board used to perform the majority of all calculations on a computer system; also known as a processor or microprocessor.

chage command — The command used to modify password expiry information for user accounts.

character devices — Storage devices that transfer data to and from the system one data bit at a time; they are represented by character device files.

chgrp (change group) command — The command used to change the group owner of a file or directory.

child process — Refers to a process that was started by another process (parent process).

chipset — The common set of computer chips on a peripheral component such as a video adapter card.

chmod (change mode) command — The command used to change the mode (permissions) of a file or directory.

chown (change owner) command — The command used to change the owner and group owner of a file or directory.

chsh command — The command used to change a valid shell to an invalid shell.

clock speed — The speed at which a processor (or any other hardware device) can execute commands related to an internal time cycle.

clockchip — The computer chip that coordinates the flow of information on a peripheral component such as a video adapter card.

closed source software — Software whose source code is not freely available from the original author. Windows 98 is an example of closed source software.

cluster — Several smaller computers that function as one large supercomputer.

clustering — The act of making a cluster. *See* cluster.

color depth — The total set of colors that can be displayed on a computer video screen.

COM ports — Rectangular nine-pin connectors that can be used to connect a variety of different peripherals to the mainboard including mice, serial printers, scanners, and digital cameras; also called serial ports.

command — A program that exists on the hard drive and is executed when typed on the command line.

command mode — One of the two input modes in the vi editor; it allows a user to perform any available text editing task that is not related to inserting text into the document.

Compact Disk–Read Only Memory (CD-ROM) — Physically durable removable storage media resistant to data corruption used in CD-ROM drives and CD-RW drives.

Complex Instruction Set Computer (CISC) processors — Processors that execute complex instructions on each time cycle.

Complimentary Metal-Oxide Semiconductor (CMOS) — A computer chip used to store the configurable information used by the BIOS ROM.

compress command — The command used to compress files using a Lempel-Ziv compression algorithm.

compression — The process in which files are reduced in size by a compression algorithm.

compression algorithm — The set of instructions used to reduce the contents of a file systematically.

compression ratio — The amount of compression that occurred during compression.

concatenation — The joining of text together to make one larger whole; in Linux, words and strings of text are joined together to form a displayed file.

control unit — The area in a processor where instruction code or commands are loaded and carried out.

copy in/out (cpio) command — A common back-up utility.

cp command — The command used to create copies of files and directories.

cracker — Someone who uses computer software maliciously for personal profit.

cron daemon (crond) — The system daemon that executes tasks repetitively in the future—it is configured using cron tables.

cron table — A file specifying tasks to be run by the cron daemon; there are user cron tables and system cron tables.

crontab command — The command used to view and edit user cron tables.

cylinder — A series of tracks on a hard disk that are written to simultaneously by the magnetic heads in a hard disk drive.

daemon — A Linux system process that provides a certain service.

daemon process — A system process that is not associated with a terminal.

data blocks — Store the information of a certain file as well as the filename.

database — An organized set of data.

Database Management System (DBMS) — Software that manages databases.

decision construct — A special construct used in a shell script to alter the flow of the program based on the outcome of a command or contents of a variable—common decision constructs include if, case, && and | |.

default gateway — The IP address of the router on the network used to send packets to remote networks.

dependencies — The prerequisites required for program execution such as shared libraries or other packages.

desktop environment — Software that works with a window manager to provide a standard GUI environment that uses standard programs and development tools.

Desktop Switching Tool — A graphical tool that allows Red Hat Linux users to set the default desktop environment or window manager.

developmental kernel — A Linux kernel whose minor number is odd and has been recently developed, but not thoroughly tested.

device driver — A piece of software that contains instructions that the kernel of an operating system uses to control and interact with a specific type of computer hardware.

device file — A file used by Linux commands that represents a specific device on the system; these files do not have a data section and use major and minor numbers to reference the proper driver and specific device on the system, respectively.

df command — A command that displays disk free space by filesystem.

Direct Memory Access (DMA) — Allows peripheral devices to bypass the CPU and talk directly with other peripheral components, enhancing performance.

directory — A special file on the filesystem used to organize other files into a logical tree structure.

disabled printer — Refers to a printer that will not accept print jobs into the print queue.

disk drive — A device that contains either a hard disk, floppy disk, CD-ROM, CD-RW disk, or zip disk.

Disk Druid — An easy-to-use graphic program used to partition or modify the partitions on an HDD.

disk mirroring — Also known as RAID 1, it consists of two identical hard disks, which are written to in parallel with the same information to ensure fault tolerance.

disk striping — A type of RAID 0, which is used to write separate information to different hard disks to speed up access time.

Disk Striping with Parity — Also known as RAID 5, it is used to write separate information to hard disks to speed up access time, and also contains parity information to ensure fault-tolerance.

distribution — A complete set of Linux operating system software including the kernel, supporting function libraries, and a variety of Open Source Software packages that can be downloaded from the Internet free of charge. These Open Source Software packages are what differentiate the various distributions of Linux.

DNS servers — Servers that resolve Fully Qualified Domain Names (FQDNs) such as *www.linux.org* to IP addresses such that one can connect to them across the Internet.

documentation — System information that is stored in a log book for future reference.

Domain Name Space (DNS) — A network service used to resolve FQDNs to the appropriate IP address.

du command — A command that displays directory usage.

dual boot — A configuration where two or more operating systems exist on the hard disk of a computer; a boot loader allows the user to choose which operating system to load at boot time.

Dual In-line Memory Modules (DIMM) — A newer connection slot having connectors (pins) along both edges allowing the array of integrated circuits comprising a stick of RAM to connect the motherboard.

dump command — The common utility used to create full and incremental back-ups.

Dynamic Host Configuration Protocol (DHCP) server — A server on the network that hands out Internet Protocol (IP) configuration to computers that request it.

Dynamic RAM (DRAM) — A type of Random Access Memory that needs to refresh its store of information thousands of times a second and is available as a SIMM or DIMM stick.

echo command — A command used to display or echo output to the terminal screen—it may utilize escape sequences.

edquota command — A command used to specify quota limits for users and groups.

egrep command — A variant of the grep command used to search files for patterns using extended regular expressions.

Electronically Erasable Programmable Read Only Memory (EEPROM) — A type of ROM whose information store can not only be erased and rewritten as a whole, but can be modified singly leaving other portions intact.

emacs (Editor MACroS) editor — A popular and wide-spread text editor more conducive to word processing than vi; developed by Richard Stallman.

enabled printer — Refers to a printer that will accept print jobs into the print queue.

Enlightenment Window Manager — A common window manager used on Linux systems.

enscript command — The command used to print Postscript formatted files.

env command — A command used to display a list of exported variables present in the current shell except special variables.

environment files — Files used immediately after login to execute commands—they are typically used to load variables into memory.

environment variables — Variables that store information commonly accessed by the system or programs executing on the system—together these variables form the user environment.

Erasable Programmable Read Only Memory (EPROM) — A type of ROM whose information store can be erased and rewritten, but only as a whole.

escape sequences — Character sequences that have special meaning inside the echo command—they are prefixed by the \ character.

Ethernet — The most common media access method used in networks today.

executable program — A file that can be executed by the Linux operating system to run in memory as a process and perform a useful function.

export command — A command used to send variables to subshells.

ext2 — A non-journaling Linux filesystem.

ext3 — A journaling Linux filesystem.

Extended Multi-User Mode — Also called run-level 3; it provides most daemons and a full set of networking daemons.

extended partition — A partition on an HDD that can be further subdivided into components called logical drives.

facility — When logging system events, refers to the area of the system from which information is gathered.

fault-tolerance — The measure of downtime a device exhibits in the event of a failure.

fdisk command — A command used to create, delete, and manipulate partitions on hard disks.

Feeble Virtual Window Manager (fvwm) — A common window manager used on Linux systems.

fgrep command — A variant of the grep command that does not allow the use of regular expressions.

file command — A Linux command that displays the file type of a specified filename.

file descriptors — Numeric labels used to define command input and command output.

File Transfer Protocol (FTP) — The most common protocol used to transfer files across the Internet.

filehandles — The connections that a program makes to files on a filesystem.

filename — The user-friendly identifier given to a file.

filename extension — A series of identifiers following a dot (.) at the end of a filename used to denote the type of the file; the filename extention .txt denotes a text file.

filesystem — The way in which an HDD partition is formatted to allow data to reside on the physical media; common Linux filesystems include ext2, ext3, REISERFS, and vfat.

filesystem corruption — Errors in a filesystem structure that prevent the retrieval of stored data.

Filesystem Hierarchy Standard (FHS) — A standard outlining the location of set files and directories on a Linux system.

filter — A command that can take from Standard Input and send to Standard Output—in other words, a filter is a command that can exist in the middle of a pipe.

find command — The command used to find files on the filesystem using various criteria.

Firewire (IEEE1394) — A mainboard connection technology developed by Apple Computer, Inc. in 1995 that supports data transfer speeds of up to 400Mb per second.

First non-destructive Interactive Partition Splitter (FIPS) — A program used to create a new partition out of the free space on an existing FAT16 or FAT32 partition.

floppy disks — Removable storage media that consist of a flexible medium coated with a ferrous material that are read by floppy disk drives.

foreground (fg) command — The command used to run a background process in the foreground.

foreground process — A process for which the BASH shell that executed it must wait for its termination.

forking — The act of creating a new BASH shell child process from a parent BASH shell process.

formatting — The process where a filesystem is placed on a disk device.

framebuffer — An abstract representation of video hardware used by programs such that they do not need to communicate directly with the video hardware.

free command — The command used to display memory and swap statistics.

Free Software Foundation — An organization started by Richard Stallman that promotes and encourages the collaboration of software developers worldwide allowing the free sharing of source code and software programs.

freeware — Computer software programs distributed and made available at no cost to the user by the developer.

Frequently Asked Questions (FAQ) — An area on a Web site where answers to commonly posed questions can be found.

fsck command — A command used to check the integrity of a filesystem and repair damaged files.

full back-up — An archive of an entire filesystem.

Fully Qualified Domain Names (FQDN) — User-friendly names used to identify machines on networks and the Internet.

fuser command — A command used to identify any users or processes using a particular file or directory.

gateway — Also known as default gateway or gateway of last resort, it specifies the address of a computer that accepts information from the local computer and will send it to other computers if the local computer cannot.

GDM Configurator — A graphical tool used to configure the appearance and behavior of the GNOME Display Manager.

gedit editor — A text editor for the GNOME desktop.

General Electric Comprehensive Operating System (GECOS) field — The field in the /etc/passwd file that contains a description of the user account.

GNOME Display Manager (gdm) — Provides a graphical login screen.

GNOME RPM Manager — A graphical tool that may be used to install RPM packages available with the GNOME desktop environment.

GNU C Compiler (gcc) command — The command used to compile source code into binary programs.

GNU Image Manipulation Program (GIMP) — An Open Source graphics manipulation program that uses the GTK+ toolkit.

GNU Object Model Environment (GNOME) — One of the two competing Graphical User Interface (GUI) environments for Linux.

GNU Project — A free operating system project started by Richard Stallman.

GNU Public License — A software license, ensuring that the source code for any Open Source Software will remain freely available to anyone who wants to examine, build on, or improve upon it.

GNU zip (gzip) command — The command used to compress files using a Lempel–Ziv compression algorithm.

GRand Unified Bootloader (GRUB) — A common boot loader used in Linux.

graphical installation — An installation method that presents interactive material in a GUI-based format, rather than a command-line text-based interface.

graphical user interface (GUI) — The component of an operating system that provides a user-friendly interface comprising graphics or icons to represent desired tasks. Users can point and click to execute a command rather than having to know and use proper command line syntax.

grep command (Global Regular Expression Print) — A program used to search one or more text files for a desired string of characters.

group — When used in the mode of a certain file or directory, it refers to group ownership of that file or directory.

Group Identifier (GID) — A unique number given to each group.

groupadd command — The command used to add a group to the system.

groupdel command — The command used to delete a group from the system.

groupmod command — The command used to modify the name or GID of a group on the system.

GRUB root partition — The partition containing the second stage of the GRUB boot loader and the /boot/grub/grub.conf file.

grub-install command — The command used to install the GRUB boot loader.

grub-md5-crypt command — The command used to generate an encrypted password for use in the /etc/grub/grub.conf file.

GTK+ toolkit — A development toolkit for C programming; it is used in the GNOME desktop and the GNU Image Manipulation Program (GIMP).

GUI environment —A GUI core component such as X Windows, combined with a window manager and desktop environment, which provides the look and feel of the GUI. Although functionality may be similar among GUI environments, users may prefer one environment to another due to its ease of use.

gunzip command — The command used to decompress files compressed by the gzip command.

hacker — Someone who explores computer science to gain knowledge. Not to be confused with cracker.

hard disk drive (HDD) — A device used to write and read data to and from a hard disk.

hard disk quotas — Limits on the number of files, or total storage space on a hard disk drive, available to a user.

hard disks — Non-removable storage media consisting of a rigid disk coated with a ferrous material and used in hard disk drives (HDD).

hard limit — A limit imposed that cannot be exceeded.

hard link — A file joined to other files on the same file system that share the same inode.

hardware — Tangible parts of a computer, such as the network boards, video card, hard disk drives, printers, and keyboards.

Hardware Compatibility List (HCL) — A list of hardware components that have been tested and deemed compatible with a given operating system.

hardware platform — A particular configuration and grouping of computer hardware, normally centered on and determined by processor type and architecture.

hashpling — The first line in a shell script, which defines the shell that will be used to interpret the commands in the script file.

head command — A Linux command that displays the first set of lines of a text file; by default the head command displays the first 10 lines.

Hexadecimal — A numerical system that represents information in base-16 format.

hidden files — Files that are not normally displayed to the user via common filesystem commands.

home directory — A directory on the file system set aside for users to store personal files and information.

hostname — A user-friendly name used to uniquely identify a computer on a network; this name is usually a FQDN.

hostname command — A command used to display and change the hostname of a computer.

hot fix — A solution for a software bug made by a closed source vendor.

hot-swappable — The ability to add or remove hardware to or from a computer while the computer and operating system are functional.

HOWTO — A task-specific instruction guide to performing any of a wide variety of tasks; freely available from the Linux Documentation Project at *http://www.linuxdoc.org*.

HP-UX — A version of UNIX developed by Hewlett-Packard.

HSync (horizontal refresh) — The rate at which horizontal elements of the video screen image are refreshed allowing for changes or animation on the screen, measured in Hertz (Hz).

Hyper Text Transfer Protocol (HTTP) — The underlying protocol used to transfer information over the Internet.

ifconfig command — A command used to display and modify the TCP/IP configuration information of a network interface.

incremental back-up — An archive of a filesystem that contains only files that were modified since the last archive was created.

Industry Standard Architecture (ISA) — An older motherboard connection slot designed to allow peripheral components an interconnect that transfers information at a speed of 8MHz.

info pages — A set of local, easy-to-read command syntax documentation available by typing the info command-line utility.

init command — The command used to change the operating system from one runlevel to another.

initialize (init) daemon — The first process started by the Linux kernel; it is responsible for starting and stopping other daemons.

initstate — *See* runlevel.

inode — That portion of a file that stores information on the file's attributes, access permissions, location, ownership, and file type.

inode table — The collection of inodes for all files and directories on a filesystem.

Input/Output (I/O) address — The small working area of RAM where the CPU can pass information to and receive information from a device.

Input/Output Statistics (iostat) command — The command that displays Input/Output statistics for block devices.

insert mode — One of the two input modes in the vi editor; it allows the user to insert text into the document but does not allow any other functionality.

insmod command — The command used to insert a module into the Linux kernel.

installation log file — A log file created at installation to record actions that occurred or failed during the installation process.

Integrated Drive Electronics (IDE) — Controllers that control the flow of information to and from up to 4 hard disks connected to the mainboard via a ribbon cable; also known as Advanced Technology Attachment (ATA).

interactive mode — Refers to the mode that file management commands use when a file may be overwritten; the system interacts with a user asking for the user to confirm the action.

Interactive System Activity Grapher (isag) command — The command used to graph system performance information stored in the /var/log/sa directory.

Internet — A large network of interconnected networks connecting company networks, home computers, and institutional networks together so that they can communicate with each other.

Internet Protocol (IP) address — The unique number that each computer participating on the Internet must have.

Internet Super Daemon (xinetd) — The daemon responsible for initializing and configuring many networking services on a Linux computer.

Interrupt Request Line (IRQ) — Specifies a unique channel from a device to the CPU.

IP forwarding — The act of forwarding TCP/IP packets from one network to another.

ISO images — Large single files that are exact copies of the information contained on a CD-ROM.

Itanium (Intel 64-bit) — A 64-bit processor architecture proprietary to Intel.

jabbering — The process by which failing hardware components send large amounts of information to the CPU.

jobs command — The command used to see the list of background processes running in the current shell.

journaling — A filesystem function that keeps track of the information that needs to be written to the hard drive in a journal; common Linux journaling filesystems include ext3 and REISER.

K Window Manager (kwm) — The window manager that works under the KDE Desktop Environment.

KDE Display Manager (kdm) — A graphical login screen for users that resembles the KDE desktop.

KDE Package Manager — A graphical tool that may be used to install RPM packages available with the KDE desktop environment.

kedit editor — A text editor for the KDE desktop.

kernel — The central, core program of the operating system. The shared commonality of the kernel is what defines Linux, the differing Open Source Software applications that can interact with the common kernel is what differentiates Linux distributions.

kill command — The command used to kill or terminate a process.

kill signal — The type of signal sent to a process by the kill command; different kill signals affect processes in different ways.

killall command — The command that kills all instances of a process by command name.

Kommon Desktop Environment (KDE) — One of the two competing Graphical User Interfaces (GUI) available for Linux.

kudzu program — The program used to detect and install support for new hardware.

Large Block Addressing 32-bit (LBA32) — A parameter that may be specified that enables Large Block Addressing in a boot loader; it is required only if a large hard disk that is not fully supported by the system BIOS is used.

ldconfig — The command that updates the /etc/ld.so.conf and /etc/ld.so.cache files.

ldd command — The command used to display the shared libraries used by a certain program.

less command — A Linux command used to display a text file page-by-page on the terminal screen; users may then use the cursor keys to navigate the file.

Level 1 (L1) cache — Cache memory stored in the processor itself.

Level 2 (L2) cache — Cache memory stored in a computer chip on the motherboard for use by the processor.

lilo command —The command used to reinstall the LILO boot loader based on the configuration information in /etc/lilo.conf.

line printer daemon (lpd) — The daemon that accepts print jobs into the print queue and prints them to the printer.

linked file — A file that represents the same data as other files.

Linus Torvalds — Finnish graduate student who coded and created the first version of Linux and subsequently distributed it under the GNU Public License.

Linux — A software operating system originated by Linus Torvalds. The common core, or kernel, continues to evolve and be revised. Differing Open Source Software bundled with the Linux kernel is what defines the wide variety of distributions now available.

Linux Documentation Project (LDP) — A large collection of Linux resources, information, and help files, supplied free of charge and maintained by the Linux community.

LInux LOader (LILO) — A common boot loader used in Linux.

Linux User Group (LUG) — An open forum of Linux users who discuss and assist each other in using and modifying the Linux operating system and the Open Source Software run on it. There are LUGs worldwide.

linuxconf — A common graphical configuration program that can configure network interfaces.

ll command — An alias for the ls –l command; it gives a long file listing.

ln (link) command — The command used to create hard and symbolic links.

Local Area Network (LAN) — A network in which the computers are all in close physical proximity.

locate command — The command used to locate files from a file database.

locking an account — Making an account temporarily unusable by altering the password information for it stored on the system.

log file — A file that contains past system events.

logical drives — The smaller partitions contained within an extended partition on an HDD.

Logical Unit Number (LUN) — Uniquely identifies each device attached to any given node in a SCSI chain.

logrotate command — The command used to rotate log files; typically uses the configuration information stored in /etc/logrotate.conf.

lpc command — The command used to view the status of and control (start, stop, enable, disable) printers on the system.

lpd command — The command used to start line printer daemon.

lpq command — The command used to view the contents of print queues.

lpr command — The command used to create print jobs in the print queue.

lprm command — The command used to remove print jobs from the print queue.

LPT port — A rectangular 25-pin connection to the mainboard used to connect peripheral devices such as printers; also called parallel ports.

ls command — A Linux command used to list the files in a given directory.

lsmod command — The command that lists modules currently used by the Linux kernel.

magnetic tape (mt) command — The command used to control tape devices.

mail delivery agent (MDA) — The service that downloads e-mail from a mail transfer agent.

mail transfer agent (MTA) — An e-mail server.

mail user agent (MUA) — A program that allows e-mail to be read by a user.

mainboard — A circuit board that connects all other hardware components together via slots or ports on the circuit board; also called a motherboard.

major number (kernel) — The number preceding the first dot in the number used to identify a Linux kernel version. It is used to denote a major change or modification.

major number (device file) — Used by the kernel to identify what device driver to call to interact properly with a given category of hardware; hard disk drives, CD-ROMs, and video cards are all categories of hardware; similar devices share a common major number.

manual pages — The most common set of local command syntax documentation, available by typing the man command-line utility. Also known as man pages.

Master Boot Record (MBR) — The area of a hard disk outside of a partition, which stores partition information and boot loaders.

maximum resolution — The best clarity of an image displayed to the screen; it is determined by the number of pixels making up the image (i.e. 640×480 pixels).

mcedit editor (Midnight Commander Editor) — A user-friendly terminal text editor that supports regular expressions and the computer mouse.

media access method — A system that defines how computers on a network share access to the physical medium.

metacharacters — Key combinations that have special meaning in the Linux operating system.

mingetty — A program used to display a login prompt on a character based terminal.

MINIX — Mini-UNIX, created by Andrew Tannenbaum. Instructions on how to code the kernel for this version of the UNIX operating system were publicly available. Using this as a starting point, Linus Torvalds improved this version of UNIX for the Intel platform and created the first version of Linux.

minor number (kernel) — The number following the first dot in the number used to identify a Linux kernel version, denoting a minor modification. If odd, it is a version under development and not yet fully tested. *See* developmental kernel and production kernel.

minor number (device file) — Used by the kernel to identify which specific hardware device, within a given category, to use a driver to communicate with; *see* **major number**.

mkbootdisk command — The command used to create a boot floppy diskette.

mkdir command — The command used to create directories.

mkfs command — A command used to format or create filesystems.

mknod command — A command used to recreate a device file provided the major number, minor number, and type (character or bock) are known.

mode — That part of the inode that stores information on access permissions.

modprobe command — The command used to insert a module and all necessary prerequisite modules into the Linux kernel.

monitoring — The process by which system areas are observed for problems or irregularities.

more command — A Linux command used to display a text file page-by-page and line-by-line on the terminal screen.

motherboard — *See* mainboard.

mount command — A command used to mount filesystems on devices to mount point directories.

mount point — The directory in a file structure to which something is mounted.

mounting — A process used to associate a device with a directory in the logical directory tree such that users may store data on that device.

mouseconfig — A command used to configure a mouse for use by X Windows.

Multi User–Mode — Also called runlevel 2; it provides most daemons and a partial set of networking daemons.

multihomed hosts — A computer that has more than one network interface.

Multiple Processor Statistics (mpstat) command — The command that displays CPU statistics.

Multiplexed Information and Computing Service (MULTICS) — A prototype time-sharing operating system that was developed in the late 1960's by AT&T Bell Laboratories.

multitasking — A type of operating system that has the ability to manage multiple tasks simultaneously.

multiuser — A type of operating system that has the ability to provide access to multiple users simultaneously.

mv (move) command — The command used to move/rename files and directories.

named pipe file — A temporary connection that sends information from one command or process in memory to another; it can also be represented by a file on the filesystem.

nedit editor — A commonly used graphical text editor available in most Linux distributions.

netconfig — A graphical utility used to configure the network card settings of a computer.

netmask — Specifies which portion of the IP address identifies the logical network the computer is on; also known as network mask or subnet mask.

network — Two or more computers joined together via network media and able to exchange information.

Network File System (NFS) — A distributed file system developed by Sun Microsystems that allows computers of differing types to access files shared on the network.

network installation — An installation where the installation source files are accessed across the network from a network share.

network interface card (NIC) — A hardware device used to connect a computer to a network of other computers and communicate or exchange information on it.

network server — A computer with files shared out on the network for other computers to access.

newgrp command — The command used to change temporarily the primary group of a user.

newsgroup — An Internet protocol service accessed via an application program called a newsreader. This service allows access to postings (e-mails in a central place accessible by all newsgroup users) normally organized along specific themes. Users with questions on specific topics can post messages, which may be answered by other users.

nice command — The command used to change the priority of a process as it is started.

nice value (NI) — The value that indirectly represents the priority of a process; the higher the value, the lower the priority.

NTLOADER — The boot loader used to boot Windows NT/2000/XP operating system kernels.

od command — A Linux command used to display the contents of a file in octal format.

Open Source Software (OSS) — Programs distributed and licensed so that the source code making up the program is freely available to anyone who wants to examine, utilize, or improve upon it.

operating system (OS) — Software used to control and directly interact with the computer hardware components.

options — Specific letters that start with a dash "-" or two and appear after the command name to alter the way the command works.

other — When used in the mode of a certain file or directory, it refers to all users on the Linux system.

overclocked — Running a processor at a higher clock speed than it has been rated for.

owner — The user whose name appears in a long listing of a file or directory and who has the ability to change permissions on that file or directory.

package manager — A system that defines a standard package format and can be used to install, query, and remove packages.

packet internet groper (ping) command — The command used to check TCP/IP connectivity on a network.

packets — Packages of data formatted by a network protocol.

parallel port — *See* LPT port.

parent process — A process that has started other processes (child processes).

parent process ID (PPID) — The PID of the parent process that created the current process.

partitions — Used to divide up a hard disk into smaller areas for ease of use; partitions may be primary or extended.

passwd command — The command used to modify the password associated with a user account.

patch command — The command used to apply a patch to the Linux kernel source cod.

PATH variable — A variable that stores a list of directories that will be searched in order when commands are executed without an absolute or relative pathname.

peripheral component — A component that attaches to the mainboard of a computer and provides a specific function such as a video card, mouse, or keyboard.

Peripheral Component Interconnect (PCI) — The most common motherboard connection slot found in computers today, which can transfer information at a speed of 33MHz and use DMA (Direct Memory Access).

permissions — A list of who can access a file or folder, and their level of access.

Personal Computer Memory Card International Association (PCMCIA) — A mainboard connection technology that allows a small card to be inserted with the electronics necessary to provide a certain function.

physical memory — A storage area for information that is directly wired through circuit boards to the processor.

pico editor — A terminal text editor with shortcut keys for common commands; pico stands for PIne COmposer.

pipe — A string of commands connected by " | " metacharacters.

Plug-and-Play (PnP) — The process allowing devices automatically to be assigned required IRQ, I/O address, and DMA information by the system BIOS.

polling — The act of querying devices to see if they have services that need to be run.

port — A number that uniquely identifies a network service.

Postscript — A non-text file format that is commonly used in documents.

Power On Self Test (POST) — An initial series of tests run when a computer is powered on to ensure that hardware components are functional.

PowerPC — A processor architecture developed by Motorola.

primary group — The group that is specified for a user in the /etc/passwd file and that is specified as group owner for all files created by a user.

primary partitions — The major unique and separate divisions into which an HDD can be divided (up to four are allowed per HDD).

print job — Information sent to a printer for printing.

print job ID — A unique numeric identifier used to mark and distinguish each print job.

print queue — A directory on the filesystem that holds print jobs that are waiting to be printed.

printer aliases — An alternate name by which a printer can be identified.

printing — The process by which print jobs are sent from a print queue to a printer.

priority — The importance of system information when logging system events.

proactive maintenance — The measures taken to reduce future system problems.

process — A program currently loaded into physical memory and running on the system.

process ID (PID) —A unique identifier assigned to every process as it begins.

process priority (PRI) — A number assigned to a process, used to determine how many time slices on the processor it will receive; the higher the number, the lower the priority.

process state — The current state of the process on the processor; most processes are in the sleeping or running state.

production kernel — A Linux kernel whose minor number (the number after the dot in the version number) is even and deemed stable for use through widespread testing.

program — A structured set of commands stored in an executable file on a filesystem; it may be executed to create a process.

Programmable Read Only Memory (PROM) — A blank ROM computer chip that can be written to once and never rewritten again.

programming language — The syntax used for developing a program. There are different programming languages that use different syntax.

protocol — A set of rules of communication used between computers on a network.

ps command — The command used to obtain information about processes currently running on the system.

PS/2 ports — Small round mainboard connectors developed by IBM with six pins that typically connect keyboards and mice to the computer.

pwconv command — The command used to enable the use of the /etc/shadow file.

pwd (print working directory) command — A Linux command used to display the current directory in the directory tree.

pwunconv command — The command used to disable the use of the /etc/shadow file.

Qt toolkit — The software toolkit used with the KDE Desktop Environment.

quota command — A command used to view disk quotas imposed on a user.

quotaoff command — A command used to deactivate disk quotas.

quotaon command — A command used to activate disk quotas.

quotas — Limits that may be imposed upon users and groups for filesystem usage.

RAM Digital Analog Converter (RAMDAC) chip — Used to convert the digital video images used by the computer to the analog format needed for the monitor.

Rambus Dynamic Random Access Memory (RDRAM) — A proprietary type of RAM developed by the Rambus Corporation.

Random Access Memory (RAM) — A computer chip able to store information, which is then lost when there is no power to the system.

rawrite — A Windows utility that can be used to create installation boot disks.

reactive maintenance — The measures taken when system problems arise.

read command — A command used to read Standard Input from a user into a variable.

Read Only Memory (ROM) — A computer chip able to store information in a static permanent manner, even when there is no power to the system.

recursive — Referring to itself and its own contents; a recursive search includes all subdirectories in a directory and their contents.

Red Hat — One of the most popular and prevalent distributions of Linux in North America, distributed and supported by Red Hat Inc.

Red Hat Package Manager (RPM) — The most commonly used package manager for Linux.

Red Hat Printer Configuration Tool — A graphical utility used to configure printers on the system.

Red Hat User Manager — A graphical utility used to manage users and groups on the system.

redirection — The process of changing the default locations of Standard Input, Standard Output, and Standard Error.

Reduced Instruction Set Computer (RISC) processors — Relatively fast processors that understand small instruction sets.

Redundant Array of Inexpensive Disks (RAID) — A type of storage that can be used to combine hard disks together for fault-tolerance.

refresh rate — The rate at which information displayed on a video screen is refreshed, measured in Hertz (Hz).

regular expressions (regexp) — Special metacharacters used to match patterns of text within text files; they are commonly used by many text tool commands such as grep.

REISER — A journaling filesystem used in Linux.

relative pathname — The pathname of a target directory relative to your current directory in the tree.

removable media — Information storage media that can be removed from a computer allowing transfer of data between machines.

renice command — The command used to alter the nice value of a process currently running on the system.

repquota command — A command used to produce a report on quotas for a particular filesystem.

resolution — The total number of pixels that can be displayed on a computer video screen horizontally and vertically.

restore command — The command used to extract archives created with the dump command.

revision number — The number after the second dot in the version number of a Linux kernel, which identifies the certain release number of a kernel.

rm command — The command used to remove files and directories.

rmdir command — The command used to remove empty directories.

rmmod command — The command that removes a module from the Linux kernel.

rogue process — A process that has become faulty in some way and continues to consume far more system resources than it should.

root filesystem — The filesystem that contains most files that make up the operating system; it should have enough free space to prevent errors and slow performance.

route table — A table of information used to indicate which networks are connected to network interfaces.

routers — Devices capable of transferring packets from one network to another.

routing — The act of forwarding data packets from one network to another.

rpm command —The command used to install, query, and remove RPM packages.

runlevel — A term that defines a certain type and number of daemons on a Linux system.

runlevel command — The command used to display the current and most recent previous runlevel.

s390 (Mainframe) — An IBM-developed Mainframe architecture.

Sawfish Window Manager — The window manager that works under the GNOME Desktop Environment.

scalability — The ability of computers to increase workload as the number of processors increases.

Scalable Processor Architecture (SPARC) — A RISC processor architecture developed by Sun Microsystems; UltraSPARC is a form of this architecture.

SCSI ID — Uniquely identifies and prioritizes devices attached to a SCSI controller.

search engine — An Internet Web site that allows one to search the World Wide Web for specific information using keywords to conduct a search.

sector — The smallest unit of data storage on a hard disk; sectors are arranged into concentric circles called tracks and may be grouped into blocks for use by the system.

serial port — *See* COM port.

server — A computer configured to allow other computers to connect to it from across a network.

server services — Services that are made available for other computers across a network.

set command — A command used to view all variables in the shell except special variables.

setserial command — The command used to set the parameters of serial device.

shareware — Programs developed and provided at minimal cost to the end user. These programs are initially free but require payment after a period of time or usage.

shell — A user interface that accepts input from the user and passes the input to the kernel for processing.

shell scripts — Text files that contain a list of commands or constructs for the shell to execute in order.

SILO — A program used to boot Linux on SPARC processor architecture computers.

Single In-line Memory Modules (SIMM) — An older type of memory stick that connects to the mainboard using connectors along only one edge.

Single User Mode — Also called runlevel 1; it provides a single terminal and a limited set of services.

skeleton directory — A directory that contains files that are copied to all new users' home directories upon creation; the default skeleton directory on Linux systems is /etc/skel.

Small Computer Systems Interface (SCSI) — Consists of controllers that can connect several SCSI HDDs to the mainboard and control the flow of data to and from the SCSI HDDs.

smbclient utility — The utility used to connect to shared resources on a Windows system.

smbmount command — A command used to mount directories from Windows computers to mount points on Linux computers.

socket file — A named pipe connecting processes on two different computers; it can also be represented by a file on the filesystem.

soft limit — A limit imposed that can be exceeded for a certain period of time.

software — Programs stored on a storage device in a computer that provide a certain function when executed.

Solaris — A version of UNIX developed by Sun Microsystems from AT&T source code.

sort command — A command used to sort lines in a file.

source code — The sets of organized instructions on how to function and perform tasks that defines or constitutes a program.

source file/directory — The portion of a command that refers to the file or directory from which information is taken.

spanning — A type of RAID level 0 that allows two or more devices to be represented as a single large volume.

special device file — A file used to identify hardware devices such as hard disks and serial ports.

spooling — The process of accepting a print job into a print queue.

standalone daemons — Daemons normally started at boot-up that configure themselves without assistance from the Internet Super Daemon.

Standard Error — Represents any error messages generated by a command.

Standard Input — Represents information inputed to a command during execution.

Standard Output — Represents the desired output from a command.

started printer — A printer that will send print jobs from the print queue to a printer.

startx — A command used to start X Windows and the associated window manager and desktop environment.

Static RAM (SRAM) — An expensive type of RAM commonly used in computer chips on the mainboard and which has a fast access speed.

stopped printer — A printer that will not send print jobs from the print queue to a printer.

strings command — A Linux command used to search for and display text characters in a binary file.

subdirectory — A directory that resides within another directory in the directory tree.

subnet mask — A series of four 8-bit numbers that determine the network and host portions of an IP address.

subshell — A shell started by the current shell.

superblock — That portion of a file system that stores critical information such as the inode table and block size.

SuperProbe — A program used to determine the computer's video adapter card properties.

superscalar — Refers to the ability of a computer processor to complete more than one command in a single cycle.

SuSE — One of the most popular and prevalent distributions of Linux in Europe.

swap memory — *See* virtual memory.

symbolic link — A pointer to another file on the same or another filesystem; commonly referred to as a shortcut.

Symmetric Multi-Processing (SMP) — Refers to a system containing more than one processor in which each processor shares tasks and memory space.

Synchronous Dynamic Random Access Memory (SDRAM) — A form of RAM that uses the standard DIMM connector and transfers data at a very fast rate.

syncing — The process of writing data to the hard disk drive that was stored in RAM.

System Activity Reporter (sar) command — The command that displays various system statistics.

system back-up — The process whereby files are copied to an archive.

system log daemon (syslogd) — The daemon that logs system events to various log files via information stored in /etc/syslog.conf.

system service — Additional functionality provided by a program that has been incorporated into and started as part of the operating system.

System Statistics (sysstat) package — A software package that contains common performance monitoring utilities such as mpstat, iostat, sar, and isag.

Tab Window Manager (twm) — One of the oldest window managers used on Linux systems.

Tab-completion — A feature of the BASH Shell that fills in the remaining characters of a unique filename or directory name when the user presses the Tab key.

tac command — A Linux command that displays a file to the screen beginning with the last line of the file and ending with the first line of the file.

tail command — A Linux command used to display the last several lines of text in a text file; by default the tail command displays the last 10 lines of the file.

tape archive (tar) command — The most common utility used to create archives.

tarball — A gzip-compressed tar archive.

target file/directory — The portion of a command that refers to the file or directory to which information is directed.

target ID — *See* SCSI ID.

tee command — A command used to take from Standard Input and send to both Standard Output and a specified file.

telinit command — An alias to the init command.

terminal — The channel that allows a certain user to log in and communicate with the kernel via a user interface.

terminator — A device used to terminate an electrical conduction medium to absorb the transmitted signal and prevent signal bounce.

test statement — A statement used to test a certain condition and generate a True/False value.

text editor — A program that allows the creation, modification, and manipulation of a text file.

text file — A file that stores information in a readable text format.

text tools — Programs that allow for the creation, modification, and searching of text files.

text-based installation — An installation method that presents interactive material in a command-line text-based format rather than a GUI-based interface.

time slice — The amount of time a process is given on a CPU in a multiprocessing operating system.

Token Ring — A popular media access method.

top command — The command used to give real-time information about the most active processes on the system; it may also be used to renice or kill processes.

Total Cost of Ownership (TCO) — The full sum of all accumulated costs, over and above the simple purchase price of utilizing a product. It includes such sundries as training, maintenance, additional hardware, and downtime.

touch command — The command used to create new files. It was originally used to update the timestamp on a file.

tr command — A command used to transform or change characters received from Standard Input.

traceroute command — A command used to trace the path a packet takes through routers to a destination host.

track — The area on a hard disk that forms a concentric circle of sectors.

trapping — The process of ignoring a kill signal.

troubleshooting procedures — The tasks performed when solving system problems.

trusted access — A configuration where computers are allowed to access a given computer without having to provide a password first.

tune2fs command — A command used to modify ext2 and ext3 filesystem parameters.

ulimit command — The command used to modify process limit parameters in the current shell.

umask — Used to alter the permissions on all new files and directories by taking select default file and directory permissions away.

umask command — The command used to view and change the umask variable.

umount command — A command used to break the association between a device and a directory in the logical directory tree.

uncompress command — The command used to decompress files compressed by the compress command.

Universal Serial Bus (USB) — A mainboard connection technology that allows data transfer speeds of up to 480Mb per second and is used for many peripheral components today such as mice, printers, and scanners.

UNIX — The first true multitasking, multiuser operating system, developed by Ken Thompson and Dennis Ritchie, from which Linux originated.

user — When used in the mode of a certain file or directory, it refers to the owner of that file or directory.

user account — Information regarding a user that is stored in a system database (/etc/passwd and /etc/shadow), which may be used to log in to the system and gain access to system resources.

User Identifier (UID) — A unique number assigned to each user account.

user interface —What the user sees and uses to interact with the operating system and application programs.

user process — A process begun by a user that runs on a terminal.

user-defined variables — Variables that are created by the user and are not used by the system—these variables are typically exported to subshells.

useradd command — The command used to add a user account to the system.

userdel command — The command used to remove a user account from the system.

usermod command — The command used to modify the properties of a user account on the system.

variable — An area of memory used to store information—variables are created from entries in environment files when the shell is first created after login and are destroyed when the shell is destroyed upon logout.

variable identifier — The name of a variable.

vfat (virtual file allocation table) — A non-journaling filesystem that may be used in Linux.

vi editor — A powerful command line text editor available on most UNIX and Linux systems.

video adapter card — A peripheral component used to display graphical images to a computer monitor.

virtual memory — An area on a hard disk (swap partition) that can be used to store information that normally resides in physical memory (RAM), if the physical memory is being used excessively.

vmlinuz-<kernel version> — The Linux kernel file.

vmstat command — The command used to display memory, CPU, and swap statistics.

volatile — Refers to information storage devices that store information only when there is electrical flow; conversely, non-volatile information storage devices store information even when there is no electrical flow.

VSync (vertical refresh) — The rate at which vertical elements of the video screen image are refreshed, measured in Hertz (Hz.)

well-known ports — Of the 65535 possible ports, the ones from 0 to 1024 used by common networking services.

which command — The command used to locate files that exist within directories listed in the PATH variable.

Wide Area Networks (WAN) — A network of computers separated geographically by large distances.

wildcard metacharacters — Metacharacters used to match certain characters in a file or directory name; they are often used to specify multiple files.

Window Maker Window Manager — A common window manager used on Linux systems.

window manager — The GUI component that is responsible for determining the appearance of the windows drawn on the screen by X Windows.

workstation — A computer used to connect to services on a server.

workstation services — Services that are used on a local computer.

X client — The component of X Windows that requests graphics to be drawn from the X server and displays them on the terminal screen.

X Display Manager (xdm) — Presents a graphical login screen to users.

X server — The component of X Windows that draws graphics to windows on the terminal screen.

X Windows — The component of the Linux GUI that displays graphics to windows on the terminal screen.

X Windows — The core component of the GUI in Linux.

Xconfigurator — A program that is used to configure video adapter card and monitor information for use by X Windows.

xedit editor — A commonly used graphical text editor available in most Linux distributions.

xemacs editor — A graphical version of the emacs text editor.

xf86config — A text-based X Windows configuration program that ships with X Windows; it allows the configuration of keyboard, mouse, video adapter card, and monitor information for use by X Windows.

XFree86 — The Open Source licensed version of X Windows version 11.

xvidtune — A program used to fine-tune the vsync and hsync video card settings for use in X Windows.

zcat command — The command used to view the contents of an archive created with compress or gzip to Standard Output.

zip disk — A removable information storage unit similar to a floppy disk that can store much more information than floppy disks and are used in zip drives.

zmore command — The command used to view the contents of an archive created with compress or gzip to Standard Output in a page-by-page fashion.

zombie process — A process that has finished executing, but whose parent has not yet released its PID; it still retains a spot in the kernel's process table.

Index

Special Characters

\~(backslash), 105
< (left angle bracket), 359
> (right angle bracket), 359
~ (tilde), 105, 127–128
! (exclamation point), 386
" (quotation mark), 105
$ (dollar sign), 105, 149
&& (double ampersands), 389–390
& (ampersand), 105
' (single quote), 105
( ) (parentheses), 105
(...|...) (parentheses with pipe), 149
* (asterisk), 105, 133, 134, 137, 149
+ (plus sign), 149
-> (arrow), 134
- (dash), 130, 134
/ (forward slash), 128, 133
= (equal sign), 133
? (question mark), 105, 137, 149
@ (at sign), 133
[ ] (square brackets), 105, 137, 149
[^] (square brackets with caret), 149
<<<>>> (input/output redirection), 105
(curly brackets), 105, 149
^ (caret), 149
_ (underscore), 130
` (backquote), 105
|| (double pipes), 389–390
| (pipe), 105, 133, 363, 364
.. (double period), 128
. (period), 128, 130, 149
; (semicolon), 105
exclamation point (!), 386

A

ABOOT, 328
absolute pathname, 126–127
Accelerated Graphics Port (AGP), 55–56
active partition, 410

advanced hardware configuration, 302–310
    mainboard flow control, 305–308
    plug-and-play, 308
    RAID, 309–310
    SCSI hard drives, 302–304
advanced installation, 301–343
    hard disk, 316–319
    hardware configuration. See advanced hardware configuration
    network-based. See network installation
    non-Intel architectures, 327–330
    text-based CD-ROM installation, 311–316
    troubleshooting. See troubleshooting installation
Advanced Power Management (APM), 57
Advanced Technology Attachment (ATA) controllers, 52
advantages of Linux, 10–15
af keyword, /etc/printcap file, 548
AGP (Accelerated Graphics Port), 55–56
AIX UNIX, 17
alert priority, system log daemon, 552
aliases, 192
    printers, 543–544
--all option, ls command, 136
--almost-all option, ls command, 136
Alpha, Linux installation, 328–330
ampersand (&), background command execution, 105
-a operator, test statements, 386
-A option
    cpio utility, 608
    fsck command, 277
    ls command, 136
    sar command, 659
    tar utility, 602
-a option
    fsck command, 277
    lpq command, 536

ls command, 135–136
    ps command, 496–497
    rpm command, 626
Apache server, 66
Apache Web server, 725
APM (Advanced Power Management), 57
apm file, 337
append= keyword, LILO, 413, 414
applications, 2
    problems related to, 648–649
application servers, 29–30
apropos command, 109
architecture, 48
archives, 601
arguments, 103
arithmetic logic unit, 48
-AR option, fsck command, 277
arrow (->), filenames, 134
Artistic License, 9
ascii command, FTP, 712
ASMP (ASymmetric Multi-Processing), 50
asterisk (*)
    executable files, 133
    regular expression, 149
    shell wildcard, 105, 134, 137
ASymmetric Multi-Processing (ASMP), 50
ATA (Advanced Technology Attachment) controllers, 52
at command, 509–512
at daemon (atd) command, 509–512
atd (at daemon) command, 509–512
at sign (@), linked files, 133
AT&T Bell Laboratories, 16, 17
a2ps command, 535
authentication, 93–94, 555–559
auth facility, system log daemon, 551
authpriv facility, system log daemon, 551
auto_irq keyword, setserial command, 653

B

background (bg) command, 504–505

background command execution (&), 105

background processes, 503–506

backquote (`), command substitution, 105

backslash (' " \) metacharacter quote, 105

back-up. *See* system back-up

bad blocks, 275

baseline, 654

bash command, 507

BASH Shell (Bourne Again Shell), 99–100, 357–391

  command input and output, 358–369

  shell scripts. *See* shell scripts

  shell variables. *See* shell variable(s)

BASH variable, 375

BASH_VERSION variable, 375

Basic Input/Output System. *See* BIOS (Basic Input/Output System) ROM

Basic Input/Output System (BIOS), 64

Beowulf clustering, 31

Berkeley Software Distribution (BSD), 17

--best option, gzip utility, 598

bfs filesystem, 248

bg (background) command, 504–505

binary command, FTP, 712

binary files

  data files, 130

  displaying contents, 145–147

binary programs, execution, 503

BIND/DNS, 725

BIND/DNS server, 66

/bin directory, 188

BIOS (Basic Input/Output System), 64

BIOS (Basic Input/Output System) ROM, 51

  problems starting installation, 331

bits, 49

block devices, 244

blocks on hard disks, 263

  bad, 275

/boot directory, 188, 410

boot disks

  creating, 78–79, 97, 324, 650

  starting installation, 80

/boot/grub/grub.conf file, 422

booting, dual. *See* dual booting Linux

boot= keyword, LILO, 413

boot loaders, 410, 411–426

  configuring, 89–90

  dual booting Linux, 419–426

  GRUB, 415–419

  LILO, 411–415

boot.log file, 341–343, 548

boot process, 410–411

-B option

  cpio utility, 608

  sar command, 659

-b option

  dump/restore utility, 611

  sar command, 659

Bourne Again Shell. *See* BASH Shell (Bourne Again Shell)

BSD (Berkeley Software Distribution), 17

bunzip2 command, 600

buses, 55

business needs, meeting with Linux, 11–12

bus mastering, 653

bye command, FTP, 712

bzcat command, 600

--bzip option, tar utility, 603

bzip2 utility, 599–601

C

caches, 49

cal command, 104

Caldera Linux, 19, 23

caret (^), regular expression, 149

case construct, 387–389

cat command, 138–139

The Cathedral and the Bazaar (Raymond), 18

cd (change directory) command, 127

  FTP, 712, 714

cdfs filesystem, 248

CD-ROM disks, 54–55, 259–261

  mounting, 260–261

text-based installation, 311–316

central processing unit (CPU), 48–50

  overclocked, 332

certification, 745–751

  Linux+ certification objectives, 746–751

  reasons to become certified, 745–746

-Cf option, fsck command, 277

CGI (Common Gateway Interface), 27

chage command, 564–565

change directory (cd) command, 127

  FTP, 712, 714

change group (chgrp) command, 204–205

change mode (chmod) command, 210–214

change owner (chown) command, 203–204

changing permissions, 210–214

character devices, 244

chgrp (change group) command, 204–205

child processes, 492

chipsets, 457

chmod (change mode) command, 210–214

chown (change owner) command, 203–204

chsh command, 565

CISC (Complex Instruction Set Computing) processors, 48

--classify option, ls command, 136

clear command, 104

clockchips, 458

clock speed, 48–49

close command, FTP, 712

closed source licenses, 9–10

closed source software, 8

cluster(s), 31

clustering, 31

cmdline file, 337

CMOS (Complementary Metal-Oxide Semiconductor) chips, 51, 308

color depth, monitors, 58

--color=n option, ls command, 136

| | command, 134

command(s). *See also specific commands*
 arguments, 103
 filter, 365–366
 halting and rebooting, 112
 help, 106–111
 input and output, BASH shell, 358–369
 options, 103
 piping, 363–369
 redirection, 359–363
 shell, 103–105
command grouping, 105
command mode, vi editor, 153, 154–156
command piping, 105
command substitution, 105
command termination, 105
Common Gateway Interface (CGI), 27
Complementary Metal-Oxide Semiconductor (CMOS) chips, 51, 308
Complex Instruction Set Computing (CISC) processors, 48
COM ports, 57
compress command, 594
compression, 594–601
 bzip2 utility, 599–601
 compress utility, 594–596
 gzip utility, 596–599
compression algorithms, 594
compress utility, 594–596
concatenation, 138–139
configure file, 618
configuring
 daemon startup, 434–436
 firewall, 90, 91
 NIC, 90, 91
 NIC interfaces, 692–699
 PPP interfaces, 699–707
 printers, 537–548
 X Windows, 97, 98, 457–475
connecting to network resources, 711–722
 accessing e-mail, 719–722
 accessing Windows files, 715–717
 FTP, 711–714
 NFS, 714–715

running remote applications, 717–719
connectors, SCSI, 304
&& construct, 389–390
|| construct, 389–390
control unit, 48
-c option
 bzip2 utility, 600
 compress command, 596
 cpio utility, 608
 gzip utility, 598
 sar command, 659
 tar utility, 602, 606
 useradd command, 563
 usermod command, 564
-C option, ls command, 136
copying, files, 253–254
copying files, 191–192
copy in/out (cpio) utility, 607–609
cost reduction with Linux, 15
cp command, 191–192, 253–254
cpio (copy in/out) utility, 607–609
CPU. *See* central processing unit (CPU)
cpuinfo file, 333–334, 337
crackers, 17
crit priority, system log daemon, 552
crond (cron daemon) command, 509, 512–516
cron facility, system log daemon, 551
cron file, 548
crontab command, 513
cron tables, 512–516
 system, 514–516
 user, 513–514
curly brackets ()
 command grouping, 105
 regular expression, 149
customizing
 ease of, 13–14
 kernel. *See* kernel, customizing
cylinders on hard disks, 263

D

daemon(s), 410
 configuring startup, 434–436
 /etc/inittab file, 429–434

standalone, 724
 system log daemon, 551
daemon processes, 492
dash (-), filenames, 130, 134
database(s), 29–30
Database Management Systems (DBMSs), 30
data blocks, 199
data files, binary, 130
date command, 104
DBMSs (Database Management Systems), 30
Debian Linux, 23
Debian Package Manager, 22
debug priority, system log daemon, 552
decision constructs, 382–390
 case construct, 387–389
 && construct, 389–390
 || construct, 389–390
 if construct, 382–387
--decompress option, gzip utility, 598
default gateway, 691
default= keyword, LILO, 413
default permissions, 214–216
deleting
 files, 193
 user accounts, 565–566
dependencies, 648
--dereference option, tar utility, 603
desktop environment, 451
desktop publishing software, 35
Desktop Switching Tool, 457
/dev directory, 188, 244–247
developmental kernel, 5
device drivers, 3
device files, 244–247
 tape, 601
devices file, 337
/dev/mouse, 469
df command, 272–273
DHCP (Dynamic Host Configuration Protocol) servers, 65
Dial In-line Memory Modules (DIMMs), 50–51
Digital Subscriber Line (DSL), PPP interface, 700, 703, 704–705
DIMMs (Dial In-line Memory Modules), 50–51

dir command, FTP, 712

Direct Memory Access (DMA), 55, 307–308

directories, 126. *See also specific directories*

changing, 127–129

creating, 189–190

home, 127

skeleton, 562

structure. *See* directory structure

users (owners), 207

directory structure, 126–129

disabled printers, 532

disable keyword, lpc command, 533

disk drives, 52–55

CD-ROM disks, 54–55

hard disk drives, 52–54

removable media, 54

zip disks, 54

Disk Druid, 87

disk mirroring, 309

disk striping, 309

Disk Striping with Parity, 310

disk usage, monitoring, 272–275

displaying. *See also* viewing

binary file contents, 145–147

text file contents, 138–145

DISPLAY variable, 375

distributions of Linux, 19, 20–23

DMA (Direct Memory Access), 55, 307–308

dmesg file, 338–341, 548

DNS (Domain Name Space), 708, 710

DNS servers, 65

DNS services, Internet servers, 38

documentation, 643

dollar sign ($)

regular expression, 149

shell variable, 105

Domain Name Space (DNS), 708, 710

-d option

bzip2 utility, 600

cpio utility, 608

sar command, 659

useradd command, 563

usermod command, 564

dot (period) (.), current directory, 128

&& construct, 389–390

double dot (double period) (..), root directory, 128

| | command, 134

| | construct, 389–390

down keyword, lpc command, 533

DRAM (Dynamic RAM), 50–51

DSL (Digital Subscriber Line), PPP interface, 700, 703, 704–705

dual booting Linux, 419–426

FIPS, 422–424

LILO or GRUB, 420–422

Windows boot loaders, 424–426

du command, 273–274

dump command, 256

dumpe2fs command, 274–275

dump/restore utility, 610–615

Dynamic Host Configuration Protocol (DHCP) servers, 65

Dynamic RAM (DRAM), 50–51

E

echo command, 381

editing text files, 152–166

emacs editor, 163

gedit editor, 165, 166

kedit editor, 165, 166

mcedit editor, 162–163

nedit editor, 164, 165

pico editor, 161–162

vi editor, 152–161

xedit editor, 164, 165

xemacs editor, 163–164

EEPROM (Electronically Erasable Programmable Read Only Memory), 51

-ef option, ps command, 495

egrep command, 149

Electronically Erasable Programmable Read Only Memory (EEPROM), 51

Emacs (Editor MACroS) editor, 66, 163

e-mail, 719–722

emerg priority, system log daemon, 552

enabled printers, 532

enable keyword, lpc command, 533

engineering workstations, 31–32

Enlightenment Window Manager, 453, 457

enscript command, 535

env command, 376

environment files, 378–379

environment variables, 369–375

ENV variable, 375

-e option

crontab command, 513

ps command, 494–495, 498

rpm command, 625, 626

useradd command, 563

usermod command, 564

EPROM (Erasable Programmable Read Only Memory), 51

equal sign (=), sockets, 133

Erasable Programmable Read Only Memory (EPROM), 51

error(s), checking filesystems, 275–278

error codes, LILO, 415

error (err) priority, system log daemon, 552

escape sequences, 381–382

/etc/cron.allow file, 513

/etc/cron.d directory, 513

/etc/cron.deny file, 513

/etc/crontab file, 513, 514–516

/etc/default/useradd file, 562

/etc directory, 188

/etc/dumpdates file, 610, 612–613

/etc/group file, 559–560, 566–567

/etc/host.conf file, 710

/etc/hosts.equiv file, 718

/etc/hosts file, 709, 710

/etc/init.d directory, 435

/etc/inittab file, 429–434

/etc/login.defs command, 561–562

/etc/logrotate.conf file, 553–555

/etc/modules.conf file, 666, 692–693

/etc/passwd file, 555, 556–557, 559, 565, 728

/etc/ppp/chap-secrets file, 706

/etc/ppp/pap-secrets file, 706

/etc/printcap file, 537, 547–548

/etc/printcap.local file, 546–547

/etc/rc.d/init.d directory, 434–435

/etc/rc.d/rc*.d directories, 434–435

/etc/rc.d/rc.local file, 666

/etc/resolv.conf file, 710

/etc/shadow file, 555, 556, 557–559, 563, 565, 728
/etc/sysconfig/iptables command, 726
/etc/sysconfig/network-scripts/ifcfg-eth0 file, 694
/etc/sysconfig/network-scripts/ifcfg-ppp1 file, 704–705
/etc/sysconfig/static-routes command, 727
/etc/sysct1.conf file, 727
/etc/syslog.conf file, 549–550
/etc/X11/gdm/gdm.conf file, 456
/etc/xinetd.conf file, 723–724
/etc/xinetd.d/telnet file, 724
/etc/X11/XF86Config file, 460
Ethernet, 691
EUID variable, 375
! command, FTP, 712
! operator, test statements, 386
exclamation point (!), test statement operator, 386
--exclude option, tar utility, 602
execdomains file, 337
executable programs, 131
execute permission, 209–210
exit command, 104
export command, 376, 377
extended partitions, 53
ext2 filesystem, 86, 248
ext3 filesystem, 248

F

facility, /etc/syslog.conf file, 550
FAQs (Frequently Asked Questions), 14
--fast option, gzip utility, 598
"fatal signal 11" error message, 332
fb file, 337
fdisk command, 266–270
Feeble Virtual Window Manager (fvwm), 453, 454, 457
fg (foreground) command, 504, 505
fgrep command, 149–150
FHS (Filesystem Hierarchy Standard), 188–189
file(s). See also specific files
   copying, 191–192, 253–254
   deleting, 193
   device, 244–247

downloading using FTP, 711–714
   environment, 378–379
   finding, 194–198
   hidden, 130
   linking, 130, 199–202
   listing, 132–137
   log. See log files
   mode, 206, 207–208
   moving, 191
   renaming, 190–191
   searching for text within. See searching for text in files
   types, 129–130. See also binary files; named pipe files; special device files; text files
   Windows, accessing, 715–717
file command, 134–135
file descriptors, 358
filehandles, 649
filename(s), 130–131
filename extensions, 131
file servers, 28–29
/ filesystem, 272
filesystem(s), 53, 86–87, 125–167. See also directories; file(s); text files
   administration. See filesystem administration
   creating (formatting), 247
   foot, 250
   Linux directory structure, 126–129
   management. See filesystem management; permissions
   monitoring. See filesystem monitoring
   root, 250
   types, 247–248
filesystem administration, 243–282
   CD-ROMs, 259–261
   /dev directory, 244–247
   filesystem types, 247–248
   floppy disks, 250–259
   hard disk quotas, 278–282
   hard disks, 262–271
   monitoring filesystems. See filesystem monitoring
   mounting, 249–250
filesystem corruption, 275–278
Filesystem Hierarchy Standard (FHS), 188–189
filesystem management, 187–221

FHS, 188–189
   finding files, 194–198
   linking files, 199–202
   managing files and directories, 189–194
   permissions. See Permissions
filesystem monitoring, 272–278
   checking for errors, 275–278
   disk usage, 272–275
filesystems file, 337
File Transfer Protocol (FTP), 711–714
   FTP server, 66
   FTP services of Internet servers, 26
   network installations, 321–322, 326
filter commands, 365–366
financial software, 35
find command, 195–197
finding, files, 194–198
finger command, 104
FIPS (First non-destructive Interactive Partition Splitter), 422–424
firewalls
   configuring, 90, 91
   Internet servers, 26–27
Firewire (IEEE1394), 57
First non-destructive Interactive Partition Splitter (FIPS), 422–424
flexibility of Linux, 12–13
floppy disks, 240–259
   mounting, 250–253
foot filesystem, 250
-F option
   ls command, 136
   rpm command, 626
-f option
   bzip2 utility, 601
   compress command, 595, 596
   dump/restore utility, 611
   fsck command, 276, 277
   gzip utility, 598
   ls command, 136
   mv command, 192
   ps command, 494, 498
   rpm command, 625, 626
   sar command, 658, 659
   tar utility, 602, 604, 606

useradd command, 563
usermod command, 564
foreground (fg) command, 504, 505
foreground processes, 503
forking, 503
formatting, 247. *See also* mounting
/ filesystem, 272
FQDNs (Fully Qualified Domain Names), 28, 65, 708, 710
framebuffers, 81
free command, 663
Free Software Foundation (FSF), 9, 17
freeware, 10
freezing during installation, 332
Frequently Asked Questions (FAQs), 14
fsck command, 263, 276–278
FSF (Free Software Foundation), 9, 17
-F switch, ls command, 132–133, 134
FTP. *See* File Transfer Protocol (FTP)
FTP server, 66
FTP services of Internet servers, 26
full back-up, 610
--full-time option, ls command, 136
Fully Qualified Domain Names (FQDNs), 28, 65, 708, 710
fuser command, 255, 257
fvwm (Feeble Virtual Window Manager), 453, 454, 457

G

gateway, 65
gathering pre-installation information, 60–66
hardware information, 61–64
software information, 65–66
Gcc (GNU C Compiler), 616
Gdm (GNOME Display Manager), 100–101, 455–456
GDM Configurator, 456
GECOS (General Electric Comprehensive Operating System), 556
gedit editor, 165, 166
General Electric Comprehensive Operating System (GECOS), 556
get command, FTP, 712, 713
GID (group Identifier), 556

GIMP (GNU Image Manipulation Program), 34, 66, 452
Global Regular Expression Print, 149
GNOME (GNU Object Model Environment), 19, 20, 451, 452
GNOME desktop, 66
GNOME Desktop Environment, 452
GNOME Display Manager (gdm), 100–101, 455–456
Gnome Office, 36
GNOME RPM Manager, 626, 627
GNU C Compiler (gcc), 616
GNU Image Manipulation Program (GIMP), 34, 66, 452
GNU Object Model Environment (GNOME), 19, 20, 451, 452
GNU Project, 17
GNU Public License (GPL), 9, 18, 753–757
GNU zip (gzip) utility, 596–599
-G option
useradd command, 563
usermod command, 564
-g option
useradd command, 563
usermod command, 564
GPL (GNU Public License), 9, 18, 753–757
GRand Unified Bootloader (GRUB), 89, 415–419
dual booting, 411–415
graphical installation, 311
Graphical User Interfaces (GUIs), 3
GUI environments, 19, 258–259
Linux, components, 450–455
graphics editing software, 34
grep command, 149–152, 366, 376
group, 207
group(s)
GIDs, 556
managing, 566–567
primary, 556
Red Hat User Manager, 568–573
groupadd command, 566
groupdel command, 567
Group Identifier (GID), 556
groupmod command, 567
groups command, 567

GRUB. *See* GRand Unified Bootloader (GRUB)
grub-install command, 419
grub-md5-crypt command, 417
GRUB root partition, 416
GTK+ toolkit, 452
GUI environments, 19
floppy devices, 258–259
GUIs. *See* Graphical User Interfaces (GUIs)
gunzip command, 597
gzip (GNU zip) utility, 596–599

H

hackers, 17–18
The Hacker's Dictionary, 18
hard disk(s), 262–271
partitioning, 85–89, 262–265
physical structure, 263
quotas, 278–282
SCSI, configuration, 302–304
working with partitions, 266–271
hard disk installation, 316–319
hard limits, hard disk quotas, 278
hard links, 199–201
hardware, 2, 48–59. *See also specific hardware*
gathering pre-installation information, 61–64
troubleshooting, 645–648
video, configuring, 95–96
Hardware Compatibility List (HCL), 60
hardware configuration, advanced. *See* advanced hardware configuration
hardware platforms, Linux flexibility, 12–13
hashplings, 379–380
HCL (Hardware Compatibility List), 60
head command, 140
help, commands, 106–111
help command, FTP, 712
hfs filesystem, 248
hidden files, 130, 135
HISTFILESIZE variable, 375
HISTFILE variable, 375
history of Linux, 16–20
hacker culture, 17–18

Linux, 19–20
UNIX, 16–17
HISTSIZE variable, 375
home directory, 127
/home directory, 188
home directory variable (~), 105,
   127–128
HOME variable, 373, 375
-h option
   du command, 274
   gzip utility, 598
   lpr command, 534
   rpm command, 623, 626
   tar utility, 603
Horizontal refresh (HSync), 59
hostname(s), 65, 708–710
hostname command, 709
HOSTNAME variable, 375
hot fixes, 12
hot-swappable devices, 57
hpfs filesystem, 248
HP-UX, 17
HSync (horizontal refresh), 59
HTTP. See Hypertext Transfer
   Protocol (HTTP)
Hypertext Transfer Protocol
   (HTTP), 27
   network installations, 323,
      326–327

I
id command, 104, 567
IDE (Integrated Drive Electronics), 52
IEEE1394 (Firewire), 57
ifconfig command, 693
if construct, 382–387
ifdown command, 694
if keyword, /etc/printcap file, 548
image= keyword, LILO, 413
IMAP (Internet Mail Access
   Protocol), 719
IMAP Server, 725
incremental back-up, 610
Industry Standard Architecture
   (ISA) slots, 55
-info option, SuperProbe
   command, 459
info priority, system log daemon, 552

information pages, 110
init command, 428
init daemon, 410, 493
initrd= keyword, LILO, 413
INN (InterNetwork News), 28
INN (InterNetwork News) server,
   66, 725
inodes, 199
inode table, 199
Input/Output (I/O) addresses, 58,
   306–307
input/output redirection
   (<<<>>>), 105
Input/Output Statistics (iostat) utility, 655–656
insert mode, vi editor, 153–154
insmod command, 665
installation log file, 332–333
INSTALL file, 615
installing Linux, 78–99
   advanced installation. See advanced
      installation
   boot loader configuration, 89–90
   choosing language, 81, 82
   creating boot disks, 78–79, 97
   firewall configuration, 90, 91
   installation methods, 78
   keyboard and mouse configura-
      tion, 81–83
   monitor settings, 97, 98
   network configuration, 90, 91
   options, 84–85
   package installation, 96
   package selection, 94–95
   partitioning the hard disk, 85–89
   preparing for installation. See
      preparing for Linux installation
   problems. See troubleshooting
      installation
   starting installation, 80–81
   system language, 91–92
   time zone, 92
   user accounts and authentication,
      93–94
   video hardware configuration,
      95–96
   X Windows settings, 97, 98
install= keyword, LILO, 413
Integrated Drive Electronics
   (IDE), 52

Integrated Services Digital Network
   (ISDN), PPP interface, 700,
   702, 703
Interactive System Activity Grapher
   (isag) command, 660–662
Internet, 2
   finding Linux resources, 759–762
Internet Mail Access Protocol
   (IMAP), 719
Internet Mail Access Protocol
   (IMAP) Server, 725
Internet Protocol (IP) addresses, 28,
   65, 691–692
Internet servers, 24–28
   DNS services, 38
   firewalls and proxy services, 26–27
   FTP services, 26
   mail services, 25
   news services, 27–28
   routing, 25
   Web services, 27
Internet Super Daemon (xinetd),
   723–724
InterNetwork News (INN), 28
InterNetwork News (INN) server,
   66, 725
Interrupt Requests (IRQs), 58,
   305–306
interrupts file, 337
I/O (Input/Output) addresses, 58,
   306–307
iomem file, 337
ioports file, 334–336, 337
-i option
   cp command, 192
   cpio utility, 608
   dump/restore utility, 611
   grep command, 151
   rpm command, 623, 626
iostat (Input/Output Statistics) utility, 655–656
IP (Internet Protocol) addresses, 28,
   65, 691–692
IP forwarding, 727
iptables command, 726
irq keyword, setserial command, 653
IRQs (Interrupt Requests), 58,
   305–306
isag (Interactive System Activity
   Grapher) command, 660–662
isapnp file, 337

ISA (Industry Standard Architecture) slots, 55
ISDN (Integrated Services Digital Network), PPP interface, 700, 702, 703
iso9660 filesystem, 248
ISO images, 316–317
Itanium, Linux installation, 328

J

jabbering, 653
-j /dev/hdc5 option, mke2fs command, 271
JetDirect printers, configuring, 540, 541
jobs command, 504, 505
-j option, tar utility, 603
journaling, 87

K

-k command, man command, 108–109
kcore file, 337
KDE (Kommon Desktop Environment), 19, 20, 451, 452
KDE Control Center, 645
KDE desktop, 66
KDE Display Manager (kdm), 456
KDE Package Manager, 627
kdm (KDE Display Manager), 456
kedit editor, 165, 166
kernel(s), 4–6, 99
  customizing. *See* kernel, customizing
  loading, 410
  new, compiling, 666–671
  patching, 671
kernel, customizing, 664–671
  compiling new kernels, 666–671
  kernel modules, 664–666
  patching kernels, 671
kernel modules, 664–666
kernel versions of Linux, 5–6
kern facility, system log daemon, 551
keyboards, 59
  choosing configuration, 81, 82
keywords. *See also specific keywords*
  /etc/printcap file, 548
killall command, 502

kill command, 500–502
killing processes, 500–502
kill signals, 500–502
  trapping, 502
kmsg file, 337
Kommon Desktop Environment (KDE), 19, 20, 451, 452
-k option
  bzip2 utility, 601
  useradd command, 563
kppp utility, 707
ksyms file, 337
kudzu program, 646–647
K Window Manager (kwm), 451
kwm (K Window Manager), 451
kwm window manager, 453

L

label= keyword, LILO, 413
language
  installation, choosing, 81, 82
  system, choosing, 91–92
LANs (Local Area Networks), 690, 692
Large Block Addressing 32-bit (LBA32) parameter, 89
lba32 keyword, LILO, 413
LBA32 (Large Block Addressing 32-bit) parameter, 89
L1 (Level 1) caches, 49
L2 (Level 2) caches, 49
lcd command, FTP, 712
ldconfig command, 649
ldd command, 648–649
LDP (Linux Documentation project), 14
left angle bracket (<), redirection symbol, 361
less command, 143–144, 273
Level 1 (L1) caches, 49
Level 2 (L2) caches, 49
-lG option, ls command, 137
-lh option, ls command, 137
-l --human-readable option, ls command, 137
/lib directory, 188
/lib/modules directory, 692
/lib/modules/<kernel-version> directory, 664, 665

licensing Linux, 6–10
  closed source licenses, 9–10
  open source licenses, 9
LILO. *See* LInux LOader (LILO)
lilo command, 414
linear keyword, LILO, 413
line printer daemon (lpd), 532, 537
link(s)
  hard, 199–201
  symbolic, 199, 201–202
link (ln) command, 200
linking files, 130, 199–202
Linux operating system, 4–15
Linux resources, finding on Internet, 759–762
Linuxconf, 698
Linux Documentation project (LDP), 14
Linux GUI, components, 450–455
LInux LOader (LILO), 89, 411–415
  dual booting, 411–415
Linux terminals, 101, 102, 103
Linux User Groups (LUGs), 15
listing files, 132–137
ln (link) command, 200
loadavg file, 337
Local Area Networks (LANs), 690, 692
local0-7 facility, system log daemon, 551
local printers, configuring, 539
locate command, 194–195
locking accounts, 565
locks file, 337
log files, 139, 548–555
  managing files, 552–555
  system log daemon, 549–552
logging in, 99–103
logical drives, 53
login command, 507
LOGNAME variable, 375
logotate command, 553–555
-L option, 565
  cpio utility, 608
  lpq command, 536
-l option
  cpio utility, 608
  gzip utility, 599
  lpq command, 536
  ls command, 136, 217–220

passwd command, 565
ps command, 495–496, 498, 506
rpm command, 623–625, 626
usermod command, 564
lpc command, 533–534
lpd (line printer daemon), 532, 537
lp keyword, /etc/printcap file, 548
lpq command, 535–536
lpr command, 532, 534–535
  system log daemon, 551
lprm command, 536
LPT ports, 57
ls command, 132–137, 217–220
  FTP, 712
lsmod command, 665–666
-l switch, ls command, 133–134
LUGs (Linux User Groups), 15
LyX, 35

M

magnetic tape (mt) command, 602
mail delivery agents (MDAs), 25
mail facility, system log daemon, 551
mail services, Internet servers, 25
mail transfer agents (MTAs), 25
mail user agents (MUAs), 25
MAIL variable, 375
mainboards, 55, 56
maintenance, 642–643
major number, 5, 245
make bzImage command, 670
make clean command, 670
make command, 616
make dep command, 670
Makefile file, 615–616, 619
make modules_install command, 670
make oldconfig command, 665
make xconfig command, 668
man command, 108–109
Mandrake Linux, 23
manual pages, 106–109
map= keyword, LILO, 413
mark facility, system log daemon, 551
Master Boot Record (MBR),
  53, 410
maximum resolution, 458
MBR (Master Boot Record),
  53, 410

mcedit editor (Midnight
  Commander Editor), 162–163
MDAs (mail delivery agents), 25
mdstat file, 337
media access method, 690
meminfo file, 334, 337
memory
  physical, 50–51
  random access, 50–51
  read only, 51
  swap, 86
  virtual, 86
  volatile, 50
message= keyword, LILO, 413
messages file, 341–342
metacharacters, 105–106
  wildcard, 137–138
mget command, FTP, 712
Midnight Commander Editor
  (mcedit editor), 162–163
MINIX, 19
minix filesystem, 248
minor number, 5, 245
misc file, 337
mkbootdisk command, 650
mkdir command, 189–190
mkdosfs command, 252
mke2fs command, 252, 271, 277
mkfs command, 250–252, 270–271
mkfs.minix command, 252
mkfs.msdos command, 252
mkfs.vfs command, 252
mkisofs command, 252
mkreiserfs command, 252
/mnt directory, 188, 249–250
modems, PPP interface, 700,
  701, 702
mode of file, 206, 207–208
modprobe command, 665
modules file, 336, 337
monitor(s), 58–59
  settings, 97, 98
  X Windows, 458
monitoring, 642
  filesystems. See filesystem
    monitoring
  performance. See performance
    monitoring
-m option, useradd command, 563
more command, 141–142, 144, 273

motherboards, 55, 56
mount command
  CD-ROMs, 260
  floppy disks, 250, 253, 255–256,
    257
mounting, 249–250
  CD-ROMs, 260–261
  floppy disks, 250–253
mount points, 249
mounts file, 337
mount -t command, 257
mouse, 59
  choosing configuration, 81, 83
mouseconfig command, 460, 461
move (mv) command, 190–191, 192
moving files, 191
Mozilla, 66, 719
mpstat (Multiple Processor
  Statistics) utility, 654–655
mput command, FTP, 712
msdos filesystem, 248
MTAs (mail transfer agents), 25
mt (magnetic tape) command, 602
MUAs (mail user agents), 25
MULTICS (Multiplexed
  Information and Computing
  Service), 16
multihomed hosts, 727
Multiple Processor Statistics
  (mpstat) utility, 654–655
Multiplexed Information and
  Computing Service
  (MULTICS), 16
multitasking operating systems, 4
multiuser operating systems, 4
-m user option, lpr command, 534
mv (move) command, 190–191, 192
mx keyword, /etc/printcap file, 548
MySQL server, 66
MYVAR variable, 376

N

named pipe files, 130
nedit editor, 164, 165
netconfig, 698
netfilter/iptables, 726
Netfilter/iptables/ipchains, 66
netmask, 65
network(s), 689–731

configuring NIC interfaces, 691–699
configuring PPP interfaces, 699–707
connecting to resources. *See* connecting to network resources
definition of, 690
name resolution, 708–710
services, 723–729
TCP/IP, 690–692
network clients, installations from, 324–327
Network File System (NFS), 714–715
network installations, 320–321, 325, 326
Network File System (NFS) server, 66, 725
Network Information Service (NIS), 709
setting up client, 729
setting up server, 728–729
Network Information Services (NIS) server, 66
network installation, 319–327
FTP, 321–322, 326
HTTP, 323, 326–327
from network clients, 324–327
NFS, 320–321, 325, 326
Network Interface Cards (NICs), 55
configuring, 90, 91
configuring NIC interfaces, 692–699
network servers, 311
network services, 723–729
newgrp command, 559, 567
news facility, system log daemon, 551
newsgroups, 27–28
news services, Internet servers, 27–28
NFS. *See* Network File System (NFS)
NFS (Network File System) server, 66, 725
NI (nice values), 496, 506–508
nice command, 507
nice values (NI), 496, 506–508
NICs. *See* Network Interface Cards (NICs)

NIS. *See* Network Information Service (NIS)
NIS (Network Information Services) server, 66
nl command, 366
--no-absolute-filenames option, cpio utility, 608
-n option
cat command, 139
dump/restore utility, 611
gzip utility, 599
sar command, 659
-#n option, lpr command, 534
notice priority, system log daemon, 552
Novell printers, configuring, 540, 541
ntfs filesystem, 248
NTLOADER, 424–426
ntsysv utility, 724

O

od command, 146–147
office productivity suites, 35–36
office workstations, 33–36
desktop publishing software, 35
financial software, 35
graphics editing software, 34
office productivity suites, 35–36
text editors, 33
word processors, 33–34
OLDPWD variable, 375
-o operator, test statements, 386
-o option
cpio utility, 608
ls command, 137
sar command, 659
-O option, cpio utility, 608
open command, FTP, 712
open source licenses, 9
Open Source Software (OSS), 6–8, 19
operating system-related problems, 649–653
operating systems (OSs), 2–4
operators, test statements, 386
-opt, mke2fs j command, 252
/opt directory, 188
-# option

bzip2 utility, 600
dump/restore utility, 611
gzip utility, 598
options, 103
OS(s) (operating systems), 2–4
OSS (Open Source Software), 6–8, 19
OSTYPE variable, 371, 375
other, 207
overclocked CPUs, 332
owner, directory, 207
ownership, files and directories, 203–206

P

package managers, 22, 615
packages, selecting, 94–95, 96
packet(s), 690
packet internet groper (ping) command, 694–696
panic priority, system log daemon, 552
parallel ports, 57
parentheses (()), command grouping, 105
parentheses with pipe ((...|...)), regular expression, 149
parent processes, 492
Parent Process ID (PPID), 492–493
partition(s), 53
active, 410
creating, 262–270
dual boot system, 420
working with, 266–271
partitioning hard disks, 85–89
partitions file, 337
passwd command, 563–564, 565
password, root, 93
password= keyword, LILO, 413
patch command, 671
pathnames
absolute, 126–127
relative, 128
PATH variable, 197–198, 374–375, 375
PCI (Peripheral Component Interconnect) connections, 55
pci file, 337

PCMCIA (Personal Computer Memory Card International Association), 57
performance monitoring, 653–664
  free command, 663
  sysstat utilities, 654–662
  top utility, 662
  vmstat command, 663–664
period (.)
  filenames, 130
  regular expression, 149
peripheral component(s), 55–58
  video adapter cards, 58
Peripheral Component Interconnect (PCI) connections, 55
permissions, 203–330
  changing, 210–214
  default, 214–216
  file and directory ownership, 203–206
  interpreting, 208–210
  mode interpretation, 207–208
  special, 216–220
Personal Computer Memory Card International Association (PCMCIA), 57
physical memory, 50–51
  RAM, 50–51
pico (PIne COmposer) editor, 161–162
PID (Process ID), 492
PIne COmposer (pine) editor, 161–162
ping (packet internet groper) command, 694–696
pipe (|)
  command piping, 105, 363, 364
  named pipes, 133
piping commands, 363–369
Plug-and-Play (PnP) devices, 58, 308
plus sign (+), regular expression, 149
PnP (Plug-and-Play) devices, 58, 308
Point to Point Protocol (PPP), 691
Point to Point Protocol (PPP) interfaces, configuring, 699–707
polling, 305
POP (Post Office Protocol), 719
POP3 Server, 725

-P option
  lpc command, 533
  lpq command, 536
  tar utility, 603, 604
port keyword, setserial command, 653
ports, 57, 723
POST (Power-on Self Test), 63–64, 410
Postgres SQL server, 66
Post Office Protocol (POP), 719
Postscript files, printing, 535
Power-on Self Test (POST), 63–64, 410
Power PC, Linux installation, 328
PPID (Parent Process ID), 492–493
PPP. See Point to Point Protocol (PPP); Point to Point Protocol (PPP) interfaces
-P printer option, lpr command, 534
preparing for Linux installation, 47–67
  gathering information. See gathering pre-installation information
  hardware. See hardware; specific hardware
PRI (process priority), 496
primary group, 203, 556
primary partitions, 53
printer(s)
  configuring, 537–548
  enabled and disabled, 532
printer administration, 532–548
  configuring printers, 537–548
  managing print jobs, 534–536
  print process, 532–534
printer aliases, 543–544
printing, 532
print job(s), 532
  managing, 534–536
print job IDs, 532
print queue, 532
print servers, 28–29
print working directory (pwd) command, 127
priorities
  /etc/syslog.conf file, 550
  processes, 506–508
  system log daemon, 551–552
proactive maintenance, 642

/proc directory, 188, 333–337
processes, 2, 491–516
  background, 503–506
  child, 492
  daemon, 492
  execution, 502–503
  foreground, 503
  killing, 500–502
  parent, 492
  priorities, 506–508
  rogue, 499
  scheduling commands. See scheduling commands
  user, 492
  viewing, 493–500
Process ID (PID), 492
process priority (PRI), 496
/proc/sys/net/ipv4/ip_forward file, 727
production kernel, 5
program(s), 2, 492. See also processes
  binary, execution, 503
Programmable Read Only Memory (PROM), 51
programming languages, 7
PROM (Programmable Read Only Memory), 51
prompt(s), logging in, 102
prompt keyword, LILO, 413
property command, 366
protocols, 690
proxy services, Internet servers, 26–27
ps command, 493–498, 506
PS/2 ports, 57
PS1 variable, 371, 373, 375
ptu command, FTP, 712
pwconv command, 555
pwd (print working directory) command, 127
pwd command, FTP, 712, 713
PWD variable, 373, 375
pwunconv command, 555

Q
-q option
  bzip2 utility, 601
  gzip utility, 599
  rpm command, 623–625, 626
  sar command, 659–660

Qt toolkit, 451–452
question mark (?)
  regular expression, 149
  shell wildcard, 105, 137
quit command, FTP, 712
quota(s), hard disks, 278–282
quota command, 281–282
quotation mark ("), metacharacter
  quote, 105

R

rad permission, 209
RAID. *See* Redundant Array of
  Independent Disks (RAID)
RAM Digital Analog Converter
  (RAMDAC) chip, 457–458
Random Access Memory (RAM),
  50–51
  adding to system, 653–654
RANDOM variable, 375
rawrite, 78–79
Raymond, Eric S., 18
reactive maintenance, 642, 643
README file, 615, 622
read-only keyword, LILO, 413
Read Only Memory (ROM), 50, 51
recursive copies, 191
--recursive option, ls command, 137
Red Hat Linux, 19, 22, 23
Red Hat Package Manager (RPM),
  22, 615, 622–627, 648, 650, 651
Red Hat Printer Configuration
  Tool, 537–546
Red Hat User Manager, 568–573
redirection of commands, 359–363
Reduced Instruction Set
  Computing (RISC) processors, 48
Redundant Array of Independent
  Disks (RAID)
  configuration, 309–310
  creating volume, 87
refresh rate of monitors, 59
regexp (regular expressions),
  147–149
regular expressions (regexp),
  147–149
REISER filesystem, 86
reiserfs filesystem, 248
relative pathnames, 128

remote applications, running,
  717–719
removable media, 54
--remove files option, tar utility,
  603602
renaming files, 190–191
renice command, 508
reset command, 104
resolution of monitors, 58
restart command, 435
restore command, 613–615
--reverse option, ls command, 137
revision numbers, 5
right angle bracket (>), redirection
  symbol, 359
RISC (Reduced Instruction Set
  Computing) processors, 48
risk reduction with Linux, 10–11
Ritchie, Dennis, 16
rlogin Daemon, 725
rm command, 193
rmdir command, 192, 193
rm keyword, /etc/printcap file, 548
rmmod command, 666
rogue processes, 499
ROM (Read Only Memory),
  50, 51
/root directory, 188
root filesystem, 250
root= keyword, LILO, 413
root password, 93
/root/.rhosts file, 718
-R option
  ls command, 137
  sar command, 659
-r option
  compress command, 595, 596
  dump/restore utility, 611
  gzip utility, 599
  lpr command, 534
  ls command, 137
  mount command, 260
  restore command, 614–615
  sar command, 659
  tar utility, 606, 603602
routers, 690
route tables, 726–727
routing, 727
  Internet servers, 25
rp keyword, /etc/printcap file, 548

RPM (Red Hat Package Manager),
  22, 615, 622–627
rpm command, 623–626
rsh Daemon, 725
runlevel(s), 427–429
runlevel command, 428, 429
running remote applications,
  717–719

S

Samba (SMB) Server, 66, 725
sar (System Activity Reporter) command, 656–660
Sawfish Window Manager, 452,
  453, 456
/sbin directory, 188
scalability, 31
scheduling commands, 509–516
  atd command, 509–512
  crond command, 512–516
scientific workstations, 31–32
SCSI. *See* Small Computer System
  Interface (SCSI)
scsi file, 337
SCSI ID, 302
sd keyword, /etc/printcap file, 548
SDRAM (Synchronous Dynamic
  Random Access Memory), 51
searching for text in files, 147–152
  grep command, 149–152
  regular expressions, 147–149
sectors on hard disks, 263
Secure Shell, 725
Secure Socket Layer (SSL), 27
security, 12
security facility, system log
  daemon, 551
segmentation faults, 332
semicolon (;), command termination, 105
Sendmail Email Server, 726
Serial Line Internet protocol
  (SLIP), 691
serial ports, 57
server services, 24. *See also* application servers; file servers; Internet
  servers; print servers
set command, 369–371, 376
Set Group ID (SGID), 216, 217
setserial command, 652–653

Set User ID (SUID), 216
SGID (Set Group ID), 216, 217
shareware, 10
shell(s), 99–100
    commands, 103–105
    functions, execution, 503
    metacharacters, 105–106
shell scripts, 379–390
    decision constructs, 382–390
    escape sequences, 381–382
    execution, 503
    reading Standard Input, 382
SHELL variable, 371, 375
shell variable ($), 105
shell variable(s), 369–379
    changing values, 372–373
    environment, 369–375
    environment files, 378–379
    UMASK, 377
    user-defined, 375–377
shell wildcard (*), 105, 134, 137
shell wildcard (?), 105, 137
shell wildcard ([ ]), 105, 137
sh keyword, /etc/printcap file, 548
shutdown command, 111–112
shutting down Linux, 111–112
SIGHUP kill signal, 501
SIGINT kill signal, 501
SIGKILL kill signal, 501
SIGQUIT kill signal, 501
SIGTERM kill signal, 501
SILO, 328
Single In-line Memory Modules
    (SIMMs), 50
single quote ('), metacharacter
    quote, 105
skeleton directory, 562
Slackware Linux, 23
slash (/)
    root directory, 128
    subdirectories, 133
SLIP (serial Line Internet
    protocol), 691
Small Computer System Interface
    (SCSI), 52
    connectors, 304
    hard disk configuration, 302–304
    standards, 303–304
smbclient utility, 716
SMB (Samba) Server, 66, 725

SMP (Symmetric Multi-
    Processing), 49
soft limits, hard disk quotas, 278
software, 2. See also operating
    systems (OSs); processes;
    program(s)
    gathering pre-installation
        information, 65–66
    installation. See software
        installation
    operating systems, 2–4
    selecting, 65–66
    troubleshooting, 648–653
software installation, 615–627
    compiling source code into pro-
        grams, 615–622
    RPM, 622–627
Solaris UNIX, 17
-S option
    gzip utility, 599
    ls command, 137
-s option
    bzip2 utility, 601
    lpq command, 536
    ls command, 137
    useradd command, 563
    usermod command, 564
sort command, 366
source code, 6
source file/directory, 191
spanning, 309
SPARC, Linux installation, 328
spd_hi keyword, setserial
    command, 653
spd_normal keyword, setserial com-
    mand, 653
spd_vhi keyword, setserial
    command, 653
special device files, 130
special permissions, 216–220
    defining, 216–217
    setting, 217–220
spooling, 532
square brackets ([ ])
    (shell wildcard), 105, 137
    regular expression, 149
square brackets with caret ([^...]),
    regular expression, 149
Squid, 27
Squid Proxy Server, 66, 726

SRAM (Static RAM), 50, 51
SSL (Secure Socket Layer), 27
-s- switch, du command, 274
stability of Linux, 12
Stallman, Richard, 17
standalone daemons, 724
Standard Error (stderr), 358
    redirection, 359–363
Standard Input (stdin), 358
    reading, 382
Standard Output (stdout), 358
    redirection, 359–363
StarOffice, 36
start kkw, lpc command, 533
startx command, 456
Static RAM (SRAM), 50, 51
stating, X Windows, 455–457
stderr. See Standard Error (stderr)
stdin. See Standard Input (stdin)
stdout. See Standard Output
    (stdout)
--stdout option, bzip2 utility, 600
-stdout option, gzip utility, 598
s390, Linux installation, 328
stop keyword, lpc command, 533
strings command, 145–146
submount command, 715
subnet mask, 691
subshells, 376
SUID (Set User ID), 216
superblock, 199
supercomputers, 30–31
SuperProbe command, 458–459
superscalar processors, 49
support, ease of obtaining, 14–16
SuSE Linux, 19, 23
swap file, 337
swap memory, 86
symbolic links, 199, 201–202
Symmetric Multi-Processing
    (SMP), 49
Synchronous Dynamic Random
    Access Memory (SDRAM), 51
syncing, 275
syslogd (system log daemon),
    549–552
syslog facility, system log daemon,
    551
sysstat (System Statistics) package,
    654–662

System Activity Reporter (sar) command, 656–660
system back-up, 601–615
    cpio utility, 607–609
    dump/restore utility, 610–615
    tar utility, 602–607
system cron table, 514–516
system documentation, 643
system initialization, 409–436
    boot loaders. *See* boot loaders
    boot process, 410–411
    configuring daemon setup, 434–436
    /etc/inittab file, 429–434
    runlevels, 427–429
system log daemon (syslogd), 549–552
system network configuration, identifying, 65
system services, 3
System Statistics (sysstat) package, 654–662

T

Tab-completion feature, 129
Tab Window Manager (twm), 453, 454, 457
tac command, 139
tail command, 140–141
tape archive (tar) utility, 602–607
tarballs, 22, 605
target file/directory, 191
target ID, 302
tar (tape archive) utility, 602–607
TCO (Total Cost of Ownership), 15
TCP/IP (Transmission Control Protocol/Internet Protocol), 691–692
telinit command, 428
telnet Daemon, 726
terminals, 99, 101, 102, 103
terminators, SCSI, 302
TERM variable, 375
--test option, rpm command, 626
test statements, 385–386
TeX, 66
text, searching for. *See* searching for text in files

text-based installation, 311–316
text editors, 33
text files, 130, 135
    displaying contents, 138–145
    editing. *See* editing text files
text tools, 147
Thompson, Ken, 16
tilde (~)
    end of file marker, 153
    home directory variable, 105, 127–128
timeout= keyword, LILO, 413
time slices, 506
time zones, 92
title keyword, GRUB, 422
/tmp directory, 188
Token Ring, 691
top command, 498–499, 662
-t option
    bzip2 utility, 601
    cpio utility, 608
    dump/restore utility, 611
    gzip utility, 599
    ls command, 137
    mkfs command, 250–251
    tar utility, 603, 606
Torvalds, Linus, 19
Total Cost of Ownership (TCO), 15
touch command, 203
traceroute command, 727–728
tracks on hard disks, 263
Transmission Control Protocol/Internet Protocol (TCP/IP), 691–692
trapping signals, 502
tr command, 366
troubleshooting, 642–653
    hardware-related problems, 645–648
    installation. *See* troubleshooting installation
    methodology, 642–644
    procedures, 643
    software-related problems, 648–653
troubleshooting installation, 330–343
    problems after installation, 332–343

problems during installation, 331–332
problems starting installation, 331
trusted access, 718–719
tune2fs command, 271
TurboLinux, 23
twm (Tab Window Manager), 453, 454, 457

U

UID (User Identifier), 556
ulimit command, 649
UltraSPARC, Linux installation, 328
UMASK variable, 377
uncompress command, 595–596
--uncompress option, gzip utility, 598
underscore (_), filenames, 130
Universal Serial Bus (USB) ports, 57
UNIX, 16–17
    configuring printers, 539, 540
unmask command, 215
unmask variable, 214
unmount command, 254–255, 257
    CD-ROMs, 260
-U option
    ls command, 137
    rpm command, 626
    sar command, 659
-u option
    cpio utility, 608
    dump/restore utility, 611
    fuser command, 257
    mount command, 263
    sar command, 659
    tar utility, 603
    useradd command, 563
    usermod command, 564
up keyword, lpc command, 533
USB (Universal Serial Bus) ports, 57
usemod command, 565
user(s), 555–573
    authentication, 555–559
    directories, 207
    Red Hat User Manager, 568–573
    UIDs, 556

user accounts, 539
  creating, 93–94, 561–564, 568, 569
  deleting, 565–566
  editing properties, 570
  locking, 565
  modifying, 564–565
useradd command, 561, 562–563
user cron tables, 513–514
user-defined variables, 375–377
userdel command, 565–566
User Identifier (UID), 556
user interfaces, 3
usermod command, 564, 566
user processes. *See* processes
/usr directory, 189, 272
usr facility, system log daemon, 551
/usr/local directory, 189
/usr/src/<kernel-version>
  directory, 665
/usr/src/linux link, 665
/usr/X11R6/bin/SuperProbe command, 458–459
/usr/X11R6/share/Xconfigurator/
  MonitorsDB file, 461
uucp facility, system log daemon, 551

V
values
  nice, 496, 506–508
  shell variables, changing, 372–373
/var directory, 189, 272
variable identifier, 376
/var/log directory, 548, 649
/var/log/logfile file, 550–551
/var/log/messages file, 552–553
/var/log/sa directory, 660
/var/spool/cron directory, 513
version file, 337
versions of Linux, 4–5
vertical refresh (VSync), 59
vfat filesystem, 86, 248
video hardware, configuring, 95–96
vi editor, 152–161
viewing. *See also* displaying
  processes, 493–500
virtual memory, 86

vmlinuz file, 99
vmlinuz-<kernel version> file, 410
vmstat command, 663–664
volatile memory, 50
-V option
  fsck command, 277
  rpm command, 626, 648
-v option
  bzip2 utility, 601
  compress command, 596
  cpio utility, 608
  dump/restore utility, 611
  grep command, 150–151
  gzip utility, 599
  rpm command, 623, 626
  sar command, 659
  tar utility, 603
VSync (vertical refresh), 59
vxfs filesystem, 248

W
WANs (Wide Area Networks),
  690, 691
warning (warn) priority, system log
  daemon, 552
wc command, 366
w command, 104
Web services, Internet servers, 27
well-known ports, 723
which command, 197
whoami command, 104, 203
who command, 104
Wide Area Networks (WANs),
  690, 691
wildcard metacharacters, 137–138
  regular expressions, 148
Window Maker Window Manager,
  453, 455, 457
window managers, 451, 453
Windows boot loaders, 424–426
Windows Device Manager, 62, 63
Windows Display applet, 62, 63
Windows files, accessing, 715–717
Windows printers, configuring,
  539, 540

Windows System Information
  Tool, 62
-W option
  sar command, 659
  tar utility, 603
-w option, tar utility, 603
word processors, 33–34
workstations, 24
  engineering, 31–32
  office, 33–36
  scientific, 31–32
workstation services, 24
write permission, 209

X
X clients, 450
.Xclients-default file, 456–457
Xconfigurator command, 460–467
X Display Manager (xdm), 456
xdm (X Display Manager), 456
xedit editor, 164, 165
xemacs editor, 163–164
xf86config program, 467–474
XFree86, 451
xinetd (Internet Super Daemon),
  723–724
-x option
  dump/restore utility, 611
  ls command, 137
  tar utility, 603
x option, ps command, 496–497
X Server, 450, 726
xvidtune utility, 475
X Windows, 19, 66, 450–451,
  455–476
  configuring, 97, 98, 457–475
  starting, 455–456

Z
zcat command, 595, 597
Zip disks, 54
zmore command, 597
zombie processes, 496
-Z option, tar utility, 603
-z option, tar utility, 603, 606